Find more online.

Auf einigen Seiten im Buch findest
du Online-Codes. Diese führen
dich zu weiteren Materialien.
Gib den Code einfach in das Suchfeld
auf www.klett.de ein.

W0083509

Story

Auf den **Story**-Seiten erwarten dich
lustige und spannende Geschichten
mit interessanten Aufgaben.

Check-out

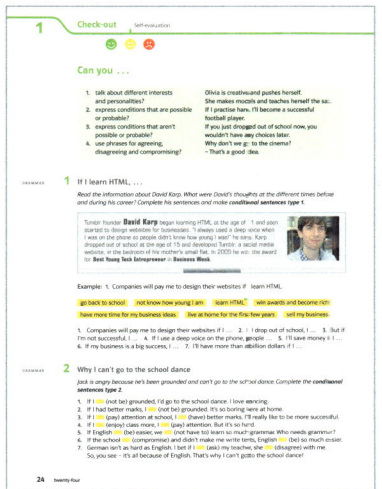

Auf den **Check out**-Seiten kannst du deine
Lernfortschritte selbst überprüfen.
Die Lösungen findest du im Anhang.

Symbole

👥	Partnerarbeit
👥👥	Gruppenarbeit
🗄	Produkt für dein Portfolio
🔊	Audios auf www.klett.de unter Code e4i9ju oder auf den Lehrer-CDs
🎞	Film
⟨ ⟩	fakultative/s Übung / Kapitel
MK	Aufgaben und Tipps zur Entwicklung und Stärkung der Medienkompetenz

Verweise →

○	Hilfestellung / zusätzliche Aufgabe
🔴	anspruchsvollere Aufgabe
WB	Übung im Workbook
G	Grammatikanhang
S	Skillsanhang

ANHANG

Text and media smart

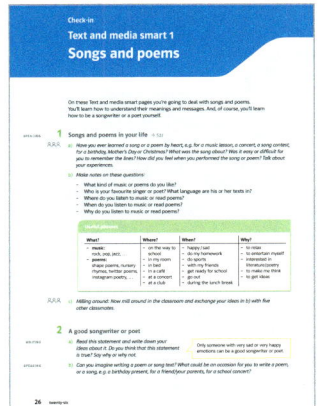

Auf den **Text and media smart**-
Seiten lernst mit bestimmten
Textsorten (z. B. Songs, Briefe)
umzugehen.

Diff pool

Im **Diff pool** findest du weitere
Übungen. Die Verweise in den
Units zeigen dir, wann du diese
am besten erledigst. Die Lösungen
findest du im Anhang.

Skills und Grammar

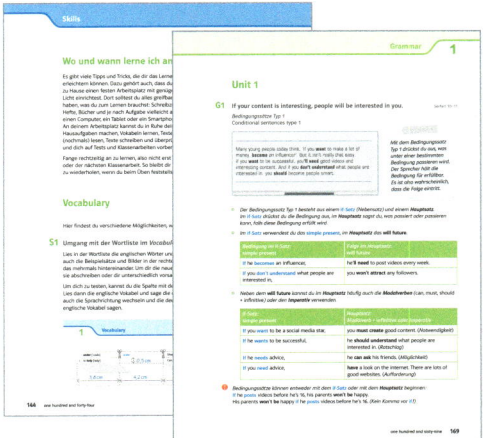

Im **Skills**-Anhang sind alle Lerntechniken, die dir
beim Lösen der Aufgaben helfen, übersichtlich
zusammengefasst. Du findest darin auch nützliche
Tipps zum Umgang mit Medien. Du erkennst sie
am **MK**-Symbol.
Auf den **Grammar**-Seiten findest du Regeln,
Beispiele, Tipps und Übungen zum grammatischen
Lernstoff aus den *Stations*. Die Lösungen findest
du im Anhang.

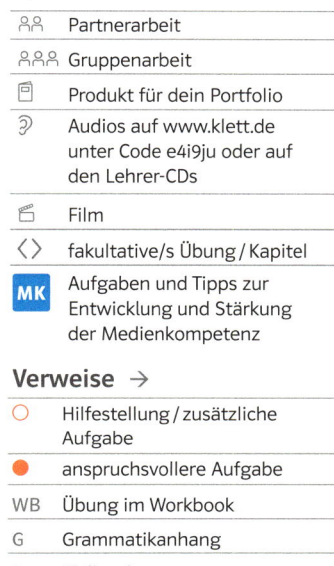

Green Line 3 G9 für Klasse 7 an Gymnasien

Zusätzliche Informationen in der Lehrerfassung:

Produktiver Lernwortschatz

Rezeptiver Wortschatz

Neue Grammatik
················

G: Hier sind Verweise auf den Grammatikanhang im Schülerbuch angegeben.

WB 4/1: Hier können Sie im Workbook Seite 4, Aufgabe 1 einsetzen.

KV 1: Hier können Sie Kopiervorlage 1 des Lehrerbuchs einsetzen.

Voc.: Hier sind Verweise auf Wortschatzhilfen im Schülerbuch und Workbook (WB) angegeben.

Lösung: Hier finden Sie Lösungen zu den geschlossenen Aufgaben.

1. Auflage

1 5 4 3 2 1 | 2025 24 23 22 21

Alle Drucke dieser Auflage sind unverändert und können im Unterricht nebeneinander verwendet werden. Die letzte Zahl bezeichnet das Jahr des Druckes.

Hinweis: Die Mediencodes enthalten zusätzliche Unterrichtsmaterialien, die der Verlag in eigener Verantwortung zur Verfügung stellt.

Herausgeber: Prof. Harald Sonntag-Weisshaar, Bisingen
Autorinnen und Autoren: Carolyn Jones M.A., Beckenham; Nilgül Karabulut-Klöppelt, Aachen; Jon Marks, Ventnor; Alison Wooder, Ventnor sowie Jennifer Baer-Engel, Göppingen; Cornelia Kaminski, Fulda; Elise-Köhler-Davidson, Exeter
Beratung: Paul Dennis M.A., Lahnstein; Cornelia Kaminski, Fulda; Nilgül Karabulut-Klöppelt, Aachen; Hartmut Klose, Seevetal; Antje Körber, Merseburg; Jörg Nieswand, Berlin; Michael Rogge, Mülheim an der Ruhr; Jörg Schulze, Dresden
Redaktion: Joanne Popp editing etc., Korntal-Münchingen (Vokabular); Gaby Bauer-Negenborn, Weßling (Lehrerfassung)

Entstanden in Zusammenarbeit mit dem Projektteam des Verlages.

Layout: Petra Michel, Essen
Umschlaggestaltung: Koma Amok, Stuttgart
Illustrationen: Peer Kramer, Düsseldorf; jani lunablau, Barcelona sowie Christian Dekelver (Karten); Denise Drews, Zürich (Timeline)
Reproduktion: Schwaben-Repro, Stuttgart
Satz: Satzkiste GmbH, Stuttgart; Fotosatz Kaufmann, Stuttgart (Lehrerfassung)
Druck: Firmengruppe APPL, aprinta druck, Wemding

Printed in Germany
ISBN 978-3-12-835032-5

Green Line

Line

Lehrerfassung

3 G9

von
Carolyn Jones
Nilgül Karabulut-Klöppelt
Jon Marks
Alison Wooder
Jennifer Baer-Engel
Cornelia Kaminski
Elise Köhler-Davidson

herausgegeben von
Harald Sonntag-Weisshaar

Ernst Klett Verlag
Stuttgart · Leipzig

Inhalt

Inhalt

Inhalt

Die in diesem Band aufbereiteten Inhalte stellen ein Angebot dar, sie sind nicht obligatorisch durchzunehmen. Maßgeblich für die Auswahl der Texte und Übungen ist der Lehrplan Ihres Bundeslandes bzw. Ihr schulinternes Curriculum.
Zu Zwecken der besseren Lesbarkeit schließt die männliche Form die weibliche Form mit ein.

Unit 1
Find your place

A

B

SPEAKING

Voc.: Continents; Countries, WB (Word bank), pp. 8–12

1 Everyone is different

a) *Look at the photos A–E. What are the teenagers' hobbies? What smart type are they? Explain why.*

b) *Read the <u>sayings</u> <u>below</u>. What's the main idea behind each saying?*

> You can't <u>judge</u> a book by its <u>cover</u>.

> Everyone is good at something.

> It <u>doesn't matter</u> if you win or lose but how you play the game.

> Life is a competition!

> I don't care if I'm in or out as long as I've got my friends.

> <u>Practice</u> makes perfect.

> You'll never know until you try.

> Don't follow the crowd.

Across cultures

"Practice makes perfect" and "You can't judge a book by its cover" are examples of **popular English sayings**. What German sayings describe the ideas and pictures on these pages?

c) *Look at the photos A–D again and match the sayings with the photos. Say which ones match and why.*
Lösung: c) saying 1 – photo C, saying 2 – all photos, saying 3 – photos B+C, saying 4 – photos B+C+D, saying 5 – all photos, saying 6 – photos B+C+D, saying 7 – all photos, saying 8 – photo A

C

D

In Unit 1 you learn

… how to talk about what you and other people would do in different situations. You learn:

- vocabulary for talking about different interests and <u>personalities</u>,
- <u>conditional sentences</u> types 1 and 2,
- phrases for <u>agreeing</u>, <u>disagreeing</u> and <u>compromising</u>.

What <u>smart</u> <u>type</u> are you?

Music Smart
Body Smart
People Smart
Word Smart
Logic Smart
Nature Smart
Self Smart
Picture Smart

LISTENING

2 A radio <u>call-in</u> → S13

WB 2/1

✓ 1: A radio call-in
B 2/1: Vocabulary
(dialogue completion)

a) *Look at the diagram above. What do you think a 'body smart' person could be good at? And what about the other seven smart types? Talk about your ideas in class.*

1/1–3

b) *Listen to a radio call-in. What's the subject today? Who are the <u>callers</u>?*

c) *Listen again. What do the callers say about …*

- *their talents / what they're good at?*
- *their <u>doubts</u> about <u>themselves</u>?*
- *what they've <u>learned about</u> themselves?*

Lösung: b) Subject: difference – people's different talents or ideas for their future; Callers: Jenna, a 15-year-old girl from Brighton and Stephen, a 16-year-old boy from London

Useful phrases

A body smart / picture smart / music smart / logic smart / … person

… is good with his / her hands / body / <u>imagination</u> / …
… is good at doing / showing / using / creating / explaining / teaching / …
… knows how to use … / play … / talk … / <u>communicate</u> … / <u>compete</u> … / …
… is creative / <u>imaginative</u> / confident / …
… likes to … / feels … / understands … / …
A … smart person would probably be a good teacher / doctor / …

WRITING

3 **Your turn: In what way are you smart?** → More help ○ 124/1 → More practice ● 124/2 → S23

WB 2/2

B 2/2: Vocabulary
(multiple choice)

a) *What smart type are you? Do any of the sayings on p. 8 <u>match</u> your personality? Or do other ones describe you better? Use the phrases in ex. 2 and write down your ideas.*

b) *Inside outside circle: Listen to different texts. Did you find out anything about your classmates that you didn't know before?*

1/4 🎧

How to be an influencer

Amalia interviewed Robert, an influencer on <u>environmental issues</u>, for *Tallis Sounds*.

Amalia:	Many young people today think, **'If you want to make a lot of money, become an influencer.'** But is it really that easy?	
5 Robert:	Of course it isn't. I don't make that much money.	
Amalia:	So, how did you become an influencer?	
Robert:	Well, I've always found it fun to make cool videos and then post them online.	
10		
Amalia:	**But if we just post videos, we can't all become influencers.** Can you give us some good tips?	
Robert:	Oh yes! You don't need a lot of <u>technical</u> skills, but you need to be 'self smart'. Your personality will be one of the main attractions to your followers. **If you're OK with that, you'll need to choose a** <u>topic</u> **that you know a lot about – for example, fashion, food, sports or computer games.**	
15		
20		
Amalia:	And what do you do then?	
Robert:	Then you need to create good content. People will only be interested in you if your content is interesting, fun and different.	
25		
Amalia:	The topics that you've just mentioned are very popular. You <u>focus on</u> environmental issues, don't you?	
30		

Robert:	That's right. When I first started my <u>channel</u>, people started to become more <u>concerned about</u> <u>climate change</u>. They wanted to know how they could <u>produce</u> less <u>waste</u>. If you want to be an influencer, you should become 'people smart'. If you don't understand what people are interested in, you won't <u>attract</u> any followers.	35 40
Amalia:	So, followers <u>trust</u> an influencer's advice. Is it difficult to make sure followers always trust your advice?	
Robert:	Yes, <u>especially</u> when money is <u>involved</u>. If you're a popular influencer, <u>companies</u> will pay you money to <u>recommend</u> or sell their <u>products</u>. This may be a problem if followers think the influencer only wants to make money. If you want to keep your followers and attract new ones, tell them what they need to know.	45 50
Amalia:	Do you have any other tips?	
Robert:	<u>Make sure</u> you choose the right social media platform for you. If most of your content is photos with comments, don't use a video platform! If you don't get many followers, try a different platform.	55
Amalia:	<u>Thank you very much</u>.	60

1   Advice on social media   → S5, S16

READING

WB 3/3

WB 3/3: Vocabulary (matching)

a) *What advice does the interview include? Choose three.*

1. How to post videos, photos and text
2. How to start as an influencer
3. What type of person can be an influencer
4. How to create interesting content
5. How to start your own website
6. How to make money as an influencer

SPEAKING   **MK**

b) *Do you follow any influencers, or have you* <u>subscribed</u> *to any channels? Say which ones and why. Do you think influencers are good* <u>role models</u>*? Explain why or why not.*

‹c)› *Make a podcast and explain how to become an influencer. Use the ideas from the text and find some on the internet too.*

Lösung: a) The interview includes advice on points 3, 4, and 6.

GRAMMAR

WB 3/4

B 3/4: Grammar
(correct sentence order)

2 **Find the rule: Conditional sentences type 1** → G1

Find the conditional sentences in the text on p. 10. Say what <u>tense</u> you use in the <u>if-clause</u>. What about the main clause? The <u>coloured</u> sentences will help you.

If ..., ... will ...	If ..., ... can / should / may ...	If ..., become ...
...	...	...

Lösung: Rule: In conditional sentences type 1 you use the simple present in the if-clause and the will future, can/should/may + infinitive or the imperative in the main clause.

GRAMMAR

WB 4/5–6
WB 5/7

B 4/5–6–5/7: Vocabulary
(survey); Listening
(environment survey);
Mediation (blog entry)

3 **Be smart!** → More practice ○ 124/3 → More practice ● 125/4 → G1

What will happen? Look at the pictures and complete the conditional sentences type 1.

1. If we turn off the lights after lessons, we ▢ energy.
2. If we ▢ to turn off the <u>tap</u>, we can save lots of water.
3. The school might save money if we ▢ the <u>heating</u> after school or at weekends.
4. We ▢ our rubbish correctly if there are different <u>bins</u> in every classroom.
5. The playground ▢ much cleaner if we all use the bins.
6. If the school ▢ <u>rainwater</u>, we can use it to <u>flush</u> the toilet.

recycle
save   be
remember
turn down
collect

Lösung: 1. 'll save/can save, 2. remember, 3. turn down, 4. can recycle, 5. will be, 6. collects

GRAMMAR

WB 5/8

B 5/8: Writing
(comment)

4 **Your turn: If ...** → S24, G1

a) *Complete the sentences with your own ideas.*

    1. If you see a light on in an empty room, ...　**2.** If I can't find a recycling bin next time I'm at a train station, ...　**3.** If there is not much <u>rain</u> next summer, ...　**4.** If we all think before we buy things that we don't need, ...　**5.** If we don't look after the environment, ...　**6.** If we look after the environment, ...

b) *Bus stop: Compare your answers.*

Lösung: a) 1. ..., you should switch it off. 2. ..., I'll take my rubbish back home. 3. ..., the grass will become brown.
4. ..., there'll be less rubbish. 5. ..., one day we won't have a place to live any more. 6. ..., we'll have a better future.

1/6 ## They wouldn't worry if they didn't care!

Jay:	Hey, look at this. A boy left school at 15 and became a <u>millionaire</u>!
Shahid:	His family were already <u>rich</u>, right?
Jay:	No, it says that he lived with his

Jay: Hey, look at this. A boy left school at
15 and became a <u>millionaire</u>!

Shahid: His family were already <u>rich</u>, right?

Jay: No, it says that he lived with his
5   mother in a small flat. At the <u>age</u> of
11, he just thought, 'If I learn HTML,
companies will pay me to <u>design</u> their
websites.' So, that's what he did.

Shahid: Well, only a few people get that kind
10   of <u>success</u> so young. Everyone would
be a millionaire if it was so easy. But it
isn't.

Jay: Well, I wouldn't feel so <u>stressed out</u> if
I had a <u>million</u> pounds.

15 Shahid: Why, what's the matter?

Jay: I got an email today. I didn't get the
<u>lead part</u> in that dance show. "You can
be a <u>backing dancer</u>," they told me.
But I want to be the *lead* dancer!
20   If I don't get a lead part soon, I'll
never become rich and famous!

Shahid: Jay, relax. If you practise a lot, you'll
get a lead part one day. But you can't
be serious about becoming rich and
25   famous. Money doesn't <u>grow</u> on trees;
you have to *work* for it!

Jay: That's the point. I can't train often
enough because Mum and Dad
always <u>want me to</u> focus on school.
If they believed in my talent, they   30
would support me.

Shahid: They're sure you'll get a good job one
day if you get better <u>marks</u> now. They
wouldn't worry if they didn't care.
And you *are* a bit <u>laid-back</u>. Anyway,   35
you know you can't leave school until
you're 18. If you just <u>dropped out</u> now,
you wouldn't have any choices later.

Jay: That's easy for you to say! Yesterday
I saw your picture on a magazine   40
again! You make easy money as a
model just because you look good.
If I didn't have to go to school, I'd go
to London and be a model too!

Shahid: But I do <u>modelling</u> just for fun! I'd be   45
stupid if I just <u>relied on</u> my <u>looks</u>, so
that's why I'm <u>studying</u> for a <u>career</u>
in IT. If I make the right plans now, I'll
have more choices later. And if *you*
make the right choices, you'll find your   50
place too.

5 Jay and Shahid: Plans and problems → S5

READING   WB 6/9

WB 6/9: Vocabulary
(crossword puzzle)

a) *What are Jay's plans for the future? And Shahid's?*

b) *Say what Jay's different problems are.
    The words on the right can help you.*

SPEAKING

c) *What advice do you have for Jay? Discuss your ideas.*
Lösung: a) Jay: be a millionaire, become a singer and dancer, rich and famous,
be a lead dancer, doesn't want to go to school any more, wants to go to
London and be a model too; Shahid: have a good job, study for a career in IT,
not just rely on good looks

> stressed out because … |
> sad/disappointed because … |
> compares himself with … |
> his parents think … |
> can't wait to …

GRAMMAR

WB 6/10

6   Find the rule: Conditional sentences type 2 → G2

a) *Go back to the text about Jay and Shahid on p. 12. Make sentences from the text.*

1. If you dropped out now,
2. If it was so easy,
3. I'd be a model too
4. If they didn't care,
5. I wouldn't be so stressed out
6. I'd be stupid

a) everyone would be a millionaire.
b) if I didn't have to go to school.
c) if I just relied on my looks.
d) you wouldn't have any choices later.
e) they wouldn't worry.
f) if I had a million pounds.

b) *Look at the sentences in a). What verb forms do you need in the **if-clause** and the **main clause**?*

c) *Now you know two types of **conditional sentences**. Look at the examples below.
What's the difference in meaning between **conditional sentences type 1** and **type 2**?*

Type 1: If I **practise** a lot, I **will be** a better dancer. So, come on! Let's start now!
Type 2: If I **practised** more often, I **would get** better parts in dance shows.
But I never find time to practise enough!

/ 2: Working with
ammar
B 6/10: Speaking
uestions and answers)

osung: a) 1. d), 2. a), 3. b),
e), 5. f), 6. c); b) Rule:
conditional sentences
pe 2 you use the simple
ast in the if-clause and
ould/could + infinitive in
e main clause. c) Rule:
u use type 1 for actions
at are probable/possible.
u use type 2 for actions
at are not probable or
t possible.

GRAMMAR

WB 7/11–12

7   What would you do <u>in Jay's shoes</u>? → More practice ○ 125/5   → More practice ● 125/6   → G2

*In a forum Jay has asked other young people for their advice about his problems. Read their advice to him. Put the verbs in the right form: **simple past** or **would/wouldn't** + infinitive.*

/ 3: What would you
 if …?
B 7/11–12: Listening
deo chat); Grammar
onditional sentences
pe 2)

calum13_leedsboy   20:05
If I 1 (be) you, I 2 (not be) sad about the backing part. I 3 (be) happy if I 4 (have) a backing part in a dance show, but I never get ANY parts!

jjm_uk14   20:50
It sounds like you want to <u>give up</u> just because you didn't get the lead part this time. But you're only 13! If every dancer 7 (give up) so quickly, nobody 8 (ever become) a star!

koolkatie14_cardiff   20:08
You 5 (not feel) so stressed out if you 6 (not think) about your brother and his modelling job so much. But it sounds like you think about it A LOT!

skater4ever15   21:14
It sounds like your parents don't know how good you are. If they 9 (know) about your talent, maybe they 10 (find) a way for you to have time for school AND for practising. So, SHOW them!

Lösung: 1. were, 2. wouldn't be, 3. would be, 4. had, 5. wouldn't feel, 6. didn't think,
7. gave up, 8. would ever become, 9. knew, 10. would find

WRITING   8

8   Your turn: A forum for teenagers → More help ○ 125/7 → S21

a) *Placemat: Think of different problems, e.g. My best friend tells others all my secrets.*

b) *Write a post in a help forum for teenagers and give advice on **one** of the problems.*

Start: Dear Gwen,
I understand how you're feeling. If my best friend told others all my secrets, she wouldn't be my friend any more! …

Lösung: … It's important that you can trust a friend. Have you asked her how she would react if you did the same thing to her? If I were you, I wouldn't tell her any more of my secrets. Karen

**Look here
for help with
your post:**
⊕ 8pv3xf

GRAMMAR

9 A <u>successful</u> young fashion designer → More practice ○ 126/8 → G2

Ivy Francis is only 19 and has already become a rich and successful fashion designer. How would her life be different if she wasn't rich and successful? Make **conditional sentences type 2.**

> not travel so often | know who liked me for me and not for my money | sleep better ✔
> not make a lot of money | not be famous | have more time for sports | not see so many great places

Lösung: 2. … we didn't travel so often. **3.** …, I wouldn't see so many great places. **4.** …, I'd have more time for sports. **5.** … I wasn't/weren't famous. **6.** … I didn't make a lot of money. **7.** …, I'd know who liked me for me and not for my money.

Example: 1. If I didn't get so nervous before big shows, …
→ If I didn't get so nervous before big shows, I**'d sleep** better.

2. My team and I would have more time for friends if …
3. But if I didn't travel so often, …
4. If I didn't work so hard, …
5. People wouldn't say hello to me if …
6. I couldn't buy what I wanted if …
7. If I didn't have a lot of money, …

MEDIATION

10 A German talent show → More help ○ 126/9 → S17

There's a girl from England who moved into the same house a few weeks ago. She's a very good singer and is going to take part in a talent show on German TV. The information she has received for her <u>audition</u> is in German. She doesn't speak much German and asks you to <u>sum up</u> the information.

Sing dich zum Star!

 Wähle einen Song aus und bereite ihn gut vor. Achtung: Wenn du einen sehr bekannten Song wie zum Beispiel von Lena oder Cro auswählst, musst du auch sehr gut sein! Die Jurymitglieder hören solche Songs ständig. Wähle einen Song aus, der nicht in der aktuellen Hitparade ist.

 Wenn du viel übst, hast du schon viel gewonnen. Stell dir vor, du würdest auf der Bühne stehen und den Songtext vergessen, dann würdest du dich ganz schön blamieren.

 Bitte denke auch an dein Äußeres. Du möchtest einen guten ersten Eindruck machen!
Wenn du unter 18 bist, muss eine erwachsene Begleitperson dabei sein.

GRAMMAR

11 The outfit → More practice ○ 126/10 → More practice ● 126/11 → G1–2

Complete the dialogue with the right verb forms for **conditional sentences type 1 or 2.**

WB 8/13–14

WB 8/13–14: Grammar (mixed tenses); Writing (If I were …)

Lisa: If I go to the audition, I `1` (have to) find a cool outfit.
Dylan: But you look good in everything. Even if you `2` (wear) <u>ugly</u> clothes, you'd look great.
Lisa: Thanks, but I won't wear ugly clothes. If you were in my shoes, what `3` (you / choose)?
Dylan: If I `4` (be) you, I'd wear something <u>comfortable</u>. Skirt, <u>dress</u>, leggings …
If I say something that you like, you `5` (tell) me, right?
Lisa: Leggings … If I `6` (wear) leggings and <u>trainers</u>, I'll feel more comfortable.
And if I feel more comfortable, I `7` (<u>perform</u>) better, right?
Dylan: You do this every time. If you just listened to me, we `8` (save) a lot of time.
Lösung: 1. will have to, 2. wore, 3. would you choose, 4. were, 5. will tell, 6. wear, 7. will perform, 8. would save

You have to push yourself!

1/8

Voc.: Reflexive
pronouns, p. 196

Olivia:	Lucy, tidy your <u>messy</u> room!
Claire:	Don't be so <u>bossy</u>, Olivia.
Lucy:	I feel tired, Mum.
Olivia:	You *always* feel tired. That's why you never tidy your room or do *anything*. When was the last time you practised your <u>recorder</u>?
5 Lucy:	Er, I can't remember.
Olivia:	<u>Exactly</u>! You never practise.
Claire:	Olivia, relax. She's only seven – she needs to have some fun. You should
10	do the same! You study so often and have so many activities. Do you ever really *enjoy* <u>yourself</u>? – Er, Olivia, are you listening to me? I'm talking to you, but I feel like I'm talking to myself.
15 Olivia:	Of course I'm listening, Claire. But isn't this about Lucy?
Lucy:	I don't like the recorder any more and I can't <u>decide on</u> a new hobby.

Claire:	Oh, you don't have to decide now.	
Olivia:	Well, I taught myself how to play the sax when I was five! Nobody taught me. If you want to be good at something, you have to push yourself!	20
Claire:	Oh, <u>saved by the bell</u>! – Girls, go and see who it is.	25
Olivia:	Oh, hi Shahid.	
Shahid:	Hey Olivia – er, are you feeling OK? Why are you and Lucy <u>giving each other funny looks</u>?	
Claire:	Hi Shahid, come in. I hope the girls can <u>behave</u> themselves for two minutes. At the moment they fight whenever they see each other. If they saw themselves like that, they'd be embarrassed! Anyway, you're here to see Desmond, right?	30
		35
Shahid:	Yeah. I need a web designer's <u>opinion</u> on a few things.	
Claire:	Girls, go and get your dad, OK?	
Shahid:	So, <u>what's up</u> with Olivia?	40
Claire:	Well, I was just telling her that she's too serious. She needs to enjoy herself more.	
Shahid:	Wow! If Jay heard you say that, he'd be so jealous! Our parents would love it if Jay had Olivia's perfect marks. They always tell him, "Olivia will be a doctor one day!" But that's just not Jay. He can't wait to be a singer or dancer!	45
Claire:	Yes … and Olivia has her own personality too. Hm, if she wasn't so busy and <u>in charge of</u> things, she wouldn't be Olivia, would she?	50
		55

READING **12** **Compare two families: the Azads and the Frasers** → More help ○ 127/12 → S5

a) *Make a grid with columns for Olivia, Claire, Lucy, Jay and Jay's parents. Write down key words about each person's personalities, opinions and problems. Then say how the two families are the same/different.*

b) *What do you think about Olivia and her personality? What would you do in her shoes?*

Lösung: a) Vgl. Lösung *Diff pool* 127/12, SB S. 294–295; **b)** On the one hand, I think Olivia is right: If you want to be good at something, you have to work hard for it. But on the other hand, I think it is also important to relax and have fun, especially when you're young. If I were in Olivia's shoes, I wouldn't react in such a hard way. I'd understand that Lucy needs some free time to do what she wants.

WRITING

13 A diary entry → S11

Imagine you're Olivia. Write a diary entry about how she feels about Claire and Lucy.

GRAMMAR

14 Find the rule: Reflexive pronouns → G3

WB 9/15–16

KV 4: Working with grammar
WB 9/15–16: Listening (do-it-yourself); Grammar (reflexive pronouns)

a) *Look at sentences 1 to 4 and the tip on the right. Then complete the sentences 5 to 8.*

1. I feel like **I**'m talking to **myself**.
2. If you want to be good at something, **you** have to push **yourself**!
3. **She** needs to enjoy **herself** more.
4. I hope **the girls** can behave **themselves**.
5. Enjoy ▭, **boys**!
6. **We**'d like to see Greenwich for ▭.
7. **Dave** introduced ▭.
8. **Your bedroom** doesn't tidy ▭.

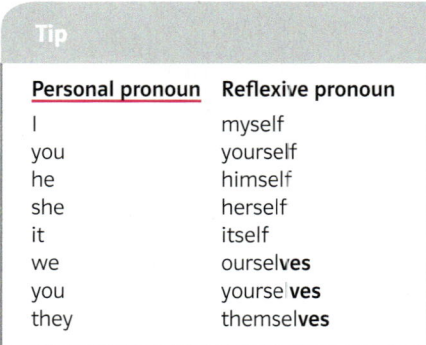

Tip	
Personal pronoun	**Reflexive pronoun**
I	myself
you	yourself
he	himself
she	herself
it	itself
we	oursel**ves**
you	yourse**lves**
they	themsel**ves**

Lösung: a) 5. yourselves, 6. ourselves, 7. himself, 8. itself **b)** Rule: You use object pronouns when the subject of the sentence is a different person to the one the pronoun stands for. You use the reflexive pronoun to show that sb did sth alone and/or without any help or when the subject and the object of the sentence are the same person.

b) *Look at the pictures and sentences. When do you use <u>object pronouns</u>, and when do you use reflexive pronouns?*

A

Mr Reed taught **me** to play the sax.

B

I taught **myself** to play the sax.

c) *Read what Olivia and Holly say. Decide if you need an object pronoun or a reflexive pronoun.*

> me | you (2x) | her (2x) | him | yourself | ourselves (2x) | herself (2x) | himself

Olivia: Claire was a bit <u>hard on</u> **1** today.
Holly: Why, what did she say to **2** ?
Olivia: Things like, "Don't be so bossy with Lucy" and "You never enjoy **3** ".
Holly: What?! You and I always enjoy **4** ! But what's the problem with Lucy?
Olivia: I worry about **5** . Her room is really messy and she'll hurt **6** with her stuff everywhere. And Claire never pushes **7** to get better, so Lucy will have to push **8** more.
Holly: Well, not *everybody* is like you.
Olivia: I know, I know. So, I *am* bossy?

Holly: No, you're my best friend. <u>Stay the way you are!</u> – But tell me more.
Olivia: Oh, what Claire said to Shahid was *really* embarrassing!
Holly: Why, what did she say?
Olivia: She said Lucy and I don't behave **9** . That's what she told **10** ! I felt like a four-year-old in front of 'Mr Cool'! Shahid probably really enjoyed **11** . It was so embarrassing.
Holly: No, he wouldn't laugh at **12** . You know how the Azads love you, <u>Miss</u> Perfect!
Olivia: Oh, stop it! You sound like Claire!

Lösung: c) 1. me, 2. you, 3. yourself, 4. ourselves, 5. her, 6. herself, 7. her, 8. herself, 9. ourselves, 10. him, 11. himself, 12. you

GRAMMAR

WB 10/17–18

4: Working with
ammar
B 10/17–18: Grammar
rror spotting);
ocabulary (multiple
oice)

15 Find the rule: *Themselves* or *each other*? → G3

a) *Write a sentence for each picture with **each other** or **themselves**.*
Use the verbs on the right.

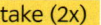 take (2x) talk to   look at

1. The girls are … 2. The brothers are … 3. They're … 4. The boys are …

b) *Now write your sentences in German. What's the rule?*

c) *Complete these sentence pairs so that they make sense.*

1. a) The children hurt themselves when …   b) The children hurt each other when …
2. a) Some students teach themselves to …   b) Some students help each other to …
3. a) Claire told the girls to look after   b) Claire told the girls to look at each other …
themselves …

Lösung: a) 1. … taking a photo of themselves. 2. … looking at themselves. 3. … talking to each other. 4. … taking a photo of each other. **b)** Rule: You use 'each other' to talk about interaction between people (when they're doing the same action).

GRAMMAR

16 Talking about each other → G3

Read what two teenagers say about boys and girls. Decide if you need an object pronoun (me, him, her etc.), a reflexive pronoun (myself, himself, herself etc.) or each other.

A. What boys think about girls

I look at **1** once in the morning and that's
enough, but girls are always looking at **2** !
They worry more about what people think
of **3** . And girls aren't good with secrets.
For example, my sister and I sometimes tell **4**
secrets. If my sister tells **5** a secret, I never
tell anyone else. If I tell **6** a secret, she can't
keep it to **7** . And they think they know
everything about boys, but they don't really
understand **8** . Keep your silly comments
about boys to **9** , girls!

B. What girls think about boys

Boys don't know how to behave **10** . I'd never
forgive **11** if I behaved like a boy. They're often
nasty to **12** , but they don't understand – you
aren't just hurting the other person. You're
hurting **13** too, because then people don't
like **14** . I think we always behave **15** – well,
most of the time! Also, boys never talk about
anything real. If a boy has a problem, he
keeps it to **16** . If you try to talk to **17** about
something serious, they just make silly jokes.
Girls share their problems with **18** .

Lösung: 1. myself, 2. themselves, 3. them, 4. each other, 5. me, 6. her, 7. herself, 8. us, 9. yourselves, 10. themselves, 11. myself, 12. each other, 13. yourself, 14. you, 15. ourselves, 16. himself, 17. them, 18. each other

SPEAKING MK

WB 11/19–20

Look here
for help with
your poll:
🌐 8pv3xf

3 11/19–20: Writing
alogue); Mediation
alogue completion)

17 Your turn: Typical statements

a) *Collect more things that parents often say to their children and make a* <u>poll</u>.

Practice makes perfect. | You have to push yourself. | Tidy up your room. |
Money doesn't grow on trees. | I feel like I'm talking to myself.

b) *Do the poll to find out which things
parents say most often.*

some | a few | lots of | most | nearly all |
almost all | a couple of | about half | … <u>per cent</u> of …

c) *Present the results in class.*

How to compromise

In the classroom, with friends, at home – it's normal to agree, to disagree and to try to find a compromise. This page can help you to practise typical situations.

Yes, you've got a point. I've never thought about it like that. – OK, I've got an idea: Why don't we …

1 The language of compromising

WB 12/21

Make a grid with the headings below. Then add the phrases in the box to your grid under the right heading:

– Asking for an opinion
– Making a suggestion
– Agreeing
– Disagreeing
– Finding a compromise

KV 5: Can we meet halfway?
Voc.: How to compromise, p. 197
WB 12/21: Skills (dialogue completion, correct order)

Useful phrases

Why don't we …? | I don't think that's a good idea / necessary. | It's not always possible to have it all. | It's not that simple. | You're right. | Yes, we should do that. | Can we meet halfway? | How do you feel about …? | I've got an idea. Can we …? | You've got a point, but … | No, I don't mind doing that. | What do you think about …? | If we did it this way, we could … | It would be better to …

2 Listening: Finding a compromise

1/10–11

a) *Listen to this family as they try to agree about something. Then answer the questions:*

1. What does Matt want to do?   2. What problems do his parents have with the idea?
3. Why does Matt feel misunderstood?   4. What compromise do they find?

b) *Listen again. Mark the phrases that they use in your grid from ex. 1.*

c) *What do you think about how the conversation ended?*
Who do you think is the happiest about the decision?
Lösung: b) What do you think about …? / I don't think that's … / I've got an idea. Can …? / I don't mind doing that. / You've got a point, but …

3 Finding a compromise   → More help ○ 127/13

KV 5: Can we meet halfway?

a) *Choose **one** of the conflicts. Write out the discussion and find a compromise.*

1. Dave wants to become an influencer for computer games, but his parents say no.
2. Jay blames his parents because he didn't get the lead part in a dance show: They don't believe in him. They want him to use his time for school and they give him little time for dance practice.
3. When Olivia isn't around, Claire talks to Lucy about her messy room and changing her hobbies too often.

b) *Role play: Act out your discussion from a). You can film it too.*

Solving a conflict

In this task, you're going to work in groups and solve a conflict. Later you're going to present the conflict in a <u>storyboard</u>.

Look here
for help:
🌐 8pv3xf

B 13/22: Writing
(matching, reaction to
comment)

Step 1

Get organised → WB 13/22

*Get into groups of four and choose **one** of the situations below.*

1. You want a tattoo / piercing / nose <u>stud</u>. Your parents disagree.
2. Your best friends don't agree with the guest list for your birthday party.
3. You have a great idea for a fun day with friends, but your friends have other ideas.
4. You've got a new hobby, but your friends think it's a bad idea.
5. You want to take part in a talent show, but your parents/friends don't believe in you / think you've got no talent.
6. You want to post videos to become a social media star. Your parents disagree.

Step 2

Collect pros → WB 13/22

Work in pairs. Two students take one side of the conflict, and the other two take the other side of the conflict.

Each pair collects pros for their side.

Step 3

Write out your discussion

Think about how many people are taking part in the discussion and then write it out. Use the pros that you collected in Step 2.
→ conditional sentences G1–2 → phrases for compromising p. 18 → <u>proofreading</u> S11

Step 4

Practise your discussion

Decide which role each of you will play and practise your discussion. Think about your voice, <u>facial expressions</u> and <u>body language</u> too.
→ pronunciation S15 → role play S16

Step 5

Your storyboard → WB 13/23

*Now make a storyboard for your conflict.
Then you can use it to make a photo story or film.
Present your result in class.*

B 13/23: Writing
(storyboard)

1/12–18 🎧 **Hang out with us instead!**

SPEAKING

1 **Before you read** → More help ○ 127/14

What kind of <u>trouble</u> have your brothers / sisters / cousins / friends <u>got into</u> before?
Was it big trouble or not so big?

A Jay was bored and <u>fed up</u>. 'Am I the only person in the world who just wants to have a bit of fun on a Saturday afternoon?' he thought to himself. He felt bad about an <u>argument</u> with
5 Luke. They couldn't agree about anything <u>these days</u>. 'What was our fight about?' Jay couldn't even remember.
'If Dave was here, he'd solve the problem in a moment,' he thought. Dave was always able
10 to find a compromise. But Dave now lived in Cornwall. For a moment, Jay thought about Holly, Olivia and Gwen. 'Maybe we could do something together,' he thought. But then he was sure he didn't need a 'girls day' today.
15 Well, Jay wasn't <u>allowed to</u> go out anyway: He was in trouble with his parents for bad marks at school, and so he was <u>grounded</u> until next Friday. What a life!
'But I need to get out of this flat now!' he
20 told himself. 'My parents are out, so why not?' He felt a bit bad because they trusted him, but it made him crazy to stay at home all day. So, he <u>put on</u> his trainers and left. "<u>Freedom</u>!" he shouted. He already felt much better.

B Jay walked towards the park and thought about the next dance show – he was sure he could get the lead part next time. When Jay reached the park, he saw them. Finn and Max. Two of the coolest boys at school. They were
30 two years older and part of the <u>in-crowd</u>. They looked so cool with their skateboards. They were laughing about something. 'About me?' Jay hoped not. As he came closer, he felt a bit nervous, but he didn't need to: The boys were
35 very friendly to him.
"Hey Jay!" said Finn, the <u>blond</u> boy. He was the in-crowd's 'boss'.
'He knows my name?!' Jay thought.
"Hey, what's up?" asked Max.
40 Jay wasn't sure how to answer. *Nothing* was up – that was the problem.

"We're going to go down to <u>the high street</u> for some coffee. Do you want to come with us and hang out?" Finn asked.
'Hanging out with the cool <u>blokes</u>. Luke 45 will be so jealous!' he thought. But Jay tried to act cool and not show how excited he really felt. "Sure. I've got an hour before I need to be somewhere else," he told them.

C When they were all in the café, Jay started to 50 relax a bit. Finn and Max were friendly and asked Jay a lot of questions. 'I can't believe they're interested in me,' he thought.
"Your brother is the model with the cool clothes, right?" Finn asked. 55
"Yeah, that's him," Jay answered.
"All the girls think he looks great," Max added.
"I don't see it myself," Jay answered, and they all laughed. They chatted about films and 60 video games and found they liked the same things. Jay told them about his problems with Luke, and how he missed Dave. Finn and Max understood.
"Jay, you need some new friends," Finn said. 65 "Your old friends are boring. Hang out with us instead!"

> **What are your ideas:**
> What's going through Jay's head?

D "Your brother Shahid isn't just a model, he's a DJ too," Max said.

70 "Yeah," Finn added, "he's got some really cool mixes. We're planning a big party for next Saturday for cool people."

"So," Max added, "would you <u>be able to</u> borrow Shahid's laptop? Just for the night?"

75 "He'll never lend it to me," Jay said.

"Hey Max, maybe you were right. Jay isn't cool enough for us," Finn said.

Not cool enough? Before he could stop himself, Jay said, "Wait! Er, Shahid is going to
80 be away next Saturday. He's got an <u>overnight</u> modelling job in Manchester."

"Great! You can just borrow his laptop and he'll never know!" Max said.

"So, come to our party with the laptop –
85 but without your boring friends," Finn said.

"Well ...," Jay didn't know what to say.

"Max wasn't sure about you, but I think you're cool. I'll give you my mobile number. Text me later if it's yes or no," Finn added.

> **What are your ideas:**
> What would you do in Jay's shoes?

E Back home, Jay didn't know what to do. Were his old friends really so boring? Were his new friends really friends at all? And how could he go behind Shahid's <u>back</u> like that? Jay had to decide. Finally, he texted Finn these words:
95 **cu on saturday. WITH the laptop.** ☺

F Jay had an awful week. Shahid knew Jay didn't feel so great, but he thought it was because of his bad marks. Shahid had more time for Jay than <u>usual</u> and told him about his
100 conversation with Claire at Olivia's house. "It's funny. Now I know that not all families are the same." Shahid <u>treated</u> Jay like an adult – and Jay only thought about his plan to take Shahid's music. He felt bad. But it was too
105 late to change things now. Before he knew it, it was Saturday evening and Jay was at Finn's front door. Finn opened the door, smiled and grabbed the laptop out of Jay's hands.

G At the party Shahid's music sounded fantastic. His brother was a great DJ! Everyone was
110 dancing, but nobody was interested in Jay. 'And I'm wearing my coolest outfit!' he thought. Finn and Max <u>ignored</u> him too. But suddenly three <u>pretty</u> girls <u>came up to</u> Jay.
He smiled at them.
115
"Ohh, <u>poor</u> baby. Have you lost your <u>mummy</u>, little boy?" one of them asked, and everyone laughed.

Jay felt so stupid. 'Where's Luke when I really need him?' Jay asked himself. He really
120 missed his friend.

Then the music suddenly stopped. People started to leave. "What a stupid party!" some of them said. "No music, no party. Let's go!" others shouted. Jay then knew that something was
125 very wrong.

"Hey Jay," Finn shouted. "Max dropped the laptop and now it's dead. So, now we haven't got any music!"

"Yeah, thanks for nothing," Max added.
130 "If your brother made real money as a model or DJ, he could buy something better than this <u>piece of junk</u> here!"

They didn't notice that Jay was white with <u>anger</u>. And they didn't care. Jay grabbed his
135 brother's laptop, ran out the door and ran all the way home.

Back in his room, he saw that Finn and Max were right: The laptop really was dead! It didn't work – at all. What would his brother
140 do when he came home? Jay had one night to think about it. 'And this is going to be one very long night,' he knew.

SPEAKING

2 **Your reaction**

What do you think about Jay's story? Share your ideas.

READING

3 **Understanding the story** → S5

WB 14/24–25

WB 14/24–25: Reading (matching pictures to text); Reading (true/false)

a) *Think of good headings for parts A–G of the story.*

b) *Which of the themes on the right are important in the story? Say why.*

Example:
Jay really wants to be popular. That's important in the story because … That's why he …

Lösung: a) A: Lonely Jay finds his freedom, B: An exciting meeting in the park, C: Hanging out with the cool boys, D: The in-crowd's rules, E: Jay wants to fit in with the in-crowd, F: The big lie, G: Nobody is interested in Jay

> **Word bank**
>
> | | |
> |---|---|
> | **Nouns:** | the in-crowd \| peer pressure \| freedom \| fun \| excitement |
> | **Verbs:** | fit in \| go behind somebody's back \| lie to somebody |
> | **Adjectives:** | lonely \| cool \| popular \| new \| old \| confused \| boring \| honest |

SPEAKING

4 **Role play: Turning points in the story** → S6

a) *First, read the skills box. Then find the other turning points for Jay in the story.*

b) *Choose **one** of the turning points from a). Imagine that Jay is having a video chat with Dave about what to do at one of the turning points. What advice would Dave give him? How would Jay react to Dave's advice? Write a short dialogue between them.*

c) *Act out your dialogues in class with your partner.*

Lösung: a) Turning points: lines 19–24, lines 65–67, lines 90–95

> **Reading skills**
>
> A **turning point** is a part of a story where a character must make a decision about what to do next. The decision can be good – or bad – for the character and for others.
>
> **Example:** In Part A you find the story's first turning point. Jay was grounded but decided to leave the house anyway. Good or bad idea?

WRITING

5 **What happens next?** → S11

WB 14/26

WB 14/26: Writing/ Speaking (options)

a) *When Shahid comes back from his modelling job in Manchester, Jay needs to tell him about his laptop. How do you think Shahid will react? Choose an idea for the story's ending and follow the instructions.*

1. Jay decides to get help from his friends.
   → Go to **A**.
2. Jay tells his parents. → Go to **B**.
3. Jay tells nobody – he helps himself. → Go to **C**.
A. Dave can ask his new friends in Cornwall.
   OR Gwen is good with computers. She's clever and knows what to do.
B. They tell Shahid.
   OR They're upset, but they promise to help.
C. Jay finds help on the internet.
   OR Jay takes Shahid's laptop to an IT expert.

> **Word bank**
>
> at first \| then \| suddenly \| finally \| feel awful / bad / sorry / scared / guilty \| be shocked / horrified \| shout angrily / loudly \| need a lot of money / more information / a really good IT expert \| explain / fix carefully \| be thankful \| relax

b) *Now write the ending. When you've finished, exchange texts with a partner and give each other feedback.*

When Sean came to visit

SPEAKING

1 **Warm-up: How would you react?**

Imagine that you aren't good at something (e.g. a sport, dancing), but you have to do it in front of other people. They can see that you're having problems, and maybe they <u>tease</u> you about it.

How would you react? Would you …

| laugh about it yourself? | feel really embarrassed? | just ignore it? | become angry? |

Or do you have other ways to deal with situations like this?

VIEWING

2 **Sean, the cousin from Northern Ireland** → S14

1

a) *Watch the film. What do you think about Sean and Nathan?*

b) *Answer the questions. The words in the box can help you.*

The basketball scene:
1. How did Nathan get on Sean's nerves?
2. How did Sean react?
3. How did Laura react?

The park <u>bench</u> scene:
1. What was so embarrassing for Nathan?
2. How could Sean help Nathan?

> **Word bank**
>
> have a <u>sense of humour</u> | <u>feel sorry for</u> somebody | be <u>optimistic</u> | <u>cheer somebody up</u> | be a <u>show-off</u> | <u>apologise</u> | mean / not mean it | post / <u>delete</u> something on a <u>wall</u> | be careful with <u>account settings</u>

The ending:
1. How did things <u>work out</u> in the end?
2. What do you think of the ending?

3 **Three different personalities** → S14, S11

VIEWING

WB 15/27

c.: Describing different
rsonalities, p. 200
3 15/27: Writing (film
ene)

a) *Watch the film again. In a grid take notes about what each person is good at, and what adjectives could describe him / her. Then look at the diagram on p. 9 again. What smart types do you think Sean, Nathan and Laura are? Share your ideas.*

WRITING

b) *Think of how you could change the basketball scene so that it shows Nathan as more 'people smart'. Write a short dialogue between Nathan and Sean.*

Lösung: a) Sean: logic smart, Nathan: body smart/self smart, Laura: people smart; **b)** Nathan is a good basketball player so maybe he could teach Sean how to play better. When Marley says, "No! Not again, Sean! I can't believe it!" Nathan tries to help Sean.

Can you . . .

1. talk about different interests and personalities?	Olivia is creative and pushes herself. She makes models and teaches herself the sax.
2. express conditions that are possible or probable?	If I practise hard, I'll become a successful football player.
3. express conditions that aren't possible or probable?	If you just dropped out of school now, you wouldn't have any choices later.
4. use phrases for agreeing, disagreeing and compromising?	Why don't we go to the cinema? – That's a good idea.

GRAMMAR

1   If I learn HTML, . . .

*Read the information about David Karp. What were David's thoughts at the different times before and during his career? Complete his sentences and make **conditional sentences type 1**.*

Tumblr <u>founder</u> **David Karp** began learning HTML at the age of 11 and soon started to design websites for businesses. "I always used a deep voice when I was on the phone so people didn't know how young I was!" he says. Karp dropped out of school at the age of 15 and <u>developed</u> Tumblr, a social media website, in the bedroom of his mother's small flat. In 2009 he won the award for **Best Young Tech Entrepreneur** in **Business Week**.

Example: 1. Companies will pay me to design their websites if I learn HTML.

go back to school	not know how young I am	learn HTML ✔	win awards and become rich

have more time for my business ideas	live at home for the first few years	sell my business

1. Companies will pay me to design their websites if I …   **2.** If I drop out of school, I …   **3.** But if I'm not successful, I …   **4.** If I use a deep voice on the phone, people …   **5.** I'll save money if I …   **6.** If my business is a big success, I …   **7.** I'll have more than <u>a billion</u> dollars if I …

Lösung: 2. …, will have more time for my business ideas. 3. …, will go back to school. 4. …, will not know how young I am. 5. … live at home for the first few years. 6. …, will win awards and become rich. 7. … sell my business.

GRAMMAR

2   Why I can't go to the school dance

*Jack is angry because he's been grounded and can't go to the school dance. Complete the **conditional sentences type 2**.*

1. If I ▨ (not be) grounded, I'd go to the school dance. I love dancing.
2. If I had better marks, I ▨ (not be) grounded. It's so boring here at home.
3. If I ▨ (pay) attention at school, I ▨ (have) better marks. I'd really like to be more successful.
4. If I ▨ (enjoy) class more, I ▨ (pay) attention. But it's so hard.
5. If English ▨ (be) easier, we ▨ (not have to) learn so much grammar. Who needs grammar?
6. If the school ▨ (compromise) and didn't make me write texts, English ▨ (be) so much easier.
7. German isn't as hard as English. I bet if I ▨ (ask) my teacher, she ▨ (disagree) with me.
   So, you see – it's all because of English. That's why I can't go to the school dance!

Lösung: 1. weren't, 'd go; 2. had, wouldn't be; 3. paid, 'd have; 4. enjoyed, 'd pay; 5. was/were, wouldn't have to, 6. compromised, would be; 7. asked, 'd disagree

GRAMMAR

3 Help! I can't do it myself!

Lucy is tidying up her room – but not alone. Complete the dialogue with the right forms.

Lucy: I'm going to tidy up my room. Can you help **1** , Olivia?

Olivia: No, I can't. Do it **2** , Lucy.

Claire: Why can't you help **3** ?

Olivia: Why should I? When I was a little girl, I always tidied up my room **4** .

Claire: Well, not exactly: I often helped **5** , remember? I tidied up your wardrobe for **6** !

Olivia: Well, maybe you're right. But it wasn't very often, believe me! And …

Lucy: Can you two please stop fighting now and show **7** where I can put my old clothes? I've already tidied up my wardrobe **8** !

Lösung: 1. me, 2. yourself, 3. her, 4. myself, 5. you, 6. you, 7. me, 8. myself

VOCABULARY

4 Different smart types

a) *Kim and John spent the day together in Lonchester. Read what they say about their day.*

Kim:
The day in Lonchester was fantastic. It's a cool place. It was my first time there, but every <u>underground</u> in every city is almost the same. You just follow the colours and numbers! I found a great place for lunch – not where all the tourists go. I watched some children our age, and then we went where they went. I didn't go to Lonchester to hang out with tourists! John wanted to go to the harbour, but the first street looked like trouble, so we took a different street, turned right, then left, then right and got there safely. I asked a few people and then we got a free tour of one of the ships!

John:
I really enjoyed our day in Lonchester. 625,000 people live there, but more than a million people work there. It's the home of a big biscuit company. It took us 37 minutes to get there by underground. In the afternoon the trains leave every hour, always at half past. A famous person designed the train station. We ate lunch at 12 o'clock and it only cost £3. The harbour was interesting because about 20 ships arrive and depart every day. It's the second biggest harbour in the south of England.
You can't usually take tours of the ships, but we were lucky! Kim just asked. I didn't know that was possible.

Lösung: b) Street smart: every underground is almost the same; just follow colours and numbers; to go to lunch how kids your age and eat what they have; don't follow tourists; if a street looks like trouble, look for a different one that is safer; ask people for help or free tours; Book smart: know facts about the big biscuit company; know about times; train station by famous architect; lunch at 12 o'clock for £3; the harbour is the biggest in the south of England and 20 ships arrive and depart every day

b) *What's the difference between 'street smart' and 'book smart'? Make a grid and put in examples from the text.*

c) *Are you more like Kim or John? Explain why you think so. Compare your ideas with a partner.*

Text and media smart 1

Songs and poems

On these Text and media smart pages you're going to deal with songs and poems. You'll learn how to understand their meanings and messages. And, of course, you'll learn how to be a songwriter or a poet yourself.

SPEAKING

1 Songs and poems in your life → S22

a) *Have you ever learned a song or a poem by heart, e.g. for a music lesson, a concert, a song contest, for a birthday, Mother's Day or Christmas? What was the song about? Was it easy or difficult for you to remember the lines? How did you feel when you performed the song or poem? Talk about your experiences.*

b) *Make notes on these questions:*

- What kind of music or poems do you like?
- Who is your favourite singer or poet? What language are his or her texts in?
- Where do you listen to music or read poems?
- When do you listen to music or read poems?
- Why do you listen to music or read poems?

Useful phrases

What?	Where?	When?	Why?
– **music:** rock, pop, jazz, … – **poems:** shape poems, nursery rhymes, twitter poems, Instagram poetry, …	– on the way to school – in my room – in bed – in a café – at a concert – at a club	– happy / sad – do my homework – do sports – with my friends – get ready for school – go out – during the lunch break	– to relax – to entertain myself – interested in literature/poetry – to make me think – to get ideas

c) *Milling around: Now mill around in the classroom and exchange your ideas in b) with five other classmates.*

2 A good songwriter or poet

WRITING

a) *Read this statement and write down your ideas about it. Do you think that this statement is true? Say why or why not.*

> Only someone with very sad or very happy emotions can be a good songwriter or poet.

SPEAKING

b) *Can you imagine writing a poem or song text? What could be an occasion for you to write a poem, or a song, e.g. a birthday present, for a friend/your parents, for a school concert?*

Say it with a song

3 A song

VOCABULARY

a) *Before you listen to the song, make a mind map about what friendship means to you.*

LISTENING 1/19

b) *Close your eyes and listen to the song. What's your first impression? Do you like it? Say why or why not.*

True Friend
by Hannah Montana (Miley Cyrus)

We sign our cards and letters BFF
You've got a million ways to make me laugh
You're lookin' out for me, you've got my back
It's so good to have you around

5 You know the secrets I could never tell
And when I'm quiet you break through my
   shell
Don't feel the need to do a rebel yell
Cause you keep my feet on the ground

10 You're a true friend
You're here till the end
You pull me aside
When something ain't right
Talk with me now and into the night
15 'Til it's alright again
You're a true friend

You don't get angry when
   I change the plans
Somehow you're never out
20 of second chances
Won't say "I told you" when
   I'm wrong again
I'm so lucky that I've found

A true friend
You're here till the end   25
You pull me aside
When something ain't right
Talk with me now and into the night
'Til it's alright again

True friends will go to the end of the earth 30
Till they find the things you need
Friends hang on through the ups and the
   downs
Cause they've got someone to believe in

A true friend   35
You're here till the end
You pull me aside
When something ain't right
Talk with me now and into the night
No need to pretend   40

You're a true friend
You're here till the end
Pull me aside
When something ain't right
Talk with me now and into the night   45
'Til it's alright again

You're a true friend
You're a true friend
You're a true friend

READING

4 **Understanding the song** → More help ○ 128/1 → More practice ● 128/2

WB 16/1

16/1: Reading (song)

a) *Read the text and say in your own words what the song is about.*

b) *What makes the singer's friend a true friend? Give examples from the song text.*

c) *Compare the examples from the text with your own ideas in ex. 3a).*

d) *Look at the title of the song and say if you think it's a good choice or not.*

Lösung: a) The song is about what it means to be a true friend. **b)** Vgl. Lösung *Diff pool* 128/1, SB S. 295; **d)** The titel 'True friend' is a good choice because the song is about true friendship. Every line of the song describes this friendship.

VOCABULARY

5 Focus on language → More help ○ 128/3 → More practice ● 128/4

a) *Look at the following lines from the song and think about their message. Explain in your own words what the singer wants to say.*

quote from the text	meaning
you break through my shell *(ll. 6–7)*	…
keep my feet on the ground *(l. 9)*	…
will go to the end of the earth *(l. 30)*	…

b) *Read the skills box and think about why the songwriter uses this kind of figurative language.*

c) *Read the lines from the text and compare them to the lines in a). Do you have to think about their meaning too? Say why or why not.*

- You know the secrets I could never tell *(l. 5)*
- You don't get angry when I change the plans *(ll. 17–18)*
- Won't say "I told you" when I'm wrong again *(ll. 21–22)*

d) *Read the phrases and match the figurative meaning with the literal meaning. Use a dictionary for help.*

1. to let the cat out of the bag
   a) to tell a secret
   b) to let the cat <u>escape</u>
   c) to <u>free</u> cats from <u>cages</u>

2. as quiet as a mouse
   a) not to tell any secrets
   b) to be very quiet
   c) only to come out when nobody is there

3. poker face
   a) good at telling <u>lies</u>
   b) a facial expression that hides your true feelings
   c) good at playing cards

4. that's music to my <u>ears</u>
   a) that hurts my ears
   b) I can hear now
   c) that's good news

5. to do it behind <u>closed</u> doors
   a) to have a surprise party when your parents are out
   b) to feel safe by closing doors
   c) to do something in secret

Lösung: a) Vgl. Lösung *Diff pool* 128/3, SB S. 295; **b)** The songwriter uses figurative language to create images/a visual impression in the reader's or listener's mind. **c)** The lines in a) use figurative language, so you have to think about their meaning. The lines in c) use literal language, so the words and phrases tell you exactly what they mean. You don't have to think about it. **d)** 1. a), 2. b), 3. b), 4. c), 5. c)

READING

6 What makes a song <u>catchy</u>?

a) *Read the definition of '<u>chorus</u>' in the skills box and find it in the song on p. 27.*

b) *What else makes the song catchy?*

> You can dance to it. | You can't <u>keep your feet or hands still!</u> | It's easy to <u>sing along</u> to. | You hear some of the words again and again. | It makes you feel happy. | You can't <u>get it out of your head</u> for a long time because the music is so great. | …

Reading skills

A **chorus** is a line or group of lines that are <u>repeated</u> a couple of times in a song. A chorus is used to make a song catchy or to <u>emphasize</u> a message in a song.

c) *Give examples of songs for the ideas you haven't used in b).*
Lösung: a) (You're) a true friend / You're here till the end / You pull me aside / When something ain't right / Talk with me now and into the night / 'Til it's alright again / (You're a true friend)

VOCABULARY

7 Taking a closer look

a) *Read the skills box. Find rhyming words at the end of the lines in the song on p. 27 and describe the <u>effect</u> that they have on you.*

MK

b) *Find more <u>rhyming</u> words for "friend".*

c) *Write a new chorus using rhyming words.*
Lösung: a) tell – shell – yell; friend – end – pretend; right – night: **b)** blend / lend / mend / send / spend / trend / recommend / …;
c) You're a true friend / I love the time that we spend / I can always trust you / We always find something fun to do / Don't leave me ever / We'll be friends forever / You're a true friend

Reading skills

Songs can have **rhymes**. They help to emphasize the <u>rhythm</u> of the song or to emphasize a part of a song like the chorus. Rhyme words also help listeners to remember the lines of the song.

LISTENING

8 Music

1/19

c.: Musical instruments, 3 (Word bank), p. 12

a) *Listen again. Does the music match the content of the song?*

Start: The music matches the content because …

| positive atmosphere | harmony | <u>rhythmic</u> <u>beat</u> | good emotions | friendly voice | … |

b) *Listen again and focus on the instruments. Which ones can you hear?*
Lösung: b) piano/keyboard, guitar, drums

WRITING

9 Your turn: Be a songwriter! → More help ○ 129/5

WB 16/2

16/2: Writing (song)

World Music Day, 21st June, celebrates music. This is the day to listen to your favourite songs or to write a song. Write a song for your best friend. You can use your ideas from your mind map in ex. 3a). Remember to use figurative and literal language and to use rhyme words and a chorus.

SPEAKING **MK** 10

Online or offline music

Do a survey among your classmates and find out about these things. Then present your results.

Look here for help with your survey:
🌐 9bw99z

6: Tandem activity: rossword

- Do they listen to music online or offline?
- Do they buy their music online or offline?
- How many hours per day do they listen to music online or offline?
- How much are your classmates happy to pay for a song / an album / a flat rate?

Media skills

Have you ever downloaded a film or music from the internet or shared it with another person? Which website did you use? Read the '<u>terms</u>' on that website. Was your action <u>legal</u>?

Say it with a poem

LISTENING **11** Twinkle, twinkle, little star!

1/20  *Jamie and his brother Oliver are in a <u>bookshop</u>. Oliver is looking for a book about poems. Listen to their conversation and do the tasks below.*

1. What are the two brothers talking about? 2. Explain why Oliver <u>prefers</u> poems. 3. Explain why Jamie prefers songs. 4. Explain what poems and songs <u>have in common</u> and what is different.
Lösung: 1. The boys are talking about songs and poems. 2. Oliver prefers poems because he enjoys the power of the words. … 3. Jamie prefers songs because music is cool. … 4. Both songs and poems can have a beat, a rhythm, a message, figurative language and rhymes, but only songs have music.

READING **12** A poem

1/21 **a)** *Read the poem. What's your first impression? Say in your own words what the poem is about too.*

Voc.: Words for talking about songs and poems, p. 203

Best Friend by Mizscorpio

You are my best friend; you belong in my heart.
We go through ups and downs, but still nothing can tear us apart.
I know you as a sister, and I will always care.
Love, respect, and <u>trust</u> are the things we share.

5 I know you as a person; I especially know you as a friend.
Our friendship is something that will never end.
Right now, this <u>second</u>, this minute, this day,
Our sisterhood is here, is here to stay.

My friendship with you is special and true.
10 When we are together, we <u>stick</u> like <u>glue</u>.
When I'm in the darkness that needs some light,
When you're by my side, I know things are all right.

Our friendship is so strong; it breaks down bars.
Our friendship is also <u>bright</u>, like the sun and the stars.
15 If we were in a competition for friendships, we would get a gold,
Because <u>responsibility</u> and <u>cleverness</u> are the keys we hold.

I met you as a <u>stranger</u>, took you as a friend.
I hope our long friendship will never end.
Our friendship is like a <u>magnet</u>; it pulls us together,
20 Because <u>no matter</u> where we are, our friendship will <u>last</u> forever!

b) *Which stanza do you like best? Explain why.*

Reading skills

A **stanza** is a <u>series</u> of lines in poems and songs. They are separated from each other by an empty line.

Useful phrases

The first/second/… stanza makes me feel … |
I like the atmosphere/language … |
The stanza sounds … | When I hear …, I think of … | The stanza <u>reminds</u> me of … .

Lösung: a) The poem is about friendship.

13 Understanding the poem → S6

a) *Read the line below and then the whole poem again. Is the speaker in the poem a boy or girl? Give <u>evidence</u> from the poem.*

> "I know you as a person; I especially know you as a friend." *(l. 5)*

b) *The poet uses figurative language. Read the skills box and find three examples from the text of a simile and one example of a metaphor.*

c) *Explain the effect that figurative language has on you.*

d) *Create figurative language yourself. Complete these sentences with a simile or a metaphor.*

1. My friendship …
2. My feelings for you are …
3. With you I am happy …
4. Being without you is …

Lösung: c) Figurative language creates emotions and pictures in our minds. **d)** 1. My friendship is a harbour. 2. My feelings for you are a s deep as the sea. 3. With you I am happy like a day in spring. 4. Being without you is like a cold and stormy winter night.

> **Reading skills**
>
> **Figurative language:**
> A **simile** is used to describe something by comparing it with something else by using the words "like" or "as."
> Example: My love is like a fire burning in my heart.
> A **metaphor** compares two things to create a visual impression but <u>leaves out</u> the words "like" or "as".
> Example: My love is a fire burning in my heart.

14 Rhymes in poetry → S6

a) *Find rhyming words at the end of the lines and describe their structure with the help of the skills box.* → More help ○ 129/6

b) *Read the poem a couple of times <u>half-aloud</u>. Then <u>read</u> it <u>out loud</u> to your partner. Take turns.*

MK

c) *This is an <u>unfinished</u> version of the third stanza. Complete it with your own ideas and rhyming words. Use a rhyming dictionary if necessary.* → More practice ● 129/7

My friendship with you is special and true.
When we are together, …
When I'm in the darkness …
When you're by my side, …

Lösung: a) AABBCCDD; **c)** …, there's just me and you. / …, you show me the way. / …, I know I'm OK.

> **Reading skills**
>
> **Rhyme** is the repetition of similar sounds. In poetry the most <u>common</u> kind of rhyme is the end rhyme. This means the last word in a line <u>rhymes</u> with the last word in another line. Common rhyme schemes are AABB; ABAB or AABBCCDD.
>
> Poems that don't rhyme or don't have a clear structure are called **free verse** poems.

15 Your turn: A friendship poem → More help ◖ 129/8

Write a short poem for your best friend. Use figurative language and a rhyme scheme.

READING

16 More poems

1/23–25

WB 18/5

WB 18/5: Reading (summary, matching)

Lösung: a) 1. The poem is about things that you do in a friendship. 2. This poem is a promise of a friendship that will last forever. 3. This poem compares a friendship to a cloud. **b)+c)** The poems in ex. 16 are examples of free verse poems. Each has a different structure. While each of the free verse poems has just one stanza and no rhyming words, the poem 'Best Friend' in ex. 12 has five stanzas and uses an AABBCCDD end rhyme scheme.

a) *Get together in groups of three. Each of you reads **one** of the poems below and the skills box. Then tell your partners what your poem is about. Do you like it? Explain why or why not.*

> ### Reading skills
>
> An **acrostic** is a type of poem in which the first letter of each line spells out one word, a message, a sentence or the alphabet.
>
> A **haiku** is a Japanese poem with a clear structure. It always has three lines. The first line has five syllables. The second has seven, and the last has five syllables.
>
> In a **shape poem** the words are arranged to look like the thing that you are writing about.

b) *Tell your partners about the structure of your poem. What is special about it?*

c) *Compare the structure of these three poems with the poem in ex. 12. Which structure do you prefer? Explain why.*

Friendship (author unknown)

F eeling for <u>one another</u>
R eading your friend's emotions
I gnoring their flaws
E ntering each other's thoughts
N ever hurting each other
D iscovering a new relation
S etting goals
H elping one another
I nterpreting what's right and wrong
P leasing one another

1

You are my true friend
Our friendship is forever
No matter what comes

2

Our friendship
is beautiful like a cloud. It is mostly pure and snowy white. But when we fight, the cloud turns black and stormy and thunderous. But the storm always passes and we fly together through the snowy white again.

3

WRITING

17 Your turn: Be a poet!

WB 19/6

WB 19/6: Writing (shape poem)

For International Friendship Day, 30th July, write an acrostic for your best friend with his or her name and describe him or her. Present all the acrostics in class.

Example: Nicole

N ice person
I nterested in music
C ool cat
O ften late
L oves chocolate
E xcellent friend

Example: Marco

M arvellous
A thletic person
R eliable
C ool
O pen-minded

WB 19/7

3 19/7: Vocabulary
ossword)

SPEAKING **18** **Let's check: Songs and poems**

a) *Now that you have learned a lot about songs and poems, let's check what you remember.*

> **Partner A:** *Make a list with all the information you have about songs.*
> **Partner B:** *Make a list with all the information you have about poems.*

Discuss the differences and similarities between songs and poems. Then copy the Venn diagram into your exercise book and fill it in.

> **poems**   **poems and songs**   **songs**

b) *Do you prefer songs or poems? Give reasons. Exchange your reasons with a partner.*

READING **19** **Option A: Present a song or a poem**

7: Present a song or
oem

a) *Find a song or poem about friendship **or** your favourite song/poem. Read it carefully and make notes on what it is about, the language, the music if it's a song and why you like it. Find a picture that goes with the song or poem too.*

b) *Use your notes in a) and write a comment on the song or poem.*

c) *Prepare your <u>findings</u> and present them in class.*

WRITING **20** **Option B: Songwriter or poet?**

*Be a songwriter or a poet. Look at the pictures and choose **one**. Then collect ideas before you write a song or poem about it. Use figurative language and rhyming words.*

Reacting to a new situation

VOCABULARY

1 Warm-up: Talking about food

WB 20/1

Voc.: Crockery; Cutlery; Others, WB (Word bank), pp. 13–14
WB 20/1: Vocabulary (odd one out)

A

B

Lösung: a) A: There's a breakfast table with toast, jam, honey and some butter. A woman is pouring tea into a cup. B: The film still shows a plate with sausages, baked beans, a fried egg, grilled tomatoes and bacon.
c) France: croissant, jam, coffee; Sweden: bread rolls, eggs, fish; China: rice/noodle soup, green tea, etc.

a) *Look at the film* <u>stills</u>. *Talk to your partner about what you can see. The word bank can help you.*

b) *Describe your typical breakfast. Compare it with your partner's breakfast. Say what's the same and what's different.*

c) *What other breakfast traditions do you know about?*

Word bank

bowl | <u>plate</u> | <u>mug</u> | <u>cup</u> | spoon | knife | fork | bread | <u>bread rolls</u> | toast | <u>butter</u> | jam | <u>marmalade</u> | <u>honey</u> | cereal | <u>muesli</u> | <u>ham</u> | bacon | tomatoes | baked beans | cheese | eggs | <u>sausages</u> | milk | tea | coffee | sugar

SPEAKING

2 Your turn: Your experiences

a) *Has anyone ever offered you food you didn't like? How did you feel? What did you say or do? Tell each other your experiences.*

b) *What do you think of how your partner reacted? Was he/she polite? Embarrassing? …*

VIEWING

3 Breakfast with the <u>host family</u> (1) → S14

2 **a)** *Watch the film and answer the questions about the two <u>exchange students</u>. Write down key words while you're watching.*

1. Who are Steffen and Brad?
2. Where are they and what are they doing?
3. What are they <u>unfamiliar</u> with? What's different from their own breakfast traditions?

b) *Why do you think there are two versions of the breakfast scene? Choose the right answer.*

A. to show different types of English breakfast
B. to give more information about the same topic
C. to show different reactions to a new situation

Lösung: b) C. to show different reactions to a new situation

4 Breakfast with the host family (2) → S14

VIEWING

a) *Watch the film again. Group A focuses on reaction 1; Group B focuses on reaction 2. Then answer the questions.*

1. Describe what's difficult for Steffen.
2. How does Steffen react?

b) *Talk to a partner from the other group. Discuss which reaction is more <u>appropriate</u>. What would you do in Steffen's situation? Look at the word bank for help.*

VOCABULARY
WB 20/2

B 20/2: Speaking (dialogue situations)

...sung: c)+d) Polite: I usually drink milk, but I'll try some tea. (A) Thank you. This looks interesting! (B) I'm sure English tea is nice too. (A) I'm surprised. It's a very big plate of food. (B) I'm not sure if I can eat it all, but I'll try. (B); ...ss polite: I don't eat hot food this early. (B) I can't eat that much in the morning. (B) ...ever drink tea. I'm not used to it. (A) What is it? I don't think I can drink it! (A) I don't want breakfast. (A+B)

c) *Look at the two stills from the film. Match the phrases in the box below to each scene.*

 A

 B

I usually drink milk, but I'll try some tea. | Thank you. This looks interesting! | I'm sure English tea is nice too. | I don't eat <u>hot</u> food <u>this early</u>. | I can't eat <u>that much</u> in the morning. | I never drink tea. I<u>'m</u> not <u>used to</u> it. | I'm surprised. It's a very big plate of food. | What is it? I don't think I can drink it! | I'm not sure if I can eat it all, but I'll try. | I don't want breakfast.

d) *Make a grid and <u>sort</u> the phrases in c) into polite and less polite ones.*

SPEAKING **5 Role play: A film scene** → S15, S16

a) *In your group from ex. 4, work with the film script. Choose **one** reaction and learn your lines by heart. <u>Rehearse</u> the scene <u>several</u> times.*

Look here for the script: 🌐 r7a6wx

b) *<u>Film</u> your scene and watch it in your group. Do you want to change anything about the way you present your scene? When everyone in your group is happy with it, act it out in class.*

1 The saxophone lessons

LISTENING 1/27
WB 21/1

WB 21/1: Listening (true/false)

a) *Listen to the conversation between Helen and her mum. Then answer the questions.*

1. What's the problem between Helen and her mum?
2. Why does Helen's mum think that it's important to practise?
3. What compromise do they reach?

SPEAKING

b) *What do you think is good or bad about the compromise between Helen and her mum?*
Give reasons for your opinion.

c) *Role play: Act out a conversation with a different compromise. You can use one of these ideas or think of your own compromise:*

> Helen will pay for part of the lessons. | Helen will do extra work around the house to help pay for the lessons. | Helen will continue[1] with the lessons but will do some extra practice for four weeks.

Lösung: b) Good: Missing sth shows you that it is important. Helen learns to practise and how important it is.
Bad: She'll have no lessons at all. Maybe she won't go back to the lessons.

WRITING

2 Follow or don't follow the crowd

WB 21/2
WB 22/3

WB 21/2–22/3: Grammar (conditional sentences type 2); Writing (forum post)

a) *Choose **one** of the cartoons and describe what you can see.*

Crying is cool now.

Lösung: b) Cartoon 1: In my opinion, the cartoon's message is that you shouldn't just follow other people. If everybody just followed the others, we'd all be the same and never be able to discover anything new. Cartoon 2: In my opinion, the cartoon's message is that we shouldn't just follow the crowd. The cartoonist wants to make fun of the fact that if something is 'in' or 'cool', everybody starts doing it, even if it's something silly.

b) *What do you think the cartoon's message is? Do you agree with it? Explain why or why not. The phrases in the box can help you.*

c) *Write a comment about **one** of the cartoons.*

Start: I think you should always try to be … /
Peer pressure can make you … /
It doesn't matter if everybody else …

Useful phrases

In my opinion, the cartoon's message is … |
I think the cartoon wants to show us that … |
The cartoonist wants us to think about … /
wants to make fun of[2] … | I agree / don't agree with the cartoon's message because …

1 to continue to do sth [kən'tɪnjuː] etw. weiterhin machen | **2 to make fun of sb/sth** [ˌmeɪk 'fʌn‿əv] sich über jmdn./ etw. lustig machen

MEDIATION **3**   **The dangers of social media**

At school you have to give a presentation in German on social media. While you're doing some research, you find this article. Take notes on the differences between direct and digital communication in German. Then prepare prompt cards for your presentation. Use a dictionary for help.

The dangers of social media

Psychologists warn that overusing social media can lead to problems with communication and self-esteem.

According to psychologists, young people are supposed to learn how to build relationships and communicate successfully as they grow up.

Before the digital age they did that mostly in direct personal interaction or on the phone. They hung out with people of the same age and could see right away how others reacted to them. Today they spend much more time looking at their phones than looking at each other face to face.

Indirect communication makes a difference: One important point is that you can't see the other person's face or body language. This can lead to problems.

Psychologists have found out that you have to take risks if you want to make friends and keep up relationships. You need to be brave to talk about problems.

Social media seem to make these risks smaller. You can hide what you really feel or even use a fake identity. It's also easier to be cruel to other people if you don't have to face them and can't see their reaction.

Psychologists say that it's important for your self-esteem to learn how to say what you think even if the other person doesn't agree with you. Young people should practise direct social interaction before they take part in more serious relationships, e.g. at work.

It's dangerous for a healthy self-esteem that most teenagers want to create a perfect image of themselves. This puts them under a lot of stress, especially if they're online on social media almost all day. They compare themselves with others and many of them would do anything to be popular with other people.

This is actually normal behaviour, but before social media existed, teenagers had more time by themselves and weren't in permanent contact with other people. With 'likes' and 'dislikes' in online media, young people get direct feedback about their personality and they never get a break from the competition.

According to a survey, social media interaction can make people feel better when they use social media for up to 1.5 hours a day, but if they use it for a longer time, the result is the opposite: People start to feel worse the longer they are online. The feeling that they aren't popular with others can hurt their self-esteem and might even lead to depression and suicide.

GRAMMAR

4 Gaming parties

a) *Read the tip.*

> **Tip**
>
> You put adverbs of indefinite time …
> – before the main verb: I **sometimes go** to parties.
> – between the modal and the main verb: I **can usually use** my parents' computer.
> – after the first auxiliary verb: I**'ve already finished** this level.
>
> In negative sentences you put adverbs of indefinite time after 'not':
> Sam **can't always** come to the party.
> Except for 'sometimes': They **sometimes don't behave** themselves very well.
>
> If 'be' is the main verb in the sentence, the adverb comes after the form of 'be':
> The parties are **always** great fun.
> Except for 'sometimes': The friends **sometimes aren't** fair when they play against each other.

b) *Put the adverbs of indefinite time into the right position.*

1. Dave can have a gaming party at home. (sometimes)
2. He and his friends try to find a new game. (always)
3. They have played this game before. (never)
4. The friends order¹ pizzas for their gaming parties. (usually)
5. The pizzas don't arrive on time. (sometimes)
6. The parties at the Prestons' house have become a big success. (already)
7. One of the rules at the party is that the friends should play fair. (always)
8. They are late for a party. (hardly ever)

5 Is e-sport really a sport?

GRAMMAR

a) *Complete the text with the simple present or the present progressive form of the verb.*

A lot of people **1** (love) sport, and a lot of people **2** (enjoy) video games, but they are two different things. Aren't they? E-sport **3** (mean) competition events for video gamers. It **4** (become) more and more popular, and we **5** (not talk) about a few teenagers in their bedrooms with laptops. In e-sport today serious professional² players **6** (take part) in big international events, and millions of people **7** (watch) their games online. E-sport isn't usually featured in other big sports events, but this **8** (change). Now the Asian Games **9** (include) e-sport, and even the organisers of the Olympic Games **10** (think about) featuring e-sport in the future. It seems³ that e-sport **11** (move) from a hobby to an important international sport.

SPEAKING

b) *Do you think that e-sport is really a sport? Give reasons for your answer.*

1 **to order** ['ɔːdə] bestellen | 2 **professionel** [prə'feʃnl] professionell | 3 **to seem** [siːm] scheinen

GRAMMAR

6 Dave didn't win …

Complete the email from Dave with verbs in the simple past. Use a positive form (+), negative form (-) or question form (?).

be (6x)   enjoy   have   lose   miss   play (2x)   say   win (3x)

Hi Luke,
Sorry I [+] your call yesterday. That's because I [+] a player in an e-sport competition, and I [-] my phone with me. I [+] three games. I [+] the first two games, but then I [+] against a girl from Brighton. She [+] amazing! I [+] for about ten minutes, and then I [+] out of the competition.
So, I [-] a prize, but I really [+] it!
How [+] your football match yesterday? You [-] anything about it in your email. [?] the weather OK?
I hope it [-] too cold! [?] your team [verb] the match?
Send me an email soon!
Dave

GRAMMAR

7 Let's dance

Alan and Ceri are talking about their plans for the weekend. Complete their conversation with **for** *or* **since** *and* **present perfect forms** *of these verbs:* **(not) be, (not) see, (not) hear, dance, love.** *Remember to use short forms.*

Alan: Hey Ceri, do you want to come to the barn dance[1] with us on Saturday? I [1] to one [2] a long time! And we'd like some girls to come too.

Ceri: Well, I [3] to one [4] last year, and I'm not even sure if I still know what to do.

Alan: I'm sure you'll remember. Just come with us on Saturday.

Ceri: OK, but let's ask Megan too.

Alan: Megan? I [5] her [6] she moved to Swansea last year.

Ceri: She's staying here with her aunt for the holidays. She [7] folk music and dancing [8] she was four years old. She knows the right steps. She [9] at festivals with a group of dancers [10] she went to Swansea.

Alan: Oh, I didn't know that. I [11] from her [12] a very long time. How long [13] (she) back?

Ceri: She [14] back [15] last Saturday. I'll text her – it'll be great to see her again!

GRAMMAR

8 Best friend?

Read about Sarah's problems with her friend Nina. Complete the text with the right tenses: **simple past** *or* **present perfect simple.**

I'm so fed up with Nina. She says she's my best friend, but she always behaves like she can do everything better. Wait – I'll give you an example. Last week at school I [1] (feel) really optimistic about our maths test. I [2] (study) a lot at the weekend, but then Nina [3] (tell) me, "If you don't push yourself more, you'll never get marks as good as mine." I have to tell you this: The worst mark Nina [4] (ever get) was a B. After maths Nina said, "I'll meet you in the cafeteria for lunch!" But during the lunch break she [5] (hang out) with Julia and [6] (ignore) me! I [7] (be) stressed out about Nina for three weeks! But I feel a little better today because I [8] (listen) to a radio call-in last night. A caller said she always relies on herself. She doesn't need other people to feel happy. So, this is my decision now: I'll chill out about Nina and I'll enjoy myself without her! I think it's time for some new friends!

1 **barn dance** ['bɑːn ˌdɑːns] Tanzveranstaltung mit ländlicher Musik

→ Solutions p. 295

Unit 2
Let's go to Scotland!

A Dunnottar Castle near Aberdeen

SPEAKING

1 **Pictures of Scotland**

WB 23/1

WB 23/1: Vocabulary (dialogue completion)

a) *Describe the photos A–E. Which one would most make you want to visit Scotland? Explain why. The phrases in the box can help you.*

b) *Imagine you're on holiday in Scotland. What do you think you can do there? Share your ideas in class.*

Lösung: b) I think in Scotland you can visit castles and festivals. I think Ben Nevis is good for hiking. Glasgow and Edinburgh are great for shopping.

> **Word bank**
>
> beautiful landscape | an old castle | <u>historic</u> houses | busy places | modern buildings | <u>traditional</u> clothes | a popular festival | amazing coastline | go hiking / climbing / mountain biking | go sightseeing / shopping | visit museums

SPEAKING **2** **Your turn: Present your country** → S16, S21

Look here for some help with your slide show:
 3746jr

a) *You want to send your exchange school a six-minute slide show to show what Germany <u>is like</u>. What kind of photos would you choose for the show? Write down your ideas in a placemat, and then agree on your top five.*

b) *Find good photos to go with your top five and use them to make a slide show. Record a comment for each photo and say why it represents Germany. Then present your <u>slide show</u> to the class.*

In Unit 2 you learn

… how to describe a place and the reasons for visiting it. You learn:

- vocabulary for talking about places and things to do,
- how to use <u>passive</u> forms,
- how to talk about past activities in progress,
- how to make a text more interesting.

B Modern Glasgow

C Ben Nevis (1,344 m)

D The Edinburgh Festival Fringe

E Going out in Edinburgh

LISTENING **3** **Ideas about Scotland** → More help ○ 130/1 → S22

a) *What do you think is 'typically Scottish'? Think of what you've read or seen about Scotland before and make notes. Then mill around in the classroom and exchange your ideas.*

1/29–31

b) *Listen to three Scottish teenagers – Jean, Stuart and Carol. What typical ideas about Scotland are they talking about? Match the speakers with the ideas.*

<mark>haggis</mark>   <mark>Scottish accents</mark>   <mark>tartan clothes / kilts</mark>   <mark>bagpipes</mark>   <mark>the Loch Ness Monster</mark>

c.: Typically Scottish, 205; Musical struments, WB ford bank), p. 12

c) *Listen again and note down what the speakers say about each of the topics.*

d) *Your turn: What are typical ideas about Germany? Do you think they're true? Explain why or why not.*

Lösung: b) Jean: the Loch Ness monster; Stuart: haggis, tartan clothes/kilts; Carol: Scottish accents, bagpipes

---

VIEWING **MK** **4** **Logan's Scotland quiz**

WB 23/2

a) *Find the Isle of Skye on a map.*

Look here for the quiz: **3746jr**

b) *Do the quiz to find out more about where Logan lives.*

c) *Would you like to live there? What would or wouldn't you like about living in Scotland?*

B 23/2: Viewing fe in Scotland)

1/32 🎧 ## Is that made with meat?

Gwen and her parents are spending their holiday in Scotland with Gwen's uncle and aunt and their son Ethan, a bagpipe player. Gwen has invited Holly and her sister Amber to come too.

"I hope you're all hungry!" said Kirsty, Gwen's aunt. "We've prepared haggis for you!" It was the girls' first day in Glasgow. Kirsty brought a plate with a large brown thing on it to
5 the table. Then she brought some bowls of vegetables.

"Is that made with meat?" asked Holly as she saw the haggis.

"Yes," said Kirsty. "It's made with meat and
10 then it's been cooked in …"

"I'm a vegetarian," said Holly. "Sorry, I forgot to mention it. I'll just have the vegetables."

"Holly has been a vegetarian since she was
ten," said Amber. "She likes to be different."
15 Ethan laughed, and the others smiled. Holly started to feel embarrassed.

"That's why she always wears pink," Amber went on. "You can see her in her pink jacket with her little pink backpack from a mile away."
20 "I don't wear pink any more. Haven't you noticed?" said Holly in a cold, quiet voice.

"I like your new house," said Gwen as she tried to change the subject. "When was it built?"

"We think it was built about 150 years ago,"
25 said James, Gwen's uncle. "There are thousands of houses like this in Glasgow, but some of them have been pulled down."

"I love your Glasgow accent," said Amber and looked at Ethan. "It sounds so musical."
30 "I like your London accent too," said Ethan. "What's it like to live there?"

"It's great," said Holly. "I like …"

"She's got me to look after her," said Amber. "I tell her and her friends about all the cool places to go. I teach them how to be cool." 35

Ethan laughed again, but nobody else did. Holly stared at the table in front of her.

"Let's play a game," said James and gave Amber a strange look. "I'll tell you something about Glasgow, and our guests must say if it's 40 right or wrong. OK, one: Most of the world's whisky is produced in Glasgow."

"Wrong!" said Holly. "Most of the world's whisky is produced in Scotland, but not in Glasgow." 45

"Correct!" said James. "Two: No ships have been built here since the 1990s."

"Wrong!" said Holly. "The shipbuilding industry isn't that important any more, but some ships are still built here." 50

"Correct again!" said James. "Two big ships were built here last year."

"I showed Holly how to find things out on the internet," said Amber quickly. "That's how she knows all this stuff." 55

Everybody looked at Amber. Then Kirsty said, "More haggis anyone?"

READING ## 1 Big sister – little sister → S5

a) *These are ways that Amber behaves. Give evidence from the text to show this.*

Example: Amber says embarrassing things about Holly: "Holly has been a vegetarian since she was ten. She likes to be different." (lines 13–14)

1. Amber makes fun of Holly   2. Amber plays the older sister   3. Amber shows off

b) *Describe the relationship between Amber and Ethan.*

c) *Why does Amber treat Holly so badly? Explain.*

Lösung: a) 1. ll. 18–19, 2. ll. 33–35, 3. ll. 53–55; **b)** Amber likes Ethan (ll. 28–29). Ethan also seems to like Amber (l. 36). **c)** Amber likes Ethan and wants him to think that she's really cool. That's why she shows off and says embarrassing things to Holly.

GRAMMAR

2 **Find the rule: Passive forms** → G4

Look for **passive forms** *in the text on p. 42 and collect them in a grid like this. Find the rule about how the passive is made in different tenses. What verb forms do you use?*

√ 8: Working with grammar

simple present			simple past			present perfect simple		
subject	'to be'	past participle	subject	…	…	subject	…	…
Haggis	is	made	The house	was		It	has been	

Lösung: Rule: Simple present passive: 'am'/'is'/'are' + past participle; Simple past passive: 'was'/'were' + past participle; Present perfect simple passive: 'have been'/'has been' + past participle

GRAMMAR

3 **Hogmanay** → More help ○ 130/2 → G4

WB 24/3

B 24/3: Grammar (simple present passive)

Write sentences in the simple present passive.

Example: 1. In Scotland people **call** the last day of the year Hogmanay.
→ In Scotland the last day of the year **is called** Hogmanay.

2. Before the new year starts, people **clean** their house.
3. They **celebrate** Hogmanay with street parties.
4. At <u>midnight</u> they **ring** bells and <u>**set off**</u> fireworks.
5. Then people **hold** hands and **sing** "Auld Lang Syne".
6. The first footer – the first person to visit a house in the new year – **gives** a black <u>bun</u> as a gift to the people that live in the house so they won't go hungry in the new year.
7. They **bring** a piece of <u>coal</u> so that the house stays warm.
8. The <u>government</u> **grants** two days of holiday to the Scottish people. (The rest of the UK just has one on New Year's Day.)

Across cultures

"Auld Lang Syne" is an old Scottish song that expresses feelings of friendship. It is sung at midnight on New Year's Eve. How do you celebrate New Year?

Lösung: 2. …, the houses are cleaned. 3. Hogmanay is celebrated …, 4. … bells are rung and fireworks are set off. 5. Then hands are held and … is sung. 6. The people that live in the house are given …, 7. A piece of coal is brought …, 8. Two days of holidays are granted …

GRAMMAR

4 **Famous <u>Scots</u>** → More help ○ 131/3 → S19 → G4

WB 24/4
WB 25/5

B 24/4–25/5: Grammar (simple past passive); Pronunciation (word stress)

a) *A lot of important <u>inventions</u> and <u>discoveries</u> were made by Scots. Use the words to make sentences in the simple past passive.*

Example: first sheep | <u>clone</u> | Scottish <u>scientists</u>
→ The first sheep **was cloned** by Scottish scientists.

Tip

In passive sentences you can use **by …** if you want to say **who** did something.

1. raincoat | <u>invent</u> | Charles Macintosh
2. Penicillin | discover | Alexander Fleming
3. first <u>steam engine</u> | build | James Watt
4. Sherlock Holmes | create | Sir Arthur Conan Doyle
5. first <u>television station</u> | start | John Logie Baird

MK
👥

b) *Find information online about three other famous Scots. Make notes about them as in a). Then exchange your notes and make sentences.*

Lösung: a) 1. The raincoat was invented by Charles Macintosh. 2. Penicillin was discovered by Alexander Fleming. 3. The first steam engine was built by James Watt. 4. Sherlock Holmes was created by Sir Arthur Conan Doyle. 5. The first television station was started by John Logie Baird. **b)** Vgl. Lösung *Diff pool* 131/3, SB S. 296

GRAMMAR

5 **Facts about haggis** → More practice ○ 131/4 → More practice ● 131/5 → G4

WB 25/6–7

KV 9: Scottish dog breeds
WB 25/6–7: Listening (festival programme); Grammar (mixed passive forms)

*Complete the text with passive forms: **simple present**, **simple past** or **present perfect simple**.*

A traditional haggis **1** (make) from a sheep's stomach. It **2** (usually <u>fill</u>) with sheep's heart and other parts of the animal, but there's a <u>vegetarian</u> <u>option</u> too. Haggis **3** (often eat) with <u>mashed</u> <u>potatoes</u> and other vegetables, but you can also find it as a burger with chips, in a pasta <u>sauce</u> or as a pizza ingredient. Most of the world's haggis **4** (make) in Scotland, but it **5** (probably not invent) there. Some say that it **6** (bring) to Britain by the Romans. Others think it came from Scandinavia. Haggis **7** (sell) around the world, but some people say it isn't healthy. That's why it **8** (<u>ban</u>) in the USA since 1971.
Lösung: 1. is made, 2. is usually filled, 3. is often eaten, 4. is made, 5. probably wasn't invented, 6. was brought, 7. is sold, 8. has been banned

GRAMMAR

6 **Active** or **passive?** → G4

WB 26/8

WB 26/8: Grammar (wrong verb forms)

a) *Look at these two sentences. Use the phrases on the right to explain why one sentence is **active** and the other is **passive**. Write down the rule.*

1. My mother makes the best haggis in Scotland.
2. Haggis is made from a sheep's stomach.

not important or clear who does the action

important who does the action

b) *Look at these examples. Say why the passive is or isn't used.*

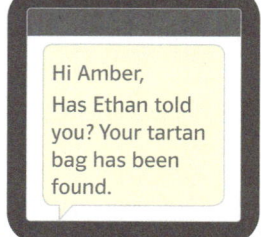

● police 3m
POLICE REPORT
Expensive bagpipes were stolen at Glasgow station.
1

Hi Amber,
Has Ethan told you? Your tartan bag has been found.
2

Hi Ethan,
Can you come and meet me after band practice in front of the cinema? Amber
3

Scottish tennis player **ANDY MURRAY** has been chosen sports star of the decade
4

Lösung: a) Rule: You use the active when it's important who does the action. You use the passive to stress what is done. Often it isn't important or clear who does the action.

GRAMMAR

7 **In Mary King's Close** → G4

WB 26/9

WB 26/9: Grammar (mixed passive forms)

Holly and Gwen are planning their trips to different places in Scotland. They've found this information about a popular attraction in Edinburgh. Put the active sentences into the passive, where possible. Decide if you need the by-agent.

<u>Hundreds of</u> years ago people built very high houses in Edinburgh. They stood on dark and <u>narrow</u> streets or '<u>closes</u>'. Sometimes they <u>named</u> a close after a person who lived there, like Mary King. Over the centuries people have told many stories about Mary King's Close. One of the most famous is about a little girl called Annie. She <u>died</u> there in 1645. People have seen her ghost many times since. She isn't scary, but she always looks sad. That's why visitors <u>leave</u> so many toys <u>behind</u> for her.
Lösung: 1. were built, 2. was named, 3. have been told, 4. has been seen, 5. are left … by visitors

WRITING

8 **Your turn: A different country** → More help ○ 132/6 → S11

WB 27/10
WB 28/11

WB 27/10–28/11: Mediation (dialogue completion); Speaking (role play)

You've learned that in Scotland some people tell scary stories, some wear kilts, even young people like traditional music and others enjoy a meal called haggis. Write a short text about a country that you've made up and describe where it is and what is typical of it.

Start: The country of Galumphia is … . Its people …
Lösung: Vgl. Lösung *Diff pool* 132/6, SB S. 297

Holly's blog

Hi everyone! Time for a new <u>update</u>. We've been so busy these last days. Got lots of news for you. Hope you like my <u>latest</u> <u>pics</u> …

I thought the biggest lake in Scotland was Loch Ness, but it's <u>actually</u> Loch Lomond (<u>in fact</u>, it's the biggest lake in Britain). I took this while we were waiting for a boat trip. I know: typical tourists! 😕

Gwen and I made some new friends! We were walking past their field when they came over and started to follow us. I don't think we have cows like this down <u>south</u>.

The Highland Games are <u>held</u> everywhere in Scotland (even in the Lowlands). I've just found some photos on the internet – what was this guy doing?! Any ideas?

I was looking for souvenirs when I discovered these. Just because Loch Ness was too far away to visit didn't mean I couldn't see the monster! Isn't she cute?

Will & Kate came to visit Glasgow – really! I tried to take a pic, but too many people were standing in front of me. So, here's an internet photo of Balmoral Castle, the Royal Family's Scottish home. Not much bigger than Ethan's house! 😊

They really love dancing here! We saw this while we were walking around Glasgow. Nice kilts, <u>gentlemen</u>! Did you know that each <u>clan</u> has its own tartan? I'd really like to know what they wear – or don't wear – under those kilts!

READING

9 Holly's quiz → S5

Holly has put a quiz for her blog online. Who can be the first to answer her questions right?

1. The Scottish word for 'lake' is …
   a) <u>ben</u>.
   b) <u>glen</u>.
   c) loch.
2. The biggest lake in Scotland is …
   a) Loch Ness.
   b) Loch Lomond.
   c) Loch Awe.
3. In the fields you can often see sheep and …
   a) squirrels.
   b) cows
   c) rabbits.
4. The Highland Games are held …
   a) in the Lowlands only.
   b) everywhere in the UK.
   c) everywhere in Scotland.

5. Balmoral Castle is …
   a) one Royal Family home.
   b) next to Ethan's house.
   c) in Glasgow.
6. In Scotland each clan has their own …
   a) bagpipes.
   b) tartan.
   c) haggis <u>recipe</u>.

> **Media skills**
>
> Holly shares her thoughts, experiences, photos and information with others on her blog. What blogs do you read? Why do you find them interesting?

Lösung: 1. c), 2. b), 3. b), 4. c), 5. a), 6. b)

GRAMMAR

WB 28/12

KV 10: Working with grammar
WB 28/12: Grammar (past progressive)

10 Find the rule: The past progressive → More practice ○ 132/7 → G5

Which sentence matches which timeline?

1. The men **were** danc**ing** in the street when it started to rain.
2. At 10:30 a.m. Holly **was** talk**ing** to her mother on the phone.

A. 10:30
   10:00   11:00

B. simple past
   past progressive

Lösung: Sentence 1 matches timeline B. Sentence 2 matches timeline A.

GRAMMAR

WB 29/13

KV 11: What were they doing when the teacher came in?
WB 29/13: Grammar (past progressive vs. simple past)

Lösung: a) At 1:30 p.m. Amber was having a burger for lunch. At 3:15 p.m. Gwen and Holly were going on a historic tour of the city. At 3:15 p.m. Ethan and Amber were listening to a bagpipe player on the High Street. At 5:30 p.m. Holly was looking for souvenirs in a shop. At 7:00 p.m. everyone was dancing at a ceilidh. At 9:00 p.m. all of them were sleeping on the train to Glasgow.
b) 1. while e), 2. while c), 3. when d), 4. while a), 5. when b)

11 What were they doing? → More practice ○ 132/8 → More practice ● 132/9 → G5

a) *Gwen and the others went to Edinburgh for a day. What was everyone doing at these times?*

Example: At 10:00 a.m. the friends were walking up to Edinburgh Castle.

> **10:00 a.m.** – the friends – walk up to Edinburgh Castle | **1:30 p.m.** – Amber – have a burger for lunch | **3:15 p.m.** – Gwen and Holly – go on historic tour of city | **3:15 p.m.** – Ethan and Amber – listen to bagpipe player on High Street | **5:30 p.m.** – Holly – look for souvenirs in shop | **7:00 p.m.** – everyone dance at a <u>ceilidh</u> | **9:00 p.m.** – all of them – sleep on train to Glasgow

b) *What else happened in Edinburgh? Make sentences with the simple past and the past progressive.*

1. We met some of Ethan's friends		a) I was looking for souvenirs. Cute, eh?
2. Amber almost lost her mobile		b) the lights went out.
3. I was taking some selfies	when	c) we were walking up to the castle.
4. I found these model bagpipes	while	d) a man in a tartan hat walked behind me.
5. Gwen and I were dancing		e) we were waiting for the train back to Glasgow.

GRAMMAR

WB 30/14–15

B 30/14–15: Grammar
ast progressive vs.
mple past); Listening
alogue completion)

3 31/16–17: Reading
orrect order, matching);
eaking (role play)

12 **A game: Act it out and guess!** → G5

*One student leaves the classroom, and 3–4 other students act out an activity **without** words. When the teacher shouts "Stop!" everyone stops. Now the student comes back in and sees the '<u>frozen</u>' students. With yes/no questions, he/she guesses what the others were doing.*

> Were you eating something?

> No, we weren't.

WRITING MK **13** **Your turn: Your travel blog** → S11

WB 31/16–17

Look here
for help with
your blog:
🌐 3746jr

a) *Look for travel blogs about Scotland on the internet and present the best one.*

b) *Write a travel blog about a funny or interesting trip. Find photos or draw pictures of the places that you visited. Think of interesting texts to go with the pictures. Use the past progressive.*

LISTENING

2/4 🎧

14 ⟨ **A song: Flower of Scotland** ⟩

O flower of Scotland
When will we see your like
again
That fought and died for
Your wee bit hill and glen
And stood against him
Proud Edward's army
And sent him homeward
Tae think again
The hills are bare now
And autumn leaves lie thick
and still

O'er land that is lost now
Which those so dearly held
And stood …
Those days are passed now
And in the past they must
remain
But we can still rise now
And be the nation again
That stood against him
Proud Edward's army
And sent him homeward
Tae think again

Across cultures 🏴󠁧󠁢󠁳󠁣󠁴󠁿

As part of the UK, Scotland's <u>official</u> **national anthem** is *God Save the King/Queen*. There are also <u>unofficial</u> anthems because Scotland has its own football and rugby teams. One of these anthems is the song *Flower of Scotland*. It's about Robert the Bruce. He <u>defeated</u> the English King Edward and his <u>soldiers</u> in 1314.

MEDIATION

2/5 🎧
WB 32/18

32/18: Mediation
nail)

15 **A Scottish legend: The spider** → S17

a) *On the internet you find the legend about Robert the Bruce. Your little sister loves scary stories and legends and you want to tell her about this one. Listen and make notes about what happens. The following words and phrases can help you:*

> Robert the Bruce   fight the English

> hide in a cave   spider's <u>web</u>   not give up

b) *Now sum up the legend for her in German.*

Lösung: a) Robert the Bruce: 14th century, king of Scotland; fight the English: war going badly, already lost many battles; Robert and 36 men: hiding from the English in a cave, not enough men to win; one night Robert saw spider make web: web broke, spider made a new one, this broke and spider began again, spider never gave up; etc.

How to write a persuasive text

When you write a text to persuade other people to do something, e. g. visit a special place or attraction, it's important to make your text interesting to grab the reader's attention.

1 Criteria for a good persuasive text

Look at the ideas on the right. Find examples for these criteria in the text. Compare your results with a partner.

talking to the reader personally   local tips

humour   longer sentences with linking words

adverbs of degree   an interesting final sentence   strong adjectives

You can't get further from London!

Well, you can, but not in the UK. Did you know that the Shetland Islands are further north than any other part of Scotland? These beautiful little islands offer great things to do and see for people of all ages.

Explore fascinating museums that tell the extremely interesting story of life on the islands from Roman times to the present day. It may not be very large, but one of the most wonderful is the Shetland Crofthouse Museum in Dunrossness. Here you can really feel what it was like to live on the islands in the 1870s. If history isn't your thing, our islands offer a huge choice of exciting outdoor activities. Take a boat trip along the amazing coastline or improve your climbing skills on one of the spectacular cliffs. But please make sure you reach the very top! After your personal adventure, you can relax and visit our tiny, world-famous Shetland ponies. Probably the best reason to visit the Shetland Islands is to meet the people. Our islands may be quite small, but we have very big hearts. So, come and see us!

Lösung: 5. Adverbs of degree: extremely, very, really, quite; 7. Strong adjectives: beautiful, great, fascinating, interesting, wonderful, huge, exciting, amazing, spectacular, tiny, world-famous

2 Strong adjectives → More help ○ 133/10

WB 33/19–20

WB 33/19–20: Skills (strong adjectives); Skills (review completion)

Strong adjectives can help you to make your text livelier and more interesting to read. Copy the grid. Then read the text in ex. 1 again and put the adjectives with similar meaning in the right category. Sometimes they belong to more than one category.

small	good	nice	big
tiny			

Lösung: Vgl. Lösung *Diff pool* 133/10, SB S. 297

3 It's amazing! → More help ○ 133/11

Improve this text to grab a tourist's attention.

Voc.: Adverbs of degree, p. 208

Glasgow is famous for its shipbuilding industry. Titan Clydebank is a crane (49m). In 1907 it was designed by the Scottish engineer Adam Hunter to build some of the biggest and nicest ships ever. Titan Clydebank has become a tourist attraction. Are you brave enough to climb up to the top and enjoy the views?

Lösung: Vgl. Lösung *Diff pool* 133/11, SB S. 297

Media skills

For a brochure, what kind of photo would you choose to go with the text to persuade tourists to come and visit the crane? Describe it.

Look here for help with your brochure or ebsite: ⊕ 3746jr

B 34/21: Writing (your ometown)

Come and visit us!

You're going to make a brochure (or website) to persuade young people from other countries to visit your hometown.

Step 1

Get organised → WB 34/21

Get into groups of 4–5. For your brochure or webseite, collect ideas for interesting things for young people to do in your hometown, e.g.

activities | attractions | festivals | food | shops

Step 2

Plan your texts

Choose the eight best ideas. Agree on who's going to find out more about what. Then write a short text about each idea. Remember to make it as interesting as possible.
→ passive G4; past progressive G5 → persuasive texts p. 48

Step 3

Check your texts

Exchange your texts and give each other feedback.
→ proofreading S11

Step 4

Rewrite your texts

Improve your text(s) and find interesting photos too.
→ stating the source S12

Step 5

Design WB 34/22

Put your texts and photos together to make your brochure or website. Organise your texts and photos so that people can find the information easily. Remember that the design needs to <u>appeal</u> to young people!
→ designing texts S12

B 34/22: Reading atching)

Step 6

Give feedback

Look at the brochures or websites of the other groups and give feedback. Which one has the most <u>convincing</u> information, photos or design?

2/6–9 🎧   # I don't believe in ghosts!

SPEAKING

1   Before you read

Have you ever been in a dangerous situation – or maybe someone you know? What happened? How did you or this other person feel? Share your experiences with a partner.

A "That last song from Ethan's band was really good," said Gwen. "I liked the part with the bagpipes. I've never heard that in a rock song." It was the end of the festival. The <u>sky</u> was
5 getting dark and people were starting to go home. "Do you want to have a look round the castle? My parents won't be here for another hour."

"OK," said Holly. "If it's still open. I don't
10 know when it closes."

They walked to the castle <u>entrance</u>. It was free to go in on the day of the festival, and there was nobody in the <u>ticket office</u>. They came through some big empty rooms with
15 <u>stone</u> walls. Suddenly the lights went out.

"I can't see!" said Holly.

"Welcome to my world," said Gwen and laughed. "Don't worry, I'll get us back to the entrance."

20 Gwen took Holly's hand, led her back to the entrance hall and tried to open the door. It was locked.

"I'll call Amber," said Holly, and took her phone from her <u>pocket</u>. "Oh, there's no <u>signal</u>.
25 Maybe because of the <u>thick</u> stone walls."

"<u>Perhaps</u> there's another way out. Let's find out."

> **What are your ideas:**
> How do you think Holly and Gwen can get out of the castle?

B "We've been <u>going round in circles</u>," said Holly. "We're at the door for the museum again." She
30 was using her mobile phone as a torch.

"Did you hear that?" said Gwen. There was a strange sound coming from another part of the castle. It sounded like a <u>wounded</u> animal.

"Yes, I heard it," Holly whispered. She was
35 starting to feel scared. The noise came again, louder this time.

"Come on," said Gwen. "Let's find out what it is. I don't believe in ghosts!"

They went through some more rooms and then through a door into a <u>tower</u>. A little 40
<u>moonlight</u> was coming through a small window.

"The sound is coming from above us," said Gwen.

The <u>stairs</u> going up the tower were very old, and some of them were missing. When they 45
carefully climbed up, the noise got louder. The stairs ended at an old, <u>wooden</u> door.

"What do you think is in there?" Gwen asked in a nervous voice.

"There's only one way to find out," said 50
Holly, and pushed open the door.

> **What are your ideas:**
> Who or what do you think is behind the door?

C At first it was too dark inside the room, but then Holly saw something moving on the other side.

"Amber!" Holly shouted. 55

Amber stopped <u>crying</u> and <u>looked up</u>. "Holly! Is it really you?"

"What are *you* doing here?" Holly asked.

"I came up here to get a better view of Ethan's band. But look at the floor!" 60

There was no floor between the door and the other side of the tower, where Amber was sitting. "It started to <u>fall down</u> when I was walking across it," said Amber.

Then Holly noticed a sign on the door: 65
<u>DANGER</u>! <u>KEEP OUT</u>!

A <u>cracking</u> sound came from where Amber was sitting.

"Oh no!" said Amber. "Now I think this part of the floor is going to fall too." 70

Holly <u>realised</u> they didn't have much time. "Got a knife?" she asked Gwen.

"I've got a little knife on my <u>key ring</u>."
Holly took the knife from Gwen and quickly
75 took the pink backpack off her back. She cut
the backpack into long pieces and <u>tied</u> them
together to make a <u>rope</u>. "Here, catch!" Holly
shouted and threw the rope across to Amber.
"<u>Hold onto</u> the rope," she said. "I'll tie it to the
80 door."

Amber caught the rope. Then there was
a big <u>crack</u>, and the floor started to fall into
the tower. Amber screamed and went down
together with pieces of old <u>wood</u>. When she
85 hit the side of the tower, she cried out in pain.

"Are you OK?" shouted Holly, as she held
onto the rope as hard as she could.

"Yeah, I'm OK," came a very scared voice
from <u>below</u>.

90 "I don't think we can pull her up," said
Gwen. "She's too heavy."

Then they heard somebody shouting from
below.

"It's Ethan!" said Gwen.

95 "I've been trying to find you since the end
of the <u>gig</u>," he called up, as he climbed the
stairs. "A man let me into the castle to look
for you and ..." He came through the door,
and realised what was happening. "I think the
100 three of us will be enough," he said, and took
the end of the rope.

D "Nothing broken," said the doctor. "You can go
home. And next time you see a sign that says
KEEP OUT, maybe you should do what it says."
105 Amber was sitting on a stone wall outside
the castle. Holly, Gwen, Ethan and Gwen's
parents were all looking at her.

"Thanks for saving my life," Amber said.

"You're welcome," Holly answered.

"I've been saying some stupid things, and   110
I'm really sorry about it. I don't know why I've
been doing it. Maybe it's just because I'm your
big sister and I always think I have to show
that. Please let's be friends again."

"Yes, let's be friends," Holly said with a   115
smile. "You see, we love each other really," she
said to the others.

"I'll buy you another backpack," said
Amber. "But not pink."

"No, <u>definitely</u> not pink," said Holly.   120

SPEAKING **2** **Your reaction**

Which parts of the story did or didn't you like? Explain why.

READING **3** **Understanding the story** → S5

WB 35/23–24

12: I don't believe in
osts
35/23–24: Reading
ue/false); Writing/
ading (questions)

a) *Describe the picture. Which part of the story does it show? Sum up what happens before and after the scene in the picture.*

b) *For each part of the story, write down what the characters feel. How does this support what you talked about in ex. 1?*

Lösung: b) Part A: Holly: happy, excited, worried; Gwen: happy, excited, confident; Part B: Holly: scared;
Gwen: confident, brave, nervous; Amber: scared; Part C: Holly: confident, brave; Gwen: worried; Amber:
scared; Ethan: confident; Part D: Holly: happy; Amber: thankful, sorry

READING

4 The climax of the story → S6

Lösung: a) Climax: ll. 81–85;
c) 1. Amber can't hold onto
the rope and falls, but Ethan
is there to catch her. 2. Gwen
and Holly say that Amber
should jump. She tries, but
can't jump that far. Holly
grabs her hand an pulls her
up. 3. The girls find a ladder
and Amber climbs down
before the floor starts to fall.

a) *Read the information in the skills box.
Explain where the climax in this story is.*

b) *Do you think the climax is realistic?
Give reasons for your opinion.*

Start: I think the climax is realistic because
the castle is very old and dangerous. /
I don't think it's realistic because …

c) *Think of ideas for a different climax. Then present them to the class.
Give feedback about how realistic your classmates' ideas are.*

Reading skills

The **climax** is the main turning point in a story,
when the suspense is highest. At this point
the main character usually gets into a difficult
situation and changes in some way, e.g.
becomes stronger and more confident.

SPEAKING

5 Role play: An interview with Holly and Amber → S16

a) *A reporter from the local newspaper wants to interview Holly and Amber about what happened.
In groups of three, think of what questions he'd like to ask the two girls and what answers they
could give.*

Useful phrases

What happened? | When / Where did it
happen? | Who was there? | Why did it
happen? | What did you feel when … | Were
you scared / upset / worried / …? | Did you
think about … / think of … | What did you
think when … | What has changed for you?

b) *Each of you takes the role of one of the characters – the reporter, Holly or Amber.
Practise the interview and then act it out in class.*

WRITING

6 An extra scene for the story → S11

WB 35/25

Voc.: Describing nature
and buildings, p. 210;
Environment, WB (Word
bank), p. 15
WB 35/25: Writing
(options)

a) *Use your ideas from ex. 5 to tell what
happened to Amber **before** Holly and Gwen
found her. Say why Amber went into the
castle and climbed up the tower. Describe
how she felt when she got into trouble.*

Start: 'Where on earth did all these people
come from?' Amber tried hard to see
Ethan and his band, but she soon
gave up. Then she had an idea …

Tip

For stories remember to use quotation
marks ("…") to show when people are
speaking. Use single quotation marks ('…')
for thoughts. Put the comma, full stop or
question mark before the closing quotation
mark, e.g. "That last song was really great,"
said Gwen.

b) *Get into groups of 3–4. Read your extra scene to the other group members.
Which of your versions do you like best? Try to improve this version if you can.
Then present it to the class.*

How times change

SPEAKING

1 Warm-up: <u>Helping out</u> in the <u>neighbourhood</u>

Have you ever helped out in your neighbourhood, e. g. <u>done the shopping</u> for someone, read books to an <u>elderly</u> person etc.? Tell your partner about your experiences. Who did you help? What did it mean to that person and what did it mean to you?

VIEWING

3
WB 36/26

36/26: Viewing (how ▸mail a photo)

2 Scotland is famous for its <u>inventors</u> → S14

a) *Watch the film. Look at the stills and find headings for the two parts. Sum up what happens in each part of the film.*

b) *Which Scottish inventors does Alva talk about? Choose from the list and match the inventors with the right invention.*

1. Alexander Graham Bell
2. John Henry Holmes
3. Robert Hooke
4. John Logie Baird

a) <u>tin can</u> telephone
b) ligℏt <u>switch</u>
c) television
d) telephone

Lösung: a) A: A video chat, B: A 'telephone radio'; **b)** 1. d), 4. c)

SPEAKING

3 Old <u>vs.</u> new

a) *The film shows one example of how communication has changed over time (<u>rotary phone</u> vs. smartphone / internet). What other inventions (old vs. new) do you know about? Look at the categories below for ideas.*

transport free time music travel media

b) *Your turn: "Scotland is famous for its inventors." What's your region / town famous for? Write 4–5 sentences.*

Can you ...

1.	describe places and things to do?	Edinburgh is a busy place with historic houses.
2.	use passive forms?	Most of the world's whisky is produced in Scotland.
3.	talk about past activities in progress?	We were walking past their field when some cows came over and started to follow us.
4.	make texts more interesting?	Visit our tiny, world-famous Shetland ponies.

GRAMMAR

1 Berlin then and now

*Use the words and phrases below to make sentences in the **present** or **past passive**.*

Example: 1. The oldest church in Berlin was built in 1230.

Lösung: 2. ... was voted the most 'fun' city in the world. 3. ... was pulled by horses. 4. ... were produced in Berlin. 5. ... are visited by millions of tourists. 6. ... was invented by Herta Heuwer. 7. ... are rented out to tourists today. 8. ... is celebrated at the Brandenburg Gate each year.

1. The oldest church in Berlin	pull	by Herta Heuwer.
2. In a survey Berlin	visit	the most 'fun' city in the world.
3. 150 years ago there were no cars, so everything	invent	by horses.
4. In the 1800s industry was growing and a lot of machines	celebrate	to tourists today.
	rent out ➕	in 1230.
5. Berlin is very popular and every year its sights	build	by millions of tourists.
6. 'Currywurst', a popular type of street food,	vote	in Berlin.
7. To make extra money, many flats	produce	at the Brandenburg Gate each year.
8. The <u>fall</u> of the Berlin Wall		

GRAMMAR

2 Only in Scotland

a) *Rewrite this dialogue. Where possible, change the active sentences to passive and the passive sentences to active to make the dialogue sound more <u>natural</u>.*

Alan: The concert last night was enjoyed by lots of people. But a storm interrupted our gig. The weather really disappointed us.

David: Oh, that doesn't matter. The storm was just ignored by most of us.

Alan: Was the rain kept out by the roof?

David: Most of it! Raincoats were put on by a lot of people.

Alan: Were they <u>rented out</u>?

David: Yeah, they usually do that at concerts. What's going on at the Highland Games tomorrow?

Alan: Some people have planned a bagpipe contest. And there's a new contest where <u>thistles</u> are walked on. Sounds dangerous!

David: Well, now we can say the Scots invented thistle-walking!

Alan: And listen to this – this is great! The thistle-walking contest is judged by the winners of the bagpipe contest. Funny, isn't it?!

David: Yes, you only find that in Scotland!

b) *Compare your dialogues in a) and practise them.*

Lösung: a) A: Lots of people enjoyed the concert last night. ... D: ... Most of us just ignored the storm. A: Did the roof keep out the rain? D: ... A lot of people put on raincoats. A: ... D: ... A: A bagpipe contest has been planned by some people. ... where people walk on thistles. ... D: ... thistle-walking was invented by the Scots! A: ... The winners of the bagpipe contest judge the thistle-walking contest. ... D: ...

GRAMMAR

3 At the ceilidh

*Look at the pictures and make sentences. Use the **simple past** and the **past progressive**.*

Start: 1. They were having dinner when …

have dinner | ring | play music at ceilidh | start to dance

sing | go red | kiss | take photos

Lösung: 1. They were having dinner when Holly's mobile rang. 2. While a band was playing music at a ceilidh, they started to dance. 3. When Ethan was singing, Amber went red. 4. When Ethan and Amber were kissing, Holly took photos of them.

VOCABULARY

4 Boring!

Make this email more interesting.
Use the ideas on the right to replace
the words and phrases in blue .

at home here | whisper it | world-famous | huge |
amazing | fascinating | thousands of | go round in
circles | traditional clothes

Dear Sue,
Edinburgh is so nice ! I love it. I really feel like I've been in this city many times before .
Well, sometimes I still get lost in the old part of the town. I start walking and then I come back to
the same place where I started .
Edinburgh is a very old city. Sometimes you can still see people in typical Scottish clothes , like kilts.
The city is full of fun things to do. Edinburgh Castle is known around the world and every August
there's a very big arts festival here.
The landscape is nice here too. If you go to the top of Calton Hill at night and look up, it feels like
you're under lots of stars and they're falling down on you. If you tell your friends about this, please
try to say it very quietly . I don't want too many tourists here – just me!
Best,
Lilian

Lösung: 1. amazing, 2. at home here, 3. go round in circles, 4. traditional clothes, 5. world-famous, 6. huge, 7. fascinating, 8. whisper it, 9. thousands of

Making small talk

SPEAKING

WB 37/1

1 What went wrong?

a) *Read the skills box about small talk.*

b) *Talk about the cartoon with a partner. What went wrong?*

Speaking skills

Small talk is a friendly way to <u>get to know</u> someone or to talk to someone you don't know well. It's **light** conversation; no serious topics! Follow this <u>pattern</u>:

A asks a question.
B answers, then asks A another question.
A answers, then asks B another question. …

- Be a good <u>talker</u> **and** listener.
  (Don't <u>hog the conversation</u>!)

- Show interest in your partner:
  Ask questions.

- When you answer questions, offer more information than just 'yes' or 'no'. But not too much information!

"I just said how are you – I didn't think you'd get on the bus to tell me."

Lösung: b) This man probably just wanted to ask a polite question to make small talk. He didn't want to know any details about the other man's health or feelings. But the other person took the question seriously and jumped on the bus to tell him everything.

SPEAKING

2 A game: <u>Keep the ball bouncing</u> → S16

a) *Choose* **one** *of these situations.*

WB 37/2

> There's a new girl at school.   It's your first day at the sports club.
>
> A new boy has <u>moved into</u> the house <u>next door</u>.

b) *Make small talk with the person in the situation from a). Each pair needs a small ball. Every time you ask a question, <u>bounce</u> the ball to your partner. Which pair can keep their ball bouncing the longest?*

Useful phrases

Hi. You're new here at / in …, right? | What do you think of …? | What's different about …? |
Do you miss anything from …? | Are you enjoying …? | Have you ever …? | Why don't we …? |
Have you tried …? | You should … | I've got a great tip: <u>Check out</u> the … I'm sure you'll like it. |
Do you feel like hanging out? | If you have any questions / If there's anything you need,
just let me know.

I'm … / My name is …| I feel (a bit) nervous / worried / excited / … | That's cool, <u>cheers</u>! |
Can you tell me more about …? | I'd like to … | Do you have any favourite places to hang out? |
What was that you mentioned about …? | Sorry, I didn't <u>catch</u> what you just said about …

VIEWING

3 **At a party** → S14

4

a) *Watch the film. Read the conversations below and then decide which one matches which stills. Explain why.*

A · 01:23

B · 03:12

C · 01:20

D · 03:09

1. **Girl:** It's interesting to compare different countries, isn't it?

   Steffen: Yes, you're right. Have you ever been on a <u>student exchange</u>?

2. **Girl:** Do you miss anything from home?

   Steffen: No, not really!

b) *Look at the skills box in ex. 1 again. Then watch (00:38–01:24) and say what goes wrong in the conversation between Steffen, Julie and Nina.*

c) *Watch the rest of the film. Discuss how Steffen improves his small talk skills.*

d) *Watch (02:18–03:09) again and take notes on the different phrases Steffen uses to keep the ball bouncing.*

WRITING

4 **Writing a film script** → S11

MK

a) *Work in groups of 3–4. Look at the situations in ex. 2 again and choose **one** of them.*

Look here for
elp with your
film script:
⊕ dd4rj2

b) *Read the skills box. Write the script for a short film scene about your situation.*

c) *Rehearse your scene several times. Then film it and present your film to the class.*

> **Writing skills**
>
> <u>Stage directions</u>: Only write what you can see or show in a film. You **can't** see a person's thoughts, but you can give <u>hints</u> at a person's feelings in the stage directions, e.g. when you give instructions for facial expressions.
>
> **Dialogues**: Keep them short and <u>to the point</u>.

WB 38/1–2: Listening (table completion); Grammar (sentence completion)

1 Landscapes

LISTENING 2/14

SPEAKING
WB 38/1–2

a) *Listen to the description of a landscape and draw it in your exercise book. Then compare your picture with a partner's. Is anything missing?*

b) *Find a picture of a landscape or a city and describe it to your partner. Your partner must draw a picture. Compare it to the original picture.*

SPEAKING

2 Role play: I'm sorry

You're staying with a family in Scotland for six weeks. Yesterday you broke one of the family's rules. Act out short dialogues: One of you is the host mother/father, the other one apologises to them for what you did wrong. Take turns. Here are some ideas for the rules which you broke:

you missed[1] a family dinner | you got home late | you didn't do your jobs around the house

MEDIATION

WB 39/3–4

WB 39/3–4: Grammar (matching, replies to phrases); Speaking (role play)

3 Let's celebrate!

You're on an exchange in Scotland and you're trying to explain the German tradition of 'Fasching'. You've found this website and show it to your host brother/sister. Tell him/her about it.

Lösung: There are different words for this festival in the different parts of Germany. Traditions and customs are different as well, but the parades are all held at the same time between 11th November and the day before Ash Wednesday. Even the Romans celebrated this festival and it has been celebrated for centuries in Germany. People celebrate 'Karneval' for different reasons. Some people are happy that the winter is over and some just want to have lots of fun before Lent. But everybody wants to be loud, to sing and dance, to be happy and celebrate in the streets.

Fasching, Fastnacht, Karneval

In Süddeutschland, Bayern und Österreich wird diese besondere Zeit des Jahres „Fasching" oder „Fastnacht" genannt, in der Mitte und im Norden Deutschlands heißt es „Karneval". Die Traditionen und Bräuche[2] sind unterschiedlich, aber die Umzüge[3] und Feiern finden überall zur gleichen Zeit statt (vom 11. November bis einen Tag vor Aschermittwoch[4]). In Deutschland wird schon seit Jahrhunderten gefeiert, aber es heißt, dass auch die Römer schon Karneval kannten.
Manche Leute feiern Fasching, um den Winter zu beenden. Andere wollen viel feiern, bevor die Fastenzeit[5] vor Ostern beginnt. Und alle, die feiern, wollen ganz schön laut sein. Sie singen, machen Musik, lachen, laufen durch die Straßen und tanzen. In manchen Gegenden gibt es sogar Schulferien[6] um diese Zeit!

1

„Seit Juni arbeiten wir an unserem Wagen für den Karnevalsumzug in Köln[7]."

2

„In meinem Dorf tragen wir seit 200 Jahren die gleichen Masken[8] und Kostüme."

3

„Meine Maske wurde schon von meinem Großvater und meinem Vater getragen!"

1 to miss [mɪs] verpassen; versäumen | **2 custom** [ˈkʌstəm] | **3 parade** [pəˈreɪd] | **4 Ash Wednesday** [ˌæʃˈwenzdeɪ] | **5 Lent** [lent] | **6 school holidays** [ˈskuːl ˌhɒlədeɪz] | **7 Cologne** [kəˈləʊn] | **8 mask** [mɑːsk]

WRITING

4 Visit Edinburgh!

In small groups choose **one** *of the attractions below and design a brochure for it.
The introductions[1] and the words can help you.*

The Edinburgh Ghost Tour

You don't believe in ghosts? Well, then you haven't been to Old Town Edinburgh yet! Get yourself ready for …

| scary | to scream | castle | to cry | close |
| trick | surprise | dead | … |

Animals in the city

Cities aren't just for people! Come to Edinburgh City Farm and spend a fantastic day with …

| creature[2] | cuddly[3] | be a farmer for a day |
| to milk | to meet | sweet | new friends | … |

VOCABULARY

5 Word puzzles

Find words and phrases in these word puzzles.

Example: **1.** I understand

STAND
I

1

2

kcap

3

PIPES

4

Lösung: 2. mashed potatoes, 3. backpack, 4. bagpipes

GRAMMAR

6 At Balmoral Castle

Adjective or adverb? Complete the text with the right forms.

I just had to see William and Kate! I thought it would be very **1** (easy). In the news it said they'd be at Balmoral Castle at the weekend. I packed[4] my backpack with **2** (warm) clothes, food and drinks. At 2 o'clock I arrived **3** (safe) at Balmoral Castle and **4** (confident) sat down in front of it. You can stay in **5** (little) houses at the castle, but it's very **6** (expensive), so I **7** (brave) decided to camp until the Royal Family arrived. I took everything out of my backpack. My plan was **8** (perfect). But then a guard came from behind and said to me **9** (rude), "What are you doing? You can't just sit there!" I answered very **10** (sweet), "I'm waiting for the Royal Family. I'd like to meet them **11** (personal)." He grabbed my arm **12** (rough[5]) and then **13** (quick) threw everything into my backpack. He walked me back to the road and that's when it happened. A car drove **14** (slow) towards the castle and then stopped **15** (quick). The guard welcomed William and Kate and I could **16** (easy) see them through the open car windows. And they gave me a **17** (friendly) smile. So, I was **18** (successful) after all!

1 introduction [ˌɪntrəˈdʌkʃn] Einleitung | **2 creature** [ˈkriːtʃə] Lebewesen | **3 cuddly** [ˈkʌdli] knuddelig | **4 to pack** [pæk] packen | **5 rough** [rʌf] grob
Lösung: 1. easy, 2. warm, 3. safely, 4. confidently, 5. little, 6. expensive, 7. bravely, 8. perfect, 9. rudely, 10. sweetly, 11. personally, 12. roughly, 13. quickly, 14. slowly, 15. quickly, 16. easily, 17. friendly, 18. successful

GRAMMAR

7 The comparison of adjectives

a) *Read the tip.*

> **Tip**
>
> For one-syllable adjectives, you add **-er / est**:
> long → longer → (the) longest; big → bi**gg**er → (the) biggest
>
> Exceptions: good → better → (the) best
> bad → worse → (the) worst
>
> You also add -er / est for two-syllable adjectives that end in -y (**y** → **ier / iest**):
> angry → angrier → (the) angriest
>
> For two or more syllables you use **more** and **most**:
> famous → more famous → (the) most famous

b) *Write down the comparative and superlative forms of these adjectives:*

amazing   hot   happy   beautiful   good

Lösung: b) amazing – more amazing – (the) most amazing, hot – hotter – (the) hottest, happy – happier – (the) happiest, beautiful – more beautiful – (the) most beautiful, good – better – (the) best

GRAMMAR

8 The best of Scotland

What do you think about the topics below?
Use comparative and superlative adjectives
to compare your ideas.

Example: a famous loch in Scotland

A: Of all the lochs I think Loch
Lomond is the most famous.

B: Really? I think Loch Ness
is more famous than Loch
Lomond.

1. an important invention by a Scot
2. a good outdoor activity
3. a popular event in Edinburgh

GRAMMAR

9 Facts about Scotland

Read these facts about Scotland and say them in different words.

Example: Scotland is **smaller than** England. (big)
Scotland **isn't as big as** England.

> 1. *Life in the Highlands isn't as noisy[1] as life in the cities. (quiet)*
> 2. *The weather this year is worse than last year. (good)*
> 3. *The Scottish accent isn't as difficult to understand as most people think. (easy)*
> 4. *Ben Nevis in Scotland is higher than Mount Snowdon in Wales. (high)*
> 5. *Edinburgh is more popular with tourists than Glasgow. (popular)*

1 noisy ['nɔɪzi] laut
Lösung: 1. is quieter than, 2. isn't as good as, 3. is easier to understand than, 4. isn't as high as, 5. isn't as popular as

GRAMMAR **10** **The comparison of adverbs**

a) *Read the tip.*

> **Tip**
>
> For one-syllable adverbs, you add **-er / -est**:
> fast → faster → (the) fastest; hard → harder → (the) hardest
>
> Exceptions: well → better → (the) best
>   badly → worse → (the) worst
>
> For adverbs that end in -y, you use **more** and **most**:
> slowly → more slowly → (the) most slowly

b) *Write down the comparative and superlative forms of these adverbs:*

easily   bad   aggressively   angrily   hard   well

Lösung: b) easily – more easily – (the) most easily, bad - worse – (the) worst, aggressively – more aggressively – (the) most aggressively, angrily – more angrily – (the) most angrily, hard – harder – (the) hardest, well – better – (the) best

GRAMMAR **11** **How well did they do?**

Pete and Tom from Edinburgh Walking Tours are looking for a new guide to join their team. They have just interviewed three young men. Complete their discussion with the words in brackets. Decide if you need the adjective or adverb form. Use the comparative or superlative form where needed.

Pete: Of the three, I think Oscar did **1** (good). He spoke **2** (slow) and **3** (clear) than both Jack and Callum. And he used **4** (simple) language that even tourists who speak **5** (little) English would understand. And to me that's really **6** (important) thing.

Tom: That's true. But Jack knew the history of the city very **7** (good). And I also thought his stories were **8** (interesting) and **9** (funny) than Oscar's.

Pete: Yes, but of the three, I think Callum was **10** (funny) and **11** (friendly). And I loved that he came in a kilt. I'm sure the tourists will find that very **12** (funny) too.

Tom: Yes, I agree. And we all know what the first question will be. But of the three, Callum spoke **13** (fast) and the tourists might find his Scottish accent **14** (hard) to understand.

Lösung: 1. best, 2. more slowly, 3. more clearly, 4. simple/simpler, 5. little, 6. the most important, 7. well, 8. more interesting, 9. funnier, 10. the funniest, 11. the most friendly, 12. funny, 13. the fastest, 14. hard/harder

GRAMMAR **12** **Dear Diary**

Holly wrote this in her diary on their first evening at Gwen's aunt and uncle's house. Complete her text with the following linking words.

as soon as   and   because   whenever   until   before   after

> Dear Diary,
>
> I'm so upset **1** Amber was so mean[1] to me at dinner this evening. **2** we sat down, everything was fine. But **3** we were at the table, she started saying the most embarrassing things about me. **4** she does it, I feel so hurt. I've tried to talk to her, but it's like she doesn't care about how I feel. I asked an agony aunt for advice last week and I felt better **5** I did that. But I haven't received an answer yet **6** I've no idea how long I will have to wait **7** I get one.

1 to be mean [biː miːn] gemein sein

→ Solutions p. 297

Lösung: 1. because, 2. Before, 3. as soon as, 4. Whenever, 5. after, 6. and, 7. until

Unit 3

2/19–22 🎧

What was it like?

Find out about the most important <u>periods</u> in British history …

A

16.000 B.C.

8.000 B.C.

7.000 B.C.

B

C

D

1 British history → S5

SPEAKING

a) *What museum is there in your area? Which historical period(s) does it focus on? What objects can you see there? What do you find interesting about them?*

VOCABULARY

WB 40/1

WB 40/1: Vocabulary (sentence completion)

b) *How do we know about history? Look at the pictures on pp. 62–64. Which objects are used to show the history of Britain? Match the words with the things in pictures A–H. You don't need all the words.*

house	painting	book	model	map	diary entry	newspaper	church

wall	letter	postcard	clothes	castle	<u>embroidery</u>

READING

c) *Read the texts to find out more about British history and match the texts with pictures A–H.*

d) *Which period are you interested in the most? Give reasons.*

Voc.: History words, p. 215

Lösung: b) A: house, B: map, C: book, D: wall, E: embroidery, F: newspaper, G: painting, castle, H: postcard; c) 1B, 2A, 3D, 4C, 5E, 6G, 7H, 8F

Across cultures 🇺🇸

The historical periods on pp. 62–65 were all important in **British history.** Which historical periods were important in your country's history? How is German history <u>connected</u> to British history?

In the beginning

The first people arrived in the British Isles at the end of the <u>Ice Age</u>. They were able to walk across the North Sea because there was a land bridge between Europe and Britain. Then this land bridge was <u>flooded</u> by <u>rising</u> <u>sea levels</u>. It <u>disappeared</u> in about 6,500 <u>BC</u> and Britain became an island.

1

In Unit 3 you learn

… how to talk about what life was like at different times in British history. You also learn to describe historical <u>objects</u> and places. You learn:

- vocabulary for history,
- how to give necessary information, (<u>defining relative clauses</u>, <u>contact clauses</u>),
- how to use the <u>prop word</u> one/ones.

The <u>Celts</u> (around 600 BC–450 <u>AD</u>)

The Celts arrived in Britain from <u>western</u> Europe in about 600 BC. They lived in <u>tribes</u>, each with its own king, and they often fought each other. They lived in <u>round</u> houses and many of them were farmers, but they also knew how to make tools from <u>metal</u>. They wore colourful clothes and <u>leather</u> shoes and designed beautiful jewellery, and they loved to sing songs and tell stories. Each year they celebrated great festivals. One of these was the Feast of Samhain. Today this festival is better known as 'Halloween'.

2

The <u>Romans</u> (43–410 AD)

Julius Caesar first came to Britain in 55 BC, and then again a year later in 54 BC, but it wasn't until 43 AD that the Romans <u>conquered</u> the lands we now call England and Wales. At first the Celts fought the Roman soldiers, but over time they became friends and lived well together. The Romans <u>founded</u> towns like London and York and connected them with roads. They built houses, baths, <u>palaces</u> and <u>forts</u> too, and they brought <u>peace</u> to the country. In 122 AD they started to build Hadrian's Wall in the north of England to protect their <u>empire</u> against the <u>Picts</u> from Scotland. When they left Britain in the early 5th century, after different tribes <u>began</u> to <u>attack</u> other parts of the Roman Empire, the Celts were sorry to <u>say goodbye</u>.

3

The <u>Anglo-Saxons</u> (410–800 AD)

The Anglo-Saxons were <u>Germanic</u> <u>peoples</u>. They began to attack Britain from about 400 AD, but they didn't conquer any land until after Roman <u>rule</u> ended. The Anglo-Saxons didn't live <u>peacefully</u> with the Celts; they attacked their houses, <u>burnt</u> down their villages and pushed them into the far corners of Britain, to Cornwall, Wales and Scotland. The Anglo-Saxons <u>divided</u> the country into seven <u>kingdoms</u>, each with its own king. Over time, these kingdoms together became known as Angleland, and then England. Codex Amiatinus, the earliest <u>complete</u> <u>Latin</u> <u>Bible</u>, also <u>dates back to</u> this time.

4

VOCABULARY

2 Odd word out → More practice ○ 134/1 → More practice ● 134/2

Three of the verbs have a similar meaning. Which word is the odd word out?

1. arrive in | connect | come to | move to
2. attack | fight | defeat | win
3. build | design | protect | found
4. leave | disappear | go | stay

Lösung: 1. connect, 2. win, 3. protect, 4. stay

WRITING

3 Other periods in British history → S19, S26

a) *Expert puzzle: Make home groups of four. Each of you chooses **one** of these periods.*

The <u>Vikings</u> (about 800–1066): who they were and why they came to Britain, Viking ships
The <u>Middle Ages</u> (1154–1485): Magna Carta, the Black Death
Civil War and <u>Revolution</u> (1603–1714): Guy Fawkes, the Great Fire of London
Empire and Sea Power (1714–1837): James Cook (and life at sea), the Battle of Trafalgar

b) *First, work alone: Find information online about the events / people of your period and take notes. Then find three students with the same period. Compare your notes and write a short text. Now go back to your home group and tell the others about what you've found out.*

E

G

BREXIT
Britain has voted to leave the EU

But thousands take to the streets to remain

F

The Promenade Pier, Dover.

H

WB 40/2: Vocabulary
(post completion)

VIEWING **4** **A visit to Bath**

WB 40/2

a) *Find Bath, an old Roman town in England, on a map. Then go on a tour to find out more.*

Look here
for the tour:
🌐 eb6iw6

b) *Bath was one of the first places in Britain to become a World Heritage Site. Explain why it is important to protect places like this.*

 5 **Your turn: Important objects** → More help ○ 135/3 → More practice ● 135/4 → S11–12

WRITING

a) *Choose the five most important objects in your life. Write a text about each of them. Say …*

WB 41/3–4

– what it is and what it looks like.
– how old you were when you got it.
– who gave it to you.
– why it is important to you.

Look here
for help with
your poster:
🌐 eb6iw6

Start: The five most important objects
in my life are …

> **Useful phrases**
>
> I chose … because … | favourite |
> (not) <u>valuable</u> | cute | colourful | <u>made of</u> wood/
> gold/stone/paper | It reminds me of … |
> It means a lot to me because … | … gave it to me

SPEAKING **b)** *Make a poster or <u>vlog</u> and then present your objects to the class.*

WB 41/3–4: Vocabulary
(multiple choice); (time line)

2/23–26

The Normans (1066–1154)
In 1066 the Normans came across the sea from France. At the Battle of Hastings their leader, William Duke of Normandy, defeated Harold, King of the Saxons. The Bayeux Tapestry shows this battle.
When William became King of England, the people in England needed to learn French to talk to the Normans. To this day there are many Saxon and French words in the English language. At this time, Norman lords gave land to the people. The people worked hard on this land and grew food, but they themselves stayed poor because the Normans took most of it.

5

The Tudors (1485–1603)
Of all the Tudor kings, King Henry VIII (1509–1547) is the most famous. He was a powerful monarch, but today most people remember him as the king with six wives. With his first wife, Catherine of Aragon, Henry had a daughter, Mary. But Henry needed a son. So, in 1533, he decided to divorce Catherine and marry Anne Boleyn. When the Pope said no, Henry founded his own church – the Church of England. With Anne Boleyn, Henry had another daughter, Elizabeth. During her reign (1558–1603), a golden age for art, literature and music started in England. It was also a time when sea captains like Francis Drake and Walter Raleigh stole gold and silver from Spanish ships in South America, and England became very rich and powerful.

6

Victorian Britain (1837–1901)
Before the Industrial Revolution most people in Britain lived in the countryside. Many worked at home, where they made products by hand. After the invention of the steam engine, however, when it became possible to make products faster, cheaper and in larger numbers, more and more people moved to the towns to work in the factories there. Because of the invention of the steam train, goods and people could now travel faster, more often and to the seaside too.
During Queen Victoria's reign, the British Empire grew bigger and bigger and the new colonies that gave Britain cheap raw materials and food made the country very rich.

7

Britain today
After the Second World War Britain's colonies became independent and Britain became less rich and powerful. However, Britain's culture, especially its music and fashion, and its political views still have an influence around the world.
In 2016, after more than 40 years as members of the European Union, the British people voted to leave. People thought it would be better for decisions to be made in the UK rather than in the EU. This became known as Brexit ('Britain' and 'exit').

8

LISTENING

6 **Claire's plan: A historical calendar** → S13

2/27–29

a) *Olivia's stepmum Claire works at a community centre, and the centre needs help. Listen to part 1 of the recording and answer these questions:*

1. How can Olivia and her friends help?
2. What do you think of the plan for the calendar?

b) *Now listen to part 2. Then answer these questions:*

1. Say which students match the different historical periods on pp. 62–65. You don't need all of them.
2. Say which different objects from the past the speakers talk about. The words below can help you.

   boots   map   axe   coin   ring   mirror   necklace   knife

   belt   sandals   hairbrush

3. Which historical period is Olivia's group going to do for the calendar?

Lösung: b) 1.+2. (Speaker: Historical period, Object): Boy 1: The Normans, axe from the Battle of Hastings; Girl 1: The Tudors, map of Tudor England; Girl 2: The Celts, her sister's Celtic necklace; Boy 2: The Romans, Roman sandals and sheets with belts; Girl 3: Victorian Britain, her grandmother's Victorian mirror; **3.** Olivia's group is going to do the Tudor period for the calendar.

The calendar **which** Claire is making

From Olivia's diary:

> *Dear Diary,*
> *I'm really happy. I'm going to be in the calendar which Claire is making. This is the calendar whose page themes are from different historical periods. I'm going to be Queen Elizabeth on the Tudor period page. She was strong and clever – just like me! (Well, I hope those are characteristics that are true for me.) She was the first queen of England that was really powerful. We can choose the people who we want to appear with. So, of course, Gwen and Holly are the girls who I'm going to be photographed with. They'll wear clothes like the women whose job it was to be with the queen all day and all night. They were called 'ladies-in-waiting'. I can understand why – I'm sure they did a lot of waiting! Now I need to think about the dress that I'm going to wear.*

Text messages between Jay and Gwen:

Me   07:04 p.m.
I still have to choose the historical person that I want to be.

> **Gwen**   07:06 p.m.
> What about someone from Tudor times, like Holly, Olivia and me? You could be Sir Walter Raleigh. In 🇺🇸 , he helped to found the first colony, and he brought potatoes 🥔 and tobacco to Europe.

Me   07:09 p.m.
So, he brought back something which has killed millions of people? No thanks!

> **Gwen**   07:11 p.m.
> How about William Shakespeare? He invented lots of those famous phrases that we learn in English lessons. You know, like 'to be or not to be' and 'all the world's a stage'.

Me   07:16 p.m.
I can't look like him. He was bald!

> **Gwen**   07:17 p.m.
> 😄 Francis Drake? Remember that famous story about him which we read in history last term?

Me   07:17 p.m.
???

> **Gwen**   07:22 p.m.
> In 1588 the Spanish Armada ⛵⛵ came to invade England. When he heard the news, Drake was in the middle of a game of bowls 🎳 . He finished his game, and *then* he went to fight the big battle which destroyed most of the Spanish ships. He was a very relaxed guy!

Me   07:24 p.m.
I can't imagine myself as a person who fought in a big battle. I think I'll join the Victorian group instead. I could be Sherlock Holmes!

> **Gwen**   07:24 p.m.
> We have to be *real* people, remember?

READING

1   Understanding the texts   → S5

Sum up Olivia's and Jay's thoughts about the calendar project and then compare them.

GRAMMAR

WB 42/5

2   Find the rule: Relative pronouns   → More help ○ 135/5   → G6

a) *Read the texts on p. 66 again and match the sentence parts.*

1. Olivia is in the Tudor period for the calendar 2. This is the calendar 3. Gwen and Holly are the girls 4. They'll wear clothes like the women 5. Jay has to choose the historical person 6. Olivia needs to think about the dress	which that who whose	a) he wants to be. b) Claire is making. c) job it was to be with the queen all day and all night. d) she's going to wear. e) Olivia is going to be photographed with. f) page themes are from different historical periods.

b) *Look at the sentences in a) again. Are the nouns before the relative pronoun people or things? When do you use which pronoun?*

c) *In which sentence can you replace the relative pronoun **that** with **who** or **which**?*

1. I hope those are characteristics that are true for me.
2. Queen Elizabeth was the first queen of England that was really powerful.

d) *Find more sentences in the texts on p. 66 which have a **relative pronoun**. Which sentences can have a different relative pronoun instead?*

> **Tip**
>
> In written formal English **whom** is sometimes used instead of **who**: Shakespeare is the man **whom** you can see in Jay's message.

GRAMMAR

WB 42/6
WB 43/7

3   People from history   → More practice ○ 136/6, 135/8   → More practice ● 136/7, 137/9   → G6

Complete the texts about people from British history with the right relative pronoun: **which**, **who** *or* **whose**.

Elizabeth I was the queen ` 1 ` is still known as one of England's greatest monarchs. She was a strong and clever woman ` 2 ` skills helped her to <u>control</u> the difficult situation in her country. However, she is often seen as a very lonely person ` 3 ` is also known as the 'Virgin Queen' because she never married.

Walter Raleigh was an English <u>explorer</u> and writer ` 4 ` good looks and <u>charm</u> made him a favourite of Queen Elizabeth I. Between 1584 and 1587 he helped to found the first English colony in America on Roanoake Island in an area ` 5 ` is now North Carolina. But it was not a success. Of the <u>colonists</u> ` 6 ` <u>settled</u> there, some returned to England. What happened to the others ` 7 ` stayed there, nobody really knows. By 1590 they were gone and were never heard of again.

Lösung: 1. who, 2. whose, 3. who, 4. whose, 5. which, 6. who, 7. who

GRAMMAR

WB 43/8

Voc.: Monarchy words, p. 217
WB 43/8: Grammar (relative pronouns)

4 〈 Relative clauses with prepositions: Shakespeare 〉 → G6

a) *Translate these sentences into German. What do you notice about the preposition?*

1. Gwen and Holly are the girls who Olivia is going to appear **with** in the calendar.
2. Jay still has to choose the historical person that he wants to appear **as**.

b) *Rewrite the sentences and put the preposition after the verb.*

Example:
I'm very interested in the period **in which** Shakespeare lived.
→ I'm very interested in the period **which** Shakespeare lived **in**.

Lösung: b) 1. The house which William lived in … 2. … which he himself appeared in. 3. … which people always got excited about. 4. … which you are looking for is from Hamlet. 5. The girls whom I want to meet with … 6. The group whom the play is performed by …

> **Tip**
>
> When **whom** or **which** have a preposition, the preposition can come before the <u>relative pronoun</u> or after the verb. When **that** or **who** have a preposition, the preposition always comes after the verb.

1. The house **in which** William lived as a boy is in Stratford-upon-Avon.
2. Shakespeare wrote lots of famous plays **in which** he himself appeared.
3. A new <u>play</u> by Shakespeare was something **about which** people always got excited.
4. The phrase 'to be or not to be, that is the question' **for which** you're looking is from *Hamlet*.
5. The girls **with whom** I want to meet live in Strateford-upon-Avon.
6. The group **by whom** the play is performed is the Royal Shakespeare Company.

WRITING

WB 44/9

WB 44/9: Writing (short biography)

5 Your turn: A calendar on German history → S11

Your class is going to make a calendar about famous Germans in history. You can choose which person you would like to be. Choose a person and find information about him or her online. Then write a short text similar in <u>style</u> to the texts on p. 67, ex. 3. Write about what the person did and why he or she is important. Here are some ideas:

| Johannes Gutenberg | Karl Friedrich Benz | Annette von Droste-Hülshoff | Clara Schumann |

MEDIATION

WB 44/10

WB 44/10: Mediation (dialogue completion)

6 A film about the Victorian period: Sherlock Holmes → S17

An exchange student is staying with your family. You're online and look for a good film to watch in English together and you find Sherlock Holmes (2009). But before you download the film, you read the German comments and tell your guest in English what the viewers think.

---

nils14_berlinboy   4 September, 20:05

Rasend schnell geht's hier zu auf dieser Reise durch das alte viktorianische London. Super unterhaltsam. Besonders klasse: Echte Schauplätze wurden auf geschickte Weise mit CGI-Bildern vermischt, was in den Action-Szenen bombastisch wirkt!

---

koolkatie16_koeln   10 September, 20:08

Ich habe den Film neulich mit meinem kleinen Bruder angeschaut, der gar keine Ahnung von den Detektiv-Geschichten über Sherlock Holmes und Dr. Watson hatte. Er fand es total spannend, in das London von vor über hundert Jahren einzutauchen. (Und die Action-Szenen mochten wir BEIDE!)

---

jcm_hh17   19 October, 19:55

Viel Action! Aber manchmal kam es mir schon ein bisschen albern vor. Man hat dem Hauptdarsteller wohl gesagt: „Spiele es wie James Bond, nicht wie der gute alte Sherlock Holmes aus der viktorianischen Zeit!"

A <u>murder</u> story

LISTENING

7   **Before you read: Where's Jay?** → S13

2/35

14: The Tudor tour

a) *Listen to the recording. What are the friends doing? Why?*

b) *What facts do they learn about the Globe Theatre? Make notes about:*

the building | the audience | the <u>actors</u>

2/36   c) *Now read how the story goes on and find out what happens to Jay.*

Across cultures

The new **Globe Theatre** is one of London's most popular attractions. The theatre was <u>rebuilt</u> very much like the first Globe of Shakespeare's time, and audiences love the special atmosphere there: There's no roof, and you can get very close to the actors! What special old buildings do you know about? What is special about their history?

"The Globe sounds really cool," Jay said to Holly and the others. They were late for the start of the tour, and they were walking fast. "The <u>Elizabethans</u> were people who really
5 knew how to have fun. During the plays, you could do anything you wanted to do! You could walk around and shout and eat and drink, and there were animals there too! How funny!"
The friends turned left into a dark, narrow
10 road and then right into another one.
"I hope you know where we're going," Jay said to the others. "I've got no idea! Anyway, did you know that Shakespeare …" He talked and talked and talked. Then he noticed that he
15 was alone. 'I'm so stupid!' he thought. 'While I was telling a silly story they probably weren't even interested in, they turned into another street. I was in my own world, and I didn't notice!' He <u>turned back</u> but soon realised that
20 he was in streets he didn't know.

Now he was quite scared. He wanted to find his friends, but how could he find people whose phones were all turned off for the tour?
Then Jay saw a small group of people. A woman who was wearing Victorian clothes 25 was standing in front of them.
"I'm going to tell you a story about a murder which happened right here in this street!" said the woman in a dramatic voice. "If there's anybody here who gets scared easily, 30 they should leave now!"
It was a tour group, but which one was it? It wasn't the Elizabethan tour, but the one about Victorian times. '<u>What luck</u>!' thought Jay.
The guide told her story. It was a story Jay 35 already knew from a school history lesson, but the guide told it in a much more exciting way. This one had cool details about <u>blood</u> and rats in it. The guide stopped talking, and a man appeared in the street. He was <u>dressed</u> 40 in Victorian clothes too. He walked past them slowly, like a ghost, then went into a house. A moment later they heard a horrible scream, then a second one and finally two quieter ones. There was <u>silence</u> for a moment, and 45 then everyone clapped.
On the ground Jay saw something small which <u>shone</u> in the moonlight. Was it the 'ghost's' <u>pipe</u>? Jay picked it up. 'Perfect!' he thought. 'This is exactly the type of thing I 50 need. It's a Victorian pipe I can use for the calendar photo!'

Lösung: a) The friends are doing a Tudor tour/an Elizabethan tour/a tour of Tudor/Elizabethan London to collect ideas for their calendar photos.

8 What do you think? → S5

READING

WB 45/11

a) *What is the Tudor tour about? And what is the Victorian tour about?*

b) *Why did Jay enjoy the Victorian tour so much?*

SPEAKING

WB 45/11: Listening (questions)

c) *Compare what you heard about the Tudor tour and the Victorian tour. Say which tour sounds more interesting to you and why.*

Lösung: a) The Tudor tour is about Shakespeare's Globe and the Victorian tour is about murder and mystery. **b)** Jay enjoyed the Victorian tour so much because the guide told them the story about murder, blood and rats in such an exciting way.

GRAMMAR

9 Find the rule: Contact clauses → G7

KV 15: Working with grammar

a) *Look at these sentences. Is the relative pronoun the <u>subject</u> or the object of the relative clause?*

> **Tip**
>
> If the word after the relative pronoun is a verb, the relative pronoun must be the subject: S-V-O!
>
> **That** is sometimes used as a <u>conjunction</u>, e.g. **hope that, know that, notice that, realise that.**

1. Jay was in streets **which** he didn't know.
2. Jay saw something small **which** shone in the moonlight.

*If the relative pronoun is **the object**, you don't need it!*
→ Jay was in streets **(which)** he didn't know.

b) *Find more contact clauses in the text on p. 69. For each clause, say which relative pronoun has been left out.*

c) *Find sentences in the text which need the relative pronoun.*

Lösung: a) 1. object, 2. subject

GRAMMAR

10 What does Jay tell Dave? → G7

WB 45/12
WB 46/13–14

WB 45/12–46/13–14: Grammar (contact clauses); Grammar (relative pronouns); Writing/Speaking (quiz)

Read what Jay tells Dave. Which sentences don't need a relative pronoun?

You know that history is a subject **which** I like very much. And the Victorian Age is a period **which** I'm really interested in. So, I didn't join the Elizabethan tour **which** the others went on. I found a Victorian tour **that** was much more exciting. A guide **who** was dressed in Victorian clothes told us about life back then. And she ended the tour with a murder story **that** was really scary. And I'm not someone **who** gets scared easily! The story was the part of the evening **that** I enjoyed the most. And <u>guess what</u>! At the end of the tour, I found a pipe **that** I'm going to use as a prop for the calendar photo.

Lösung: The sentences 1 (which), 2 (which), 3 (which), 8 (that), 10 (that) don't need a relative pronoun.

GRAMMAR

11 At History Club → More help ○ 137/10 → G7

WB 47/15

KV 16: William Shakespeare
WB 47/15: Grammar (relative pronouns)

Replace the words in bold with a relative pronoun and make a new sentence. Put the relative pronouns that can be left out in brackets.

Examples: The History Club organises different activities. **They** are really exciting.
→ The History Club organises different activities **which / that** are really exciting.
Last month we talked about a famous writer of plays. We all know **him**.
→ Last month we talked about a famous writer of plays **(who / that)** we all know.

1. Last week we watched a modern film about Shakespeare. **It** was very interesting.
2. Yesterday we did a tour of a London theatre. We really enjoyed **it**.
3. The guide told us that in the old days they needed light. **The light** came through an open roof.
4. He said that all the actors were men and boys. **They** also played the roles of women and girls.
5. After the backstage tour, we met an actor. We'll never forget **him**.

Lösung: 1. … Shakespeare which/that was very interesting. 2. … theatre (which/that) we really enjoyed. 3. … light which/that came through an open roof. 4. … men and boys who/that also played the roles of women and girls. 5. … actor (who/that) we'll never forget.

WB 47/16

47/16: Reading
atching)

SPEAKING

12 **Your turn: A visit to a museum** → S16

a) *You are in London on holiday and would like to visit a museum. Go online and find a museum you would both like to visit.*

b) *Role play: Act out these scenes at the museum.*

1. A: You want to buy tickets for your family.
   B: You work at the ticket office.
2. A: You want to get a museum map.
   B: You work at the museum shop.
3. A: You can't find the room(s) about …
   B: You are a museum guide.
4. Your ideas

> **Useful phrases**
>
> May / Can I ask you a question? |
> Excuse me, … | How much are the tickets? |
> Are there special prices for families …? |
> Where can I get …? | Can you tell me the way
> to …? | May I have / take …?

GRAMMAR

WB 48/17

17: Working with
mmar

48/17: Grammar
op word one/ones)

13 **Find the rule: The prop word one/ones** → G8

a) *If you don't want to repeat a noun, you can use* **one** *or* **ones**. *Compare these sentences:*

1. They heard a horrible scream and then a second **scream** and finally two quieter **screams**.
2. They heard a horrible scream and then a second **one** and finally two quieter **ones**.

b) *Find two more sentences in the text on p. 69 with* **one/ones**. *What nouns do they replace?*

c) *Jay wants to hire a costume from a drama club in Greenwich. Rewrite the dialogue and replace the nouns with* **one/ones** *where possible.*

sung: a) In sentence 1 the
rds 'scream/screams' are
eated. In sentence 2 they
n't repeated but replaced
h 'one/ones'.

: How about this one?
hat one … Have you got
ler ones? A: This one is very
e. J: Which one? … I like
t one. A: … The ones on
t shelf … J: … I can wear
se ones. A: … Pipes like
se ones … J: … already got
e. I found one in the street!

Jay: I want to <u>hire</u> a costume for a Victorian gentleman.
Assistant: How about this costume?
Jay: That costume is a bit boring. Have you got any cooler costumes?
Assistant: This costume is very nice.
Jay: Which costume? … Oh yes! I like that costume.
Assistant: Do you need shoes too? The shoes on that shelf would go well with your costume.
Jay: No, it's OK. I can wear these shoes.
Assistant: Would you like a pipe? Pipes like these pipes were very popular then.
Jay: Thanks, but I've already got a pipe. I found a pipe in the street!

14 **Olivia hires a costume** → G8 → S11, S16

WRITING

WB 48/18–19

48/18–19: Speaking
esentation); Vocabulary
d completion)

a) *Olivia wants to hire a costume for Queen Elizabeth I at a costume hire shop. She needs a dress, a crown and shoes. One student takes Olivia's role and the other the role of the shop assistant. Write the dialogue so that you can replace some of the nouns with* **one/ones**.

SPEAKING

b) *Role play: Act out your dialogue in front of another pair who give feedback. Take turns.*

How to talk about history

For the unit task you're going to present a historical object to your class and you need language to help you with this. This page will give you some useful phrases and help you with a prompt card.

1 Useful phrases for presenting facts and figures → More help ○ 137/11

WB 49/20

WB 49/20: Skills (error spotting)

Lösung: a) Vgl. Lösung *Diff pool* 137/11, SB S. 299; **b)** Times and dates: for 200 years, at the beginning of, from 1066 to 1154, at the end of; Descriptions of places/objects: was worn by, it has, was given to, it looks, you can see a/an, was brought from; Biographical information: at the beginning of, invented, at the end of; Typical history verbs: invented, was brought from, was given to

a) *The text below is part of what a guide tells a tour group in London. Read what he says, and then find examples of phrases in the text and put them under the right heading in the grid. The phrases in bold help you to start.*

"… Now we're on Bankside and **in the 16th century** there were four theatres here along the river. In a moment – just around the corner – you'll see the famous Globe Theatre. It **was built in 1599** and it **was used for** all kinds of <u>entertainment</u> – plays, musical events and animal fights. Of course, William Shakespeare **wrote** and **acted** here while Elizabeth I <u>reigned</u>. He **was born** in Stratford-upon-Avon **in 1564** but moved to London as a young man. The diary in my hand probably belonged to Shakespeare himself! But, anyway, it's sad to say that the first Globe was made of wood, and when a fire **started** 400 years ago, the theatre **burnt down** in just two hours. That was in 1613. It was rebuilt the following year but pulled down again in 1644–45. The modern Globe was opened in 1997 …"

times and dates	descriptions of places / objects	biographical information	typical history verbs
in 1599	… was used for …	… was born in 1564	was built

b) *Add these phrases to the right categories in your grid.*

> for 200 years | at the beginning of | was worn by | it has | invented | was given to | from 1066 to 1154 | it looks | you can see a / an | at the end of | was brought from

2 Be a guide! → S11

WB 49/21

Voc.: Describing objects, p. 218
WB 49/21: Skills (picture description)

The key words on this prompt card are from the same categories as ex. 1. Use the key words to write a short speech for a tour guide.

- In this picture, you can see …
- Victorian student / 1890s / writing letter
- <u>quills</u> used for writing / no pens
- made from feathers / difficult to use

Our historical gallery walk

Go for a walk through history! Each of you presents a historical object (or a picture of one) to the rest of the class. The best part: You **are** the historical person who presents the object. The best speech along the gallery walk wins! You can be young or old, rich or poor, famous or not famous. Here's an example of things to say in a **one- or two-minute presentation** about a famous ring:

Look here for help with your presentation:
🌐 eb6iw6

"My name is Elizabeth and this is my ring. As you can see, it's made of gold and jewels. When you open it, you can see two pictures: one of me and one of my mother, Anne Boleyn. The pictures were actually a secret nobody knew about: I was only a little girl when my mother died and I never talked much about her. My mother was the second of my father's six wives. He wanted a son to become the next king. If you close the ring, you'll see the letters 'ER' – Elizabeth Regina. Elizabeth the Queen. That's me!"

Step 1

50/22: Reading
(matching)

Choose a period, character and object → WB 50/22

Find a photo of your object. Then make notes about what historical period it's from, what kind of object it is, and who it belonged to.
This person is the character you'll play. In the grid you can find some ideas to start with.
→ Check-in pp. 62–65

historical period	object	character
Celtic Britain	clothes	a famous person
Roman Britain	axe	a child
Norman Britain	jewellery	a rich / poor person
Tudor Britain	tool	a king / queen
Victorian Britain	…	…

Step 2

Write a prompt card

On your card remember to include these things:

times and dates | a description of your object | biographical information | typical history words / phrases
→ How to talk about history p. 72 → prompt cards S11

Step 3

50/23: Speaking
(correct order)

Make your speech → WB 50/23

Now give your one- or two-minute speech about your object to your classmates. Answer any questions they ask you as a 'historical person'.
→ How to talk about history p. 72 → defining relative clauses G6 → contact clauses G7
→ prop word one/ones G8 → pronunciation S15 → presentation S16

It's a mystery!

VOCABULARY

KV 18: It's a mystery!

1 Before you read: What could go wrong?

*Think about what happens at a photoshoot.
In a few sentences, describe some things
that could go wrong, and say why.
Think of the people and things on the right.*

models · photographer

other people / things on the set · props

equipment · accidents

A Jim slowly tried to open his eyes, but he
couldn't look into the lights; they really hurt
his eyes. Where was he? In hospital? Why was
he there? He closed his eyes again. He had a
5 really bad headache.

'Think!' Jim said to himself. 'Try to focus.'

Slowly, pictures started to come back:
Claire … the community centre … historical
periods … 'OK,' he thought, 'so, I took some
10 photos for the history calendar Claire is
making. I remember the Victorian picture and
the boy – was his name Jay? – who wanted to
be the centre of attention.' More memories
started to come back …

B "Quiet, please!" Claire shouted. "I know you're
excited, but we need to get organised now!"
Almost everyone was at the community centre
for the calendar photoshoot, and everything
was in chaos. "This is our photographer, Jim,"
20 said Claire. "Do you want to know how you
can help him? Be in the right place at the
right time and in the right costume! I see
some people who are in the wrong group!
The Romans and the Normans need to be in
25 their own groups. Don't mix up the historical
periods!"

C "Where's Holly?" said Olivia. "She can't be late
today. I need her now!"

"Well, she isn't your lady-in-waiting in real
30 life!" Gwen said. "I'm sure you can put your
dress on by yourself!"

"Yes, but I'll need her in the photo," said
Olivia. "I won't look really important if there's
only one person who's taking care of me."

35 "Drama queen!" said Jay as he walked past
the Tudor group. Olivia didn't even hear him;
she was still in her own world as the queen.

Then the door opened.

"Sorry I'm late!" Holly shouted.

Everyone stopped what they were doing 40
and stared at her. Then they all started talking
at the same time. Chaos again. "Oh no!" –
"Look at you!" – "What happened?!"

"I fell over in my skates and broke my arm,"
Holly answered, and showed them her plaster 45
cast. "Who wants to write their name on it?"
Olivia was the only quiet one; she didn't say a
word.

"Great!" she said at last. "That's going to
look really good in the photo! I mean, they 50
didn't even *have* plaster casts back then!"

"Thanks a lot," said Holly. "My best friend
doesn't even ask me if I'm OK!"

D In the Victorian room, Jay was having fun
in front of the camera. He was a Victorian 55
gentleman, and his partner in the photo was
a fine Victorian lady. "Zoom in on me more,"
Jay shouted as the girl rolled her eyes.

"That's enough!" said Jim finally, "I've got
plenty of nice shots of you two now." 60
Then Jay wanted to look at the photos on the
camera. "Hey, I look really cool in that one!"
he said. "And that one, and that one …"

"You both look cool," Jim added. "Now
I just need to go out to the car to get some 65
equipment I need for the Tudor group.
Back in two minutes …"

> **What are your ideas:**
> What do you think is 'Victorian' about
> the photo of Jay with the girl on the next
> page? How do you know? Give examples
> from the unit or from your own sources.

E "I just don't understand," said Claire. "Where on earth is Jim? He went out <u>half an</u>
70 <u>hour</u> ago – it's a mystery! I'll just have to try to take the photo myself. I hope the camera in my phone is good enough. Olivia and Holly, stop fighting! Gwen, please stand still, or the photo will be <u>out of focus</u>. And Jay, no <u>photobombing</u>
75 – you're a Victorian!" Finally, everything was quiet and there was a <u>FLASH</u>. They had a photo they could use, Claire hoped.

F "Would you like a glass of water?" asked the <u>nurse</u>, but Jim couldn't focus on anything.
80 "So, I went down to the car and looked in the <u>boot</u> for my equipment … but after that I can't remember anything. Are they all still waiting for me? I should
85 call Claire – but where's my phone? Oh, my head! Nurse, could you call the community centre and tell Claire I'm in <u>hospital</u>?"

G "Jim is going to be OK," said the nurse on the phone to Claire. "He can see you now if you want to come to the hospital."
95 Claire jumped in her car and <u>drove off</u>. She was happy that Jim was OK, but she still had a problem: the Tudor photo!

"So," Claire finished telling her story to Jim, 100 as he sat in his bed, "that's all I know."
"Show me your photo," he said.
"Oh no! It's awful," Claire answered.
Jim looked. "No, it's fine – maybe a bit dark, but I've got some tricks to fix that," he said. 105 "And I can easily <u>edit out</u> the mistakes and <u>crop the photo</u> a bit – it'll be perfect. But I'd still like to know why I'm in hospital."

> **What are your ideas:**
> What do you think happened to Jim?

H In another part of the hospital, a girl with a broken leg was sitting on a bed. 110
"I was on my bike," she told her parents, "when a man ran out of a building and opened his car boot. I heard a lot of noise from inside the building, so I looked up at the window to see why. I wasn't looking where I was 115 going, and I <u>crashed into</u> him. The next thing I remember, I was in the <u>ambulance</u> that brought me here. But who was that man, and what happened to him?"

> **What are your ideas:**
> How many mistakes do you think Jim will have to edit out of this Tudor photo?

VOCABULARY

2 What belongs, what doesn't belong in the scene? → S5

a) *Did any of the problems you mentioned in ex. 1 come up in the story? Tell the class.*

MK

Look here to edit a photo:
🌐 eb6iw6

b) *On the right you can see Claire's photo **after** Jim has improved it. Say which mistakes he has edited out. How has Holly solved the problem with her arm? Explain why these changes were important for the Tudor photo. The word bank can help you.*

Example: Jay photobombed the Tudor scene as a Victorian!

Word bank

out of focus | wrong period | modern objects | crop / lighten a photo | zoom in on | edit out | photobomb a scene

Lösung: b) The mistakes in the photo were modern things that don't belong to the Tudor period. The changes to the photo were important to make the scene look real.

READING

3 Flashbacks and the order of events → S6

WB 51/24

WB 51/24: Reading (error spotting, text evidence)

a) *First, read the skills box. Then find other examples of flashbacks in the story.*

b) *In groups of eight, each person chooses **one** of these moments from the story (A–H). Your group then lines up in the order you think they happened. Then compare with other groups. If there are differences, explain what's right and wrong.*

A. Jim opened his eyes in hospital.
B. Everyone arrived.
C. Holly broke her arm.
D. Jim went to his car.
E. The nurse called Claire.
F. Claire took the Tudor photo.
G. The girl crashed into Jim.
H. Jim took the Victorian photo.

c) *Your turn: What books, films or TV shows do you know that use flashbacks? In a few sentences, describe a key scene.*

Reading skills

A **flashback** is a part of a story that describes what a character suddenly remembers from an earlier time.

Example:

Part A: Jim tries to remember what happened earlier in the day. His first flashback to the events at the photoshoot is described in Parts B–D.

Flashbacks are often used to make a story more interesting, like a puzzle for the reader.

Lösung: a) Parts A–D, ll. 7–67: Jim remembers what happened at the photoshoot. Part C, ll. 44–46: Holly tells everyone about her accident. Part H: ll. 111–119: The girl with the broken leg remembers the accident. **b)** C – B – H – D – G – F – A – E

SPEAKING

4 Key moments from the story: Freeze frames

WB 51/25

WB 51/25: Writing (options)

*Your group chooses **one** of these three scenes from the story. Discuss how you can present your scene as a freeze frame. Talk about what each of the characters is thinking / feeling / doing?*

A. Holly arrives with her arm in plaster.
B. Jay has fun in front of the camera for his Victorian photo.
C. Claire tries to organise the friends for the Tudor photo.

The girl from the past

SPEAKING **1** **School or work?**

Many years ago, children from poorer families in Britain and Europe often needed to work to earn money for their family. Lots of parents didn't have money to send their children to school.

In the film you're going to watch, Marley says, "I'd rather work than go to school and do this history homework." Can you identify with Marley's statement? Explain why or why not.

VIEWING **2** **This is the year 1888?** → S14

5 🎬
WB 52/26

c.: Time words, p. 219
52/26: Vocabulary
ble completion)

a) *Watch the film. What happens? Think of Violet, her problem and how Marley can help her.*

b) *Read the skills box and look at the stills. How is the dream sequence shown in the film? And how does Marley travel through time? What other details in the film make you think of time travel?*

c) *Your turn: Talk about another film that you've seen with a dream sequence and/or time travel. Tell your partner how it's done in that film.*

> ### Word bank
>
> pawn shop | school fees | travel through time |
> tea bag | pineapple | vitamins

> ### Viewing skills
>
> A **dream sequence** is often used to show **time travel** in films. **Audio-visual effects** like music or blurred pictures mark the start and end of the sequence. The viewer (and the film character too) usually only realises at the end of the sequence that it's been a dream – when the character wakes up.

A

B

WRITING **3** **Violet's diary** → S11

Write a diary entry from Violet's point of view. How did she experience her trip to the 21st century? Remember to write about feelings too.

Can you . . .

1.	describe historical objects and places?	This object was my first toy. His name is Thomas and he's a brown bear. He is really old now.
2.	use vocabulary for history?	In 43 AD the Romans conquered Britain.
3.	use the right relative pronouns?	Olivia's going to be in the calendar which Claire is making.
4.	make contact clauses?	It was a story (which / that) Jay already knew.
5.	use the prop word one / ones?	This costume is very nice. – Yes, I like that one.

GRAMMAR

1 Quiz time!

a) *Complete the sentences with a relative pronoun.*

1. She was a British queen ▢ name began with V.
2. It's the place ▢ has been the British king or queen's London home since 1837.
3. It's a Spanish word ▢ means 'a big group of ships'.
4. It was the theatre in ▢ many of Shakespeare's plays were first performed.
5. He was a very important Elizabethan sailor ▢ name rhymes with 'make'.
6. It's the thing ▢ Victorian pipes were made of.

b) *What are the answers to the questions in a)?*
Lösung: a) 1. whose, 2. that/which, 3. that/which, 4. which, 5. whose, 6. (that/which);
b) 1. Victoria, 2. Buckingham Palace, 3. armada, 4. the Globe Theatre, 5. Francis Drake, 6. wood

GRAMMAR

2 Victorian inventions

*Put in a relative pronoun **if one is needed**.*

'Victorian' describes people ▢**1**▢ lived in Britain when Victoria was queen (1837–1901). It is also used to describe things ▢**2**▢ happened in Britain and in other countries during this period. The Victorians were people for ▢**3**▢ new inventions were very exciting. They invented many things ▢**4**▢ we still use today.
For example, Alexander Cumming was the Scottish inventor ▢**5**▢ patented the modern toilet. It made Victorian cities much healthier places to live in. Thomas Edison was an American ▢**6**▢ inventions really changed the world. He helped to invent something without ▢**7**▢ life today would be very different: the light bulb. The light bulb ▢**8**▢ Edison developed in 1879 was similar to the ones ▢**9**▢ we used until just a few years ago.

There were lots of other Victorian inventors ▢**10**▢ we are very thankful for. It was people from this time ▢**11**▢ invented the car, the telephone, the radio and the bicycle.

Thomas Edison

But there were also inventors ▢**12**▢ hoped to make a lot of money, but ▢**13**▢ inventions didn't become famous because people didn't need them. In the late 19th century, somebody invented an umbrella ▢**14**▢ was also a pair of glasses. Another crazy invention was a machine ▢**15**▢ brushed your hair.

Lösung: 1. who/that, 2. which/that, 3. whom, 4. (which/that), 5. who/that, 6. whose, 7. which, 8. (which/that), 9. (which/that), 10. (who/that), 11. who/that, 12. who/that, 13. whose, 14. which/that, 15. which/that

GRAMMAR

3 **Tidying up the community centre**

Claire, Olivia and Holly are tidying up the community centre after the photoshoot.
*Find the nouns which you can replace with **one/ones**.*

sung: O: … I think people
ok a clean glass/one … H:
d these are just the ones
e brought … O: … C: The
all glasses/ones go in the
pboard, and the big ones
… O: … C: The one over
ere, … H: … C: Well, it may
t be the best one in the …
… I think the best photos/
es from the shoot are the
es which … C: Well, it's the
ly photo/one we've …

Olivia: So many glasses! I think people took
         a clean glass every time they wanted
         some more lemonade!
Holly: And these are just the glasses I've
         brought into the kitchen. There are
         still some in the Roman room. And the
         Romans were the people who drank the
         most lemonade!
Olivia: Where should I put them, Claire?
Claire: The small glasses go in the cupboard,
         and the big glasses go on the shelf.
Olivia: Which shelf?

Claire: That shelf over there, next to the
         door.
Holly: I hope our Tudor photo is OK.
Claire: Well, it may not be the best photo
         in the calendar, but Jim says it'll be
         good enough.
Holly: Gwen and I are smiling in it. I think
         the best photos from the shoot are
         the photos which are more serious.
Claire: Well, it's the only photo we've got
         with you in your costumes. I'm sure
         it'll be fine.

VOCABULARY

4 **Which one doesn't belong?**

a) *Find the word in each group that doesn't belong. Match each of these words to one of the other
    five groups. Write down the six new groups.*

1	2	3
Roman	lady-in-waiting	(to) attack
bath	play	Spanish Armada
empire	Globe Theatre	battle
French	writer	Industrial Revolution

4	5	6
(to) defeat	heating	Norman
factory	dress	William the Conqueror
British Empire	(to) take care of	food
steam engine	queen	entertainment

b) *For each group of words, write 1–3 sentences. Use all four words.*

c) *Give your sentences to a partner. Add one of these words to each of your partner's six sentences or
    write a new sentence with the word.*

    to this day   mystery   lifestyle   back then   new   axe

Lösung: a) 1. Roman, bath, empire, heating; 2. entertainment, Globe Theatre, play, writer; 3. (to) attack,
Spanish Armada, battle, (to) defeat; 4. Industrial Revolution, factory, British Empire, steam engine;
5. lady-in-waiting, dress, (to) take care of, queen; 6. Norman, William the Conqueror, food, French

On- & offline communication

KV 19: Find someone who …

On the following pages you're going to learn about formal and informal types of messages. At the end you'll write your own messages in the appropriate style. The messages you're going to deal with are all related to the calendar project in Unit 3.

1 Types of messages → More practice ● 138/1, 138/3 → More practice ○ 138/2

VOCABULARY
WB 53/1

WB 53/1: Vocabulary (table completion)

a) *What kinds of written online and offline communication do you use? Copy the grid and fill it in. Then compare your answers: What are the most popular kinds of communication in your class?*

  email   invitation   letter   postcard   text message

type of message	online	offline	both
email	✔		

b) *Which type of message is the best for the following situations? You want to …*

send greetings from a holiday destination | send a message and receive a direct answer quickly | explain something in detail in a more formal way | let somebody know about your next party | write a short letter and receive an answer quickly

READING

c) *Read these messages. What type of message are they? How do you know?*

A Dear Mum and Dad,
The weather here is great, and I'm having lots of fun. I hope you get this before I arrive home!
See you soon,
Jay

C Hi Dave,
Just a quick message. We hope that you're enjoying life in Cornwall. Things are the same here, except you're not here! We wanted to send you a text message, but we haven't got your new mobile number. Can you email it to us?
All the best,
Gwen, Holly, Jay, Luke and Olivia

E Dear Olivia,
Please come to my birthday party on Saturday 16th April at 3 p.m.
Address: 305 Canberra Road, Greenwich
Theme: Pirates!
Love,
Emma

B Dear parents,
I am writing to inform you that from Monday 2nd May the school day will start five minutes later at 8.50 a.m. This is because of a change in the local bus timetable.
Yours sincerely,
Jeanette Wilson
Head teacher

D WHERE RU? I'm waiting 4U!

Writing skills

In English you start your message with **Hi / Hello / Dear**, and you finish your message with **All the best / Love / See you / Yours sincerely**. Remember to start the sentence after the greeting with a capital letter.
When do you use which greeting or ending? There's one type of message where you needn't use a greeting or an ending. Which one is it?

Lösung: a) online: email, text message; offline: letter, postcard; both: invitation; **b)** 1. postcard, 2. text message, 3. letter, 4. invitation, 5. email; **c)** A: postcard, B: letter, C: email, D: text message, E: invitation

Formal emails

From: claire.fraser@parkstreetcentre.org.uk	✕
To: jim@jimevansphotos.co.uk	
Subject: Photos for a charity calendar	

Dear Mr Evans,

5   I read on your website that you are a photographer and that you live in Greenwich.
I am the <u>manager</u> of Park Street Community Centre. We plan to produce a charity calendar with
historical scenes that feature local children in costumes. There will be twelve scenes,
one for each month of the year.

Would you be interested in taking the photographs for us, and how much would it cost?

10   The children are at the centre every Saturday from 10 a.m. to 12:30 p.m.
Would you be <u>available</u> on any Saturday in April?

Yours sincerely,

Claire Fraser
Manager, Park Street Community Centre

READING

2 Understanding the email

Read the email and answer the questions.

1. What is Claire's reason for sending the email?   2. What information does she give to Mr Evans?
3. What information does she want to get in Mr Evans' reply?

WRITING

3 A formal email → More help ○ 138/4

WB 53/2

‹ 53/2: Reading
rmal vs. informal)

a) *Are these statements about Claire's email true or false?*

1. It is organised into <u>paragraphs</u>.
2. It uses short forms.
3. It is written in a clear and simple way.
4. Only the <u>recipient</u> will see the date and time that it was written.
5. It uses an informal, friendly style of English.
6. It <u>contains</u> a lot of <u>unnecessary</u> information.
7. It has a clear <u>purpose</u>.
8. It doesn't use the <u>postal address</u>.
9. The greeting is formal.

b) *Think – pair: What is the purpose of each paragraph?*
Lösung: **a)** True: 1, 3, 7, 8, 9; False: 2, 4, 5, 6; **b)** Vgl. Lösung *Diff pool* 138/4, SB S. 299

WRITING MK

4 Mr Evans' reply → More help ○ 138/5 → More practice ○ 139/6 → More practice ● 139/7 → S11

WB 54/3

‹ 54/3: Writing (email)

Write Jim's reply to Claire. Include the following information.

– available on Sat., 9th April
– happy to support the community centre
– without <u>payment</u>
– visit the community centre before
– will decide what equipment he needs

Lösung: Vgl. Lösung *Diff pool* 138/5, SB S. 299–300

Look here
for help with
your email:
⊕ jj59te

Across cultures

Greetings for formal letters and emails:
– Man: Dear Mr Smith, ['mɪstə]
– Woman who is <u>married</u>: Dear Mrs Smith, ['mɪsɪz]
– Woman who is not married: Dear Miss Smith, [mɪs]
– You don't know if the woman is married or not:
  Dear <u>Ms</u> Smith, [mɪz]

Formal letters

> Park Street Community Centre
> Park Street
> Greenwich
> SE9 4ZQ
>
> 5 Ms S Richardson
> 127 Brook Lane
> Greenwich
> SE3 8AS
>
> 20th March 2021
>
> 10 Dear Ms Richardson,
>
> I am writing to ask for your <u>permission</u> for Holly to appear in a
> calendar. Each month will feature a photo of local children in
> historical costumes. The children will act in scenes from local
> history. The purpose of the calendar will be to raise money to
> 15 support the work of the community centre.
>
> Yours sincerely,
>
> *Claire Fraser*
>
> Claire Fraser
> Manager

READING

5 Understanding the letter

Read the letter and answer the questions.

1. What is Claire's reason for sending the letter? **2.** What does she want Holly's mum to do?
Lösung: 1. Claire is sending this letter to Holly's mum because she needs her permission for Holly to appear in the charity calendar.
2. She wants Holly's mum (to reply to her and) to give her permission.

WRITING

6 A formal letter → More help ○ 139/8

WB 54/4

WB 54/4: Reading
(formal/polite phrases)

a) *In which lines do you find these things in the letter?*

> the <u>signature</u> | the <u>sender</u>'s name and job | the sender's address | the recipient's address |
> the date | the greeting | the ending | the main part of the letter

b) *Compare the structure of the letter with the email on p. 81. How is it different?*
Lösung: a) 1. l. 17; 2. ll. 18–19; 3. ll. 1–4; 4. ll. 5–8; 5. l. 9; 6. l. 10; 7. l. 16; 8. ll. 11–15;
b) Differences: addresses, date, format, written signature in letter

WRITING MK

7 Ms Richardson's reply → S11

Look here
for help with
your letter:
 jj59te

Read the dialogue. What type of message does Holly's mum need to write? Write her reply.

Mum: I got a letter from the manager of the community centre.
   She wants me to give my permission for you to be in the calendar.
Holly: Is that OK? I'd really like to be in the calendar.
Mum: Yes! But she hasn't given her phone number or email address, so I'll have to write ▨ !
Holly: I'll go and get an <u>envelope</u> and a <u>stamp</u>.
Lösung: a letter

Semi-formal emails

From: claire.fraser@parkstreetcentre.org.uk

To: jay.azad@email123.com

Subject: Re: Photoshoot on Saturday

Hi Jay,

5 Thanks for your email. Yes, that's <u>absolutely</u> fine. I'm looking forward to meeting your cousin.

See you at the centre,

Claire

- -

From: jay.azad@email123.com

Date: 2/4/2021   4:26 p.m.

10 To: claire.fraser@parkstreetcentre.org.uk

Subject: Photoshoot on Saturday

Dear Mrs Fraser,

Next weekend my cousin Amir from Bradford is going to visit my family. He's 14, and he's very interested in history. Is it OK for him to come to the community centre on Saturday morning too?

15 He doesn't want to be in the photoshoot. He just wants to watch.

<u>Best wishes</u>,

Jay Azad

READING

8 Understanding the emails

WB 55/5

Read the emails and choose the right answer.

55/5: Reading (ice completion)

1. Jay sends the email because …
    a) he can't come to the photoshoot because he's going to visit his cousin.
    b) he wants to know if Amir can be in the photoshoot.
    c) his cousin wants to watch them.
    Lösung: 1. c), 2. c)

2. Claire replies that …
    a) she's sorry to hear that Jay can't come.
    b) Amir can be in the calendar too.
    c) she's happy about Amir coming to the photoshoot.

WRITING

9 A semi-formal email

Think – pair – share: Read Jay's and Claire's email and answer the questions.

WB 55/6

55/6: Writing (ni-formal email)

1. How is the style different from the formal email and letter (pp. 81–82)?
2. Why do Jay and Claire use a semi-formal style?
3. Why do you think that Jay begins with 'Dear …', but Claire begins with 'Hi …'?

WRITING

10 Jay's reply → More practice ● 139/9 → S11

Write a reply from Jay to Claire. Thank her for her email. Say that you and your cousin are both looking forward very much to the photoshoot on Saturday morning. Ask if there is anything else you can do to help with the photoshoot.

Lösung: Dear Mrs Fraser, Thanks for your quick reply. It's great that Amir can come and watch. We're both looking forward very much to the photoshoot on Saturday morning! Let me know if there's anything we can do to help. See you on Saturday, Jay

Text messages

Jay   10:02 a.m.

No problem about coming 2 the 📷 on Sat. Come & see me dressed as a fine
Victorian gentleman with a 🚬 ! I know ur <u>gonna</u> laugh! R u sure u don't wanna b
in the photos???

Amir   10:05 a.m.

No, I'll just 👀 . Don't like being in pics. Could b difficult 2 get a costume 4 me.
But I'm sure it's gonna b <u>loads of</u> fun. Looking forward 2 it already!!!
Say ✋ 2 Shahid & ur mum & dad.

READING

11   Understanding the text messages

Read the text messages. Are the statements true or false? Correct the false statements.

1. Amir can come to the photoshoot.
2. Jay is going to wear a Victorian costume.
3. Jay tells his cousin that he can't be in the photos.
4. Amir is sad that he can't be in the pictures.
5. The boys don't think that they will enjoy the photoshoot.

Lösung: True 1, 2; False 3. Jay asks his cousin if he is sure that he doesn't want to be in the photos. 4. Amir doesn't
like being in pictures. 5. Jay thinks Amir is going to laugh and Amir is already looking forward to the photoshoot.

WRITING

12   Text messages   → More help ○ 139/10

WB 56/7

WB 56/7: Writing
(text messages)

Lösung: a) Vgl. Lösung
Diff pool 139/10, SB S. 300;
b) 1. Saturday, 2. you're (you
are), 3. your, 4. be, 5. for,
6. pictures, 7. are, 8. to

a) *Compare the text messages with formal messages. Explain how the style is different
and give examples.*

b) *Look at these abbreviations from the text messages. What words are <u>abbreviated</u>?*

   Sat   u   ur   b   4   pics   r   2

c) *The boys also use the words 'gonna' and 'wanna'. What should they say in formal communication?*

d) *What words do the <u>icons</u> <u>replace</u>?*

e) *Why do you think the boys sent each other text messages and not emails?*

Lösung: c) gonna – going to, wanna – want to; **d)** 1. photoshoot, 2. pipe, 3. watch, 4. hello; **e)** It's quicker and easier
to write text messages. It's a very informal way of communication.

WRITING MK

13   A group chat   → S11

Look here
for help with
your chat:
🌐 jj59te

*Jay is texting Holly, Luke, Olivia and Gwen. Put these entries in the right order and write their
group chat.*

Holly: That's great! Is he going to be in the pictures too?
Jay: No, he isn't. He doesn't like being in pictures.
Jay: My cousin is going to come to the photoshoot on Saturday.
         I've asked Claire. It's OK with her.
Gwen: If he is, we'll need to find a costume for him, won't we?
Olivia: Good. I'm Queen Elizabeth and I don't need a <u>husband</u>!
Luke: I'm looking forward to seeing him again!

Lösung: J: My cousin … H: That's great! … G: If he is, we … J: No, he isn't. He … O: Good. I'm … L: I'm looking forward …

Greetings cards

Jim had an accident outside the community centre. Claire gives him a 'Get well soon' card when she visits him in hospital. Olivia and her friends have added messages too.

Get **well** soon

Very sorry about your accident.
Best wishes for a quick return to health. Claire

Sorry about the accident! Get well soon! Jay

Bad luck! But thanks for the great photos! Olivia

I hope you get better very soon! Gwen

Hope you feel better soon. Luke

Sorry to hear about your bad luck. Get better soon! Holly

WRITING **MK** **14**   **Your turn: A digital greetings card**

Look here for material: 🌐 jj59te

Imagine your English teacher is ill. Find a digital greetings card on the internet: What would be a good motif? Then write your message.

VOCABULARY **15**   **Other occasions**

Match the wishes to the cards.

So happy for you!   Hugs and kisses and my best birthday wishes.   Great job at school!

Life is better when you're together!   May all your dreams come true this year!

Sorry you're leaving!   Sending you lots of love on your special day!   Hooray! You did it!

It won't be the same without you!   A new family member … how happy you must be!

You're off to new places. Good luck!

WRITING

16 Register

a) *Register shows how formal or informal the language in a text is. Match text types A–H with 1–8 on the line.*

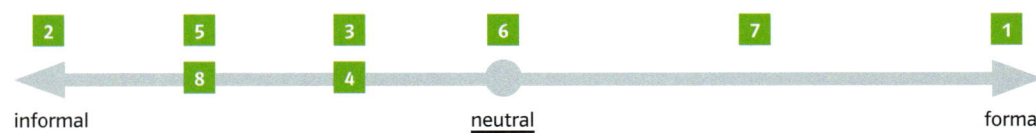

```
  2      5        3        6            7            1
         8        4
◄───────────────────────●──────────────────────────►
informal              neutral                    formal
```

A an email to all the people in a school club
B a business letter
C a text message to your best friend
D a message on a greetings card to your favourite teacher

E a postcard to your grandparents
F an email from a child to an aunt or uncle
G an email asking for information from an online shop
H a letter from a school to parents

b) *Decide if each phrase is informal, semi-formal or formal.*

1. You're the best.
2. That's really cool news!
3. Are you available next Friday?
4. We are writing to inform you of some important news.

5. Thank you for your letter of 17th April.
6. I look forward to receiving your reply.
7. We're gonna have loads and loads of laughs.
8. Many thanks for inviting me to your party.

c) *Compare your answers from a) and b) in class.*

Lösung: a) 1B, 2C, 3D, 4A, 5E, 6G, 7H, 8F; **b)** informal: 1, 2, 7; semi-formal: 3, 8; formal: 4, 5, 6

VIEWING **MK 17** 〈 **How to: Make a tutorial** 〉 → S11

a) *Make expert groups. Focus on these types of messages:*

WB 56/8

WB 56/8: Writing (formal letter)

Group A: *How to write an email.*
Group B: *How to write a formal letter.*
Group C: *How to write a text message.*

b) *Find tutorials for your type of message on the internet and takes notes on …*

– reasons for using the type of text
– how the information is organised
– the register
– useful words and phrases
– what you shouldn't do

> **Tip**
>
> Use the information in the Options on p. 87 and what you've learned from these **Text and media smart** pages to make your own tutorial.

c) *Watch the tutorial again. Which of these devices are used to pass on the information?*

different colours are used

not too much information is given on one screen

examples are provided

not all information is shown at once

information is highlighted   …

December

Mon	Tue	Wed	Thur	Fri	Sat	Sun
1	2	3	4	5	6	7
8	9	10	11	12	13	14
15	16	17	18	19	20	21
22	23	24	25	26	27	28
29	30	31				

WRITING

18 Writing options

Now that you know more about writing different types of messages, <u>try out</u> your new skills with the writing options below.

20: A game

Writing skills

Remember …
- that the message should have a clear purpose.
- to use an appropriate register.
- to organise the information so that it is clear and easy to understand.
- to be polite.
- to set out your text correctly for the type of message you're writing.

Group A:
Claire has asked Olivia to write an email to a local bookshop. She wants the bookshop to sell the community centre calendars. Step into Olivia's role and write the email. Ask …

- if they will sell the calendars.
- how many they think they can sell.
- if they want to keep some of the money from selling them.

Group B:
Your family bought one of the community centre calendars while they were on holiday in London. Write a letter to Claire Fraser, the manager of the community centre. Tell her that you like …

- the idea of a calendar with photos that show local history.
- the pictures of the children in their costumes.
- the fact that the money goes to people in need.

Group C:
It is the day of the photoshoot in the community centre. Everybody has to be quiet so that the photographer can give instructions. Holly, Olivia and Amir have a group chat and send each other text messages. They comment on people in the scenes, costumes, what's happening, how they feel etc. This is how you can start:

Olivia	10:06 a.m.
Check out Jay's costume and 🔲! Looks like Sherlock Holmes! 😄	

	Holly	10:08 a.m.
	I think he looks gr8! Ur costume is …	

Amir	10:09 a.m.
…	

WRITING MK

19 ⟨ Your turn: A tutorial ⟩

Use your texts from ex. 18 or other texts from pp. 81–84 and make a tutorial for your type of text.

Useful phrases

In this tutorial you're going to learn how to write … | Here are some rules to follow. | Step 1: … | start / close with | write / type / include / use | write to friends / family / people you know well / strangers / adults | name / address / date / greeting / reason / ending | paragraph / empty line | icon / abbreviation / short form

Dos and don'ts

SPEAKING

1 **Good or bad <u>behaviour</u>?** → S16

WB 57/1

WB 57/1: Listening (matching)

a) *Look at the situations in the pictures. Then look at the dos and don'ts below which are typical of English-speaking countries (and for others too). Which ones can you use to describe each situation? Explain why.*

Lösung: a) A: The picture shows some teenagers who are getting off a bus. They're saying thank you to the bus driver. (Say thank you.; Be polite.) B: The picture shows a man and a woman in a park. The man is throwing a paper cup to the ground. (Don't litter.) C: The picture shows a man who is jumping the queue. (Don't jump the queue.) D: The picture shows a boy who is holding the door open for a man. (Hold the door open for others.; Be polite.)

> Say thank you.   Don't stare.   Don't point.   Be polite.   Don't stand in the way.
>
> <u>Hold</u> the door <u>open</u> for others.   Don't jump the queue.   Don't talk with your mouth full.
>
> Smile.   Say hello back.   Don't <u>litter</u>.   Don't stand too close to others.

b) *What counts as good or bad behaviour in your family / your school / <u>among</u> your friends? You can look at the dos and don'ts in a) for help.*

SPEAKING

2 **Your turn: Your experiences**

WB 57/2

WB 57/2: Reading (logical order)

Can you remember a situation in which someone behaved differently to what you'd normally expect (in Germany or in another country)? Tell your partner about what happened. How did you feel about it? How did you react?

Useful phrases

Just imagine what happened to me when … | I saw something really funny / strange / <u>odd</u> when … | I was really surprised. | I couldn't believe my eyes / ears. | I didn't understand what was <u>going on</u>. | Well, I <u>guess</u> every country has its own <u>customs</u>. | To me, it looked like good / bad behaviour, but then I realised …

VIEWING

3 **Aliens in London!** → S14

6

Just imagine: Aliens have landed in central London. It's a strange experience for everyone. Find out more!

a) *Watch the film. What did the aliens do wrong from a British point of view? Take notes.*

b) *Look at the stills. What's the situation and what goes wrong? Work with your notes from a).*

ung: a) no small talk,
rt answers, staring,
nding too close to
ple, not smiling

A   B

SPEAKING

4 **Role play: Breaking the ice** → S16

a) *You're at a station and your train is late. Another person is waiting for the train too. The person looks friendly and smiles at you. Write down a conversation you could have with him / her. Look at the icebreakers in the box for ideas. Remember: Question tags are a good way to start a conversation and to get feedback too.*

b) *Act out your conversation in class.*

> **Useful phrases**
>
> **Icebreakers**
> I hope the train will arrive soon. | How long do you think we'll have to wait for …? | How long have you been …? | I'm glad it isn't so crowded / busy / hot / cold here today. Yesterday it was so …, wasn't it? | Cool T-shirt! You must be a … fan. | I've heard the film / show / band / … is really good. | Have you seen the latest film with …?

WRITING

5 **Tips for aliens** → S11–S12

WB 57/3

Work in groups of 3–4. Write a short chapter of a travel guide for aliens who have come to visit earth. The chapter includes a list of tips about how to behave.

57/3: Grammar
r spotting)

> *Tips for aliens*
> It's good / bad manners to …
> You should always …
> You shouldn't ever …
> People here (don't) usually … when …
> It's a good / bad idea to … because …
> People (don't) like it when you …

LISTENING

1 At the museum

3/2

a) *Listen to the conversation between a teacher and a group of students at the British Museum. There are ten things the teacher tells the students to do. Make a list.*

Start: 1. pick up the audio guide   2. …

b) *Which group at the museum would you choose? Explain why.*
Lösung: a) 2. test the audio guide, 3. ask the museum assistant to help, 4. don't be too loud, 5. put things in locker, 6. look at museum map, 7. listen to audio guide, 8. complete worksheet, 9. take back audio guide, 10. meet at 4:00, don't be late

SPEAKING

2 Be a history detective[1]

WB 58/1
WB 59/2–4

Find out about something that happened in Roman times near where you live (or in other parts of Germany). Prepare prompt cards and give a one-minute speech to the class.

WB 58/1–59/2–4: Reading (correct order, mediation); Listening (multiple choice); Grammar (relative pronouns); Writing (report)

VOCABULARY

3 What's new?

a) *Olivia has to do a presentation. She has found this article about the history of different foods. Complete the text with the words below. Make sure to use the right form of the verbs.*

bring   coffee   Europe   produce   grow   chocolate

know   make   century   Spanish   travel   popular

There's a saying in English that goes like this: 'as American as apple pie'. But did you know that before the 17th ⬛1️⃣ , apples were not ⬛2️⃣ in America? They were first ⬛3️⃣ in Asia thousands of years ago, brought to Europe and only introduced into America much later. And the same thing happened with oranges and bananas. The first oranges probably came from China and arrived in the Americas on ⬛4️⃣ ships in the 1500s and 1600s, while bananas from Southeast Asia weren't introduced into America until the second half of the 19th century. And what about ⬛5️⃣ ? It's the same story: It was ⬛6️⃣ in Yemen in the 15th century long before it spread[2] to ⬛7️⃣ and was finally ⬛8️⃣ to South America by the French and to North America by the British.
Things ⬛9️⃣ in the other direction too. ⬛🔟 , for example, was very popular in South America among the Mayan Indians[3] and the Aztecs[4] for hundreds of years. Spanish explorers discovered it much later when they brought cocoa beans[5] back with them in 1528. The Spanish served[6] it as a drink too, but they ⬛1️⃣1️⃣ it sweeter with sugar and honey. It wasn't until 1847 that a British company ⬛1️⃣2️⃣ the first chocolate bar[7]. Other foods travelled too: potatoes, tomatoes, pineapples and beans, for example.

b) *Find out about five other foods and drinks you can buy in Germany. Where did they come from? How did they get here? Make notes and present your results to the class.*

1 detective [dɪˈtektɪv] Detektiv/-in | **2 to spread, spread, spread** [spred, spred, spred] (sich) verbreiten | **3 the Mayan Indians** [ðə ˈmaɪən ˈɪndɪənz] die Maya-Indianer | **4 the Aztecs** [ðiˈæzteks] die Azteken | **5 cocoa beans** [ˈkəʊkəʊ ˌbiːnz] Kakaobohnen | **6 to serve** [sɜːv] servieren | **7 bar** [bɑː] Riegel
Lösung: 1. century, 2. known, 3. grown, 4 Spanish, 5. coffee, 6. popular, 7. Europe, 8. brought, 9. travelled, 10. Chocolate, 11. made, 12. produced

MEDIATION

4 **Who said it and why?**

a) *While you were on a class trip to England, you read these quotes in the brochure of a museum you visited. Back home your grandparents have a look at the brochure and ask you about the quotes. Explain their meaning in German. Why did the people say it? What did they mean?*

> "All the world's a stage."
>
> **William Shakespeare, 1599, from the play *As You Like It***
>
> 1

> "I came. I saw. I conquered."
>
> **Julius Caesar, 46 BC**
>
> 2

> "Rome wasn't built in a day."
>
> **Queen Elizabeth, 1563, in a speech in Cambridge**
>
> 3

> "The important thing is not what they think of me, but what I think of them."
>
> 4 **Queen Victoria**

> "History is written by the winners."
>
> **George Orwell, 1944, Tribune**
>
> 5

> "History is herstory too."
>
> **Unknown**
>
> 6

b) *Your exchange partner asks you about famous German quotes. Find quotes on the internet. Then explain their meaning in English.*

VOCABULARY

5 **French words in English**

a) *The Normans brought their language, a kind of French, to England. Lots of French words became part of the English language. Look at these modern French words and say what they are in English.*

acteur	arriver	changer	cousin	grands-parents	départ
dialogue	histoire	danser	excuser	famille	différent
problème	répéter	visiteur	musique	théâtre	station

b) *Say the English words out loud. Compare the way you say them in French and English. You can use a dictionary for help or listen to the words in an online dictionary.*
Lösung: 1. actor, 2. (to) arrive, 3. (to) change, 4. cousin, 5. grandparents, 6. (to) depart, 7. dialogue, 8. history, 9. (to) dance, 10. (to) excuse, 11. family, 12. different, 13. problem, 14. (to) repeat, 15. visitor, 16. music, 17. theatre, 18. station

WRITING

6 **Plan a visit to a museum**

a) *Think of a museum you want to visit in or near your town. Write down five things you want to find out at the museum.*

b) *Discuss which kind of object you'd like to add to the museum. It can be an object about a topic you thought of in a), or something completely different. Then write a short text for the object.*

GRAMMAR

7 Exciting news

a) *Read the tip.*

> **Tip**
>
> You use **will** and **be going to** to talk about things in the future.
>
> You use **will** 1) for general facts, 2) when you decide to do something at the time of speaking, or 3) to talk about things you think will probably happen in the future.
>
> Claire: I'm making a historical calendar for the community centre, but **I'll need** some help.
> Olivia: What a great idea! **I'll help** you. And **I'll ask** my friends if they**'ll** help you too. I'm sure they **will** all **say** yes.
>
> You use **be going to** 1) for plans and intentions, or 2) when you are almost certain that something will happen, often because you can see the signs now.
>
> Olivia and her friends **are going to** appear in a historical calendar.
> It**'s going to** be a lot of fun.

b) *Complete the text with the right form of the verb:* **will future** *or* **going-to future**.

Olivia: Claire, you ▮1▮ (never / guess) what happened at school today.
Claire: Well, why don't you just tell me?
Olivia: Our next school play ▮2▮ (be) about Elizabeth I. Mr Day told me today. I'm so excited.
Claire: Sounds great. Have they already decided who ▮3▮ (play) the role of Elizabeth I?
Olivia: No, not yet. But Mr Day thinks that I ▮4▮ (have) a good chance. He saw me in your calendar and thought I looked great. And if get the role, I ▮5▮ (choose) my ladies-in-waiting. Of course, I ▮6▮ (ask) Gwen and Holly. I can't wait. I just know we ▮7▮ (have) a lot of fun together.

Lösung: b) 1. 'll never guess, 2. is going to be, 3. is going to play, 4. 'll have, 5. 'm going to choose/'ll choose, 6. 'm going to ask,'ll ask, 7. 'll going to have

GRAMMAR

8 Before the class trip to the Globe

Before Mr Benson takes his class on a trip to the Globe, he gives them some important information. Complete the text with the right form of the verb: **will future** *or* **going-to future**.

Now, everybody, I ▮1▮ (say) a few words about our trip to the Globe Theatre on Thursday, so please listen carefully. We ▮2▮ (catch[1]) the 9:30 train from Greenwich, so you must be at the station by 9:15. If you are late, we can't wait for you. In the morning we ▮3▮ (take) a tour of the theatre with a guide. These guides know a lot about Shakespeare's life and about London as it was in his time, so I hope you ▮4▮ (have) lots of interesting questions for him. After the tour I'm sure you ▮5▮ (be) hungry and thirsty[2]. So, make sure you have enough to eat and drink. In the afternoon we ▮6▮ (watch) Romeo and Juliet. As you know, the Globe doesn't have a roof and we ▮7▮ (be) outside. I've checked the weather forecast and, luckily, it ▮8▮ (not rain) on Thursday. But it ▮9▮ (be) cold, so you must bring warm clothes with you. Any questions?

1 catch, caught, caught [kætʃ, kɔːt, kɔːt] nehmen (Bus, Zug) | **2 thirsty** [ˈθɜːsti] durstig

Lösung: 1. 'm going to say, 2. 're going to catch, 3. 're going to take, 4. 'll have, 5. 'll be, 6. 're going to watch, 7. 'll be, 8. won't rain/isn't going to rain, 9. 'll be/'s going to be

GRAMMAR **9** ## A visit to Madame Tussauds

You can see a lot of important people from British history at the World Stage at Madame Tussauds wax museum in London. Match the sentences.

1. Here's a museum guide. If you want, you
2. The faces are made of wax. They
3. This dress is very beautiful. It
4. Today captains of British ships
5. If our teacher says yes, we
6. Is Daniel Radcliffe here? I
7. I've got a map of the 'World Stage', so you

a) can do a workshop at the Globe Theatre.
b) mustn't steal from other ships.
c) needn't ask a guide.
d) can't see him anywhere.
e) can ask him a question.
f) must be very expensive.
g) mustn't get too hot.

Lösung: 1. e), 2. g), 3. f), 4. b), 5. a), 6. d), 7. c)

GRAMMAR **10** ## An interview with a Celtic warrior

Imagine you're living in the year 2231. People have invented a time machine and you go back in time to interview a Celtic warrior in 400 AD. Complete the dialogue with the modals below.

can   may   must   can't   needn't   should(n't)   could(n't)   mustn't

You: Excuse me, I've just arrived from the 23rd century in my time machine here. **1** I ask you some questions?

Celt: Yes, of course you **2** . What would you like to know?

You: Well, my first question is: **3** you tell me why you aren't wearing any paint on your body? I've heard that Celtic warriors didn't wear any clothes. They painted their bodies instead.

Celt: Oh, you **4** believe everything you hear about us. We don't wear paint on our bodies every day, only when we need to frighten[1] our enemies.[2]

You: But the Romans are your enemies, aren't they? And you **5** fight them every day, **6** you?

Celt: Oh no. Not now. When they first conquered our lands in 43 AD, we often fought them. But we **7** do that any more. It's 400 AD and we're friends now.

You: Really? **8** you tell me how that happened?

Celt: They've helped us a lot. They've built towns, roads, baths and palaces. Before they arrived, we Celts knew how to use tools and we **9** make lots of things like weapons[3] and fine jewellery. But we **10** build roads or towns or baths. And now their soldiers are helping us to fight the Anglo-Saxons. We Celts are brave warriors but we **11** fight the Anglo-Saxons on our own. If you come from the 23rd century, perhaps I **12** ask you what is going to happen to our country.

You: I'm sorry, I wish I **13** help you, but I really **14** go now. I promised to be back in the 23rd century for dinner. And I **15** be late. But thanks for all the information you've given me. Now I **16** tell everybody what life was really like for you. And don't worry! You'll be fine.

1 to frighten [ˈfraɪtn] erschrecken; Angst machen | **2 enemy** [ˈenəmi] Feind/-in | **3 weapon** [ˈwepən] Waffe

Lösung: 1. May/Can, 2. may/can, 3. Can/Could, 4. mustn't/shouldn't, 5. must, 6. mustn't, 7. needn't, 8. Can/Could, 9. could, 10. couldn't, 11. can't, 12. can/should, 13. could, 14. must, 15. mustn't, 16. can

→ Solutions p. 300

Unit 4
On the move

A

SPEAKING

WB 60/1

1 Reasons for travelling

WB 60/1: Vocabulary (reasons)

a) *Look at the photos A–D. What are the people doing? What might they be thinking?*

b) *Why do you think these people are travelling? Share your ideas in class. The words and phrases in the box can help you.*

c) *Collect more reasons for travelling.*

Lösung: c) business trips, university studies abroad, high school year, spend the holidays together, research for an article/a book, etc.

> **Word bank**
>
> class trip | family holiday | have fun |
> escape from hard life | get to know other
> cultures | hope for a better future |
> visit family | learn a foreign language |
> have a break | meet exchange partners

LISTENING

2 Travel situations → S13

a) *What can happen when you're travelling to another country? Share your ideas in class.*

3/4–8 b) *Listen to the different travel situations. Match the speakers with the problems they're talking about. You don't need all of these ideas.*

feel seasick   get lost   have too much luggage   have communication problems

be scared of flying   lose money   forget tickets   miss train / plane

Lösung: b) 1. have communication problems, 2. feel seasick, 3. miss train, 4. get lost, 5. lose money

In Unit 4 you learn

… how to talk about <u>travel</u> experiences and the pros and cons of travelling. You learn:

- to talk about the future with the simple present and the present progressive,
- to plan and write a travel <u>itinerary</u>,
- words and phrases for talking about travel.

D

VOCABULARY

WB 60/2–3

60/2–3: Vocabulary (crossword); Vocabulary (matching)

3 Travel words → S1–S4

a) *Make a grid and sort the words into these categories:*

transport | places | people | things you need

b) *Can you think of more travel words? Add them to the grid.*

> <u>departure lounge</u> | by bike / train / bus / car / plane | <u>passport</u> | <u>boarding card</u> | check-in <u>desk</u> | on foot | <u>visa</u> | <u>passenger</u> | <u>flight attendant</u> | train station | <u>customs</u> | <u>suitcase</u> | public transport | tickets | guide | <u>airport</u> | by boat / <u>ferry</u> / ship | tourist | passport <u>control</u> | <u>arrivals hall</u> | luggage | <u>foreign currency</u> | duty-free shop | <u>environmentally friendly</u> | pollution | <u>CO$_2$ emissions</u> | trip | journey | destination

c) *Your turn: Choose 5–10 words from your grid. Use them to write a short text about your last holiday or trip.* → More help ○ 140/1

Example: Last summer we spent the <u>holidays</u> at my grandparents' house. We went there by train. It's a long journey, so we left for the train station very early. …

SPEAKING

Nouns and verbs the same form, 4

4 Ways of travelling → More help ○ 140/2

Look at the <u>means of transport</u> which you collected in ex. 3. In groups of 3–4, discuss the pros and cons. Think of things like time, money, <u>convenience</u> and the environment. Present your main points to the class.

3/9 🕮 # What time do we get there?

The Clarkson family were on a ferry. In the distance they could see the French <u>coast</u>.

"France here we come!" said Charlie.

"Uh-huh. What time do we get there?"
5 asked Charlie's older brother Benjamin with zero <u>enthusiasm</u>.

"Oh, Benjamin!" said their mother. "In 30 minutes we arrive in a foreign country! Aren't you even a little bit excited?"

10   "All my friends are meeting at the leisure centre later this afternoon. I won't be there! I'll be in boring France, and we don't get back until late in the evening two weeks from now. My friends will forget who I am!"

15   "Teenagers!" said Dad as he rolled his eyes.

Charlie didn't think that was fair. He was looking forward very much to visiting France. They were staying in a *gîte*, a <u>holiday home</u> on a farm in the countryside.

20   At that moment there was an announcement.

"This is the captain speaking. The ferry arrives at 3:15 <u>local time</u>. You may want to put your watches <u>ahead</u> one hour."

Charlie looked at the time on his phone: 25
1:47. Something was wrong.

"Guys, …" he said to his family. "We found out it takes five hours to drive to the *gîte* …."

"Yeah," said Benjamin. "I can't believe we're going to sit in the car for five hours just to go   30
to some farm in the middle of nowhere. Are we stopping for a break?"

Charlie ignored him. "We can leave the <u>port</u> and be on the road about forty-five minutes after the ferry arrives, and we're meeting the   35
owners at about 7:30 …"

"That's right," said Dad.

"We forgot the time difference!" said Charlie. "We won't get there until about 8:30. The owners won't be very pleased if we're an   40
hour late."

"Hmmm," said Mum. "We should call them." They all looked at Charlie.

"No!" said Charlie. "I'm not making a phone call in French!"   45

He loved French, but speaking it on the phone wasn't easy.

"You're the best at speaking French," said Mum. "Just tell them we're arriving an hour later. Easy."   50

"OK, OK," Charlie <u>mumbled</u> as he <u>dialled</u> the number on his phone.

"*Allô?*" said a woman.

Charlie explained the situation. It wasn't easy, and he made some mistakes, but he   55
said what he needed to say. At the end, he apologised for his French.

"Don't worry about the delay. And about your French – it's not too bad," said the woman with a London accent. "It's better than mine   60
was when I moved here ten years ago!"

1 Understanding the text → S5

READING

a) *What is happening at these times in the future?*

2:15 p.m. UK time   about 3:30 p.m. French time   about 7:30 p.m. UK time

b) *How do Charlie and Benjamin feel about the trip to France? Make a grid and write down what you find out about the two characters in the text.*

SPEAKING

c) *Your turn: Can you identify more with Benjamin or Charlie? Say what's important to you when you go on holiday.*

Lösung: a) 2:15 p.m. UK time: The ferry is arriving at the port. About 3:30 p.m.
French time: They're leaving the ferry. About 7:30 p.m. UK time: They're arriving at the holiday home.

GRAMMAR

WB 61/4

21: Working with
grammar
61/4: Listening
(true/false)

2 Find the rule: Simple present and present progressive with future meaning → G9

a) *Find examples of both forms in the text.*

simple present with future meaning	present progressive with future meaning
The ferry **arrives** at 3:15 local time.	All my friends **are meeting** at the leisure centre later this afternoon.

b) *Think about when you use the **simple present** and when you use the **present progressive** to talk about the future. Write down the rule.* → More help ○ 140/3

Lösung: b) Rule: You use the simple present for actions in the future which are related to timetables or programmes. You use the present progressive to talk about plans or arrangements which you have made for the (near) future.

GRAMMAR

WB 61/5

22: Tandem activity:
concert
61/5: Grammar
(simple present vs.
present progressive)

3 Simple present or present progressive? → G9

Choose the best form for each situation.

1. My train **arrives / is arriving** at 10:45.
2. Your grandparents **come / are coming** to lunch next Sunday.
3. The film **starts / is starting** at 7:30 this evening.
4. Hurry up! The bus **leaves / is leaving** in three minutes!
5. **Does Luke play / Is Luke playing** football tomorrow evening?
6. What time **do you meet / are you meeting** your friends this afternoon?
7. What time **does the concert start / is the concert starting**?

Lösung: 1. arrives, 2. are coming, 3. starts, 4. leaves, 5. Is Luke playing, 6. are you meeting, 7. does the concert start

GRAMMAR

WB 62/6–7

62/6–7: Grammar
(simple present vs.
present progressive);
grammar (future vs.
present)

4 Benjamin's post → More practice ● 140/4 → G9

*Read Benjamin's latest post from France. Put in the right form of the verb: **simple present** or **present progressive**.*

There are still lots of things to look forward to on this holiday. We **1** (go) pony trekking tomorrow. I've never done it before, but it's with a group, and you don't need any experience. The group **2** (leave) at 8 o'clock tomorrow morning – that's a bit early for me! We **3** (not do) anything in the afternoon, so I can relax then. In the evening we **4** (see) a show in a local theatre. It'll be in French, of course. It **5** (start) at 7:30, and it **6** (finish) at 11. That's a lot of French! But there'll be music and dancing too, so that's OK! The day after tomorrow, we **7** (take) a boat trip on the river. We **8** (have) lunch on the boat too! The boat tour **9** (end) at about 3 o'clock, and then we **10** (go) to the supermarket to buy lots of French food to take home. We can't do that on the last day because the ferry **11** (depart) in the afternoon, and we won't have time to drive to the ferry port and go shopping. We **12** (not leave) the gîte early, because we **13** (enjoy) a last nice French breakfast before we go! At first I didn't want to come to France, but I've really enjoyed it. I'm sorry we **14** (go) home on Saturday. I'd like to stay for another two or three weeks!

Lösung: 1. are going, 2. leaves, 3. aren't doing, 4. are seeing, 5. starts, 6. finishes, 7. are taking, 8. are having, 9. ends, 10. are going, 11. departs, 12. aren't leaving, 13. are enjoying, 14. are going

SPEAKING

👥
WB 62/8
WB 63/9

WB 62/8–63/9:
Vocabulary (text completion); Speaking (answers to questions)

5 Role play: Around the world → S16

a) **A:** *You're a film star. For your next film you're going to act in some amazing places around the world. First, make notes about where you're going, what you're doing and how you're getting there. What times do your* <u>flights</u>/trains/buses arrive?

B: *You're a magazine reporter who wants to interview the film star. It's your job to call him/her and ask about what he/she is doing for the next few weeks. First, make notes about the questions you're going to ask.*

Start: B: Thank you for giving me the chance to interview you. May I ask you about …?
A: …

b) *Now <u>switch</u> roles: B is the film star and A is the reporter.*

WRITING **MK**

WB 63/10
WB 64/11–12

Look here for help with your blog: 🌐 36c8a4

WB 63/10–64/11–12:
Writing (travel blog); Mediation (dialogue); Speaking (phone call)

SPEAKING 👥👥

6 What happened? → S11, S22

a) *The Jones family had some problems during their holiday. In their blog they tell their friends about everything that went wrong. Look at the pictures and write the blog entries.*
→ More help ○ 141/5

1   2   3

b) *Your turn: Mill around the classroom. Think of a funny, scary or embarrassing situation which you experienced during your last holiday or on a trip. Tell your partner about it. Try to make it as interesting as possible.* → More help ○ 141/6
Lösung: a) Vgl. Lösung *Diff pool* 141/5, SB S. 301; **b)** Vgl. Lösung *Diff pool* 141/6, SB S. 301

LISTENING

3/11 🎧
WB 65/13

WB 65/13: Listening (answers to questions)

7 ⟨ A song: Island in the sun ⟩ Weezer → S13

When you're on a holiday
You can't find the words to say
All the things that come to you
And I wanna feel it too

On an island in the sun
We'll be playing and having fun
And it makes me feel so fine
I can't control my brain

When you're on a golden sea
You don't need no memory
Just a place to call your own
As we drift into the zone

On an island in the sun
…

We'll run away together
We'll spend some time forever
We'll never feel bad any more

Lösung: a) Words/Phrases: 1. We'll be playing and having fun, 2. And it makes me feel so fine I can't control my brain, 3. We'll never feel bad any more; Feelings: 1. happy, relaxed; 2. fine, happy; 3. happy, free

a) *Listen to the song. Which words / phrases tell you how the main character feels?*

b) *Write an extra verse for the song. First, think of words that rhyme.*

Start: When you're on a lonely beach … / When you're feeling really cool …

3/13 🎧 ## At passport control

Rafiq lives in London. His parents are from Bangladesh, but up to now he hasn't been able to visit their family there.

"Can we visit Aunt Sadia and Uncle Dhanu
5 this summer?" Rafiq asked his parents. "Sorry, Rafiq, we can't. We have to work," his mother replied.

"Why can't I go alone then? I wasn't allowed to fly on my own last year, but now
10 I'm 14 and now I can." Rafiq was getting really excited.

"Well, it would be nice if you finally got to know Bangladesh," his father said. "But we'll need to make sure that you have all
15 the necessary documents first. I think your passport photo is about four years old," he continued. "You don't look anything like that now. You'll have to get a new passport."

"I'm sure I won't have to get a new
20 passport. It's still valid for one year, that's what's important. I don't even think I'll be allowed to get one before the old one expires," Rafiq insisted.

"I think you can apply for a new one," his
25 mother replied. "But you'll have to check to be sure. You'll need to do it right away!"

Rafiq looked up the regulations on the internet. He was right – he didn't have to get a new passport before this one expired.

30 It was a long flight from London to Dhaka, the capital of Bangladesh. Rafiq had to change planes in India, and he was very tired when he arrived.

'I hope I'll be able to stay awake until I
35 get to my aunt and uncle's flat,' he thought to himself.

At the passport control desk he opened his passport at the photo page.

The man looked at the photo and frowned. "Is this really you? Your passport photo has to 40 look like you. Because I can't identify you, I'm not allowed to let you go through."

Rafiq started to feel nervous. What would happen if he wasn't allowed to enter the country? 45

The man looked at Rafiq's tired, nervous face. "I'll have to call somebody about this," the man said and picked up the phone. Now Rafiq felt really scared.

A few minutes later, Rafiq was in a side 50 room and had to answer more questions. Luckily, he had his uncle and aunt's address and phone number with him and was allowed to call them. When they came to the airport, they were able to identify Rafiq, and the 55 immigration officer finally said, "You can go through now. But please get a new passport as soon as you can. It'll save everybody a lot of trouble in the future. OK?"

"OK, thank you!" said Rafiq with great 60 relief. 'Now I'll be able to enjoy my holiday in Bangladesh after all,' he thought to himself.

READING ## **8** At passport control → S5

a) *Explain Rafiq's problem when he arrives in Bangladesh.*

b) *How do you think Rafiq felt during his conversation with the man at passport control? How do you think he felt when he left the airport?* → More help ○ 141/7

Start: Rafiq felt … because …
He was worried that …

c) *Role play: Act out the scene at passport control. What does Rafiq tell the immigration officer? Which questions does Rafiq have to answer in the side room?*

Lösung: a) When Rafiq arrives in Bangladesh, the officer at passport control tells him that he isn't allowed to let him into the country because Rafiq doesn't look anything like his passport photo and he can't identify him.
b) Vgl. Lösung *Diff pool* 141/7, SB S. 301

GRAMMAR   **9** *Be able to, be allowed to, have to* → G10

Read the text on p. 99 again and make sentences.

Rafiq His parents The immigration officer Rafiq's aunt and uncle	➕	isn't allowed to aren't able to have to is allowed to are able to doesn't have to	➕	go to Bangladesh for the summer. fly on his own. work. let Rafiq go through passport control. get a new passport. identify Rafiq.

Lösung: His parents aren't able to go to Bangladesh … / Rafiq is allowed to fly on his own. / His parents have to work. / The immigration officer isn't allowed to let Rafiq go … / Rafiq doesn't have to get a new passport. / Rafiq's aunt and uncle are able to identify Rafiq.

GRAMMAR   **10** **Find the rule: The substitute form of modals** → G10

WB 65/14
WB 66/15

KV 23: Working with grammar
WB 65/14–66/15: Grammar (substitute forms); Grammar (matching)

a) *Find more examples in the text of **be able to**, **be allowed to** and **have to** in the simple present and the simple past.*

b) *In which sentence (A or B) does **can** mean **be able to** ('können', 'fähig sein') and in which does it mean **be allowed to** ('dürfen')?*

A: I **can** fly on my own because I'm 14 now.
B: His aunt and uncle **can** identify him.

c) *In which sentence (A or B) does **have to** mean **must** ('müssen') and in which does it mean **needn't** ('nicht zu brauchen')?*

A: Rafiq's parents **have to** work.
B: He doesn't **have to** get a new passport before the old one expires.

Lösung: b) A: be allowed to, B: be able to; **c)** A: must, B: needn't

GRAMMAR   **11** **Getting around in Dhaka** → G10

WB 66/16

KV 24: Tandem activity: School rules
WB 66/16: Grammar (jumbled sentences)

Rafiq is talking to Masud, his cousin from Dhaka, the capital of Bangladesh. What does Masud tell Rafiq to do? Rewrite the dialogue with the substitute form of the modals in the simple present.

Start: Masud: You **have to** visit the old centre of Dhaka. …

Masud: You **must** visit the old centre of Dhaka. It's quite small, but it's very interesting.
Rafiq: Sounds good. Is it OK if I go on my own?
Masud: Yes, of course. You **needn't** worry about that. But you **must** be careful of the <u>traffic</u>!
Rafiq: And what's the best way to get there?
Masud: Walk. The traffic here is very slow. People here **can** get to places more quickly if they walk.
Rafiq: But it's so hot! I don't want to walk. **May** I take a taxi? Will your parents be OK with that?
Masud: Sure, but we'll ask them.
Rafiq: In London it's expensive to take a taxi. What about here?
Masud: Taxis are very cheap. But you **must** agree on the price first.
Rafiq: Oh, I've never done that. I don't know if I **can** <u>bargain</u>. Maybe I should walk after all?
Masud: Good idea! I'm sorry I **can't** come with you, but I **mustn't** miss classes.

Lösung: 2. don't have to worry, 3. have to be careful, 4. are able to get, 5. Am I allowed to take, 6. have to agree on, 7. I'm able to bargain, 8. I'm not able to come, 9. I'm not allowed to miss

GRAMMAR
WB 67/17–18
WB 68/19–20

67/17–18–68/19–20:
mmar (simple past
ns of substitute
ms); Grammar (future
ns of substitute
ns); Grammar (mixed
ses of substitute
ns); Speaking (tips on
toms)

12 Rafiq's school day in Dhaka → More practice ○ 142/8 → More practice ● 142/9 → G10

*Rafiq is writing to his friend in London. Use **have to**, **be able to** or **be allowed to** in the right tense (present, past or future).*

It was a busy day today. I ▮1▮ (be allowed to) go to school with Masud. I really like his school! Classes were mostly in English, so I ▮2▮ (be able to) understand almost everything. As you can imagine, all the classrooms are smart classrooms: The students ▮3▮ (not have to) take a lot of books to school and they ▮4▮ (be allowed to) do a lot of research. In history, the students ▮5▮ (have to) write a test on Victorian Britain, and, of course, I ▮6▮ (not allowed to) help anybody. To tell you the truth, I ▮7▮ (not be able to) answer half of the questions anyway. But Masud and his classmates did a really good job. During the lunch break some of the students taught me a bit of the Bengali alphabet. Not easy, but at the end of the break, I ▮8▮ (be able to) write my name! I really enjoyed this school day, but tomorrow I ▮9▮ (have to) stay at home and relax. I'm still on holiday!

Lösung: 1. was allowed to, 2. was able to, 3. don't have to, 4. are allowed to, 5. had to, 6. wasn't allowed to, 7. wasn't able to, 8. was able to, 9. will have to

SPEAKING
👥
WB 68/21

68/21: Writing (tips
travel forum)

13 Your turn: When I was . . .

What were you (not) able/allowed to do in the past? What did you (not) have to do in the past? What's it like now? Tell your partner.

Example: When I was four, I **wasn't able to** swim. Now I can.
When I was ten, I **wasn't allowed to** have my own phone. Now I have one.
When I was five, I **didn't have to do homework**. Now I have to do lots.

Lösung: When I was two, I wasn't able to ride a bike. Now I can. / When I was seven, I wasn't allowed to take the train to my grandparents' house without my parents. Now I can visit them on my own. / etc.

MEDIATION
3/14 🎧
WB 69/22

25: Airport
ouncements
69/22: Vocabulary
tching)

14 Airport announcements → S17

a) *After a holiday in Great Britain, you're waiting with your family at London Heathrow for your flight back to Berlin. You're taking British Airways flight BA 0982 at 9:15. While you're waiting, you hear different announcements. First, read the skills box. Then listen to the announcements. Which of them are important for you? Take notes. The key words in the box can help you.*

b) *Your parents didn't hear the announcements. Tell them the most important points in German.*

Lösung: a) Important: 2, 3, 5; 2. Passengers must keep their luggage with them at all times. 3. Boarding time for Flight 0982 to Berlin has been delayed until 9:35. 5. Flight 0982 is ready for boarding but will now leave from Gate 14.

> ### Mediation skills
>
> **Announcements** at airports or train stations often contain new words, and background sounds make them difficult to understand. It can help you to focus on important words, e.g. names of people or places, numbers or times, nouns and verbs.

flight number | boarding time | gate |
delay / why? | luggage

SPEAKING 👥
WB 69/23

9/23: Writing
ing competition)

 15 Your turn: Destinations for a school trip → More help ○ 142/10 → S16

Choose a European capital you'd both like to visit with your class on your next school trip. Use websites in English and find out about two different ways of getting there (e.g. by train or by coach). Compare the means of transport. Think of time, money and environmental issues. Then decide how you would like to get there and why. Present your ideas to the class.

How to plan a travel itinerary

For the unit task you're going to plan and write an itinerary for a class trip.
On this skills page you'll get helpful tips on what makes a good itinerary.

LISTENING

3/16
WB 70/24

WB 70/24: Skills (correct order)

1 Trips and itineraries: A travel expert's tips → S13

a) *Listen to an interview with Amy Lassiter, the owner of a British tour operator, knowB4Ugo. What does the reporter think is the 'real' problem on group trips? What does Amy say about it?*

b) *Look at the word bank. Then listen again and take notes on these questions:*

1. Amy talks about planning a trip from two perspectives. Describe each one.
2. Which tips did you find helpful? Give reasons.

> **Word bank**
>
> eco-friendly | flexible | practical | realistic | wasteful | highlight | illness | locals | ways of travelling | means of transport | package tour | souvenir | structure | theme days

Lösung: a) The reporter thinks that lost passports and illnesses are the biggest problems. Amy says the real problem is bad planning before the trip.

WRITING

WB 70/25

WB 70/25: Skills (strong adjectives)

Lösung: a) The written itinerary has got motivating descriptions and photos. The trip will take the tourists to some of London's top attractions and each day has got a highlight. The time frame is clear and realistic and there are fixed meeting times and places. However, Tube stops are not always given and there's no detailed information on the means of transport that will be used.

2 A typical itinerary → S11

a) *On the right you can read part of a tour operator's itinerary for a trip to London. Compare what you see here with Amy's tips for good itineraries. What does this itinerary do well, what could be better in your opinion? Explain.*

b) *You can only see Days 1 and 2 of the itinerary, but there are two more days on the tour. Work with a partner. One of you writes an itinerary for Day 3, one of you for Day 4. Follow the examples. Peer-edit each other's texts. What can you improve?*

A **LOOK AT LONDON**

Discover London, the capital of the United Kingdom! With only four days to spend in one of the world's most spectacular cities, is it any surprise you aren't sure about where, how or what to start with? But trust us: We've done our homework and know the perfect mix for an unforgettable class trip!

DAY 1

After arrival and hotel check-in, discover London at your own pace and get on a sightseeing bus. On the tour you'll get an overall view of the city and see some of its amazing attractions on your first day! Later, enjoy dinner at the tasty Tandoori restaurant we've chosen for you in the popular Covent Garden area.

▷ 1:00 p.m.: ticket pick-up for bus tours
▷ 5:15 p.m.: meet in lobby
▷ 6:00 p.m.: Taj Mahal Tandoori (Tube: Holborn)

DAY 2

First, the Tower of London with the amazing crown jewels is a must-see historical attraction. But many prisoners died horrible deaths here, so don't come face-to-face with a ghost! Enjoy a private tour with the Raven Master and his famous ravens. But that isn't all: Shop at the colourful market stalls at Camden Lock Market, a favourite for visitors and locals.

▷ 11:30 a.m.: picnic lunch, view of Tower at City Hall
▷ 12:30 p.m.: guided tour of Tower (across the bridge)
▷ 4:30 p.m.: Camden Market + dinner (Tube: Camden Town)

MK ## Our class trip

A tour operator in Britain wants to add class trips to its <u>catalogue</u>. At the moment they're asking Year 7 students to send in **itinerary suggestions** for four-day class trips to anywhere in Europe. The prize for the best trip idea? All the Year 7 classes at the winning school will go on that same trip – for free!

Look here for help with your itinerary:
🌐 **36c8a4**

Step 1

Decide on a destination → WB 71/26

Get into groups of 5–6. Collect ideas for the class trip you would like to design an itinerary for. Think about which destinations would need more/less research time.

71/26: Matching (places to photos)

Step 2

Do your research → WB 71/27

*The tour operator has given <u>criteria</u> which **every** trip must include. Do research on your destination <u>based on</u> these criteria:*

1. Activities must include something:	2. Each day must include:	3. Ways of travelling must include:
historical | surprising | free | with action | cultural	a theme | plans for lunch and dinner | one group activity	an eco-friendly <u>alternative</u> – Think of the environment!

→ internet research S19

71/27: Transport (correct order)

Step 3

What to do and when → WB 71/28

You now have lots of input and need to choose what you do on what day and at what time. Also: Don't forget how you get to your destination and back home!
→ substitute form of modals G10

71/28: Four-day trip (correct order)

Step 4

<u>Draw up</u> your itinerary

Draw up an itinerary with an <u>introduction</u>, descriptions, important time information and also pictures. Make your itinerary interesting enough for Year 7 students.
→ future tenses G9 → travel itineraries S11

Step 5

Present your itinerary

Present your trip idea. Make sure you're <u>motivating</u> and convincing.
→ presentations S16

Step 6

Discuss and vote

Which trip will your class send in for the competition? Why? Discuss and vote.

3/17–20 🎧 **Where I belong**

1 **Before you read**

👥 *Talk about reasons why people might want to leave their country.*

KV 26: Questioning the text

A My father grabbed my arms and looked down at me. "Listen," he said. "You can't do anything here. It's getting harder and harder for people like us who travel around with our
5 animals. Soon we'll have nothing left. If you go to England, you'll be able to help the whole family. And maybe, one day, you can come back and help Somalia too."

A week ago, I'd been nothing but a girl
10 who would <u>lead</u> the same kind of life as her mother. I thought I would have a husband one day, and children to look after and teach. But now, suddenly, I was <u>responsible</u> for my whole family – and the future of my country too.

15 For a moment I was too scared to answer my father. But I knew he wouldn't <u>change</u> his <u>mind</u>. He had chosen me for this task and I had to <u>accept</u> it. "Yes," I said. "Yes, I will."

There was no time for anything else. My
20 father jumped back into his car, turned round quickly and drove off, his face like a <u>mask</u>. I walked down the road to join the man who was taking me away.

What are your ideas:
What do you think the narrator's journey will be like?

B The <u>smuggler</u> first took me to Kenya in a boat.
25 Those journeys are very dangerous because the boats are always <u>overloaded</u> and the sea

is full of <u>sharks</u>. Many people have died while they were trying to do what I was doing. But I didn't know that until much later. While we were at sea, I had other things to worry about. 30

It was a little boat, and I was <u>crushed</u> between men I had never seen before. It was the first time I had ever been in a boat, and Uncle didn't tell me that it would <u>rock</u> so badly as the waves <u>smashed</u> against it. I was scared, 35 and I thought every moment that I was going to be sick.

I closed my eyes and repeated the things that Uncle had told me to learn.

My name is Khadija Ahmed Mussa. I'm 40 *thirteen years old. I'm going to England to join my mother and my brother and sisters. My sisters' names are Fowsia, Maryan and Sabra. Fowsia is eleven, Maryan is seven and Sabra is four. And my brother Abdi is fourteen.* 45

I didn't try to imagine their faces or what they were like. They weren't people at all, just words that I had to learn. *My name is Khadija …*

Those hours in the boat were the worst hours of my life. I <u>survived</u> by <u>closing</u> myself 50 <u>away from</u> what was happening, and when we landed in Kenya, I felt like a different person.

C What happened to me is called piggyback. Uncle was <u>giving</u> me <u>a 'piggyback'</u> to England. That was his business, and he did exactly what 55 my father had paid for. Nothing else.

After we had left the boat, we travelled by road and then by plane, and every time we went through a <u>checkpoint</u> Uncle smiled at me. That was part of his routine. When we 60 were through, the smile was put away together with my passport and he ignored me again, even when we were sitting next to each other.

I could have run away when we changed planes in Dubai. He showed me a seat in the 65 airport and told me to sit there until he came back. But where would I have run to? I didn't know anything about that place and I had no

passport except the one in Uncle's pocket.
70 My father had paid for me to go to England
and that was where I had to go.

I felt cold in the air-conditioning, and I
<u>concentrated</u> on repeating the same words
inside my head. *My name is Khadija …*

> **What are your ideas:**
> How do you think Britain will
> be different for the narrator?

D When we landed in England, the sky was grey,
and it was raining. Not clean, heavy rain, like
the *gu*, but a <u>steady</u>, <u>depressing</u> <u>drizzle</u>. I didn't
see how it was going to make anything grow
because everywhere I looked the ground was
80 <u>covered</u> with <u>concrete</u>. I felt hard and cold,
like that concrete ground. If I hadn't, maybe
everything would have happened differently
and the <u>officials</u> would have sent me home.
But they didn't. They looked at my face and
85 then at my passport and let me into the
country.

On the train, there were people from all
over the world – they were all taking care
not to look at each other. Was the whole city
90 like that? Thousands of people who were all
pretending that nobody else was there?

We travelled through streets of tall, yellow-
grey buildings, and all the time the <u>useless</u>
rain went on falling. When I looked up at the
95 sky, I couldn't see any sign of the sun. Was it
always <u>invisible</u> here?

I thought Uncle would take me to my new
family's house. But when we got off the train,
he took some coins out of his pocket and gave
100 them to me. "Can you use a telephone?" he said.

I looked at him. "Of course I can!"

"You see the phone there?" He pointed
down the road. "Call the number I give you.
Then stay in the <u>phone box</u>. The person who
answers the phone will come and <u>fetch</u> you." 105

I was too surprised to do anything except
stare at him. "Don't waste time," he said.
"People will notice you. Go!" The piggyback
was over and suddenly I was <u>on my own</u>,
walking down this strange road. 110

The phone was different from the phones
I had used before, but it was easy to see how
to use it. I <u>pressed</u> the <u>buttons</u> very carefully:
I had no more money to put in if I made a
mistake the first time. 115

"Hello," said a boy's voice. He spoke
<u>Somali</u>, but his accent was very strange. "Are
you in the phone box?"

"Yes," I said. "But I don't know where –"
"Just wait," he said. "I'm coming." 120

I knew it was him as soon as he came
round the corner. A tall Somali boy who came
<u>straight</u> towards me. He opened the door and
stared at me.

"I'm Abdi," he said. When I <u>hesitated</u>, he 125
said his full name this time. "I'm Abdirahman
Ahmed Mussa."

He was much older than my brother
Mahmoud, and tall too, but he was – more
of a boy. That was when I really understood 130
how far I had travelled. I was far away from
Somalia, and far from myself, in a place where
the people were going to be different. And I
had to learn how to live there.

I stared straight back at Abdi. "And I'm 135
Khadija Ahmed Mussa," I said.

From: *Where I belong* by Gillian Cross

SPEAKING

2 Your reaction

a) *Do you like the story? Explain why or why not.*

b) *Have you heard or read about people who try to come to Europe as <u>refugees</u>? How are these stories similar to the narrator's experience? The ideas from pp. 94–95 can help you.*

3 Understanding the story → S5–6

READING
WB 72/29–30

WB 72/29–30: Reading (headings); Reading (multiple choice)

a) *Explain why the narrator must leave her country.*

b) *Look at the map on p. 104 and the text again. How does the narrator get from Somalia to England? Copy the grid and fill in the first line.*

	Part B	Part C	Part D
How?	by boat, overloaded		
Feelings?	I was scared … (l. 35)		

c) *How does the narrator feel during her journey? Find lines in the text that tell you about her feelings. Add them to your grid from b).*

SPEAKING

d) *Imagine you have to go on a journey like the narrator in the story. What would be the scariest part for you? Share your ideas with a partner.*

Lösung: a) The narrator's family is poor and life in Somalia is getting harder and harder. It's difficult to find work. So the narrator's father tells her that she must leave the country and go to England to earn some money to support the family.

READING

4 Reading between the lines → More practice ○ 143/11 → More practice ● 143/12 → S5–6

First, read the skills box. Then find information in the text that answers these questions.

1. What's the situation of the <u>narrator</u>'s family?
2. What do you think the relationship is between the narrator and her father?
3. What kind of person is Uncle, the smuggler who takes the narrator to England?

> ### Reading skills
>
> Sometimes important information is not mentioned directly in a text. You need to **read between the lines** to get ideas about the characters and their relationships.
>
> **Example:** When the narrator's father drives away, his face is like a mask. (l. 21) That might tell us that he is trying to hide his feelings.

WRITING
 **5 More thoughts about the story** → S11

WB 72/31

Voc.: Travel words, p. 228
WB 72/31: Writing (options)

a) *After she was picked up by Abdi at the phone box, the narrator meets her 'new' family. What do you think will happen? What might be new for the narrator compared with her old life? Make notes. The ideas in the box can help you.*

> ### Useful phrases
>
> different culture | new <u>gadgets</u> | modern house | different <u>climate</u> | no friends | <u>be homesick</u> | go to school | new rules

b) *Get into groups of 3–4. Work with your ideas from a). Together write a new paragraph for the story.*

The <u>guitar</u> lesson

SPEAKING

1 Warm-up

What do you think of when you hear the words "<u>I go wherever the wind takes me</u>"?

VIEWING

2 Ciara and Hayley → S14

7 🎬

WB 73/32

a) *Watch the film and collect information about Ciara and Hayley. Think of the topics below. Then compare the two women.*

future plans / dreams   origin   work

travel destinations (past and future)

b) *What do you think of Ciara and Hayley? Would you like to meet them? Say why / why not.*

> **Word bank**
>
> friendly | <u>outgoing</u> | interesting | nice |
> boring | cool | sad | <u>easy-going</u> |
> strange | silly | rude | funny | happy |
> quiet | clever | crazy | odd

VIEWING

3 Film <u>genres</u> → S14

a) *Read the skills box. What elements match the film 'The guitar lesson'?*

b) *Make a list with the genres from the box and add two films you've already seen (or heard of) for each genre.*

> **Film skills**
>
> There are many different **kinds of films**, or 'film genres'. Films from one genre usually have similar **main elements**. Here are some examples:
>
> **Science fiction**: inventions in science / technology; often <u>set in</u> the future; time travel; aliens; <u>unreal</u> atmosphere
>
> **<u>Romance</u>**: relationship between two characters; love; adventure; happy ending
>
> **Historical**: set in <u>specific</u> historical <u>era</u>; often about a real historical person / event; often <u>lavish</u> costumes / props
>
> **Fantasy**: story about <u>magic</u> or <u>supernatural</u> <u>forces</u>; set in <u>mythical</u> time; often tells the story of a hero / heroine

WRITING   MK **4** A film poster → S11–12

Look here
for help with
your poster:
🌐 **36c8a4**

Design a film poster for your favourite film from ex. 3b). Include the title of the film, the name of the main actors, the date when it comes out and a photo of the main characters or an important scene. Present your poster in a gallery walk.

Can you ...

1. talk about travel experiences / reasons for travelling / ways of travelling?	It's exciting to get to know other cultures and learn a foreign language. / To me it's important to travel in an environmentally friendly way.
2. plan and write an itinerary for a (class) trip?	After arrival and hotel check-in, discover London at your own pace. / First, the Tower of London is a must-see historical attraction.
3. talk about the future with the simple present and the present progressive?	We're visiting my grandparents on Sunday. The film starts at 5.30 p.m.
4. use substitute forms of modals?	I have to get a new passport. / He wasn't allowed to go through passport control. / They haven't been able to visit Bangladesh.

GRAMMAR

1 What is happening next week?

Pauline is taking part in a school exchange programme. Her German exchange partner Anna is visiting her in England next week. Pauline has got the programme for the week and talks to her parents about it. What does she tell them? Choose the right tense to talk about the future: simple present or present progressive.

MON		arrive in the UK
TUES	(a.m.)	(go) to classes with partner / school only (start) at 10 a.m. that day
	(p.m.)	(visit) leisure centre
WED		(spend) whole day in London / train (depart) 7 a.m. / (not come back) before 10 p.m.
THURS	(a.m.)	(stay) with family
	(p.m.)	(see) musical at school theatre
FRI		(enjoy) day trip to seaside
SAT		(return) to Germany. Bus (leave) from the front of the school at 5:30 a.m!

Start: On Monday they arrive in the UK. | On Tuesday morning Anna is ... |
In the afternoon they ...

GRAMMAR

2 The worst day of our trip

*Anna is on holiday with her parents. She writes an email to her friend Lisa. Use **have to**, **be able to** or **be allowed to** in the right tense.*

Dear Lisa,
Yesterday was the worst day of our trip! The weather forecast was bad, but my father wanted to go on a bicycle tour with all of us anyway. So, we **1** cycle through the rain the whole day! And we **2** (not) say anything, of course! My silly brother took lots of photos and posted them on his blog, so soon everybody **3** see those stupid pictures of me on a bike in the rain! But it got even worse. The road was so wet that I fell off my bike and into a small river. Luckily, there was a café around the corner and I **4** change my clothes and have a cup of very hot tea there. My mother got so angry with my father! That's why from now on, I **5** decide what to do for the rest of our holiday! And what is even better: You and I **6** (not) wait long to see each other – we're coming back home on Saturday.
See you,
Anna

Lösung: 1. had to, 2. weren't allowed to, 3. will be able to/was able to, 4. was able to, 5. 'll be allowed to, 6. won't have to

MEDIATION

3 Welcome to our home

Your family and an English family have agreed to spend the holidays in each other's houses. When you arrive, you find a note from the English family. Your English is best, so you have to explain the information in it. In German write down the important instructions about the things in the pictures for your family members.

Welcome! Please feel at home. Here's a bit of information for you:

— *There's a list of <u>emergency</u> numbers next to the phone But we hope you won't have to use them!*
— *If you need instructions for the washing machine etc., you'll be able to find information in the <u>booklets</u> on the kitchen shelf.*
— *Sorry, but the TV is broken. It broke yesterday, so we weren't able to get it fixed.*
  But you can use the computer in the children's room to watch TV online.
— *Rubbish collection day is Tuesday. Please remember that you must <u>sort</u> the rubbish correctly between the green and yellow boxes. The neighbours will explain the system to you.*
— *Don't hesitate to use the bikes in the garage. But you mustn't forget to ride on the left!*
— *If you see a black cat, please chase it away. It's not allowed to come into our garden or house because it always brings dead mice to us!*

Enjoy England! We're looking forward to Germany!

4 Travel advice

VOCABULARY

a) *Mr Wood needs to go to Panitania on business. He's found this advice on the internet. Complete the text.*

flights   delays   get in   passport control   land   purpose   look   suggest

traffic   passengers   coast   foreign

Travel advice for Panitania

Panitania is a dangerous country for `1` visitors, and we `2` you only go there if your visit is really necessary.

Arrival: The country's main airport is at Panville, the capital city, but some `3` also `4` at Napada, a town on the west `5` . `6` at both airports have written about very long `7` to go through `8` . People who have visited the country in the last few months have said that the officials were very rude and asked them a lot of questions about the `9` of their visit. The officials also told these visitors to open all their bags because they wanted to `10` through them. The road from the airport to Panville city centre is not good, and the `11` is often very bad. Taxis are cheap, but do not `12` any "taxi" which does not have an official blue and white sign on its roof.

WRITING

b) *Write more advice for visitors to the fictional country of Panitania for the website. You can use **one** of these ideas: hotels, public transport, money, weather, visas and crime.*

Lösung: a) 1. foreign, 2. suggest, 3. flights, 4. land, 5. coast, 6. Passengers, 7. delays, 8. passport control, 9. purpose, 10. look, 11. traffic, 12. get in

Walking in the Highlands feels great!

Last year Matt and his brother Andrew went on a long walk across the Scottish Highlands. After their <u>return</u> Adam, a reporter, asked Matt about their experience.

Adam: Hi Matt, thanks for being here today. How do you feel after your 230-mile walk across the Scottish Highlands?

Matt: When we arrived at Cape Wrath, our
5 final stop, we felt fantastic and tired at the same time. I could <u>hardly</u> walk <u>any longer</u>.

Adam: You took the <u>trail</u> from Fort William to Cape Wrath. What were your <u>daily</u>
10 distances?

Matt: That's hard to tell. We often turned off our phones to save the batteries, so we couldn't count our steps. But I guess we walked about 12 to 15 miles daily.

15 Adam: Wow, that's amazing! It's early spring now, so I'm sure you sometimes felt very cold.

Matt: Yes, we did. Most of the time we camped in <u>the wild</u>. One night the wind
20 was so strong that we thought our <u>tent</u> might <u>fly</u> away. The <u>howling</u> wind sounded scary, and it was very cold.

Adam: Did you take your food with you?

Matt: Yeah, we took lots of tinned food
25 with us. In the evenings we collected <u>firewood</u> and <u>warmed</u> our food over the <u>fire</u>. Have you ever <u>tasted</u> haggis from a <u>tin</u>? Believe me, it looks horrible but tastes very good!

30 Adam: Hmm, not sure about that. But tell us: What was the most dangerous thing on your tour?

Matt: I guess it was the rivers. Some of them have no bridges, and that can be quite
35 difficult because the rivers <u>carry</u> so

much water at this time of year. We tried to cross very fast. Another dangerous thing was when we climbed over a <u>fence</u> into a <u>military firing range</u>. We had a fast jog to get 40 out again.

Adam: I heard that the trail to Cape Wrath is completely <u>unmarked</u>. How did you find your way?

Matt: We used our map and a <u>compass</u>. And 45 we met other <u>hikers</u> – they all helped us in a friendly way.

Adam: And what did you like most about your adventure?

Matt: The landscape. It looked beautiful. 50 The last days were very sunny, and the <u>air</u> <u>smelt</u> wonderful. Finally, we could wash in the water without getting too cold. We arrived at Cape Wrath late in the evening. That was our best 55 moment!

Adam: And tomorrow we'll hear how the trip changed the relationship between you and your brother …

READING **1** **Matt and Andrew's adventure** → S5

a) *On their tour Matt and Andrew <u>experienced</u> positive things, but they also had difficult or dangerous moments. Make two lists.*

b) *Would you like to go on a tour across the Scottish Highlands? Explain why or why not.*

GRAMMAR

2 Revision: Adjectives and adverbs → G11

You already know the difference between adjectives and adverbs. Say what the rule is.

In the end Andrew and I were very **slow**. | We walked down the mountain **slowly**.
Sometimes it wasn't an **easy** walk. | We climbed over the fence **easily**.
Lösung: Rule: You make regular adverbs with the adjective + -ly. You use adjectives to describe nouns.
They say how sb/sth is. You use adverbs to describe verbs. They say how sb/sth does sth.

GRAMMAR

WB 74/1

74/1: Grammar
(multiple choice)

3 Adverbs with the same form as adjectives → G11

Some adverbs have the same form as their adjectives.
Find three more examples in the text on p. 110.

Example: A tour across the Highlands **is hard**. (adjective)
We **tried hard** to find the right trail. (adverb)
Lösung: daily, fast, late

> **Tip**
>
> The adverb **hard** has two forms:
> We worked **hard** to dry our boots.
> … *schwer* …
>
> I could **hardly** walk any longer.
> … *kaum* …

GRAMMAR

WB 74/2

74/2: Grammar
(verbs of perception and
adjectives)

4 Adjectives after verbs of perception → G11

a) *After the verbs of perception* **feel, look, sound, taste** *and* **smell** *there's sometimes an adjective after the verb. Find more examples in the text on p. 110.*

Example: We **felt fantastic** and **tired** at the same time.

b) *Think of your last class trip or family trip. Write about your experience (8–10 sentences).*
Use the verbs of perception **feel, look, sound, taste, smell** *and your own* **adjectives**.

Start: Last summer I went to Italy with my parents. The food tasted …
Lösung: a) 2. sometimes felt, 3. sounded scary, 4. looks horrible, 5. tastes very good, 6. looked beautiful, 7. smelt wonderful

GRAMMAR

5 Lost in the Highlands: Adjective or adverb? → G11

a) *Daniel went on a day tour in the Highlands, but he wasn't very well* prepared. *Read what happened to him on his tour. Decide if you need an* **adjective** *or an* **adverb**.

dark | late (2x) | long (2x) | big | scary | fast | great | hard | strong
amazing | quick | dramatic

Getting lost in the Highlands can be dangerous. I learned this the **1** way when I walked up Cairngorm Mountain near Inverness. I left my hostel **2** after breakfast and didn't take a lot of food because it's not a **3** walk. At least that's what I thought. When I reached the top, I felt **4** . The view from up there was **5** . But I didn't know the weather in the Highlands can change so **6** ! I was still enjoying the **7** landscape when the clouds moved in. They looked **8** and **9** . Within a few moments the fog was so thick that I couldn't see my hand in front of my face. It was already **10** and the last bus to town left at 5 p.m.! I turned and walked down the mountain as **11** as I could. Suddenly my heart stopped. I heard a **12** sound very close to me. Then I remembered the Highland cows. I guessed there were quite a few of them because they smelt very **13** . I tried to relax. From there it didn't take **14** to walk back down. On the way the fog cleared. That's when I saw that I was on the wrong trail!

b) *Write your own ending for Dave's adventure. Use* **adjectives** *and* **adverbs**.
Lösung: a) 1. hard, 2. late, 3. long, 4. great/amazing, 5. great/amazing, 6. quickly/fast, 7. dramatic,
8. big/dark, 9. big/dark, 10. late, 11. fast/quickly, 12. scary, 13. strong, 14. long

Robin Hood's diary

SPEAKING

1 Before you read

Have you seen any films or read any stories about Robin Hood? Tell the class what you already know about him.

Sherwood Forest, April 1190

The poor people here in England really hate the Normans, which I can understand. I hate them too! The king
5 *and his men have all the power and money while the people have nothing, which I don't think is fair at all. And that stupid Sheriff of Nottingham is the worst! He goes from house to*
10 *house, farm to farm and takes from people who have so little to give, which makes me very angry. One woman lost her husband last month, but she still has five children to feed. The Sheriff*
15 *wanted all her money. "No, these are my last coins, please don't take them all," she cried. "Silly woman, they're mine." He laughed in her face. "And whose house is this?" he asked.*
20 *"My children and I live here, it's ours." – "You mean it WAS yours. Now it's mine. Get out!"*
Men like the Sheriff do things like this every day. We must stop it. So, I take
25 *from the rich Normans and give to the poor Saxons, which the people love me for. The powerful Normans have taken*

the people's money, their houses, their land – so, why not give them back what's theirs? But now I'm an outlaw, 30 *and the Sheriff and his men have often tried to kill me. But my men and I are good with weapons and always escape. "Robin Hood should turn himself in," the Sheriff tells the people. "He* 35 *shouldn't think we won't catch and kill him. It's only a question of time, ha-ha!"*
Yes, it's only a question of time before they kill me, which will make the people very sad. This morning I 40 *asked one of my men, "What should I do? Should I turn myself in? I can't hide in Sherwood Forest forever." His answer was wise: "You should do what your heart tells you." I gave him a big* 45 *smile, and he knew what that meant. He smiled back and asked, "So, shall I tell the men we're ready for our next adventure?"*

READING

2 Understanding the text → S5

a) *What kind of person is Robin Hood? Describe him with examples from the text.*

b) *"You should do what your heart tells you," one of Robin's men tells him. Explain what this means and say how Robin reacts.*

c) *Your turn: When has your heart told you to do something even if your head still had doubts? Write about it (8–10 lines).*

Lösung: b) This statement means that Robin should do what he believes is right. When he hears this advice, Robin smiles. This shows that he will not turn himself in and will continue to take money from the rich and give it to the poor.

2: The relative pronoun which to comment on the main clause
3: Possessive pronouns
Giving extra information with *which*; possessive pronouns; *shall/should*

⟨ **Trailer 2** ⟩

T

GRAMMAR

3 Giving extra information with *which* → G12

WB 75/1

a) *Find the sentences with* **which** *in the text. Then write them in German.*

b) *Complete a student's sentences with the 'which' comments in the box below.*

1. Robin liked to fight for the poor people, …
2. The people were very poor and the rulers were very rich in the 12th century, …
3. Robin and his men lived deep in the forest

| which was very typical of that time |
| which made it easier to hide from the Sheriff | which made him very popular |

Lösung: b) 1. …, which made him very popular. 2. …, which was very typical of that time. 3. …, which made it easier to hide from the Sheriff.

GRAMMAR

4 Possessive pronouns → G13

WB 75/2

The Sheriff and one of his men are talking. Complete the text with **possessive pronouns**.

| mine (2x) | yours | his | hers | ours | theirs |

"This beautiful ring is perfect for my wife. Yes, it's ⬛**1** . – Oh, I like these gold coins! They're ⬛**2** now." – "No, Sheriff. My men and I attacked that house, we did all the work! So, they're ⬛**3** ." – "Well, OK. But whose sword is this? Very nice." – "That's Robin's. He lost it in the fight last night." – "It's ⬛**4** ?! But Robin *never* loses his sword! Well, it's ⬛**5** now." – "Yes, keep it. But look, these rings belonged to his men." – "The rings are ⬛**6** ?" – "They *were*. Now they're ⬛**7** , Sheriff!"

Lösung: 1. hers, 2. mine, 3. ours, 4. his, 5. mine, 6. theirs, 7. yours

VOCABULARY

5 Suggestions and advice: *Shall* or *should*?

WB 75/3

a) *Look at the two questions below. Which is a suggestion and which is asking for advice?*

1. Should I turn myself in?　2. Shall I tell the men we're ready for our next adventure?

b) *How can Robin's men react to his statements? Answer with* **should/shall** *and a verb.*

1. "I don't want to be an outlaw any more." you / turn in
2. "Men, I'm hungry for a big meal in tonight!" we / hunt for food
3. "The Sheriff was horrible to that mother with the five kids." we / help her

Lösung: a) 1. asking for advice, 2. suggestion;
b) 1. You should turn yourself in. 2. Shall we hunt for food? 3. We should help her.

GRAMMAR

6 Visit Nottingham, the home of Robin Hood! → G12–13

Complete the text for visitors. Use **possessive pronouns, which, shall** *and* **should**.

A mother has a suggestion for her husband: "Tim and Amy watched that Robin Hood film last weekend and now it's all they talk about! ⬛**1** we take the kids to Nottingham next weekend?" The answer to that question ⬛**2** always be "YES!" Kids <u>all over</u> Britain love Robin Hood and his Merry Men. Robin was an outlaw, but to the people he was a hero and a very popular man. His life was dangerous but also full of adventure, ⬛**3** is what Nottingham can give your family too. Just click on the links below and begin to discover the world of Robin Hood, ⬛**4** you'll really love. So, be our guests in Nottingham: The <u>pleasure</u> will be ⬛**5** , the fun will be ⬛**6** !

Lösung: 1. watched, 2. Shall, 3. should, 4. which, 5. which, 6. ours, 7. yours

A trip to Dublin

Jessica is visiting Dublin with her mum and she has posted a blog entry about their trip. Emily, her classmate, is reading the post.

Hi friends and followers!

This is Jessica, and right now I'm in cool Dublin! I hope that you aren't too jealous of me! I'm here with my mum for the <u>bank holiday</u> – and we're having lots of fun! She knows Dublin really well because this is where she studied, and she has told me so much about this cool city. I couldn't wait to come here. And now I'll tell you about this great place:

🏠 First, our <u>accommodation</u>: We're staying in a flat <u>right</u> in the city centre, close to the River Liffey. I can even see it from our window. These lights at night are really <u>GRAND</u> – as they say here!

🧁 <u>Yummy</u> food: Last night we went to a popular restaurant. Mum had Irish <u>stew</u> and I tried '<u>boxty</u>'. Do you know what boxty is? It's a traditional Irish potato <u>pancake</u> – very yummy! I'll take the restaurant's <u>secret</u> recipe home with me. 😂

🎻 <u>Last but not least</u> great music: It's everywhere! We went to this <u>cosy</u> <u>pub</u> in Temple Bar – yes, I'm allowed to go into a pub as long as I'm with an adult! – and there was <u>live</u> music, like in most pubs here. The band played typical Irish music with the <u>tin whistle</u>, the <u>Bodhrán</u> and the <u>fiddle</u>. They also sang Gaelic songs (I didn't <u>get</u> one word of it), and in the end we all joined in and learned a bit of Irish dancing. It was so much fun!

Tomorrow is our last day and we're planning to visit the Emigration Museum. Bye! – Slán libh!

While Emily is reading Jessica's post, she gets a call from Karen, another classmate.

Karen: Hi Em, what's going on?

Emily: I'm reading Jess' post from Dublin.

Karen: Oh, she's in Ireland?

Emily: Yeah, she writes that she's there with her mum and that her mum knows Dublin really well because that is where she studied. Jess couldn't wait to go there.

Karen: Hm, isn't it a bit boring?

Emily: Well, no, she even says that she and her mum are having lots of fun. And she says she hopes that we aren't too jealous of her.

Karen: Typical Jess! So, what else does she write about?

Emily: The usual stuff. Where they're staying, food … Oh, wow, they even went to a pub. There was live music, like in most pubs there, and …

Karen: What? Is she allowed to go into a pub?

Emily: She writes that she's allowed to as long as she's with an adult.

Karen: Cool! I guess they had nice food there too.

Emily: No, not in the pub, but in a popular restaurant – Irish stew and boxty.

Karen: Box… what?

Emily: Ha, in her post Jess actually asks if we know what boxty is. It's a traditional Irish potato pancake. She really liked it, and she says she'll bring the restaurant's recipe back home with her.

Karen: Good, then she can make this boxty thingy for us! Can't wait.

GRAMMAR   **1**   **Find the rule: From direct to indirect speech** → G14

WB 76/1

76/1: Grammar rsonal pronouns)

a) *Copy the grid and put in the sentences in direct speech and in indirect speech. Underline the words that change and find the rule.*

Direct speech	Indirect speech
1. Jessica: **I'm here** with **my** mum.	Jessica writes that **she**'s **there** with **her** mum.
2. **I** hope that **you** aren't too jealous of **me**!	She says **she** hopes that **we** aren't too jealous of **her**!
3. **These** lights at night are really grand.	She says **those** lights at night are really grand.

4. My mum and I are having lots of fun.   6. Do you know what boxty is?
5. This is where my mum studied.   7. I'll take the restaurant's recipe home with me.

b) *Put more examples from Jessica's post into indirect speech.*
Lösung: a) 4. She writes that her mum and she are … 5. She says that is where her mum …
6. She asks if I know what … 7. She writes that she will take … with her.

GRAMMAR   **2**   **A message from London** → G14

WB 76/2

76/2: Grammar oorted versions)

Emily sends Jessica a message with a selfie. Jessica tells her mum about it. What does she say?

Em   1:05 p.m.

Hi Jess! Just read your post. Grand! 😊 Life here is really boring. This is me in my room, still in my pyjamas! Karen and I were really excited about your pub post. Please send us some more photos and a video of the Irish dancing! Oh, and we must try this boxty <u>thingy</u> when you're back – we love pancakes. 😊 Maybe you can also bring some typical Irish sweets home from Dublin? And: You mustn't forget to go on a shopping tour so that you can tell us about the cool clothes shops there. Or are shops in Ireland closed on bank holidays? XXX Em.

WRITING   **3**   **St Patrick's Day** → S6

a) *Read the poem. What do you think St Patrick's Day is about? Then read the Across cultures box below.*

b) *The poem about St Patrick is a so-called "limerick". A limerick is a small, funny poem with five lines. Its rhyme scheme is AABBA. Write a limerick about a special holiday you celebrate in your region or with your family or about a hero/heroine from your favourite legend.*

> Saint Patrick would have never believed
> How his memory would become <u>perceived</u>
> In the Emerald Isle
> They do it in style
> With green outfits, green hats and green <u>sleeves</u>.

Across cultures

St Patrick's Day is an Irish holiday and it's celebrated in Ireland (and many other English-speaking countries like the US) on 17th March. St Patrick is the <u>patron saint</u> of Ireland and he brought <u>Christianity</u> to Ireland. People go to street <u>parades</u> in the towns and celebrate with friends and family at home or in pubs. What **holidays** do you celebrate in your region or with your family and what traditions do you have?

3/21 # Claire's Devil   by Dave Draper

WB 77/1–4

WB 77/1–4: Reading (summary); Reading (matching); Reading (questions); Reading (freeze frame)

You're going to read different scenes from a play about a teenage girl and a dilemma she's facing[1].

The characters are:
- Claire, the story's protagonist[2]
- Rob, a friend
- Claire's mum
- Claire's dad
- Claire's devil[3]
- Claire's angel[4]

Scene 1

Rob and Claire are walking home from school.

Rob: Listen, there's a party in West Street tomorrow night. It'll be fantastic: Do you fancy coming with us?

5

Claire: In West Street? Isn't that on the other side of town? It's a pretty rough area, isn't it?

Rob: We'll be okay! The station is only a
10 few minutes away. Nearly everyone we know will be there. What do you say?

Claire: I'll phone you tonight. At about six, OK?

15 Rob: If you're worried about what your parents will say, then there's a simple solution – don't tell them. Say you're staying over at my house with my sister. My mum will cover up[5] for us –
20 she does what I tell her!

Claire: I'll phone you.

Rob goes off. Claire is alone with her conscience[6].

Scene 2

25 Claire's The trouble with you is that you
devil: never take risks[7]. You always worry about what your parents tell you. What's the matter with you? Just have a little fun!

30 Claire's What if something bad happened?
angel: What if there's a fight? And you're not old enough to go. They'll see that you're not old enough; you'll end up embarrassed and miserable in front
35 of Rob. Tell him you're sorry, but you can't go.

Claire's How boring can you get?! Do you
devil: want to lose all your friends? They'll *all* be there, and you'll be at home in front of the TV, like a good little girl. 40

Claire's Rob is exaggerating[8] as usual. Most
angel: of your school friends won't be allowed to go because their parents are as sensible[9] as yours.

Claire's Let's face it[10] – you're scared! You 45
devil: always back down[11] from things.

Claire's It wouldn't be right to lie to your
angel: parents. You know they love you and only want what's best for you. If they found out you had lied, they'd never 50 trust you again.

Claire's All kids lie to their parents. And it
devil: would only be a small lie, a white lie[12]. Say you're going to stay with Rob's sister; that's partly true: 55 You can sleep at their house after the party.

Scene 3

Later at Claire's house. Claire is talking to her mum and dad. 60

Claire: Mum, is it okay if I stay over at Jenny's house on Saturday night?

Mum: I didn't know you two were friendly.

Claire: Well, I like her a lot.

Mum: I hope you're not getting involved 65 with that brother of hers. Rob isn't the sort of boy you should be mixing with.

Claire: Rob isn't as bad as people think.

Mum: From what I've heard, he's heading 70 for trouble. So, be warned!

---

1 to face [feɪs] konfrontiert werden mit | **2** protoganist [prəʊˈtægnɪst] Hauptfigur | **3** devil [ˈdevl] Teufel | **4** angel [ˈeɪndʒl] Engel | **5** to cover up for sb [ˌkʌvərˌʌp fə] jdn. decken | **6** conscience [ˈkɒnʃns] Gewissen | **7** to take a risk [ˌteɪkˌə ˈrɪsk] ein Risiko eingehen | **8** to exaggerate [ɪgˈzædʒreɪt] übertreiben | **9** sensible [ˈsensɪbl] vernünftig

Claire: Rob has his own circle of friends – we hardly[13] ever speak to each other. Is it okay then, Mum?

75 Mum: All right. But check with your dad first.

Claire's mother goes out. Claire is alone with her conscience.

Angel: See! So many lies already. She'll be
80 terribly[14] hurt if she finds out you've been so dishonest[15]. She trusts you, Claire!

Devil: She'll sleep easy and you can have a great time. Now you need a good
85 story to convince your dad.

Later Claire is with her dad.

Claire: Dad, Mum says it's okay for me to stay at Jenny Costello's on Saturday, as long as you agree too.

90 Dad: As long as her parents don't mind, then, that's fine! Have I met her?

Claire: No, she's new in my class. We're working on a design project and I need money for materials.

95 Dad: What sort of design work is it?

Claire: Er … it's a dress design project. Could I have £25?

Dad: That's a lot! What's this dress going to be made out of? Silk[16]?

100 Claire: Of course not. But we'd like to do really well on the project, so we're buying a couple of books to help us.

Dad: Well, I don't mind paying out if it's to help with schoolwork. Here you are.

105 *He gives Claire £25 and leaves.*

Scene 4

Devil: Easy, wasn't it? Now everyone's happy: Your parents think you're a really keen student and that they're
110 supporting you. What could be better?

Angel: But you've been dishonest and you'll have to live with that on your conscience. Once you start being dishonest, it is hard to stop. One lie 115 nearly always leads to another.

Devil: It's their own fault. If they were a bit more tolerant and easy-going then there'd be no need to lie to them.

Angel: Wouldn't you feel safer if your 120 parents knew where you were and what time to expect you?

Devil: Safer? Where's the danger? A lively night out with a group of friends: Sounds safe enough to me. You've 125 got to make the most of your youth[17] while you still have it! Enjoy yourself while you've got the chance.

Claire: Yes! It's time I started living.

On Saturday evening at Claire's house with 130 *her mum and dad.*

Claire: Bye, then. I'll see you tomorrow lunchtime.

Mum: Have a good time. Why not bring Jenny round here next weekend? 135 It would be nice to meet your new friend. Perhaps I should ring Jenny's mother later this evening. Just to check it's still okay for you to stop the night. It'll give me the chance to 140 thank her.

Claire: There's no need. Anyway, you can't. Their phone is out of order.

Mum: But I thought Jenny rang you a little while ago. You did say it was Jenny, 145 didn't you?

Claire: Er … Yes, it was. She had to ring from somewhere else. Bye, now.

Angel: See? What did I tell you? Lies lead to more lies. It never stops. 150

Devil: Stop preaching[18]! It was an excellent piece of quick thinking. Well done, Claire! Now for a night out on the town! Let's go!

10 **Let's face it.** [lets ˈfeɪsˌɪt] Machen wir uns doch nichts vcr. | 11 **to back down** [ˌbæk ˈdaʊn] nachgeben | 12 **white lie** [ˌwaɪt ˈlaɪ] Notlüge | 13 **hardly** [ˈhɑːdli] kaum | 14 **terribly** [ˈterəbli] furchtbar | 15 **dishonest** [dɪˈsɒnɪst] unehrlich | 16 **silk** [sɪlk] Seide | 17 **youth** [juːθ] Jugend | 18 **to preach** [priːtʃ] predigen

3/22

WB 78/1–3

WB 78/1–3: Reading
(matching, true/false);
Reading (correct order);
Writing (report)

The Spaniards[1] are coming

A   I am an old man now, but I will never forget that hot evening in July 1588. I remember every minute! And every minute is a picture full of life – and
5 adventure.

All was quiet at Plymouth harbour where the English fleet[2] lay at anchor[3]. Everyone in England knew that the Spaniards wanted to attack us with the
10 greatest fleet in the world. They called it the Great Armada. The only question was: When would they come? The Spaniards had a large army in the Netherlands[4], and they wanted to bring it *here*, to England.
15 But our ships were ready for them.

On that evening Sir Francis Drake and a few other officers[5] were busy with a game of bowls on a hill above the town, where the bowling green[6] was. I was a very young officer and it was my job to take care of[7] Sir
20 Francis' ship when he was gone.

Suddenly I heard the shouts[8] of our men on land.

I ran to the side of the ship and looked down. "What is it?" I asked.
25

"The Spaniards, sir," a sailor shouted. "Some of our men have seen their ships in the English Channel. Over a hundred!"

Over a hundred! There was only one thing to do. I left the ship and ran all the
30 way through the town to the bowling green. Sir Francis and Lord Howard, the commander[9] of the English fleet, were standing with a group of officers. I ran up to them.
35

"My Lord Howard! Sir Francis!" I said. "The Spaniards are coming up the Channel! The Armada is almost here!"

---

1 **Spaniard** ['spænɪəd] Spanier /-in | 2 **fleet** [fli:t] Flotte | 3 **to lie at anchor** [ˌlaɪ ət 'æŋkə] vor Anker liegen |
4 **the Netherlands** [ðə 'neðələndz] Niederlande | 5 **officer** ['ɒfɪsə] Offizier | 6 **bowling green** ['bəʊlɪŋ gri:n]
Rasenfläche zum Bowlen | 7 **to take care of** [teɪk 'keə ˌəv] *hier:* bewachen | 8 **shout** [ʃaʊt] Ruf; Schrei |
9 **commander** [kə'mɑ:ndə] Kommandant

2

Lord Howard threw down his bowl,
40 and all the other officers – but not Drake –
looked very worried.

"Back to your ships, gentlemen," said
Lord Howard. "There is no time to lose!"

"One moment, my Lord," Drake said
45 quietly. "There is time to finish the game
and defeat the Spaniards too. Let the
Spaniards go by[10], and with the help of God,
we can follow them and defeat them. We'll
finish the game first."

50 That was the way of Sir Francis Drake.
He never became excited or worried. He
smiled, took his bowl, which he still held in
his hands, and continued[11] the game.

B When we left the harbour we soon
55 sighted[12] the Armada. Many, many heavy
ships were sailing up[13] the channel in the
shape of a great half-moon. I heard later
that there were 130 of them, with 30,000
men on them.

60 Our little ships were not even half the
size of the big Spanish ships. But we could
sail much faster. We followed Drake's plan
and attacked them from behind. First,
we fired off[14] our cannonballs[15], then we
65 turned away before the Spaniards could fire
theirs.

This is the way we followed the Armada
up the Channel, until the Spaniards turned
towards the French coast and entered the
70 harbour of Calais. It was difficult to attack
them there, but Drake, as always, knew
what to do. We filled six of our oldest ships
with pitch[16] and tar[17]. Then, in the night,
we set fire to[18] them and let them drift[19]
75 towards the Spanish fleet.

It was terrible to see those burning
Spanish ships in the night. We could hear
the shouts of the Spaniards as they tried to
sail off[20].

That was the chance we needed. 80
We surrounded[21] a few of the largest ships
and sank[22] them. The rest of the ships
sailed out into the North Sea. We followed
them and fired off our cannons again and
again. Soon we had no more cannonballs, 85
and then we turned back.

C Then, on our way home, we got into a
great storm. The Armada had no choice
but to sail farther and farther[23] north on a
course round Scotland and Ireland, where 90
they lost most of their ships. Only 54 out of
130 ships returned to Spain.

There was great joy[24] in all of Queen
Elizabeth's land. When we returned to
England, bonfires[25] were burning, church 95
bells were ringing, and all the people
were dancing in the streets. Everyone was
celebrating the greatest victory[26] in English
history. I was a very young officer, so I
danced on the deck with the other men. 100
Sir Francis stood there and watched us, and
I could see that he was smiling.

---

10 to go by [gəʊ ˈbaɪ] vorbeiziehen | **11 to continue** [kənˈtɪnjuː] fortfahren; weitermachen | **12 to sight** [saɪt]
sichten | **13 sail up** [seɪl ˈʌp] hinaufsegeln | **14 to fire off** [faɪə ˈɒf] abfeuern | **15 cannonball** [ˈkænənbɔːl] Kanonen-
kugel | **16 pitch** [pɪtʃ] Pech | **17 tar** [tɑː] Teer | **18 to set fire to** [set ˈfaɪə tə] in Brand stecken | **19 to drift** [drɪft]
driften | **20 to sail off** [seɪl ˈɒf] davonsegeln | **21 to surround** [səˈraʊnd] umstellen; umzingeln | **22 sink, sank, sunk**
[sɪŋk, sæŋk, sʌŋk] versenken | **23 farther and farther** [ˈfɑːðə ənd ˈfɑːðə] immer weiter | **24 joy** [dʒɔɪ] Freude |
25 bonfire [ˈbɒnfaɪə] Freudenfeuer | **26 victory** [ˈvɪktri] Sieg

3/23–24

MK

WB 79/1–3

WB 79/1–3: Reading (true/false); Reading (matching), Reading (reasons)

Screen enemies[1] by Jon Marks and Alison Wooder

Grace Evans is a 14-year-old schoolgirl whose family has just moved to Cardiff, Wales. At her new school she has trouble making new friends. To become popular with other students, she starts sending nasty messages to a girl called Charlotte.

A bad day for Grace

Another breakfast, another day.

Grace was at the kitchen table in her family home. Her mother and brother were
5 eating breakfast. Her father came to the table with some pieces of hot toast on a plate.

"I can't find the jam," he said.

"There isn't any jam," Grace's mother
10 replied. "We didn't go to the supermarket at the weekend, remember? Why not? Because we haven't got any money. And why's that? Because *you* haven't got a job."

"Hey, that's not fair!" said her father. "It's
15 not my fault. The factory closed, and I'm looking for another job."

Grace didn't want to listen. She'd heard it all before. She took her phone and looked at her reflection[2] in the black screen. Grace
20 Evans: a typical 14-year-old schoolgirl from Cardiff. There wasn't much interesting or special about her, she thought.

She looked across the table at her older brother Owen. He wasn't listening to their
25 parents' argument either. He was busy looking at his own phone. He seemed[3] to get hundreds of messages every day.

Grace decided to check her phone too. No new messages for her. So, she read the
30 latest posts from her 'friends'. Most of them were people she hardly[4] knew. 'Friend collectors' Grace called them: people with hundreds of online friends who still wanted more. But Grace always accepted
35 their friend requests[5]. It made her feel good to have lots of online friends too, even if she didn't really know who they were.

There was another post from Charlotte Jones, a girl in Grace's class. In the photo she was playing hockey again. Winning
40 the match, probably. And even in a sports outfit, she looked amazing. Tall, long blond hair, big smile. And then there was another photo of her. This time she was with a group of friends, singing and playing her
45 guitar. She was good at everything. She was even good at Welsh, one of the world's most difficult languages! Grace was terrible[6] at Welsh.

• • •

"Bore da, Grace. Sut wyt ti?"
50 It was later the same morning. Grace was at school. The Welsh teacher was waiting for her answer. No problem. The question was just, 'Good morning, Grace. How are you?'
55 "Iawn da, diolch." she replied.

There was a laugh from the desk[7] behind her. It was Charlotte.

The teacher smiled and shook[8] his head. Charlotte's hand was in the air. "Bore da,
60 Charlotte. Sut wyt ti?" he said.

"Da iawn, diolch," said Charlotte. 'I'm fine, thanks.' with the words in the correct order. "A chi?" she continued.

The teacher smiled. "Da iawn, diolch,
65 Charlotte," he replied.

Grace felt awful. She'd made a basic mistake in the first two minutes of the lesson!

• • •

---

1 **enemy** ['enəmi] Feind/-in | 2 **reflection** [rɪ'flekʃn] Spiegelbild | 3 **to seem** [siːm] scheinen | 4 **hardly** ['hɑːdli] kaum | 5 **friend request** [frend rɪ'kwest] Freundschaftsanfrage | 6 **terrible** ['terəbl] furchtbar | 7 **desk** [desk] Tisch | 8 **to shake, shook, shaken** [ʃeɪk, ʃʊk, 'ʃeɪkn] schütteln

70 It was lunchtime. Grace stood in the school cafeteria queue. She only had £3.10 left on her lunch card. A hot meal was £2.80, but there was no drink with that. OK, there was free water, but Grace *loved*
75 the chocolate milkshakes. It had been a difficult morning, and she deserved a treat[9]! For £2.65 she could get a nice sandwich and a delicious chocolate milkshake.

A few minutes later she was carrying
80 her lunch to an empty table. She sat down and started to take the top[10] off the milkshake. Suddenly something hit her arm. The milkshake fell over and went all over[11] the sandwich.

85 "I'm *so* sorry!" It was Charlotte again. Her sports bag had hit Grace's arm while she was running across the room. "I'm really in a hurry. It's hockey in PE this afternoon, and I want to practise a bit
90 before the match."

"It doesn't really matter[12], does it?" said Grace in a small voice[13]. But it did matter to her. It mattered a lot, but she didn't want Charlotte to know that.

95 "That's *really* nice of you," said Charlotte with a big smile. "You're my *best* friend! See you at PE!"

'Best friend? You don't know anything about me,' thought Grace. She looked at
100 her sandwich. Half of it was covered[14] in chocolate milkshake, but she could still eat the other half. She stood up and went to get a glass of water.

• • •

There was one thing Grace knew she
105 was good at: she was the best hockey goalkeeper[15] in the school.

It was later that afternoon and near the end of the PE lesson. Grace was glad it was near the end. It was raining, and the pitch
110 was covered in mud.

The teacher had put Charlotte and Grace into different hockey teams. Grace had stopped all the other team's goals so far, but their goalkeeper was good too. The score was still zero for both teams. 115

Charlotte was the captain of the other team, and had nearly scored[16] two goals: those had been the most difficult to stop. Grace was worried that the next time Charlotte tried to score a goal, it would go 120 into the net. Grace didn't like Charlotte, but she had to agree[17] that Charlotte was a very good hockey player.

Grace looked at the big clock on the school wall next to the hockey pitch. Now 125 there were only two minutes left. The match was sure to be a no-score draw[18]. That was OK. No winners, no losers. Everybody would be happy enough with that. Then she could go home, and it 130 would be the end of an awful day. The embarrassing Welsh lesson, the spilt[19] milkshake …

Suddenly Grace saw Charlotte running towards her fast. Grace realised that she 135 had stopped paying attention[20] to the match. Now Charlotte was running towards the goal, pushing the ball forward with her stick[21]. She wanted to score a goal! Grace realised that Charlotte was aiming[22] at the 140 right side of the goal. She was at the left side, and she wasn't ready to stop the ball at the right side.

Whack! Charlotte hit the ball hard.

Grace tried to reach the ball as it came 145 towards the goal, but it was too fast. She fell over in the mud, and the ball went into the net. Grace was lying face-down on the ground with mud in her mouth, in her eyes and in her hair. 150

The PE teacher blew her whistle[23], and the match was over. Everybody in

9 **treat** [triːt] Belohnung | 10 **top** [tɒp] Deckel, Verschluss | 11 **to go all over sth/sb** [ɡəʊ ɔːl ˈəʊvə] sich ergießen/verteilen über etw./jmdn. | 12 **to matter** [ˈmætə] ausmachen | 13 **in a small voice** [ɪn ə smɔːl vɔɪs] mit leiser Stimme | 14 **be covered** [bi ˈkʌvəd] bedeckt sein | 15 **goalkeeper** [ˈɡəʊlˌkiːpə] Torhüter/-in | 16 **to score** [skɔː] schießen; erzielen | 17 **to agree** [əˈɡriː] *hier:* zugeben | 18 **no-score draw** [nəʊ-skɔː drɔː] Null zu Null | 19 **spilt** [spɪlt] verschüttete/r/s | 20 **to pay attention** [peɪ əˈtenʃn] *hier:* verfolgen | 21 **stick** [stɪk] Schläger | 22 **to aim** [eɪm] zielen | 23 **to blow the whistle** [bləʊ ðə ˈwɪsl] *hier:* abpfeifen

Charlotte's team was cheering. Everybody in Grace's team looked disappointed.

155 "Don't worry, Grace," said her team's captain while they were walking back to the changing rooms[24]. "It wasn't your fault. That was a really great goal from Charlotte."

"Thanks," said Grace. But she knew that 160 it *was* her fault. It wasn't really a great goal. If she hadn't stopped paying attention, she could have stopped it.

• • •

"How was your day, Grace?"

"Terrible, Lewis! Worse than terrible!"

165 Grace was walking home from school with her friends. There was Jack who was in the year above, a girl with long dark hair called Becky and a tall boy with very short hair called Lewis. Then there were Molly 170 and Lauren. People called them 'the terrible twins'. They weren't twins or even sisters, but they were *always* together.

None of[25] them was from her class. Grace's family had moved house a few 175 months earlier. Jack and the others lived in the same area, and so she usually walked home with them. Were they really her friends? They had all known each other for a long time, and Grace still felt that she was 180 the new member of the group. She knew that the others often sent messages to each other, but they never sent messages to her.

"Bad luck about the hockey match," said Jack.

"How do you know about that?" asked 185 Grace.

Jack took out his phone and tapped at the screen. Then he showed it to Grace. There was a photo of her, lying face-down in the mud in front of the hockey goal. 190 Who had taken that?

"You're a star," he said. "There are already lots of comments. And they aren't from us!"

Jack gave the phone to Grace, and she started to read the comments below the 195 photo.

Bad luck[26], Grace. You *mud* be very disappointed!

Yes, Grace. You *mud* try harder[27] in the next match. 200

Arrghh! It's the mud monster of Year 9!

I thought it was a hippo[28] who was having a mud bath.

She didn't want to read any more and gave the phone back to Jack. Suddenly 205 Grace felt angry. Why had this happened to her?

"It wasn't my fault," said Grace. "Well, maybe the goal was my fault. I wasn't playing as well as I could, but I'd had an 210 awful morning. That Charlotte Jones made fun of[29] me in Welsh. And then I didn't have much lunch because she spilt my milkshake all over my sandwich."

That's why Grace felt angry. It was 215 Charlotte! It was all Charlotte's fault, not hers.

"Do you know Charlotte?" she asked.

"Yes!" said Jack and Lewis at the same time. 220

---

24 **changing rooms** [tʃeɪndʒɪŋ ruːmz] Umkleidekabine | 25 **none of** [nʌn əv] kein/e/r | 26 **bad luck** [bæd lʌk] Pech; dumm gelaufen | 27 **to try hard** [traɪ haːd] sich bemühen | 28 **hippo** (*kurz für* hippopotamus) [ˈhɪpəʊ] Nilpferd | 29 **to make fun of sb/sth** [ˌmeɪk ˈfʌn əv] sich über jmdn./etw. lustig machen

"She's awful," said Becky. Then she pretended to be Charlotte. "Oh, look at me! I'm so pretty, I'm so perfect! All the boys love me, don't you Jack? Don't you, Lewis? Eh?"

"Well, no, erm …," said Lewis

"Er, no, well, I mean …," said Jack.

"We hate her, don't we, Molly?" said Lauren.

"Yes, we do," said Molly. "We think she's the horriblest person in our year."

"Most horrible[24]," said Lewis.

"What?" said Molly.

"It's 'most horrible', not 'horriblest'," said Lewis.

"Yeah," said Becky to Molly. "You're so stupid, you don't even know that. You don't know *anything*! Stupid! Stupid! Stupid! OW!"

Molly had hit Becky with her schoolbag.

"That really hurt!" said Becky.

The others laughed.

"Hit her again," said Lewis to Molly. "She deserves it!"

Grace looked at them. Did she even like them? But what choice did she have? She didn't really have any other friends.

"Hey, hey," said Jack. "Let's not fight with each other. What are we going to do about this Charlotte girl? She made our friend Grace have a bad day[30]. We must do something!"

Jack had called Grace 'friend'! Perhaps she belonged with this group after all.

"Has anybody got her email address?" asked Lauren. "We could send her, you know, a nasty message or something."

"Ha ha! Yes! That would show her that not *everybody* thinks she's perfect!" said Becky.

"I've got her email address," said Grace. "She put it on a hockey club list. But she'll know who sent it, won't she?"

"We can just start a new email account[31]," said Becky. "It'll take two minutes. What name are we going to use?"

They had nearly arrived at their homes.

"Let's sit down here and do it now," said Jack, and pointed at a long bench in front of a charity shop.

Grace felt great. This was the first time she had actually done something with them, apart from just walking home and chatting. An idea came to her.

"What about 'screen enemies', written as one word," she said.

"I like it," said Lauren.

"Me too," said Molly.

"Yeah, that's good," said Jack. "I mean, it's not very nice, but that's what we want, don't we?"

Grace quickly set up a new email account with her phone.

"Now we need a message," she said.

"What about, 'You're horrible and we hate you,'" said Lewis.

"No, that's rubbish," said Becky. "Are you seven? We need something much better than that."

Another idea came into Grace's head.

"What about, 'Hey Miss Perfect. Everybody thinks you're so special, don't they?' What do you think about that?"

"Oooh, that's good," said Becky. "It's nasty!"

"Yeah, that'll worry her," said Molly. "She'll think, 'Oh no, who sent me this weird[32] message?'"

"Yeah, do it," said Lewis.

"Ha ha! That's great, Grace," said Jack. "You're so cool and funny!"

Grace felt better than she had for a long time. She started to type the message.

---

30 **to make sb have a bad day** [meɪk hæv ə bæd deɪ] jmdn. den Tag vermiesen | **31** **to start an account** [stɑːt ən əˈkaʊnt] ein Konto anlegen | **32** **weird** [wɪəd] komisch; seltsam

Legende

Diese Symbole und Erklärungen zeigen dir, wie du mit den Aufgaben auf den Diff pool-Seiten arbeitest. Die Lösungen findest du ab Seite 294.

More help ○ p. 9/3 Diese Aufgabe hilft dir beim Lösen der Aufgabe in der Unit.

More practice ○ p. 11/3 Mit dieser Aufgabe kannst du den Lernstoff aus der Unit noch einmal üben.

More practice ● p. 11/3 Diese Aufgabe ist eine zusätzliche Herausforderung.

Unit 1

○ **1 Your turn: In what way are you smart?** → More help Check-in, p. 9/3

Here is what Julie wrote. Maybe her text and the useful phrases in **bold** *can help you with your own text.*

I think I'm body smart because **I'm very good at** sport.
I like running, cycling and playing volleyball.
And **I never have problems when** I learn a new sport.

Also, I'm self smart:
I know what I'm good at, and **I often think about** what I want to do before I start something.
If you are self smart, you often learn from your mistakes.
That's what I do too.

● **2 Your turn: In what way are you smart?** → More practice Check-in, p. 9/3

What do you remember about the characters in your book – Gwen, Holly, Olivia, Dave, Jay and Luke. Choose **one** *character and make a mind map of his or her hobbies and personality. What smart type is he/she?*

○ **3 What will the future bring?** → More practice Station 1, p. 11/3

a) *Complete the sentences. Use the simple present and the will future.*

1. If Olivia ▭ a lot, she ▭ in front of a big audience. (practise / play)
2. If Holly ▭ hard, she ▭ become a vet. (study[1] / become)
3. If Luke ▭ himself, he ▭ in the Premier League. (push / play)
4. If Dave ▭ his pocket money, he ▭ a snack bar. (save / open)

b) *Your turn: Write if-sentences that are true for you.*

Start: If I …

1 to study [ˈstʌdi] lernen; studieren
Lösung: 1. practises, 'll play; 2. studies, 'll become; 3. pushes, 'll play; 4. saves, 'll open

4 What will the future bring? → More practice Station 1, p. 11/3

Look at the pictures and make conditional sentences type 1.

practise a lot   **play in front of a big audience**   **study¹ hard**   **become a vet**

push himself   **play in Premier League**   **save pocket money**   **open a snack bar**

Lösung: 1. practises, she'll play; 2. studies, she'll become; 3. pushes, he'll play; 4. saves, he'll open

5 More advice for Jay → More practice Station 2, p. 13/7

Read this advice for Jay. Put the verbs in the right form.

---

mr_know_it_all_14   19:27

If I **1** (be) you, I **2** (not worry) about dancing and singing.
I **3** (worry) about SCHOOL! I mean, if your brother **4** (be) smarter, he **5** (not earn) his money
as a model – what kind of a career is THAT?! No magazine **6** (put) his photo on the cover if he
7 (not look) good and young, but you can't stay young FOREVER. If I **8** (be) your father, I **9**
(make sure) that you worked harder. And I **10** (stop) paying for your dancing lessons!

Lösung: 1. were, 2. wouldn't worry, 3. 'd/would worry, 4. was/were, 5. wouldn't earn, 6. would put, 7. didn't look, 8. was/were, 9. 'd/would make sure, 10. 'd/would stop

6 What would an adult say? → More practice Station 2, p. 13/7

*Read the advice on p. 13 again. How do you think advice from an adult would be different?
Write a comment from the point of view of an adult, e.g. a sports star, a famous singer, a teacher,
an uncle / aunt. Use **conditional sentences type 2**.*

7 Your turn: A forum for teenagers → More help Station 2, p. 13/8

*Here are some problems to start with and some ideas for advice. Use **conditional sentences type 2**.*

My friend always wants to copy my homework!

> tell him / her to do it himself / herself | ask to
> copy his / her homework next time | suggest
> to do it together | look for new friends

My parents don't let me go out with my friends!

> promise to take your phone and not to turn it
> off | try to find a compromise | explain that
> friends are important

○ **8** **Ivy's model** → More practice Station 2, p. 14/9

*Read what one of Ivy's models tells a fashion magazine. Complete his sentences with **conditional sentences type 2**.*

"If I ▊**1**▊ (not love) fashion so much, I ▊**2**▊ (not be) a model. I'm lucky that there aren't so many boys or young men in the modelling business[1]. I ▊**3**▊ (find) it a lot harder to get a job if I ▊**4**▊ (be) a girl! It's also great that I can choose who I work for. If I ▊**5**▊ (not like) Ivy's clothes, I ▊**6**▊ (not work) for her. We all love Ivy. If we ▊**7**▊ (not be) a great team, we ▊**8**▊ (have) less success, I'm sure!"

Lösung: 1. didn't love, 2. wouldn't be, 3. 'd/would find, 4. was/were, 5. didn't like, 6. wouldn't work, 7. weren't, 8. 'd/would have

○ **9** **A German talent show** → More help Station 2, p. 14/10

*Look at this list of things to do and **not** to do at an audition. The words can help you to sum up the information.*

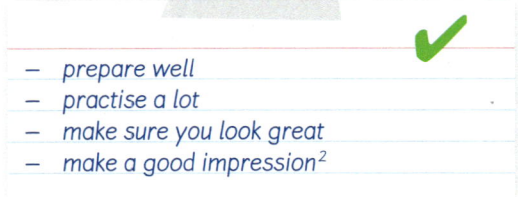

✔	✘
– prepare well	– choose a popular song
– practise a lot	– come without an adult
– make sure you look great	– do embarrassing things on stage[3]
– make a good impression[2]	

○ **10** **Different jobs** → More practice Station 2, p. 14/11

Look at these groups of words. Which job do they describe – influencer, designer, model or dancer?

1. self and picture smart | like to perform | love fashion | like travelling | work in a team
2. good technical skills | communicate well | people and self smart | post videos | give advice
3. body and self smart | practise hard | imaginative | confident | perform in front of an audience
4. creative | like drawing | good at working with his/her hands | people smart | good at working in a team

Lösung: 1. model, 2. influencer, 3. dancer, 4. designer

● **11** **Different jobs** → More practice Station 2, p. 14/11

Make a mind map for each of the jobs: influencer, designer, model, dancer. What do these people do? What do they have to be good at?

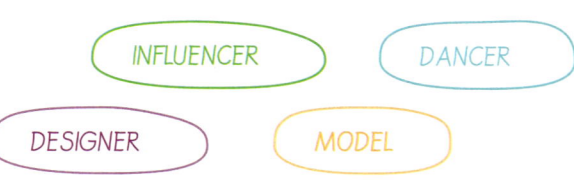

INFLUENCER   DANCER

DESIGNER   MODEL

1 business ['bɪznɪs] Geschäft | **2 impression** [ɪm'preʃn] Eindruck | **3 stage** [steɪdʒ] Bühne

○ **12** **Compare two families: the Azads and the Frasers** → More help Station 3, p. 15/12a)

Copy the grid and complete it.

	personality	opinions	problems
Olivia			
Claire			
…			

Here are some ideas to help you:

Personality:	bossy │ strong │ serious │ messy │ clever │ creative │ is good at … │ likes to get organised │ likes to dream (about the future) │ likes to play … │ likes to have fun
Opinions:	school is important │ hobbies are good for you │ find time to enjoy yourself │ you must work hard and get good marks │ no good job without good marks at school │ you should teach yourself new things │ you're too laid-back
Problems:	can't agree with parents │ room is messy │ gets bad marks │ can't focus on important things │ can only focus on important things like school

○ **13** **Act it out!** → More help Skills, p. 18/3b)

a) *Look at the words for feelings and match them with the photos, if possible. Then try to make the same face. Work with a partner. Can he/she guess which feeling you're acting?*

<mark>disappointed</mark>   <mark>angry</mark>   <mark>sad</mark>   <mark>not sure what to do</mark>   <mark>happy / excited</mark>   <mark>shocked[1]</mark>

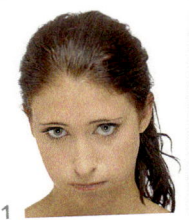 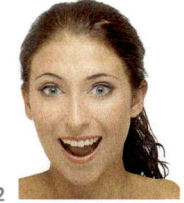  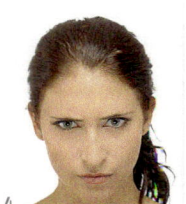 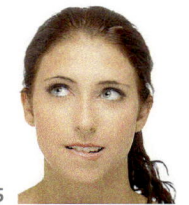

1   2   3   4   5

b) *Which words can you use in your dialogue on p. 18? Can you think of more?*
Lösung: a) Picture 1: disappointed; Picture 2: happy/excited; Picture 3: shocked; Picture 4: angry; Picture 5: not sure what to do

○ **14** **Before you read** → More help Story, p. 20/1

What kind of trouble have your brothers/sisters/cousins/friends got into before? Was it big trouble, or not so big? Maybe some of the phrases in the box can help you.

1 shocked [ʃɒkt] schockiert │ **2 to tell lies** [tel ˈlaɪz] lügen │ **3 to tease sb** [tiːz] jmdn. ärgern; jmdn. hänseln

> **Useful phrases**
>
> – One of my friends always gets into trouble for telling lies[2] / making nasty comments / …
> – My friend / cousin breaks the rules at home / at school / in our team / …
> – There's always trouble when …
> – He / She likes to start fights / tease[3] people / …

Text and media smart 1

○ **1** **Understanding the song** → More help Station 1, p. 27/4a)

Look at the mind map of reasons for being friends. Can you find them in the song text?

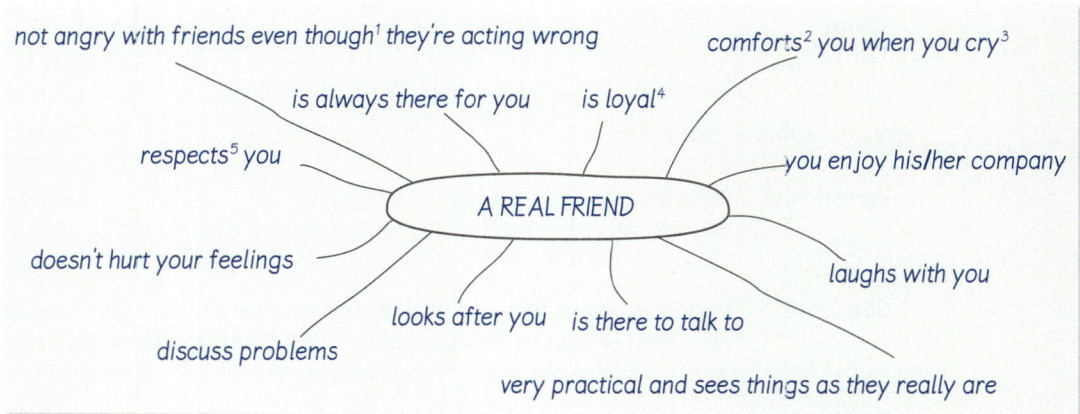

not angry with friends even though[1] they're acting wrong

comforts[2] you when you cry[3]

is always there for you   is loyal[4]

respects[5] you

you enjoy his/her company

A REAL FRIEND

doesn't hurt your feelings

laughs with you

looks after you   is there to talk to

discuss problems

very practical and sees things as they really are

Lösung: laughs with you (l. 2), looks after you (l. 3), you enjoy his/her company (l. 4),
is loyal (l. 5), is always there for you (ll. 11, 30, 32–33), is there to talk to (l. 14)

● **2** **Understanding the song** → More practice Station 1, p. 27/4a)

Bus stop: Look at the lyrics and focus on spelling and punctuation[6]. Share your results with a partner.
Think of reasons why the text is presented that way.
Lösung: In a song the writer often leaves out commas, full stops and letters. Each line or idea starts with a capital letter.

○ **3** **Focus on language** → More help Station 1, p. 28/5

Read the phrases on the left and match them with the phrases on the right.

quote from the text	meaning
1. you break through my shell *(ll. 6–7)*	a) to do everything to achieve[7] something, no matter[8] how long it takes
2. keep my feet on the ground *(l. 9)*	b) somebody makes you become more interested in other people and more willing[9] to talk and take part in social activities
3. will go to the end of the earth *(l. 30)*	c) to let somebody see things as they really are

Lösung: 1. b), 2. c), 3. a)

● **4** **Focus on language** → More practice Station 1, p. 28/5

Read the phrases below and say what they mean in your own words.

friends stick together like glue   a shoulder to cry on   speak the same language

know someone inside out[10]   be on the same page

1 even though [ˌiːvn ˈðəʊ] obwohl **|** **2 to comfort sb** [ˈkʌmfət] jmdn. trösten **|** **3 to cry** [kraɪ] weinen **|** **4 loyal** [ˈlɔɪəl]
loyal; treu **|** **5 to respect sb** [rɪˈspekt] jmdn. respektieren **|** **6 punctuation** [ˌpʌŋktʃuˈeɪʃn] Zeichensetzung **|** **7 to achieve**
[əˈtʃiːv] erreichen **|** **8 no matter** [nəʊ ˈmætə] egal **|** **9 more willing** [wɪlɪŋ] eher bereit **|** **10 inside out** [ɪnˈsaɪd aʊt]
in- und auswendig

5 Be a songwriter! → More help Station 1, p. 29/9

*Look at the images and describe them in figurative
or literal language for your song.*

> **Word bank**
>
> helps you to get back on your feet | helps you to
> reach your goals | supports you when you are down |
> helps you to carry your burdens[1] | supports you so
> you can take the next step | shares everything with
> you | helps you to meet challenges | never leaves
> you when you are in trouble

Lösung: left to right: 1. helps you to get back to your feet; 2./5. helps you to carry your burdens; 3. supports you when you are
down; 4. helps you to reach your goals; 6./8. shares everything with you; 7. supports you so you can take the next step

6 Rhymes in poetry → More help Station 2, p. 31/14a)

Read the first eight lines of the poem out loud. Which rhyme scheme is right?

a) AABB AABB
b) ABAB ABAB
c) AABBCCDD

Lösung: c)

7 Writing a stanza → More practice Station 2, p. 31/14c)

One more stanza is missing in the poem. Write a new stanza with the same rhyme scheme.

8 Your turn: A friendship poem → More help Station 2, p. 31/15

*Write a short poem for your best friend. Read the idioms and their meaning. Choose three and create
a poem for a friend. Use a dictionary for help.*

- birds of a feather flock together = people with the same interests come together
- like two peas in a pod = very similar
- through thick and thin = through all circumstances no matter how difficult
- to build bridges = to create friendly relations between people or groups
- to bury the hatchet = to end a conflict
- to get on like a house on fire = to get on very well with someone
- to make strange bedfellows = to be unlikely companions
- to see eye to eye with someone = to agree with someone

Here are some ideas for rhyming words:

together – forever   pod – odd   thin – pin   bridges – fridges   hatchet – match it

fire – hire   bedfellows – dear fellows   someone – become one

1 burden ['bɜːdn] Last

Unit 2

1 **Typically German?** → More help Check-in, p. 41/3d)

The picture and phrases can help you to talk about typical ideas people have about Germany.

Start: People from other countries believe / think that most / many Germans …

Word bank

good / great at football | like beer | love fast / good / expensive cars | drive fast | work hard / a lot | wear lederhosen and dirndls | are never late | make high-quality products

2 **Hogmanay** → More help Station 1, p. 43/3

Write sentences in the simple present passive.

Example: 1. In Scotland people **call** the last day of the year Hogmanay.
→ In Scotland the last day of the year **is called** Hogmanay.

2. Before the new year starts people **clean** their house.
→ Before the new year starts houses ▨ .
3. They **celebrate** Hogmanay with street parties.
→ Hogmanay ▨ with street parties.
4. At midnight they **ring** bells and **set off** fireworks.
→ At midnight bells ▨ and fireworks ▨ .
5. Then people **hold** hands and **sing** 'Auld Lang Syne'.
→ Then hands ▨ and 'Auld Lang Syne' ▨ .
6. The first footer – the first person to visit you in the new year – **gives** a black bun as a gift to the people that live in the house so they won't go hungry in the new year.
→ The people that live in the house ▨ a black bun as a gift so they won't go hungry in the new year.
7. They **bring** a piece of coal so that the house stays warm.
→ A piece of coal ▨ so that the house stays warm.
8. The government **grants** two days of holiday to the Scottish people. (The rest of the UK just has one on New Year's Day.)
→ Two days of holiday ▨ to the Scottish people.

Lösung: 2. are cleaned; 3. is celebrated; 4. are rung, (are) set off; 5. are held, is sung; 6. are given; 7. is brought; 8. are granted

Tip

Look at the new subject in the passive sentence carefully. Is it singular or plural? Think about the verb forms carefully too – are they regular or irregular?

3 Famous Scots → More help Station 1, p. 43/4b)

Here are some ideas to help you with the exercise:

radar[1] – invent – Robert Wattson-Watt   tunnels, canals[2] and roads – build – Thomas Telford

Scottish castles – design – Robert Adams   James Bond – play – Sean Connery

lots of money – give to charity – Andrew Carnegie   *Treasure Island* – write – Robert Louis Stevenson

Lösung: 1. Radar was invented by … 2. Tunnel, canals and roads were built by … 3. Scottish castles were designed by …
4. James Bond was played by … 5. Lots of money was given to charity by … 6. *Treasure Island* was written by …

4 Scottish heroes and heroines → More practice Station 1, p. 44/5

Complete the text with passive forms: **simple present**, *simple past* or ***present perfect simple***.

Stories about heroes and heroines **1** (tell) in Scotland for centuries. There is even a story about a dog.

In 1872 a statue[3] of Greyfriar's Bobby **2** (put up) in a park in Edinburgh. Bobby, a Skye terrier, was so sad about his owner's death[4] that he sat on his grave[5] for 14 years, and the people of Edinburgh brought him food and drink. His story **3** (tell) in a number of books and films. When you go to Edinburgh, you can see his statue in the Old Town or have a drink in the bar[6] "Greyfriar's Bobby".

Another Scottish heroine is Flora MacDonald. Her father died when she was a child, and her mother **4** (kidnap[7]) – so Flora **5** (bring) to her father's cousin, the chief[8] of the MacDonald clan[9]. Later Flora **6** (tell) to move to the island of Benbecula. Today Flora **7** (always describe) in stories as a very brave young woman. And so she was! Bonnie Prince Charlie wanted to become King of Scotland, but he **8** (defeat[10]) by British soldiers[11]. He then escaped to Benbecula and **9** (hide) by Flora.

Lösung: 1. have been told, 2. was put up, 3. has been told, 4. was kidnapped, 5. was brought, 6. was told, 7. is always described, 8. was defeated, 9. was hidden

5 Scottish heroes and heroines → More practice Station 1, p. 44/5

Complete the text with passive forms: simple present, simple past or present perfect simple.

Stories about heroes and heroines **1** (tell) in Scotland for centuries. There is even a story about a dog.

In 1872 a statue[3] of Greyfriar's Bobby **2** (put up) in a park in Edinburgh. Bobby, a Skye terrier, was so sad about his owner's death[4] that he sat on his grave[5] for 14 years, and the people of Edinburgh brought him food and drink. His story **3** (tell) in a number of books and films. When you go to Edinburgh, you can see his statue in the Old Town or have a drink in the bar[6] "Greyfriar's Bobby".

Another Scottish heroine is Flora MacDonald. Her father died when she was a child, and her mother **4** (kidnap[7]) – so Flora **5** (bring) to her father's cousin, the chief[8] of the MacDonald clan[9]. Later Flora **6** (tell) to move to the island of Benbecula. Today Flora **7** (always describe) in stories as a very brave young woman. And so she was! Bonnie Prince Charlie wanted to become King of Scotland, but he **8** (defeat[10]) by British soldiers[11]. He then escaped to Benbecula and **9** (hide) by Flora.

Lösung: 1. have been told, 2. was put up, 3. has been told, 4. was kidnapped, 5. was brought, 6. was told, 7. is always described, 8. was defeated, 9. was hidden

1 radar ['reɪdɑː] Radar | **2 canal** [kə'næl] Kanal | **3 statue** ['stætʃuː] Statue | **4 death** [deθ] Tod | **5 grave** [greɪv] Grab | **6 bar** [bɑː] Bar; Kneipe | **7 to kidnap** ['kɪdnæp] entführen | **8 chief** [tʃiːf] Anführer; Oberhaupt | **9 clan** [klæn] Clan | **10 to defeat** [dɪ'fiːt] besiegen | **11 soldier** ['səʊldʒə] Soldat

○ **6** **Your turn: A different country** → More help Station 1, p. 44/8

When you write your text, use this structure:

At the beginning say the name of the country and where it is. In the main part of the text describe the people, where they live, their hobbies, what they eat etc. At the end explain why everyone should visit this country.

These words can help you too:

| tall | small | rich | poor | tree house | palace | island | forest | colourful clothes | hat | crown | jewellery | king | queen | sweets | fruit | vegetables | party | sports | job

○ **7** **What were Olivia and her family doing?** → More practice Station 2, p. 46/10

Put in the right verb forms.

It's Saturday, 10:00
1. Olivia: I **am** play**ing** the saxophone.
2. Lucy **is** tidy**ing** her room.
3. Hey Lucy, why ▨ (you) my mp3 player?
4. Claire and Desmond **are** preparing lunch.
5. We ▨ on the internet for tips on how to spend the weekend.

Last Saturday, 10:00
1. Olivia: I **was** play**ing** the saxophone.
2. Lucy ▨ her room.
3. Hey Lucy, why **were** you us**ing** my mp3 player?
4. Claire and Desmond ▨ lunch.
5. We **were** look**ing** on the internet for tips on how to spend the weekend.

Lösung: Present progressive (left side): 3. are you using, 5. are looking;
Past progressive (right side): 2. was tidying, 4. were preparing

○ **8** **When or while?** → More practice Station 2, p. 46/11b)

*Complete the sentences with **when** or **while**.*

1. We were watching a film ▨ Mum came home.
2. ▨ I saw my brother, he was buying lots of sweets.
3. I read a whole magazine ▨ I was waiting for the bus.
4. ▨ my dog was sleeping, my cat stole his dinner!
5. My sister was preparing a presentation ▨ her phone rang.
6. ▨ the friends were walking home from school, it started to rain.

Lösung: 1. when, 2. When, 3. while, 4. While, 5. when, 6. While

> **Tip**
>
> Use **while** for the action that was already going on and **when** for the new action that started.

● **9** **A crazy day at home** → More practice Station 2, p. 46/11b)

Use these photos and write a short story about a crazy day at home. Think of your own crazy ideas too. Use the simple past and the past progressive.

Start: First, breakfast was crazy. While Mum was…, our dog … her breakfast! Then, while Mum and Dad were …, we … in the kitchen. But when …

○ **10** **Strong adjectives** → More help Skills, p. 48/2

Strong adjectives can help you to make your text livelier and more interesting to read.
Copy the grid. Put the adjectives with similar meaning in the right category. Sometimes they
belong to more than one category.

beautiful   little   great   fascinating   interesting   large   wonderful   exciting

amazing   spectacular   tiny   huge

small	good	nice	big

Lösung: small: little, tiny; good: great, amazing, spectacular, fascinating, interesting, wonderful, exciting;
nice: great, beautiful, amazing, interesting, spectacular, fascinating, wonderful; big: large, huge

○ **11** **It's amazing!** → More help Skills, p. 48/3

a) *Improve the text to grab a tourist's attention. Choose the right word.*

Did you know that Glasgow is **1** (well-known / world-famous) for its shipbuilding industry?
Titan Clydebank is a **2** (tall / big) shipbuilding crane (49m). In 1907 it was designed by
the Scottish engineer Adam Hunter to build some of the **3** (biggest / largest) and **4**
(nicest / most beautiful) ships ever.
  Titan Clydebank has become an **5** (exciting / interesting) tourist attraction. Are you
brave **6** (too / enough) to climb up to the **7** (complete / very) top and enjoy the **8**
(amazing / nice) views across Glasgow?

b) *Which photo would you choose to persuade tourists to come and visit the crane?*
Give reasons for your answer.

A   B   C

Lösung: a) 1. world-famous, 2. tall, 3. largest, 4. most beautiful, 5. exciting, 6. enough, 7. very, 8. amazing; **b)** I'd choose picture C.
In this picture you can see that the crane is really tall. Also, the sky is blue, and good weather makes people want to go outside
and do and see things.

Unit 3

○ 1 Vocabulary → More practice Check-in, p. 63/2

a) *Match the verbs with their opposite meaning.*

1. win   a) make peace
2. arrive   b) leave
3. appear   c) divorce
4. fight   d) lose
5. marry   e) disappear

b) *Complete the sentence with one verb from each pair in a). Use the verb in the right tense.*

1. The Normans ▮ the battle against the Saxons.
2. By the time the Angles and Saxons ▮ in Britain, there were already roads there.
3. Since the Industrial Revolution, much of the countryside has ▮ .
4. Back then they ▮ over land.
5. King Henry VIII ▮ six times. There's a rhyme to remember what happened to each of his wives: "Divorced, Beheaded[1], Died: Divorced, Beheaded, Survived[2]".

c) *Find the nouns for the verbs in each group. Use a dictionary for help. What is similar for the nouns in each group?*

Group 1	Group 2	Group 3
attack | defeat | fight | design	build | kill | feel | paint	invent | protect | connect | decide | invade

● 2 Vocabulary → More practice Check-in, p. 63/2

a) *Find the opposite meaning of these verbs. Look at the texts on pp. 63–65 for help.*

▮ arrive ▮ win ▮ appear ▮ fight ▮ marry

b) *Look at the pictures and write a sentence for each. Use one verb from each pair in a).*

1 2 3 4 5

c) *Find the nouns for the verbs. Use a dictionary for help. Then put them into three groups: What is similar for the nouns in each group?*

connect \| attack \| decide \| build \| defeat \| fight \| kill \| protect \| design \| feel \| paint \| invent \| invade

1 **beheaded** [bɪˈhedɪd] geköpft; enthauptet |
2 **survived** [səˈvaɪvd] überlebt

3 Your turn: The five most important objects → More help Check-in, p. 64/5

a) *Put the sentences in a good order.*

1. He's a happy childhood[1] memory.
2. His name is Thomas and he's a brown bear.
3. My grandparents gave him to me when I was a baby.
4. I played with him a lot and I went to bed with him too.
5. I chose this object because it was my first cuddly toy[2].
6. Thomas is really old now, but I still like him very much.

b) *Here are some ideas for objects:*

> ring | bracelet | necklace | doll[3] | car | photo | ticket for a concert / the cinema / the zoo | a pair of shoes | book | kindergarten drawing | instrument

Lösung: a) 5. – 2. – 3. – 4. – 6. – 1.

4 The oldest thing → More practice Check-in, p. 64/5

What's the oldest thing in your house? Describe it in a short text. Then tell the class about it.

Lösung: The oldest thing [in] our house is this doll. [It] belonged to my grandma. [It] was very important to [her] because it was her only [toy]. She used to take it [ev]erywhere when she was [a c]hild and she never threw [it a]way. Today it's sitting on [our] sofa in the living room – [a m]emory of my grandma.

Useful phrases

I found this in … | It belonged to my grandad / grandma / … | He / She used it to … | It was very important to my …, so he / she didn't throw it away. | Today we use … instead.

Word bank

baking moulds[4] / pots[5] / pans[6] | old toys (china doll[7] / cuddly toy) | a pair of snowshoes[8] | old photos / letters / postcards | a telescope[9] | keys | jewellery | chair / table / wardrobe / …

5 Find the rule: Relative pronouns → More help Station 1, p. 67/2

a) *Read the text on p. 66 again and complete these sentences. Use **which, that, who** or **whose**.*

1. Olivia is in the Tudor period for the **calendar** ▨ Claire is making.
2. This is the **calendar** ▨ page themes are from different historical periods.
3. Gwen and Holly are the **girls** ▨ Olivia is going to be photographed with.
4. They'll wear clothes like the **women** ▨ job was to be with the queen all day and all night.
5. Jay has to choose the historical **person** ▨ he wants to be.
6. Olivia needs to think about the **dress** ▨ she's going to wear.

b) *Look at the sentences in a) again. Are the nouns before the relative pronoun people or things? When do you use which pronoun? Now go on with exercises 2c) and d) on p. 67.*

1 childhood [ˈtʃaɪldhʊd] Kindheit; Kindheits- | **2** cuddly toy [ˌkʌdli ˈtɔɪ] Plüschtier | **3** doll [dɒl] Puppe | **4** baking mould [ˈbeɪkɪŋ ˌməʊld] Backform | **5** pot [pɒt] Topf | **6** pan [pæn] Pfanne | **7** china doll [ˌtʃaɪnə ˈdɒl] Porzellanpuppe | **8** snowshoes [ˈsnəʊʃuːz] Schneeschuhe | **9** telescope [ˈtelɪskəʊp] Teleskop

Lösung: a) 1. calendar which, 2. calendar whose, 3. girls who, 4. women whose, 5. person that, 6. dress that; **b)** You use 'which' or 'that' for things. You use 'who' or 'that' for people. You use 'whose' for people or things.

6 People from history → More practice Station 1, p. 67/3

*Complete the text about Francis Drake with the right relative pronoun: **which**, **who** or **whose**.*

Francis Drake was the first Englishman ⬛**1** sailed¹ around the world. On his way he attacked Spanish ships ⬛**2** carried² gold and spices³. In 1587 the Spanish were preparing to attack England, but it was Drake ⬛**3** led a surprise attack and burnt the Spanish ships. When the Spanish ships (known as the Armada) attacked in 1588, Drake was one of the people ⬛**4** defeated them in the English Channel. The battle was won by the side ⬛**5** ships were lighter and faster. It was the first sea battle ⬛**6** involved⁴ large numbers of ships.

Lösung: 1. who, 2. which, 3. who, 4. who, 5. whose, 6. which

7 People from history → More practice Station 1, p. 67/3

Write a text about Francis Drake. Use these notes and relative clauses.

- first Englishman / sailed¹ around the world
- attacked Spanish ships / carried² gold and spices³
- 1587 Spanish prepared to attack England / but Drake led surprise attack / burnt the Spanish ships
- Spanish ships (known as the Armada) attacked in 1588
- Drake one of the people / defeated Armada
- the English won against the Spanish
- was won by the side / ships lighter and faster
- first sea battle / involved⁴ large numbers of ships

Lösung: 1. the first Englishman who sailed, 2. Spanish ships which carried gold, 3. it was Drake who led a surprise attack, 4. the people who defeated them, 5. the side whose ships were lighter, 6. the first sea battle which involved large

8 Sherlock Holmes → More practice Station 1, p. 67/3

Choose the right relative pronoun.

1. Sherlock Holmes is a character **who / whose** name will always be famous.
2. *A Study in Scarlet* was the story **that / who** introduced Sherlock Holmes to the world in 1887.
3. Sir Arthur Conan Doyle was the writer **which / who** created Sherlock Holmes.
4. Dr John Watson is the character **that / whose** Sherlock Holmes has most of his adventures with.
5. *The Strand Magazine* was the magazine **which / whom** most of the Sherlock Holmes stories first appeared in.
6. "The Final Problem" is the story **who / which** many people think is the best Sherlock Holmes adventure.

Lösung: 1. whose, 2. that, 3. who, 4. that, 5. which, 6. which

1 to sail [seɪl] segeln | **2 to carry** [ˈkæri] befördern | **3 spice** [spaɪs] Gewürz | **4 to involve** [ɪnˈvɒlv] beteiligen

9 **Sherlock Holmes** → More practice Station 1, p. 67/3

a) *Complete the sentences with a relative pronoun:* **which, who** *or* **whose**.

1. Sherlock Holmes is a character 🟨 name will always be famous.
2. *A Study in Scarlet* was the book 🟨 introduced Sherlock Holmes to the world in 1887.
3. Sir Arthur Conan Doyle was the writer 🟨 created Sherlock Holmes.
4. Dr John Watson is the character 🟨 Sherlock Holmes has most of his adventures with.
5. *The Strand Magazine* was a magazine 🟨 most of the Sherlock Holmes short stories first appeared in.
6. "The Final Problem" is the story 🟨 many people think is the best Sherlock Holmes adventure.

b) *In which sentence can't you change the relative pronoun to* **that**?
Lösung: a) 1. whose, 2. which, 3. who, 4. who, 5. which, 6. which; **b)** 1.

10 **At History Club** → More help Station 2, p. 70/11

a) *Choose the right relative pronoun.*

Examples: The History Club organises different activities **which** ✔/ **who** are really exciting.
Last month we talked about a famous writer of plays **who** ✔/ **which** we all know.

1. Last week we watched a modern film about Shakespeare **which / who** was very interesting.
2. Yesterday we went to a theatre **that / whose** we really liked.
3. The guide told us that in the old days they needed light **which / who** came through an open roof.
4. He said that all the actors were men and boys **which / who** also played the roles of women and girls.
5. After the backstage tour, we met an actor **whose / who** we'll never forget.

b) *Look at the sentences in a) again. Put the relative pronoun that can be left out in brackets.*
Lösung: a)+b) 1. which, 2. (that), 3. which, 4. who, 5. (who)

11 **Useful phrases for presenting facts and figures** → More help Skills, p. 72/1

In this version of the text the phrases you need are in **bold**.

sung: 1. times and dates: 1599, in the 16th century, 0 years ago, in just two urs, the following year; escription of places/ ects: was used for, onged to, was made of; biographical information: s born in 1564, wrote, ed, moved to, reigned; ical history verbs: was lt, started, was rebuilt, s opened, burnt down, led down

"… Now we're on Bankside and **in the 16th century** there were four theatres here along the river. In a moment – just around the corner – you'll see the famous Globe Theatre. It **was built in 1599** and it **was used for** all kinds of entertainment – plays, musical events and animal fights. Of course, William Shakespeare **wrote** and **acted** here while Elizabeth I **reigned**. He **was born** in Stratford-upon-Avon **in 1564** but **moved to** London as a young man. The diary in my hand probably **belonged to** Shakespeare himself! But, anyway, it's sad to say that the first Globe **was made of** wood, and when a fire **started 400 years ago**, the theatre **burnt down in just two hours**. That was in 1613. It **was rebuilt the following year** but **pulled down** again in 1644–45. The modern Globe **was opened** in 1997 …"

Text and media smart 2

1 Types of messages → More practice Check-in, p. 80/1

a) *Which types of messages do you reply to with the same type of message?*

b) *Which type of message don't you reply to with the same type of message?*

c) *For which type of message don't you expect a reply?*
Lösung: a) C, D; **b)** E; **c)** A, B

2 Write a reply → More practice Check-in, p. 80/1

Write a reply to the email or text message on page 80.

Email:
Thank[1] your friends for their email and give them your new mobile phone number – 0977 905844. Then say a little about your latest life in Cornwall, e.g. school, activities, friends, family and plans to visit Greenwich.
Lösung: text message (D): Sorry, just left home. Will b there in 10 min. CU

Text message:
Say where you are now. Say when you will see the other person (in a text message, 'see you' can be CU.) You don't need a greeting (Hi …) an ending (All the best), or your name.

3 Write a reply → More practice Check-in, p. 80/1

Write a reply to the email, text message or invitation on page 80.
Lösung: invitation (E): Dear Emma, Thank you for inviting me to your party. I'm sorry, but I can't come. My grandma's birthday is on the same day. I hope you have a nice party. Love, Olivia

4 Formal emails → More help Station 1, p. 81/3b)

Match the purpose to each paragraph in the formal email.

header[2]   greeting   ending   reason for writing   giving information   asking for information

Lösung: ll. 1–3 header, l. 4 greeting, ll. 5–8 reason for writing, l. 9 asking for information, ll. 10–11 giving information, ll. 12–14 ending

5 Mr Evans' reply → More help Station 1, p. 81/4

Mr Evans' email is too informal. Rewrite it in a more formal style. Remember your answer from p. 81, ex. 3.

> Hi Claire,
>
> It was wonderful to get your email! I can come on Sat, 9th April, and it wouldn't be a problem to take the photos for your calendar – it sounds amazing! I'd love to help your community centre, and you don't need to pay me anything. Just make me a nice cup of tea while I'm taking the photos!
>
> If it's OK, I'd like to come to the centre before I take the photos. That'll help me to decide what stuff I'll need to bring. It's going to be really great – I can't wait!
>
> Lots of love,
> Jim

1 to thank [θæŋk] danken | **2 header** [ˈhedə] Kopfzeile

6 Mrs, Miss or Ms? → More practice Station 1, p. 81/4

Complete the text with the words.

`formal`   `greeting`   `married`   `Miss`   `Mrs`   `Ms`   `recipient`   `surname`

It can be difficult to choose the best **1** for a **2** email or letter. If the **3** is a woman, should you use Mrs, Miss or Ms? In the UK only 65% of **4** women under 40 use their husband's[1] **5**. If you know that a woman prefers Mrs, Miss or Ms, then use that. If you do not know which they prefer, it may be best to use **6**. Many women now prefer it to **7** or **8**.

Lösung: 1. greeting, 2. formal, 3. recipient, 4. married, 5. surname, 6. Ms, 7. Miss/Mrs, 8. Mrs/Miss

7 Claire's reply to Mr Evans → More practice Station 1, p. 81/4

*Write Claire's reply to Mr Evans. She thanks him for his help and says he can come to the community centre any time it's open – the times are on the website **www.parkstreetcentre.org.uk**.*

8 Parts of a letter → More help Station 1, p. 82/6

Match the words to the parts of the letter (1–8).

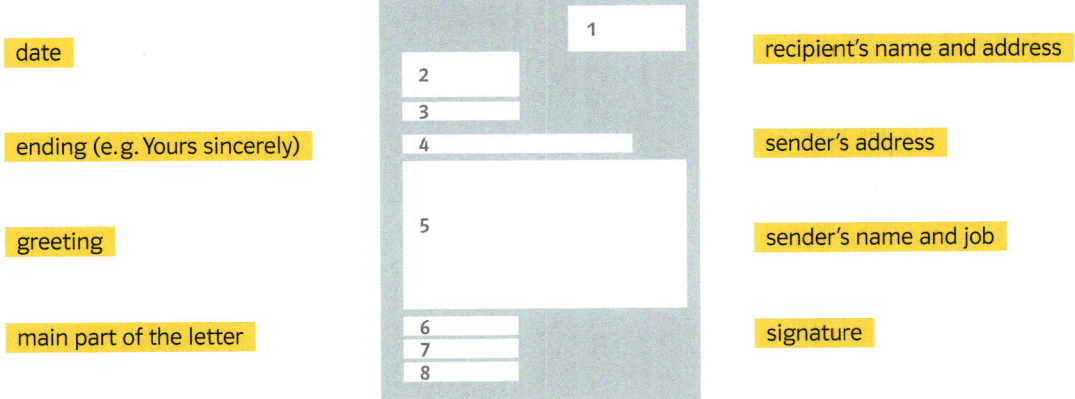

`date`   `ending (e.g. Yours sincerely)`   `greeting`   `main part of the letter`

`recipient's name and address`   `sender's address`   `sender's name and job`   `signature`

Lösung: 1. sender's address, 2. recipient's name and address, 3. date, 4. greeting, 5. main part of the letter, 6. ending, 7. signature, 8. sender's name and job

9 A semi-formal email → More practice Station 2, p. 83/10

Write another email from Claire to Jay. Thank him for his offer to help. Ask him to come an hour before the photoshoot starts to help set up the rooms.

10 Informal communication → More help Station 2, p. 84/12a)

These ideas can help you to say how the English is different in text messages and formal messages.

(in)complete[2] sentences | punctuation[3] | abbreviations | (no) greeting |
short/long forms | icons

1 **husband** [ˈhʌzbənd] Ehemann | 2 **incomplete** [ˌɪnkəmˈpliːt] unvollständige/-r/-s | 3 **punctuation** [ˌpʌŋktʃuˈeɪʃn] Zeichensetzung

Lösung: Text messages: incomplete sentences; no punctuation or punctuation like ?!/!!!; abbreviations like u, ur; no greeting; short forms; icons; Formal messages: complete sentences; correct punctuation; abbreviations like Re:/Mr/Mrs;

Unit 4

1 Vocabulary → More help Check-in, p. 95/3c)

Complete the text with the words in the box. Make sure you use the right tense of the verb.

> train station   destination   tickets   get on   journey   taxi   train   car

Last summer we spent the holidays at my grandparents' house. The holiday was nice, but the ⬛**1** was really chaotic. We travelled by ⬛**2** . It's a long trip, and we left for the ⬛**3** very early. When we arrived there, my parents couldn't find the ⬛**4** anymore. As we still had time before the train left, my father took a ⬛**5** back home and got the tickets. He ⬛**6** the train just as the doors were closing[1]. But it got even worse. When we arrived at our ⬛**7** my tablet was gone – it was still on the train! Next time I want to travel by ⬛**8** !

Lösung: 1. journey, 2. train, 3. train station, 4. tickets, 5. taxi, 6. got on, 7. destination, 8. car

2 Ways of travelling → More help Check-in, p. 95/4

The ideas in the boxes can help you to talk about different ways of travelling.

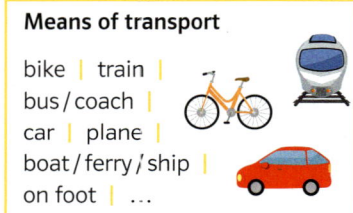

Means of transport

bike | train |
bus / coach |
car | plane |
boat / ferry / ship |
on foot | …

Word bank

I prefer to travel by … because it's cheaper / faster / more convenient[2] … | I don't like travelling by … / go on foot. | It's not convenient. | I get sick / tired … | You mustn't just think of money and time. You have to think of the environment too. | Travelling by … is better / is worse for the environment.

3 Find the rule → More help Station 1, p. 97/2b)

Look at the examples which you collected in ex. 2a) on p. 97. Then read the two rules below.
For which rule do you use the simple present? For which rule do you use the present progressive?
Write down the rules.

> 1. You use the ⬛ for actions in the future which are related to timetables (trains, buses …) or programmes (of cinemas, theatres …).
> 2. You use the ⬛ to talk about plans or arrangements[3] which you have made for the (near) future.

Lösung: 1. simplete present, 2. present progressive

4 Simple present or present progressive? → More practice Station 1, p. 97/4

Compare your calendar for the next few days with a partner and make an arrangement.
Use the simple present and the present progressive to talk about the future.

Example: A: School ends at 11:00 on Friday. Let's go to the leisure centre together!
B: Sorry, but I'm already …

1 to close [kləʊs] (sich) schließen | **2 convenient** [kənˈviːniənt] praktisch; bequem; zweckmäßig | **3 arrangement** [əˈreɪndʒmənt] Absprache; Vereinbarung

5 What happened? → More help, Station 1, p. 98/6a)

These words and phrases can help you to write about the experiences of the Jones family.

Picture 1:

in Italy – go to the beach – want to take the bus to the beach – be little bit late – arrive at bus stop – bus leave – next bus only in one hour

Picture 2:

go swimming – leave everything on the beach – come back – all things gone – see thief[1] – can't catch – too far away

Picture 3:

camp – long day – tired – sleep in tent[2] – suddenly hear noise – tent start to shake – open – cow looked at us

ung: 1. In Italy we
[wa]nted to go to the
[bea]ch by bus. We were
[li]ttle bit late and when
[we] arrived at the bus
[sto]p, the bus was just
[lea]ving. The next bus
[was] only in one hour!
[L]ater when we were
[at t]he beach, somebody
[stol]e our clothes so we
[wen]t back to our tent in
[our] swimsuits. 3. In the
[eve]ning we were trying
[to s]leep in our tent when
[cow] looked inside it.
[It w]as scary!

6 Travel situations → More help Station 1, p. 98/6b)

These phrases can help you to talk about your travel experiences:

When I was in … last year … | During the holidays I … | I felt very stupid / embarrassed / scared when … | Everyone / Someone was staring / looking at me / trying to explain something to me. | I was confused / upset / angry because … | I wanted to …, but I couldn't … | Next time I'll use my mobile / ask someone about … / remember to …

7 At passport control → More help Station 2, p. 99/8b)

How do you think Rafiq felt during his conversation with the man at passport control? How do you think he felt when he left the airport? Make sentences.

Rafiq felt nervous	when he left the airport.
He was worried	that he was allowed to call his aunt and uncle.
He felt lucky	because he would be able to enjoy his holiday after all.
But he was happy	when the man at passport control called somebody.
Rafiq was tired	that he wouldn't be allowed to enter the country.

1 thief [θiːf] Dieb/-in | **2** tent [tent] Zelt

Lösung: 1. Rafiq felt nervous when the man at passport … 2. He was worried that he wouldn't be allowed to enter… 3. He felt lucky that he was allowed to call… 4. Rafiq was tired when he left … 5. But he was happy because he would be able to enjoy …

○ **8** **After the holiday** → More practice Station 2, p. 101/12

*When Rafiq comes back from Bangladesh, his mother has a lot of questions. Complete the questions and answers with **have to**, **be able to** or **be allowed to** in the right tense (present, past or future).*

Mum: Did Masud take you to the old centre of Dhaka?
Rafiq: No, he **1** (not able to) go with me. He **2** (have to) go to school.
Mum: Did you go there all alone? Wasn't that dangerous?
Rafiq: Mum, you **3** (not have to) worry about me all the time!
Mum: But **4** (be able to) find your way around?
Rafiq: Of course I **5** (be able to). It was easy!
Mum: OK, OK. And **6** (be allowed to) go to school with Masud?
Rafiq: Yes, I was. That was really interesting.
Mum: Did Aunt Sadia cook black rice[1] for you? Her rice is the best!
Rafiq: Yes, she did. She even showed me how to cook it, so now I **7** (be able to) cook it for you at the weekend!
Mum: Good idea. And what about the saree[2] for me? Did you buy one?
Rafiq: Sorry, Mum. We **8** (have to) do and see so many things that we didn't have time to go shopping.

Lösung: 1. wasn't able to, 2. had to, 3. don't have to, 4. were you able to, 5. was able to,
6. were you allowed to, 7. I'll be able to, 8. had to

● **9** **After the holiday** → More practice Station 2, p. 101/12

*When Rafiq comes back from Bangladesh, his mother has a lot of questions. Complete the questions and answers with **have to**, **be able to** or **be allowed to** in the right tense (present, past or future).*

Mum: Did Masud take you to the old centre of Dhaka?
Rafiq: No, he **1** go with me. He **2** go to school.
Mum: Did you go there all alone? Wasn't that dangerous?
Rafiq: Mum, you **3** worry about me all the time!
Mum: But **4** find your way around?
Rafiq: Of course I **5** . It was easy!
Mum: OK, OK. And **6** go to school with Masud?
Rafiq: Yes, I was. That was really interesting.
Mum: Did Aunt Sadia cook black rice[1] for you? Her rice is the best!
Rafiq: Yes, she did. She even showed me how to cook it, so now I **7** cook it for you at the weekend!
Mum: Good idea. And what about the saree[2] for me? Did you buy one?
Rafiq: Sorry, Mum. We **8** do and see so many things that we didn't have time to go shopping.

Lösung: 1. wasn't able to, 2. had to, 3. don't have to, 4. were you able to, 5. was able to,
6. were you allowed to, 7. I'll be able to, 8. had to

○ **10** **Destinations for a school trip** → More help Station 2, p. 101/15

You can choose from these European cities to find ideas for your plans:

	Madrid	Dublin	Vienna
flights from Frankfurt / Munich	duration[3]: 1 h 55 / 2 h 05 | price (single/group ticket): …	2 h 05 / 2 h 35 | …	1 h 20 / 1 h 05 | …
train / ferry from …	… | …	… | …	… | …
coach from …	…	…	…

1 rice [raɪs] Reis \| **2 saree** [ˈsɑːri] Sari \| **3 duration** [djʊˈreɪʃn] Dauer

○ **11** **Reading between the lines** → More practice Story, p. 106/4

Read these short texts. Then decide which important information can be found between the lines.

1. It was wet outside. Very wet. Ryan looked at the kitchen clock: football practice was at 4 p.m., and now it was already 3:50. He picked up his shoes and jacket and with a sigh[1] walked out into the rain.
   a) Ryan lives close to the football stadium.
   b) Ryan hates playing football in the rain.
   c) The kitchen clock doesn't show the right time.

2. Kimberly ran all the way home, her maths test still in her hand and a big smile on her face. "Mum!" she shouted. "You won't believe this!"
   a) Kimberly hurries home to help her mum in the kitchen.
   b) Kimberly is a very good student, especially in maths.
   c) She has a good mark in a maths test, which is a surprise to her.

3. Mrs Lynch looked at the students who were playing outside the school building. Laura was standing all by herself under what looked like 'her' tree now. She was staring down at her feet, as usual.
   a) Laura is unhappy because the other students don't talk to her.
   b) Mrs Lynch likes trees and students.
   c) The weather is great, so everyone can play outside.

4. Ethan checked his mobile for the tenth time – still no message. He played with the empty glass in front of him and asked himself if he should ask for another drink or give up and go home.
   a) Ethan likes drinks in restaurants and cafés.
   b) Ethan doesn't know what to do when he is alone in a restaurant.
   c) Ethan is waiting for someone, but that person hasn't come.

Lösung: 1. b), 2. c), 3. a), 4. c)

● **12** **Reading between the lines** → More practice Story, p. 106/4

Write a short text for your partner (4–5 sentences). Think of one important piece of information which you want to give in your text but which isn't there directly. Then give your text to a partner. Can he/she read between the lines and guess the important piece of information? The example can help you to write your text.

Example: Ethan checked his mobile for the tenth time – still no message. He played with the empty glass in front of him and asked himself if he should ask for another drink or give up and go home.

Important information (which isn't in the text directly):
Ethan is waiting for someone, but that person hasn't come.

1 sigh [saɪ] Seufzer

Wo und wann lerne ich am besten?

Es gibt viele Tipps und Tricks, die dir das Lernen erleichtern können. Dazu gehört auch, dass du dir zu Hause einen festen Arbeitsplatz mit genügend Licht einrichtest. Dort solltest du alles greifbar haben, was du zum Lernen brauchst: Schreibzeug, Hefte, Bücher und je nach Aufgabe vielleicht auch einen Computer, ein Tablet oder ein Smartphone. An deinem Arbeitsplatz kannst du in Ruhe deine Hausaufgaben machen, Vokabeln lernen, Texte (nochmals) lesen, Texte schreiben und überprüfen und dich auf Tests und Klassenarbeiten vorbereiten.

Fange rechtzeitig an zu lernen, also nicht erst am Tag oder Abend vor einem Test oder der nächsten Klassenarbeit. So bleibt dir ausreichend Zeit, den Lernstoff nochmals zu wiederholen, wenn du beim Üben feststellst, dass du noch nicht alles kannst.

Vocabulary

Hier findest du verschiedene Möglichkeiten, wie du Vokabeln lernen kannst.

S1 Umgang mit der Wortliste im *Vocabulary*

Lies in der Wortliste die englischen Wörter und ihre deutsche Übersetzung. Schau dir auch die Beispielsätze und Bilder in der rechten Spalte genau an. Am besten machst du das mehrmals hintereinander. Um dir die neuen Wörter besser einzuprägen, kannst du sie abschreiben oder dir unterschiedlich vorsagen, z. B. laut, leise oder singend.

Um dich zu testen, kannst du die Spalte mit der deutschen Übersetzung abdecken. Lies dann die englische Vokabel und sage die deutsche Übersetzung. Du kannst natürlich auch die Sprachrichtung wechseln und die deutsche Übersetzung lesen und dann die englische Vokabel sagen.

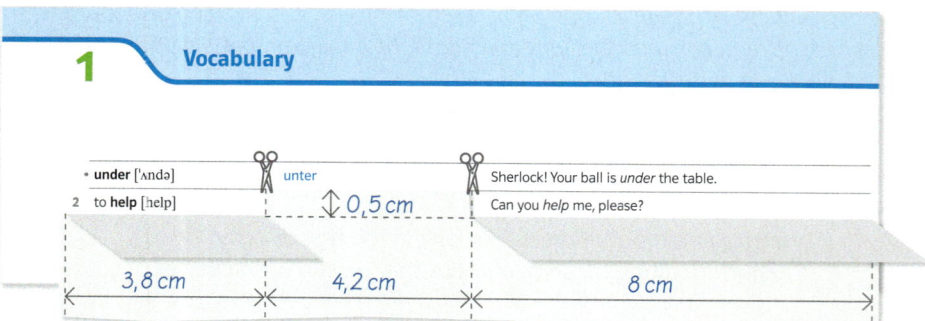

S2 Vokabellernkarten

Vokabeln kannst du gut mithilfe von Vokabellern-
karten lernen. Dazu brauchst du Karteikarten und
einen Karton oder Kasten mit mehreren Fächern.
Schreibe jeweils das englische Wort auf die Vorder-
seite der Karteikarte. Als Merkhilfe kannst du auch
ein Bild dazu malen oder einen Beispielsatz aus
deinem Buch mit aufschreiben. Auf die Rückseite der
Karte schreibst du dann die deutsche Übersetzung.

Nimm zum Lernen eine Karte nach der anderen
heraus und prüfe, ob du die Übersetzung noch weißt,
und zwar deutsch – englisch und englisch – deutsch.
Hast du die Vokabel richtig gewusst, steckst du
sie ins nächste Fach und wiederholst sie an einem
anderen Tag noch einmal.

MK Vokabellernkarten gibt es auch digital. Meistens sind
die Wörter vertont. So lernst du nicht nur die richtige
Schreibweise, sondern auch die Aussprache.

S3 Vokabelheft

Das Abschreiben von neuen Vokabeln ist für viele
eine gute Methode, sich Wörter einzuprägen.
Verwende dazu ein Vokabelheft, das mindestens
DIN A5 groß ist und lege drei Spalten an: eine für das
englische Wort, eine für die deutsche Übersetzung
und eine für einen Beispielsatz. Zur besseren
Orientierung kannst du dir auch die Lektion, der
Lektionsteil und ggf. die Seitenzahl notieren.

Zusätzliche neue Wörter (*personal vocabulary*)
kannst du ebenfalls in deinem Vokabelheft notieren.
Wenn du möchtest, kannst du dein Vokabelheft
um *mind maps*, Bildwörter, Beziehungen zwischen
Wörtern und Ähnlichkeiten zu anderen Sprachen
(→ S4) erweitern.

Um deinen Lernfortschritt zu dokumentieren, kannst
du neben richtig gewusste Vokabeln einen grünen
Punkt setzen.

S4 Methoden

Du hast schon mehrere Methoden gelernt, wie du dir Vokabeln besser einprägen kannst:

- Klebezettel mit englischen Wörtern an die entsprechenden Gegenstände in deinem Zimmer kleben

- Wörter als Bildwörter oder mit passenden Bildern aufmalen

- Wörter mit anderen Begriffen, die zu einem Thema gehören, anhand von Überbegriffen in *mind maps* oder Tabellen strukturieren

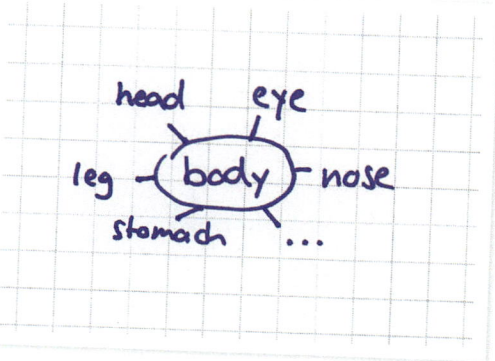

- Wörter pantomimisch darstellen und gegenseitig erraten lassen

- Wörter aussprechen, zusammen mit ihrer Übersetzung und vielleicht einem Beispielsatz aufnehmen und immer wieder anhören

- Wörter mit ähnlichen Wörtern in anderen Sprachen notieren

- Wörter, die miteinander in Beziehung stehen, zusammen notieren, z. B. verwandte Wörter, Gegensatzpaare, zusammengehörige Paare
  Zum Beispiel:

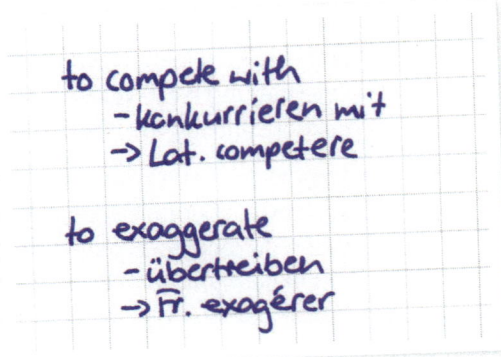

tiny	*tiny ⇔ huge*
friendly	*friendly → friend → friendship*
bike	*go by bike*
have	*have breakfast, have a shower*

Reading

S5 Texte verstehen und bearbeiten

Wenn du einen unbekannten Text nicht verstehst, kann es helfen, dir den Text mehrmals durchzulesen und schrittweise vorzugehen:

Vor dem ersten Lesen
Lies die Überschrift und schau dir die Bilder zum Text an. Sie geben oft schon Hinweise zum Inhalt des Textes.

Während des ersten Lesens
Lies den Text einmal am Stück durch. Dabei musst du nicht jedes Wort verstehen, um herauszufinden, worum es hauptsächlich im Text geht. Am Ende des ersten Lesens solltest du die W-Fragen beantworten können: *Who?* (Wer ist beteiligt?), *What?* (Was geschieht?), *Where?* (Wo?), *When?* (Wann?).

Nach dem ersten Lesen
Lies dir die Arbeitsanweisung und die Aufgaben/Fragen zum Text genau durch.

Während des zweiten Lesens
Suche beim zweiten Lesen im Text gezielt nach den Informationen, die du zur Bearbeitung der Aufgaben/Fragen benötigst. Mache Notizen oder markiere dir diese wichtigen Textstellen, wenn das Buch dir gehört. Achte beim Lösen der Aufgabe darauf, wie die Fragen gestellt sind, und beantworte sie entsprechend, z. B.:

*What **are** they good at?*	→ *They **are** good at …*
*What **have** they **learned**?*	→ *They**'ve learned** …*

Diese Techniken können dir helfen einen Text zu lesen, wenn du nur begrenzt Zeit hast:

Skimming	Scanning
Wenn du danach gefragt wirst, worum es in einem Text geht, sollst du das Wichtigste *(gist)* zusammenfassen. Dazu kannst du den ganzen Text überfliegen und darauf achten, ob bestimmte Wörter *(key words)* oder Personen häufiger vorkommen. Auch die Überschrift und die Bilder können dir helfen einzuschätzen, was wichtig ist und was nicht.	Wenn du nach bestimmten Einzelheiten *(details)* in einem Text gefragt wirst, musst du den Text überfliegen und die Stellen mit der benötigten Information finden. Dazu suchst du gezielt nach bestimmten Stichwörtern *(key words)*. Sie zeigen an, welche Textpassage du genauer lesen solltest, um die Frage zu beantworten.

S6 Wichtige Merkmale von Erzähltexten und Gedichten erkennen

1. Story

Wenn du eine Geschichte genauer liest oder analysierst, solltest du nicht nur über die Handlung (*plot*) selbst nachdenken, sondern auch darüber, wie die Geschichte erzählt wird. Zu den wichtigsten Erzähltechniken (*narrative techniques*) gehören:

atmosphere / mood	Bestimmte Wörter und Beschreibungen schaffen in einer Geschichte eine gewisse Stimmung (*atmosphere* oder *mood*). Stimmung entsteht z.B. dadurch, dass die fünf Sinne (*five senses*) angesprochen werden: Wenn man liest, was die Figuren sehen, hören, riechen, schmecken und fühlen, ist es leichter, sich in sie hineinzuversetzen.
climax	Der Höhepunkt (*climax*) ist der Hauptwendepunkt in einer Geschichte. Die Spannung ist hier am höchsten. Die Hauptfigur befindet sich oft in einer schwierigen Situation und macht Veränderungen durch, sie wird z.B. stärker oder selbstbewusster. (Siehe auch *turning point*.)
flashback	Eine Rückblende (*flashback*) erzählt Ereignisse, die vor einem bestimmten Zeitpunkt in der Geschichte stattgefunden haben, z.B. wird die Erinnerung einer Figur an etwas Vergangenes beschrieben.
narrative perspective	Die Wirkung, die eine Geschichte auf den Leser hat, wird stark von der Erzählperspektive (*narrative perspective*) beeinflusst. Wer ist der Erzähler und wie ist seine Einstellung zu den Figuren der Geschichte? Was erzählt er und wann? Die häufigsten Erzählperspektiven sind: 1. **Ich-Erzähler** *(first-person narrator)* Der Ich-Erzähler erzählt die Geschichte aus seiner Perspektive. Oft (aber nicht immer) ist der Ich-Erzähler die Hauptfigur der Geschichte. Der Leser und der Ich-Erzähler erleben die Geschichte sozusagen „gemeinsam". 2. **Er- / Sie-Erzähler** *(third-person narrator)* Dieser Erzähler erzählt die Geschichte „von außen". Die Perspektive ist nicht die der Hauptfigur.
suspense	Spannung (*suspense*) ist eine wichtige Erzähltechnik, um den Leser in die Geschichte hineinzuziehen. Spannung kann direkt in den ersten Zeilen der Geschichte aufgebaut werden oder aber langsam im Verlauf der Geschichte. Sie wird z.B. durch starke, dramatische Sprache erzeugt oder durch das Zurückhalten von Informationen.
turning point	Ein Wendepunkt (*turning point*) ist der Teil einer Geschichte, in dem eine Figur eine wichtige Entscheidung treffen muss. Diese Entscheidung beeinflusst den weiteren Verlauf der Geschichte. Sie kann für die Hauptfigur und die anderen Figuren gut oder schlecht sein. (Siehe auch *climax*.)

2. Poetry

Ein Gedicht ist wie eine Zeichnung oder ein Gemälde, das mit Wörtern „gemalt" wurde. In einem Gedicht ist jedes einzelne Wort wichtig. Denke daran: Beim Verständnis von Gedichten geht es nicht darum, die „richtige" Bedeutung zu finden – das gleiche Gedicht kann von verschiedenen Menschen ganz unterschiedlich verstanden werden. Wichtig ist aber, dass du deine Deutung am Text belegen kannst. Dazu ist es hilfreich, auch formale Merkmale zu untersuchen und mit dem Inhalt in Verbindung zu bringen. Zu den wichtigsten Merkmalen von Gedichten gehören:

rhyme scheme	Gedichte, die sich reimen, folgen immer einem bestimmten Reimschema (*rhyme scheme*). Typische Reimschemata sind: **AABB** und **ABAB** sowie **ABCB**. Es gibt aber auch Gedichte, die sich nicht reimen, sogenannte *free verse poems*.
rhythm / stress	Ein Gedicht funktioniert nur mit dem richtigen Rhythmus (*rhythm*). Er bestimmt, welche Stelle in jeder Zeile betont wird. Die Betonung (*stress*) liegt dann immer an der gleichen Stelle. Bei Gedichten, die sich nicht reimen (*free verse poems*), ist es wichtig, dass du selbst entscheidest, wo die Betonung liegt oder wo eine Pause gemacht werden sollte.
symbol / simile / metaphor	In Gedichten spielen Symbole eine wichtige Rolle. Ein Symbol (*symbol*) steht stellvertretend für etwas anderes, z. B. für ein Gefühl, eine Idee oder eine Handlung. So ist das Herz ein Symbol für die Liebe. Bei einem Vergleich (*simile*) werden Dinge oder Personen mit etwas anderem verglichen, um auszudrücken, dass sie die gleichen Eigenschaften besitzen. Dabei wird *like* oder *as* verwendet: *My love is like a fire burning in my heart.* Eine Metapher (*metaphor*) ist ein verkürzter Vergleich ohne *like* oder *as*: *My love is a fire burning in my heart.*

S7 Texte gliedern

Um einen Text besser zu verstehen, kann es dir helfen, ihn in mehrere Abschnitte zu gliedern. Orientiere dich dabei am Inhalt und an Absätzen. Überlege, was in den einzelnen Abschnitten jeweils das Wichtigste ist und formuliere kurze passende Überschriften. Dies erleichtert es dir, den Text im Anschluss zusammenzufassen.

S8 Umgang mit neuen Wörtern

Viele Wörter kannst du schon verstehen, obwohl du sie noch nicht gelernt hast.

1. **Ähnlichkeit mit Wörtern, die du schon kennst**
   Oft haben verwandte Wörter den gleichen Stamm, aber andere Vorsilben oder Endungen.
   Wenn du z.B. *appear* oder *invent* schon kennst, wirst du *disappear* oder *invention*
   sicher auch verstehen. Englische Wörter haben oft keine Endungen, aber es gibt sie in
   verschiedenen Wortarten, z.B. *to fight – fight*. Wenn du das Wort *guide* als Nomen kennst,
   kannst du dir bestimmt denken, was das Verb *to guide* oder die Zusammensetzung *travel
   guide* bedeutet.

2. **Ähnlichkeit mit Wörtern, die du aus einer anderen Sprache kennst**
   Viele englische Wörter gibt es genauso oder ähnlich auch im Deutschen, z.B. *computer,
   hobby* oder *pony*. Manchmal hilft dir auch ein Wort, das du aus einer anderen Sprache
   kennst (Französisch, Latein, …) ein englisches Wort zu verstehen, z.B. weil es ähnlich
   geschrieben wird oder ähnlich klingt.

3. **Verstehen der Wörter im Zusammenhang**
   Manchmal kannst du dir anhand eines Bildes oder einer Überschrift denken, was ein
   Wort in einem Text bedeutet. Und wenn du alle Wörter in einem Satz verstehst außer
   einem, kann dieses oft nur eine bestimmte Bedeutung haben. Was bedeutet z.B. *return*
   in diesem Satz?
   *My dog ran away and I was really happy when he **returned** after three days.*

Und wenn du doch im Wörterbuch nachschlagen musst, helfen dir die Tipps im Abschnitt → S18.

S9 Textbearbeitung mit Markierungen und Notizen

Im geliehenen Buch darfst du das zwar nicht, aber auf Kopien oder in Arbeitsheften solltest du dir angewöhnen, wichtige Stellen in Texten zu markieren und Randnotizen zu machen (z.B. Fragen oder Anmerkungen). Verwende am besten verschiedene Farben: Markiere z.B. wichtige inhaltliche Punkte grün und Informationen zu den Personen blau. Wörter, die du nachschlagen musst, solltest du auch hervorheben. Unterstreiche sie beispielsweise und notiere die richtige Übersetzung am Rand. So fällt dir das erneute Lesen leichter.

> *characters*
>
> "Ha! I hit you!" said Dave. He had headphones on
> his head. This made him speak in a loud voice.
> On the TV, a wizard fell off a skateboard.
> "Ohhhhhh!" cried Luke. He had headphones on
> his head too.
> "I win, you lose! I win, you lose!" Dave shouted.
> "I'm always the winner!"
> "A winner with a very big head! You say that
> whenever you win, but you don't always win," said
> Luke. He took off his headphones, and Dave did
> the same. "Anyway, you play it more than I do so
> you don't need to show off. Do you want to play   *angeben*
> again?"

S10 Karten lesen

 Auch Stadtpläne und Landkarten – egal ob gedruckt oder digital – musst du lesen und verstehen können. Sie sind eine besondere Textsorte mit wenig Text, aber vielen Symbolen, Farben und Linien.

Mithilfe von Karten kannst du herausfinden, wo sich ein Land, eine Stadt, eine Straße, ein Fluss, ein Gebirge oder eine Sehenswürdigkeit befindet oder wo du lang musst, um von A nach B zu gelangen.

Die wichtigsten Symbole sind:

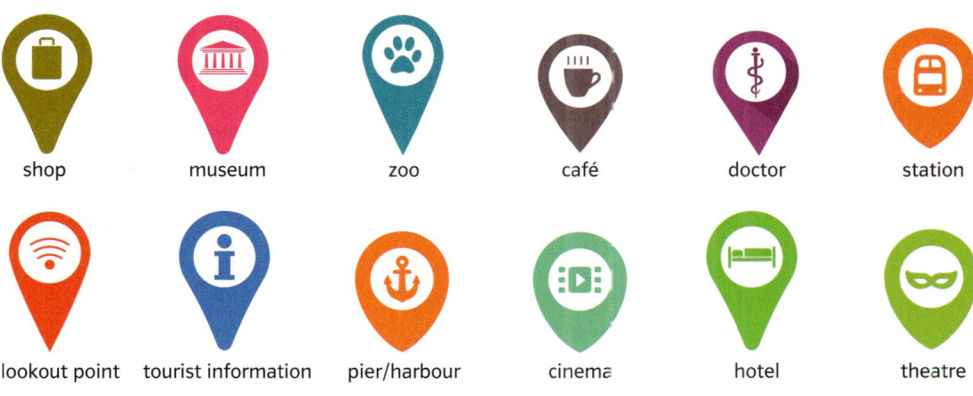

| shop | museum | zoo | café | doctor | station |

| lookout point | tourist information | pier/harbour | cinema | hotel | theatre |

Die wichtigsten Farben und Linien sind:

| river/lake | park/forest | mountains | road | railway | border |

Digitale Karten schlagen dir auch Routen vor, also den besten Weg von einem Ort zum anderen. Manche zeigen außerdem die Entfernung zwischen den beiden Orten an und berechnen, wie lange du zu Fuß, mit dem Bus oder mit der Bahn zum Ziel benötigst. Manchmal wird dir sogar die nächste Bus- oder Bahnverbindung angezeigt.

❗ Wenn du auf der Straße unterwegs bist, schaue nicht nur in die Karte oder auf das Smartphone. Achte unbedingt auf deine echte Umgebung, also andere Fußgänger, Radfahrer, Ampeln, Straßenbahnen und den Straßenverkehr.

Writing

S11 Texte planen, schreiben und überprüfen

Bevor du mit dem Schreiben deines Textes beginnst, solltest du dir die Arbeitsanweisung genau durchlesen. Darin steht meistens, an wen du schreiben sollst (Adressat), das Thema und die Textsorte.

Überlege dir dann, was du schreiben willst, und mache dir Notizen. Bringe deine Notizen anschließend in eine logische Reihenfolge. Denke beim Schreiben daran, dass es nicht nur auf den Inhalt und deine Ideen, sondern auch auf die Rechtschreibung und die Grammatik ankommt.

Lies deinen Text zum Schluss noch einmal durch und überprüfe ihn auf Fehler. Dabei kann dir ein Wörterbuch (→ S18), die Grammatik im Anhang oder eine Nachschlagegrammatik helfen. Du kannst auch einen Mitschüler darum bitten, ihn zu überprüfen und höflich Feedback zu geben.

MK Wenn du deinen Text am Computer oder auf dem Tablet geschrieben hast, kann dir die Rechtschreib- und Grammatikprüfung im Textverarbeitungsprogramm helfen. Stelle dazu die Sprache auf Englisch um.

Checkliste

Rechtschreibung:
- Wörter richtig geschrieben?
- Am Satzanfang groß?
- Bei Unsicherheiten im Wörterbuch nachgeschaut?

Grammatik:
- Formen richtig gebildet?
- Wortstellung beachtet?
- Bei Unsicherheiten in der Grammatik nachgeschaut?

Zeichensetzung:
Apostrophe, Kommata, Satzpunkte, Fragezeichen, Anführungszeichen gesetzt?

Inhalt:
- Alle wesentlichen Punkte enthalten?
- Text logisch aufgebaut?

Textsorten und ihre Haupteigenschaften im Überblick:

blog (Blog)	Ein Blog ist eine Art Online-Tagebuch, das in chronologischer Reihenfolge fortgeschrieben werden kann. Darin teilt eine Person ihre Gedanken, Erlebnisse, Fotos und Informationen mit anderen auf einer spezifischen Webseite. Leser können die Einträge kommentieren. Es gibt unterschiedliche Arten von Blogs, z. B. Reiseblogs, Musikblogs, Nachrichtenblogs.
brochure (Broschüre)	Eine Broschüre ist ein gefaltetes Blatt oder ein dünnes, kleines Heft. Um Neugier zu wecken, benutzt du auf der Titelseite ein großes Bild und einen Titel. Für den Innenteil schreibst du kurze, informative Texte. Auf der letzten Seite gibst du Kontaktdaten an, z. B. die Internetseite und E-Mail-Adresse. Vergiss nicht, die Quelle (→ S12) deiner Bilder anzugeben. Diese schreibst du entweder direkt unter das Bild oder auf die letzte Seite.

dialogue (Dialog)	In Dialogen benutzt du echte mündliche Sprache wie z.B. Kurzformen (*she's* statt *she is*; *they've got* statt *they have got*) und Füllwörter wie *er …*, *well …*. Denke daran, die Sprecher vom Text abzusetzen (vgl. Dialog auf S. 10), damit der Leser erkennt, wer was sagt.
diary entry (Tagebuch- eintrag)	Ein Tagebucheintrag beginnt mit dem Datum und der Anrede *Dear Diary, …* . Er erzählt und kommentiert Ereignisse aus einer ganz persönlichen Sicht und ist normalerweise nicht für andere Leser bestimmt. Verwende Adjektive und Adverbien, um Ereignisse oder Gefühle zu beschreiben und *linking words*, um deine Sätze logisch miteinander zu verknüpfen.
email (E-Mail)	E-Mails sind meist längere Nachrichten mit vielen Informationen. Sie bestehen häufig aus ganzen Sätzen. Beim Schreiben der E-Mail musst du darauf achten, an wen du schreibst. In formellen E-Mails (z.B. an erwachsene und fremde Personen) verwendest du *Dear Mr/Mrs/Miss/Ms …*, oder *Dear Sir or Madam*, als Begrüßung. Du benutzt Langformen und unterteilst die E-Mail in Abschnitte. Typische Wendungen der Verabschiedung sind *Yours sincerely, … und Best wishes, …* . In informellen E-Mails (z.B. an Freunde oder Familie) benutzt als Begrüßung *Hi/Hello …*. Du verwendest Kurzformen und fügst auch kleine Bilder ein, um Informationen oder Gefühle auszudrücken. Verabschieden kannst du dich mit *Bye./Love, …/See you, …/XOXO*. Denke beim Schreiben von E-Mails immer daran, dass nach der Begrü- ßung ein Komma steht, und der erste Satz mit einem Großbuchstaben anfängt sowie an den Betreff, der den Inhalt der E-Mail (ähnlich wie eine Überschrift) kurz zusammenfasst.
FAQs (Häufig gestellte Fragen)	FAQs (*frequently asked questions*) sind eine Liste häufig gestellter Fragen zu einem Thema. Im Anschluss an die Frage erfährt man die dazugehörige Antwort. Du findest solche Listen z.B. auf der Internetseite von Sehenswürdigkeiten.
film script (Filmskript)	`EXT. CAFÉ – DAY`
	Diese Angaben brauchen die Filmcrew und Darsteller, um zu wissen wo und wann die Szene spielt. INT. steht für *interior* (innen) und EXT. steht für *exterior* (draußen).
	`BOY 1 (20) and PENNY (20) outside getting coffee. Boy at front of queue; Penny arrives at back of queue, gives Boy 1 big smile.`
	Wenn ein Charakter zum ersten Mal im Film auftritt, wird dieser großgeschrieben, die Altersangabe steht in Klammern. Außerdem werden Mimik, Gestik und Requisiten (wie z.B. Kaffeebecher) definiert. Diese Angaben stehen linksbündig.

	`BOY 1`
	`Coffee?`
	
	`PENNY`
	`I'm Penny.`

	Zentriert steht, welcher Darsteller welchen Text spricht. Verwende für den Text gesprochene Sprache wie z.B. *short forms* und *question tags*.

flyer (Flyer)	Ein Flyer sollte alle wichtigen Informationen *(Who?, What?, Where?, When?, Why?)* enthalten, gut lesbar und passend zum Inhalt gestaltet sein (→ S12). Formuliere außerdem einen ansprechenden Slogan, d.h. einen kurzen einprägsamen Spruch.
instructions, recipe (Anleitung, Rezept)	Eine Anleitung kann z.B. eine Spielanleitung oder ein Rezept sein. Darin beschreibst du, was nach und nach in kleineren Schritten passiert. Meist werden dabei der Imperativ und Modalverben verwendet, z.B. **Buy** *a small present. You* **must** *wrap it ten times.* oder *First,* **break** *the cake into small pieces. Then* **slice** *the fruit.*
invitation (Einladung)	Wenn du jemanden zu einem Geburtstag oder einer Veranstaltung einladen möchtest, kannst du per Karte, E-Mail oder Textnachricht eine Einladung versenden. Beginne mit der Anrede *(Dear …,)*. Sage, was der Anlass der Einladung ist, wann und wo die Party stattfindet und frage, ob die Person kommen kann. Du kannst die Person auch bitten, etwas mitzubringen. Verabschiede dich dann höflich.

itinerary (Reiseplan, Reiseroute)	Einem Reiseplan kann man entnehmen, wie die Reise verlaufen wird, d.h. wann man in welchem Ort sein wird. In der Einleitung *(introduction)* weckst du das Interesse des Lesers. Du gibst kurze Informationen über das Reiseziel. Anschließend führst du die Planung für jeden einzelnen Tag der Reise an. Du solltest dabei darauf achten, dass man gut von einem Stopp zum nächsten kommt und die Aktivitäten zeitlich schaffbar sind. Zum Beispiel:
	Discover London, the capital of the United Kingdom!
	With only four days to spend in one of the world's most spectacular cities, is it any surprise you aren't sure about where, how or what to start with? But trust us: We've done our homework and know the perfect mix for an unforgettable class trip!
	Day 1: After arrival and hotel check-in, discover London at your own pace and get on a sightseeing bus. On the tour you'll get an overall view of the city and see some of its amazing attractions on your first day! Later, enjoy dinner at the tasty Tandoori restaurant we've chosen for you in the popular Covent Garden area.
	  – **1:00 p.m.:** ticket pick-up for sightseeing bus tour
	  – **5:15 p.m.:** meet in lobby
	  – **6:00 p.m.:** Taj Mahal Tandoori (Tube: Holborn)

letter (Brief)	In formellen Briefen schreibst du oben rechtsbündig den Namen und die Adresse des Absenders. Darunter schreibst du linksbündig die Anschrift des Empfängers und mit etwas Abstand das Datum, an dem der Brief erstellt wird. Den eigentlichen Inhalt beginnst du mit der Anrede *Dear Mr / Mrs / Miss / Ms …,* oder wenn du nicht weißt, an wen du schreibst mit *Dear Sir or Madam, …* . Denke beim Schreiben von Briefen immer daran, dass nach der Begrüßung ein Komma steht, und der erste Satz mit einem Großbuchstaben anfängt. Nach der Begrüßung, nennst du den Anlass, also warum du schreibst, und was du erfahren möchtest. Anschließend verabschiedest du dich mit *Yours sincerely, …* oder *Best wishes, …* und unterschreibst den Brief. Denke bei Briefen ins Ausland daran, dass die Anschrift anders aufgebaut sein kann als in Deutschland (→ *postcard*).

poster **(Poster)**	Für ein Poster brauchst du ein großes Blatt Papier, verschiedenfarbige Stifte, einen Klebestift, Bilder und eine Schere. Wähle eine Überschrift, die gut zum Thema des Posters passt. Diese schreibst du am besten oben mittig auf dein Blatt. Formuliere kurze Texte oder Stichpunktlisten mit eigener Überschrift. Am besten schreibst du deine Texte erst auf ein anderes Blatt und überträgst sie später gut leserlich auf dein Poster. Du kannst deine Texte auch auf dem Computer oder Tablet schreiben (→ S12). Wähle große Bilder aus, die man auch aus etwas Entfernung gut sehen kann und die zum Inhalt deiner Texte passen. Schneide sie aus und ordne sie zusammen mit deinen Texten auf dem Poster an, ehe du sie aufklebst. Bei den Bildern kannst du kurze Bildunterschriften ergänzen.
postcard **(Postkarte)**	Postkarten schreibst du meist an Familienmitglieder oder Freunde, wenn du irgendwo unterwegs bist. Darin berichtest du kurz, was du schon erlebt hast und was du noch machen möchtest. Oft schreibt man auch wie die Unterkunft und das Wetter ist. Achte auf die richtige Anrede, z. B. *Dear …,* und Grußformel am Ende, z. B. *Love,* / *See you soon.* Denke bei Postkarten ins Ausland daran, dass die Anschrift anders aufgebaut sein kann als in Deutschland. In Großbritannien steht die Hausnummer beispielsweise vor dem Straßennamen und die Postleitzahl unter dem Ort.
prompt cards **(Karteikarten)**	Wenn du dich auf eine Präsentation vorbereitest, dann notiere auf Karteikarten nur Stichwörter, die dich an die einzelnen Punkte deines Vortrags erinnern. Schreibe z. B. wichtige Namen, Ereignisse, Orte und Daten unter die Überschriften *What?, Who?, When?, Where?, Why?*
report **(Bericht)**	Wenn du z. B. einen Reisebericht schreibst, berichtest du sachlich, informativ und objektiv, was der Reihe nach passiert ist. In der Einleitung nennst du das Ereignis (*What?*), wer beteiligt war (*Who?*), wann es stattfand (*When?*), wohin die Reise ging (*Where?*), wie du dorthin gekommen bist (*How?*) und den Anlass der Reise (*Why?*). Im Hauptteil beschreibst du, was du auf der Reise gesehen oder gemacht hast sowie ein besonderes Erlebnis. Schließe deinen Bericht, indem du sagst, wie die Reise oder das Erlebnis endete. Verwende für deinen Bericht Zeitformen der Vergangenheit (*simple past, past progressive*) und strukturiere ihn mit Wörtern wie *then, after that, in the end, the next day*. Adjektive können dir helfen, den Bericht interessant und anschaulich zu gestalten, z. B. *old, grey building, busy streets, a friendly man*. Falls du wörtliche Rede verwendest, benutze im Englischen beide Anführungszeichen oben und setze das Satzzeichen vor dem hinteren Anführungszeichen, z. B. *"Don't talk," said Will.*
story **(Geschichte)**	In einer Geschichte erzählst du nacheinander, was passiert. Dabei helfen dir Bindewörter wie z. B. *and, because, but, before, first, then, later, after that*. Versuche deine Geschichte interessant und abwechslungsreich zu gestalten. Benutze dazu Adjektive wie z. B. *awful, big, boring, funny*, um Personen und Gegenstände zu beschreiben. Gedanken von Personen setzt du in einfache Anführungszeichen, z. B. *'I'm very unlucky,' Jay thinks.*

summary (Zusammen-fassung)	Wenn du eine Zusammenfassung von einem Text schreiben sollst, lies zuerst den gesamten Text. Lies ihn anschließend noch einmal Abschnitt für Abschnitt durch und notiere dir dabei die wichtigsten Informationen in Stichwörtern. Schreibe dann in ganzen Sätzen was der Reihe nach passiert ist. Verbinde sie logisch mit Wörtern wie *and, but, because, so, then, when*. Verwende für deine Zusammenfassung das Präsens *(simple present)*.
text message (Text-nachricht)	Textnachrichten sind sehr kurze Texte mit oft unvollständigen Sätzen. Der Absender verwendet meist kleine Bilder, um Informationen oder seine Gefühle auszudrücken, und Abkürzungen wie z. B. *u = you; ur = your; 2morrow = tomorrow, cu = see you, XOXO = Hugs and kisses*.

S12 Texte am PC oder auf dem Tablet gestalten

MK

Mit der passenden Schriftgröße, Schriftart und Schriftfarbe kannst du deinen Text passend zur Textsorte gestalten. Außerdem kannst du deinen Text unterschiedlich auf der Seite verteilen und Bilder einfügen.

1. **Schriftgröße**
   Die Schriftgröße sollte der Textsorte angemessen sein. Bei Texten wie z. B. einem Dialog oder Brief, einer Geschichte, E-Mail oder Broschüre verwendest du 10 pt bis 12 pt. Bei Postern und Präsentationen hingehen musst du eine größere Schrift (mindestens 18 pt) wählen, damit die Informationen darin auch aus etwas Entfernung gelesen werden können. Achte darauf, dass deine Texte bzw. Stichpunkte auf Postern und Folien möglichst kurz und prägnant sind.

2. **Schriftart**
   Verwende für deinen Text eine Schriftart, die leicht zu lesen ist, z. B. Arial, Helvetica oder Verdana, und bleibe bei dieser Schriftart! Bei kreativen Texten wie Einladungen kannst du auch eine Schriftart benutzen, die deiner Handschrift ähnelt.

3. **Schriftfarbe**
   Als Schriftfarbe verwendest du in E-Mails, Briefen, Dialogen und Geschichten am besten schwarz. Bei Postern und Flyern kannst du wichtige Wörter im Text ggf. in einer anderen gut sichtbaren Farbe hervorheben – verwende aber niemals Gelb oder Hellblau auf weißem Papier, weil die Schrift sonst schlecht lesbar ist.

4. **Ausrichtung**
   Deinen Text kannst du je nach Textsorte verschieden ausrichten. Normalerweise verwendet man linksbündig (1) oder Blocksatz (4). Gedichte kannst du aber auch zentrieren (2).

5. **Textgliederung**

Für die Gliederung eines Textes hast du – je nach Textsorte – verschiedene Möglichkeiten:

a) Überschrift:

Für die Überschrift wählst du am besten einen größeren Schriftgrad aus als für deinen Text. Du kannst sie **fett** machen, <u>unterstreichen</u> oder eine **Schriftfarbe** wählen.

b) Absätze:

Mit der Eingabetaste (auch Return-Taste genannt) kannst du einen neuen Absatz beginnen.
Absätze fügst du beispielsweise ein:

- nach der Überschrift deines Textes,
- wenn ein neuer Sinnabschnitt in deinem Text beginnt,
- nach der Begrüßung oder Verabschiedung in einer E-Mail oder in einem Brief:
  Hi Pia, ↵
  Thanks for … ↵
  See you, ↵
  Olivia

c) Aufzählungszeichen:

Du kannst deine Notizen oder deine Präsentation gliedern, indem du Aufzählungszeichen verwendest. Klicke dazu auf das entsprechende Symbol in deinem Textverarbeitungsprogramm. Dort werden dir verschiedene Möglichkeiten angezeigt.

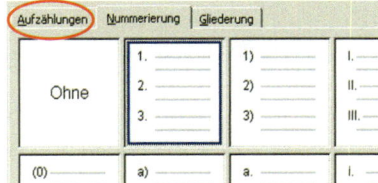

6. **Bilder**

Für Flyer oder Präsentationen benötigst du meist Bilder. Wenn du selbst Fotos machst, überlege, was genau darauf zu sehen sein soll. Überlege auch, ob du ein Foto im Hoch- oder Querformat brauchst. Um ein gutes, nicht verwackeltes Foto zu erhalten, nimm deine Oberarme eng an deinen Körper oder lehne dich gegen eine Wand. Fotografiere nicht gegen das Licht. Auf Smartphones, Kameras und PCs oder Tablets gibt es normalerweise die Möglichkeit, Fotos zu bearbeiten. Das heißt, du kannst sie zurecht-schneiden oder die Helligkeit verändern.

❗ Wenn Personen mit auf das Foto sollen, musst du sie vorher fragen, ob es okay ist, sie zu fotografieren. Sag ihnen auch, wofür du das Bild verwenden möchtest. Nur wenn sie einverstanden sind, darfst du das Foto auch wirklich verwenden. Wenn du ein Bild verwenden möchtest und ganz sicher gehen willst, dass nichts passiert, dann lass dir am besten eine schriftliche Einverständniserklärung geben.

❗ Du hast im Internet ein gutes Bild gefunden und willst es benutzen? Das geht leider nicht immer, weil viele Bilder urheberrechtlich geschützt sind. Für die Verwendung im Unterricht kannst du Bilder mancher Fotoagenturen benutzen, wenn du den Urheber, die Webadresse der Seite, auf der das Foto steht (nicht die Adresse des Fotos selbst) und das Zugriffsdatum nennst, z. B.: Jason Franck, http://www…, 20 April 2020.

Außerhalb des Unterrichts darfst du die Bilder aber niemals ohne das Einverständnis des Urhebers veröffentlichen, z. B. in der Schülerzeitung, in Textnachrichten oder im Internet.

Wenn du ein Bild gespeichert hast, aber nicht mehr weißt, wo du es gefunden hattest, dann kannst du es in eine Suchmaschine hochladen und eine Bildsuche starten. Diese Funktion gibt es aber nicht bei allen Anbietern.

Listening

S13 Hörtexte verstehen

Bei Hörverstehensaufgaben hörst du meist ein oder mehrere Gespräche oder Durchsagen. Gehe beim Hören am besten so vor:

Vor dem ersten Hören
Schau dir die Überschrift und die Bilder zum Hörverstehenstext an. Sie geben oft Hinweise zum Inhalt: Wer spricht? Worüber? Wo? Lies dir dann die Arbeitsanweisung und alle Aufgaben/Fragen genau durch. Beginne erst dann mit dem Abspielen des Audios.

Während des ersten Hörens
Beantworte die Aufgaben/Fragen, deren Lösung du schon weißt.

Während des zweiten Hörens
Achte jetzt gezielt auf die Inhalte, die dir noch unklar sind, und beantworte die restlichen Aufgaben/Fragen.

Viewing

S14 Filme verstehen

Wenn du einen Film anschaust, geht es nicht nur darum, dass du das Gesagte verstehst, sondern auch die Handlung. Achte auf die folgenden Punkte:

1. Welche Personen spielen mit?
2. Was passiert in welcher Reihenfolge?
3. Wo und wann spielt die Szene/der Film?

Wie verhalten sich die Personen?
-- ➤ Achte vor allem auf Sprache, Mimik und Gestik.

Wie werden Handlungsort und -zeit *(setting)* dargestellt?
-- ➤ Achte auf Landschaften, Gebäude und Innenräume, Kleidung, Frisuren und Gegenstände.

Wie wird eine bestimmte Atmosphäre *(atmosphere)* geschaffen?
-- ➤ Achte auf Licht, Farben, Musik, Geräusche.

Wie unterstützt die Musik *(music)* den Inhalt des Films?
-- ➤ Beachte, wann welche Musik ertönt und wann sie wechselt.

Wie helfen bestimmte Kameraeinstellungen *(shot)* den Inhalt deutlicher darzustellen?
-- ➤ Achte z. B. auf Nahaufnahmen *(close-ups)*.

Wie wird Spannung *(suspense)* erzeugt?
-- ➤ Achte auf Vorandeutungen, Musik, Licht, Geräusche und natürlich die Gestik und Mimik der Schauspieler.

 Bei vielen Filmen kann man den deutschen oder englischen Untertitel einschalten. Probiere es einmal aus! Am Anfang braucht es etwas Gewöhnung, da dein Gehirn mit dem Ton, Bild und den Untertiteln viele Informationen gleichzeitig bekommt.

Speaking

S15 Wörter richtig aussprechen

Wichtig ist beim Sprechen die richtige Aussprache der Wörter. Dabei kann dir die Lautschrift in der Vokabelliste (ab Seite 192) helfen. Sage dir die Wörter immer wieder laut vor. Du kannst dich auch aufnehmen, um deine Aussprache anschließend zu überprüfen.

Auch die Audios zu deinem Buch, Online-Wörterbücher und digitale Vokabellern-karten, bei denen du jedes Wort anklicken und anhören kannst, können dir bei der Aussprache helfen.

Achte beim Üben besonders auf schwierig auszusprechende Laute, die anders sind als im Deutschen, z.B. das stimmhafte oder stimmlose *th*, das *w* im Kontrast zu *v* oder ein stimmhaftes *d* oder *g* am Wortende.

Wenn du ganze Texte hörst, bekommst du ein Gefühl dafür, wie die Wörter im Textzusammenhang ausgesprochen werden. Die Aussprache unterscheidet sich manchmal stark von der Aussprache der Einzelwörter. Aufeinander treffende Laute werden z.B. häufig miteinander verbunden.

They **th**ink of **th**e **th**ree **th**ousand **th**ankful **th**ieves.

Why **w**ork **w**ith **v**ocabulary **w**hen you can **v**isit a **w**onderful **v**illage **w**orld?

Dad says: Coul**d** I have my chil**d**'s ba**g** back? It has a bi**g** do**g** on it.

This is th**e end of t**he story. They know over**_**a hundred different stories.

S16 Gespräche führen und Vorträge halten

Im Englischunterricht wirst du verschiedenen Arten des Sprechens begegnen, z.B. Rollenspielen, Umfragen, Interviews, Telefonaten und Vorträgen. Um welche Art es geht, steht in der Arbeitsanweisung. Allgemein gilt: Sprich langsam und deutlich, sodass man dich gut verstehen kann.

interview **(Interview)**	In einem Interview befragt ein Journalist eine andere Person, um Informationen oder eine Meinung in Erfahrung zu bringen. Dabei stellt er offene Frage (*Who? What? Where? When? Why? How?*), um möglichst viel herauszufinden und das Gespräch am Laufen zu halten. Achtet bei der Durchführung von Interviews auf Fragen und Antworten in der richtigen Zeitform und das richtige Hilfsverb. Denkt auch daran, höflich zu sein und nachzufragen, wenn ihr etwas nicht verstanden habt, z.B. mit *Excuse me, can you repeat that, please? / I'm sorry, could you repeat that?*
news report **(Nachrichten-** **beitrag)**	Bei einem Nachrichtenbeitrag gibt es zumeist drei beteiligte Personen, den Fernseh- oder Radiomoderator, den Reporter und die Augenzeugen vor Ort. Der Moderator führt kurz und sachlich in das Thema ein, indem er zusammenfasst, was, wo und wann passiert ist und wer beteiligt war. Der Reporter vor Ort berichtet sachlich von dem neusten Stand der Informationen und interviewt Augenzeugen. Diese berichten meist emotional in Umgangssprache über das Gesehene / Erlebte.
phone call **(Telefonat)**	Im Gegensatz zur Sprachnachricht gibt es beim Telefonat zwei Personen, die miteinander sprechen. Zu Beginn des Gesprächs begrüßen sie sich und stellen sich kurz vor, z.B. *Hello. This is … .* Danach sagt der Anrufer, warum er anruft und man bespricht das Thema / die Themen gemeinsam. Am Ende verabschieden sie sich, z.B. mit *Talk to you later. Bye.*
podcast **(Podcast)**	Ein Podcast ist eine Audiodatei, die man im Internet herunterladen und am Computer oder auf dem Smartphone anhören kann. Um selbst einen Podcast zu produzieren, brauchst du einen Computer, einen Laptop oder ein Smartphone mit Aufnahmefunktion. Überlege dir ein interessantes Thema und deine Zielgruppe. Sammle dann Informationen und bringe sie in eine logische Reihenfolge. Achte darauf, dass die Sätze und der Beitrag insgesamt nicht zu lang (max. drei Minuten) wird, damit Zuhörer leichter folgen und sich an die Informationen besser erinnern können. Dein Podcast kann monologisch sein oder du kannst Aussagen eines Experten einfügen. Wenn du mit deinem Ergebnis nicht zufrieden bist, kannst du den Podcast noch einmal aufnehmen oder aber mit entsprechenden Werkzeugen bearbeiten.
presentation **(Vortrag)**	Bereite deinen Vortrag gut vor. Recherchiere Informationen (→ S19) und überlege, welche davon wichtig sind. Mache dir dann Notizen auf Karteikarten (→ S11). Erstelle oder besorge dir auch Material, dass du zeigen möchtest, z.B. Flyer, Bilder (→ S12), und überlege gut, wann du dieses Material in deinem Vortrag einsetzen möchtest. Denke während deines Vortrags daran, frei, ruhig, laut und verständlich zu sprechen und mit deinen Zuhörern Blickkontakt zu halten. Übe deinen Vortrag am besten ehe du ihn vor der Klasse hältst und stoppe die Zeit, die du brauchst. Diese Wendungen können dir während deines Vortrags helfen: *Hello and welcome to …, My name is …, and today I'd like to talk to you about …, First, … / Secondly, … / Thirdly, …, After that / Next …, Let's take a look at …, It's really interesting / fantastic because …*

role play **(Rollenspiel)**	Versetze dich in deine Rolle und versuche nachzufühlen, was die Person in der jeweiligen Situation denkt und fühlt. Du kannst dir dazu auch Notizen machen. Verwende typische Merkmale der gesprochenen Sprache (Bestätigungsfragen, Kurzformen, *er ...*, *well ...*). Klinge wütend, traurig, erstaunt etc., wenn deine Rolle es verlangt. Setze auch Mimik und Gestik ein.
slide show **(Diashow)**	Eine Diashow kannst du mit Hilfe einer Software- oder Online-Anwendung erstellen. Wähle zunächst Bildmaterial aus und füge es in deine Anwendung ein. Gib dann jedem Bild eine Bildunterschrift, d.h. nenne, was darauf zu sehen ist. Während der Präsentation kannst du entweder mit Hilfe von *prompt cards* erklären, was auf den Bildern zu sehen ist, oder du kannst vorab deine Erläuterungen aufnehmen und in die Anwendung als Tondatei einbinden. Achte darauf, dass du deutlich und weder zu schnell, noch zu langsam sprichst. Nützliche Wendungen zur Bildbeschreibung sind: *I'd like to show you this photo of ...*; *I found it on/in ...*; *In the foreground/background/middle you can see ...*, *On the right/left there is/are ...* Gehe bei der Bildbeschreibung immer in einer bestimmten Reihenfolge vor, z.B. von links nach rechts oder von oben nach unten.
survey/poll **(Umfragen)**	Sei höflich, wenn du jemanden befragst. Scheue dich nicht davor nachzufragen, wenn du etwas nicht verstanden hast: *Sorry, but can you say that again?/Excuse me, but what does that mean?* Achte bei der Fragestellung auf die richtige Wortstellung und das richtige Hilfsverb. Gehe sicher, dass die Antwort die Frage auch wirklich beantwortet. Im Gegensatz zu Interviews werden in Umfragen meist Entscheidungsfragen verwendet, um eine kurze Antwort zu erhalten.
voice message **(Sprach-nachricht)**	Wenn du jemandem eine Sprachnachricht schicken möchtest, denke daran, sie kurz und knapp zu formulieren. Sie sollte maximal eine Minute lang sein. Höre sie noch einmal an, bevor du sie abschickst: Ist sie gut zu verstehen oder sind die Hintergrundgeräusche zu laut? Denke auch daran, dass beim Abspielen der Nachricht andere mithören könnten – willst du den Inhalt wirklich verschicken? Wenn du Quatsch erzählt hast, nimm die Nachricht lieber noch einmal neu auf.

MK Tonaufnahmen können dich beim Lernen unterstützen. Indem du Rollenspiele oder deinen Vortrag aufnimmst und die Tondatei anschließend anhörst, kannst du deine Aussprache und Sprachmelodie kontrollieren. Solltest du mit dem Ergebnis nicht zufrieden sein, kannst du es einfach noch einmal probieren!

1. Achte bei der Aufnahme auf Folgendes:
   - Sprich deutlich und nicht zu schnell.
   - Stehe oder sitze während der Aufnahme ruhig.
   - Halte deinen Mund nah an das Aufnahmegerät.
     Dein Mund sollte jedoch das Gerät nicht berühren.
   - Achte auf die passende Sprachmelodie:
     Handelt es sich um einen Aussagesatz oder eine Frage?
     Bist du glücklich oder wütend?

2. Für eine gute Aufnahme brauchst du eine geräuschfreie Umgebung:
   - Mache deine Aufnahme in einem geschlossenen Raum.
     Schließe die Zimmertür und alle Fenster.
   - Bitte Personen, die sich im Raum oder außerhalb des Raums aufhalten,
     sich leise zu verhalten.
   - Schalte andere Geräte wie Radio oder Fernseher aus und dein
     Smartphone auf stumm.

🛑 Nimm niemals jemanden ohne sein Einverständnis oder gar heimlich auf!

Mediation

S17 Mediationsaufgaben bearbeiten

Bei *Mediation*-Aufgaben überträgst
du wichtige Informationen aus einem
gesprochenen oder geschriebenen Text in
eine andere Sprache, z.B. vom Englischen
ins Deutsche oder umgekehrt. Das machst
du, wenn jemand den Ausgangstext nicht
versteht.

1. **Konzentriere dich auf wesentliche Inhalte**
   Achte auf die in der Arbeitsanweisung
   beschriebene Situation: Was möchte der
   Adressat wissen oder erfahren? Welche
   Informationen aus dem Ausgangstext
   sind für ihn wichtig und welche kannst du
   weglassen?

2. **Lange Sätze teilen**
   Du kannst einen längeren Satz einfacher in die andere Sprache übertragen, wenn du
   ihn in mehrere kurze Sätze unterteilst, z.B. kannst du den Satz „Pia geht montags in
   die Tanzschule und macht anschließend ihre Hausaufgaben." mit zwei kurzen Sätzen
   wiedergeben: *"On Mondays Pia goes to Dance Club. After that she does her homework."*

3. **Wörter umschreiben**

   Wenn du ein Wort nicht weißt oder es dir nicht einfällt, kannst du versuchen, es zu umschreiben, z. B. indem du „Wie wär's mit einem Fußballspiel?" mit *"Let's play football."* wiedergibst.

4. **Perspektive wechseln**

   Denke daran, dass du manchmal die Perspektive ändern musst, z. B.:
   Pia: Montags gehe **ich** in den Tanzverein.
   Du (zu Emma): *On Mondays **she** goes to Dance Club.*

   Es kann auch vorkommen, dass du die Satzform ändern musst, also z. B. aus einem Satz eine Frage wird:
   Emma: Frage ihn, wie alt er ist.
   Du (zu Luke): *How old are you?*

5. **Unterschiede zwischen Englisch und Deutsch**

   Beachte die Unterschiede zwischen Englisch und Deutsch, z. B. in der Wortstellung, bei Präpositionen und Zeitformen.

   Luke geht **oft** mit Sherlock **in** den Park.
   ⟶ *Luke **often** goes **to** the park with Sherlock.*
     (*simple present*, weil er dies regelmäßig tut)
   Er **geht gerade** mit Sherlock in den Park.
   ⟶ *He **is going** to the park with Sherlock now.*
     (*present progressive*, weil er es jetzt gerade tut).

Study skills

S18 Mit dem Wörterbuch arbeiten

Wenn du die Bedeutung eines Wortes nachschlagen willst, dann benutzt du am besten ein zweisprachiges Wörterbuch (Englisch-Deutsch bzw. Deutsch-Englisch) beim Erstellen von eigenen Texten oder *Mediation*-Aufgaben.

Die Leitwörter (*running heads*) oben auf der Seite helfen dir, schnell zu finden, was du suchst. Links steht das erste Stichwort, rechts das letzte Stichwort auf der Seite.

cousin	152	153	driver

Hier findest du das Stichwort *(headword)*. Die Stichwörter sind alphabetisch geordnet.

Diese Ziffern zeigen an, dass ein Stichwort unterschiedliche Bedeutungen hat.

Einem Stichwort sind häufig Redewendungen und typische *phrases* zugeordnet.

Unregelmäßige Verb-, Plural- und Steigerungsformen stehen oft in Klammern.

> **show** [ʃəʊ, AM ʃoʊ] **I.** *n* ① *(showing)* Demonstration *f geh;* ~ **of solidarity** Solidaritätsbekundung *f gen* ② *no pl (display, effect)* Schau *f;* **just for** ~ nur der Schau wegen ③ *(exhibition, event)* Schau *f,* Ausstellung *f;* **slide** ~ Diavortrag *m;* ■**to be on** ~ ausgestellt sein ④ *(entertainment)* Show *f; (on TV a.)* Unterhaltungssendung *f; (at a theatre)* Vorstellung *f* ▶ PHRASES: **let's get this** ~ **on the road** *(fam)* lasst uns die Sache [endlich] in Angriff nehmen; **the** ~ **must go on** *(saying)* die Show muss weitergehen **II.** *vt* <showed, shown *or* showed> ① *(display, project, express) film* zeigen; *(exhibit)* ausstellen; *(perform,* vorführen; *(produce) passport* vorzeigen; **to** ~ **sb respect** jdm Respekt erweisen ② *(expose)* sehen lassen; **this carpet** ~**s all the dirt** bei dem Teppich kann man jedes bisschen Schmutz sehen ③ *(reveal)* zeigen; **he started to** ~ **his age** man konnte ihm langsam sein Alter sehen; **to** ~ **common sense** gesunden Menschenverstand beweisen ④ *(explain)*

Die Lautschrift zeigt dir, wie das Wort ausgesprochen und betont wird.

Die kursiv gedruckten Hinweise helfen dir, die für deinen Text passende Bedeutung zu finden.

Die römischen Ziffern machen deutlich, dass ein Stichwort unterschiedlichen Wortarten angehört.

Beachte bei der Arbeit mit einem Wörterbuch folgende Punkte:

– Du findest meist mehrere Bedeutungen für ein Wort. Achte also auf den Zusammenhang, wenn du ein Wort nachschlägst:
Take the second street on the right. That's the right way to the station.
– Achte darauf, welche Wortart du suchst – Nomen, Verb, Adjektiv, …?
– Lies auch immer die besonderen Ausdrücke, denn das Wort könnte Teil einer Redewendung sein: *to take place* bedeutet nicht 'Platz nehmen'; es bedeutet 'stattfinden'!

S19 Im Internet recherchieren

Im Internet findest du eine Reihe verschiedener Webseiten, z. B. Bildagenturen, Enzyklopädien, Foren, Reiseportale und Suchmaschinen, die meist frei zugänglich sind.

1. Wenn du nach Informationen zu einem Thema suchst, überlege dir zunächst gute Stichwörter, die du in eine Suchmaschine eingibst. Je genauer deine Stichwörter, umso besser das Suchergebnis!

2. Schau dir die Adresse der Webseiten in der Suchergebnisliste an: Welche Art von Webseite kann am ehesten die gesuchten Informationen liefern? Wie glaubwürdig ist die Quelle? Handelt es sich beispielsweise um einen Lexikon-Eintrag, die Webseite eines Museums, eines bekannten Radio- oder Fernsehsenders oder einer Tageszeitung? Oder spiegelt das Suchergebnis eher eine persönliche Meinung z. B. in einem Forum oder sozialen Netzwerk wider?

3. Lies die Informationen auf der Webseite / den Webseiten und notiere wichtige Punkte, um dann eigene Sätze zu formulieren. Kopiere niemals ganze Sätze oder gar den ganzen Artikel! Übrigens haben viele Webseiten Suchfelder, um die Webseite genauer nach Informationen zu durchsuchen.

Kooperative Lernformen

Hier findest du die Erklärung für einige ausgewählte Methoden der kooperativen Arbeit.

S20 Think – Pair – Share

1. *Think:* Du sammelst still mögliche Lösungen zu der Aufgabe. Du kannst deine Ideen in Stichpunkten notieren.
2. *Pair:* Zusammen mit deinem Partner besprichst du leise deine gesammelten Ideen.
3. *Share:* Im Klassengespräch meldet ihr euch und teilt euren Mitschülern die Ergebnisse eurer Partnergespräche mit.

S21 Placemat (Platzdeckchen)

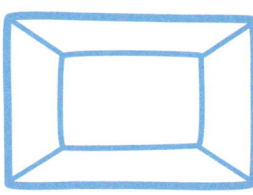

Look here for a placemat: 🌐 w67f59

Die *Placemat-Methode* ist eine Variante von Think – Pair – Share. Jedes der vier Gruppenmitglieder notiert mögliche Lösungen oder Ideen in seinem Feld. Anschließend werden diese innerhalb der Gruppe besprochen. Die Lösung bzw. Idee auf die sich die Gruppe geeinigt hat, wird in der Mitte der *Placemat* festgehalten.

Placemat in Vierergruppen

S22 Milling around (Marktplatz)

Du gehst durch das Klassenzimmer, erfragst von deinen Mitschülern bestimmte Informationen und gibst auch selbst Auskunft. Versuche mit möglichst vielen Mitschülern zu sprechen und verschiedene Informationen zu sammeln. Ihr könnt auch ein Signal vereinbaren, zu dem ihr eure Gesprächspartner wechselt.

S23 Inside outside circle (Kugellager)

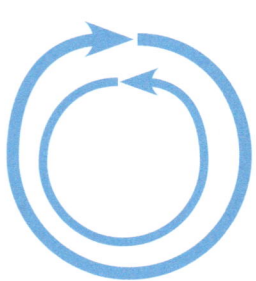

1. Bildet zwei Stuhlkreise, einen inneren und einen äußeren.
2. Setzt euch in den Stuhlkreisen so hin, dass immer ein Schüler des äußeren und des inneren Stuhlkreises sich gegenüber sitzen.
3. Stellt euch gegenseitig eure Fragen und beantwortet diese.
4. Rutscht im inneren oder äußeren Kreis nach dem Ende der Gesprächsrunde einen Platz weiter und beginnt ein Gespräch mit einem neuen Mitschüler.

S24 Bus stop (Lerntempoduett)

Sobald du deine Aufgabe fertig bearbeitet hast, gehst du zu einem verein-barten Treffpunkt, dem *bus stop*. Dort wartest du auf den nächsten Mitschüler, der fertig ist, und zusammen besprecht und vergleicht ihr eure Lösungen. Anschließend verlasst ihr den *bus stop* und bearbeitet die nächste Aufgabe.

S25 Gallery walk (Museumsgang)

1. *Group work:* In der Gruppe erarbeitet ihr ein Thema und haltet euer Ergebnis, z. B. auf einem Poster, fest.
2. *Gallery walk:* Es werden neue Gruppen gebildet. In jeder Gruppe ist ein Schüler jeder Ausgangsgruppe. Jede Gruppe betrachtet die verschiedenen Ergebnisse der Gruppenarbeiten. Jeder präsentiert nun in der neuen Gruppe das Ergebnis seiner Ausgangsgruppe.

S26 Expert puzzle (Expertenpuzzle)

1. Bildet Gruppen zu je vier Schülern.
2. Jeder Schüler aus der Gruppe wählt ein Thema und bearbeitet es selbstständig.
3. Jeder Schüler findet einen Partner mit dem gleichen Thema aus einer anderen Gruppe. Die Paare vergleichen ihre Ergebnisse.
4. Jeder Schüler kehrt in seine Gruppe zurück und stellt seine Ergebnisse aus der Partnerarbeitsphase vor.

Grammar

Liebe Schülerin, lieber Schüler,
in dieser *Grammar* findest du ausführliche Erklärungen zu allen grammatischen Themen in Green Line 3.
Die Grammatikkapitel (**G**) helfen dir, die Grammatik zu verstehen, einzelne Punkte nachzuholen, wenn
du im Unterricht gefehlt hast, oder bestimmte Regeln für Hausaufgaben und die Vorbereitung von Tests
und Klassenarbeiten nachzuschlagen. Regeln sind mit einem grünen Punkt (**o**) gekennzeichnet.
Ein Ausrufezeichen (**!**) bedeutet, dass du hier besonders aufpassen musst. Die **English summary** fasst die
wichtigsten Regeln auf Englisch zusammen. Am Ende jedes Kapitels überprüfst du mit **Test yourself**,
ob du alles verstanden hast. Die Lösungen findest du ab Seite 294.

Grammatical terms

English term		Example	Deutsche Bezeichnung
‹adjectives after verbs of perception›	G11	After the long walk they **felt terrible**.	Adjektive nach Verben der Sinneswahrnehmung
conditional sentence type 1	G1	If you **want** to be successful, you**'ll need** good videos.	Bedingungssatz Typ 1
conditional sentence type 2	G2	**If** I **had** the choice, I **would drop out of** school.	Bedingungssatz Typ 2
defining relative clause	G6	The Globe is a theatre **that** was popular in Shakespeare's days.	notwendiger Relativsatz – mit Relativpronomen
contact clause	G7	**The man Jay** saw was a ghost.	– ohne Relativpronomen
‹indirect speech›	G14	She **writes (that) she's** in Dublin with **her** mum.	indirekte Rede
passive	G4	Haggis **is made** with meat.	Passiv
past progressive	G5	Holly **was looking** for souvenirs when she found the Loch Ness Monsters.	Verlaufsform der Vergangenheit
‹possessive pronouns›	G13	This isn't your ring. It's **mine**.	Possessivpronomen
present progressive with future meaning	G9	My friends **are meeting** this afternoon.	Verlaufsform der Gegenwart mit Zukunftsbedeutung
prop word one/ones	G8	There was a scream and then another **one**.	Stützwort
simple present with future meaning	G9	The train **leaves** at 6:10 a.m.	Gegenwart mit Zukunftsbedeutung
substitute forms of modals	G10	He **was allowed to** visit his aunt and uncle in Bangladesh.	Ersatzform der Modalverben
reflexive pronouns	G3	Come to northwest Scotland – and enjoy **yourself**!	Reflexivpronomen
‹which to comment on the main clause›	G12	They take from the poor people, **which makes me angry**.	which *mit Satzbezug*

Unit 1

G1 **If your content is interesting, people will be interested in you.** Seiten 10–11

Bedingungssätze Typ 1
Conditional sentences type 1

Many young people today think, 'If you **want** to make a lot of money, **become** an influencer'. But it isn't really that easy. If you **want** to be successful, you**'ll need** good videos and interesting content. And if you **don't understand** what people are interested in, you **should** become people smart.

Mit dem Bedingungssatz Typ 1 drückst du aus, was unter einer bestimmten Bedingung passieren wird. Der Sprecher hält die Bedingung für erfüllbar. Es ist also wahrscheinlich, dass die Folge eintritt.

○ *Der Bedingungssatz Typ 1 besteht aus einem* **if-Satz** *(Nebensatz) und einem* **Hauptsatz**. *Im* **if-Satz** *drückst du die Bedingung aus, im* **Hauptsatz** *sagst du, was passiert oder passieren kann, falls diese Bedingung erfüllt wird.*

○ *Im* **if-Satz** *verwendest du das* **simple present**, *im* **Hauptsatz** *das* **will future**.

Bedingung im if-Satz: simple present	Folge im Hauptsatz: will future
If he **becomes** an influencer,	he**'ll need** to post videos every week.
If you **don't understand** what people are interested in,	you **won't attract** any followers.

○ *Neben dem* **will future** *kannst du im* **Hauptsatz** *häufig auch die* **Modalverben** *(can, must, should + infinitive) oder den* **Imperativ** *verwenden.*

if-Satz: simple present	Hauptsatz: Modalverb + infinitive *oder Imperativ*
If you **want** to be a social media star,	you **must create** good content. (*Notwendigkeit*)
If he **wants** to be successful,	he **should understand** what people are interested in. (*Ratschlag*)
If he **needs** advice,	he **can ask** his friends. (*Möglichkeit*)
If you **need** advice,	**have** a look on the internet. There are lots of good websites. (*Aufforderung*)

❗ *Bedingungssätze können entweder mit dem* **if-Satz** *oder mit dem* **Hauptsatz** *beginnen:*
If he **posts** videos before he's 16, his parents **won't be** happy.
His parents **won't be** happy **if** he **posts** videos before he's 16. (*Kein Komma vor* **if**!)

❗ *Verwechsle nicht **if** (wenn / falls = Bedingung) mit **when** (wenn = zeitlicher Zusammenhang)!*
If his parents tell him to focus on school again, he'll go crazy.
Wenn / Falls seine Eltern ihm noch einmal sagen, dass er sich auf die Schule konzentrieren soll, wird er durchdrehen.
He hates it **when** they do that.
Er hasst es, wenn sie das tun.

English summary

A conditional sentence has two parts: an **if-clause** and a **main clause**.

You use **type 1** for actions that are **probable / possible**. The verb in the **if-clause** is in the **simple present**; the verb in the **main clause** is in the **will future**, **a modal verb + infinitive**, or an **imperative**.

If your content is interesting or fun, people will be interested in you.
If you need new ideas for topics, you can ask your friends.
If you need feedback, ask your followers.

Test yourself *Robert and his friend want to go to the cinema together. They want to catch the train at 5:30 p.m., but his friend isn't ready. This is what Robert says. Complete his sentences.*

1. If we (not leave) now, we (miss) our train.
2. If we (miss) our train, we (be) late for the film.
3. If we (be) late for the film, they probably (not let) us in.
4. And I (be) really upset if that (happen). So, please hurry up!

G2 They wouldn't worry if they didn't care.

Seiten 12–14

Bedingungssätze Typ 2
Conditional sentences type 2

I know you want to become a famous dancer. But **if** you **didn't think about** dancing all the time, you **would have** better marks. **If** you **had** better marks, Mum and Dad **would support** you. So, **if** I **were** you, I **would listen** to them and try harder at school.

If I **had** the choice, I **would drop out of** school.

Mit dem Bedingungssatz Typ 2 drückst du aus, was unter einer bestimmten Bedingung passieren könnte. Der Sprecher hält diese Bedingung für nicht oder nicht so einfach erfüllbar. Es ist also (zur Zeit) eher unwahrscheinlich, dass die Folge eintritt.

○ *Für die Bedingung im **if-Satz** verwendest du das **simple past**, für die Folge im **Hauptsatz** **would(n't) / could(n't) + infinitive**.*
*Die entsprechende Kurzform von would lautet **'d** (I'd / you'd / he'd …).*

Bedingung im if-Satz: simple past	Folge im Hauptsatz: conditional (would / could + infinitive)
If I **had** the choice,	I **would / I'd drop out of** school.
Wenn ich die Wahl hätte, würde ich die Schule abbrechen.	
If I **didn't have to** go to school,	I **could dance** all day.
Wenn ich nicht zur Schule gehen müsste, könnte ich den ganzen Tag tanzen.	
If Jay **looked** as good as Shahid,	he**'d work** as a model too.
Wenn Jay so gut aussehen würde wie Shahid, würde er auch als Model arbeiten.	
If I **were** Jay,	I**'d take** Shahid's advice.
Wenn ich Jay wäre, würde ich Shahids Rat annehmen.	

○ *Nach I / he / she / it kannst du **was** oder **were** verwenden.*
If I **were / was** rich, I**'d** …
If he / she / it **were / was** famous, he**'d** …

❶ *Achte darauf, dass du **would** nur für die **Folge im Hauptsatz** verwendest! Die **Bedingung** im* **if-Satz** *steht immer im **simple past**.*
If Shahid **didn't work** as a model, he **wouldn't** have so much money.
*Wenn Shahid **nicht** als Model **arbeiten würde**, **hätte** er nicht so viel Geld.*

English summary

A conditional sentence has two parts: an **if-clause** and a **main clause**.

You use **type 2** for actions that are **not probable** or **not possible**. The verb in the **if-clause** is in the **simple past**; the verb in the **main clause** is in the **conditional** tense.

If Jay had the chance, he'd drop out of school now.
If I had a million pounds, I could travel the world.

Test yourself   *Jay has had another fight with his parents. He's talking to Shahid about his problems with them now. Complete this part of their conversation.*

Jay: If Mum and Dad **1** (try) to understand me, we **2** (not fight) so often.

Shahid: They're just worried about you, Jay. You **3** (not have) so many fights if you **4** (work) harder at school and **5** (get) better marks.

Jay: The problem is that they don't believe in me, Shahid. If they **6** (believe) in me, they **7** (not worry) about my marks.

Shahid: They only worry because they care about you, Jay. Maybe if you **8** (not be) so laid-back, they **9** (not have to) worry so much.

G3   You have to push yourself!

Seiten 15–17

Reflexivpronomen
Reflexive pronouns and each other

> Wow! Olivia plays the sax really well. Did **you** teach **her**?

> No, I didn't. **She** taught **herself**.
> And **she** even wrote the music **herself**.

*Im Englischen verwendest du die Reflexivpronomen (Pronomen auf -self / -selves), wenn das **Objekt** sich auf das **Subjekt** im Satz zurückbezieht. Subjekt und Objekt sind dabei **dieselbe Person.***
Du verwendest die Reflexivpronomen auch, wenn du eine Person oder Sache im Satz hervorheben willst.

○   *Die Singularformen der Reflexivpronomen enden auf -self (herself); die Pluralformen auf -selves (themselves).*

	1. Person	**2. Person**	**3. Person**
Singular:	(I) … mysel**f**	(you) … yoursel**f**	(he, she, it) … himsel**f**, hersel**f**, itsel**f**
Plural:	(we) … oursel**ves**	(you) … yoursel**ves**	(they) … themsel**ves**

○   *Die -self-Pronomen kommen im Englischen als Reflexivpronomen (rückbezügliche Pronomen) und als verstärkende Pronomen vor.*

a)   *Reflexiver Gebrauch*

○   *Im Englischen verwendest du die Pronomen auf -self / -selves, wenn das **Objekt dieselbe Person** bezeichnet wie das **Subjekt**. In diesem Fall entsprechen sie den deutschen Pronomen mich / mir, dich / dir, sich (selbst), usw. Vergleiche:*

Did **you** teach **her**?   *her = andere Person (Objektpronomen)*
She taught **herself**.   *herself = dieselbe Person (Reflexivpronomen)*

	Subjekt	Verb	Objekt / Reflexivpronomen	Deutsch
	I	cut	**myself** with a knife.	ich – mich
Did	**you**	hurt	**yourself**?	du – dich / du – dir
Jay wants to become a famous singer.	**He**	really pushes	**himself** with singing and dancing.	er – sich (selbst)
Claire often feels like	**she**'s	talking to	**herself**.	sie – (mit) sich (selbst)
	We	always enjoy	**ourselves**.	wir – uns
Why can't	**you**	behave	**yourselves**?	ihr – euch
Don't worry about the boys.	**They**	can look after	**themselves**.	sie – sich (selbst)

❗ Die Reflexivpronomen werden im Englischen wesentlich seltener gebraucht als im Deutschen.
*Viele Verben, die **im Deutschen reflexiv** sind, werden **im Englischen ohne** -self oder -selves gebildet.*
How do you feel today? – *Wie fühlst du **dich** heute?*
I'm looking forward to the weekend. – *Ich freue **mich** auf das Wochenende.*

to change	*sich (ver)ändern*	to meet	*sich treffen*
to decide	*sich entscheiden*	to move	*sich bewegen*
to feel	*sich fühlen*	to relax	*sich entspannen*
to get dressed	*sich anziehen*	to remember	*sich erinnern*
to hide	*sich verstecken*	to sit down	*sich hinsetzen*
to hurry	*sich beeilen*	to wash (face/hands/hair)	*sich waschen*
to imagine	*sich vorstellen*	to wonder	*sich wundern*
to look forward to	*sich freuen auf*	to worry	*sich Sorgen machen*

b) *Verstärkender Gebrauch*

○ *Mit den Reflexivpronomen kannst du auch eine Person oder eine Sache im Satz besonders hervorheben. In diesem Fall entspricht* myself, yourself, himself … *dem deutschen **selbst / allein**:*
Wow, that's a cool song. – Thanks, **I** wrote it **myself**. *(selbst)*
You don't have to help us. **We** can do it **ourselves**. *(allein, ohne fremde Hilfe)*

c) Themselves *oder* **each other?**

○ *Wenn du ausdrücken möchtest, dass zwischen Personen etwas wechselseitig geschieht oder es um Gegenseitigkeit geht, verwendest du **each other** (auf Deutsch „sich", „einander", „gegenseitig").*

They're looking at **themselves**.

They're looking at **each other**.

English summary

1. The singular forms of the reflexive pronouns end
   in -**self** (myself); the plural forms end in -**selves**
   (ourselves). You use the reflexive pronoun
   a) when the subject and object of the sentence   *He hurt himself.*
      are the same person.
   b) as an emphasizing (*hervorhebendes*) pronoun.   *Nobody helped me. I did it myself.*
2. You use **each other** to talk about an interaction   *We talk to each other every day.*
   between people.

Test yourself *Olivia and Lucy are fighting again. Complete these sentences. Do you need an object pronoun,
a reflexive pronoun or each other?*

Olivia: Claire, I'm hungry. Can I make **1** a sandwich?
Lucy: That's a good idea, Olivia. Can you make **2** one too?
Olivia: No, I can't. You can do that **3** .
Claire: Hey, you two, please behave **4** . You know I hate it when you fight with **5** .

Unit 2

G4 Is haggis made with meat?

Seiten 42–44

Das Passiv
The passive

Active: **They build** ships in Scotland.

Passive: Ships **are built** in Scotland.

*Du benutzt das Passiv, wenn der Ausführende einer Handlung unwichtig oder nicht
bekannt ist. Damit rückt die Handlung selbst in den Vordergrund. Das Passiv wird
häufig in Zeitungsberichten, Sachtexten und technischen Beschreibungen verwendet.*

a) *Das Passiv bildest du mit einer Form von* **be** *in der jeweiligen Zeitform und dem* **past participle** *des Vollverbs (Verb + -ed oder unregelmäßige Form).*

Zeitform	Form von be + past participle	Beispiel
simple present	am / is / are + past participle	Haggis **is made** with meat. … *wird … gemacht.*
simple past	was / were + past participle	The house **was built** 20 years ago. … *wurde … gebaut.*
present perfect simple	have / has been + past participle	Whisky **has been produced** in Scotland for 500 years. … *wird … hergestellt.*

❗ *Im Deutschen verwendest du für das Passiv eine Form von „werden".*

b) *Wenn du in einem Passivsatz sagen möchtest, von wem die Handlung ausgeführt wird, verwendest du die Präposition* **by** *(auf Deutsch „von"). Der Ausführende der Handlung wird* **by-agent** *genannt. Du entscheidest im Einzelfall, ob dieser wichtig ist oder nicht:*
Gaelic **is only spoken by** a few people today.
Gälisch **wird** *heute nur* **von** *wenigen Menschen* **gesprochen**.
The broken engine was fixed (**by** a worker).
*Der kaputte Motor wurde (**von** einem Arbeiter) repariert.*

c) *Wenn du einen Aktivsatz in einen Passivsatz umwandelst, musst du Folgendes beachten:*
1. *Das* Objekt *des Aktivsatzes wird zum* Subjekt *im Passivsatz. Aus* **Objektpronomen** *werden* **Subjektpronomen**: me, you, him, her, it, us, you, them → I, you, he, she, it, we, you, they.
2. *Die Aktivform des Verbs wird zur Passivform, indem du die passende Form von* **be** *mit dem* **past participle** *des Aktivverbs verbindest:* take → are taken.
3. *Das Subjekt des Aktivsatzes wird nicht genannt. Ist der Ausführende der Handlung jedoch für den Kontext wichtig, wird das Subjekt mit dem* **by-agent** *angefügt.*

Aktiv:	Passiv:
People all over the world **have read** the Sherlock Holmes stories.	The Sherlock Holmes stories **have been read by** people all over the world.
The Scottish author Sir Arthur Conan Doyle **wrote** them.	They **were written by** the Scottish author Sir Arthur Conan Doyle.
Every year thousands of fans **visit** Sherlock Holmes' home in London.	Every year Sherlock Holmes' home in London **is visited by** thousands of fans.

❗ *Die Zeitform im Aktivsatz und im Passivsatz bleibt gleich.*

English summary

You form the passive voice with a form of **be** and the **past participle**.

1. You use the active voice to stress what the subject does. You use the passive to stress what is done. Often you don't know who has done the action, or you think this is not important.
2. If it's important to say who does the action, you use the **by-agent**.

*The raincoat **was invented** by Charles Macintosh.*

Test yourself   *Complete this short text about the Scottish game of shinty. Use passive forms of the verbs in brackets and be careful with the tenses.*

Shinty[1] is one of the oldest games in the world. Some people think that it (invent) in Ireland 2,000 years ago and that it (bring) to Scotland by the Irish in the 6th century. Others say that it (play) in Scotland since Celtic times. Shinty is similar to field hockey but faster and more dangerous. In the past whole villages played against each other. Today shinty is a club sport. It (play) between two teams of 12 players.

G5   **What were they doing when Holly took the picture?**   Seiten 45–47

Die Verlaufsform der Vergangenheit
The past progressive

Look at this picture. Isn't it funny? I took it while we **were walking** around Glasgow.

Oh, and look at these cute little monsters here. I **was looking for** souvenirs when I found these.

Das **past progressive** *ist die Verlaufsform der Vergangenheit. Mit dieser Zeitform drückst du aus, dass* **eine Handlung zu einem bestimmten Zeitpunkt in der Vergangenheit gerade ablief** *und* **noch nicht zu Ende** *war. Häufige Signalwörter hierfür sind* while *und* still.

1 shinty [ˈʃɪnti]

○ *Du bildest das* **past progressive** *aus der Vergangenheitsform von* **be (was/were)** *und dem* **present participle** *(= Verb + -ing).*

Aussage:	The two men in Holly's picture **were wearing** kilts.
Verneinung:	They **weren't wearing** skirts.
Ergänzungsfrage:	What **was** the guy on the right **doing**?
Entscheidungsfrage mit Kurzantwort:	**Were** the girls **dancing** too? – Yes, they **were**. / No, they **weren't**.

○ *Mit dem* **past progressive** *betonst du den Verlauf einer Handlung, die zu einem bestimmten Zeitpunkt in der Vergangenheit bereits angefangen hatte und noch nicht zu Ende war.*

9 p.m. → → 7 a.m. ⌇⌇⌇⌇⌇⌇➤ 6 a.m.	At 6 a.m. Holly **was** still **sleeping**.
	Um 6 Uhr schlief Holly noch.

○ *Mit dem* past progressive *kannst du auch ausdrücken, dass zwei Handlungen gleichzeitig in der Vergangenheit abliefen:*
While Holly **was looking for** souvenirs in a shop, the others **were waiting** outside.

○ *Du verwendest es auch, wenn sich in der Vergangenheit eine Handlung noch im Verlauf befand, als etwas Neues einsetzte. Diese neu eintretende Handlung steht dann im* **simple past**.

Past progressive: *gerade ablaufende Handlung*	Simple past: *neu eintretende Handlung*
Holly **was looking for** souvenirs	when she **found** the Loch Ness Monsters.
While Holly **was looking for** souvenirs,	she **found** the Loch Ness Monsters.

❗ *Das* past progressive *gibt es im Deutschen nicht. Du kannst es mit „gerade dabei sein, etwas zu tun" oder mit „während" wiedergeben.*

❗ *Die* progressive-*Form kannst du nur von* **Tätigkeitsverben** *bilden (z.B.* dance, go, listen, look for, sleep, take, wait, walk*), nicht aber von Verben, die einen Zustand ausdrücken (z.B.* be, believe, find, know, see*).*

> **English summary**
>
> You use the past progressive
>
> 1. to describe an action that was **still happening** at a certain time **in the past**.
> 2. to describe actions that were still happening at the same time in the past.
> 3. to describe an action that was going on at a time when something else happened.
>
> *At 4 p.m. yesterday afternoon, Gwen and Holly were walking around Glasgow.*
> *While Gwen was waiting for Holly, a man was playing the bagpipes in the street.*
> *They were walking around Glasgow when it started to rain.*

Test yourself *Write dialogues. Use the past progressive and the simple past.*

Example:
1. Holly sleep / Gwen take photo? – No / she write blog.
    A: Was Holly sleeping when Gwen took a photo?
    B: No, she wasn't. She was writing her blog.

2. William and Kate visit Edinburgh / Holly and Gwen see them? – No / visit Glasgow.
3. Gwen run in park / she fall over? – No / run down the road.
4. Holly and Gwen walk through field / cows start to follow them? – No / walk past it.

Unit 3

G6 **I'm in the calendar which Claire is making.**   Seiten 66–68

Notwendige Relativsätze
Defining relative clauses

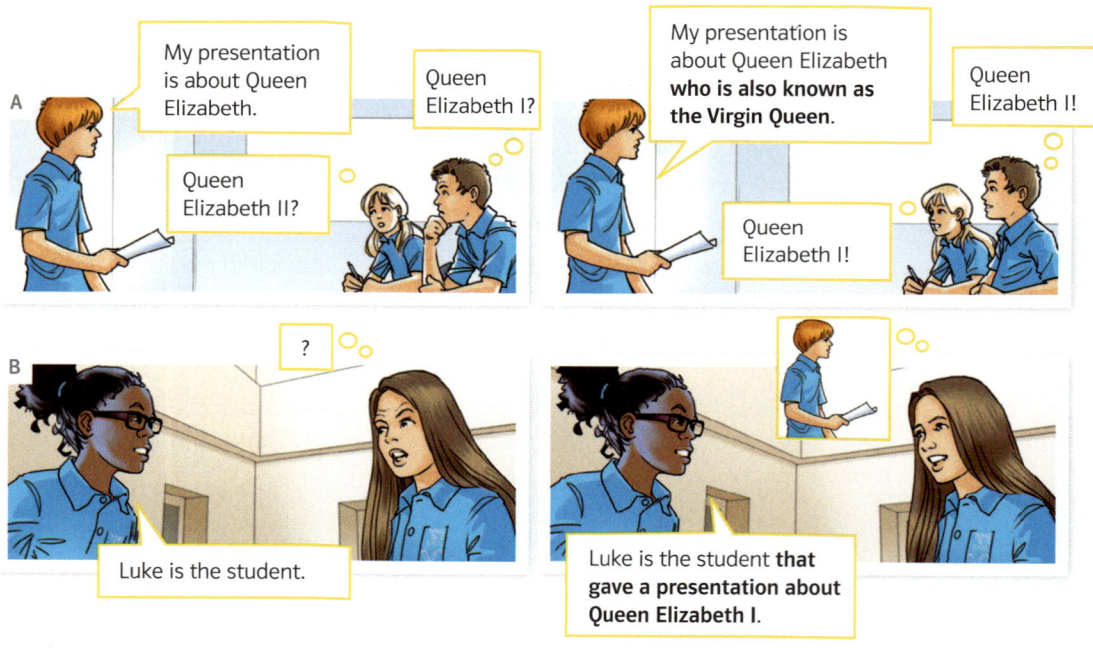

> *Relativsätze sind Nebensätze, die ein Nomen (Bezugswort) näher beschreiben oder definieren.*
> *Notwendige Relativsätze werden deshalb so genannt, weil der Hauptsatz ohne die im Relativsatz*
> *enthaltene Information nicht eindeutig (A) oder nicht verständlich wäre (B).*

○ *Relativsätze leitest du durch ein Relativpronomen ein. Du verwendest …*

who *für Personen*

which *für Sachen*

that *für Personen oder Sachen*

○ *Das Relativpronomen steht meist direkt nach dem* Bezugswort *und leitet den Relativsatz ein. Danach folgt die* notwendige Information .
From his journey to America, Sir Walter Raleigh brought back potatoes . They were different from modern potatoes .
From his journey to America, Sir Walter Raleigh brought back potatoes which / that were different from modern potatoes .

○ *Das Relativpronomen* **whose** *(deren / dessen) benutzt du, um Besitz oder Zugehörigkeit auszudrücken, z. B.:*
James Watt was the man **whose** ideas changed the world.
The tribes **whose** land the Romans took needed to find new homes.

○ *Das Relativpronomen* **whom** *ist die Objektform von* who. *Es wird oft in der förmlichen Schriftsprache benutzt. Gebräuchlicher ist* who, *z. B.:*
Queen Elizabeth I is the woman **whom / who** I want to tell you about.

❗ *Im Gegensatz zum Deutschen trennst du notwendige Relativsätze nicht durch Kommas vom Hauptsatz ab.*

❗ *Im notwendigen Relativsatz steht die Präposition (about, with, to, …) meist hinter dem Verb. Sie kann auch vor dem Relativpronomen* whom *und* which *stehen. Nur beim Relativpronomen* that *und* who **muss** *sie hinter dem Verb stehen.*

Shakespeare wrote lots of plays	that	students learn **about** at school.	*Shakespeare hat viele Theaterstücke geschrieben,* **über die …**
	which	students learn **about** at school.	
	about which	students learn at school.	
Gwen and Holly are the girls	that	Olivia wants to be photographed **with**.	Gwen und Holly sind die Mädchen, **mit denen …**
	who	Olivia wants to be photographed **with**.	
	with whom	Olivia wants to be photographed.	

English summary

Defining relative clauses tell you which person or thing the speaker is talking about.

Defining relative clauses begin with a relative pronoun. You use **who / that** for people, **which / that** for things and **whose** for people or things. You do not use a comma between the noun and the relative clause.

Jay saw a man who was wearing Victorian clothes.
He heard a scary story about a murder which happened in the street.
How can you call people whose mobiles are turned off?

Test yourself
Lisa got a Celtic bracelet for her birthday from her aunt. Complete the information that came with it in a box. Choose the right relative pronoun: who, which or whose.

Your bracelet – a piece of Celtic history

The bracelet in this box is a design `1` is over 2,000 years old. The people `2` lived in Britain at that time were Celtic tribes, and objects `3` have survived[1] from those days give us information about them. Although the Celts often fought, they loved beautiful things. They used different colours for the clothes `4` they wore, and they had many clever people. This bracelet is an example of the wonderful work `5` they did. When the Angles and Saxons arrived in Britain from Germany 1,500 years ago, they were too strong for the Celts. The tribes `6` land they took found new homes in the west. That is why many people `7` you meet in Wales today are of Celtic origin[2]. Here the old culture lives on in our Welsh language and in our music and art. Your Celtic bracelet is a part of our history.

G7 Jay was in streets he didn't know.

Seite 69–70

Notwendige Relativsätze ohne Relativpronomen
Contact clauses

Guide:
… The theatre **that** was rebuilt looks very much like the first Globe Theatre. Back then the audience could do anything **that** they wanted to do during plays. So the Elizabethans were people **who** really knew how to have fun. That's the end of our tour. But come back and see a play here. It's an experience **which** you'll never forget!

Contact clauses *sind eine besondere Form von notwendigen Relativsätzen, bei denen das Relativpronomen weggelassen werden kann. Du verwendest sie vor allem in der Umgangssprache.*

1 to survive [sə'vaɪv] überleben; überdauern | **2 origin** ['ɒrɪdʒɪn] Abstammung

○ *Relativpronomen können Subjekt oder Objekt des notwendigen Relativsatzes sein:*

a) *Relativpronomen als Subjekt*

○ *Die Relativpronomen who, which und that darfst du nie weglassen, wenn sie Subjekt im Relativsatz sind.*

Hauptsätze	Hauptsatz + Relativsatz
The guide was **an expert** . She knew everything about Elizabethan times.	The guide was **an expert** who / that knew everything about Elizabethan times.
Jay found **a Victorian tour** . It was very exciting.	Jay found **a Victorian tour** which / that was very exciting.

b) *Relativpronomen als Objekt*

○ *Die Relativpronomen who, which und that kannst du weglassen, wenn sie Objekt im Relativsatz sind. Das erkennst du am neuen Subjekt nach dem Relativpronomen. Solche Relativsätze nennt man contact clauses, weil sie ohne Relativpronomen in direktem Kontakt zum Hauptsatz stehen.*

Hauptsätze	Hauptsatz + Relativsatz
Shakespeare was a writer. We talked about him in English.	Shakespeare was a writer (who / that) **we** talked about in English.
The pipe is a thing. Jay found it in the street.	The pipe is a thing (which / that) **Jay** found in the street.

❗ *Im* contact clause *steht die Präposition (about, with, to, …) immer hinter dem Verb.*
Shakespeare wrote lots of plays students learn **about** at school.
Gwen and Holly are the girls Olivia wants to be photographed **with**.

English summary

Defining relative clauses tell you which person or thing the speaker is talking about.

If the relative pronoun **who / which / that** is the object of the relative clause, you can leave it out and make a contact clause.

Jay thought that the Victorian pipe (which) he found in the street would be perfect for the calendar photo.

Test yourself   *Go back to the Test yourself exercise in G6. Read the text again and say where the relative pronoun can be left out.*

G8 They heard a scream and then another one.

Seite 71

Das Stützwort one/ones
The prop word one/ones

Woman:	Hello, we'd like to go on a tour of the Globe.
Assistant:	Which **one** would you like to go on?
Woman:	The **one** that is for children, please.
Assistant:	How many children are there in your group?
Woman:	Ten. … Erm, sorry, twelve. Those **ones** over there are my students too.
Assistant:	An adult and 12 children. That's £120, please.
Woman:	Here you are.
Assistant:	Thank you. Can you see the two doors over there? Please wait for the guide in front of the red **one**.

Wenn du im Englischen ein zählbares Nomen nicht wiederholen möchtest, dann kannst du es durch one/ones ersetzen. Man nennt das Stützwort.

○ *Mit* **one** *ersetzt du ein zählbares Nomen im* **Singular***, und mit* **ones** *ein zählbares Nomen im* **Plural***. Du benutzt es nach …*

einem Adjektiv:	Jay doesn't need **new shoes** for the calendar project. He can wear his **old ones**.
the:	Do you want to see my new **dress**? – **The one** that you're going to wear for the photoshoot?
den Demonstrativpronomen **this / that / these / those:**	Holly wants to buy a **crown**. She thinks she'll buy **this one**.
which *in Fragen:*	There are two different tours, the Elizabethan **tour** and the Victorian **tour**. Which **one** would you like to go on?

❗ *Anders als im Deutschen kann im Englischen das Adjektiv, Demonstrativpronomen und Fragewort* **which** *nicht allein stehen. Vergleiche:*

Jay doesn't need new shoes. He can wear his **old ones**.
Er kann seine **alten** *anziehen.*
Holly wants to buy a crown. She thinks she'll buy **this one.**
Sie denkt, dass sie **diese** *kaufen wird.*
The Elizabethan tour or the Victorian tour. **Which one** would you like to go on?
An **welcher** *wollen Sie teilnehmen?*

English summary

If you don't want to use the same countable noun again, you can use the prop word **one** for nouns in the **singular** and **ones** for nouns in the **plural**.

Is this your hat?
– No, I've got a blue one.
Those shoes are great!
– Which ones do you mean?
– The/Those ones over there.

Test yourself

a) *You're visiting the Globe Theatre. At the souvenir shop you want to buy a T-shirt for your aunts. Complete the dialogue. Use one or ones.*

You: Do you have any T-shirts?
Shop assistant: Yes, we do. Which **1** do you mean? The **2** that have 'Globe Theatre' on them?
You: No, I mean the **3** with 'All the world's a stage'.
Shop assistant: How many would you like?
You: Two, please.
Shop assistant: Here you are.
You: I'm sorry, but I think these **4** are too small. Do you have any bigger **5** ?
Shop assistant: Sure. We've got them in medium, large and extra large too.
You: Great! I'll have **6** in medium and **7** in large.
Shop assistant: That's 20 pounds, please.

b) *Work with a partner and make another dialogue at the souvenir shop. Here are some ideas for things you could buy: a poster, a hat, a bag, a book or a cup.*

Unit 4

G9 The ferry arrives at 3:15 local time.

Seiten 96–97

Das Präsens mit Futurbedeutung
The simple present and present progressive with future meaning

I'm not making a phone call in French.

The ferry **arrives** at 3:15. We**'re arriving** at the gîte about 8:30.

Neben dem will future *und dem* going-to future *werden im Englischen häufig auch das* **simple present** (it arrives) *und das* **present progressive** (we're arriving) *verwendet, um über zukünftige Handlungen zu sprechen.*

○ *Das* simple present *verwendest du für zukünftige Handlungen, die durch* **Fahrpläne**, **Programme** *oder andere* **offizielle Vorgaben** *festgelegt sind. Solche Handlungen werden häufig mit Verben wie* arrive, leave, start, finish, open, close, land, take etc. *gebraucht, z.B.* The film starts *at 8:00 p.m.*

○ *Das* present progressive *verwendest du für zukünftige Handlungen, wenn es sich um* **Pläne** *oder* **Vereinbarungen** *handelt, die persönlich vereinbart wurden. Solche Handlungen werden häufig mit Verben wie* meet, come *und* go *gebraucht, z.B.* My friends are meeting *at the leisure centre later this afternoon.*

❗ *Das* present progressive *mit Futurbedeutung bietet eine Alternative zum* going-to future, *die von englischen Muttersprachlern häufig verwendet wird, z.B.* My grandparents are coming *for lunch next Saturday. statt* My grandparents **are going to come** *for lunch next Saturday.*

English summary

You use the **simple present** to talk about timetables, programmes etc.

You use the **present progressive** to talk about something that you've arranged to do in the future.

When does the train leave? – It leaves at 6:10 a.m.

What are you doing this weekend? – I'm doing my homework on Saturday. On Sunday I'm going to the beach with some friends.

Test yourself *Use the* **simple present** *or the* **present progressive** *to complete the dialogue.*

Ella: What ⬛**1** (you – do) tomorrow?
Mia: I ⬛**2** (meet) my cousin at the new shopping centre. It ⬛**3** (open) tomorrow at 10:00. Why don't you come with us?
Ella: That sounds like a great idea. How ⬛**4** (you – get) there?
Mia: By bus or by Tube. I haven't decided yet. The bus is cheaper, but it ⬛**5** (leave) earlier and it ⬛**6** (take) a lot longer.
Ella: I've got a better idea. My brother ⬛**7** (drive) into town tomorrow morning. I'm sure he can take us with him. But let me ask him first what time he ⬛**8** (go).

G10   Your passport photo has to look like you.

Seiten 99–101

Modalverben und ihre Ersatzformen
Modals and their substitute forms

Officer: May I see your passport, please?
Rafiq: Yes, sure.
Officer: Is that really you? Your passport photo **has to** look like you. Because I can't identify you, I'**m not allowed to** let you go through.

Die Modalverben can, may, can't, mustn't, must *und* needn't *kannst du nur im* simple present *benutzen. Ihre Ersatzform verwendest du vor allem für alle anderen Zeitformen.*

Modalverb	Ersatzform im **simple present**	Ersatzform im **simple past**
can	Rafiq **is allowed to** go to Bangladesh.	He **was allowed to** visit his aunt and uncle.
can't / mustn't	They **aren't allowed to** enter the country because their passport isn't valid.	We **weren't allowed to** fly on our own last year.
may	**Am** I **allowed to** call my aunt and uncle?	**Were** you **allowed to** travel on your own?
can	Rafiq **is able to** find some information on the internet.	His family **was able to** identify him.
can't	The officers **aren't able to** identify him.	His parents **weren't able to** travel to Bangladesh.
must	My parents **have to** work. He **has to** get a new passport.	Rafiq **had to** change planes in India. They **had to** pick him up at the airport.
needn't	I **don't have to** get a new passport – it's still valid. He **doesn't have to** look at a map – he knows the way.	Rafiq and his cousin **didn't have to** be in bed before 9:30 p.m. He **didn't have to** speak any Bengali.

The rows are grouped on the left as:
- **Erlaubnis / Verbot** — be allowed to (can; can't / mustn't; may)
- **(Un)Fähigkeit** — be able to (can; can't)
- **(keine) Notwendigkeit** — have to (must; needn't)

Die Ersatzformen verwendest du auch für die übrigen Zeitformen der Vergangenheit und Zukunft:

present perfect simple:	He **hasn't been allowed to** play cricket since he broke his arm. They **haven't been able to** visit their parents' home country yet. He **has had to** buy a new rucksack for the trip because his old one was too small.
will future:	We **won't be allowed to** use a dictionary in the test. At the end of the trip, I**'ll be able to** speak some Bengali. The students **will have to** do a test tomorrow.

English summary

In the simple present, modal verbs have only one form that's followed by the infinitive of another verb without to.
You usually use substitute forms (have to, be allowed to, be able to) for other tenses.

We can't go on holiday this summer.

I was able to find some interesting information on Bangladesh on the internet.

Test yourself   *Rafiq is calling his parents. Complete the conversation. Use the right tense.*

Dad: Hi, have you arrived yet?

Rafiq: Yes, but I'm still in the airport.

Dad: Why, what happened?

Rafiq: When I arrived, I `1` (*musste*) show my passport. But the officer `2` (*konnte nicht*) identify me because I look so young in the photo. And because he couldn't identify me, he `3` (*nicht erlauben*) let me go through.

Mum: So, do you `4` (*musst*) catch the next plane back to London?

Rafiq: No, no. The officer made a phone call and then I `5` (*musste*) answer some questions and I `6` (*durfte*) call Aunt Sadia and Uncle Dhanu. They `7` (*müssen*) come to the airport and pick me up. But they should be here any minute now. Oh, here they are. Speak to you later. Bye.

Dad: Yes, say hello to them.

‹ Trailer 1 ›

G11   When we arrived, we felt fantastic.   Seiten 110–111

Die Verwendung von Adjektiven nach Verben der Wahrnehmung
The use of adjectives after verbs of perception

Reporter: Matt, thanks for being here today. How do you feel after your long walk across the Scottish Highlands?

Matt: When we arrived at Cape Wrath, we **felt fantastic and tired** at the same time.

Reporter: Tell us what you liked most about your adventure.

Matt: The landscape. It **looked beautiful**. The last days were sunny, and the air **smelt wonderful**.

> Während mit Adjektiven Lebewesen, Sachen oder auch Verben der Sinneswahr-nehmung näher beschrieben werden, beschreiben Adverbien andere Verben näher. Mit ihnen kannst du Texte interessanter und lebhafter gestalten.

○ *Wie im Deutschen steht ein Adjektiv vor dem Nomen, auf das es sich bezieht (we went on a long walk) oder nach einer Form des Verbs be (there was a strong wind).*

○ *Neben dem Verb* be *gibt es auch* **Verben der Wahrnehmung,** *nach denen nicht ein Adverb, sondern ein* **Adjektiv** *steht:*

feel	We **felt** fantastic and tired at the same time.
sound	The howling wind **sounded** scary.
look	Food from a tin **looks** terrible.
taste	If you're hungry, food from a tin **tastes** good.
smell	The air **smelt** wonderful.

❗ *In einigen Fällen gleicht die Form des Adjektivs, der des Adverbs:*
hard *(schwierig, mühevoll):* A tour across the Highlands is **hard**. *(Adjektiv)*
                             We tried **hard** to find the right path. *(Adverb)*
daily *(täglich, pro Tag):* What were your **daily** distances? *(Adjektiv)*
                             We walked about 12 to 15 km **daily**. *(Adverb)*
fast *(schnell):* We had a **fast** jog to get out of the military firing range. *(Adjektiv)*
                             Rivers carry so much water at this time of year, so we tried to cross **fast**. *(Adverb)*

❗ *Beachte, dass* hardly *dem Deutschen „kaum" entspricht:*
There was **hardly** any food left.   *Es war* **kaum** *noch Essen übrig.*

❗ *Beachte die Sonderform:*
Hikers are friendly people. *(Adjektiv)* They help each other **in a friendly way**. *(Adverb)*

> ### English summary
>
> You use adjectives to give more information about a noun or a pronoun. They tell you what people or things are like. You use adverbs to describe how something is done.
>
> Adjectives are used before nouns. They are also used after verbs like *be, feel, look* etc. These verbs don't describe an activity but tell you what someone or something is like or how they feel.
>
> *It wasn't comfortable sleeping in a cold tent. After the long walk they felt terrible but also happy.*

Test yourself   *Use an adjective or an adverb to complete what Dave tells Jay about a new member of the Cooking Club.*

There's a **1** (new) boy at the Cooking Club. He's a bit older than me and really **2** (nice). He can cook **3** (good). No matter what ingredients you give him, he **4** (quick) decides what to cook. Last week he made a chicken pie that tasted **5** (great). I was so **6** (happy) to help him that I cut the onions[1] and carrots **7** (fast) but very **8** (careful). They looked **9** (perfect), but they made me cry **10** (terrible). We're a **11** (fantastic) team because we like each other very much. We work **12** (hard) together, and everything we cook tastes and smells **13** (fantastic) and looks **14** (amazing) too!

1 onion [ˈʌnjən] Zwiebel

⟨Trailer 2⟩

G12 **He takes from people who have little to give, which makes me angry.** Seiten 112–113

Which *mit Satzbezug*
The relative pronoun which to comment on the main clause

> The poor people here in England really hate the Normans, **which I can understand**.
> That stupid Sheriff of Nottingham goes from house to house and takes from people who have little to give, **which makes me angry**.

Ein Relativsatz mit which kann auch verwendet werden, um den Hauptsatz zu kommentieren.

○ *Du kennst schon das Relativpronomen* which, *das sich auf eine Sache bezieht und diese näher definiert (→ G6).*

○ *Das Relativpronomen* **which** *kann sich aber auch* **auf einen Hauptsatz beziehen und diesen kommentieren***. Es entspricht zumeist dem deutschen Wort „was".*

○ *Da es sich um einen nachgestellten Kommentar in Form eines nicht notwendigen Relativsatzes handelt, musst du diesen vom Hauptsatz abtrennen.*

Hauptsatz	*nicht notwendiger Relativsatz*
It's only a question of time before they kill me,	**which** will make the people very sad. *was die Menschen traurig stimmen wird.*
I take from the rich Normans and give to the poor Saxons,	**which** the people love me for. *wofür mich die Menschen lieben.*

English summary

You can use a non-defining relative clause with **which** to comment on the main clause.

Robin Hood has lent me his bow and arrow, which was very nice of him.

Test yourself *Complete the text and comment on the main clause.*

which was great for his fans   which makes it one of the most successful historical drama films

which was too bad   which came as a surprise to his fans

In 2011 the film *The King's Speech* won four Oscars, `1`. Although Colin Firth is a busy man, he came to the film festival, `2`. He even signed autographs while he was walking along the red carpet, `3`. But he only gave a short interview for a TV station. `4`.

G13 My children and I live in this house. It's ours.

Seiten 112–113

Possessivpronomen
Possessive pronouns

Woman: No, these are my last coins, please don't take them all.
Sheriff: Silly woman, they're **mine**. And whose is this house?
Woman: My children and I live here. It's ours.
Sheriff: You mean it was **yours**. Now it's **mine**. Get out!

Ein Possessivpronomen zeigt Besitz oder Zugehörigkeit an und kann für ein Nomen stehen, das nicht wiederholt werden soll.

– Du kennst schon Possessivbegleiter, die vor einem Nomen stehen. Zu jedem gibt es das entsprechende Possessivpronomen, das statt des bekannten Nomens verwendet wird.

Possessivbegleiter + Nomen	Possessivpronomen
Please don't take **my money**.	It's **mine**.
Take **your bow**, Robin.	It's **yours**.
Is this **his sword**?	Yes, it's **his**.
This looks like **her ring**.	Yes, it's **hers**.
This is **our house**.	It's **ours**.
Take **your arrows**, Robin.	They're **yours**.
Why don't we give them back **their land**?	It's **theirs**.

○ *Häufig werden Possessivpronomen als Antwort auf eine Frage mit* Whose …? *benutzt, z.B.:*
Whose house is this? – Mine.
Whose are those coins? – They aren't mine.

Test yourself

Complete the dialogue at the snack bar with the right possessive pronoun.

Assistant:	Who wanted the hamburger?
Tim:	It's `1` .
Cheryl:	No, it's not `2` , it's `3` . `4` is the cheeseburger.
Tim:	You're right. I'm sorry.
Assistant:	And who had the chips? I've got two plates.
Tim and Cheryl:	They're `5` .
Assistant:	And the salad?
Dad:	My son wanted it. It's `6` .

⟨Trailer 3⟩

G14　**She writes that she's in Dublin.**　Seiten 114–115

Die indirekte Rede mit Einführungsverb im Präsens
Indirect speech without backshift

Karen　　10:02 a.m.
Have you heard from Jessica?

Emily　　10:04 a.m.
Yes, she posted something on her blog a few minutes ago. **She writes that** she's in Dublin with her mum. **She says** her mum knows that place well.

Mit der indirekten Rede berichtest du, was jemand sagt oder vor kurzem gesagt hat.

Direkte Rede	Indirekte Rede
"I hope that you aren't too bored without me."	Jessica **writes (that)** she hopes that we aren't too bored without her.
"I'm in Dublin with my mum."	She **says (that)** she's in Dublin with her mum.
"Do you know what boxty is?"	She **asks if** we know what boxty is.

○ *Die indirekte Rede leitest du durch einen Einleitungssatz mit* say, write, tell sb, promise *oder* ask if *ein. Darauf folgt ein Nebensatz, der mit oder ohne* that *eingeleitet werden kann.* That *wird oft in der gesprochenen Sprache weggelassen.*

○ *Steht das Verb im Einleitungssatz im* simple present, *wird die Zeitform aus der direkten Rede in den Nebensatz der indirekten Rede übernommen.*

❗ *Anders als im Deutschen steht nach* that *kein Komma.*

○ *Pronomen, Zeit- und Ortsangaben ändern sich in der indirekten Rede:*
"**I** hope that **you** aren't bored without **me**."
→ She says **she** hopes **we** aren't bored without **her**.
"There's live music like in most pubs **here**."
→ She says there's live music like in most pubs **there**.
"**You** should look at **these** photos."
→ She tells us that **we** should look at **those** photos.
"**This** is **my** favourite type of food.
→ He writes that **that**'s **his** favourite type of food.

○ *Auch einige Verben ändern sich in der indirekten Rede:*
"I couldn't wait to **come** here."
→ She says that she couldn't wait to **go** there.
"I'll **take** the recipe home with me!"
→ She tells us that she'll **bring** the recipe home with her.

English summary

If you report what someone has just said or what you've just read, you use indirect speech. You start with a sentence in the simple present. What you report is in the same tense as in direct speech. Make sure you use the right pronouns and phrases of time and place.

"My mum and I went to a pub here. The musicians were playing Irish instruments."
→ *Jessica writes that she and her mum went to a pub there. She says the musicians were playing Irish instruments.*

Test yourself *Report what his woman says about greyhound[1] races.*

Reporter: Why do you bring your dog to greyhound races like this one in Dublin?
Woman: Well, my dog likes to move. The origin of the sport dates back centuries, and in my family this tradition has been passed down from one generation to the next.
Reporter: Do you agree that greyhounds are dangerous?
Woman: No, my dog is very nice. In fact, most owners treat their greyhounds as friends.
Reporter: So, you don't enter competitions to make money?
Woman: No, I don't. If he didn't enjoy racing so much, I'd stop right away.

Start: The woman says that she … because …

1 greyhound ['greɪhaʊnd] Windhund

Vocabulary

Im *Vocabulary* findest du alle wichtigen englischen Wörter und Redewendungen aus *Green Line* 3 G9. Sie stehen in der Reihenfolge, in der sie im Buch vorkommen. Diese Wörter solltest du lernen und anwenden können. Mager gedruckte Einträge musst du nicht auswendig lernen. Sie helfen dir, Texte zu verstehen. Weitere nützliche Wörter und Begriffe (z. B. Arbeitsanweisungen), die du nicht auswendig lernen musst, findest du ab S. 288. Auf das *Vocabulary* folgt das ***Dictionary (English – German, German – English)***. Falls du ein Wort vergessen hast, kannst du in diesen alphabetischen Wortlisten nachsehen.

Englische Begriffe wie *blog* oder *cartoon*, die du auch im Deutschen verwendest, stehen nicht im *Vocabulary*. Du kannst ihre Aussprache und Übersetzung aber im *Dictionary* nachschlagen. Das gleiche gilt für Wörter, die auf Englisch und Deutsch fast gleich geschrieben und ausgesprochen werden, wie z. B. *park* oder *partner*.

In den beiden Teilen ***Text and media smart*** musst du nicht alle neuen Vokabeln auswendig lernen. Die Wörter und Ausdrücke, die im *Vocabulary* aufgelistet sind, sind die wichtigsten und sie solltest du lernen und anwenden können. Alle anderen neuen Wörter aus *Text and media smart* kannst du ebenfalls hinten im *Dictionary* ab S. 233 nachschlagen.

Abkürzungen und Zeichen

pl	Mehrzahl (Plural)	↔	ist das Gegenteil von
sg	Einzahl (Singular)	→	ist verwandt mit
coll/ugs	umgangssprachlich	=	entspricht
5	In dieser Übung kommen die Wörter vor.	╪	entspricht nicht
!	Achtung!	*Fr./Lat.*	verwandte Wörter in anderen Fremdsprachen

---

Englische Laute

Konsonanten

[b]	**b**ed	[p]	**p**icture
[d]	**d**ay	[r]	**r**ed
[ð]	**th**e	[s]	**s**ix
[f]	**f**amily	[ʃ]	**sh**e
[g]	**g**o	[t]	**t**en
[ŋ]	morni**ng**	[tʃ]	**ch**air
[h]	**h**ouse	[v]	**v**ideo
[j]	**y**ou	[w]	**w**e, **o**ne
[k]	**c**an, mil**k**	[z]	ea**s**y
[l]	**l**etter	[ʒ]	revi**s**ion
[m]	**m**an	[dʒ]	**p**age
[n]	**n**o	[θ]	**th**ank you

Vokale

[ɑ:]	c**ar**	[i]	happ**y**
[æ]	**a**pple	[i:]	t**ea**cher
[e]	p**e**n	[ɒ]	d**o**g
[ə]	**a**gain	[ɔ:]	b**a**ll
[ɜ:]	g**ir**l	[ʊ]	b**oo**k
[ʌ]	b**u**t	[u]	J**a**nuary
[ɪ]	**i**t	[u:]	t**oo**, tw**o**

Doppellaute

[aɪ]	**I**, m**y**
[aʊ]	n**ow**, m**ou**se
[eɪ]	n**a**me, th**ey**
[eə]	th**ere**, p**air**
[ɪə]	h**ere**, id**ea**
[əʊ]	hell**o**
[ɔɪ]	b**oy**
[ʊə]	s**ure**

[:]	der vorangehende Laut ist lang, z. B. *you* [ju:]	[']	die folgende Silbe trägt den Hauptakzent
[‿]	der Bindebogen zeigt, dass zwei Wörter in der Aussprache verbunden werden	[ˌ]	die folgende Silbe trägt den Nebenakzent

Unit 1 Find your place

Check-in

personality [ˌpɜːsnˈælətɪ]	Persönlichkeit; Charakter	*personality* → person
to **agree** [əˈgriː]	zustimmen; einer Meinung sein; sich einigen	Sorry, I don't *agree*.
to **disagree** [ˌdɪsəˈgriː]	anderer Meinung sein; nicht einverstanden sein	*to disagree* ↔ to agree
to **compromise** [ˈkɒmprəmaɪz]	einen Kompromiss eingehen	It isn't always easy to *compromise*.
smart type [ˈsmɑːt ˌtaɪp]	Lerntyp; Intelligenztyp	What *smart type* are you? Are you more nature smart or more people smart?
smart [smɑːt]	schlau; klug; intelligent	*smart* ↔ stupid
body [ˈbɒdi]	Körper	Hands, legs, feet etc. are parts of the *body*.
self [self]	das Selbst	A *self* smart person knows what he/she is good (or not so good) at.
logic [ˈlɒdʒɪk]	Logik	Who is *logic* smart in this class?
saying [ˈseɪɪŋ]	Sprichwort; Redensart	"When the cat's away, the mice will play" is an English *saying*.
to **judge** [dʒʌdʒ]	beurteilen; bewerten	Never *judge* people by their clothes.
cover [ˈkʌvə]	Titelseite; Einband; Cover	I like the *cover* of this book. It looks interesting and I want to read the book.
It doesn't matter. [ɪt ˌdʌznt ˈmætə]	es spielt keine Rolle; das macht nichts; das ist nicht wichtig	*It doesn't matter* if you win or lose!
practice [ˈpræktɪs]	Übung; Training	= training *practice* → to practise
call-in [ˈkɔːlɪn]	*Sendung, bei der sich das Publikum telefonisch beteiligen kann*	My father often takes part in radio *call-ins*.
imagination [ɪˌmædʒɪˈneɪʃn]	Fantasie; Vorstellungskraft	*imagination* → to imagine *Fr.* imagination (f)
to **communicate** [kəˈmjuːnɪkeɪt]	kommunizieren; sich verständigen	An easy way to *communicate* with people is to speak to them. *Lat.* communicare
to **compete (with)** [kəmˈpiːt (wɪð)]	konkurrieren (mit); sich messen (mit); in Wettbewerb treten (mit)	*to compete (with)* → competition *Lat.* competere
imaginative [ɪˈmædʒɪnətɪv]	einfallsreich; fantasievoll	*imaginative* → imagination → to imagine
doubt [daʊt]	Zweifel	Claire isn't sure if she's made the right choice. She has *doubts*.
themselves [ðəmˈselvz]	sie (selbst); sich (selbst); selbst; selber	The kids didn't want any help. They wanted to solve the problem *themselves*.
to **learn about, learnt about, learnt about** [ˈlɜːn əˌbaʊt; ˈlɜːnt əˌbaʊt; ˈlɜːnt əˌbaʊt]	erfahren über	What did they *learn about* themselves?

Station 1: How to be an influencer

environmental issues [ɪnˌvaɪrnməntl 'ɪʃuːz]	Umweltprobleme	*environmental issues* → environment
technical ['teknɪkl]	technisch; fachlich; hand-werklich	She's really interested in *technical* things.
topic ['tɒpɪk]	Thema	The *topic* we want to discuss today is the environment.
to **focus (on)** ['fəʊkəs (ˌɒn)]	sich konzentrieren (auf)	Let's *focus on* the most important points.
channel ['tʃænl]	Kanal *(TV)*; Programm *(Radio)*	What's your favourite TV *channel*?
to **be concerned (about)** [bɪ kən'sɜːnd (ˌəˌbaʊt)]	besorgt sein (um); beunruhigt sein (wegen)	Some people are very *concerned about* the environment.
climate change ['klaɪmət ˌtʃeɪndʒ]	Klimawandel	*Climate change* is causing more and more problems in the world.
to **produce** [prə'djuːs]	produzieren; erzeugen; herstellen	We can *produce* more if we work together.
waste [weɪst]	Abfall; Müll; Verschwendung	We all have to produce less *waste*.
to **attract** [ə'trækt]	anziehen; anlocken	He *attracts* lots of followers to his channel. *to attract* → attraction
to **trust** [trʌst]	vertrauen	I know what I'm doing. Please *trust* me.
especially [ɪ'speʃli]	besonders; vor allem	*especially* → special
to **be involved** [bɪ ɪn'vɒlvd]	beteiligt sein; involviert sein	It sometimes gets more difficult when money *is involved*.
company ['kʌmpəni]	Gesellschaft; Firma; Unter-nehmen	My dad works for an American *company*.
to **recommend** [ˌrekə'mend]	empfehlen	You did a good job. I will *recommend* you on my website.
product ['prɒdʌkt]	Produkt; Erzeugnis	! Achtung Schreibung und Aussprache *product* → to produce
to **make sure, made sure, made sure** [ˌmeɪk 'ʃɔː; ˌmeɪd 'ʃɔː; ˌmeɪd 'ʃɔː]	sichergehen; achten auf	*Make sure* you don't share too much personal information on social media.
Thank you very much! [ˌθæŋk ju veri 'mʌtʃ]	Vielen Dank!; Herzlichen Dank!	*Thank you very much* for your help!
1 to **subscribe** [səb'skraɪb]	abonnieren	I've *subscribed* to a a a new online channel.
role model ['rəʊl ˌmɒdl]	Vorbild	*Role models* are very important to young people.
3 **tap** [tæp]	Wasserhahn	The *tap* is broken. We must call a plumber.
to **turn down** [ˌtɜːn 'daʊn]	abdrehen; niedriger stellen	It's too loud. Please *turn down* the music.
heating ['hiːtɪŋ]	Heizung	Our new house has modern *heating*.
bin [bɪn]	Mülleimer; Abfalleimer; Mülltonne	There's a special *bin* for paper in our classroom.
rainwater ['reɪnˌwɔːtə]	Regenwasser	*rainwater* → to rain
to **flush** [flʌʃ]	spülen; die Wasserspülung betätigen	Don't forget to *flush* the toilet!
4 **rain** [reɪn]	Regen	*rain* → to rain

Station 2: They wouldn't worry if they didn't care!

millionaire [ˌmɪljə'neə]	Millionär/-in	! Achtung Schreibung
rich [rɪtʃ]	reich	*Fr.* riche
age [eɪdʒ]	Alter; Zeitalter	at the *age* of 11 = when he was 11
to **design** [dɪ'zaɪn]	entwerfen; gestalten	Companies will pay me to *design* their websites.
success [sək'ses]	Erfolg	He had no *success* in his career.
to **be stressed out** [bi ˌstrest 'aʊt]	völlig gestresst sein	Why are you so *stressed out*? Just relax.
a million [ə 'mɪljən]	Million	*a million* → millionaire
lead part [ˌli:d 'pɑːt]	Hauptrolle	Hasn't he had the *lead part* in lots of films?
backing dancer ['bækɪŋ ˌdɑːnsə]	Backgroundtänzer/-in	You can be a *backing dancer*.
lead dancer ['li:d ˌdɑːnsə]	Vortänzer/-in	Jay wanted to be the *lead dancer* in the show.
to **grow, grew, grown** [grəʊ; gru:; grəʊn]	wachsen; anbauen; züchten	Money doesn't *grow* on trees.
to **want sb to do sth** [ˌwɒnt tə 'du:]	wollen, dass jmd. etw. tut	My parents always *want me to focus on* school.
mark [mɑːk]	Note	What was your worst *mark* in English?
laid-back [leɪd'bæk]	entspannt; locker	= very relaxed
to **drop out (of)** [drɒp 'aʊt (ˌəv)]	abbrechen; ausscheiden; aussteigen	She *dropped out of* school when she was 14. = She didn't finish school.
modelling ['mɒdəlɪŋ]	Modeln	Shahid does *modelling* just for fun.
to **rely (on)** [rɪ'laɪ (ˌɒn)]	sich verlassen (auf); vertrauen (auf)	Can I *rely on* you?
looks *(pl)* [lʊks]	Aussehen	If you want to be a model, you need good *looks*.
to **study** ['stʌdi]	lernen; studieren	If you *study* a subject, you learn a lot about it.
career [kə'rɪə]	Beruf; Laufbahn; Karriere	I'm studying for a *career* in IT.
7	**in ... shoes** [ɪn 'ʃu:z]	an ... Stelle	I wouldn't want to be *in his shoes*.
	to **give up, gave up, given up** [ˌgɪv 'ʌp; ˌgeɪv 'ʌp; ˌgɪvn 'ʌp]	aufgeben	I can't play this game. I *give up*.
9	**successful** [sək'sesfl]	erfolgreich	*successful* → success
10	**audition** [ɔː'dɪʃn]	Vorsprechen; Vorsingen; Vortanzen	She didn't get the lead part in the dance show because her *audition* didn't go well.
11	**ugly** ['ʌgli]	hässlich; scheußlich; übel	*ugly* ↔ beautiful
	comfortable ['kʌmftəbl]	bequem; komfortabel	This sofa is really *comfortable*.
	dress [dres]	Kleid	My sister doesn't like *dresses*. She only wears jeans.
	trainer ['treɪnə]	Turnschuh	I like to wear *trainers* every day, not only for sport.
	to **perform** [pə'fɔːm]	auftreten; etw. vorführen; aufführen; vortragen; spielen	I *performed* better at my last audition.

Station 3: You have to push yourself

to **push oneself** ['pʊʃ wʌnˌself]	sich alles abverlangen; sich Mühe geben	Olivia's parents don't push her. She *pushes herself*.
messy ['mesi]	unordentlich	Lucy must tidy up her room because it's *messy*.
bossy ['bɒsi]	bestimmend; rechthaberisch; herrisch	My brother always tells me what to do. He's really *bossy*.
recorder [rɪ'kɔːdə]	Flöte	Lucy plays the *recorder*.
exactly [ɪg'zæktli]	genau	I don't understand. What *exactly* do you mean? *Lat.* exactus/-a/-um
to **enjoy oneself** [ɪn'dʒɔɪ]	Spaß haben; sich amüsieren	= to have a good time
to **decide (on)** [dɪ'saɪd (ˌɒn)]	(sich) entscheiden (für)	Lucy can't *decide on* a new hobby.
to **be saved by the bell** [bi 'seɪvd baɪ ðə ˌbel]	noch mal Glück haben	We nearly had a fight, but we *were saved by the bell*.
to **give sb funny looks** [ˌgɪv fʌni 'lʊks]	jmdn. schief anschauen; jmdn. komisch anschauen	Olivia *is giving* Lucy *funny looks*.
each other [ˌiːtʃ'ʌðə]	einander; sich; sich gegenseitig	We looked at *each other* and laughed.

Reflexive pronouns

myself	**I** made this cake **myself**.
yourself	Did **you** write this text **yourself**?
herself	**She** took photos of **herself** on holiday.
himself	**He** planned the tutorial **himself**.
itself	My phone is on. **It** turned **itself** on.
ourselves	**We** wrote the article for the website **ourselves**.
yourselves	Did **you** watch **yourselves** on TV last night?
themselves	The kids have solved the problem. **They** solved it **themselves**.

funny ['fʌni]	komisch; merkwürdig; seltsam	= strange
to **behave** [bɪ'heɪv]	sich benehmen; sich verhalten	You're silly! You *behave* like a little child.
opinion [ə'pɪnjən]	Meinung; Ansicht; Einstellung	In my *opinion* … = I think … *Lat.* opinio (f)
What's up? [ˌwɒts'ʌp]	Was ist los?	Why are you shouting at each other? *What's up?*
to **be in charge (of)** [bi ˌɪn 'tʃɑːdʒ (ˌəv)]	zuständig sein (für); die Verantwortung tragen (für)	Who *is in charge of* the food for the party?
12	to **react** [rɪ'ækt]	reagieren	*to react* → reaction
14	to **be hard on sb** [bi 'hɑːd ˌɒn]	streng mit jmdm. sein	Don't *be* so *hard on him*.
	Stay the way you are. [ˌsteɪ ðə weɪ ju 'ɑː]	Bleib wie du bist.	Don't change. *Stay the way you are.*

Miss [mɪs]	Fräulein *(veraltete Anrede)*	*Miss* Perfect – Mr Perfect
17 **per cent** [pə ˈsent]	Prozent	60 *per cent* of 10 students = 6 students

Skills: How to compromise

to **have a point** [ˌhæv ə ˈpɔɪnt]	nicht ganz Unrecht haben	Yes, you *have a point*. I've never thought about it like that.
1 **necessary** [ˈnesəsri]	nötig; notwendig; erforderlich	I don't think that's *necessary*.
possible [ˈpɒsəbl]	möglich	It's not always *possible* to have it all.
simple [ˈsɪmpl]	einfach; simpel	*simple* ↔ difficult *Fr.* simple
to **meet halfway** [ˌmiːt hɑːfˈweɪ]	sich auf halbem Weg treffen	I don't agree! But I don't want to fight, so let's *meet halfway*.
I don't mind (+ …*ing*) [ˌaɪ dəʊnt ˈmaɪnd]	Ich habe nichts dagegen (zu …); Mir macht es nichts aus (zu …)	*I don't mind doing* that.

How to compromise

Asking for/Giving an opinion:
What do you think about …?
How do you feel about …?
What's your opinion on …?
I think …
In my opinion …

Making a suggestion:
Why don't we …?
If we did it this way, we could …
I've got an idea. Can we …?
It would be better to …

Agreeing:
Yes, we should do that.
No, I don't mind doing that.
I agree with you.
Yes, you're right.

Disagreeing:
I don't think that's a good idea.
You've got a point, but …
I don't think we can do that.
I disagree.
I think you're wrong there.
I don't think you're right.

Finding a compromise:
Can we meet halfway?
The compromise (between the two
   suggestions) is …

Nach einer Meinung fragen/Seine Meinung sagen:
Was denkst du über …?
Was hältst du von …?
Wie ist deine Meinung zu …?
Ich glaube/denke …
Meiner Meinung nach …

Einen Vorschlag machen:
Warum machen/… wir nicht …?
Wenn wir es so machen würden, dann könnten wir …
Ich habe eine Idee. Können wir …?
Es wäre besser, wenn wir …

Zustimmen:
Ja, das sollten wir tun.
Nein, es macht mir nichts aus, das zu tun.
Ich stimme dir zu.
Ja, du hast recht.

Nicht zustimmen:
Ich halte das für keine gute Idee.
Da hast du recht, aber …
Ich glaube nicht, dass wir das machen können.
Da bin ich anderer Meinung.
Ich glaube, du liegst hier falsch.
Ich glaube nicht, dass du recht hast.

Einen Kompromiss finden:
Können wir uns in der Mitte treffen?
Der Kompromiss (zwischen den beiden Vorschlägen)
   lautet …

You want to go to the cinema and the film ends at nine in the evening. Your parents think that's too late.
Discuss and find a compromise.

2	**misunderstood** [ˌmɪsʌndəˈstʊd]	missverstanden	Every time I talk to my parents I feel *misunderstood*.
	to **end** [end]	enden; beenden	*to end* ↔ to start *to end* → end
	decision [dɪˈsɪʒn]	Entscheidung	*decision* → to decide
3	**conflict** [ˈkɒnflɪkt]	Konflikt; Auseinandersetzung	**!** Achtung Schreibung und Aussprache
	to **blame** [bleɪm]	verantwortlich machen; beschuldigen	Don't *blame* me. It's not my fault. **!** *to blame* ≠ blamieren

Unit task: Solving a conflict

storyboard [ˈstɔːrɪbɔːd]	Szenenbuch; Storyboard	Let's make a *storyboard* to help us.
stud [stʌd]	Stecker	What do you think of nose *studs*?
facial expression [ˌfeɪʃl ɪkˈspreʃn]	Gesichtsausdruck	The *facial expression* of people sometimes tells you more than what they say.
body language [ˈbɒdi ˌlæŋgwɪdʒ]	Körpersprache	*body language* → body

Story: Hang out with us instead!

to **hang out (with)**, **hung out (with)**, **hung out (with)** *(infml)* [ˌhæŋ ˈaʊt (wɪð); ˌhʌŋ ˈaʊt (wɪð); ˌhʌŋ ˈaʊt (wɪð)]	rumhängen (mit); sich herumtreiben (mit)	When you *hang out* with friends, you meet them and spend time with them.
instead [ɪnˈsted]	stattdessen	If the weather is too cold for swimming, we could go for a walk *instead*.
to **get into trouble** [ˌget ˌɪntə ˈtrʌbl]	in Schwierigkeiten geraten	I *got into trouble* with my parents when I was late.
to **be fed up (with)** [bi fed ˈʌp (wɪð)]	sauer sein (auf); die Nase voll haben (von)	Jay *was fed up* with his friends.
argument [ˈɑːɡjəmənt]	Auseinandersetzung; Streit	= fight The boys didn't agree with each other. They had a big *argument*.
these days [ˌðiːz ˈdeɪz]	heute; heutzutage; zurzeit	*these days* ↔ in the past
to **be allowed to (do sth)** [bi ˌəˈlaʊd tə]	dürfen	Students *aren't allowed to* use mobiles at school.
to **be grounded** [bi ˈɡraʊndɪd]	Hausarrest haben	Jay *was grounded* for five days.
to **put on**, **put on**, **put on** [ˌpʊt ˈɒn; ˌpʊt ˈɒn; ˌpʊt ˈɒn]	anziehen	We're going out now. *Put on* your shoes, please.
freedom *(no pl)* [ˈfriːdəm]	Freiheit; Unabhängigkeit	*freedom* → free
in-crowd [ˈɪnkraʊd]	die Angesagten; die Beliebten; Szene	Finn and Max are part of the *in-crowd*.

blond [blɒnd]	blond	She's *blond*. Her hair is almost yellow.
the high street [ðə ˈhaɪ ˌstriːt]	die Haupteinkaufsstraße	Let's go to *the high street* for some burgers.
		! In größeren Städten wie London gibt es in jedem Viertel eine *high street*.
bloke *(fam)* [bləʊk]	Typ *(ugs.)*	Jay thinks that Finn and Max are cool *blokes*.
to be able to (do sth) [bɪ ˈeɪbl tə]	fähig sein zu; können; dürfen	When my grandma lived in the next town, we *were able to* see her often. Now she lives in another town.
overnight [ˌəʊvəˈnaɪt]	über Nacht	Shahid won't be back until tomorrow. He's got an *overnight* modelling job.
back [bæk]	Rücken; Rückseite	I must sit down. My *back* is really painful.
usual [ˈjuːʒl]	üblich	*usual* → usually
to treat [triːt]	behandeln	If you don't *treat* your dog right, you'll have trouble with it.
to ignore [ɪgˈnɔː]	ignorieren; außer Acht lassen	If you don't look at sth and don't listen to it, even if you know it's there, you *ignore* it.
pretty [ˈprɪti]	hübsch	*pretty* ↔ ugly
to come up to sb, came up to, come up to [kʌmˈʌp tə; keɪmˈʌp tə; kʌmˈʌp tə]	auf jmdn. zukommen	The girls *came up to* Jay. = The girls walked towards Jay.
poor [pɔː; pʊə]	arm	*poor* ↔ rich
mummy [ˈmʌmi]	Mama; Mami; Mutti	*mummy* → mum
piece of junk [ˌpiːs əv ˈdʒʌŋk]	Stück Schrott	After the party Shahid's laptop was a *piece of junk*.
anger *(no pl)* [ˈæŋgə]	Zorn; Wut	Jay was white with *anger*! *anger* → angry
3 **peer pressure** [ˈpɪə ˌpreʃə]	Gruppenzwang	*Peer pressure* can be very hard for some teenagers.
to fit in [ˌfɪtˈɪn]	dazupassen; sich einfügen	Not everyone *fits in* with everyone else.
excitement *(no pl)* [ɪkˈsaɪtmənt]	Aufregung	*excitement* → excited → exciting
confused [kənˈfjuːzd]	verwirrt; wirr; konfus	What happened? Why is Jay so *confused*?
honest [ˈɒnɪst]	ehrlich	Don't lie. Be *honest*! *Lat.* honestus
4 **turning point** [ˈtɜːnɪŋ ˌpɔɪnt]	Wendepunkt	The *turning point* in the story was very surprising.

Action UK! When Sean came to visit

1 **to tease sb** [tiːz]	jmdn. aufziehen; jmdn. hänseln; jmdn. ärgern	Olivia sometimes *teases* Lucy.
2 **sense of humour** *(no pl)* [ˌsens əv ˈhjuːmə]	Sinn für Humor	She's funny – everyone says that she's got a good *sense of humour*.
to feel sorry for, felt sorry for, felt sorry for [ˌfiːl ˈsɒri fɔː; felt ˈsɒri fɔː; felt ˈsɒri fɔː]	Mitleid haben mit; bedauern	I *felt sorry for* him. = Er hat mir leid getan.

optimistic [ˌɒptɪˈmɪstɪk]	optimistisch	Everything will be fine, let's be *optimistic*.
to **cheer sb up** [ˌtʃɪərˈʌp]	jmdn. aufheitern	Are you sad? What can I do to *cheer you up*?
show-off [ˈʃəʊˌɒf]	Angeber/-in	*show-off* → to show off
to **apologise** [əˈpɒlədʒaɪz]	sich entschuldigen	= to say sorry
to **delete** [dɪˈliːt]	löschen	They *deleted* all the music on Shahid's laptop.
wall [wɔːl]	*hier:* Online-Pinnwand	They deleted the messages on the *wall*.
account settings [əˈkaʊnt ˌsetɪŋz]	Profileinstellungen	Check your *account settings* for your social network carefully.
bench [benʃ]	Bank; Sitzbank	Let's sit down on this *bench*.
to **work out** [ˌwɜːkˈaʊt]	funktionieren; klappen	How did things *work out* in the end?

Describing different personalities

to **have a sense of humour**	(einen Sinn für) Humor haben
to **be a show-off**	angeberisch sein
to **be creative/confident/ honest/funny/bossy/ messy/laid-back/ optimistic/smart**	kreativ/selbstsicher/selbstbewusst/ ehrlich/lustig/rechthaberisch/ unordentlich/locker/optimistisch/ klug sein
to **never give up**	nie aufgeben
to **always get into trouble**	immer in Schwierigkeiten geraten
to **start arguments**	Streit anfangen
to **push oneself**	sich alles abverlangen; sich Mühe geben
to **follow the crowd**	der Masse folgen
to **compare oneself with**	sich vergleichen mit
to **be good with/at**	gut sein bei/in
…	…

Describe your friend's personality.

Check-out

1	**founder** [ˈfaʊndə]	Gründer/-in	David Karp was the *founder* of Tumblr.
	to **develop** [dɪˈveləp]	(sich) entwickeln	He *developed* a social media website.
	a billion [ə ˈbɪliən]	Milliarde	= 1,000,000,000
2	to **pay attention, paid attention, paid attention** [ˌpeɪ əˈtenʃn; ˌpeɪd əˈtenʃn; ˌpeɪd əˈtenʃn]	aufmerksam sein; aufpassen; jmdn./etw. beachten	You have to *pay attention* at school.
4	**underground** [ˈʌndəgraʊnd]	U-Bahn	Let's go by *underground*.

Aufgabe **Sounds and spelling**
Laute und Rechtschreibung

3/25 **a)** *Which word in each group has a different sound? Compare your answers with the audio.*

1. lose | shoes | does | use
2. follow | tiptoe | know | now
3. nice | practice | price | advice

4. care | hair | are | share
5. everyone | sun | done | phone
6. idea | sea | she | tree

3/26 **b)** *Listen to these new words. Repeat them, write them down and put them in the right group 1–6 in a). You can use a dictionary for help.*

lice   bunny   hare   flea   doe   kangaroos

Text and media smart 1 Songs and poems

Check-in

songwriter [ˈsɒŋˌraɪtə]	Liedermacher/-in; Songschreiber/-in	*songwriter* → song	
poet [ˈpəʊɪt]	Dichter/-in	A *poet* writes poems.	
1	**concert** [ˈkɒnsət]	Konzert	! Achtung Schreibung und Aussprache
	shape poem [ˈʃeɪp ˌpəʊɪm]	Formgedicht; Gestaltgedicht	= a certain kind of poem
	nursery rhyme [ˈnɜːsri ˌraɪm]	Kinderreim; Kinderlied	What was your favourite *nursery rhyme* when you were little?
	poetry [ˈpəʊɪtri]	Lyrik; Poesie; Dichtung; Gedichte	*poetry* → poet → poem
	to **get ready** [ˌget ˈredi]	sich vorbereiten; sich fertig machen	I listen to music while I'*m getting ready* for school.
	to **entertain sb** [ˌentəˈteɪn]	jmdn. unterhalten; jmdn. beschäftigen	Actors *entertain* their audience.
	literature [ˈlɪtrətʃə]	Literatur	! Achtung Schreibung und Aussprache
2	**emotion** [ɪˈməʊʃn]	Gefühl; Emotion	Some people like to show their *emotions*, some people don't.
	occasion [əˈkeɪʒn]	Anlass; Ereignis; Gelegenheit	A birthday is a special *occasion*.

Station 1: Say it with a song

3	**impression** [ɪmˈpreʃn]	Eindruck; Impression	What is your *impression* of the poem? What do you think of it?
	to **sign** [saɪn]	unterschreiben; unterzeichnen	Please *sign* the letter. *Fr.* signer; *Lat.* signare

laugh [lɑːf]	Lachen	*laugh* → to laugh
you've got my back [bæk]	du stehst hinter mir	Whatever happens, *you've got my back*.
shell [ʃel]	Schale; Muschel	I can't open the *shell* of this nut.
ground [graʊnd]	Boden; Erdboden	You help me to keep my feet on the *ground*.
to **be out of chances** [bi ˌaʊt̬ əv ˈtʃɑːnsɪz]	keine Chance mehr haben	This is the end. I'*m out of chances*.
to **hang on** [ˌhæŋ ˈɒn]	warten; durchhalten	*to hang on* = to wait
ups and downs [ˌʌps ̬ən ˈdaʊnz]	Höhen und Tiefen	Life has lots of *ups and downs*.
to **pretend** [prɪˈtend]	tun als ob; vortäuschen	Let's *pretend* to be on holiday.
5	to **escape** [ɪˈskeɪp]	fliehen; entfliehen; flüchten; entkommen	= to run away from sth or sb
to **free** [friː]	befreien; freilassen	They cut the net and *freed* all the birds.
cage [keɪdʒ]	Käfig	The bird got out of the *cage*.
lie [laɪ]	Lüge	*lie* → to lie
ear [ɪə]	Ohr	I can't hear you very well. My *ears* are blocked.
closed [kləʊzd]	geschlossen; zu	*closed* ↔ open *closed* → to close
6	**catchy** [ˈkætʃi]	eingängig; einprägsam	If a song is *catchy*, it's easy to remember.
chorus [ˈkɔːrəs]	Refrain	You sing the *chorus* three times in this song.
to **repeat** [rɪˈpiːt]	wiederholen	Can you *repeat* that, please? = Can you say that again, please?
to **emphasize** [ˈemfəsaɪz]	betonen; hervorheben	We try to *emphasize* the positive aspects of using social networks.
to **keep one's feet or hands still** [ˌkiːp wʌnz ˈfiːt̬ ɔː ˈhændz stɪl]	die Beine und Hände ruhig halten	My brother can't *keep his feet and hands still*!
to **sing along, sang along, sung along** [ˌsɪŋ əˈlɒŋ; ˌsæŋ əˈlɒŋ; ˌsʌŋ əˈlɒŋ]	mitsingen	I always *sing along* to my favourite songs.
to **get sth out of one's head** [get ˌaʊt̬ əv wʌnz ˈhed]	etw. aus dem Kopf bekommen; von einem Gedanken loskommen	The song is really catchy. I can't *get it out of my head*.
7	**effect** [ɪˈfekt]	Effekt; Wirkung	You should always think of the *effects* of your actions before you do something. *Fr.* effet *(m)*
rhythm [ˈrɪðm]	Rhythmus	I like music with a fast *rhythm*.
8	**rhythmic** [ˈrɪðmɪk]	rhythmisch; gleichmäßig	This song has a great *rhythmic* background. *rhythmic* → rhythm
beat [biːt]	Takt; Schlag	Songs are catchy if they have a rhythmic *beat*.

| 10 | **terms** [tɜːmz] | Bestimmungen; Bedingungen | Always read the *terms* on a website before you download or post something. |
| | **legal** ['liːgl] | legal; rechtlich; Rechts- | *Lat.* lex, legis *(f)* |

Station 2: Say it with a poem

11	**bookshop** ['bʊkʃɒp]	Buchhandlung	Our *bookshop* has got books and CDs, but it hasn't got magazines.
	to **prefer** [prɪ'fɜː]	vorziehen; bevorzugen	= to like more/better *Fr.* préférer
	to **have in common** [ˌhæv ɪn 'kɒmən]	gemein haben	Friends usually *have* a lot *in common*. *to have in common* ↔ to be different
12	**trust** [trʌst]	Vertrauen	*trust* → to trust
	second ['seknd]	Sekunde	There are sixty *seconds* in a minute.
	to **stick, stuck, stuck** [stɪk; stʌk; stʌk]	kleben; stecken	*Stick* the pictures on your poster.
	glue [gluː]	Klebstoff	The pictures won't stick. You'll have to use more *glue*.
	bright [braɪt]	leuchtend; strahlend; hell	In summer the sun is very *bright*.
	responsibility [rɪˌspɒnsə'bɪləti]	Verantwortung	I have a lot of *responsibility* in my job.
	cleverness ['klevənəs]	Schlauheit; Klugheit; Cleverness	*cleverness* → clever
	stranger ['streɪndʒə]	Fremde/-r	I don't know that man – he's a *stranger*.
	magnet ['mægnət]	Magnet	! Achtung Aussprache
	no matter [nəʊ 'mætə]	egal; ganz gleich	*No matter* what the problem is, just call me if you need my help.

Words for talking about songs and poems

acrostic	Akrostichon	rhyme	Reim
author	Autor/-in	rhyme scheme	Reimschema
beat	Takt; Schlag	rhythm; rhythmic	Rhythmus; rhythmisch
chorus	Refrain	simile	Vergleich; Gleichnis
metaphor	Metapher; bildhafte Sprache	stanza	Strophe
poetry	Lyrik; Poesie; Dichtung; Gedichte	syllable	Silbe
repetition	Wiederholung	verse	Vers; Strophe

	to **last** [lɑːst]	dauern; andauern; anhalten	Our friendship will *last* forever. = We'll stay friends forever.
	to **remind (sb of sth/sb)** [rɪ'maɪnd (ˌəv)]	(jmdn. an etw./jmdn.) erinnern	! I didn't remember Dad's birthday. Mum *reminded* me.
13	**evidence** *(no pl)* ['evɪdns]	Beweis; Beleg; Beweismaterial	The witness gave the police good *evidence*.

	to **leave out** [ˌliːvˈaʊt]	weglassen; auslassen	He didn't *leave out* any details.
14	**common** [ˈkɒmən]	üblich; gewöhnlich; (weit) verbreitet; gebräuchlich	CDs aren't *common* any more.
	to **rhyme** [raɪm]	(sich) reimen	'Bee' *rhymes* with 'sea'.
16	**one another** [ˌwʌn_əˈnʌðə]	einander; gegenseitig	= each other

Across cultures 1 Reacting to a new situation

1	**plate** [pleɪt]	Teller	There's too much food on the *plate*.
	mug [mʌg]	Becher	I like to drink tea from a *mug*.
	cup [kʌp]	Tasse	Put the *cups* into the cupboard, please.
	bread roll [ˌbred ˈrəʊl]	Brötchen	*bread roll* → bread
	butter [ˈbʌtə]	Butter	milk – cheese – *butter*
	marmalade [ˈmɑːməleɪd]	Orangenmarmelade	! *marmalade* = Orangenmarmelade jam = Marmelade; Konfitüre
	honey [ˈhʌni]	Honig	We get *honey* from bees.
	muesli [ˈmjuːzli]	Müsli	I always eat *muesli* on Sundays.
	ham [hæm]	Schinken	I'd like a sandwich. – With cheese and tomato? Or *ham*?
	sausage [ˈsɒsɪdʒ]	Wurst; Bratwurst	In Britain people often eat *sausages* for breakfast.
3	**host family** [ˈhəʊst ˌfæmli]	Gastfamilie	While I'm in Greenwich, I'll be at the Jacksons' house. The Jacksons are my *host family*.
	exchange student [ɪksˈtʃeɪndʒ ˌstjuːdnt]	Austauschschüler/-in	Our *exchange student* comes from England and wants to learn German.
	unfamiliar [ˌʌnfəˈmɪliə]	nicht vertraut; unbekannt	Staying with a host family is an *unfamiliar* situation for Brad.
4	**appropriate** [əˈprəʊpriət]	angemessen	Don't do that! It's not *appropriate* in a situation like this.
	to **make sb angry** [meɪk ˈæŋgri]	jmdn. wütend machen; jmdn. verärgern	Don't *make me angry*!
	to **upset, upset, upset** [ʌpˈset; ʌpˈset; ʌpˈset]	aus der Fassung bringen	My friends *upset* me. They made me really angry.
	gratitude [ˈgrætɪtjuːd]	Dankbarkeit	If you want to say thank you to somebody, you can show your *gratitude* in different ways.
	impolite [ˌɪmpˈlaɪt]	unhöflich	*impolite* ↔ polite
	hot [hɒt]	heiß	*hot* ↔ cold
	this early [ˈðɪs ˌɜːli]	so früh	Do you really have to go home *this early*?
	that much [ðæt ˈmʌtʃ]	so viel	Sorry, I can't eat *that much* in the morning.
	to **be used to** [bi ˈjuːs_tə]	gewöhnt sein an; gewohnt sein	I'm not *used to* drinking coffee.

Unit 2 Let's go to Scotland!

Check-in

1	**historic** [hɪˈstɒrɪk]	historisch	*historic* → history
	traditional [trəˈdɪʃnl]	traditionell	*traditional* → tradition
2	to **be like sb/sth** [bi ˈlaɪk]	wie jmd./etw. sein	Please tell me more about your school. What *is* it *like*?
3	**haggis** [ˈhægɪs]	Haggis *(schottisches Gericht aus in einem Schafsmagen gekochten Schafsinnereien und Haferschrot)*	I ate *haggis* in Scotland. I liked it.
	tartan [ˈtɑːtn]	Schottenkaro *(bestimmtes Muster eines Clans)*; karierter Schottenstoff	Different families have *tartans* of different colours, e. g. with a red, blue or green background.
	kilt [kɪlt]	Kilt; Schottenrock	= a traditional skirt for Scottish men
	bagpipes *(pl)* [ˈbægpaɪps]	Dudelsack	= a Scottish instrument
	loch [lɒx; lɒk]	See *(in Schottland)*	! Achtung Aussprache: In Schottland wird das „ch" in *loch* wie ein deutsches „ch" ausgesprochen.

Typically Scottish

the **Scottish flag**

bagpipes

a **thistle**

a **kilt**

tartan

haggis

Station 1: Is that made with meat?

meat *(no pl)* [miːt]	Fleisch	Holly doesn't eat *meat*.
son [sʌn]	Sohn	Ethan is the *son* of Gwen's uncle and aunt.

large [lɑːdʒ]	groß; riesig	London is one of the *largest* cities in Europe.
vegetable ['vedʒtəbl]	Gemüse	Carrots are *vegetables*.
vegetarian [ˌvedʒɪ'teəriən]	Vegetarier/-in	*Vegetarians* don't eat meat.
thousands of ['θaʊzndz ̩əv]	tausende (von)	*Thousands of* people live in Greenwich.
to **pull down** [ˌpʊl ̩'daʊn]	abreißen	They *pulled down* the house and built a new one.
musical ['mjuːzɪkl]	musikalisch; Musik-	*musical* → music
shipbuilding ['ʃɪpbɪldɪŋ]	Schiffsbau	*shipbuilding* → ship
industry ['ɪndəstri]	Industrie; Branche; Gewerbe	Scotland still has a shipbuilding *industry*. **!** Achtung Schreibung und Aussprache
3 **midnight** ['mɪdnaɪt]	Mitternacht	= twelve o'clock at night
to **set off fireworks** [set ̩ɒf 'faɪəwɜːks]	ein Feuerwerk zünden	At midnight we *set off* lots of *fireworks*.
bun [bʌn]	Brötchen; Gebäckstück	= bread roll
coal [kəʊl]	Kohle	They put more *coal* on the fire.
government ['gʌvnmənt]	Regierung	The people of a country vote for their *government*.
to **grant** [grɑːnt]	gewähren; zusprechen; geben	The government *grants* the Scottish people two days holiday every year.
4 **Scot** [skɒt]	Schotte/Schottin	*Scot* → Scottish → Scotland
invention [ɪn'venʃn]	Erfindung	Lots of *inventions* came from Scotland.
discovery [dɪ'skʌvri]	Entdeckung	*discovery* → to discover
by [baɪ]	von	I bought a CD *by* Beyoncé.
to **clone** [kləʊn]	klonen	It's possible to *clone* animals.
scientist ['saɪəntɪst]	Wissenschaftler/-in	*scientist* → science
to **invent** [ɪn'vent]	erfinden	*to invent* → invention
steam engine ['stiːm ̩endʒɪn]	Dampfmaschine	The *steam engine* was the most important invention of the 18th century.
television ['telɪvɪʒn]	Fernsehen; Fernseher	*television* → TV
station ['steɪʃn]	Sender	What's your favourite radio *station*?
to **start** [stɑːt]	*hier:* gründen	John Logie Baird *started* the first television station.
5 to **fill** [fɪl]	füllen	She *filled* her glass with water.
vegetarian [ˌvedʒɪ'teəriən]	vegetarisch	Today you can even buy *vegetarian* sausages.
option ['ɒpʃn]	Möglichkeit; Option; Wahl	There's a vegetarian *option* too.
mashed potatoes *(pl)* [ˌmæʃt pə'teɪtəʊz]	Kartoffelpüree; Kartoffelbrei	Haggis is often eaten with *mashed potatoes*.
sauce [sɔːs]	Soße	I love ice cream with chocolate *sauce*.
to **ban** [bæn]	bannen; verbieten; sperren	If sth *has been banned*, you mustn't do it or use it.

6	**decade** ['dekeɪd]	Jahrzehnt	= 10 years
7	**hundreds of** ['hʌndrədzˌəv]	hunderte (von)	*Hundreds of* years ago people built very high houses in Edinburgh.
	narrow ['nærəʊ]	eng; schmal	a *narrow* street, a *narrow* bridge
	close [kləʊs]	schmaler Durchgang	The people in Edinburgh call the narrow streets '*closes*'.
	to **name** [neɪm]	nennen; benennen	*to name* → a name
	to **die** [daɪ]	sterben	Robert has only got one grandma. His other grandma *died* four years ago.
	to **leave behind** [ˌliːv bɪˈhaɪnd]	zurücklassen	Never *leave* your rubbish *behind* after a picnic.

Station 2: Holly's blog

	update ['ʌpdeɪt]	Aktualisierung; Update	It's time for a new *update* from Scotland.
	latest ['leɪtɪst]	neueste/-r/-s	What's the *latest* news from your brother in Scotland?
	pic (= picture) [pɪk]	Foto	= picture
	actually ['æktʃuəli]	tatsächlich; wirklich; eigentlich	! *actually* ≠ aktuell
	in fact [ɪn 'fækt]	tatsächlich; eigentlich; genau genommen	*in fact* → fact
	south [saʊθ]	südlich; im Süden	We don't have cows like this down *south*.
	to **hold, held, held** [həʊld; held; held]	abhalten	They *hold* a garden party here every summer.
	gentleman, gentlemen (pl) ['dʒentlmən; 'dʒentlmen]	Gentleman; feiner Herr	There were lots of nice *gentlemen* at the dance.
	clan [klæn]	Clan; Sippe	= the Scottish name for a family group
9	**ben** [ben]	hoher Berg	*Ben* Nevis is in Scotland.
	glen [glen]	Schlucht	'*Glen*' is a Scottish word.
	recipe ['resɪpi]	Rezept	! Achtung Aussprache
11	**ceilidh** ['keɪli]	*schottisches Fest, bei dem getanzt und musiziert wird*	! Achtung Aussprache
14	**official** [əˈfɪʃl]	offiziell	Did you read the *official* letter from school?
	national anthem [ˌnæʃnl 'ænθəm]	Nationalhymne	Can you sing the German *national anthem*?
	unofficial [ˌʌnəˈfɪʃl]	inoffiziell	*unofficial* ↔ official
	to **defeat** [dɪˈfiːt]	besiegen	= to beat
	soldier ['səʊldʒə]	Soldat/-in	Robert the Bruce defeated King Edward and his *soldiers*.
15	**web** [web]	Netz; Spinnennetz	Spiders make *webs*.

Skills: How to write a persuasive text

1	**final** [ˈfaɪnl]	letzte/-r/-s	= last
	further [ˈfɜːðə]	weiter (weg)	far → further → (the) furthest Wales is far from London, but Scotland is *further* and the Shetland Islands are the furthest.
	north [nɔːθ]	nördlich; im Norden	Which is further *north*: Scotland or Ireland?
	fascinating [ˈfæsɪneɪtɪŋ]	faszinierend	= very interesting
	extremely [ɪkˈstriːmli]	äußerst; sehr	= very much
	present [ˈpreznt]	heutig; Gegenwarts-	The museum shows life on the islands from Roman times to the *present* day.
	huge [hjuːdʒ]	riesig; riesengroß; gewaltig	Berlin is a big city. London is a *huge* city.
	to improve [ɪmˈpruːv]	(sich) verbessern	I want to *improve* my English.
	tiny [ˈtaɪni]	klein; winzig	A mouse looks *tiny* next to a horse. *tiny* ↔ huge
3	**crane** [kreɪn]	Kran	If you want to fix the roof of that tall building, you'll need a *crane*.
	engineer [ˌendʒɪˈnɪə]	Ingenieur/-in; Techniker/-in	My father builds bridges. He's an *engineer*.

Adverbs of degree

Adverbs of degree modify the meaning of a verb, adjective or adverb.
Adverbs of degree are: very, terribly, really, extremely, completely, quite, too, almost, enough.

We walked up the hill to the castle **extremely** slowly.	(adverb + adverb)
The guide's story was **quite** dramatic.	(adverb + adjective)
The guide **completely** ignored my question at the end.	(adverb + verb)
! The castle was fascinating **enough**.	(adjective + adverb)

Unit task: Come and visit us!

to **appeal to sb** [əˈpiːl tə]	jmdm. zusagen; jmdm. gefallen; jmdn. ansprechen; jmdn. reizen	Your design needs to *appeal* to young people.
convincing [kənˈvɪnsɪŋ]	überzeugend	The story doesn't sound *convincing*.

Story: I don't believe in ghosts!

1	**sky** [skaɪ]	Himmel	At the end of the festival the *sky* was getting dark.
	entrance [ˈentrəns]	Eingang; Eintritt	*entrance* → to enter
	ticket office [ˈtɪkɪt ˌɒfɪs]	Kartenausgabestelle; Vorverkaufsschalter; Fahrkartenschalter	The *ticket office* is at the entrance.
	stone [stəʊn]	Stein; Stein-	The castle has a *stone* floor and *stone* walls.

pocket ['pɒkɪt]	Tasche; Hosentasche	He put his smartphone into his trouser *pocket*.
signal ['sɪgnl]	Empfang; Signal; Zeichen	I can't use my phone because there's no *signal*.
thick [θɪk]	dick	The stone walls of the castle are very *thick*.
perhaps [pə'hæps]	vielleicht	= maybe
to go round in circles [gəʊ ˌraʊnd ɪn 'sɜːklz]	sich im Kreis drehen	They couldn't find the way out. They *went round in circles*.
wounded ['wuːndɪd]	verletzt; verwundet	We found a small bird in the garden. It was *wounded* so we took it to the vet.
tower [taʊə]	Turm	The castle has got four high *towers*.
moonlight ['muːnlaɪt]	Mondlicht	There's no *moonlight* tonight because the sky is cloudy.
stairs *(pl)* [steəz]	Treppe	*stairs* → downstairs → upstairs
wooden ['wʊdn]	hölzern; aus Holz	Our house has *wooden* stairs.
to cry [kraɪ]	weinen	*to cry* ↔ to laugh
to look up [ˌlʊkˈʌp]	aufschauen; hochschauen	Amber stopped crying and *looked up*. She was very happy to see Holly.
to fall down [ˌfɔːlˈdaʊn]	einstürzen; zusammenfallen; hinunterfallen	The wall started to *fall down*.
danger ['deɪndʒə]	Gefahr	*danger* → dangerous
to keep out (of) [ˌkiːpˈaʊt (ˌəv)]	draußen bleiben (von); draußen halten (von)	Parents must *keep out* of my room!
cracking ['krækɪŋ]	knackend; brechend	There was a *cracking* sound and then the floor fell down.
to realise ['rɪəlaɪz]	erkennen; realisieren	Holly *realised* they didn't have much time.
key ring ['kiː ˌrɪŋ]	Schlüsselbund; Schlüssel-anhänger	*key ring* → key
to tie (to) ['taɪ (tə)]	binden (an); festbinden (an)	If you *tie* a dog *to* something, it can't run away.
rope [rəʊp]	Seil	She tied the pieces together to make a *rope*.
to hold onto [ˌhəʊldˈɒntə]	(sich) festhalten an	Amber caught the rope and *held onto* it.
crack [kræk]	Knacken; Krachen	*crack* → cracking
wood [wʊd]	Holz	*wood* → wooden
below [bɪ'ləʊ]	unten; unter; unterhalb (von)	*below* ↔ above
gig [gɪg]	Auftritt; Gig	Ethan and his band play *gigs* every weekend.
definitely ['defɪnətli]	definitiv; bestimmt; eindeutig	Do you want a pink backpack? – No, *definitely* not.
climax ['klaɪmæks]	Höhepunkt	What do you think about the *climax* of the story?

4

Describing nature and buildings

nature	cliff, mountain, hill, park, island, coastline, …	beautiful, amazing, fascinating, wonderful, fantastic, spectacular, …	
buildings	castle, museum, church, tower, …	old, modern, big, huge, nice, tiny, interesting, fascinating, stone, wood/wooden, stairs, wall, …	

Describe your school building. Write 3–5 sentences.

Action UK! How times change

1	to **help out** [ˌhelpˈaʊt]	aushelfen	Our neighbour couldn't look after her garden, so I *helped out*.
	neighbourhood [ˈneɪbəhʊd]	Nachbarschaft	*neighbourhood* → neighbour
	to **do the shopping** [ˌduː ðə ˈʃɒpɪŋ]	einkaufen; einkaufen gehen	*to do the shopping* → shopping → shop
	elderly [ˈeldəli]	ältere/-r/-s	= a more polite word for 'old' (when you talk about people)
2	**inventor** [ɪnˈventə]	Erfinder/-in	*inventor* → invention → to invent
	tin can [ˈtɪn kæn]	Blechdose	You can buy most drinks in *tin cans*.
	switch [swɪtʃ]	Schalter	I can't see anything. Where's the light *switch*?
3	**versus (vs.)** [ˈvɜːsəs]	gegen	old *vs.* new old *vs.* young
	rotary phone [ˈrəʊtri fəʊn]	Telefon mit Wählscheibe	In the past all phones were *rotary phones*.

Check-out

1	**fall** [fɔːl]	Sturz	*fall* → to fall
2	**natural** [ˈnætʃrl]	natürlich; Natur-	! Achtung Aussprache *natural* → nature
	to **rent (out)** [ˌrent (ˈaʊt)]	(ver)mieten	Last year our friends *rented* their house in England *out* to us.
	thistle [ˈθɪsl]	Distel	A *thistle* is a plant with beautiful pink flowers.
3	to **kiss** [kɪs]	(sich) küssen	Amber and Ethan *kissed* after the gig.
4	to **be known (as)** [bi ˈnəʊn (ˌəz)]	bekannt sein (als)	The building *is known* around the world. It's very famous.

Aufgabe **Syllable stress**
Silbenbetonung

Say the words. Where's the stress? Copy the grid and then write the words in the right box.

historic	traditional	vegetable	musical	competition
shipbuilding	historical	unofficial	interrupt	entertain
spectacular	engineer	impolite	communicate

●○○	○●○	○○●	○●○○	○○●○

Across cultures 2 Making small talk

1	to **get to know** [ˌget tə ˈnəʊ]	kennen lernen	I would like to *get to know* your friends.
	light [laɪt]	leicht	Small talk is *light* conversation.
	pattern [ˈpætn]	Muster	= how sth is done or repeated
	talker [ˈtɔːkə]	Sprecher/-in	*talker* → to talk
	to **hog a conversation** [ˌhɒg ə kɒnvəˈseɪʃn]	ein Gespräch für sich in Beschlag nehmen; ein Gespräch dominieren	You shouldn't *hog a conversation*, you should also listen to your partner.
2	to **keep the ball bouncing** [ˌkiːp ðə bɔːl ˈbaʊntsɪŋ]	*hier:* das Gespräch am Laufen halten	= to keep the conversation going
	to **move in/into** [ˌmuːv ˈɪn/ˈɪntə]	einziehen in	Dave and his parents *moved into* a new house in Cornwall.
	next door [ˌnekst ˈdɔː]	(von) nebenan	Your neighbours live *next door*.
	to **bounce** [baʊnts]	springen; hüpfen	The ball *bounced* away and broke the window.
	to **check out** *(coll)* [ˌtʃek ˈaʊt]	abchecken; auschecken; prüfen	I've got a great tip: *Check out* the new BMX shop in Greenwich.
	Cheers! [tʃɪəz]	Danke!	Young people in Britain often say "*Cheers!*" when they want to say "Thanks!".
	to **catch, caught, caught** [kætʃ; kɔːt; kɔːt]	mitbekommen *(ugs.)*; mitkriegen *(ugs.)*	I didn't *catch* what you said. Can you repeat it, please?
3	**student exchange** [ˌstjuːdnt ɪksˈtʃeɪndʒ]	Schüleraustausch	I went on a *student exchange* to France last year.

4	stage direction ['steɪdʒ dɪˌrekʃn]	Regieanweisung	A *stage direction* is an instruction in a script. It tells the actors what to do.
	hint [hɪnt]	Hinweis; Andeutung; Tipp	Can't you give me just a little *hint* about my birthday present? Please!
	to the point [tə ðə 'pɔɪnt]	prägnant; treffend	Keep your dialogues short and *to the point*.

Unit 3 What was it like?

Check-in

What was . . . like? [ˌwɒt wɒz 'laɪk]	Wie war . . . ?	*What was* life *like* in the 18th century?
object ['ɒbdʒɪkt]	Gegenstand; Objekt	Describe a historical *object*.
period ['pɪəriəd]	Periode; Zeitspanne; Zeitraum	! Achtung Schreibung und Aussprache
Ice Age ['aɪs ˌeɪdʒ]	Eiszeit	= a historical period when there was ice over most of Northern Europe
to flood [flʌd]	überfluten; fluten; überschwemmen	The rain *flooded* all the fields.
to rise, rose, risen [raɪz, rəʊz, 'rɪzn]	steigen; sich erheben; aufstehen	= to go up; to go higher
sea level ['siː ˌlevl]	Meeresspiegel	The *sea level* rises at high tide.
to disappear [ˌdɪsə'pɪə]	verschwinden	My bike *has disappeared*. Perhaps someone stole it.
BC (= before Christ) [ˌbiː'siː]	vor Christus	The land bridge disappeared about 6,500 *BC*.
Celt [kelt]	Kelte/Keltin	*Celt* → Celtic
AD (= Anno Domini) [ˌeɪ'diː]	nach Christus	*AD* ↔ BC
western ['westən]	westlich; West-	The Celts arrived from *western* Europe.
tribe [traɪb]	Stamm; Volksstamm	*Fr.* tribu (f)
round [raʊnd]	rund	The Celts lived in *round* houses.
metal ['metl]	Metall	Tools are usually made from *metal*.
leather ['leðə]	Leder	*Leather* shoes are good for your feet.
to conquer ['kɒŋkə]	erobern	The Normans *conquered* England in 1066.
to found [faʊnd]	gründen	! *to found, founded, founded* = gründen *to find, found, found* = finden
palace ['pælɪs]	Palast	Buckingham Palace is a famous *palace*.
fort [fɔːt]	Fort; Festung	The Romans built a lot of *forts* to protect their soldiers.
peace [piːs]	Frieden	The Celts fought the Romans at first. But over time the Romans brought *peace* to the country.
empire ['empaɪə]	Reich; Kaiserreich	the Roman *Empire*, the British *Empire*

Picts [pɪkt]	Pikten *(schottischer Volks-stamm)*	The *Picts* lived in Scotland.
to **begin, began, begun** [bɪˈgɪn; bɪˈgæn; bɪˈgʌn]	anfangen; beginnen	My name *begins* with 'B'.
to **attack** [əˈtæk]	angreifen	Yesterday a cat *attacked* my dog but he wasn't badly hurt.
to **say goodbye (to)** [ˌseɪ gʊdˈbaɪ (tə)]	sich verabschieden (von)	*to say goodbye* → goodbye
Anglo-Saxon [ˌæŋgləʊˈsæksn]	Angelsachse; Angelsächsin; angelsächsisch	The *Anglo-Saxons* came to Britain from continental Europe.
Germanic [dʒəˈmænɪk]	germanisch	There were different *Germanic* tribes in the past.
people *(pl)* [ˈpiːpl]	Volk	! a *people* = ein Volk people = Leute; Menschen
rule [ruːl]	Herrschaft; Regierungszeit	Roman *rule* in Britain began in 43 AD.
peaceful [ˈpiːsfl]	in Frieden; friedlich	*peaceful* → peace
to **burn, burnt, burnt** [bɜːn, bɜːnt, bɜːnt]	brennen; verbrennen	Dry wood *burns* very well.
to **divide (up/into)** [dɪˈvaɪd (ʌp/ɪntə)]	aufteilen (in)	The pizza was so big that we *divided* it *into* three pieces.
kingdom [ˈkɪŋdəm]	Königreich	*kingdom* → king
complete [kəmˈpliːt]	vollständig; komplett; völlig	Is this the *complete* version of the story or only part of it?
Latin [ˈlætɪn]	Latein; lateinisch	Do you learn *Latin* at school?
bible [ˈbaɪbl]	Bibel	! Achtung Schreibung und Aussprache
to **date back to** [ˈdeɪt ˌbæk tə]	zurückgehen auf; stammen aus	Hadrian's Wall *dates back to* Roman times.
Norman [ˈnɔːmən]	Normanne/Normannin; normannisch	The *Normans* came to Britain in the 11th century.
leader [ˈliːdə]	Führer/-in; Anführer/-in	William the Conqueror was the *leader* of the Normans.
duke [djuːk]	Herzog	The *Duke* of Normandy defeated Harold.
Saxon [ˈsæksn]	Sachse/Sächsin; sächsisch	Harold was king of the *Saxons*.
battle [ˈbætl]	Schlacht; Kampf	Armies fight in *battles*.
to **this day** [ˌtə ðɪs ˈdeɪ]	bis heute	*To this day* I don't know what happened.
at this time [ˌət ðɪs ˈtaɪm]	zu dieser Zeit	= back then
lord [lɔːd]	Lord; Herr	*lord* – prince – king
Tudor [ˈtjuːdə]	Tudor; Tudor-	King Henry VIII was a famous *Tudor* king.
monarch [ˈmɒnək]	Monarch/-in	*monarchs* = kings and queens
daughter [ˈdɔːtə]	Tochter	How many *daughters* did Henry VIII have? – Two: Mary I and Elizabeth I.
to **divorce** [dɪˈvɔːs]	sich scheiden lassen	Henry *divorced* Catherine in 1533.
to **marry** [ˈmæri]	heiraten	Henry VIII *married* six times. *to marry* ↔ to divorce

the Pope [ðə ˈpəʊp]	der Papst	*The Pope* wouldn't let Henry VIII marry Anne Boleyn.
reign [reɪn]	Herrschaft; Regierungszeit	Queen Elizabeth I's *reign* was from 1558 to 1603.
golden age [ˌgəʊldn ˈeɪdʒ]	goldenes Zeitalter	Queen Elizabeth's reign was a *golden age* for art, literature and music.
Spanish [ˈspænɪʃ]	spanisch; Spanisch; die Spanier	Drake and Raleigh stole gold and silver from *Spanish* ships.
Victorian [vɪkˈtɔːriən]	viktorianisch; Viktorianer/-in	The *Victorian* period was in the 19th century.
Industrial Revolution [ɪnˌdʌstriəl revlˈuːʃn]	die industrielle Revolution	The *Industrial Revolution* began in Britain.
by hand [ˌbaɪ ˈhænd]	von Hand; manuell	Before the Industrial Revolution, people worked at home and made things *by hand*.
however [haʊˈevə]	jedoch	He had lots of money. *However*, he wasn't happy with his life.
number [ˈnʌmbə]	Anzahl	*in larger numbers* = more
factory [ˈfæktri]	Fabrik; Werk	Cars, washing machines and cookers are all made in *factories*.
goods *(pl)* [gʊdz]	Güter; Waren	The *goods* were moved from the factories by steam train.
seaside [ˈsiːsaɪd]	Küste; Meeresküste	We went to the *seaside* for the weekend.
colony [ˈkɒləni]	Kolonie	In the 19th century Germany had *colonies* too. *Fr.* colonie *(f)*; *Lat.* colonia *(f)*
raw material [ˌrɔː məˈtɪəriəl]	Rohstoff; Rohmaterial	You need *raw materials* to make products.
independent [ˌɪndɪˈpendənt]	unabhängig	*Fr.* indépendant/e
political [pəˈlɪtɪkl]	politisch	Do you like watching TV programmes about *political* topics?
view [vjuː]	Ansicht; Einstellung; Standpunkt	*view* → point of view
influence [ˈɪnfluəns]	Einfluss	How people behave has an *influence* on what you think of them.
to vote [vəʊt]	abstimmen; wählen	In 2016 the UK *voted* to leave the EU.
rather than [ˈrɑːðə ðən]	eher als	The UK wanted to make their own decisions *rather than* do what the EU said.
exit [ˈeksɪt]	Ausgang; Abgang; Ausfahrt; Ausstieg	*exit* ↔ entrance
1 **embroidery** [ɪmˈbrɔɪdri]	Stickerei	You need to be patient to do *embroidery*. It can take months.
to connect (to) [kəˈnekt (tə)]	verbinden (mit); vermitteln; anschließen	You can *connect* two words to make other words: 'school' and 'bag' make 'schoolbag'.
3 **Viking** [ˈvaɪkɪŋ]	Wikinger	The *Vikings* arrived in ships.
Middle Ages [ˌmɪdl ˈeɪdʒɪz]	Mittelalter	= the time in history from about 500 to 1500
revolution [ˌrevlˈuːʃn]	Revolution	! Achtung Aussprache
5 **valuable** [ˈvæljuəbl]	wertvoll	It isn't *valuable* but I like it.
to be made of [bi ˈmeɪd əv]	bestehen aus; gemacht sein aus; hergestellt sein aus	Windows *are made of* glass.

History words

Ice age	Eiszeit	at the end of the Ice Age people from Europe used a land bridge across the North Sea to get to the British Isles
Celts	Kelten	people that came to the British Isles from Europe
Roman Empire	Römisches Reich	Rome and the area the Romans invaded from the 8th century BC to the 7th century AD
Romans	Römer	
Julius Caesar	(100 BC–44 BC)	
Anglo-Saxons	Angelsachsen	
Vikings	Wikinger	
Normans	Normannen	people that lived in France and fought against the English in 1066
Battle of Hastings	Schlacht bei Hastings	1066
Middle Ages	Mittelalter	
Tudors		family of kings and queens that ruled England and Wales
Church of England		official Christian church in England – its head is the British king or queen
Henry VIII	(1491–1547)	King of England from 1509 to 1547, King of Ireland from 1541 to 1547
Catherine of Aragon	(1485–1536)	first wife of Henry VIII
Anne Boleyn	(1501/1507–1536)	second wife of Henry VIII, mother of Elizabeth I
Elizabeth I	(1533–1603)	Queen of England from 1558 to 1603
Elizabethan	elisabethanisch	the time when Elizabeth I ruled
Sir Walter Raleigh	(1552/1554–1618)	favourite of Queen Elizabeth I.
Sir Francis Drake	(1540–1596)	English sailor that fought against the Spanish Armada
Spanish Armada	spanische Armada	the Spanish navy that attacked England in the 16th century
Guy Fawkes	(1570–1606)	
William Shakespeare	(1564–1616)	famous English writer
Civil War	Bürgerkrieg	
Great Fire of London	Großer Brand von London (1666)	
Captain James Cook	(1728–1779)	
Battle of Trafalgar	Schlacht von Trafalgar	1805
Queen Victoria	(1819–1901)	Queen of Great Britain from 1837 to 1901
Victorian Age	viktorianisches Zeitalter	the time of Queen Victoria's reign
Industrial Revolution	Industrielle Revolution	the period between 1750 and 1914 when important inventions (e.g. the steam engine) were made
British Empire	britisches Königreich	
Second World War	zweiter Weltkrieg	
European Union	Europäische Union (EU)	
Brexit	Austritt von GB aus der EU	

6	**calendar** [ˈkæləndə]	Kalender	You can find all the dates in a *calendar*. **!** Achtung Schreibung und Aussprache
	axe [æks]	Axt	An *axe* is a tool.
	mirror [ˈmɪrə]	Spiegel	If you look in a *mirror*, you can see yourself.
	necklace [ˈnekləs]	Halskette	A *necklace* is a piece of jewellery.
	sandal [ˈsændl]	Sandale	**!** Achtung Schreibung und Aussprache
	hairbrush [ˈheəbrʌʃ]	Haarbürste	*hairbrush* → hair

Station 1: The calendar which Claire is making

	which [wɪtʃ]	der; die; das; dem; den *(Relativpronomen)*	The subject *which* I like most is English.
	characteristic [ˌkærəktəˈrɪstɪk]	Eigenschaft; typisches Merkmal	Tell me about your *characteristics*.
	that [ðæt]	der; dem; den; die; das *(Relativpronomen)*	The TV was an invention *that* came from Scotland.
	who [huː]	der; dem; den; die *(Relativpronomen)*	Pia is the only girl *who* comes from Germany.
	to **photograph (sb/sth)** [ˈfəʊtəɡrɑːft]	jmdn./etw. fotografieren	*to photograph* → photographer → photo
	lady-in-waiting [ˌleɪdiɪnˈweɪtɪŋ]	Hofdame	Queens usually have *ladies-in-waiting*.
	potato, potatoes *(pl)* [pəˈteɪtəʊ; pəˈteɪtəʊz]	Kartoffel	Sir Walter Raleigh brought *potatoes* from America to Europe.
	tobacco *(no pl)* [təˈbækəʊ]	Tabak	*Tobacco* isn't good for your health.
	to **kill** [kɪl]	töten; umbringen	Tobacco has *killed* millions of people.
	bald [bɔːld]	glatzköpfig; kahl	= without hair
	term [tɜːm]	Trimester; Semester; Halbjahr	= the time when students are at school or at college
	to **invade** [ɪnˈveɪd]	einmarschieren (in); einfallen in	The Spanish tried to *invade* England.
	bowls [ˈbəʊlz]	Bowling	Drake was in the middle of a game of *bowls*.
	to **destroy** [dɪˈstrɔɪ]	zerstören; vernichten; auslöschen	The storm *destroyed* a lot of buildings and roads. **Fr.** détruire
	relaxed [rɪˈlækst]	entspannt; locker; gelassen	*relaxed* → to relax
2	**whom** [huːm]	der; die; das	Shakespeare is the man *whom* you can see in Jay's message.
	instead of [ɪnˈsted əv]	statt; anstatt; an Stelle von	This year we're going to go on holiday in the winter *instead of* the summer.
3	to **control** [kənˈtrəʊl]	kontrollieren; beherrschen; steuern	Queen Elizabeth I *controlled* England very well.
	explorer [ɪkˈsplɔːrə]	Forscher/-in; Forschungsreisende/-r	Sir Walter Raleigh was an English *explorer*.
	charm [tʃɑːm]	Charme	He had good looks and *charm*.
	colonist [ˈkɒlənɪst]	Siedler/-in; Kolonist/-in	*colonist* → colony

to **settle** ['setl]	siedeln; sich niederlassen	The colonists *settled* in America.
4 **play** [pleɪ]	Theaterstück	William Shakespeare wrote lots of *plays*.

Monarchy words

empire	(Kaiser-)Reich
emperor/empress	Kaiser/-in
lord	Adeliger
monarch	Monarch/Monarchin
king/queen	König/Königin
crown	Krone
reign	Herrschaft, Regierungszeit
to reign	regieren; herrschen
lady-in-waiting	Hofdame

Station 2: A murder story

murder ['mɜːdə]	Mord	The guide told a scary story about a *murder*.
7 to **rebuild, rebuilt, rebuilt** [ˌriːˈbɪld; ˌriːˈbɪlt; ˌriːˈbɪlt]	wieder aufbauen	The Globe Theatre was *rebuilt* in the 20th century. *to rebuild* → building → to build
actor/actress ['æktə]	Schauspieler/Schauspielerin	*actor/actress* → to act
Elizabethan [ɪˌlɪzəˈbiːθən]	Elisabethaner/-in; elisabethanisch	The *Elizabethans* were people who lived during the reign of Queen Elizabeth I.
to **turn back** [tɜːn ˈbæk]	umkehren; zurückgehen	*turn back* → turn (a)round
What luck! [wɒt ˈlʌk]	Was für ein Glück!	I lost my mobile but my brother found it. *What luck!*
blood [blʌd]	Blut	There's *blood* on your T-shirt. Did you hurt yourself?
dressed [drest]	angezogen; gekleidet; angekleidet	The man was *dressed* in Victorian clothes.
silence *(no pl)* ['saɪləns]	Stille; Schweigen; Ruhe	There was no noise, just *silence*.
to **shine, shone, shone** [ʃaɪn; ʃɒn; ʃɒn]	glänzen; scheinen	Jay saw something on the ground. It *was shining*.
pipe [paɪp]	Pfeife	Jay found the ghost's *pipe* on the ground.
10 **Guess what!** [ges ˈwɒt]	Stell dir vor!; Rate mal!	*Guess what!* You'll never believe what happened!
13 to **hire** [haɪə]	mieten; ausleihen	Jay wants to *hire* a costume for the photo.

Skills: How to talk about history

1 **entertainment** *(no pl)* [ˌentəˈteɪnmənt]	Unterhaltung	The Globe Theatre was used for different kinds of *entertainment*.
to **reign** [reɪn]	herrschen; regieren	*to reign* → reign
to **be born** [bi ˈbɔːn]	geboren werden	*to be born* ↔ to die

to **burn down** [ˌbɜːn ˈdaʊn]	abbrennen; niederbrennen	The first Globe Theatre *burnt down* in 1613.
description [dɪˈskrɪpʃn]	Beschreibung	*description* → to describe
biographical [ˌbaɪəʊˈɡræfɪkl]	biografisch	What do we know about his life? How much *biographical* information do we have?
2 **quill** [kwɪl]	Federkiel	In Victorian times people wrote with *quills*.

Describing objects

It's **(very) old/big/small/expensive** …	Es ist (sehr) alt/groß/klein/teuer/…
It **has** …	Es hat …
It's **made of gold/wood/metal/paper/ silver/leather** …	Es ist aus Gold/Holz/Metall/Papier/ Silber/Leder… (gemacht).
It **looks like** …	Es sieht aus wie …
It **dates back to the year/period** …	Es stammt aus dem Jahr/der Zeit …
People **used it for** …	Man verwendete es für …
We **got it from** …	Wir haben es von/vom … (bekommen).

Describe a family object you like.

Story: It's a mystery!

mystery [ˈmɪstri]	Geheimnis; Rätsel	Nobody knew about the *mystery* behind the ring.
1 **photoshoot** [ˈfəʊtəʊʃuːt]	Fotoshooting; Fotoaufnahmen	Have you ever been to a *photoshoot*?
chaos [ˈkeɪɒs]	Chaos; Durcheinander; Unordnung	When everything goes wrong at the same time, there's *chaos*.
to **mix (up)** [mɪks (ˈʌp)]	mischen; vermischen	Don't *mix up* the historical periods.
to **take care of sb/sth** [teɪk ˈkeər əv]	sich um jmdn./etw. kümmern; für jmdn. sorgen	While my neighbours were on holiday, I *took care* of their cats.
drama queen (coll) [ˈdrɑːmə ˌkwiːn]	Tussi (abwertend); Zicke (abwertend)	I don't like her. She's a real *drama queen*.
plaster cast [ˈplɑːstə kɑːst]	Gipsverband	If you break your leg or arm, it has to be put in a *plaster cast*.
to **zoom in (on)** [zuːmˈɪn (ɒn)]	heranzoomen (auf)	If the camera *zooms in on* somebody, you get a close-up picture of that person.
to **roll one's eyes** [ˌrəʊl wʌnzˈaɪz]	die Augen verdrehen	The girl *rolled her eyes*. Jay was getting on her nerves.
half an hour [ˌhɑːf ənˈaʊər]	eine halbe Stunde	= 30 minutes
out of focus [ˌaʊt əv ˈfəʊkəs]	unscharf	The photo was *out of focus* because Gwen didn't stand still.
to **photobomb** [ˈfəʊtəʊbɒm]	ins Foto laufen	No *photobombing*!
flash [flæʃ]	Blitz; Lichtblitz	You need a *flash* when you take a picture in the dark.
nurse [nɜːs]	Krankenschwester; Kranken-pfleger	= sb who looks after people who need a doctor

boot [buːt]	Kofferraum	I've put all the bags into the *boot* of the car. We're ready to leave now.
hospital ['hɒspɪtl]	Krankenhaus; Hospital	Later they used the house as a *hospital*. *Fr.* hôpital (*m*)
to **drive off** [draɪv ˈɒf]	wegfahren	She jumped into the car and *drove off*.
to **edit out** [ˌedɪt ˈaʊt]	herausschneiden	Jim could *edit out* the mistakes in the photo.
to **crop (a photo)** [krɒp]	(ein Foto) zurechtschneiden	The photo doesn't fit, we'll have to *crop* it.
to **crash (into)** [ˌkræʃ (ˈɪntə)]	zusammenstoßen (mit)	The girl *crashed* into Jim.
ambulance ['æmbjələns]	Krankenwagen	**!** Achtung Aussprache
2 to **lighten** ['laɪtn]	aufhellen	*to lighten* → light
3 flashback ['flæʃbæk]	Rückblende; Flashback	*Flashbacks* are often used in films and books to show an event that happened in the past.

Action UK! The girl from the past

1 **I'd rather** [aɪd ˈrɑːðə]	ich würde lieber	I don't want to watch the film on TV. *I'd rather* watch it at the cinema.
to **identify (with)** [aɪˈdentɪfaɪ (wɪð)]	sich identifizieren (mit)	I love the book because it's easy to *identify with* the characters.
2 **pawn shop** ['pɔːn ʃɒp]	Pfandhaus; Pfandleihe	People who need money sometimes take their jewellery or other expensive things to the *pawn shop*.
school fees (*pl*) ['skuːl fiːz]	Schulgeld; Schulgebühren	In the past parents had to pay *school fees* to send their children to school. Today most schools are free.
teabag ['tiːbæg]	Teebeutel	*teabag* → tea
pineapple ['paɪnæpl]	Ananas	*Pineapple* is my favourite fruit.
vitamin ['vɪtəmɪn]	Vitamin	There are lots of *vitamins* in fruit and vegetables.
sequence ['siːkwəns]	Sequenz; Szene	A film is made of lots of *sequences*.
blurred [blɜːd]	verschwommen; verwischt	In dream sequences the pictures are often *blurred*.
to **wake up, woke up, woken up** [ˌweɪk ˈʌp; ˌwəʊk ˈʌp; ˌwəʊkn ˈʌp]	aufwachen; aufwecken	It's 7:30 and he *has* just *woken up*.

Time words

AD (Anno Domini)	nach Christus	in the future	in der Zukunft
at this time	zu dieser Zeit	nowadays, today	heutzutage; heute; jetzt
back then	damals	period	Periode; Zeitspanne; Zeitraum
BC (before Christ)	vor Christus	to this day	bis heute
in the past	in der Vergangenheit		

Write three sentences about the time when your great-grandparents were born.

Check-out

2	**patent** [ˈpeɪtnt]	patentieren	Alexander Cumming *patented* the modern toilet.
	light bulb [ˈlaɪt ˌbʌlb]	Glühbirne	*light bulb* → light
	umbrella [ʌmˈbrelə]	Regenschirm	It's raining. Where's my *umbrella*?
	to **brush** [brʌʃ]	bürsten	I *brush* my hair with a hairbrush.

Aufgabe   **The phonetic alphabet**
Die Lautschrift

a) *Read the words in green out loud and match them to the pictures.*

A   B   C   D   E

1. [flʌd]
When does this happen?

2. [ˈmɒnək]
Is there one in Germany?

3. [ˈmæri]
Where can you do this?

4. [ˈkæləndə]
What do you write in this?

5. [ʌmˈbrelə]
When do you need this?

b) *Take turns to answer the questions below the pictures.*

Text and media smart 2   On- & offline communication

Check-in

	informal [ɪnˈfɔːml]	informell; zwanglos; inoffiziell	*informal* ↔ formal
	to **be related to** [bi rɪˈleɪtɪd ˌtə]	sich beziehen auf; verwandt sein mit	The messages *are related to* the calendar project.
1	**destination** [ˌdestɪˈneɪʃn]	Ziel; Reiseziel	Where are you travelling to? What's your *destination*?
	direct [dɪˈrekt]	direkt; unmittelbar	I needed a *direct* answer to my text message.
	to **inform** [ɪnˈfɔːm]	informieren	*to inform* → information

Yours sincerely, [ˌjɔːz sɪnˈsɪəli]	Mit freundlichen Grüßen,	= used at the end of a formal letter
head teacher [ˌhed ˈtiːtʃə]	Schulleiter/-in	Jeanette Wilson is the *head teacher* at my school.

Station 1: Formal communication

2	**manager** [ˈmænɪdʒə]	Geschäftsführer/-in; Leiter/-in; Manager/-in	Claire is the *manager* of the community centre.
	available [əˈveɪləbl]	verfügbar; erhältlich	Claire asked if the photographer was *available*. He replied that he had time to do the photoshooting.
3	**paragraph** [ˈpærəɡrɑːf]	Absatz; Paragraf	word – sentence – *paragraph* – text
	recipient [rɪˈsɪpiənt]	Empfänger/-in	= the person who receives a letter or message
	to **contain** [kənˈteɪn]	enthalten	What does this box *contain*? = What's in the box?
	unnecessary [ʌnˈnesəsri]	unnötig; überflüssig; verzichtbar	*unnecessary* ↔ necessary
	purpose [ˈpɜːpəs]	Ziel; Absicht; Zweck	If you have a *purpose*, you have a reason to do something.
	postal address [ˈpəʊstl əˌdres]	Postanschrift	You send letters to *postal addresses*.
4	**payment** [ˈpeɪmənt]	Bezahlung; Vergütung	*payment* → to pay
	married [ˈmærid]	verheiratet	*married* → to marry
	Ms [mɪz]	Frau *(Anrede)*	If you don't know if a woman is married, you use '*Ms*' before her name.
5	**permission** [pəˈmɪʃn]	Erlaubnis; Genehmigung	We need your parents' *permission* to take the photos.
6	**signature** [ˈsɪɡnətʃə]	Unterschrift	Someone's *signature* is at the bottom of a letter.
	sender [ˈsendə]	Absender/-in	The *sender* sends a letter.
7	**envelope** [ˈenvələʊp]	Umschlag; Briefumschlag	Put the letter in the *envelope*, please.
	stamp [stæmp]	Briefmarke	You have to put a *stamp* on the envelope too.
8	**semi-** [ˈsemi]	halb-; Halb-	An email can be *semi*-formal.
	absolutely [ˌæbsəˈluːtli]	völlig; absolut	It's *absolutely* fine if Amir comes to watch the film with us.
	Best wishes, [ˌbest ˈwɪʃɪz]	Viele Grüße,; Herzliche Grüße,	= used at the end of a formal letter

Station 2: Informal communication

11	**gonna** (= going to) *(coll)* [ˈɡɒnə]	werden	I know ur *gonna* laugh.
	loads (of) [ˈləʊds (ˌəv)]	viel/-e; jede Menge	= a lot of
12	to **abbreviate** [əˈbriːvieɪt]	abkürzen	*to abbreviate* → abbreviation
	icon [ˈaɪkɒn]	Symbol; Ikone	= small pictures you can use in texts
	to **replace (by/with)** [rɪˈpleɪs (baɪ/wɪð)]	ersetzen (durch)	*Icons replace* words in texts.
13	**husband** [ˈhʌzbənd]	Ehemann	My dad is my mum's *husband*.

14	**Get well soon!** [ˌget wel ˈsuːn]	Gute Besserung!	You send a 'Get well soon' card to someone who is not well.
	Congratulations! [kənˌgrætʃəˈleɪʃnz]	Glückwunsch!; Gratuliere!	*Congratulations!* You won the competition.
	hug [hʌg]	Umarmung	Luke gave Sherlock a big *hug*.
	kiss [kɪs]	Kuss	a *kiss* → to kiss When they said goodbye, she gave him a *kiss*.
	Hooray! [hʊˈreɪ]	Hurra!	*Hooray*, you did it!
16	**neutral** [ˈnjuːtrl]	neutral	The language should be *neutral* – not formal or informal.

Across cultures 3 Dos and don'ts

	dos and don'ts [ˌduːz ənd ˈdəʊnts]	Ge- und Verbote; was man tun und was man nicht tun sollte	= the things you should and shouldn't do
1	**behaviour** *(no pl)* [bɪˈheɪvjə]	Verhalten; Benehmen; Betragen	*behaviour* → to behave
	to **hold open** [ˌhəʊld ˈəʊpn]	aufhalten	It's polite to *hold* the door *open* for others.
	to **litter** [ˈlɪtə]	verschmutzen; Müll herumliegen lassen; verunreinigen	Don't *litter* the playground. Take your rubbish home with you.
	among [əˈmʌŋ]	unter; inmitten	**!** *among* ≠ under He stood *among* his friends. He stood under a tree.
2	**odd** [ɒd]	seltsam; komisch	= strange
	to **go on** [gəʊ ˈɒn]	geschehen; los sein; ablaufen	I didn't understand what was *going on*.
	to **guess** [ges]	annehmen; vermuten; raten; erraten	You look tired. I *guess* you want to go home.
	custom [ˈkʌstəm]	Gewohnheit; Brauch; Sitte	People often wear funny costumes at Halloween. It's a *custom*.
4	**icebreaker** [ˈaɪsˌbreɪkə]	Eisbrecher *(Sätze, um mit jmdm. ins Gespräch zu kommen)*	= phrases which people use to start a conversation
	glad [glæd]	froh; dankbar	I'm *glad* you aren't angry with me.
	crowded [ˈkraʊdɪd]	überfüllt	= full of people
5	**chapter** [ˈtʃæptə]	Kapitel	This book has got 15 *chapters*.
	manners *(pl)* [ˈmænəz]	Manieren; Benehmen	It's good *manners* to say hello.

Unit 4 On the move

Check-in

	on the move [ˌɒnˌðə 'muːv]	unterwegs	He has to travel a lot in his job. He's always *on the move*.
	travel ['trævl]	Reise-	I read an interesting *travel* report yesterday.
	itinerary [aɪ'tɪnrri]	Reiseplan; Reiseroute; Reiseweg	The *itinerary* for our holiday looks interesting.
1	**foreign language** [ˌfɒrɪn 'læŋgwɪdʒ]	Fremdsprache	A lot of British schools teach French as a first *foreign language*.
2	**seasick** ['siːsɪk]	seekrank	People sometimes feel *seasick* when they're travelling on boats or ships in bad weather.
	luggage *(no pl)* ['lʌgɪdʒ]	Gepäck	We've got too much *luggage*. What shall we do?
	flying [flaɪ]	Fliegen	I'm not scared of *flying*.
	to **miss** [mɪs]	verpassen; versäumen	We were late and *missed* the train.
	plane [pleɪn]	Flugzeug	The *plane* was flying very low.
3	**departure lounge** [dɪ'pɑːtʃə ˌlaʊndʒ]	Abflughalle	We waited in the *departure lounge* because our plane was late.
	passport ['pɑːspɔːt]	Pass; Reisepass	If you want to travel from Germany to New York, you'll need a *passport*.
	boarding card ['bɔːdɪŋ ˌkɑːd]	Bordkarte	You need a *boarding card* to get on a plane.
	desk [desk]	Schalter; Schreibtisch	The check-in *desk* was closed when we arrived.
	visa, visas *(pl)* ['viːzə, 'viːzəz]	Visum, Visa *(Pl.)*; Einreisebewilligung	I can't travel to the US. I didn't get a *visa*.
	passenger ['pæsndʒə]	Passagier/-in; Fahrgast	= a person who is travelling by plane, train, bus etc.
	flight attendant ['flaɪtˌəˌtendnt]	Flugbegleiter/-in	A *flight attendant* looks after the passengers on a plane.
	customs *(sg)* ['kʌstəmz]	Zoll	! *Customs* **is** on your right.
	suitcase ['suːtkeɪs]	Koffer	Have you packed your *suitcase* yet?
	airport ['eəpɔːt]	Flughafen	London has got five *airports*. *Fr.* aéroport *(m)*
	ferry ['feri]	Fähre	= a boat that takes passengers and cars across a river or a narrow part of the sea
	control [kən'trəʊl]	Kontrolle	If you want to travel by plane, you have to go through passport *control*.
3	**arrivals hall** [ə'raɪvlz ˌhɔːl]	Ankunftshalle	*arrivals hall* → to arrive
	foreign ['fɒrɪn]	ausländisch; fremd	*foreign* → foreign language
	currency ['kʌrnsi]	Währung	The *currency* in the UK is the British pound.
	environmentally friendly [ɪnˌvaɪrnˌmentli 'frendli]	umweltfreundlich	*environmentally friendly* → environmental issues

CO₂ (carbon dioxide) [ˌsiːəʊˈtuː (ˌkɑːbn daɪˈɒksaɪd)]	Kohlendioxid; CO_2	CO_2 is bad for the environment.
emission [ɪˈmɪʃn]	Emission; Ausstoß	Scientists check CO_2 *emissions* in cities.
holidays *(pl)* [ˈhɒlədeɪz]	Ferien; Schulferien	*Holidays*! Great! No school.
means of transport *(sg or pl!)* [ˌmiːnz ˌəv ˈtrænspɔːt]	Transportmittel; Verkehrsmittel	= cars, buses, trains, planes etc.
convenience [kənˈviːniəns]	Zweckmäßigkeit; Annehmlichkeit; Komfort	The issue of *convenience* is important when you look at means of transport.

(marker: 4 at "means of transport" row)

Nouns and verbs with the same form

answer	to answer	exchange	to exchange	name	to name
change	to change	film	to film	plan	to plan
chat	to chat	fight	to fight	plant	to plant
compromise	to compromise	help	to help	post	to post
control	to control	hope	to hope	rain	to rain
dance	to dance	interview	to interview	reply	to reply
design	to design	joke	to joke	run	to run
dream	to dream	land	to land	show	to show
drink	to drink	lie	to lie	smile	to smile
email	to email	look	to look	travel	to travel
end	to end	love	to love	work	to work

Station 1: What time do we get there?

coast [kəʊst]	Küste	= where the land meets the sea *coast* → coastal path
enthusiasm [ɪnˈθjuːziæzm]	Begeisterung; Enthusiasmus	She talks about her city with so much *enthusiasm*.
holiday home [ˈhɒlədeɪ ˌhəʊm]	Ferienhaus	The *holiday home* we stayed in last summer was perfect.
local time [ˈləʊkl ˌtaɪm]	Ortszeit	We will arrive at 1:30 p.m. *local time*.
ahead [əˈhed]	vor; vorn; voraus	In France the time is one hour *ahead* of English time.
port [pɔːt]	Hafen	The ferry arrived at the *port* late.
to mumble [ˈmʌmbl]	murmeln; nuscheln	Charlie wasn't very happy and he *mumbled* quietly.
to dial [ˈdaɪəl]	wählen	I *dialled* the number and waited for someone to answer the phone.
flight [flaɪt]	Flug	*flight* → flight attendant

(marker: 5 at "flight" row)

Station 2: At passport control

to fly, flew, flown [flaɪ; fluː; fləʊn]	fliegen	We *flew* from Berlin to London for the weekend.
document [ˈdɒkjəmənt]	Dokument; Urkunde	A ticket and passport are important travel *documents*.

to **continue** [kən'tɪnju:]	fortfahren; andauern; weitermachen	He didn't stop. He just *continued* talking.	
valid ['vælɪd]	gültig	My passport is *valid* until next year.	
to **expire** [ɪk'spaɪə]	ablaufen	I don't need a new passport before my old one *expires*.	
to **insist (on)** [ɪn'sɪst (ɒn)]	bestehen (auf); insistieren	I *insisted* that we buy enough to drink.	
to **apply for** [ə'plaɪ fə]	beantragen; sich bewerben um	I have to *apply for* a new passport before I travel.	
regulation [ˌregjə'leɪʃn]	Vorschrift; Regelung; Regulierung	I'll look up the *regulations* on the internet.	
awake [ə'weɪk]	wach	I'm so tired. We stayed *awake* all night.	
to **frown** [fraʊn]	die Stirn runzeln	He *frowned* because he didn't believe me.	
to **enter** ['entə]	einreisen; hineingehen; betreten; eintreten; mitmachen	The teacher *entered* the room. *Fr.* entrer	
side room ['saɪd ˌrʊm]	Nebenraum	We celebrated my birthday in a *side room* in the restaurant.	
luckily ['lʌkɪli]	glücklicherweise	*Luckily* we still had enough money and could pay for our lunch.	
immigration officer [ɪmɪ'greɪʃn ˌɒfɪsə]	Grenzschutzbeamter/-beamtin; Einwanderungsbeamter/-beamtin	The *immigration officer* checked the documents very carefully.	
relief [rɪ'li:f]	Erleichterung; Linderung	"Thank you " Rafiq said with *relief*.	

11	**traffic** ['træfɪk]	Verkehr	= all the cars, buses etc. that are moving on a road
	to **bargain** ['bɑ:gɪn]	verhandeln	I'm not sure if I can *bargain* with a taxi driver.
12	**research** *(no pl)* [rɪ'sɜ:tʃ]	Recherche; Forschung; Untersuchung	The students did a lot of *research*.
	truth [tru:θ]	Wahrheit	*truth* ↔ lie *truth* → true
	Bengali [beŋ'gɔ:li]	Bengale/Bengalin; bengalisch	The *Bengali* alphabet was hard to learn.
15	**European** [ˌjʊərə'pi:ən]	Europäer/-in; europäisch; aus Europa	*European* → Europe

Skills: How to plan a travel itinerary

1	**tour operator** ['tʊərˌɒpreɪtə]	Reiseveranstalter	Which *tour operator* did you book your holiday with?
	flexible ['fleksɪbl]	flexibel	**!** Achtung Schreibung und Aussprache
	practical ['præktɪkl]	praktisch	*Fr.* pratique
	wasteful ['weɪstfl]	verschwenderisch	Don't be *wasteful* with water!
	illness ['ɪlnəs]	Krankheit	I felt really bad for two weeks. I don't know what kind of *illness* I had.
	local ['ləʊkl]	Ortsansässige/-r; Einheimische/-r	I'm not from here. I'm not a *local*.
	package tour ['pækɪdʒ ˌtʊə]	Pauschalreise	The *package tour* included everything we wanted.

perspective [pə'spektɪv]	Perspektive; Blickwinkel	When you look at a problem from two *perspectives* you look at it from two sides.
2 **mix** [mɪks]	Mischung	The meal was a perfect *mix* of meat and vegetables.
unforgettable [ˌʌnfə'getəbl]	unvergesslich	*unforgettable* → to forget
arrival [ə'raɪvl]	Ankunft	*arrival* → to arrive
pace [peɪs]	Geschwindigkeit; Gangart	We wanted to discover London at our own *pace*.
overall [ˌəʊvr'ɔ:l]	allgemein; Gesamt-	The bus tour gave us an *overall* view of the city.
tasty ['teɪsti]	lecker; schmackhaft	This sandwich is *tasty*.
a must-see [ə ˌmʌst 'si:]	unbedingt empfehlenswert	The Tower of London is *a must-see* in London.
prisoner ['prɪznə]	Gefangene/-r; Häftling; Sträfling	*prisoner* → prison
death [deθ]	Tod	*death* → dead
stall [stɔ:l]	Stand; Bude	There were lots of clothes *stalls* in the market.

Unit task: Our class trip

catalogue ['kætlɒg]	Katalog; Broschüre	We looked at lots of travel *catalogues* for a holiday.
to **require** [rɪ'kwaɪə]	benötigen; erfordern	= to need
based on ['beɪst ˌɒn]	basierend auf; beruhend auf	Their decision was *based on* their feelings.
criterion, criteria *(pl)* [kraɪ'tɪəriən; kraɪ'tɪəriə]	Kriterium; Kriterien *(Pl.)*	What *criteria* is your research based on?
alternative [ɔ:l'tɜ:nətɪv]	Alternative	! Achtung Aussprache
to **draw up, drew up, drawn up** [drɔ: 'ʌp; dru: 'ʌp; drɔ:n 'ʌp]	entwerfen	*Draw up* an interesting itinerary.
introduction [ˌɪntrə'dʌkʃn]	Einführung; Einleitung	the *introduction* of a report = the first part of a report

Story: Where I belong

where I belong [ˌweər ˌaɪ bɪ'lɒŋ]	wo ich hingehöre	Sometimes I ask myself *where I belong*.
1 to **lead, led, led** [li:d; led; led]	führen; anführen	I followed my dad and he *led* the way to the beach.
responsible [rɪs'pɒnsəbl]	verantwortlich; zuständig	Who is *responsible* for the pets?
to **change one's mind** [ˌtʃeɪndʒ wʌnz 'maɪnd]	seine Meinung ändern	I hated the film at first, but now I like it. I've *changed my mind* about it.
to **accept** [ək'sept]	akzeptieren; hinnehmen; annehmen	I had to *accept* my parents' decision.
mask [mɑ:sk]	Maske	He showed no feelings. His face looked like a *mask*.
smuggler ['smʌglə]	Schmuggler/-in	I'm reading an exciting adventure story about *smugglers*.

overloaded [ˌəʊvəˈləʊdɪd]	überladen	The bus was completely *overloaded*.
shark [ʃɑːk]	Hai	You can't go swimming here. There are *sharks* everywhere!
crushed [krʌʃt]	eingequetscht; eingeklemmt	The doors were closing and the man was *crushed*.
to **rock** [rɒk]	schaukeln	The wind was very strong and the boat *rocked* badly.
to **smash** [smæʃ]	zerschlagen; zerschmettern	The waves *smashed* against the boat.
to **survive** [səˈvaɪv]	überleben	I don't know how I *survived* my exams.
to **close oneself away from** [ˌkləʊz əˈweɪ frəm]	sich abschotten von	I *closed myself away from* what was happening around me.
to **give sb a piggyback** [gɪv ə ˈpɪgibæk]	jmdn. Huckepack nehmen	My legs were tired and my dad *gave me a piggyback*.
checkpoint [ˈtʃekpɔɪnt]	Kontrollpunkt	*checkpoint* → to check
to **concentrate (on)** [ˈkɒnsntreɪt (ɒn)]	(sich) konzentrieren (auf)	Stop talking and *concentrate* on your work!
steady [ˈstedi]	kontinuierlich; unaufhörlich	The rain was *steady* and it didn't stop.
depressing [dɪˈpresɪŋ]	deprimierend; bedrückend	It rained for more than a week, which was very *depressing* for everyone.
drizzle [ˈdrɪzl]	Nieselregen	= fine rain
to **cover** [ˈkʌvə]	abdecken; bedecken; zudecken	I *covered* my head because it was raining.
concrete [ˈkɒnkriːt]	Beton	The streets in a city are covered with *concrete*.
official [əˈfɪʃl]	Beamter/Beamtin	The *officials* just looked at her passport and then let her into the country.
useless [ˈjuːsləs]	nutzlos	*useless* ↔ useful
invisible [ɪnˈvɪzəbl]	unsichtbar	If something becomes *invisible*, you can't see it any more.
phone box [ˈfəʊn ˌbɒks]	Telefonzelle	There are not a lot of *phone boxes* any more because almost everybody has got a mobile phone.
to **fetch** [fetʃ]	holen; abholen	Wait at the station. I'm going to *fetch* you.
on one's own [ɒn wʌnz ˈəʊn]	allein; für sich	If you're *on your own*, you're alone.
to **press** [pres]	drücken; pressen	She *pressed* her lips together.
button [ˈbʌtn]	Knopf	How do I open this? – It's easy. Just press the *button*.
Somali [səˈmɑːli]	Somali; somalisch	In Somalia people speak *Somali*.
straight [streɪt]	gerade; direkt; geradewegs	Go *straight* to school. You're late.
to **hesitate** [ˈhezɪteɪt]	zögern	She *hesitated* for a few seconds, then she entered the room.
2 **refugee** [ˌrefjʊˈdʒiː]	Flüchtling	I'm a *refugee*. I had to leave my country.
4 **narrator** [nəˈreɪtə]	Erzähler/-in	The *narrator* of a story is the person who tells it.
5 **gadget** [ˈgædʒɪt]	Gerät; technische Spielerei	Smartphones and play stations are *gadgets*.
climate [ˈklaɪmət]	Klima	= the kind of weather that is typical of a country or area
to **be homesick** [bi ˈhəʊmsɪk]	Heimweh haben	*Are* you *homesick* when you're away from home?

Travel words

Means of transport

bus	Bus
car	Auto
coach	Reisebus
ferry	Fähre
plane	Flugzeug
taxi	Taxi

Equipment

boarding card	Bordkarte
foreign currency	Fremdwährung
luggage	Gepäck
passport	Pass; Reisepass
suitcase	Koffer
ticket	Ticket; Fahrkarte
valid documents	gültige Unterlagen
visa	Visum

Others

climate	Klima
flight	Flug
foreign language	Fremdsprache
itinerary	Reiseplan; Reisebeschreibung
local time	Ortszeit
regulations	Vorschriften; Regelungen; Regulierungen

Write 4–5 sentences about your last holiday.

People

flight attendant	Flugbegleiter/-in
passenger	Passagier/-in; Fahrgast
security guard	Sicherheitsdienst
taxi driver	Taxifahrer/-in
tour operator	Reiseveranstalter

Places

airport	Flughafen
arrivals hall	Ankunftshalle
check-in	Einchecken; Gepäckaufgabe
checkpoint	Kontrollpunkt
customs	Zoll
departure lounge	Abflughalle
desk	Schalter
destination	Reiseziel
gate	Gate; Flugsteig; Ausgang
holiday home	Ferienhaus
hotel	Hotel
lobby	Empfangsbereich; Eingang
passport control	Passkontrolle
port	Hafen
station (bus/train)	Bahnhof

Action UK! The guitar lesson

guitar [gɪˈtɑː]	Gitarre	My favourite instrument is the *guitar*.
1 **I go wherever the wind takes me.** [aɪ ˌgəʊ weəˌrevə ðə wɪnd ˈteɪks miː]	Ich lasse mich treiben.	Let's *go wherever the wind takes us.*
2 **future** [ˈfjuːtʃə]	zukünftig; Zukunfts-	Talk about your *future* plans.
origin [ˈɒrɪdʒɪn]	Ursprung; Herkunft; Abstammung	The girl is of American *origin*.
outgoing [ˈaʊtˌgəʊɪŋ]	kontaktfreudig	*outgoing* ↔ shy
easy-going [ˈiːzɪˌgəʊɪŋ]	locker; unkompliziert	Who is more *easy-going* – your dad or your mum?
3 **genre** [ˈʒɑ̃ːnrə]	Gattung; Genre	Which film *genre* do you like best?

to **be set in** [bɪ ˈset ɪn]	spielen in	The film *is set in* London in the 1990s.
unreal [ˌʌnˈrɪəl]	unwirklich	*unreal* ↔ real
romance [ˈrəmæns]	Liebesgeschichte; Liebesfilm	I don't like *romances*.
specific [spəˈsɪfɪk]	spezifisch; speziell	*specific* → special
era [ˈɪərə]	Ära; Zeitalter	The Industrial Revolution was an exciting *era* in British history.
lavish [ˈlævɪʃ]	üppig; verschwenderisch	We don't need *lavish* meals on holiday. We like simple food.
magic [ˈmædʒɪk]	Magie; Zauberei	*magic* → magical
supernatural [ˌsuːpəˈnætʃrl]	übernatürlich	Fantasy stories are usually about people with magical or *supernatural* powers.
force [fɔːs]	Kraft; Macht	The hero couldn't beat the supernatural *forces*.
mythical [ˈmɪθɪkl]	sagenhaft; sagenumwoben	Fantasy stories are set in a *mythical* place.

Check-out

2	**the rest** [rest]	der Rest	We aren't going to cycle for *the rest* of the holiday.
3	**emergency** [ɪˈmɜːdʒnsi]	Notfall; Notlage	The *emergency* numbers are next to the phone.
	booklet [ˈbʊklət]	Broschüre; Heft	*booklet* → book
	to **sort** [sɔːt]	sortieren	Please *sort* your socks.

Aufgabe **Sounds and spellings**
Laute und Rechtschreibung

a) *Write these words in your exercise book. Say them out loud and underline the letters you don't speak (the 'silent letters').*

autumn   birds   castle   could   fascinating   foreign   frown

guess   ghost   island   know   lambs   local   travel

b) *Write the sentences in your exercise book and complete them with the words from a).*

1. We went to an amazing ▮ in the middle of the sea.
2. The ▮ in the ▮ was very scary.
3. The ▮ in the Tower are ravens.
4. ▮ are born in the spring not in the ▮.
5. Did you ▮ the answer? I didn't. I had to ▮.
6. You need to speak a ▮ language when you ▮ to some countries.
7. Find out the ▮ time at your destination before you leave.
8. It was a ▮ museum we went to yesterday.
9. Why did you ▮ at me? ▮ we talk about the problem, please?

‹Trailer 1 Walking in the Highlands feels great!›

return [rɪ'tɜːn]	Rückkehr	*return* → to return
travel ['trævl]	Reise-	I read an interesting *travel* report.
hardly ['hɑːdli]	kaum	I can *hardly* believe it.
(not) any longer [(nɒt‿)ˌeni 'lɒŋgə]	(nicht) mehr; (nicht) länger	At the end I could hardly walk *any longer*.
trail [treɪl]	Weg; Pfad	We took the *trail* from Fort William to Cape Wrath.
daily ['deɪli]	täglich	We walked 12 miles *daily*.
the wild [ðə 'waɪld]	Wildnis; freie Wildbahn	*the wild* → wild
tent [tent]	Zelt	We slept in a *tent*.
to fly, flew, flown [flaɪ; fluː; fləʊn]	fliegen	The wind was so strong that we thought the tent would *fly* away.
howling ['haʊlɪŋ]	heulend	I didn't like the *howling* wind at night.
firewood ['faɪəwʊd]	Brennholz	fire + wood = *firewood*
to warm [wɔːm]	aufwärmen	We *warmed* our food over the fire.
fire [faɪə]	Feuer	*fire* → firewood
to taste [teɪst]	probieren; kosten; schmecken	I've never *tasted* haggis. What's it like?
tin [tɪn]	Dose; Büchse	The *tins* are really heavy.
to carry ['kæri]	*hier:* befördern; mit sich tragen	The rivers *carry* a lot of water at this time of year.
fence [fens]	Zaun	Farmers put *fences* around their fields.
military ['mɪlɪtri]	militärisch	It was dangerous in the *military* areas.
firing range ['faɪrɪŋ ˌreɪndʒ]	Schießplatz	I didn't know there were *firing ranges* in the Highlands.
unmarked [ʌn'mɑːkt]	nicht gekennzeichnet	The trail was completely *unmarked*.
compass ['kʌmpəs]	Kompass	We got lost, but luckily we had a *compass*.
hiker ['haɪkə]	Wanderer/-in	*hiker* → hiking
air [eə]	Luft	Let's go for a walk and get some fresh *air*.
to smell, smelt, smelt [smel; smelt; smelt]	riechen; duften	The air in the Highlands *smelt* wonderful.
1	to experience [ɪk'spɪəriəns]	erleben; erfahren	We *experienced* some great things on the trip. *to experience* → an experience
3	to dry [draɪ]	trocknen	Our boots were wet so we *dried* them.
5	lost [lɒst]	verloren	'*Lost* in the Highlands' is a dramatic title.
prepared [prɪ'peəd]	vorbereitet	I wasn't very well *prepared* for the trip.
hostel ['hɒstl]	Herberge	A *hostel* is cheaper than a hotel.

at least [ət ˈliːst]	zumindest; mindestens; wenigstens	It wasn't late, *at least* I didn't think it was.	
view [vjuː]	Aussicht; Sicht; Ausblick; Blick	There's a fantastic *view* from the top.	
within [wɪˈðɪn]	innerhalb (von)	We were totally wet *within* five minutes.	
fog [fɒg]	Nebel	We couldn't see through the *fog*.	
to clear [klɪə]	aufklaren	On the way down the fog *cleared*.	

⟨Trailer 2 Robin Hood's diary⟩

1	power [paʊə]	Kraft; Macht; Stärke	The king and his men have all the *power*.
	little [ˈlɪtl]	wenig	**!** *little* = not much; almost nothing: The poor people have so *little* to give. a *little* = some: They have to save a little food every month.
	husband [ˈhʌzbənd]	Ehemann	My dad is my mum's *husband*.
	ours [aʊəz]	unser/-er/-e/-es	This isn't your house. It's *ours*.
	to get out (of) [ˌget ˈaʊt (_əv)]	verschwinden (von/aus)	Let's *get out of* Sherwood Forest and look for the Sheriff.
	theirs [ðeəz]	ihre/-r/-es	This money belongs to them. It's *theirs*.
	to be good with [bi ˈgʊd wɪð]	gut umgehen können mit	I'm *good with* animals.
	to turn in [ˌtɜːn ˈɪn]	sich stellen	The Sheriff thinks Robin Hood should *turn* himself *in*.
	wise [waɪz]	weise	The woman gave me a very *wise* answer.
5	to hunt [hʌnt]	jagen	Robin Hood and his men *hunted* for food.
	terrible [ˈterəbl]	furchtbar; schrecklich; schlimm	Should we help that woman? The Sheriff was *terrible* to her.
6	all over [ˌɔːlˈəʊvə]	überall (in)	*all over* the country = im ganzen Land
	pleasure [ˈpleʒə]	Freude; Vergnügen	Come and visit us! The *pleasure* will be ours!

⟨Trailer 3 A trip to Dublin⟩

bank holiday [ˌbæŋk ˈhɒlɪdeɪ]	Feiertag	Jessica visited Dublin for the *bank holiday*.	
accommodation [əˌkɒməˈdeɪʃn]	Unterkunft; Unterbringung	A place where you can stay (e.g. for a holiday) or live.	
right [raɪt]	direkt; genau	Our flat is *right* in the city centre.	
grand [grænd]	großartig; prächtig; o.k.	In Ireland people use '*grand*' to say 'just fine'.	
yummy [ˈjʌmi]	lecker	= delicious	

	stew [stjuː]	Eintopf	Irish *stew* is a typical meal in Ireland.
	boxty [ˈbɒksti]	*irische Pfannkuchen aus Kartoffeln*	*Boxty* is a traditional Irish potato pancake.
	pancake [ˈpænkeɪk]	Pfannkuchen	I love *pancakes* with sugar on them.
	secret [ˈsiːkrət]	geheim; Geheim-	It's *secret*. = It's a secret.
	last but not least [ˌlɑːst bʌt nɒt ˈliːst]	zu guter Letzt	*Last but not least*: There was great music.
	cosy [ˈkəʊzi]	gemütlich; kuschelig	The café we went to was small and *cosy*.
	pub [pʌb]	Kneipe; Gasthaus	The *pub* wasn't far from the hotel.
	live [laɪv]	live	! Achtung Aussprache: *live* ↔ to live
	tin whistle [ˈtɪn ˌwɪsl]	Blechflöte	The *tin whistle* is really small and hard to play.
	Bodhrán [ˈbɒdrən]	*traditionelle irische Trommel*	Have you ever seen or heard a *Bodhrán*?
	fiddle [ˈfɪdl]	Geige	I can play the *fiddle*.
	to get [ɡet]	verstehen; begreifen	I liked the songs but didn't *get* the meaning because I don't understand Gaelic.
2	thingy [ˈθɪŋi]	Dingsda	What's the name of that *thingy* again?
3	to perceive [pəˈsiːv]	wahrnehmen; empfinden; betrachten	How do you *perceive* this story?
	sleeve [sliːv]	Ärmel	A jumper has got two *sleeves*.
	patron saint [ˈpeɪtrn ˌseɪnt]	Nationalheiliger	St Patrick is the *patron saint* of Ireland.
	Christianity [ˌkrɪstiˈænəti]	Christentum	St Patrick brought *Christianity* to Ireland too.
	parade [pəˈreɪd]	Parade; Umzug	There are lots of street *parades* on St Patrick's Day.

Dictionary

In dieser alphabetischen Wortliste findest du das gesamte Vokabular von *Green Line* 1 G9, *Green Line* 2 G9 und *Green Line* 3 G9. Namen stehen in einer extra Liste am Ende des **Dictionary**.
Einträge, die aus mehreren Wörtern bestehen, kannst du meist unter verschiedenen Stichwörtern nachschlagen.
So ist z.B. *front door* unter *front* und unter *door* eingetragen. Die Fundstellen stehen immer hinter dem jeweiligen Wort und zeigen dir an, wo es zum ersten Mal vorkommt, z. B.:
airport ['eəpɔ:t] Flughafen III U4, 95 kommt zum ersten Mal vor in Band III, Unit 4, Seite 95
absolutely [ˌæbsə'lu:tli] völlig; absolut III TMS2, 83 kommt zum ersten Mal vor in Band III, Text and media smart 2, Seite 83
U = Unit, TMS = Text and media smart, AC = Across cultures, ⟨TR⟩ = Trailer
Die mit * gekennzeichneten Verben sind unregelmäßig. Eine Übersicht der *irregular verbs* findest du ab S. 292.
Die mit ° gekennzeichneten Vokabeln sind rezeptiv.
Die mit ⟨ ⟩ gekennzeichneten Vokabeln beziehen sich auf fakultative Übungen oder Buchteile oder sind nur zum Nachschlagen im **Dictionary**.

A

a [ə] ein/-e I
a bag of … [ə 'bæɡ əv] eine Tüte … I
a bit [ə 'bɪt] ein bisschen; ein wenig II
a box of … [ə 'bɒks əv] eine Schachtel …; eine Kiste …; ein Karton … I
a couple of [ə 'kʌpl əv] ein paar I
a cup of … [ə 'kʌp əv] eine Tasse … I
a few [ə 'fju:] ein paar; wenige; einige I
a little [ə 'lɪtl] ein wenig; etwas I
a lot [ə 'lɒt] viel; oft I
a lot of [ə 'lɒt əv] viel/-e; eine Menge I
a piece of … [ə 'pi:s əv] ein Stück … I
a.m. [eɪ'em] vormittags (*Uhrzeit*); morgens (*Uhrzeit*) I
to abbreviate [ə'bri:vieɪt] abkürzen III TMS2, 84
abbreviation [əˌbri:vi'eɪʃn] Abkürzung I
*****to be able to (do sth)** [bi 'eɪbl tə] fähig sein zu; können; dürfen III U1, 21
aboard [ə'bɔ:d] an Bord I
about [ə'baʊt] ungefähr; circa; etwa I
out and **about** [ˌaʊt ən ə'baʊt] unterwegs I
about [ə'baʊt] über; von I
What **about** …? ['wɒt əbaʊt] Was ist mit …?; Wie wär's mit …? I
above [ə'bʌv] über; oberhalb (von); oben II
absolutely [ˌæbsə'lu:tli] völlig; absolut III TMS2, 83
accent ['æksnt] Akzent II
to accept [ək'sept] akzeptieren; hinnehmen; annehmen III U4, 104
accident ['æksɪdnt] Unfall II
accommodation [əˌkɒmə'deɪʃn] Unterkunft; Unterbringung ⟨III TR3, 114⟩
account settings [ə'kaʊnt ˌsetɪŋz] Profileinstellungen III U1, 23
across [ə'krɒs] auf der anderen Seite von; über; hinüber; herüber; quer durch I
acrostic [ə'krɒstɪk] Akrostichon (*Gedicht, bei der die Anfangsbuchstaben hintereinander gelesen einen Sinn ergeben*) III TMS1, 32

to **act** [ækt] spielen (*Theater*) II
acting ['æktɪŋ] Schauspielen II
action ['ækʃn] Handlung; Action; Aktion I
active ['æktɪv] aktiv °III U2, 44
activity [æk'tɪvəti] Aktivität I
actor/**actress** ['æktə] Schauspieler/Schauspielerin III U3, 69
actually ['æktʃuəli] tatsächlich; wirklich; eigentlich III U2, 45
AD (= Anno Domini) [eɪ'di:] nach Christus III U3, 63
to **add** [æd] hinzufügen; ergänzen; addieren I
addiction [ə'dɪkʃn] Sucht; Abhängigkeit II
additional [ə'dɪʃnl] zusätzlich II
address [ə'dres] Adresse I
postal **address** ['pəʊstl əˌdres] Postanschrift III TMS2, 81
admission [əd'mɪʃn] Einlass; Zutritt II
adult ['ædʌlt] Erwachsene/-r II
adventure [əd'ventʃə] Abenteuer II
adverb ['ædvɜ:b] Adverb II
adverb of degree [ˌædvɜ:b əv dɪ'gri:] Gradadverb °III U2, 48
advice (*no pl*) [əd'vaɪs] Rat; Ratschlag I
piece of **advice** [ˌpi:s əv əd'vaɪs] Rat; Ratschlag; Hinweis II
after ['ɑ:ftə] nach (*zeitlich*) I
after all [ˌɑ:ftər 'ɔ:l] doch; schließlich; immerhin II
after that [ˌɑ:ftə 'ðæt] danach I
afternoon [ˌɑ:ftə'nu:n] Nachmittag I
this **afternoon** [ðɪs ˌɑ:ftə'nu:n] heute Nachmittag II
again [ə'gen] wieder; noch einmal; noch mal I
against [ə'genst] gegen II
age [eɪdʒ] Alter; Zeitalter III U1, 12
Bronze **Age** ['brɒnz eɪdʒ] Bronzezeit (*ca. 2200–800 v. Chr.*) II
golden **age** [ˌgəʊldn 'eɪdʒ] goldenes Zeitalter III U3, 65
Middle **Ages** [ˌmɪdl 'eɪdʒɪz] Mittelalter III U3, 63

ages ago ['eɪdʒɪz əˌgəʊ] vor langer Zeit; vor einer Ewigkeit II
travel **agent's** ['trævl ˌeɪdʒnts] Reisebüro II
aggressive [ə'gresɪv] aggressiv II
ago [ə'gəʊ] vor (*zeitlich*) II
ages **ago** ['eɪdʒɪz əˌgəʊ] vor langer Zeit; vor einer Ewigkeit II
agony aunt ['æɡəni ˌɑ:nt] Kummerkastentante II
to **agree** [ə'gri:] zustimmen; einer Meinung sein; sich einigen III U1, 9
ahead [ə'hed] vor; vorn; voraus III U4, 96
first **aid kit** [ˌfɜ:st eɪd 'kɪt] Erste-Hilfe-Kasten I
ain't (= isn't/aren't) [eɪnt] ist nicht; sind nicht ⟨III TMS1, 27⟩
air [eə] Luft ⟨III TR1, 110⟩
air-conditioning [eəkən'dɪʃnɪŋ] Klimaanlage III U4, 105
airport ['eəpɔ:t] Flughafen III U4, 95
album ['ælbəm] Album III TMS1, 29
alien ['eɪliən] Außerirdische/-r; außerirdisches Wesen II
all [ɔ:l] alle/-s; ganz I
after **all** [ˌɑ:ftər 'ɔ:l] doch; schließlich; immerhin II
all night [ɔ:l 'naɪt] die ganze Nacht II
all over [ˌɔ:l 'əʊvə] überall (in) ⟨III TR2, 112⟩
all the time [ɔ:l ðə 'taɪm] die ganze Zeit II
(not) at **all** [ət 'ɔ:l] überhaupt (nicht) II
all of us ['ɔ:l əv ˌʌs] wir alle II
bowling **alley** ['bəʊlɪŋ ˌæli] Bowlingbahn II
to **allow** [ə'laʊ] erlauben; gestatten II
*****to be allowed** to (do sth) [bi ə'laʊd tə] dürfen III U1, 20
almost ['ɔ:lməʊst] fast; beinahe II
alone [ə'ləʊn] allein; ohne fremde Hilfe I
along [ə'lɒŋ] entlang II
*****to sing along** [ˌsɪŋ ə'lɒŋ] mitsingen III TMS1, 29
alphabet ['ælfəbet] Alphabet II
alphabetical [ˌælfə'betɪkl] alphabetisch II
already [ɔ:l'redi] schon; bereits I

alright (= all right) [ɔːlˈraɪt] in Ordnung; alles klar ⟨III TMS1, 27⟩

also [ˈɔːlsəʊ] auch II

alternative [ɔːlˈtɜːnətɪv] Alternative III U4, 103

always [ˈɔːlweɪz] immer; ständig I

amazing [əˈmeɪzɪŋ] unglaublich; toll; erstaunlich II

ambulance [ˈæmbjələns] Krankenwagen III U3, 75

American [əˈmerɪkən] Amerikanisch; amerikanisch; aus Amerika; Amerikaner/-in II

among [əˈmʌŋ] unter; inmitten III AC3, 88

an [ən] ein/-e I

and [ænd; ənd] und I

anger (no pl) [ˈæŋgə] Zorn; Wut III U1, 21

Anglo-Saxon [ˌæŋgləʊˈsæksn] Angelsachse; Angelsächsin; angelsächsisch III U3, 63

angry [ˈæŋgri] wütend; zornig; verärgert; böse I
  *to make sb **angry** [meɪk ˈæŋgri] jmdn. wütend machen; jmdn. verärgern III AC1, 35

animal [ˈænɪməl] Tier I

ankle [ˈæŋkl] Fußgelenk; Fußknöchel II
  to twist your **ankle** [ˌtwɪst jɔːr ˈæŋkl] sich den Knöchel verrenken II

announcement [əˈnaʊnsmənt] Ankündigung; Durchsage II

annoying [əˈnɔɪɪŋ] ärgerlich; lästig II

anonymous [ənˈɒnɪməs] anonym II

another [əˈnʌðə] ein/-e andere/-r/-s; noch ein/-e I
  one **another** [ˌwʌn əˈnʌðə] einander; gegenseitig III TMS1, 32

answer [ˈɑːnsə] Antwort II

to answer [ˈɑːnsə] antworten; beantworten I

national **anthem** [ˌnæʃnl ˈænθəm] Nationalhymne III U2, 47

any [ˈeni] irgendein/-e/-er; irgendwelche I
  not **any** more [ˌnɒt eni ˈmɔː] nicht mehr I
  not … **any** [ˌnɒt eni] kein/-e/-en I

anybody [ˈeniˌbɒdi] jeder (beliebige); irgendjemand II

anyone [ˈeniwʌn] jeder (beliebige); irgendjemand II
  anyone else [ˌeniwʌn ˈels] jemand anderes II

anything [ˈeniθɪŋ] irgendetwas II
  not … **anything** [ˌnɒt ˈeniθɪŋ] nichts I
  Anything else? [ˌeniθɪŋ ˈels] Sonst noch etwas? I

anyway [ˈeniweɪ] jedenfalls; trotzdem; sowieso II

anywhere [ˈeniweə] irgendwo; überall (egal, wo) II

*to tear **apart** [ˌteər əˈpɑːt] auseinanderreißen; zerreißen ⟨III TMS1, 30⟩

to apologise [əˈpɒlədʒaɪz] sich entschuldigen III U1, 23

app (= application) [æp; ˌæplɪˈkeɪʃn] App; Anwendung II

---

to appeal to sb [əˈpiːl tə] jmdm. zusagen; jmdm. gefallen; jmdn. ansprechen; jmdn. reizen III U2, 49

to appear [əˈpɪə] erscheinen; auftauchen II

apple [ˈæpl] Apfel I

to apply for [əˈplaɪ fə] beantragen; sich bewerben um III U4, 99

appropriate [əˈprəʊpriət] angemessen III AC1, 35

April [ˈeɪprl] April II

area [ˈeəriə] Gegend; Gebiet; Areal; Fläche II

argument [ˈɑːgjəmənt] Auseinandersetzung; Streit III U1, 20

arm [ɑːm] Arm II

army [ˈɑːmi] Armee ⟨III U2, 47⟩

around [əˈraʊnd] um … herum; umher I
  to turn **around** [ˌtɜːn əˈraʊnd] (sich) umdrehen; wenden II
  around the house [əˌraʊnd ðə ˈhaʊs] rund ums Haus; ums Haus herum I

to arrest [əˈrest] festnehmen; verhaften II

arrival [əˈraɪvl] Ankunft III U4, 102
  arrivals hall [əˈraɪvlz ˌhɔːl] Ankunftshalle III U4, 95

to arrive [əˈraɪv] ankommen II

arrow [ˈærəʊ] Pfeil II

art [ɑːt] Kunst; Kunstunterricht I

artist [ˈɑːtɪst] Künstler/-in II

as [æz; əz] wie II
  as … **as** [əz ˌəz] so … wie I

as [æz; əz] da; weil II
  as soon **as** [əz ˈsuːn əz] sobald II

aside [əˈsaɪd] beiseite ⟨III TMS1, 27⟩

to ask [ɑːsk] fragen; bitten I
  to **ask** for [ˈɑːsk fə] fragen nach; bitten um I

*to be **asleep** [bi əˈsliːp] schlafen II

*to fall **asleep** [ˌfɔːl əˈsliːp] einschlafen I

assembly [əˈsembli] Schülerversammlung II

at [æt; ət] in; auf; bei; an; um (bei Uhrzeitangaben) I
  at first [ət ˈfɜːst] zuerst; zunächst II
  at home [ət ˈhəʊm] zu Hause I
  at last [ət ˈlɑːst] endlich; schließlich I
  at least [ət ˈliːst] zumindest; mindestens; wenigstens ⟨III TR1, 111⟩
  at once [ət ˈwʌns] gleichzeitig; sofort ⟨III TMS2, 86⟩
  at the moment [ət ðə ˈməʊmənt] im Moment; gerade I
  at the same time [ət ðə ˌseɪm ˈtaɪm] gleichzeitig; zur selben Zeit II
  at the weekend [ət ðə ˌwiːkˈend] am Wochenende I
  (not) **at** all [ət ˈɔːl] überhaupt (nicht) II
  at this time [ˌət ðɪs ˈtaɪm] zu dieser Zeit III U3, 65

athletic [æθˈletɪk] athletisch ⟨III TMS1, 32⟩

atmosphere [ˈætməsfɪə] Atmosphäre; Stimmung II

to attack [əˈtæk] angreifen III U3, 63

---

flight **attendant** [ˈflaɪt əˌtendnt] Flugbegleiter/-in III U4, 95

attention [əˈtenʃn] Aufmerksamkeit; Beachtung II
  *to pay **attention** [ˌpeɪ əˈtenʃn] aufmerksam sein; aufpassen; jmdn./etw. beachten III U1, 24

attic [ˈætɪk] Dachboden II

to attract [əˈtrækt] anziehen; anlocken III U1, 10

attraction [əˈtrækʃn] Attraktion; Sehenswürdigkeit II

audience [ˈɔːdiəns] Publikum II

audio [ˈɔːdiəʊ] Audio-; Hör- I

audition [ɔːˈdɪʃn] Vorsprechen; Vorsingen; Vortanzen III U1, 14

August [ˈɔːgəst] August II

aunt [ɑːnt] Tante I
  agony **aunt** [ˈægəniˌɑːnt] Kummerkastentante II

author [ˈɔːθə] Autor/-in III TMS1, 32

autumn [ˈɔːtəm] Herbst ⟨III U2, 47⟩

available [əˈveɪləbl] verfügbar; erhältlich III TMS2, 81

awake [əˈweɪk] wach III U4, 99

award [əˈwɔːd] Auszeichnung; Preis II

away [əˈweɪ] weg I
  far **away** [ˌfɑːr əˈweɪ] weit weg I
  *to put **away** [ˌpʊt əˈweɪ] wegstellen; weglegen I
  right **away** [ˌraɪt əˈweɪ] sofort; gleich I
  *to run **away** [ˌrʌn əˈweɪ] wegrennen I
  *to throw **away** [ˌθrəʊ əˈweɪ] wegwerfen I

awful [ˈɔːfl] schrecklich; furchtbar I

axe [æks] Axt III U3, 65

B

baby [ˈbeɪbi] Baby; Säugling II

back [bæk] Rücken; Rückseite III U1, 21
  you've got my **back** [juːv gɒt maɪ ˈbæk] du stehst hinter mir III TMS1, 27

back [bæk] zurück I
  back then [bæk ˈðen] damals II
  *to go right **back** to [ˌgəʊ raɪt ˈbæk tə] zurückgehen auf II
  to turn **back** [tɜːn ˈbæk] umkehren; zurückgehen III U3, 69
  to date **back** to [ˈdeɪt ˌbæk tə] zurückgehen auf; stammen aus III U3, 63

backache [ˈbækeɪk] Rückenschmerzen; Rückenweh II

background [ˈbækgraʊnd] Hintergrund II

backing [ˈbækɪŋ] Hintergrund-; Background- III U1, 12
  backing dancer [ˈbækɪŋ ˌdɑːnsə] Backgroundtänzer/-in III U1, 12

backpack [ˈbækpæk] Rucksack II

backstage [ˌbækˈsteɪdʒ] Backstage; hinter der Bühne III U3, 70

bacon [ˈbeɪkn] Schinkenspeck; Speck I

bad [bæd] schlecht; böse; schlimm (ugs.) I
  Too **bad**! [ˌtuː ˈbæd] Zu dumm!; Schade! I

badminton ['bædmɪntən] Badminton I

bag [bæg] Tasche; Tüte I

a **bag** of … [ə 'bæg əv] eine Tüte … I

bagpipes (pl) ['bægpaɪps] Dudelsack
III U2, 41

baked beans (pl) [ˌbeɪkt 'biːnz] weiße
Bohnen in Tomatensoße I

bald [bɔːld] glatzköpfig; kahl **III U3**, 66

ball [bɔːl] Ball I

*to keep the **ball** bouncing [ˌkiːp ðə bɔːl
'baʊntsɪŋ] hier: das Gespräch am Laufen
halten **III AC2**, 56

to **ban** [bæn] bannen; verbieten; sperren
III U2, 44

banana [bə'nɑːnə] Banane I

band [bænd] Band; Musikgruppe **III U2**, 50

bank [bæŋk] Ufer II

bank holiday [ˌbæŋk 'hɒlɪdeɪ] Feiertag
⟨**III TR3**, 114⟩

piggy **bank** ['pɪgi bæŋk] Sparbüchse;
Spardose; Sparschwein I

word **bank** ['wɜːd ˌbæŋk] Wortsammlung
°**III AC1**, 34

bar [bɑː] Schranke; Gitterstab ⟨**III TMS1**, 30⟩
snack **bar** ['snæk ˌbɑː] Café; Imbissstube I

bare [beə] nackt; bloß ⟨**III U2**, 47⟩

bargain ['bɑːgɪn] Schnäppchen I

to **bargain** ['bɑːgɪn] verhandeln **III U4**, 100

to **bark** [bɑːk] bellen I

based on ['beɪst ɒn] basierend auf;
beruhend auf **III U4**, 103

basic ['beɪsɪk] grundlegend; Grund- II

basketball ['bɑːskɪtbɔːl] Basketball I

bath [bɑːθ] Bad; Badewanne I

bathroom ['bɑːθrʊm] Bad; Badezimmer I

battery ['bætri] Batterie; Akku II

battle ['bætl] Schlacht; Kampf **III U3**, 65

BC (= before Christ) [biː'siː] vor Christus
III U3, 63

*to **be** [biː] sein I

*to **be** able to (do sth) [bi ˈeɪbl tə] fähig
sein zu; können; dürfen **III U1**, 21

*to **be** about [bi ə'baʊt] sich handeln um;
handeln von I

*to **be** allowed to (do sth) [bi ə'laʊd tə]
dürfen **III U1**, 20

*to **be** asleep [bi ə'sliːp] schlafen II

*to **be** born [bi 'bɔːn] geboren werden
III U3, 72

*to **be** concerned (about) [bi kən'sɜːnd
(əˌbaʊt)] besorgt sein (um); beunruhigt
sein (wegen) **III U1**, 10

*to **be** fed up (with) [bi fed 'ʌp (wɪð)]
sauer sein (auf); die Nase voll haben
(von) **III U1**, 20

*to **be** gone [bi gɒn] verschwunden sein;
weg sein II

*to **be** good at [bi 'gʊd ət] gut sein in I

*to **be** good with [bi 'gʊd wɪð] gut umgehen können mit ⟨**III TR2**, 112⟩

*to **be** grounded [bi 'graʊndɪd] Hausarrest haben **III U1**, 20

*to **be** hard on sb [bi 'hɑːd ɒn] streng mit
jmdm. sein **III U1**, 16

*to **be** homesick [bi 'həʊmsɪk] Heimweh
haben **III U4**, 106

*to **be** impressed [bi ɪm'prest] beeindruckt sein II

*to **be** in [bi ˈɪn] dabei sein; mitmachen II

*to **be** in charge (of) [bi ɪn 'tʃɑːdʒ (ˌəv)]
zuständig sein (für); die Verantwortung
tragen (für) **III U1**, 15

*to **be** in the way [bi ɪn ðə 'weɪ] im Weg
sein/stehen I

*to **be** interested in [bi 'ɪntrəstɪd ɪn] interessiert sein an; sich interessieren für II

*to **be** into [bi'ɪntə] mögen; stehen auf I

*to **be** involved [bi ɪn'vɒlvd] beteiligt sein;
involviert sein **III U1**, 10

*to **be** known (as) [bi 'nəʊn (ˌəz)] bekannt
sein (als) **III U2**, 55

*to **be** late [bi 'leɪt] zu spät dran sein; zu
spät kommen I

*to **be** like sb/sth [bi 'laɪk] wie jmd./etw
sein **III U2**, 40

*to **be** lucky [bi 'lʌki] Glück haben I

*to **be** made of [bi 'meɪd əv] bestehen
aus; gemacht sein aus; hergestellt sein
aus **III U3**, 64

*to **be** on [bi 'ɒn] an sein; laufen II

*to **be** on one's way [bi ɒn wʌnz 'weɪ] auf
dem Weg sein; unterwegs sein I

*to **be** out of chances [bi ˌaʊt əv 'tʃɑːnsɪz]
keine Chance mehr haben **III TMS1**, 27

*to **be** related to [bi rɪ'leɪtɪd tə] sich beziehen auf; verwandt sein mit **III TMS2**, 80

*to **be** right [bi 'raɪt] Recht haben I

*to **be** saved by the bell [bi 'seɪvd baɪ ðə
ˌbel] noch mal Glück haben **III U1**, 15

*to **be** scared (of) [bi 'skeəd əv] Angst
haben (vor) I

*to **be** set in [bi 'set ɪn] spielen in
III U4, 107

*to **be** sick [bi 'sɪk] sich übergeben II

*to **be** sorry [bi 'sɒri] leid tun I

*to **be** stressed out [bi ˌstrest 'aʊt] völlig
gestresst sein **III U1**, 12

*to **be** sure [bi 'ʃʊə] sicher se n II

*to **be** surprised [bi sə'praɪzd] überrascht
sein II

*to **be** unlucky [bi ʌn'lʌki] Pech haben II

*to **be** used to [bi 'juːs tə] gewöhnt sein
an; gewohnt sein **III AC1**, 35

*to **be** worried [bi 'wʌrid] beunruhigt sein;
besorgt sein II

*to **be** worth [bi 'wɜːθ] wert sein I

*to **be** wrong [bi 'rɒŋ] unrecht haben; sich
irren I

*to **be** out [bi 'aʊt] hier: draußen sein II

Here you are. [ˌhɪə ju 'ɑː] Bitte schön. I

How **are** you? [ˌhaʊ 'ɑː jə] Wie geht es dir/
euch/Ihnen?; Wie geht es euch?; Wie geht
es Ihnen? II

How much **is/are** …? [ˌhaʊ mʌtʃ (ˌɪz/ɑː)]
Wie viel (kostet/kosten) .. ? I

What **was** … like? [ˌwɒt wɒz 'laɪk] Wie
war … ? **III U3**, 62

beach [biːtʃ] Strand II

baked beans (pl) [ˌbeɪkt 'biːnz] weiße
Bohnen in Tomatensoße I

bear [beə] Bär II

polar **bear** ['pəʊlə ˌbeə] Eisbär II

beat [biːt] Takt; Schlag **III TMS1**, 29

*to **beat** [biːt] schlagen; besiegen II

beautiful ['bjuːtɪfl] schön; hübsch; wunderbar II

because [bɪ'kɒz] weil; da I

because of [bɪ'kɒz ˌəv] wegen II

*to **become** [bɪ'kʌm] werden II

bed [bed] Bett I

*to go to **bed** [ˌgəʊ tə 'bed] ins Bett
gehen I

bedroom ['bedrʊm] Schlafzimmer I

bee [biː] Biene I

before [bɪ'fɔː] vor (zeitlich); bevor I; vorher;
zuvor; schon einmal II

*to **begin** [bɪ'gɪn] anfangen; beginnen
III U3, 63

beginning [bɪ'gɪnɪŋ] Anfang; Beginn II

to **behave** [bɪ'heɪv] sich benehmen; sich
verhalten **III U1**, 15

behaviour (no pl) [bɪ'heɪvjə] Verhalten;
Benehmen; Betragen **III AC3**, 88

behind [bɪ'haɪnd] hinter II

*to leave **behind** [ˌliːv bɪ'haɪnd] zurücklassen **III U2**, 44

to **believe** [bɪ'liːv] glauben I

I couldn't **believe** my eyes. [ai ˌkʊdnt
bɪˌliːv mai 'aɪz] Ich traute meinen Augen
nicht. II

bell [bel] Glocke; Klingel I

*to be saved by the **bell** [bi 'seɪvd baɪ ðə
ˌbel] noch mal Glück haben **III U1**, 15

to **belong** (to) [bɪ'lɒŋ (tə)] gehören (zu) II

where I **belong** [ˌweər aɪ bɪ'lɒŋ] wo ich
hingehöre **III U4**, 104

below [bɪ'ləʊ] unten; unter; unterhalb (von)
III U2, 51

belt [belt] Gürtel I

ben [ben] hoher Berg **III U2**, 46

bench [bentʃ] Bank; Sitzbank **III U1**, 23

Bengali [beŋ'gɔːli] Bengale/Bengalin; bengalisch **III U4**, 101

besides [bɪ'saɪdz] neben II

(the) **best** [best] (der/die/das) Beste II

best [best] beste/-r/-s; am besten I

Best wishes, [ˌbest 'wɪʃɪz] Viele Grüße,;
Herzliche Grüße, **III TMS2**, 83

*to **bet** [bet] wetten II

better ['betə] besser; lieber II

between [bɪ'twiːn] zwischen II

BFF (best friend forever) [biː'efef (ˌbest
frend fə'revə)] BFF ⟨**III TMS1**, 27⟩

bible ['baɪbl] Bibel **III U3**, 63

bicycle ['baɪsɪkl] Fahrrad II

bicycle motocross (BMX) [ˌbaɪsɪkl
'məʊtəʊkrɒs] Fahrradmotocross (=BMX)
II

big [bɪg] groß **I**
bike [baɪk] Fahrrad **I**
mountain **biking** [ˈmaʊntɪn ˌbaɪkɪŋ] Mountainbikefahren **II**
a billion [ə ˈbɪliən] Milliarde **III U1**, 24
bin [bɪn] Mülleimer; Abfalleimer; Mülltonne **III U1**, 11
biographical [ˌbaɪəʊˈgræfɪkl] biografisch **III U3**, 72
bird [bɜːd] Vogel **I**
birdwatching [ˈbɜːdˌwɒtʃɪŋ] Vogelbeobachtung **II**
birthday [ˈbɜːθdeɪ] Geburtstag **II**
  Happy **Birthday**! [ˌhæpi ˈbɜːθdeɪ] Alles Gute zum Geburtstag!; Herzlichen Glückwunsch zum Geburtstag! **II**
biscuit [ˈbɪskɪt] Keks **I**
a bit [ə ˈbɪt] ein bisschen; ein wenig **II**
  wee **bit** [ˈwiː bɪt] klitzeklein ⟨**III U2**, 47⟩
black [blæk] schwarz **I**
  *to go **black** [ˌgəʊ ˈblæk] schwarz werden **II**
to blame [bleɪm] verantwortlich machen; beschuldigen **III U1**, 18
to block [blɒk] blockieren; abblocken **II**
blog [blɒg] Blog; Internettagebuch **III U2**, 45
bloke (fam) [bləʊk] Typ (ugs.) **III U1**, 20
blond [blɒnd] blond **III U1**, 20
blood [blʌd] Blut **III U3**, 69
*to blow [bləʊ] pusten; blasen; wehen **II**
  *to **blow** out [ˌbləʊˈaʊt] ausblasen; auspusten **II**
blue [bluː] blau **I**
blurred [blɜːd] verschwommen; verwischt **III U3**, 77
BMX [ˌbiːemˈeks] BMX **II**
boarding [ˈbɔːdɪŋ] Boarding; an Bord gehen **III U4**, 101
  boarding card [ˈbɔːdɪŋ ˌkɑːd] Bordkarte **III U4**, 95
boat [bəʊt] Boot **I**
  sailing **boat** [ˈseɪlɪŋ ˌbəʊt] Segelboot **II**
Bodhrán [ˈbɒdrɑːn] traditionelle irische Trommel ⟨**III TR3**, 114⟩
body [ˈbɒdi] Körper **III U1**, 9
  body language [ˈbɒdi ˌlæŋgwɪdʒ] Körpersprache **III U1**, 19
  human **body** [ˌhjuːmən ˈbɒdi] menschlicher Körper **II**
exercise book [ˈeksəsaɪz ˌbʊk] Übungsheft **I**
  guide **book** [ˈgaɪd ˌbʊk] Reiseführer **II**
to book [bʊk] buchen; reservieren **II**
booklet [ˈbʊklət] Broschüre; Heft **III U4**, 109
bookshop [ˈbʊkʃɒp] Buchhandlung **III TMS1**, 30
to boom [buːm] dröhnen **II**
boot [buːts] Stiefel **I**
boot [buːt] Stiefel **I**; Kofferraum **III U3**, 75
  walking **boot** [ˈwɔːkɪŋ ˌbuːt] Wanderschuh **II**
bored [bɔːd] gelangweilt **II**
boring [ˈbɔːrɪŋ] langweilig **I**

*to be born [bi ˈbɔːn] geboren werden **III U3**, 72
to borrow [ˈbɒrəʊ] (sich) ausleihen **II**
boss [bɒs] Boss; Chef **III U1**, 20
bossy [ˈbɒsi] bestimmend; rechthaberisch; herrisch **III U1**, 15
both [bəʊθ] beide **II**
bottle [ˈbɒtl] Flasche **I**
to bounce [baʊnts] springen; hüpfen **III AC2**, 56
  *to keep the ball **bouncing** [ˌkiːp ðə bɔːl ˈbaʊntsɪŋ] hier: das Gespräch am Laufen halten **III AC2**, 56
bow [bəʊ] Bogen **II**
bowl [bəʊl] Schale; Schälchen; Schüssel **II**
bowling alley [ˈbəʊlɪŋ ˌæli] Bowlingbahn **II**
bowls [bəʊlz] Bowling **III U3**, 66
box [bɒks] Box; Kasten; Schachtel; Kiste **I**
  a **box** of … [ə ˈbɒks ˌɒv] eine Schachtel …; eine Kiste …; ein Karton … **I**
  phone **box** [ˈfəʊn ˌbɒks] Telefonzelle **III U4**, 105
round of boxing [ˌraʊnd ˌəv ˈbɒksɪŋ] Boxrunde **II**
boxty [ˈbɒksti] irische Pfannkuchen aus Kartoffeln ⟨**III TR3**, 114⟩
boy [bɔɪ] Junge **I**
  cabin **boy** [ˈkæbɪn ˌbɔɪ] Schiffsjunge **I**
bracelet [ˈbreɪslət] Armband **I**
brain [breɪn] Gehirn; Verstand ⟨**III U4**, 98⟩
brave [breɪv] mutig; tapfer **I**
bread [bred] Brot **I**
  bread roll [ˌbred ˈrəʊl] Brötchen **III AC1**, 34
break [breɪk] Pause **I**
  *to have a **break** [ˌhæv ə ˈbreɪk] eine Pause machen **I**
  lunch **break** [ˈlʌnʃ breɪk] Mittagspause **I**
  spring **break** [ˈsprɪŋ breɪk] Frühlingsferien **I**
*to break [breɪk] brechen; zerbrechen **II**
  *to **break** down [ˌbreɪk ˈdaʊn] zerstören; auflösen; niederreißen ⟨**III TMS1**, 30⟩
breakfast [ˈbrekfəst] Frühstück **I**
  *to have **breakfast** [ˌhæv ˈbrekfəst] frühstücken **I**
to breathe [briːð] atmen **II**
bridge [brɪdʒ] Brücke **II**
bright [braɪt] leuchtend; strahlend; hell **III TMS1**, 30
*to bring [brɪŋ] bringen; mitbringen **I**
  *to **bring** to life [ˌbrɪŋ tə ˈlaɪf] zum Leben erwecken; veranschaulichen **II**
British [ˈbrɪtɪʃ] britisch; Brite/Britin **I**
brochure [ˈbrəʊʃə] Broschüre; Prospekt **I**
broken [ˈbrəʊkn] gebrochen; kaputt **I**
Bronze Age [ˈbrɒnz eɪdʒ] Bronzezeit (ca. 2200–800 v. Chr.) **II**
brother [ˈbrʌðə] Bruder **I**
brown [braʊn] braun **I**
to brush [brʌʃ] bürsten **III U3**, 78
bucket [ˈbʌkɪt] Eimer **II**
*to build [bɪld] bauen **II**
building [ˈbɪldɪŋ] Gebäude **I**

light bulb [ˈlaɪt ˌbʌlb] Glühbirne **III U3**, 78
cyber bully [ˌsaɪbə ˈbʊli] jemand, der andere in sozialen Netzwerken belästigt oder mobbt **II**
to bully (sb) [ˈbʊli] (jmdn.) tyrannisieren; (jmdn.) drangsalieren; (jmdn.) mobben **II**
*to give sb the bumps [ˌgɪv ðə ˈbʌmps] jmdn. hochleben lassen **II**
bun [bʌn] Brötchen; Gebäckstück **III U2**, 43
burger [ˈbɜːgə] Hamburger **I**
*to burn [bɜːn] brennen; verbrennen **III U3**, 63
  *to **burn** down [ˌbɜːn ˈdaʊn] abbrennen; niederbrennen **III U3**, 72
bus [bʌs] Bus **I**
  bus station [ˈbʌs ˌsteɪʃn] Busbahnhof **I**
  bus stop [ˈbʌs ˌstɒp] Bushaltestelle **I**
business [ˈbɪznɪs] Geschäft; Business **III U1**, 24
busy [ˈbɪzi] belebt; beschäftigt **I**
but [bʌt] aber **I**
butter [ˈbʌtə] Butter **III AC1**, 34
button [ˈbʌtn] Knopf **III U4**, 105
*to buy [baɪ] kaufen **I**
buyer [ˈbaɪə] Käufer/-in **I**
by [baɪ] bei; neben; an **II**; von **III U2**, 43
  by (bike) [baɪ] mit (dem Fahrrad) **I**
  by hand [ˌbaɪ ˈhænd] von Hand; manuell **III U3**, 65
  by now [baɪ ˈnaʊ] inzwischen; mittlerweile **II**
  by my side [ˌbaɪ maɪ ˈsaɪd] an meiner Seite ⟨**III TMS1**, 30⟩
bye [baɪ] tschüss **I**

C

cabin boy [ˈkæbɪn ˌbɔɪ] Schiffsjunge **I**
cache [kæʃ] Versteck; geheimes Lager **I**
café [ˈkæfeɪ] Café **I**
cafeteria [ˌkæfəˈtɪəriə] Cafeteria **I**
cage [keɪdʒ] Käfig **III TMS1**, 28
cake [keɪk] Kuchen; Torte **I**
calendar [ˈkæləndə] Kalender **III U3**, 65
(phone) call [ˈfəʊn ˌkɔːl] Anruf; Telefonanruf **I**
to call [kɔːl] nennen; anrufen; rufen **I**
caller [ˈkɔːlə] Anrufer/-in °**III U1**, 9
call-in [ˈkɔːlɪn] Sendung, bei der sich das Publikum telefonisch beteiligen kann **III U1**, 9
to calm down [ˌkɑːm ˈdaʊn] sich beruhigen **II**
camel racing [ˈkæml ˌreɪsɪŋ] Kamelrennen **II**
camera [ˈkæmrə] Fotoapparat; Kamera **II**
  caught on **camera** [ˌkɔːt ɒn ˈkæmrə] ertappt; mit der Kamera festgehalten **II**
to camp [kæmp] campen; zelten **II**
can [kæn] Dose; Büchse **I**
  tin **can** [ˈtɪn kæn] Blechdose **III U2**, 53
can [kæn; kən] können; dürfen **I**
  can't [kɑːnt] kann nicht; können nicht; darf nicht; dürfen nicht **I**

candle ['kændl] Kerze II
candlelight (no pl) ['kændlaɪt] Kerzenlicht II
cannot ['kænɒt] kann nicht; können nicht; darf nicht; dürfen nicht II
cap [kæp] Kappe; Mütze II
cape [keɪp] Umhang II
capital ['kæpɪtl] Hauptstadt II
captain ['kæptɪn] Kapitän/-in; Mannschaftsführer/-in I
car [kɑː] Auto I
card [kɑːd] Karte; Spielkarte I
    boarding card ['bɔːdɪŋ ˌkɑːd] Bordkarte III U4, 95
    prompt card ['prɒmpt kɑːd] Stichwortkarte; Rollenkarte II
cardigan ['kɑːdɪgən] Strickjacke I
*to take care of sb/sth [teɪk ˈkeər əv] sich um jmdn./etw. kümmern; für jmdn. sorgen III U3, 74
to care (about) ['keə (r ə'baʊt)] wichtig nehmen; sich kümmern (um); sich interessieren (für) II
career [kə'rɪə] Beruf; Laufbahn; Karriere III U1, 12
careful ['keəfl] vorsichtig; sorgfältig II
carrot ['kærət] Karotte; Möhre I
to carry ['kæri] tragen II; befördern; mit sich tragen ⟨III TR1, 110⟩
cartoon [kɑː'tuːn] Cartoon; Zeichentrickfilm III AC2, 56
in case [ɪn 'keɪs] falls; für den Fall, dass … II
pencil case ['pensl ˌkeɪs] Federmäppchen; Mäppchen I
plaster cast ['plɑːstə kɑːst] Gipsverband III U3, 74
castle ['kɑːsl] Schloss; Burg II
cat [kæt] Katze I
catalogue ['kætlɒg] Katalog; Broschüre III U4, 103
*to catch [kætʃ] fangen II; mitbekommen (ugs.); mitkriegen (ugs.) III AC2, 56
catchy ['kætʃi] eingängig; einprägsam III TMS1, 29
category ['kætəgri] Kategorie; Klasse II
caught on camera [ˌkɔːt ɒn 'kæmrə] ertappt; mit der Kamera festgehalten II
to cause [kɔːz] verursachen II
'cause [kɒz] weil; da ⟨III TMS1, 27⟩
cave [keɪv] Höhle II
CD [ˌsiː'diː] CD II
ceilidh ['keɪli] schottisches Fest, bei dem getanzt und musiziert wird III U2, 46
to celebrate ['seləbreɪt] feiern II
Celt [kelt] Kelte/Keltin III U3, 63
Celtic ['keltɪk; 'seltɪk] keltisch II
cent [sent] Cent (Währung) I
    per cent [pə 'sent] Prozent III U1, 17
central ['sentrl] zentral; Zentral- II
centre ['sentə] Zentrum; Center I
    community centre [kə'mjuːnəti ˌsentə] Gemeindezentrum I
    leisure centre ['leʒə ˌsentə] Freizeitzentrum I

tourist information centre [ˌtɔːrɪst ɪnfə'meɪʃn ˌsentə] Touristeninformation I
century ['sentʃri] Jahrhundert II
cereal (no pl) ['sɪərɪəl] Frühstückszerealie; Getreideprodukt (z. B. Cornflakes oder Müsli) I
certain ['sɜːtn] bestimmt; sicher; gewiss II
chair [tʃeə] Stuhl; Sessel I
challenge ['tʃælɪndʒ] Herausforderung II
chance [tʃɑːns] Chance; Gelegenheit; Möglichkeit III TMS1, 27
    *to be out of chances [bi ˌaʊt əv 'tʃɑːnsɪz] keine Chance mehr haben III TMS1, 27
change [tʃeɪndʒ] Änderung; Veränderung; Wechsel II
    climate change ['klaɪmət ˌtʃeɪndʒ] Klimawandel III U1, 10
to change [tʃeɪndʒ] (sich) ändern; wechseln II
    to change (onto) [tʃeɪndʒ ('ɒntə)] umsteigen (in) II
    to change one's mind [ˌtʃeɪndʒ wʌnz 'maɪnd] seine Meinung ändern III U4, 104
channel ['tʃænl] Kanal (TV); Programm (Radio) III U1, 10
chant [tʃɑːnt] Sprechgesang II
chaos ['keɪɒs] Chaos; Durcheinander; Unordnung III U3, 74
chaotic [keɪ'ɒtɪk] chaotisch II
chapter ['tʃæptə] Kapitel III AC3, 89
character ['kærəktə] Charakter; Figur II
characteristic [ˌkærəktə'rɪstɪk] Eigenschaft; typisches Merkmal III U3, 66
charge [tʃɑːdʒ] Gebühr II
    *to be in charge (of) [bi ɪn 'tʃɑːdʒ (əv)] zuständig sein (für); die Verantwortung tragen (für) III U1, 15
charity ['tʃærɪti] Wohltätigkeitsverein; wohltätige Zwecke; Wohlfahrt I
    charity shop ['tʃærɪti ʃɒp] Second-Hand-Laden I
charm [tʃɑːm] Charme III U3, 67
    lucky charm [ˌlʌki 'tʃɑːm] Glücksbringer; Talisman I
to chase [tʃeɪs] jagen; nachjagen I
chat [ˌtʃæt] Chat II
    video chat ['vɪdiəʊ ˌtʃæt] Videochat II
to chat [tʃæt] plaudern; chatten (sich online unterhalten) I
cheap [tʃiːp] billig; preiswert I
to check [tʃek] überprüfen; prüfen; kontrollieren I
    to check out (coll) [tʃek 'aʊt] abchecken; auschecken; prüfen III AC2, 56
check-in ['tʃekɪn] Einchecken; Gepäckaufgabe III U4, 95
checkpoint ['tʃekpɔɪnt] Kontrollpunkt III U4, 104
to cheer on [tʃɪə (r ɒn)] jubeln; anfeuern II
    to cheer sb up [tʃɪər 'ʌp] jmdn. aufheitern III U1, 23
Cheers! [tʃɪəz] Danke! III AC2, 56
cheese [tʃiːz] Käse I

chess [tʃes] Schach II
chewing gum ['tʃuːɪŋ ˌgʌm] Kaugummi I
chicken ['tʃɪkɪn] Huhn; Hähnchen I
child, children (pl) ['tʃaɪld; 'tʃɪldrən] Kind I
    only child ['əʊnli ˌtʃaɪld] Einzelkind I
chimney ['tʃɪmni] Kamin; Schornstein II
chips (pl) [tʃɪps] Pommes frites I
chocolate ['tʃɒklət] Schokolade I
choice [tʃɔɪs] Wahl; Auswahl II
*to choose [tʃuːz] auswählen; wählen II
chorus ['kɔːrəs] Refrain III TMS1, 29
Christianity [ˌkrɪsti'ænəti] Christentum ⟨III TR3, 115⟩
Christmas ['krɪsməs] Weihnachten III TMS1, 26
church [tʃɜːtʃ] Kirche I
cinema ['sɪnəmə] Kino I
circle ['sɜːkl] Kreis; Ring II
    *to go round in circles [gəʊ ˌraʊnd ɪn 'sɜːklz] sich im Kreis drehen III U2, 50
city ['sɪti] Stadt; Großstadt I
clan [klæn] Clan; Sippe III U2, 45
to clap [klæp] klatschen II
class [klɑːs] Klasse; Schulklasse I; Unterricht; Unterrichtsstunde II
classmate ['klɑːsmeɪt] Klassenkamerad/-in; Mitschüler/-in I
classroom ['klɑːsrʊm] Klassenzimmer I
contact clause ['kɒntækt ˌklɔːz] Relativsatz ohne Relativpronomen °III U3, 63
    defining relative clause [dɪ'faɪnɪŋ 'relətɪv ˌklɔːz] notwendiger Relativsatz °III U3, 63
    if-clause ['ɪfˌklɔːz] if-Satz °III U1, 11
clay pipe ['kleɪ ˌpaɪp] Tonpfeife II
to clean [kliːn] putzen; säubern; reinigen II
clean [kliːn] sauber II
to clear [klɪə] aufklären ⟨III TR1, 111⟩
    to clear out [klɪər 'aʊt] ausräumen; entrümpeln I
clear [klɪə] klar; deutlich I
clever ['klevə] schlau; klug I
cleverness ['klevənəs] Schlauheit; Klugheit; Cleverness III TMS1, 30
click [klɪk] Klicken; Klick II
to click on ['klɪk ɒn] anklicken II
cliff [klɪf] Klippe; Kliff II
climate ['klaɪmət] Klima III U4, 106
    climate change ['klaɪmət ˌtʃeɪndʒ] Klimawandel III U1, 10
climax ['klaɪmæks] Höhepunkt III U2, 52
to climb [klaɪm] klettern; besteigen; steigen I
climbing ['klaɪmɪŋ] Kletter-; Klettern II
clock [klɒk] Uhr I
    o'clock [ə'klɒk] Uhr (Zeitangabe bei vollen Stunden) I
to clone [kləʊn] klonen III U2, 43
close [kləʊs] schmaler Durchgang III U2, 44
to close [kləʊz] schließen; zumachen I
    to close oneself away from [ˌkləʊz ə'weɪ frəm] sich abschotten von III U4, 104
close [kləʊs] eng; knapp I; nahe II

That was **close**! [ˌðæt wəz 'kləʊs] Das war knapp! I

closed [kləʊzd] geschlossen; zu III TMS1, 28

close-up ['kləʊsʌp] Nahaufnahme II

clothes *(pl)* [kləʊðz] Kleider; Kleidung I

clotted cream [ˌklɒtɪd 'kriːm] *stichfester Rahm* II

cloud [klaʊd] Wolke II

cloudy ['klaʊdi] bedeckt; bewölkt II

clown [klaʊn] Clown II

club [klʌb] Klub; Verein; AG I
cooking **club** ['kʊkɪŋ ˌklʌb] Koch-AG II

clue [kluː] Hinweis; Spur II

CO₂ (carbon dioxide) [ˌsiːˈəʊˈtuː: (ˌkɑːbn daɪˈɒksaɪd)] Kohlendioxid; CO₂ III U4, 95

coach [kəʊtʃ] Trainer/-in I; Reisebus II

coal [kəʊl] Kohle III U2, 43

coast [kəʊst] Küste III U4, 96

coastal path [ˌkəʊstl 'pɑːθ] Küstenweg II

coastline ['kəʊstlaɪn] Küste; Küstenverlauf II

coconut ['kəʊkənʌt] Kokosnuss II

coffee ['kɒfi] Kaffee I

coin [kɔɪn] Münze I

coke ['kəʊk] Cola I

cold [kəʊld] Erkältung II

cold [kəʊld] kalt I
I'm **cold**. [aɪm 'kəʊld] Mir ist kalt. I

to **collect** [kəˈlekt] sammeln II

collection [kəˈlekʃn] Sammlung; Kollektion II

colonist ['kɒlənɪst] Siedler/-in; Kolonist/-in III U3, 67

colony ['kɒləni] Kolonie III U3, 65

colour ['kʌlə] Farbe I
What **colour** is …? [ˌwɒt 'kʌlər ˌɪz] Welche Farbe hat …? I

coloured ['kʌləd] farbig; bunt °III U1, 11

colourful ['kʌləfl] farbenfroh; bunt II

*to **come** [kʌm] kommen I
*to **come** down [ˌkʌm 'daʊn] herunterkommen I
*to **come** in [ˌkʌm ˌ'ɪn] hereinkommen I
*to **come** up to sb [kʌm ˌʌp tə] auf jmdn. zukommen III U1, 21
Come in. [ˌkʌm ˌ'ɪn] Komm/Kommt rein. I
Come on! [ˌkʌm ˌ'ɒn] Komm schon!; Komm jetzt! I

comedian [kəˈmiːdiən] Komiker/-in; Comedian II

comedy ['kɒmədi] Komödie II
comedy show ['kɒmədi ˌʃəʊ] Comedy Show II

comfortable ['kʌmftəbl] bequem; komfortabel III U1, 14

comic ['kɒmɪk] Comicheft II

comma ['kɒmə] Komma °III U2, 52

comment ['kɒment] Kommentar II

to **comment** (on) ['kɒment (ˌɒn)] kommentieren II

common ['kɒmən] üblich; gewöhnlich; (weit) verbreitet; gebräuchlich III TMS1, 31

*to have in **common** [ˌhæv ˌɪn 'kɒmən] gemein haben III TMS1, 30

to **communicate** [kəˈmjuːnɪkeɪt] kommunizieren; sich verständigen III U1, 9

communication [kəˌmjuːnɪˈkeɪʃn] Kommunikation III U2, 53

community centre [kəˈmjuːnəti ˌsentə] Gemeindezentrum I

company ['kʌmpəni] Gesellschaft; Firma; Unternehmen III U1, 10

to **compare** (with/to) [kəmˈpeə] vergleichen (mit) II

compass ['kʌmpəs] Kompass ⟨III TR1, 110⟩

to **compete** (with) [kəmˈpiːt (wɪð)] konkurrieren (mit); sich messen (mit); in Wettbewerb treten (mit) III U1, 9

competition [ˌkɒmpəˈtɪʃn] Wettbewerb; Turnier II

complete [kəmˈpliːt] vollständig; komplett; völlig III U3, 63

completely [kəmˈpliːtli] völlig II

compromise ['kɒmprəmaɪz] Kompromiss II

to **compromise** ['kɒmprəmaɪz] einen Kompromiss eingehen III U1, 9

computer [kəmˈpjuːtə] Computer I

con [kɒn] Argument dagegen II

to **concentrate** (on) ['kɒnsntreɪt (ɒn)] (sich) konzentrieren (auf) III U4, 105

*to be **concerned** (about) [bi kənˈsɜːnd (ˌəˌbaʊt)] besorgt sein (um); beunruhigt sein (wegen) III U1, 10

concert ['kɒnsət] Konzert III TMS1, 26

concrete ['kɒnkriːt] Beton III U4, 105

concrete ['kɒnkriːt] konkret; eindeutig °III U4, 102

condition [kənˈdɪʃn] Kondition; Bedingung °III U1, 12

conditional sentence [kənˌdɪʃnl 'sentəns] Bedingungssatz °III U1, 9

confident ['kɒnfɪdnt] selbstsicher; selbstbewusst II

conflict ['kɒnflɪkt] Konflikt; Auseinandersetzung III U1, 18

confused [kənˈfjuːzd] verwirrt; wirr; konfus III U1, 22

Congratulations! [kənˌgrætʃəˈleɪʃnz] Glückwunsch!; Gratuliere! III TMS2, 85

conjunction [kənˈdʒʌŋkʃn] Konjunktion °III U3, 70

to **connect** (to) [kəˈnekt (tə)] verbinden (mit); vermitteln; anschließen III U3, 62

connection [kəˈnekʃn] Verbindung II

to **conquer** ['kɒŋkə] erobern III U3, 63

contact ['kɒntækt] Kontakt II
contact clause ['kɒntækt ˌklɔːz] *Relativsatz ohne Relativpronomen* °III U3, 63

to **contact** sb ['kɒntækt] sich mit jmdm. in Verbindung setzen; jmdn. kontaktieren II

to **contain** [kənˈteɪn] enthalten III TMS2, 81

content ['kɒntent] Inhalt II

contest ['kɒntest] Wettkampf; Wettbewerb I

to **continue** [kənˈtɪnjuː] fortfahren; andauern; weitermachen III U4, 99

contraction [kənˈtrækʃn] Verkürzung; Zusammenziehung ⟨III TMS2, 87⟩

control [kənˈtrəʊl] Kontrolle III U4, 95

to **control** [kənˈtrəʊl] kontrollieren; beherrschen; steuern III U3, 67

convenience [kənˈviːniəns] Zweckmäßigkeit; Annehmlichkeit; Komfort III U4, 95

conversation [ˌkɒnvəˈseɪʃn] Konversation; Gespräch; Unterhaltung II
to hog a **conversation** [ˌhɒg ə kɒnvəˈseɪʃn] ein Gespräch für sich in Beschlag nehmen; ein Gespräch dominieren III AC2, 56

convincing [kənˈvɪnsɪŋ] überzeugend III U2, 49

to **cook** [kʊk] kochen II

cooker ['kʊkə] Herd I

cooking ['kʊkɪŋ] Kochen I
cooking club ['kʊkɪŋ ˌklʌb] Koch-AG II

*to leave sth to **cool** [liːv tə 'kuːl] etw. kalt stellen II

cool [kuːl] cool; super I

corner ['kɔːnə] Ecke II

Cornish ['kɔːnɪʃ] in Cornwall; kornisch; Kornisch II

correct [kəˈrekt] richtig; korrekt III U1, 11

*to **cost** [kɒst] kosten II

costume ['kɒstjuːm] Kostüm; Verkleidung II

cosy ['kəʊzi] gemütlich; kuschelig ⟨III TR3, 114⟩

cough [kɒf] Husten II

could [kʊd] konnte/-n II

to **count** (on) ['kaʊnt (ˌɒn)] zählen (auf) II

country, countries *(pl)* ['kʌntri; 'kʌntriz] Land I

countryside ['kʌntrisaɪd] Land II

a **couple** of [ə 'kʌpl əv] ein paar I

course [kɔːs] Kurs II
*to do a **course** (in) [duː ə 'kɔːs (ɪn)] einen Kurs belegen II
of **course** [əv 'kɔːs] natürlich; selbstverständlich I

court [kɔːt] Spielfeld II

cousin ['kʌzn] Cousin/Cousine I

cover ['kʌvə] Titelseite; Einband; Cover III U1, 8

to **cover** ['kʌvə] abdecken; bedecken; zudecken III U4, 105

cow [kaʊ] Kuh I

cowboy ['kaʊbɔɪ] Cowboy; Rinderhirte II

crack [kræk] Knacken; Krachen III U2, 51

cracking ['krækɪŋ] knackend; brechend III U2, 50

cramp [kræmp] Krampf II

crane [kreɪn] Kran III U2, 48

to **crash** [kræʃ] abstürzen II

to **crash** (into) [kræʃ ('ɪntə)] zusammenstoßen (mit) III U3, 75

crazy ['kreɪzi] verrückt I
*to go **crazy** [ˌgəʊ 'kreɪzi] ausflippen; durchdrehen; verrückt werden II

cream [kri:m] Creme; Sahne II
  clotted **cream** [ˌklɒtɪd 'kri:m] *stichfester Rahm* II
  cream tea [kri:m 'ti:] Cream Tea *(südwestenglische Spezialität: Tee mit süßen Brötchen, die mit stichfestem Rahm und Marmelade serviert werden)* II
  ice **cream** [ˌaɪs 'kri:m] Eis; Eiscreme II
to **create** [kri'eɪt] schaffen; erschaffen; erfinden II
creative [kri'eɪtɪv] kreativ II
credit ['kredɪt] Guthaben II
cress [kres] Kresse II
cricket ['krɪkɪt] Cricket II
crime [kraɪm] Verbrechen; Kriminalität II
crisp [krɪsp] Kartoffelchip I
criterion, criteria (pl) [kraɪ'tɪəriən; kraɪ'tɪəriə] Kriterium, Kriterien *(Pl.)* °III U2, 48; III U4, 103
to **crop** (a photo) [krɒp] (ein Foto) zurechtschneiden III U3, 75
cross [krɒs] Kreuz II
to **cross** [krɒs] überqueren; kreuzen I
  *to keep your fingers **crossed** [ˌki:p jɔ: ˌfɪŋɡəz 'krɒst] die Daumen drücken I
crowd [kraʊd] Zuschauer; Menschenmenge II
crowded ['kraʊdɪd] überfüllt III AC3, 89
crown [kraʊn] Krone II
  crown jewels [ˌkraʊn 'dʒu:əlz] Kronjuwelen II
cruel ['kru:əl] grausam II
crushed [krʌʃt] eingequetscht; eingeklemmt III U4, 104
to **cry** [kraɪ] schreien; rufen II; weinen III U2, 50
CU (= See you) ['si: ju] Bis dann!; Bis … I
culture ['kʌltʃə] Kultur I
cup [kʌp] Tasse III AC1, 34
  a **cup** of … [ə 'kʌp əv] eine Tasse … I
cupboard ['kʌbəd] Küchenschrank; Schrank I
currency ['kʌrnsi] Währung III U4, 95
curry ['kʌri] Curry (Gewürz oder Gericht) I
curtain ['kɜ:tn] Vorhang II
custard ['kʌstəd] Vanillesoße; Vanillepudding II
custom ['kʌstəm] Gewohnheit; Brauch; Sitte III AC3, 88
customs (sg) ['kʌstəmz] Zoll III U4, 95
*to **cut** (off) [kʌt (ˈɒf)] abschneiden; schneiden II
cute [kju:t] niedlich; süß I
cyber bully ['saɪbə ˈbʊli] *jemand, der andere in sozialen Netzwerken belästigt oder mobbt* II
cyberbullying ['saɪbəˈbʊliɪŋ] Cyber-Mobbing II
to **cycle** ['saɪkl] Fahrrad fahren I
cycling ['saɪklɪŋ] Radfahren I

D

dad [dæd] Papa; Vati I
daily ['deɪli] täglich ⟨III TR1, 110⟩
dance (no pl) [dɑ:ns] Tanz; Tanzveranstaltung II
  dance move ['dɑ:ns ˌmu:v] Tanzschritt I
to **dance** [dɑ:ns] tanzen I
  everyone was **dancing** [ˌevriwʌn wəz 'dɑ:nsɪŋ] alle tanzten ⟨III U1, 21⟩
dancer ['dɑ:nsə] Tänzer/-in III U1, 12
  backing **dancer** ['bækɪŋ ˌdɑ:nsə] Backgroundtänzer/-in III U1, 12
  lead **dancer** ['li:d ˌdɑ:nsə] Vortänzer/-in III U1, 12
dancing ['dɑ:nsɪŋ] Tanz I
danger ['deɪndʒə] Gefahr III U2, 50
dangerous ['deɪndʒrəs] gefährlich I
the **dark** [ðə 'dɑ:k] Dunkelheit II
dark [dɑ:k] dunkel II
darkness ['dɑ:knəs] Dunkelheit II
date [deɪt] Datum II
  to **date** back to ['deɪt ˌbæk tə] zurückgehen auf; stammen aus III U3, 63
daughter ['dɔ:tə] Tochter III U3, 63
day [deɪ] Tag I
  day out [ˌdeɪ 'aʊt] Ausflug II
  one **day** [wʌn 'deɪ] eines Tages I
  these **days** [ˌði:z 'deɪz] heute; heutzutage; zurzeit III U1, 20
  the next **day** [ðə ˌnekst 'deɪ] am nächsten Tag II
  to this **day** [ˌtə ðɪs 'deɪ] bis heute III U3, 65
dead [ded] tot II
*to **deal** (with) [di:l] sich befassen (mit); umgehen (mit) II
Oh **dear**! [ˌəʊ 'dɪə] Oje! II
Dear … [dɪə] Lieber …; Liebe … I
dearly ['dɪəli] lieb ⟨III U2, 47⟩
death [deθ] Tod III U4, 102
decade ['dekeɪd] Jahrzehnt III U2, 44
December [dɪ'sembə] Dezember II
to **decide** (on) [dɪ'saɪd (ˌɒn)] (sich) entscheiden (für) III U1, 15
decision [dɪ'sɪʒn] Entscheidung III U1, 18
deck [dek] Deck I
to **decorate** ['dekəreɪt] dekorieren; schmücken; verzieren II
decorations (pl) [ˌdekə'reɪʃnz] Dekoration; Schmuck II
deep [di:p] tief II
to **defeat** [dɪ'fi:t] besiegen III U2, 47
defining relative clause [dɪ,faɪrɪŋ 'relətɪv ˌklɔ:z] notwendiger Relativsatz °III U3, 63
definitely ['defɪnətli] definitiv; bestimmt; eindeutig III U2, 51
definition [ˌdefɪ'nɪʃn] Definition II
adverb of **degree** [ˌædvɜ:b əv dɪ'gri:] Gradadverb °III U2, 48
delay [dɪ'leɪ] Verspätung; Verzögerung II
to **delete** [dɪ'li:t] löschen III U1, 23
delicious [dɪ'lɪʃəs] köstlich II
to **depart** [dɪ'pɑ:t] abfahren II

departure lounge [dɪ'pɑ:tʃə ˌlaʊndʒ] Abflughalle III U4, 95
to **depend** (on) [dɪ'pend (ˌɒn)] abhängen von II
depressing [dɪ'presɪŋ] deprimierend; bedrückend III U4, 105
to **describe** [dɪ'skraɪb] beschreiben II
description [dɪ'skrɪpʃn] Beschreibung III U3, 72
to **deserve** [dɪ'zɜ:v] verdienen II
to **design** [dɪ'zaɪn] entwerfen; gestalten III U1, 12
designer [dɪ'zaɪnə] Designer/-in III U1, 14
  web **designer** ['web dɪˌzaɪnə] Webdesigner III U1, 15
desk [desk] Schalter; Schreibtisch III U4, 95
dessert [dɪ'zɜ:t] Dessert; Nachspeise II
destination [ˌdestɪ'neɪʃn] Ziel; Reiseziel III TMS2, 80
to **destroy** [dɪ'strɔɪ] zerstören; vernichten; auslöschen III U3, 66
detail ['di:teɪl] Detail; Einzelheit II
to **develop** [dɪ'veləp] (sich) entwickeln III U1, 24
device [dɪ'vaɪs] Gerät; Vorrichtung I
  GPS **device** [dʒi:pi:ˌes dɪ'vaɪs] GPS-Gerät I
diagram ['daɪəgræm] Diagramm III U1, 9
to **dial** ['daɪəl] wählen III U4, 96
dialect ['daɪəlekt] Dialekt II
dialogue ['daɪəlɒg] Dialog; Gespräch III U2, 54
diary ['daɪəri] Tagebuch III U3, 66
  diary entry ['daɪəri ˌentri] Tagebucheintrag II
dictionary ['dɪkʃnri] Wörterbuch II
to **die** [daɪ] sterben III U2, 44
difference ['dɪfrəns] Unterschied II
  *to make a **difference** [ˌmeɪk əˈdɪfrns] etw. verändern; einen Unterschied machen II
different ['dɪfrnt] anders; unterschiedlich; verschieden I
difficult ['dɪfɪklt] schwierig I
digital ['dɪdʒɪtl] digital II
dinner ['dɪnə] Abendessen I
dinosaur (dino) ['daɪnəsɔ:; 'daɪnəʊ] Dinosaurier II
direct [dɪ'rekt] direkt; unmittelbar III TMS2, 80
stage **direction** ['steɪdʒ dɪˌrekʃn] Regieanweisung III AC2, 57
directory [dɪ'rektri] Verzeichnis II
dirty ['dɜ:ti] dreckig; schmutzig II
to **disagree** [ˌdɪsə'gri:] anderer Meinung sein; nicht einverstanden sein III U1, 9
to **disappear** [ˌdɪsə'pɪə] verschwinden III U3, 63
disappointed [ˌdɪsə'pɔɪntɪd] enttäuscht I
disappointment [ˌdɪsə'pɔɪntmənt] Enttäuschung II
disaster [dɪ'zɑ:stə] Desaster; Katastrophe; Unglück II
to **discover** [dɪ'skʌvə] entdecken II

discovery [dɪˈskʌvri] Entdeckung III U2, 43
discussion [dɪˈskʌʃn] Diskussion II
disgusting [dɪsˈɡʌstɪŋ] ekelhaft: widerlich I
display [dɪˈspleɪ] Ausstellung II
distance [ˈdɪstns] Distanz; Entfernung II
diversity [daɪˈvɜːsəti] Vielfalt; Verschiedenheit II
to divide (up/into) [dɪˈvaɪd (ʌp/ɪntə)]
aufteilen (in) III U3, 63
to divorce [dɪˈvɔːs] sich scheiden lassen
III U3, 65
DJ [ˌdiːˈdʒeɪ] DJ; Discjockey III U1, 21
*to do [duː] machen; tun I
  *to do a course (in) [ˌduː ə ˈkɔːs (ɪn)]
  einen Kurs belegen II
  *to do our hair [ˌduː aʊə ˈheə] uns fri-
  sieren; unsere Haare machen II
  *to do the shopping [ˌduː ðə ˈʃɒpɪŋ] ein-
  kaufen; einkaufen gehen III U2, 53
  Don't worry! [ˌdəʊnt ˈwʌri] Keine Sorge! I
  dos and don'ts [ˌduːz ənd ˈdəʊnts] Ge-
  und Verbote; was man tun und was man
  nicht tun sollte III AC3, 88
  We did it! [ˌwi ˈdɪd ɪt] Wir haben es
  geschafft! II
doctor [ˈdɒktə] Arzt/Ärztin II
document [ˈdɒkjəmənt] Dokument; Urkunde III U4, 99
dog [dɒɡ] Hund I
dog-tired [ˌdɒɡˈtaɪəd] hundemüde I
dollar [ˈdɒlə] Dollar (Währung) III U1, 24
door [dɔː] Tür I
  front door [ˌfrʌnt ˈdɔː] Haustür II
  next door [ˌnekst ˈdɔː] (von) nebenan
  III AC2, 56
double [ˈdʌbl] Doppel-; zweimal I
doubt [daʊt] Zweifel III U1, 9
down [daʊn] nach unten; herunter; hinunter I
  *to break down [breɪk ˈdaʊn] zerstören;
  auflösen; niederreißen ⟨III TMS1, 30⟩
  *to come down [kʌm ˈdaʊn] herunter-
  kommen I
  *to go down [ɡəʊ ˈdaʊn] entlanggehen;
  hinuntergehen; nach unten gehen I
  to pull down [pʊl ˈdaʊn] abreißen
  III U2, 42
  *to sit down [ˌsɪt ˈdaʊn] sich hinsetzen;
  sich setzen I
  to turn down [tɜːn ˈdaʊn] abdrehen;
  niedriger stellen III U1, 11
to download [ˈdaʊnˌləʊd] herunterladen
(aus dem Internet) I
ups and downs [ˌʌps ən ˈdaʊnz] Höhen und
Tiefen III TMS1, 27
downstairs [daʊnˈsteəz] nach unten; im
Untergeschoss; unten II
drama queen (coll) [ˈdrɑːmə ˌkwiːn]
Tussi (abwertend); Zicke (abwertend) III U3, 74
drama [ˈdrɑːmə] Theater; Drama II
dramatic [drəˈmætɪk] dramatisch II
*to draw [drɔː] zeichnen I

*to draw up [drɔː ˈʌp] entwerfen
III U4, 103
dream [driːm] Traum; Traum- I
*to dream [driːm] träumen II
dress [dres] Kleid III U1, 14
  fancy dress (no pl) [ˌfænsi ˈdres] Verkleidung; Kostüm II
dressed [drest] angezogen; gekleidet;
angekleidet III U3, 69
to drift [drɪft] schweben; treiben ⟨III U4, 98⟩
drink [drɪŋk] Getränk I
*to drink [drɪŋk] trinken I
*to drive [draɪv] fahren II
  *to drive off [draɪv ˈɒf] wegfahren
  III U3, 75
driver [ˈdraɪvə] Fahrer/-in II
drizzle [ˈdrɪzl] Nieselregen III U4, 105
to drop [drɒp] fallen (lassen) II
  to drop out (of) [drɒp ˈaʊt (əv)] abbrechen; ausscheiden; aussteigen III U1, 12
to dry [draɪ] trocknen ⟨III TR1, 111⟩
duck [dʌk] Ente I
duke [djuːk] Herzog III U3, 65
during (+ noun) [ˈdjʊərɪŋ] während (+ Nomen) II
duty-free [ˌdjuːtiˈfriː] zollfrei III U4, 95
DVD [ˌdiːviːˈdiː] DVD I

E

e.g. (= for example) [iːˈdʒiː] z.B. (= zum
Beispiel) I
each [iːtʃ] jede/-r/-s II
  each other [iːtʃ ˈʌðə] einander; miteinander; sich; sich gegenseitig II
each [iːtʃ] pro Person; pro Stück I
ear [ɪə] Ohr III TMS1, 28
early [ˈɜːli] früh I
  this early [ˈðɪs ˌɜːli] so früh III AC1, 35
to earn [ɜːn] verdienen I
earth [ɜːθ] Erde; die Erde; Erdboden II
  What on earth …? [ˌwɒt ɒn ˈɜːθ] Was um
  alles in der Welt …? II
east [iːst] Osten; Ost- I
easy [ˈiːzi] einfach; leicht I
easy-going [ˈiːziˌɡəʊɪŋ] locker; unkompliziert III U4, 107
*to eat [iːt] essen; fressen I
Eco [ˈiːkəʊ] Öko- II
ecology [iˈkɒlədʒi] Ökologie II
to edit out [ˌedɪt ˈaʊt] herausschneiden
III U3, 75
education (no pl) [ˌedʒʊˈkeɪʃn] Erziehung;
Bildung II
effect [ɪˈfekt] Effekt; Wirkung III TMS1, 29
egg [eɡ] Ei I
  Scotch egg [skɒtʃ ˈeɡ] hart gekochtes Ei in
  Wurstbrät II
eight [eɪt] acht I
not … either [nɒt □ ˈaɪðə; nɒt □ ˈiːðə] auch
nicht II
elderly [ˈeldəli] ältere/-r/-s III U2, 53
electrician [elɪkˈtrɪʃn] Elektriker/-in II

electricity [ˌelɪkˈtrɪsəti] Elektrizität; Strom II
electrics [ɪˈlektrɪks] Elektrik II
element [ˈelɪmənt] Element II
eleven [ɪˈlevn] elf I
Elizabethan [ɪˌlɪzəˈbiːθn] Elisabethaner/-in;
elisabethanisch III U3, 69
else [els] andere/-r/-s; sonst noch II
  Anything else? [ˌeniθɪŋ ˈels] Sonst noch
  etwas? I
  nobody else [ˈnəʊbədi ˌels] niemand
  anderes II
  what else [ˌwɒt ˈels] was sonst; was noch II
email [ˈiːmeɪl] E-Mail II
to email [ˈiːmeɪl] mailen; per E-Mail
schicken II
embarrassed [ɪmˈbærəst] verlegen II
embarrassing [ɪmˈbærəsɪŋ] peinlich II
embroidery [ɪmˈbrɔɪdri] Stickerei III U3, 62
emergency [ɪˈmɜːdʒnsi] Notfall; Notlage
III U4, 109
emission [ɪˈmɪʃn] Emission; Ausstoß
III U4, 95
emoji [ɪˈməʊdʒi] Emoji I
emotion [ɪˈməʊʃn] Gefühl; Emotion
III TMS1, 26
to emphasize [ˈempfəsaɪz] betonen II
to emphasize [ˈemfəsaɪz] betonen; hervorheben III TMS1, 29
empire [ˈempaɪə] Reich; Kaiserreich
III U3, 63
empty [ˈemti] leer II
encyclopedia [ɪnˌsaɪkləˈpiːdiə] Lexikon II
end [end] Ende; Schluss I
  in the end [ˌɪn ðɪ ˈend] schließlich; zum
  Schluss I
to end [end] enden; beenden III U1, 18
  to end up [ˌend ˈʌp] enden; landen II
ending [ˈendɪŋ] Ende; Schluss (einer
Geschichte) I
energy [ˈenədʒi] Energie; Kraft II
search engine [ˈsɜːtʃˌendʒɪn] Suchmaschine
II
steam engine [ˈstiːmˌendʒɪn] Dampfmaschine III U2, 43
engineer [ˌendʒɪˈnɪə] Ingenieur/-in; Tech-
niker/-in III U2, 48
English [ˈɪŋɡlɪʃ] englisch; Englisch; aus
England; Engländer/-in I
  English-speaking [ˈɪŋɡlɪʃˌspiːkɪŋ] englischsprachig I
to enjoy [ɪnˈdʒɔɪ] genießen II
  to enjoy oneself [ɪnˈdʒɔɪ] Spaß haben;
  sich amüsieren III U1, 15
enough [ɪˈnʌf] genug; genügend I
to enter [ˈentə] hineingehen; betreten; eintreten; mitmachen; einreisen III U4, 99
to entertain sb [ˌentəˈteɪn] jmdn. unterhalten; jmdn. beschäftigen III TMS1, 26
entertainment (no pl) [ˌentəˈteɪnmənt]
Unterhaltung III U3, 72
enthusiasm [ɪnˈθjuːziæzm] Begeisterung;
Enthusiasmus III U4, 96

entrance ['entrəns] Eingang; Eintritt **III U2**, 50

entry ['entri] Eintritt; Eintrag **II**
diary **entry** ['daɪəri ˌentri] Tagebucheintrag **II**

envelope ['envələʊp] Umschlag; Briefumschlag **III TMS2**, 82

environment [ɪn'vaɪrnmənt] Umwelt; Umgebung **II**

environmental issues [ɪnˌvaɪrnmentl 'ɪʃuːz] Umweltprobleme **III U1**, 10

environmentally friendly [ɪnˌvaɪrnˌmentli 'frendli] umweltfreundlich **III U4**, 95

equipment [ɪ'kwɪpmənt] Ausstattung; Ausrüstung **II**

era ['ɪərə] Ära; Zeitalter **III U4**, 107

escalator ['eskəleɪtə] Rolltreppe **I**

to escape [ɪ'skeɪp] fliehen; entfliehen; flüchten; entkommen **III TMS1**, 28

especially [ɪ'speʃli] besonders; vor allem **III U1**, 10

etc. (= et cetera) [ɪt'setrə] usw. (= und so weiter) **II**

euro ['jʊərəʊ] Euro (Währung) **I**

European [jʊərə'piːən] Europäer/-in; europäisch; aus Europa **III U4**, 101

even ['iːvn] sogar; selbst **I**

even (+ comparative) ['iːvn] noch (+ Komparativ) **II**

evening ['iːvnɪŋ] Abend **I**
in the **evenings** [ɪn ði 'iːvnɪŋz] abends **I**

event [ɪ'vent] Veranstaltung; Ereignis **II**

ever ['evə] jemals **II**

every ['evri] jede/-r/-s **I**

everybody ['evribɒdi] jeder; alle **II**

everyone ['evriwʌn] jeder; alle **I**
everyone was dancing [ˌevriwʌn wəz 'dɑːnsɪŋ] alle tanzten ⟨**III U1**, 21⟩

everything ['evriθɪŋ] alles **I**

everywhere ['evriweə] überall **I**

evidence (no pl) ['evɪdns] Beweis; Beleg; Beweismaterial **III TMS1**, 31

exactly [ɪg'zæktli] genau **III U1**, 15

example [ɪg'zɑːmpl] Beispiel **II**
for **example** [fər ɪg'zɑːmpl] zum Beispiel **II**

except [ɪk'sept] außer; bis auf **II**

exchange [ɪks'tʃeɪndʒ] Austausch-; Austausch **II**
exchange student [ɪks'tʃeɪndʒ ˌstjuːdnt] Austauschschüler/-in **III AC1**, 34
student **exchange** [ˌstjuːdnt ɪks'tʃeɪndʒ] Schüleraustausch **III AC2**, 57

excited [ɪk'saɪtɪd] aufgeregt; begeistert **I**

excitement (no pl) [ɪk'saɪtmənt] Aufregung **III U1**, 22

exciting [ɪk'saɪtɪŋ] spannend; aufregend **I**

Excuse me … [ɪk'skjuːz mi] Entschuldigung!; Entschuldigen Sie! **I**

exercise ['eksəsaɪz] Übung; Aufgabe **I**
exercise book ['eksəsaɪz ˌbʊk] Übungsheft **I**

exhibition [ˌeksɪ'bɪʃn] Ausstellung; Vorführung **II**

exit ['eksɪt] Ausgang; Abgang; Ausfahrt **III U3**, 65

to expect [ɪk'spekt] erwarten **II**

expensive [ɪk'spensɪv] teuer **I**

experience [ɪk'spɪəriəns] Erfahrung **II**

to experience [ɪk'spɪəriəns] erleben; erfahren ⟨**III TR1**, 110⟩

to expire [ɪk'spaɪə] ablaufen **III U4**, 99

to explain [ɪk'spleɪn] erklären **II**

to explore [ɪk'splɔː] auf Entdeckungsreise gehen; sich umschauen; erkunden; erforschen **I**

explorer [ɪk'splɔːrə] Forscher/-in; Forschungsreisende/-r **III U3**, 67

to express [ɪk'spres] ausdrücken **II**

facial expression [ˌfeɪʃl ɪk'spreʃn] Gesichtsausdruck **III U1**, 19

extra ['ekstrə] extra; zusätzlich **I**

extremely [ɪk'striːmli] äußerst; sehr **III U2**, 48

eye [aɪ] Auge **II**
to roll one's **eyes** [ˌrəʊl wʌnz 'aɪz] die Augen verdrehen **III U3**, 74
I couldn't believe my **eyes**. [aɪ ˌkʊdnt bɪˌliːv maɪ 'aɪz] Ich traute meinen Augen nicht. **II**

eyewitness ['aɪwɪtnəs] Augenzeuge/Augenzeugin **II**

F

face [feɪs] Gesicht **I**

face-to-face [ˌfeɪstə'feɪs] persönlich; von Angesicht zu Angesicht **II**

facial expression [ˌfeɪʃl ɪk'spreʃn] Gesichtsausdruck **III U1**, 19

fact [fækt] Fakt; Tatsache **II**
in **fact** [ɪn 'fækt] tatsächlich; eigentlich; genau genommen **III U2**, 45

factory ['fæktri] Fabrik; Werk **III U3**, 65

factual ['fæktʃʊəl] sachlich **II**

fair [feə] gerecht; fair **I**

to fake [feɪk] vortäuschen; fälschen **II**

fake [feɪk] falsch; gefälscht **II**

fall [fɔːl] Sturz **III U2**, 54

***to fall** [fɔːl] fallen; hinfallen **I**
***to fall** asleep [ˌfɔːl ə'sliːp] einschlafen **I**
***to fall** down [ˌfɔːl 'daʊn] einstürzen; zusammenfallen; hinunterfallen **III U2**, 50
***to fall** off [ˌfɔːl 'ɒf] herunterfallen; hinunterfallen **I**
***to fall** over [ˌfɔːl 'əʊvə] hinfallen; umkippen **I**

family ['fæmli] Familie **I**
host **family** ['həʊst ˌfæmli] Gastfamilie **III AC1**, 34

famous ['feɪməs] berühmt **II**

fan [fæn] Fan; Anhänger/-in **III AC3**, 89

fancy dress (no pl) [ˌfænsi 'dres] Verkleidung; Kostüm **II**

fantastic [fæn'tæstɪk] fantastisch; großartig **II**

fantasy ['fæntəsi] Fantasie; Traum- **I**; Fantasy **III U4**, 107

far [fɑː] weit **II**
far away [ˌfɑːr ə'weɪ] weit weg **I**
so **far** [ˌsəʊ 'fɑː] bis jetzt **II**

fare [feə] Fahrpreis **II**

farm [fɑːm] Farm; Bauernhof **I**

farmer ['fɑːmə] Bauer/Bäuerin; Landwirt/-in **II**

fascinating ['fæsɪneɪtɪŋ] faszinierend **III U2**, 48

fashion ['fæʃn] Mode **I**

fast [fɑːst] schnell **I**

father ['fɑːðə] Vater **I**

(my) **fault** [ˌmaɪ 'fɔːlt] (meine) Schuld **II**

favourite ['feɪvrɪt] Lieblings- **I**
My **favourite** … is … [ˌmaɪ 'feɪvrɪt ɪz] Mein Lieblings… ist … **I**
What's your **favourite** …? ['wɒts jə ˌfeɪvrɪt] Was ist dein/-e Lieblings …? **I**

fear [fɪə] Angst; Furcht; Befürchtung **II**

feather ['feðə] Feder **II**

to feature ['fiːtʃə] zeigen; aufweisen **II**

February ['februri] Februar **II**

***to be fed up (with)** [bi fed ˈʌp (wɪð)] sauer sein (auf); die Nase voll haben (von) **III U1**, 20

fee [fiː] Gebühr **II**
school **fees** (pl) ['skuːl fiːz] Schulgeld; Schulgebühren **III U3**, 77

***to feed** [fiːd] füttern; ernähren **II**

feedback ['fiːdbæk] Feedback; Rückmeldung **II**

***to feel** [fiːl] fühlen; sich fühlen **I**
***to feel** left out [ˌfiːl left 'aʊt] sich ausgeschlossen fühlen **II**
***to feel** sick [ˌfiːl 'sɪk] Übelkeit verspüren; sich schlecht fühlen **II**
***to feel** sorry for [ˌfiːl 'sɒri fɔː] Mitleid haben mit; bedauern **III U1**, 23

feeling ['fiːlɪŋ] Gefühl **II**

fence [fens] Zaun ⟨**III TR1**, 110⟩

ferry ['feri] Fähre **III U4**, 95

to fetch [fetʃ] holen; abholen **III U4**, 105

fever ['fiːvə] Fieber **II**

few [fjuː] wenige **II**
a **few** [ə 'fjuː] ein paar; wenige; einige **I**

science fiction [ˌsaɪəns 'fɪkʃn] Science-Fiction (Zukunftsdichtung) **III U4**, 107

fictional ['fɪkʃnl] fiktional; fiktiv; erdichtet **III U4**, 109

fiddle ['fɪdl] Geige ⟨**III TR3**, 114⟩

field [fiːld] Feld; Spielfeld; Wiese; Weide; Acker **II**

fifteen [ˌfɪf'tiːn] fünfzehn **I**

fight [faɪt] Schlacht; Kampf; Streit **II**

***to fight** [faɪt] kämpfen; (sich) streiten **II**

figurative ['fɪgjrətɪv] bildlich; figurativ °**III TMS1**, 28

figure ['fɪgə] Ziffer; Zahl **III U3**, 72

wax **figure** ['wæks ˌfɪɡə] Wachsfigur II
to **fill** [fɪl] füllen III U2, 44
  to **fill** in [ˌfɪl ˈɪn] ausfüllen II
film [fɪlm] Film I
to **film** [fɪlm] filmen; drehen °III AC1, 35
filmmaker ['fɪlmˌmeɪkə] Filmemacher/-in II
to **filter** ['fɪltə] filtern II
final ['faɪnl] letzte/-r/-s III U2, 48
finally ['faɪnli] schließlich; endlich; zum Schluss; letztlich II
*to **find** [faɪnd] finden; herausfinden I
  *to **find** out [ˌfaɪnd ˈaʊt] herausfinden I
findings (pl only) ['faɪndɪnz] Ergebnisse °III TMS1, 33
fine [faɪn] gut; in Ordnung; schön I
  I'm **fine**. [ˌaɪm ˈfaɪn] Mir geht's gut. I
finger ['fɪŋɡə] Finger I
  finger food ['fɪŋɡə ˌfuːd] Fingerfood (Essen, das man mit den Fingern essen kann) I
  *to keep your **fingers** crossed [ˌkiːp jɔː ˌfɪŋɡəz ˈkrɒst] die Daumen drücken I
finish line ['fɪnɪʃ ˌlaɪn] Ziellinie II
to **finish** ['fɪnɪʃ] beenden; enden; fertigstellen; aufhören II
fire [faɪə] Feuer ⟨III TMS1, 31⟩; ⟨III TR1, 110⟩
firewood ['faɪəwʊd] Brennholz ⟨III TR1, 110⟩
*to set off **fireworks** [setˌɒf ˈfaɪəwɜːks] ein Feuerwerk zünden III U2, 43
firing range ['faɪrɪŋ ˌreɪndʒ] Schießplatz ⟨III TR1, 110⟩
first [fɜːst] erste/-r/-s; zuerst; als Erstes I; erstens II
  at **first** [ət ˈfɜːst] zuerst; zunächst II
  first aid kit [ˌfɜːstˌeɪd ˈkɪt] Erste-Hilfe-Kasten I
  first name [ˌfɜːst ˈneɪm] Vorname I
fish, fish (pl) [fɪʃ; fɪʃ] Fisch I
fishing ['fɪʃɪŋ] Angeln; Fischen; Fischerei II
to **fit in** [ˌfɪt ˈɪn] dazupassen; sich einfügen III U1, 22
fitness ['fɪtnəs] Fitness II
five [faɪv] fünf I
to **fix** [fɪks] reparieren; befestigen II
flair [fleə] Flair; Atmosphäre II
flash [flæʃ] Blitz; Lichtblitz III U3, 75
flashback ['flæʃbæk] Rückblende; Flashback III U3, 76
flat [flæt] Wohnung I
flat rate ['flæt reɪt] Flatrate; Einheitspreis III TMS1, 29
flaw [flɔː] Fehler; Mangel; Defekt ⟨III TMS1, 32⟩
flea market ['fliː ˌmɑːkɪt] Flohmarkt I
flexible ['fleksɪbl] flexibel III U4, 102
flight [flaɪt] Flug III U4, 98
  flight attendant ['flaɪtˌəˌtendnt] Flugbegleiter/-in III U4, 95
to **flood** [flʌd] überfluten; fluten; überschwemmen III U3, 63
floor [flɔː] Fußboden I
to **flow** [fləʊ] fließen; strömen II
flower ['flaʊə] Blume II

to **flush** [flʌʃ] spülen; die Wasserspülung betätigen III U1, 11
*to **fly** [flaɪ] fliegen III U4, 99
flyer ['flaɪə] Flyer I
flying [flaɪ] Fliegen III U4, 94
out of **focus** [ˌaʊt əv ˈfəʊkəs] unscharf III U3, 75
to **focus** (on) ['fəʊkəs (ˌɒn)] sich konzentrieren (auf) III U1, 10
fog [fɒɡ] Nebel ⟨III TR1, 111⟩
to **follow** ['fɒləʊ] folgen; befolgen; hinterhergehen I
follower ['fɒləʊə] Follower; Anhänger/-in III U1, 10
the **following** [ðə ˈfɒləʊɪŋ] folgende/-r/-s °III TMS2, 80
food [fuːd] Essen; Lebensmittel I
  finger **food** ['fɪŋɡə ˌfuːd] Fingerfood (Essen, das man mit den Fingern essen kann) I
foot, feet (pl) [fʊt; fiːt] Fuß I
  *to keep one's **feet** or hands still [ˌkiːp wʌnz ˈfiːtˌɔː ˈhændz stɪl] die Beine und Hände ruhig halten III TMS1, 29
  on **foot** [ɒn ˈfʊt] zu Fuß II
football ['fʊtbɔːl] Fußball I
for [fɔː; fə] zum; für I; wegen II
  for example [fər ɪɡˈzɑːmpl] zum Beispiel II
force [fɔːs] Kraft; Macht III U4, 107
weather **forecast** ['weðə ˌfɔːkɑːst] Wettervorhersage II
foreign ['fɒrɪn] ausländisch; fremd III U4, 95
  foreign language [ˌfɒrɪn ˈlæŋɡwɪdʒ] Fremdsprache III U4, 94
forest ['fɒrɪst] Wald II
forever [fəˈrevə] für immer; ewig II
*to **forget** [fəˈɡet] vergessen I
*to **forgive** [fəˈɡɪv] vergeben; verzeihen II
fork [fɔːk] Gabel I
form [fɔːm] Formular II
formal ['fɔːml] formal; formell; förmlich II
fort [fɔːt] Fort; Festung III U3, 63
forum ['fɔːrəm] Forum II
to look **forward** to [ˌlʊk ˈfɔːwəd tə] sich freuen auf II
to **found** [faʊnd] gründen III U3, 63
founder ['faʊndə] Gründer/-in III U1, 24
four [fɔː] vier I
to **free** [friː] befreien; freilassen III TMS1, 28
free [friː] frei; kostenlos I
  free time (no pl) [ˌfriː ˈtaɪm] Freizeit I
freedom (no pl) ['friːdəm] Freiheit; Unabhängigkeit III U1, 20
free-time ['friːˌtaɪm] Freizeit- II
French [frenʃ] Französisch; französisch II
fresh [freʃ] frisch II
Friday ['fraɪdeɪ] Freitag I
fridge [frɪdʒ] Kühlschrank I
friend [frend] Freund/-in I
  *to make **friends** [ˌmeɪk ˈfrendz] Freundschaft schließen I

  That's what **friends** are for. [ˌðæts wɒt ˈfrendzˌɑː ˌfɔː] Dafür sind Freunde da. I
friendly ['frendli] freundlich; nett I
  environmentally **friendly** [ɪnˌvaɪrnˌmentli ˈfrendli] umweltfreundlich III U4, 95
friendship ['frendʃɪp] Freundschaft II
from [frɒm; frəm] aus; von I
  from … to [frəmˌtə] von … bis I
  Where … **from**? [ˌweə ☐ ˈfrɒm] Woher …? I
front door [ˌfrʌnt ˈdɔː] Haustür II
in **front** of [ɪn ˈfrʌntˌəv] vor I
to **frown** [fraʊn] die Stirn runzeln III U4, 99
frozen ['frəʊzn] eingefroren; erstarrt °III U2, 47
fruit [fruːt] Frucht; Obst I
full [fʊl] ganz; vollständig II
  full (of) [fʊl (ˌəv)] voll (mit/von) I
full stop [ˌfʊl ˈstɒp] Punkt °III U2, 52
fun [fʌn] Freude; Spaß I
  *to have **fun** [ˌhæv ˈfʌn] Spaß haben; sich amüsieren I
  It's **fun**. [ɪts ˈfʌn] Es macht Spaß. I
fun [fʌn] lustig; witzig; fröhlich I
funny ['fʌni] lustig; witzig I; komisch; merkwürdig; seltsam III U1, 15
further ['fɜːðə] weiter (weg) III U2, 48
future ['fjuːtʃə] Zukunft II
future ['fjuːtʃə] zukünftig; Zukunfts- III U4, 107

G

gadget ['ɡædʒɪt] Gerät; technische Spielerei III U4, 106
Gaelic ['ɡeɪlɪk] gälisch; Gälisch II
gallery ['ɡælri] Kunstgalerie; Galerie II
game [ɡeɪm] Spiel I
garage ['ɡærɑːʒ] Garage I
garden ['ɡɑːdn] Garten I
gate [ɡeɪt] Gate; Flugsteig; Ausgang III U4, 101
genius ['dʒiːniəs] Genie II
genre ['ʒɑːnrə] Gattung; Genre III U4, 107
gentleman, gentlemen (pl) ['dʒentlmən; 'dʒentlmen] Gentleman; feiner Herr III U2, 45
geocaching ['dʒiːəʊkæʃɪŋ] Geocaching I
geography [dʒiˈɒɡrəfi] Geografie; Erdkunde II
German ['dʒɜːmən] deutsch; Deutsch; aus Deutschland; Deutsche/-r I
Germanic [dʒɜːˈmænɪk] germanisch III U3, 63
*to **get** [ɡet] holen; bringen; bekommen I; werden II; verstehen; begreifen ⟨III TR3, 114⟩
  *to **get** away with sth [ˌɡetˌəˈweɪ wɪð] davonkommen; durchkommen mit II
  *to **get** here [ˌɡet ˈhɪə] hinkommen II
  *to **get** in the way [ˌɡetˌɪn ðə ˈweɪ] stören; im Weg stehen II

*to **get** into [ˌget ˈɪntə] einsteigen; hineingelangen **II**

*to **get** into trouble [ˌget ˌɪntə ˈtrʌbl] in Schwierigkeiten geraten **III U1**, 20

*to **get** lost [ˌget ˈlɒst] verloren gehen; sich verirren **II**

*to **get** off (a bus/train) [ˌget ˈɒf] aussteigen (aus einem Bus/Zug) **II**

*to **get** on (the bus) [ˌget ˈɒn] einsteigen (in den Bus) **II**

*to **get** on somebody's nerves [ˌget ɒn sʌmbɒdiz ˈnɜːvz] jmdm. auf die Nerven gehen **I**

*to **get** out (of) [ˌget ˈaʊt (ˌəv)] verschwinden (von/aus) ⟨**III TR2**, 112⟩

*to **get** out of [ˌget ˈaʊt əv] aussteigen; herauskommen aus **II**

*to **get** ready [ˌget ˈredi] sich vorbereiten; sich fertig machen **III TMS1**, 26

*to **get** sth out of one's head [get ˌaʊt əv wʌnz ˈhed] etw. aus dem Kopf bekommen; von einem Gedanken loskommen **III TMS1**, 29

*to **get** through sth [ˌget ˈθruː] etw. überstehen **II**

*to **get** to [ˈget tə] kommen zu; kommen nach; erreichen **I**

*to **get** to know [ˌget tə ˈnəʊ] kennen lernen **III AC2**, 56

*to **get** up [ˌget ˈʌp] aufstehen (aus dem Bett) **I**

Get well soon! [get wel ˈsuːn] Gute Besserung! **III TMS2**, 85

Get out of his way. [get ˌaʊt əv hɪz ˈweɪ] Geh ihm aus dem Weg. **I**

Time to **get** up! [ˌtaɪm tə ˌget ˈʌp] Es ist Zeit aufzustehen! **I**

you've **got** my back [ˌjuːv gɒt maɪ ˈbæk] du stehst hinter mir **III TMS1**, 27

ghost [gəʊst] Geist; Gespenst **II**

gift [gɪft] Geschenk **I**

gig [gɪg] Auftritt; Gig **III U2**, 51

girl [gɜːl] Mädchen **I**

girlfriend [ˈgɜːlfrend] Freundin *(in einer Paarbeziehung)* **II**

gite [ʒiːt] *französisches Ferienhaus* ⟨**III U4**, 96⟩

*to **give** [gɪv] geben; schenken **I**

*to **give** sb a piggyback [gɪv ˌə ˈpɪgibæk] jmdn. Huckepack nehmen **III U4**, 104

*to **give** sb funny looks [ˌgɪv fʌni ˈlʊks] jmdn. schief anschauen; jmdn. komisch anschauen **III U1**, 15

*to **give** sb the bumps [ˌgɪv ðə ˈbʌmps] jmdn. hochleben lassen **II**

*to **give** up [gɪv ˈʌp] aufgeben **III U1**, 13

glad [glæd] froh; dankbar **III AC3**, 89

glass [glɑːs] Glas **I**

magnifying **glass** *(no pl)* [ˈmægnɪfaɪɪŋ ˌglɑːs] Lupe **II**

glasses *(pl)* [ˈglɑːsɪz] Brille **II**

glen [glen] Schlucht **III U2**, 46

glove [glʌv] Handschuh **II**

glue [gluː] Klebstoff **III TMS1**, 30

*to **go** [gəʊ] gehen; fahren **I**

*to **go** black [ˌgəʊ ˈblæk] schwarz werden **II**

*to **go** crazy [ˌgəʊ ˈkreɪzi] ausflippen; durchdrehen; verrückt werden **II**

*to **go** down [ˌgəʊ ˈdaʊn] entlanggehen; hinuntergehen; nach unten gehen **I**

*to **go** for a walk [ˌgəʊ fər ə ˈwɔːk] spazieren gehen **II**

*to **go** on [ˌgəʊ ˈɒn] geschehen; los sein; ablaufen **III AC3**, 88

*to **go** out [ˌgəʊ ˈaʊt] ausgehen; hinausgehen **II**

*to **go** over to [ˌgəʊ ˈəʊvə tə] hinübergehen zu; zu jmdm. nach Hause gehen **II**

*to **go** right back to [ˌgəʊ raɪt ˈbæk tə] zurückgehen auf **II**

*to **go** round in circles [gəʊ ˌraʊd ɪn ˈsɜːklz] sich im Kreis drehen **III U2**, 50

*to **go** shopping [ˌgəʊ ˈʃɒpɪŋ] einkaufen gehen **I**

*to **go** to bed [ˌgəʊ tə ˈbed] ins Bett gehen **I**

*to **go** together [ˌgəʊ təˈgeðə] zueinander passen; zueinander gehören **I**

*to **go** wrong [ˌgəʊ ˈrɒŋ] schiefgehen **II**

*to let **go** (of) [ˌlet ˈgəʊ (əv)] loslassen **II**

Here you **go**. [ˌhɪə ju ˈgəʊ] Bitte schön!; Bitte sehr! **I**

It's **gone**. [ɪts ˈgɒn] Es ist weg. **II**

goal [gəʊl] Tor; Ziel **II**

goat [gəʊt] Ziege **I**

gold [gəʊld] Gold **I**

golden [ˈgəʊldn] golden; Gold- ⟨**III U4**, 98⟩

golden age [ˌgəʊldn ˈeɪdʒ] goldenes Zeitalter **III U3**, 65

golf [gɒlf] Golf **II**

*to be **gone** [bi ˈgɒn] verschwunden sein; weg sein **II**

gonna (= going to) *(coll)* [ˈgɒnə] werden **III TMS2**, 84

good [gʊd] gut **I**

*to be **good** at [bi ˈgʊd ət] gut sein in **I**

*to be **good** with [bi ˈgʊd wɪð] gut umgehen können mit ⟨**III TR2**, 112⟩

Good morning. [gʊd ˈmɔːnɪŋ] Guten Morgen. **I**

goodbye [gʊdˈbaɪ] auf Wiedersehen **I**

*to say **goodbye** (to) [ˌseɪ gʊdˈbaɪ (tə)] sich verabschieden (von) **III U3**, 63

goods *(pl)* [gʊdz] Güter; Waren **III U3**, 65

gorge scrambling [ˈgɔːdʒ ˌskræmblɪŋ] Schluchtenklettern **II**

government [ˈgʌvnmənt] Regierung **III U2**, 43

GPS device [dʒiːpiːˌes dɪˈvaɪs] GPS-Gerät **I**

to **grab** [græb] greifen; ergreifen; schnappen **II**

grand [grænd] großartig; prächtig; o.k. ⟨**III TR3**, 114⟩

grandad [ˈgrændæd] Opa; Opi **I**

grandchild *(sg)* **grandchildren** *(pl)* [ˈgræntʃaɪld; ˈgræntʃɪldrn] Enkel/-in; Enkelkind **II**

grandma [ˈgrænmɑː] Oma; Omi **I**

grandpa [ˈgrænpɑː] Opa; Opi **II**

grandparents *(pl)* [ˈgrænˌpeərənts] Großeltern **I**

granny [ˈgræni] Oma; Omi **I**

to **grant** [grɑːnt] gewähren; zusprechen; geben **III U2**, 43

gratitude [ˈgrætɪtjuːd] Dankbarkeit **III AC1**, 35

great [greɪt] großartig; toll; super **I**

green [griːn] grün **I**

Greenwich Mean Time *(= GMT)* [ˌgrenɪdʒ ˈmiːn ˌtaɪm] westeuropäische Zeit **I**

greeting [ˈgriːtɪŋ] Gruß **I**

grey [greɪ] grau **I**

ground [graʊnd] Boden; Erdboden **III TMS1**, 27

*to be **grounded** [bi ˈgraʊndɪd] Hausarrest haben **III U1**, 20

group [gruːp] Gruppe; Klasse **I**

tutor **group** [ˈtjuːtə ˌgruːp] Klasse *(in einer englischen Schule)* **I**

*to **grow** [grəʊ] wachsen; anbauen; züchten **III U1**, 12

guard [gɑːd] Wache; Wächter/-in **II**

to **guess** [ges] annehmen; raten; erraten **III AC3**, 88

Guess what! [ges ˈwɒt] Stell dir vor!; Rate mal! **III U3**, 70

guest [gest] Gast **II**

guide [gaɪd] Führer/-in; Reiseführer **II**

guide book [ˈgaɪd ˌbʊk] Reiseführer **II**

guided [ˈgaɪdɪd] geführt **II**

guinea pig [ˈgɪni ˌpɪg] Meerschweinchen **I**

guitar [gɪˈtɑː] Gitarre **III U4**, 107

chewing **gum** [ˈtʃuːɪŋ ˌgʌm] Kaugummi **I**

guy [gaɪ] Typ; Kerl; *(Pl.)* Leute **II**

gym(nasium) [dʒɪm; dʒɪmˈneɪziəm] Turnhalle; Sporthalle **II**

H

haggis [ˈhægɪs] Haggis *(schottisches Gericht aus in einem Schafsmagen gekochten Schafsinnereien und Haferschrot)* **III U2**, 41

haiku [ˈhaɪkuː] Haiku *(japanisches Gedicht mit drei Zeilen, in dem es eine unterschiedliche Anzahl an Silben gibt)* **III TMS1**, 32

hair [heə] Haar; Haare **II**

*to do our **hair** [ˌduː ˌaʊə ˈheə] uns frisieren; unsere Haare machen **II**

hair straightener [ˈheə ˌstreɪtnə] Haarglätter **I**

hairbrush [ˈheəbrʌʃ] Haarbürste **III U3**, 65

half (of), **halves** *(pl)* [hɑːf (ˌəv); hɑːvz] die Hälfte **I**

half an hour [ˌhɑːf ən ˈaʊər] eine halbe Stunde **III U3**, 75

half [hɑːf] halb I
  half past [ˌhɑːf ˈpɑːst] halb *(bei Uhrzeit-angaben)* I
  half-sister [ˈhɑːfˌsɪstə] Halbschwester I
half-aloud [hɑːfəˈlaʊd] halblaut °III TMS1, 31
*to meet halfway [ˌmiːt hɑːfˈweɪ] sich auf halbem Weg treffen III U1, 18
hall [hɔːl] Halle; Saal; Flur; Diele; Korridor II
  arrivals **hall** [əˈraɪvlz ˌhɔːl] Ankunftshalle III U4, 95
ham [hæm] Schinken III AC1, 34
hand [hænd] Hand II
  by **hand** [ˌbaɪ ˈhænd] von Hand; manuell III U3, 65
  On the one **hand** …, (but) on the other **hand** … [ɒn ðəˈwʌn ˌhænd (bʌt) ɒn ðiˌʌðə ˌhænd] Einerseits …, (aber) andererseits … II
handwritten [ˌhændˈrɪtn] handgeschrieben; handschriftlich II
*to hang on [ˌhæŋˈɒn] warten; durchhalten III TMS1, 27
  *to **hang** out (with) *(infml)* [ˌhæŋˈaʊt wɪð] rumhängen (mit); sich herumtreiben (mit) III U1, 20
to happen [ˈhæpn] geschehen; passieren I
happy [ˈhæpi] glücklich; froh; fröhlich I
  Happy Birthday! [ˌhæpi ˈbɜːθdeɪ] Alles Gute zum Geburtstag!; Herzlichen Glückwunsch zum Geburtstag! II
harbour [ˈhɑːbə] Hafen II
hard [hɑːd] schwierig; schwer; hart; fest; stark II
  *to be **hard** on sb [bi ˈhɑːd ɒn] streng mit jmdm. sein III U1, 16
hardly [ˈhɑːdli] kaum ⟨III TR1, 110⟩
harmony [ˈhɑːməni] Harmonie III TMS1, 29
hat [hæt] Hut II
to hate [heɪt] nicht mögen; hassen I
*to have [hæv] haben I
  *to **have** *(a sweet)* [hæv] *(ein Bonbon)* nehmen; *(ein Bonbon)* essen I
  *to **have** a break [ˌhæv ə ˈbreɪk] eine Pause machen I
  *to **have** a look (at) [ˌhæv ə ˈlʊk (ət)] anschauen I
  *to **have** a look (at) [ˌhæv ə ˈlʊk] anschauen II
  *to **have** a point [ˌhæv ə ˈpɔɪnt] nicht ganz Unrecht haben III U1, 18
  *to **have** breakfast [ˌhæv ˈbrekfəst] frühstücken I
  *to **have** fun [ˌhæv ˈfʌn] Spaß haben; sich amüsieren I
  *to **have** got [hæv ˈgɒt] besitzen; haben I
  *to **have** in common [ˌhæv ɪn ˈkɒmən] gemein haben III TMS1, 30
  *to **have** to [ˈhæv tə] müssen II
he [hiː] er I
head [hed] Kopf I
  *to get sth out of one's **head** [get ˌaʊt əv wʌnz ˈhed] etw. aus dem Kopf bekom-

men; von einem Gedanken loskommen III TMS1, 29
  head teacher [ˌhed ˈtiːtʃə] Schulleiter/-in III TMS2, 80
  With a very big **head**! [ˌwɪð ə ˌveri bɪg ˈhed] Und ein Angeber! II
headache [ˈhedeɪk] Kopfschmerzen; Kopfweh II
heading [ˈhedɪŋ] Überschrift; Titel I
headphones *(pl)* [ˈhedfəʊnz] Kopfhörer II
headset [ˈhedset] Kopfhörer II
health [helθ] Gesundheit II
healthy [ˈhelθi] gesund I
*to hear [hɪə] hören I
  I **hear** … [aɪ ˈhɪə] Ich habe gehört, dass … I
heart [hɑːt] Herz; Zentrum II
  *to learn … by **heart** [ˌlɜːn baɪ ˈhɑːt] auswendig lernen III TMS1, 26
heating [ˈhiːtɪŋ] Heizung III U1, 11
heavy [ˈhevi] schwer; stark II
Hello. [helˈəʊ] Hallo. I
  *to say **hello** (to) [ˌseɪ helˈəʊ (tə)] grüßen I
helmet [ˈhelmət] Helm I
help [help] Hilfe I
to help [help] helfen I
  to **help** out [ˌhelp ˈaʊt] aushelfen III U2, 53
helpful [ˈhelpfl] hilfsbereit; hilfreich I
helpless [ˈhelpləs] hilflos I
her [hɜː] ihr/-e; sie I
here [hɪə] hier I
  right **here** [ˌraɪt ˈhɪə] genau hier II
  Here you are. [ˌhɪə juˈɑː] Bitte schön. I
  Here you go. [ˌhɪə juˈgəʊ] Bitte schön!; Bitte sehr! I
  Here's … [ˌhɪəz] Hier ist … I
hero, heroes *(pl)* [ˈhɪərəʊ, ˈhɪərəʊz] Held II
heroine [ˈherəʊɪn] Heldin II
herself [hɜːˈself] (sie) selbst; sich (selbst) III U1, 15
to hesitate [ˈhezɪteɪt] zögern III U4, 105
Hey! [heɪ] Hi.; He!; Hallo. I
Hi. [haɪ] Hi.; Hallo. I
*to hide [haɪd] (sich) verstecken II
high [haɪ] hoch; groß II
  high tide [ˈhaɪ ˌtaɪd] Flut II
  the **high** street [ðə ˈhaɪ ˌstriːt] die Haupteinkaufsstraße III U1, 20
highlight [ˈhaɪlaɪt] Highlight; Höhepunkt II
highlighted [ˈhaɪlaɪtɪd] markiert ⟨III TMS2, 86⟩
hiker [ˈhaɪkə] Wanderer/-in ⟨III TR1, 110⟩
hiking [ˈhaɪkɪŋ] Wandern II
hill [hɪl] Berg; Hügel II
him [hɪm] ihn; ihm I
himself [hɪmˈself] er/sich (selbst); selber II
hint [hɪnt] Hinweis; Andeutung; Tipp III AC2, 57
to hire [haɪə] mieten; ausleihen III U3, 71
his [hɪz] sein/-e I
historic [hɪˈstɒrɪk] historisch III U2, 40
historical [hɪˈstɒrɪkl] historisch; geschichtlich II

history [ˈhɪstri] Geschichte II
  living **history** show [ˌlɪvɪŋ ˈhɪstəri ˌʃəʊ] *Show, in der historischer Alltag nachgespielt wird* II
*to hit [hɪt] schlagen; treffen I
hobby, hobbies *(pl)* [ˈhɒbi; ˈhɒbiz] Hobby I
hockey [ˈhɒki] Hockey II
to hog a conversation [ˌhɒg ə kɒnvəˈseɪʃn] ein Gespräch für sich in Beschlag nehmen; ein Gespräch dominieren III AC2, 56
*to hold [həʊld] halten; festhalten I; abhalten III U2, 45
  *to **hold** onto [ˌhəʊld ˈɒntə] (sich) festhalten an III U2, 51
  *to **hold** open [ˌhəʊld ˈəʊpn] aufhalten III AC3, 88
holiday [ˈhɒlədeɪ] Urlaub; Feiertag I
  bank **holiday** [ˌbæŋk ˈhɒlədeɪ] Feiertag ⟨III TR3, 114⟩
  holiday home [ˈhɒlədeɪ ˌhəʊm] Ferienhaus III U4, 96
holidays *(pl)* [ˈhɒlədeɪz] Ferien; Schulferien III U4, 95
home [həʊm] Zuhause; Heim I
  at **home** [ət ˈhəʊm] zu Hause I
  holiday **home** [ˈhɒlədeɪ ˌhəʊm] Ferienhaus III U4, 96
home [həʊm] nach Hause I
homepage [ˈhəʊmpeɪdʒ] Homepage I
*to be homesick [bi ˈhəʊmsɪk] Heimweh haben III U4, 106
hometown [ˈhəʊmtaʊn] Heimatstadt; Heimatort II
homeward [ˈhəʊmwəd] heimwärts ⟨III U2, 47⟩
homework *(no pl)* [ˈhəʊmwɜːk] Hausaufgabe(n) I
honest [ˈɒnɪst] ehrlich III U1, 22
honey [ˈhʌni] Honig III AC1, 34
Hooray! [hʊˈreɪ] Hurra! III TMS2, 85
hope [həʊp] Hoffnung II
to hope [həʊp] hoffen I
hopeful [ˈhəʊpfl] hoffnungsvoll I
horrible [ˈhɒrəbl] schrecklich; furchtbar II
horrified [ˈhɒrɪfaɪd] entsetzt I
horse [hɔːs] Pferd I
hospital [ˈhɒspɪtl] Krankenhaus; Hospital III U3, 75
host family [ˈhəʊst ˌfæmli] Gastfamilie III AC1, 34
hostel [ˈhɒstl] Herberge ⟨III TR1, 111⟩
hot [hɒt] heiß III AC1, 35
hotel [həʊˈtel] Hotel III U4, 102
hour [aʊə] Stunde I
  half an **hour** [ˌhɑːf ən ˈaʊər] eine halbe Stunde III U3, 75
house [haʊs] Haus I
  to move (**house**) [muːv (ˈhaʊs)] umziehen II
  around the **house** [əˌraʊnd ðə ˈhaʊs] rund ums Haus; ums Haus herum I
how [haʊ] wie I

How many …? [ˌhaʊ ˈmeni] Wie viele
…? I

How are you? [ˌhaʊ ˈɑː jə] Wie geht es dir/
euch/Ihnen?; Wie geht es euch?; Wie geht
es Ihnen? II

How much (is/are) …? [ˌhaʊ ˈmʌtʃ ˌɪz/
ɑː)] Wie viel (kostet/kosten) …? I

How old are you? [haʊˌəʊld ə ˈjuː] Wie
alt bist du?; Wie seid ihr?; Wie alt sind
Sie? I

how to … [ˈhaʊ tə] wie man … I
that's **how** [ˌðæts ˈhaʊ] so I

however [haʊˈevə] jedoch III U3, 65

howling [ˈhaʊlɪŋ] heulend ⟨III TR1, 110⟩

hug [hʌg] Umarmung III TMS2, 85

to **hug** [hʌg] umarmen I

huge [hjuːdʒ] riesig; riesengroß; gewaltig
III U2, 48

human body [ˌhjuːmən ˈbɒdi] menschlicher
Körper II

humanities (pl) [hjuːˈmænətiz] Sozialwissenschaften II

humour (no pl) [ˈhjuːmə] Humor; Stimmung; Laune III U1, 23
sense of **humour** (no pl) [ˌsens əv ˈhjuːmə]
Sinn für Humor III U1, 23

hundreds of [ˈhʌndrədz ˌəv] hunderte (von)
III U2, 44

hungry [ˈhʌŋgri] hungrig II

to **hunt** [hʌnt] jagen ⟨III TR2, 112⟩

to **hurry** [ˈhʌri] eilen; sich beeilen II

*to be **hurt** [hɜːt] verletzen; weh tun II

hurt [hɜːt] verletzt II

husband [ˈhʌzbənd] Ehemann III TMS2, 84

I

I [aɪ] ich I

I don't know! [aɪ ˌdəʊnt ˈnəʊ] Ich weiß
(es) nicht! I

I hear … [aɪ ˈhɪə] Ich habe gehört, dass
… I

I spy with my little eye [aɪ spaɪ wɪð ˌmaɪ
lɪtl ˈaɪ] Ich sehe was, was du nicht siehst
II

I was just telling [aɪ wəz dʒʌst ˈtelɪŋ] ich
habe gerade gesagt ⟨III U1, 15⟩

I'd like to … (= I would like to) [aɪd ˈlaɪk
tə] Ich möchte …; Ich würde gern … I

I'd rather [aɪd ˈrɑːðə] ich würde lieber
III U3, 77

I'm (not) scared of … [aɪm (nɒt) ˈskeəd ˌ
əv] Ich habe (keine) Angst vor … I

I'm fine. [aɪm ˈfaɪn] Mir geht's gut. I

I'm sorry! [aɪm ˈsɒri] Tut mir leid! I

ice [aɪs] Eis II

ice cream [ˌaɪs ˈkriːm] Eis; Eiscreme II

ice rink [ˈaɪs ˌrɪŋk] Eisbahn; Schlittschuhbahn II

icebreaker [ˈaɪsˌbreɪkə] Eisbrecher (Sätze,
um mit jmdm. ins Gespräch zu kommen)
III AC3, 89

icon [ˈaɪkɒn] Symbol; Ikone III TMS2, 84

idea [aɪˈdɪə] Idee; Einfall I
No **idea**. [nəʊ aɪˈdɪə] Keine Ahnung. I

to **identify** (with) [aɪˈdentɪfaɪ (wɪð)] sich
identifizieren (mit) III U3, 77

idiot [ˈɪdiət] Idiot/-in II

if [ɪf] wenn; falls; ob I
if-clause [ˈɪfˌklɔːz] if-Satz °III U1, 11

to **ignore** [ɪgˈnɔː] ignorieren; außer Acht
lassen III U1, 21

illness [ˈɪlnəs] Krankheit III U4, 102

to **illustrate** [ˈɪləstreɪt] illustrieren; veranschaulichen; darstellen II

image [ˈɪmɪdʒ] Bild; Abbildung °III TMS1, 28

imagination [ɪˌmædʒɪˈneɪʃn] Fantasie;
Vorstellungskraft III U1, 9

imaginative [ɪˈmædʒɪnətɪv] einfallsreich;
fantasievoll III U1, 9

to **imagine** [ɪˈmædʒɪn] sich (etwas) vorstellen II

immigration officer [ɪmɪˈgreɪʃn ˌɒfɪsə] Gren-
zschutzbeamter/-beamtin; Einwander-
ungsbeamter/-beamtin III U4, 95

imperative [ɪmˈperətɪv] Imperativ; Befehlsform II

impolite [ˌɪmpˈlaɪt] unhöflich III AC1, 35

important [ɪmˈpɔːtnt] wichtig I

*to be **impressed** [bi ɪmˈprest] bee ndruckt
sein II

impression [ɪmˈpreʃn] Eindruck; Impression
III TMS1, 27

improbable [ɪmˈprɒbəbl] unwahrscheinlich
°III U1, 12

to **improve** [ɪmˈpruːv] (sich) verbessern
III U2, 48

in [ɪn] in; im; rein; herein I
in case [ɪn ˈkeɪs] falls; für den Fall, dass
… II
in fact [ɪn ˈfækt] tatsächlich; eigentlich;
genau genommen III U2, 45
in front of [ɪn ˈfrʌnt əv] vor I
in need [ɪn ˈniːd] bedürftig; in Not II
in pairs [ɪn ˈpeəz] zu zweit; mit einem
Partner/einer Partnerin I
in secret [ɪn ˈsiːkrət] heimlich I
in the end [ɪn ði ˈend] schließlich; zum
Schluss I
in the evenings [ɪn ði ˈiːvnɪŋz] abends I
in the middle of [ɪn ðə ˈmɪdl əv] mitten
in II
in the north of [ˌɪn ðə ˈnɔːθ əv] im Norden
von I
in the street [ˌɪn ðə ˈstriːt] auf der Straße I
in … shoes [ɪn ˈʃuːz] an … Stelle III U1, 13

to **include** [ɪnˈkluːd] beinhalten; einschließen II

in-crowd [ˈɪnkraʊd] die Angesagten; die
Beliebten; Szene III U1, 20

independent [ˌɪndɪˈpendənt] unabhängig
III U3, 65

Indian [ˈɪndiən] Inder/-in; indisch I

indirect speech [ˌɪndɪrekt ˈspiːtʃ] indirekte
Rede ⟨III TR3, 115⟩

industry [ˈɪndəstri] Industrie; Branche;
Gewerbe III U2, 42

influence [ˈɪnfluəns] Einfluss III U3, 65

influencer [ˈɪnfluənsə] Influencer/-in; Ein-
flussnehmer/-in III U1, 10

to **inform** [ɪnˈfɔːm] informieren III TMS2, 80

informal [ɪnˈfɔːml] informell; zwanglos;
inoffiziell III TMS2, 80

information (no pl) [ˌɪnfəˈmeɪʃn] Information; Informationen I

ingredient [ɪnˈgriːdiənt] Zutat II

injury [ˈɪndʒəri] Verletzung II

inline skating [ˈɪnlaɪn ˌskeɪtɪŋ] Inlineskatefahren I

input [ˈɪnpʊt] Input; Beitrag III U4, 103

inside [ɪnˈsaɪd] innen; im Innern; hinein;
nach drinnen; in; drin II

to **insist** (on) [ɪnˈsɪst (ɒn)] bestehen (auf);
insistieren III U4, 99

instead [ɪnˈsted] stattdessen III U1, 20
instead of [ɪnˈsted əv] statt; anstatt; an
Stelle von III U3, 67

instruction [ɪnˈstrʌkʃn] Instruktion; Anweisung III AC2, 57

instructor [ɪnˈstrʌktə] Lehrer/-in; Betreuer/
-in II

instrument [ˈɪnstrəmənt] Instrument
III TMS1, 29

interactive [ˌɪntəˈæktɪv] interaktiv °III U2, 41

interest [ˈɪntrəst] Interesse II

*to be **interested** in [bi ˈɪntrəstɪd ɪn] interessiert sein an; sich interessieren für II

interesting [ˈɪntrəstɪŋ] interessant I

international [ˌɪntəˈnæʃnl] international II

internet [ˈɪntənet] Internet I

to **interpret** [ɪnˈtɜːprɪt] interpretieren
⟨III TMS1, 32⟩

to **interrupt** [ˌɪntəˈrʌpt] unterbrechen II

interview [ˈɪntəvjuː] Interview; Befragung I

to **interview** [ˈɪntəvjuː] interviewen; befragen II

into [ˈɪntə] in; in … hinein I
*to be **into** [bi ˈɪntə] mögen; stehen auf I

to **introduce** [ˌɪntrəˈdjuːs] vorstellen II

introduction [ˌɪntrəˈdʌkʃn] Einführung;
Einleitung III U4, 103

to **invade** [ɪnˈveɪd] einmarschieren (in);
einfallen in III U3, 66

to **invent** [ɪnˈvent] erfinden III U2, 43

invention [ɪnˈvenʃn] Erfindung III U2, 43

inventor [ɪnˈventə] Erfinder/-in III U2, 53

invisible [ɪnˈvɪzəbl] unsichtbar III U4, 105

invitation [ˌɪnvɪˈteɪʃn] Einladung II

to **invite** [ɪnˈvaɪt] einladen II

*to be **involved** [bi ɪnˈvɒlvd] beteiligt sein;
involviert sein III U1, 10

inward [ˈɪnwəd] ankommend II

Irish [ˈaɪrɪʃ] irisch; Irisch II

is [ɪz] ist I

island [ˈaɪlənd] Insel II

environmental **issues** [ɪnˌvaɪrnˈmentl ˈɪʃuːz] Umweltprobleme **III U1**, 10
it [ɪt] er; sie; es **I**
  It's fun. [ɪts ˈfʌn] Es macht Spaß. **I**
  It's your turn. [ɪts ˈjɔː tɜːn] Du bist dran. **I**
  It's …/They're … [ɪts/ðeə] Es kostet …/ Sie kosten … **I**
IT (= *Information Technology*) [aɪˈtiː] Informatik; Informationstechnik **III U1**, 12
itinerary [aɪˈtɪnrri] Reiseplan; Reiseroute; Reiseweg **III U4**, 95
its [ɪts] sein/-e; ihr/-e **I**
itself [ɪtˈself] (sich) selbst **III U1**, 16

J

jacket [ˈdʒækɪt] Jacke **I**
jam [dʒæm] Marmelade; Konfitüre **II**
January [ˈdʒænjuri] Januar **II**
Japanese [ˌdʒæpənˈiːz] japanisch; Japanisch **III TMS1**, 32
jazz [dʒæz] Jazz (*Musik*) **III TMS1**, 26
jealous [ˈdʒeləs] eifersüchtig; neidisch **II**
jeans (*pl*) [dʒiːnz] Jeans **I**
jelly [ˈdʒeli] Götterspeise; Wackelpudding; Tortenguss; Gelee **II**
crown **jewels** [ˌkraʊn ˈdʒuːəlz] Kronjuwelen **II**
jewellery [ˈdʒuːəlri] Schmuck **I**
job [dʒɒb] Arbeit; Aufgabe; Job **I**
to join [dʒɔɪn] beitreten; sich anschließen; verbinden **II**
joke [dʒəʊk] Witz **I**
to joke [dʒəʊk] scherzen **II**
journey [ˈdʒɜːni] Reise; Fahrt **II**
to judge [dʒʌdʒ] beurteilen; bewerten **III U1**, 8
juice [dʒuːs] Saft **I**
July [dʒʊˈlaɪ] Juli **II**
to jump [dʒʌmp] springen **I**
  to jump the queue [ˌdʒʌmp ðə ˈkjuː] sich vordrängeln **I**
jumper [ˈdʒʌmpə] Pullover; Pulli **I**
June [dʒuːn] Juni **II**
piece of **junk** [ˌpiːs əv ˈdʒʌŋk] Stück Schrott **III U1**, 21
just [dʒʌst] gerade; nur; einfach **I**
  just then [ˌdʒʌst ˈðen] genau in dem Moment **I**

K

karaoke [ˌkæriˈəʊki] Karaoke **II**
*to **keep** [kiːp] behalten; aufbewahren; halten **II**
  *to **keep** away from [ˌkiːp əˈweɪ frəm] (sich) fernhalten von **II**
  *to **keep** one's feet or hands still [ˌkiːp wʌnz ˈfiːt ɔː ˈhændz stɪl] die Beine und Hände ruhig halten **III TMS1**, 29
  *to **keep** out (of) [ˌkiːp ˈaʊt (əv)] draußen bleiben (von); draußen halten (von) **III U2**, 50

*to **keep** sth going [ˌkiːp ˈgəʊɪŋ] etw. aufrechterhalten **II**
  *to **keep** the ball bouncing [ˌkiːp ðə bɔːl ˈbaʊntsɪŋ] *hier*: das Gespräch am Laufen halten **III AC2**, 56
  *to **keep** up (with) [ˌkiːp ˈʌp (wɪð)] mithalten (mit); Schritt halten (mit) **II**
  *to **keep** your fingers crossed [ˌkiːp jɔː ˌfɪŋgəz ˈkrɒst] die Daumen drücken **I**
key [kiː] Schlüssel **II**
  key ring [ˈkiː ˌrɪŋ] Schlüsselbund; Schlüsselanhänger **III U2**, 51
to kick [kɪk] schießen; treten **II**
kid [kɪd] Jugendliche/-r; Kind **II**
to kill [kɪl] töten; umbringen **III U3**, 66
kilometre (km) [ˈkɪləˌmiːtə; kɪˈlɒmɪtə] Kilometer **II**
kilt [kɪlt] Kilt; Schottenrock **III U2**, 41
kind (of) [kaɪnd (ˌəv)] Art; Sorte **II**
kind [kaɪnd] nett; freundlich **II**
king [kɪŋ] König **I**
kingdom [ˈkɪŋdəm] Königreich **III U3**, 63
kiss [kɪs] Kuss **III TMS2**, 85
to kiss [kɪs] sich küssen **III U2**, 55
first aid **kit** [ˌfɜːst ˌeɪd ˈkɪt] Erste-Hilfe-Kasten **I**
kitchen [ˈkɪtʃɪn] Küche **I**
kite [kaɪt] Drachen **I**
knife, **knives** (*pl*) [naɪf; naɪvz] Messer **I**
knight [naɪt] Ritter **II**
knob [nɒb] Griff; Knopf **II**
*to **know** [nəʊ] kennen; wissen **I**
  *to be **known** (as) [bi ˈnəʊn (ˌəz)] bekannt sein (als) **III U2**, 55
  *to get to **know** [ˌget tə ˈnəʊ] kennen lernen **III AC2**, 56
  I don't **know**! [aɪ ˌdəʊnt ˈnəʊ] Ich weiß (es) nicht! **I**
Korean [kəˈriːən] koreanisch; Koreanisch; Koreaner/-in **II**

L

lady [ˈleɪdi] Lady; Dame **II**
lady-in-waiting [ˌleɪdiɪnˈweɪtɪŋ] Hofdame **III U3**, 66
laid-back [leɪdˈbæk] entspannt; locker **III U1**, 12
lake [leɪk] See **I**
lamb [læm] Lamm; Lämmchen **I**
land [lænd] Land **I**
to land [lænd] landen **III AC3**, 89
landscape [ˈlændskeɪp] Landschaft **II**
language [ˈlæŋgwɪdʒ] Sprache **II**
  body **language** [ˈbɒdi ˌlæŋgwɪdʒ] Körpersprache **III U1**, 19
  foreign **language** [ˌfɒrɪn ˈlæŋgwɪdʒ] Fremdsprache **III U4**, 94
  sign **language** [saɪn] Gebärdensprache; Zeichensprache **II**
laptop [ˈlæptɒp] Laptop **II**
large [lɑːdʒ] groß; riesig **III U2**, 42
lassi [ˈlʌsi] Lassi **II**

to last [lɑːst] dauern; andauern; anhalten **III TMS1**, 30
last [lɑːst] letzte/-r/-s **I**
  at **last** [ət ˈlɑːst] endlich; schließlich **I**
  last but not least [ˌlɑːst bʌt nɒt ˈliːst] zu guter Letzt ⟨**III TR3**, 114⟩
late [leɪt] spät; zu spät **I**
  *to be **late** [bi ˈleɪt] zu spät dran sein; zu spät kommen **I**
later [ˈleɪtə] später **I**
latest [ˈleɪtɪst] neueste/-r/-s **III U2**, 45
Latin [ˈlætɪn] Latein; lateinisch **III U3**, 63
laugh [lɑːf] Lachen **III TMS1**, 27
to laugh [lɑːf] lachen
  they were **laughing** [ˌðeɪ wər ˈlɑːfɪŋ] sie lachten gerade ⟨**III U1**, 20⟩
lavish [ˈlævɪʃ] üppig; verschwenderisch **III U4**, 107
*to **lead** [liːd] führen; anführen **III U4**, 104
lead [liːd] Haupt- **III U1**, 12
  lead dancer [ˈliːd ˌdɑːnsə] Vortänzer/-in **III U1**, 12
  lead part [ˈliːd ˌpɑːt] Hauptrolle **III U1**, 12
leader [ˈliːdə] Führer/-in; Anführer/-in **III U3**, 65
leaf [liːf], **leaves** [liːvz] (*pl*) Blatt ⟨**III U2**, 47⟩
*to **learn** [lɜːn] lernen **I**; erfahren **II**
  *to **learn** about [ˈlɜːn əˌbaʊt] erfahren über **III U1**, 9
  *to **learn** … by heart [ˌlɜːn baɪ ˈhɑːt] auswendig lernen **III TMS1**, 26
at **least** [ət ˈliːst] zumindest; mindestens; wenigstens ⟨**III TR1**, 111⟩
leather [ˈleðə] Leder **III U3**, 63
*to **leave** [liːv] verlassen; lassen; abfahren **I**
  *to **leave** behind [ˌliːv bɪˈhaɪnd] zurücklassen **III U2**, 44
  *to **leave** out [ˌliːv ˈaʊt] weglassen; auslassen **III TMS1**, 31
  *to **leave** sth to cool [ˌliːv tə ˈkuːl] etw. kalt stellen **II**
left [left] (nach) links; linke/-r/-s **I**
  on the **left** [ɒn ðə ˈleft] auf der linken Seite; links **I**
left [left] übrig **I**
leg [leg] Bein **II**
legal [ˈliːgl] legal; rechtlich; Rechts- **III TMS1**, 29
legend [ˈledʒənd] Legende; Sage **II**
leggings (*pl*) [ˈlegɪŋz] Leggings **I**
leisure (*no pl*) [ˈleʒə] Freizeit; Freizeit- **I**
  leisure centre [ˈleʒə ˌsentə] Freizeitzentrum **I**
lemon [ˈlemən] Zitrone **II**
lemonade [ˌleməˈneɪd] Limonade **I**
*to **lend** (to) [ˈlend (tə)] leihen; verleihen **II**
lesson [ˈlesn] Unterrichtsstunde; Schulstunde; Unterricht **I**
*to **let** [let] lassen **II**
  *to **let** go (of) [ˌlet ˈgəʊ (əv)] loslassen **II**
  Let's … [lets] Lass/Lasst uns … **I**
letter [ˈletə] Brief; Buchstabe **II**

sea level ['siː ˌlevl] Meeresspiegel **III U3**, 63
lie [laɪ] Lüge **III TMS1**, 28
to **lie** [laɪ] lügen **II**
***to lie** [laɪ] liegen ⟨**III U2**, 47⟩
life, lives (pl) [laɪf, laɪvz] Leben **II**
 ***to bring to life** [ˌbrɪŋ təˈlaɪf] zum Leben erwecken; veranschaulichen **II**
lifeboat ['laɪfbəʊt] Rettungsboot **I**
lifebuoy ['laɪfbɔɪ] Rettungsring **I**
lifestyle ['laɪfstaɪl] Lifestyle; Lebensstil **III U3**, 79
light [laɪt] Licht; Lampe **I**
 light bulb ['laɪt ˌbʌlb] Glühbirne **III U3**, 78
 traffic light ['træfɪk ˌlaɪt] Ampel **I**
light [laɪt] leicht **III AC2**, 56
to **lighten** ['laɪtn] aufhellen **III U3**, 76
lightning (no pl) ['laɪtnɪŋ] Blitz **II**
to **like** [laɪk] mögen; gern haben **I**
 would **like** [wʊd 'laɪk] würde/-st/-n/-t gern; hätte/-st/-n/-t gern **I**
 I'd **like** to … (= I would like to) [aɪd 'laɪk tə] Ich möchte …; Ich würde gern … **I**
like [laɪk] wie **I**
 ***to be like** [bi 'laɪk] wie jmd./etw. sein **III U2**, 40
 like that [ˌlaɪk 'ðæt] so **I**
 like this [ˌlaɪk 'ðɪs] so **II**
 like me [ˌlaɪk 'miː] wie ich **I**
 What was … **like**? [ˌwɒt wɒz 'laɪk] Wie war … ? **III U3**, 62
limerick ['lɪmrɪk] Limerick (bestimmte Form eines fünfzeiligen Gedichts) ⟨**III TR3**, 115⟩
line [laɪn] Zeile; Linie **I**; Text **II**
 finish **line** ['fɪnɪʃ ˌlaɪn] Ziellinie **II**
link [lɪŋk] Link; Verbindung **II**
linking word ['lɪŋkɪŋ ˌwɜːd] Bindewort °**III U2**, 48
lip [lɪp] Lippe °**III TMS1**, 28
list [lɪst] Liste **II**
to **listen** (to) ['lɪsn (tə)] zuhören; anhören **I**
 to **listen** for ['lɪsn fə] horchen auf **I**
listener ['lɪsənə] Zuhörer/-in **II**
literal ['lɪtrətʃə] wörtlich; buchstäblich °**III TMS1**, 28
literature ['lɪtrətʃə] Literatur **III TMS1**, 26
to **litter** ['lɪtə] verschmutzen; Müll herumliegen lassen; verunreinigen **III AC3**, 88
little ['lɪtl] klein **I**
little ['lɪtl] wenig ⟨**III TR2**, 112⟩
 a **little** [ə 'lɪtl] ein wenig; etwas **I**
to **live** [lɪv] wohnen; leben **I**
live [laɪv] live ⟨**III TR3**, 114⟩
lively ['laɪvli] lebendig; lebhaft; munter °**III U2**, 48
living room ['lɪvɪŋ rʊm] Wohnzimmer **I**
loads (of) ['ləʊds (ˌəv)] viel/-e; jede Menge **III TMS2**, 84
lobby ['lɒbi] Empfangsbereich; Eingang **III U4**, 102
local ['ləʊkl] Ortsansässige/-r; Einheimische/-r **III U4**, 102
local ['ləʊkl] örtlich; lokal **II**
 local time ['ləʊkl ˌtaɪm] Ortszeit **III U4**, 96

location [ləʊˈkeɪʃn] Handlungsort; Lage; Standort **II**
loch [lɒx; lɒk] See (in Schottland) **I** / **I U2**, 41
locked [lɒkt] abgeschlossen **II**
locker ['lɒkə] Schließfach; Spind **II**
loft [lɒft] Dachboden **I**
logic ['lɒdʒɪk] Logik **III U1**, 9
LOL (= laughing out loud) [lɒl] LOL **I**
Londoner ['lʌndənə] Londoner/-in **I**
lonely ['ləʊnli] einsam **II**
long [lɒŋ] lang **I**
 (not) any **longer** [(nɒt ˌ)eni 'lɒŋɡə] (nicht) mehr; (nicht) länger ⟨**III TR1**, 110⟩
look [lʊk] Blick **II**
 ***to give sb funny looks** [ˌɡɪv fʌni 'lʊks] jmdn. schief anschauen; jmdn. komisch anschauen **III U1**, 15
 ***to have a look** (at) [ˌhæv ə 'lʊk] anschauen **II**
to **look** [lʊk] schauen; sehen; aussehen **I**
 Look! [lʊk] Schau/Schaut mal! **I**
 to **look** after [ˌlʊk 'ɑːftə] aufpassen auf; hüten; sich kümmern um **I**
 to **look** at ['lʊk ət] anschauen; ansehen **I**
 to **look** for ['lʊk fɔː] suchen nach **I**
 to **look** forward to [ˌlʊk 'fɔːwəd tə] sich freuen auf **II**
 to **look** out [ˌlʊk 'aʊt] aufpassen **II**
 to **look** up [ˌlʊk 'ʌp] nachschlagen; nachschauen **II**; aufschauen; hochschauen **III U2**, 50
 what the man **looked** like [ˌwɒt ðə mæn 'lʊkt laɪk] wie der Mann aussah **II**
looks (pl) [lʊks] Aussehen **III U1**, 12
lord [lɔːd] Lord; Herr **III U3**, 65
***to lose** [luːz] verlieren **II**
lost [lɒst] verloren ⟨**III U2**, 47⟩; ⟨**III TR1**, 111⟩
 ***to get lost** [ˌɡet 'lɒst] verloren gehen; sich verirren **II**
a **lot** [ə 'lɒt] viel; oft **I**
a **lot** of [ə 'lɒt ˌəv] viel/-e; eine Menge **I**
lots (of) [ˌlɒts ˌəv] viel/-e; jede Menge **I**
loud [laʊd] laut **I**
 ***to read/sing out loud** [ˌriːd/sɪŋ ˌaʊt 'laʊd] laut vorsingen °**III TMS1**, 31
departure **lounge** [dɪˈpɑːtʃə ˌlaʊndʒ] Abflughalle **III U4**, 95
love [lʌv] Liebe **II**
 Love … [lʌv] Liebe Grüße (am Briefende); Herzliche Grüße (am Briefende) **II**
to **love** [lʌv] lieben; gern mögen **I**
 would **love** [wʊd 'lʌv] würde/-st/-n/-t sehr gern; hätte/-st/-n/-t sehr gern **II**
lovebirds (pl) ['lʌvˌbɜːdz] Turteltauben **II**
low [ləʊ] niedrig **II**
 low tide [ˌləʊ ˌtaɪd] Ebbe **II**
What luck! [wɒt 'lʌk] Was für ein Glück! **III U3**, 69
luckily ['lʌkɪli] glücklicherweise **III U4**, 99
lucky … ['lʌki] … der/die Glückliche **I**
 ***to be lucky** [bi 'lʌki] Glück haben **I**
 lucky charm [ˌlʌki 'tʃɑːm] Glücksbringer; Talisman **I**

lucky number [ˌlʌki 'nʌmbə] Glückszahl **I**
luggage (no pl) ['lʌɡɪdʒ] Gepäck **III U4**, 94
lunch [lʌntʃ] Mittagessen **I**
 lunch break ['lʌntʃ breɪk] Mittagspause **I**

M

machine [məˈʃiːn] Automat; Maschine; Apparat; Gerät **I**
 washing **machine** ['wɒʃɪŋ məˌʃiːn] Waschmaschine **II**
mad [mæd] verrückt **II**
magazine [ˌmæɡəˈziːn] Zeitschrift **I**
magic ['mædʒɪk] Magie; Zauberei **III U4**, 107
magical ['mædʒɪkəl] magisch; Zauber- **II**
magnet ['mæɡnət] Magnet **III TMS1**, 30
magnifying glass (no pl) ['mæɡnɪfaɪɪŋ ˌɡlɑːs] Lupe **II**
main [meɪn] Haupt- **II**
***to make** [meɪk] machen; tun; bilden; hier: ergeben **I**
 ***to be made of** [bi ˈmeɪd ˌəv] bestehen aus; gemacht sein aus; hergestellt sein aus **III U3**, 64
 ***to make** a difference [ˌmeɪk ə 'dɪfrns] etw. verändern; einen Unterschied machen **II**
 ***to make** a wish [ˌmeɪk ə 'wɪʃ] sich etwas wünschen **II**
 ***to make** friends [ˌmeɪk 'frendz] Freundschaft schließen **I**
 ***to make** money [ˌmeɪk 'mʌni] Geld verdienen **I**
 ***to make** sb angry [meɪk 'æŋɡri] jmdn. wütend machen; jmdn. verärgern **III AC1**, 35
 ***to make** sb do something [ˌmeɪk sʌmbədi 'duː sʌmθɪŋ] jmdn. dazu bringen, etw. zu tun **II**
 ***to make** sure [ˌmeɪk 'ʃɔː] sichergehen; achten auf **III U1**, 10
 ***to make** trouble [ˌmeɪk 'trʌbl] Ärger machen; in Schwierigkeiten bringen **I**
man, men (pl) [mæn; men] Mann **I**
 what the **man** looked like [ˌwɒt ðə mæn 'lʊkt laɪk] wie der Mann aussah **II**
manager ['mænɪdʒə] Geschäftsführer/-in; Leiter/-in; Manager/-in **III TMS2**, 81
mango ['mæŋɡəʊ] Mango **I**
manners (pl) ['mænəz] Manieren; Benehmen **III AC3**, 89
many ['meni] viele **I**
 How **many** …? [ˌhaʊ 'meni] Wie viele …? **I**
map [mæp] Stadtplan; Landkarte **I**
marathon ['mærəθn] Marathon **II**
March [mɑːtʃ] März **II**
mark [mɑːk] Note **III U1**, 12
 question **mark** ['kwestʃən ˌmɑːk] Fragezeichen °**III U2**, 52
 quotation **marks** [kwəˈteɪʃn ˌmɑːks] Anführungszeichen °**III U2**, 52
market ['mɑːkɪt] Markt **I**

flea **market** ['fli: ˌmɑːkɪt] Flohmarkt I

marmalade ['mɑːməleɪd] Orangenmarmelade **III AC1**, 34

married ['mærid] verheiratet **III TMS2**, 81

to **marry** ['mæri] heiraten **III U3**, 65

marvellous ['mɑːvləs] wunderbar; wundervoll; großartig ⟨**III TMS1**, 32⟩

mashed potatoes (pl) [ˌmæʃt pə'teɪtəʊz] Kartoffelpüree; Kartoffelbrei **III U2**, 44

mask [mɑːsk] Maske **III U4**, 104

raven **master** ['reɪvn ˌmɑːstə] Aufseher über die Raben II

match [mætʃ] Spiel; Match II

to **match** [mætʃ] passen zu; entsprechen °**III U1**, 9

mate [meɪt] Schiffsoffizier; Maat I

raw **material** [ˌrɔː mə'tɪəriəl] Rohstoff; Rohmaterial **III U3**, 65

maths [mæθs] Mathematik; Mathe II

no **matter** [nəʊ 'mætə] egal; ganz gleich **III TMS1**, 30

What's the **matter**? [ˌwɒts ðə 'mætə] Was ist los?; Was hast du? II

It doesn't **matter**. [ɪt ˌdʌznt 'mætə] es spielt keine Rolle; das macht nichts; das ist nicht wichtig **III U1**, 8

May [meɪ] Mai II

may [meɪ] (vielleicht) können; dürfen I

maybe ['meɪbi] vielleicht I

me [miː] mich; mir I

like **me** [ˌlaɪk 'miː] wie ich I

me too [miː tuː] ich auch I

meal [miːl] Mahlzeit; Essen II

ready **meal** [ˌredi 'miːl] Fertiggericht I

*to **mean** [miːn] bedeuten; meinen I

meaning ['miːnɪŋ] Bedeutung; Sinn II

means (pl only) [miːnz] Mittel; Weg **III U4**, 95

means of transport (sg or pl) [ˌmiːnz əv 'trænspɔːt] Transportmittel; Verkehrsmittel **III U4**, 95

meat (no pl) [miːt] Fleisch **III U2**, 42

mechanic [mə'kænɪk] Mechaniker/-in; Kfz-Mechaniker/-in II

media (pl) ['miːdiə] Medien II

social **media** [ˌsəʊʃl 'miːdiə] soziale Netzwerke **III U1**, 10

to **mediate** ['miːdieɪt] vermitteln II

medieval [ˌmedi'iːvl] mittelalterlich II

*to **meet** [miːt] treffen; sich treffen I; (sich) treffen; (sich) begegnen; (sich) kennenlernen II

*to **meet** halfway [ˌmiːt hɑː'fweɪ] sich auf halbem Weg treffen **III U1**, 18

member ['membə] Mitglied II

memory ['memri] Erinnerung; Gedächtnis II

to **mention** ['menʃn] erwähnen II

message ['mesɪdʒ] Botschaft; Nachricht I

*to take a **message** [ˌteɪk ə 'mesɪdʒ] eine Nachricht entgegennehmen; jmdm. etw. ausrichten I

text (**message**) ['tekst ˌmesɪdʒ] SMS; Kurznachricht I

voice **message** ['vɔɪs ˌmesɪdʒ] Sprachnachricht I

messy ['mesi] unordentlich **III U1**, 15

metal ['metl] Metall **III U3**, 63

metaphor ['metəfə] Metapher; bildhafte Sprache **III TMS1**, 31

metre ['miːtə] Meter II

middle ['mɪdl] Mitte II

in the **middle** of [ɪn ðə 'mɪdl̩ əv] mitten in II

Middle Ages [ˌmɪdl̩'eɪdʒɪz] Mittelalter **III U3**, 63

midnight ['mɪdnaɪt] Mitternacht **III U2**, 43

might [maɪt] könnte/-n (vielleicht) II

mile [maɪl] Meile (brit. Längenmaß) II

military ['mɪlɪtri] militärisch ⟨**III TR1**, 110⟩

milk [mɪlk] Milch I

to **milk** [mɪlk] melken II

to **mill** around [ˌmɪl ə'raʊnd] umherlaufen °**III TMS1**, 26

a **million** [ə 'mɪljən] Million **III U1**, 12

I've done this a **million** times before. [aɪv dʌn ðɪs ə ˌmɪljən taɪmz bɪ'fɔː] Ich habe das schon eine Million Mal gemacht. II

millionaire [ˌmɪljə'neə] Millionär/-in **III U1**, 12

mind [maɪnd] Kopf; Geist; Verstand °**III TMS1**, 28

to change one's **mind** [ˌtʃeɪndʒ wʌnz 'maɪnd] seine Meinung ändern **III U4**, 104

I don't **mind** (+ …ing) [aɪ dəʊnt 'maɪnd] Ich habe nichts dagegen (zu …); Mir macht es nichts aus (zu …) **III U1**, 18

mine [maɪn] Mine II

mine [maɪn] mein/-er/-e/-es I

mineral ['mɪnrl] Mineral II

mini ['mɪni] Mini- II

mining ['maɪnɪŋ] Bergbau II

minute ['mɪnɪt] Minute I

mirror ['mɪrə] Spiegel **III U3**, 65

Miss [mɪs] Fräulein (veraltete Anrede) **III U1**, 16

to **miss** [mɪs] vermissen II; verpassen; versäumen **III U4**, 94

missing ['mɪsɪŋ] fehlend; verschwunden II

mistake [mɪ'steɪk] Fehler II

misunderstood [ˌmɪsʌndə'stʊd] missverstanden **III U1**, 18

mix [mɪks] Mischung **III U4**, 102

to **mix** (up) [mɪks (ˌʌp)] mischen; vermischen **III U3**, 74

mobile ['məʊbaɪl] Handy; Mobiltelefon II

model ['mɒdl] Modell; Tonmodell; Model I

role **model** ['rəʊl ˌmɒdl] Vorbild **III U1**, 10

modelling ['mɒdəlɪŋ] Modeln **III U1**, 12

modern ['mɒdn] modern II

moment ['məʊmənt] Moment; Augenblick II

at the **moment** [ət ðə 'məʊmənt] im Moment; gerade I

monarch ['mɒnək] Monarch/-in **III U3**, 65

Monday ['mʌndeɪ] Montag I

on **Mondays** [ɒn 'mʌndeɪz] montags I

money ['mʌni] Geld I

*to make **money** [ˌmeɪk 'mʌni] Geld verdienen I

pocket **money** ['pɒkɪt ˌmʌni] Taschengeld I

to raise **money** [ˌreɪz 'mʌni] Geld sammeln II

monster ['mɒnstə] Monster; Ungeheuer I

month [mʌnθ] Monat II

monument ['mɒnjəmənt] Monument; Denkmal II

mood [muːd] Stimmung; Laune II

moonlight ['muːnlaɪt] Mondlicht **III U2**, 50

more [mɔː] mehr; weitere I

not any **more** [ˌnɒt eni 'mɔː] nicht mehr I

more … than ['mɔː ðən] mehr … als I

morning ['mɔːnɪŋ] Morgen; Vormittag I

Good **morning**. [gʊd 'mɔːnɪŋ] Guten Morgen. I

(the) **most** [ðə 'məʊst] der/die/das meiste; die meisten II

mostly ['məʊstli] meistens; größtenteils; hauptsächlich ⟨**III TMS1**, 32⟩

mother ['mʌðə] Mutter I

motif ['məʊtɪf] Motiv °**III TMS2**, 85

motivating ['məʊtɪveɪtɪŋ] motivierend °**III U4**, 103

mountain ['maʊntɪn] Berg II

mountain biking ['maʊntɪn ˌbaɪkɪŋ] Mountainbikefahren II

mouse, mice (pl) [maʊs; maɪs] Maus/Mäuse I

move [muːv] Bewegung II

dance **move** ['dɑːns ˌmuːv] Tanzschritt I

on the **move** [ɒn ðə 'muːv] unterwegs **III U4**, 94

to **move** [muːv] (sich) bewegen II

to **move** (house) [muːv ('haʊs)] umziehen II

to **move** in/into [ˌmuːv 'ɪn/'ɪntə] einziehen in II

Mr ['mɪstə] Herr (Anrede) I

Mrs ['mɪsɪz] Frau (Anrede) I

Ms [mɪz] Frau (Anrede) **III TMS2**, 81

much [mʌtʃ] viel I

that **much** [ðæt 'mʌtʃ] so viel **III AC1**, 35

mud [mʌd] Schlamm II

muddy ['mʌdi] schlammig II

muesli ['mjuːzli] Müsli **III AC1**, 34

mug [mʌg] Becher **III AC1**, 34

multi-ethnic [ˌmʌlti'eθnɪk] Vielvölker- I

mum [mʌm] Mama; Mutti I

to **mumble** ['mʌmbl] murmeln; nuscheln **III U4**, 96

mummy ['mʌmi] Mama; Mami; Mutti **III U1**, 21

murder ['mɜːdə] Mord **III U3**, 69

museum [mjuː'ziːəm] Museum I

music ['mjuːzɪk] Musik I

musical ['mjuːzɪkl] Musical **III U4**, 108

musical ['mjuːzɪkl] musikalisch; Musik- **III U2**, 42

musician [mjuːˈzɪʃn] Musiker/-in **II**

a **must**-see [ə ˌmʌst ˈsiː] unbedingt emp-fehlenswert **III U4**, 102

must [mʌst] müssen **I**

mustn't [ˈmʌsnt] nicht dürfen **II**

my [maɪ] mein/-e **I**

(**my**) fault [ˌmaɪ ˈfɔːlt] (meine) Schuld **II**

My favourite … is … [ˌmaɪ ˈfeɪvrɪt ɪz] Mein Lieblings… ist … **I**

My name is … [maɪ ˈneɪm ɪz] Ich heiße … **I**

myself [maɪˈself] ich/mir/mich (selbst); selber **II**

mysterious [mɪˈstɪəriəs] mysteriös; geheimnisvoll **II**

mystery [ˈmɪstri] Geheimnis; Rätsel **III U3**, 74

mythical [ˈmɪθɪkl] sagenhaft; sagenumwoben **III U4**, 107

N

name [neɪm] Name **I**

first **name** [ˌfɜːst ˈneɪm] Vorname **I**

My **name** is … [maɪ ˈneɪm ɪz] Ich heiße … **I**

What's your **name**? [ˌwɒts jə ˈneɪm] Wie heißt du?; Wie heißen Sie? **I**

to **name** [neɪm] nennen; benennen **III U2**, 44

narrator [nəˈreɪtə] Erzähler/-in **III U4**, 106

narrow [ˈnærəʊ] eng; schmal **III U2**, 44

nasty [ˈnɑːsti] garstig; gemein **II**

nation [ˈneɪʃn] Nation ⟨**III U2**, 47⟩

national anthem [ˌnæʃnl ˈænθəm] Nationalhymne **III U2**, 47

natural [ˈnætʃrl] natürlich; Natur- **III U2**, 54

nature [ˈneɪtʃə] Natur **II**

near [nɪə] nahe; in der Nähe von **I**

nearly [ˈnɪəli] fast; annähernd **II**

necessary [ˈnesəsri] nötig; notwendig; erforderlich **III U1**, 18

necklace [ˈnekləs] Halskette **III U3**, 65

in **need** [ɪn ˈniːd] bedürftig; in Not **II**

with special **needs** [wɪð ˌspeʃl ˈniːdz] mit Behinderung; mit speziellen Bedürfnissen **II**

to **need** [niːd] brauchen; benötigen **I**

to **need** to (do) [niːd tə] (tun) müssen **I**

needn't [ˈniːdnt] nicht brauchen; nicht müssen **II**

negative [ˈnegətɪv] negativ; verneint **II**

neighbour [ˈneɪbə] Nachbar/-in **I**

neighbourhood [ˈneɪbəhʊd] Nachbarschaft **III U2**, 53

*to get on somebody's **nerves** [ˌget ɒn sʌmbɒdiz ˈnɜːvz] jmdm. auf die Nerven gehen **I**

nervous [ˈnɜːvəs] nervös; aufgeregt **II**

net [net] Netz **I**

netball [ˈnetbɔːl] Korbball **I**

social **network** [ˌsəʊʃl ˈnetwɜːk] soziales Netzwerk **II**

neutral [ˈnjuːtrl] neutral **III TMS2**, 8€

never [ˈnevə] nie; niemals **I**

new [njuː] neu **I**

New Year's Eve [ˌnjuː ˌjɪəz ˈiːv] Silvester **III U2**, 43

news (sg) [njuːz] Nachrichten; Neuigkeiten **I**

newspaper [ˈnjuːzˌpeɪpə] Zeitung **I**

next [nekst] nächste/-r/-s; der/die Nächste(n) **I**

next door [nekst ˈdɔː] (von) nebenan **III AC2**, 56

next to [ˈnekst tə] neben **I**

the **next** day [ðə ˌnekst ˈdeɪ] am nächsten Tag **II**

next [nekst] als Nächstes **I**

nice [naɪs] nett; schön; lieb **I**

night [naɪt] Nacht; Abend **II**

all **night** [ɔːl ˈnaɪt] die ganze Nacht **II**

night walk [ˈnaɪt wɔːk] Nachtwanderung **II**

nine [naɪn] neun **I**

2nite (= tonight) [təˈnaɪt] heute Abend **I**

no [nəʊ] kein/-e **I**

no matter [nəʊ ˈmætə] egal; ganz gleich **III TMS1**, 30

No idea. [ˌnəʊ aɪˈdɪə] Keine Ahnung. **I**

no such thing as [ˌnəʊ sʌtʃ θɪŋ ˈæz] nicht so etwas wie **II**

No way! [ˌnəʊ ˈweɪ] Auf keinen Fall!; keineswegs **I**

no [nəʊ] nein **I**

nobody [ˈnəʊbədi] niemand **II**

nobody else [ˈnəʊbədi ˌels] niemand anderes **II**

noise [nɔɪz] Lärm; Geräusch **II**

non- [nɒn] nicht- **II**

normal [ˈnɔːml] normal **II**

Norman [ˈnɔːmən] Normanne/Normannin; normannisch **III U3**, 62

north [nɔːθ] Norden; Nord- **I**

in the **north** of [ˌɪn ðə ˈnɔːθ əv] im Norden von **I**

north [nɔːθ] nördlich; im Norden **III U2**, 48

nose [nəʊz] Nase **II**

not [nɒt] nicht **I**

not any more [ˌnɒt eni ˈmɔː] nicht mehr **I**

not … any [nɒt ˌeni] kein/-e/-en **I**

not … anything [ˌnɒt ˈeniθɪŋ] nichts **I**

not … either [nɒt ˈaɪðə; nɒt ˈiːðə] auch nicht **I**

not … yet [nɒt ˈjet] noch nicht **II**

(**not**) at all [ət ˈɔːl] überhaupt (nicht) **II**

note [nəʊt] Notiz; Anmerkung **II**

nothing [ˈnʌθɪŋ] nichts **II**

to notice [ˈnəʊtɪs] bemerken; wahrnehmen **II**

noticeboard [ˈnəʊtɪsbɔːd] schwarzes Brett **II**

November [nəˈvembə] November **II**

now [naʊ] jetzt; nun **I**

by **now** [baɪ ˈnaʊ] inzwischen; mittlerweile **I**

right **now** [raɪt ˈnaʊ] im Moment; gleich jetzt; sofort **II**

nowhere [ˈnəʊweə] nirgendwo; nirgendwohin **II**

number [ˈnʌmbə] Zahl; Nummer **I**; Anzahl **III U3**, 65

lucky **number** [ˌlʌki ˈnʌmbə] Glückszahl **I**

phone **number** [ˈfəʊn ˌnʌmbə] Telefon-/Handynummer **I**

nurse [nɜːs] Krankenschwester; Krankenpfleger **III U3**, 75

nursery rhyme [ˈnɜːsri ˌraɪm] Kinderreim; Kinderlied **III TMS1**, 26

nut [nʌt] Nuss **I**

O

o'clock [əˈklɒk] Uhr (Zeitangabe bei vollen Stunden) **I**

o'er [ˈəʊə] über ⟨**III U2**, 47⟩

object [ˈɒbdʒɪkt] Gegenstand; Objekt **III U3**, 63

object pronoun [ɒbdʒɪkt ˈprəʊnaʊn] Objektpronomen °**III U1**, 16

occasion [əˈkeɪʒn] Anlass; Ereignis; Gelegenheit **III TMS1**, 26

October [ɒkˈtəʊbə] Oktober **II**

odd [ɒd] seltsam; komisch **III AC3**, 88

of [ɒv; əv] von **I**

of course [əv ˈkɔːs] natürlich; selbstverständlich **I**

off [ɒf] von … weg/ab/herunter **I**

*to take **off** [ˌteɪk ˈɒf] abnehmen; herunternehmen; ausziehen **II**

to turn **off** [ˌtɜːn ˈɒf] abschalten; ausschalten **II**

offer [ˈɒfə] Angebot **I**

special **offer** [ˌspeʃl ˈɒfə] Sonderangebot **I**

to offer [ˈɒfə] anbieten **II**

office [ˈɒfɪs] Büro **I**

post **office** [ˈpəʊst ˌɒfɪs] Postamt **I**

ticket **office** [ˈtɪkɪt ˌɒfɪs] Kartenausgabestelle; Vorverkaufsschalter; Fahrkartenschalter **III U2**, 50

immigration **officer** [ɪmɪˈgreɪʃn ˌɒfɪsə] Grenzschutzbeamter/-beamtin; Einwanderungsbeamter/-beamtin **III U4**, 99

official [əˈfɪʃl] Schiedsrichter/-in **II**; Beamter/Beamtin **III U4**, 105

official [əˈfɪʃl] offiziell **III U2**, 47

offline [ˈɒflaɪn] offline **II**

often [ˈɒfn] oft; häufig **I**

oh [əʊ] null (bei Telefonnummern und Uhrzeitangaben) **I**

Oh! [əʊ] O! **I**

Oh dear! [əʊ ˈdɪə] Oje! **II**

ointment [ˈɔɪntmənt] Salbe **II**

OK [əʊˈkeɪ] o.k.; in Ordnung **I**

old [əʊld] alt **I**

How **old** are you? [haʊ ˌəʊld ə ˈjuː] Wie alt bist du?; Wie alt seid ihr?; Wie alt sind Sie? **I**

11-year-**old** [ɪˌlevnˈjɪərəʊld] 11-Jährige/-r **II**

to turn **on** [ˌtɜːn ˈɒn] einschalten **II**

on [ɒn] auf; an; am; in; im **I**; mit **II**

*to be on [bi ˈɒn] an sein; laufen II
on Mondays [ɒn ˈmʌndeɪz] montags I
on one's own [ɒn wʌnz ˈəʊn] allein; für sich III U4, 105
on the left [ɒn ðə ˈleft] auf der linken Seite; links I
on the right [ɒn ðə ˈraɪt] auf der rechten Seite; rechts I
on time [ɒn ˈtaɪm] pünktlich II
on top [ɒn ˈtɒp] oben; obendrauf II
on TV [ɒn ˌtiːˈviː] im Fernsehen II
on the move [ɒn ðə ˈmuːv] unterwegs III U4, 94
once [wʌns] einmal; einst II
at once [ət ˈwʌns] gleichzeitig; sofort ⟨III TMS2, 86⟩
once [wʌns] sobald II
one [wʌn] eins I
one another [ˌwʌn əˈnʌðə] einander; gegenseitig III TMS1, 32
one-way ticket [ˈwʌnweɪ ˌtɪkɪt] einfache Fahrkarte II
one, ones (pl) [wʌn, wʌnz] ein/eine II
online [ɒnˈlaɪn] online II
only [ˈəʊnli] einzige/-r/-s II
only [ˈəʊnli] erst; bloß; nur I
only child [ˈəʊnli ˌtʃaɪld] Einzelkind I
onto [ˈɒntə] auf … hinauf II
Oops! [uːps] Hoppla!; Huch! I
to open [ˈəʊpn] öffnen; aufmachen I
open [ˈəʊpn] offen; geöffnet; aufgeschlagen I
*to hold open [ˌhəʊld ˈəʊpn] aufhalten III AC3, 88
opening times [ˈəʊpnɪŋ ˌtaɪmz] Öffnungszeiten II
open-minded [ˌəʊpnˈmaɪndɪd] aufgeschlossen; unvoreingenommen; vorurteilsfrei ⟨III TMS1, 32⟩
tour operator [ˈtʊər ˌɒpreɪtə] Reiseveranstalter III U4, 102
opinion [əˈpɪnjən] Meinung; Ansicht; Einstellung III U1, 15
opposite [ˈɒpəzɪt] gegenüber; auf der anderen Seite von I
optimistic [ˌɒptɪˈmɪstɪk] optimistisch III U1, 23
option [ˈɒpʃn] Möglichkeit; Option; Wahl III U2, 44
or [ɔː] oder I
orange [ˈɒrɪndʒ] Orange I
orange [ˈɒrɪndʒ] orange I
order [ˈɔːdə] Reihenfolge; Ordnung II
to organise [ˈɔːgənaɪz] organisieren I
origin [ˈɒrɪdʒɪn] Ursprung; Herkunft; Abstammung III U4, 107
other [ˈʌðə] anders; andere/-r/-s; weitere I
each other [iːtʃ ˈʌðə] einander; miteinander; sich; sich gegenseitig II
(the) others [(ði) ˈʌðəz] (die) anderen II
Ouch! [aʊtʃ] Aua! II
our [aʊə; ɑː] unser/-e I
ours [aʊəz] unser/-er/-e/-es ⟨III TR2, 112⟩

ourselves [ˌaəˈselvz] selber; wir (selbst); uns (selbst); selbst III U1, 16
out [aʊt] außerhalb; heraus; hinaus; nach draußen I
to clear out [klɪər ˈaʊt] ausräumen; entrümpeln I
to drop out (of) [drɒp ˈaʊt (ˌəv)] abbrechen; ausscheiden; aussteigen III U1, 12
*to hang out (with) (infml) [ˌhæŋ ˈaʊt wɪð] rumhängen (mit); sich herumtreiben (mit) III U1, 20
*to leave out [liːv ˈaʊt] weglassen; auslassen III TMS1, 31
out and about [ˌaʊt ən əˈbaʊt] unterwegs I
out of focus [aʊt əv ˈfəʊkəs] unscharf III U3, 75
outdoor [aʊtˈdɔː] Freiluft-; Outdoor- II
outfit [ˈaʊtfɪt] Outfit; Kleidung II
outgoing [ˈaʊtˌgəʊɪŋ] kontaktfreudig III U4, 107
outlaw [ˈaʊtlɔː] Geächtete/-r; Gesetzlose/-r II
outside [aʊtˈsaɪd] nach draußen; draußen; außerhalb I; vor II
outward [ˈaʊtwəd] abfahrend II
over [ˈəʊvə] hinüber; über I
*to go over to [ˌgəʊ ˈəʊvə tə] hinübergehen zu; zu jmdm. nach Hause gehen II
over there [ˌəʊvə ˈðeə] da drüben; dort drüben; nach dort drüben I
overall [ˌəʊvrˈɔːl] allgemein; Gesamt- III U4, 102
overloaded [ˌəʊvəˈləʊdɪd] überladen III U4, 104
overnight [ˌəʊvəˈnaɪt] über Nacht III U1, 21
to overreact [ˌəʊvəriˈækt] überreagieren II
own [əʊn] eigene/-r/-s I
on one's own [ɒn wʌnz ˈəʊn] allein; für sich III U4, 105
owner [ˈəʊnə] Besitzer/-in I

P

p.m. [ˌpiːˈem] nachmittags (Uhrzeit); abends (Uhrzeit) I
pace [peɪs] Geschwindigkeit; Gangart III U4, 102
package tour [ˈpækɪdʒ ˌtʊə] Pauschalreise III U4, 102
packet [ˈpækɪt] Päckchen; Paket; Packung I
page [peɪdʒ] Seite II
web page [ˈweb ˌpeɪdʒ] Website; Internetauftritt II
pain [peɪn] Schmerz II
paint [peɪnt] Farbe II
to paint [peɪnt] anmalen; malen I
painting [ˈpeɪntɪŋ] Malerei; Gemälde; Malen II
pair [peə] Paar I
in pairs [ɪn ˈpeəz] zu zweit; mit einem Partner/einer Partnerin I
palace [ˈpælɪs] Palast III U3, 63

palm tree [ˈpɑːm ˌtriː] Palme II
pancake [ˈpænkeɪk] Pfannkuchen ⟨III TR3, 114⟩
paper [ˈpeɪpə] Papier II
parade [pəˈreɪd] Parade; Umzug ⟨III TR3, 115⟩
paradise [ˈpærədaɪs] Paradies II
paragraph [ˈpærəgrɑːf] Absatz; Paragraf III TMS2, 81
to paraphrase [ˈpærəfreɪz] paraphrasieren; umschreiben II
parcel [ˈpɑːsl] Paket; Päckchen II
parents (pl) [ˈpeərənts] Eltern I
park [pɑːk] Park I
parrot [ˈpærət] Papagei II
part [pɑːt] Teil; Stadtteil I; Rolle III U1, 12
lead part [liːd ˈpɑːt] Hauptrolle III U1, 12
*to take part (in) [teɪk ˈpɑːt (ɪn)] teilnehmen (an) II
partially sighted [ˌpɑːʃəli ˈsaɪtɪd] sehbehindert II
past participle [ˌpɑːst pɑːˈtɪsɪpl] Partizip °III U2, 43
partner [ˈpɑːtnə] Partner/-in I
party [ˈpɑːti] Party; Feier II
to pass [pɑːs] zupassen; zuspielen II; weitergehen; vorbeigehen ⟨III TMS1, 32⟩
to pass (on) [ˌpɑːs ˈɒn] weitergeben II
passenger [ˈpæsndʒə] Passagier/-in; Fahrgast III U4, 95
passive [ˈpæsɪv] Passiv °III U2, 41
passport [ˈpɑːspɔːt] Pass; Reisepass III U4, 95
password [ˈpɑːswɜːd] Passwort II
past [pɑːst] Vergangenheit II
past participle [ˌpɑːst pɑːˈtɪsɪpl] Partizip °III U2, 43
past [pɑːst] nach (bei Uhrzeitangaben); vorbei (an); vorüber (an) I
half past [ˌhɑːf ˈpɑːst] halb (bei Uhrzeitangaben) I
quarter past/to [ˈkwɔːtə ˌpɑːst/tə] Viertel nach/vor I
pasta [ˈpæstə] Pasta; Nudeln I
pasty [ˈpæsti] Fleischpastete II
patent [ˈpeɪtnt] patentieren III U3, 78
coastal path [ˌkəʊstl ˈpɑːθ] Küstenweg II
patient [ˈpeɪʃnt] geduldig II
patron saint [ˈpeɪtrn ˌseɪnt] Nationalheiliger ⟨III TR3, 115⟩
pattern [ˈpætn] Muster III AC2, 56
pavement [ˈpeɪvmənt] Bürgersteig I
pawn shop [ˈpɔːn ʃɒp] Pfandhaus; Pfandleihe III U3, 77
*to pay (for) [peɪ] bezahlen I
*to pay attention [ˌpeɪ əˈtenʃn] aufmerksam sein; aufpassen; jmdn./etw. beachten III U1, 24
payment [ˈpeɪmənt] Bezahlung; Vergütung III TMS2, 81
PE (= Physical Education) [ˌpiːˈiː; ˌfɪzɪkl edʒʊˈkeɪʃn] Sportunterricht II
peace [piːs] Frieden III U3, 63

peaceful ['pi:sfl] in Frieden; friedlich
III U3, 63

peer pressure ['pɪə ˌpreʃə] Gruppenzwang
III U1, 22

pen [pen] Füller I

penny, pence (pl) ['peni; pens] Penny
(brit. Währungseinheit); Pence (brit.
Währungseinheit) I

pencil ['pensl] Bleistift; Buntstift I
pencil case ['pensl ˌkeɪs] Federmäppchen;
Mäppchen I

penicillin [ˌpenɪ'sɪlɪn] Penicillin **III U2**, 43

penny, pence (pl) ['peni; pens] Penny
(brit. Währungseinheit); Pence (brit.
Währungseinheit) I

people (pl) ['pi:pl] Leute; Menschen I
people (pl) ['pi:pl] Volk **III U3**, 63

per [pɜ:; pə] pro II
per cent [pə 'sent] Prozent **III U1**, 17

to **perceive** [pə'si:v] wahrnehmen; empfinden; betrachten ⟨**III TR3**, 115⟩

perception [pə'sepʃn] Wahrnehmung
⟨**III TR1**, 110⟩

present **perfect** [ˌpreznt 'pɜ:fɪkt] das Perfekt
°**III U2**, 44

perfect ['pɜ:fɪkt] perfekt; vollkommen I

to **perform** [pə'fɔ:m] auftreten; etw.
vorführen; aufführen; vortragen; spielen
III U1, 14

perhaps [pə'hæps] vielleicht **III U2**, 50

period ['pɪəriəd] Periode; Zeitspanne;
Zeitraum **III U3**, 62

permission [pə'mɪʃn] Erlaubnis; Genehmigung **III TMS2**, 82

person, people (pl) ['pɜ:sn; 'pi:pl] Person;
Mensch I
a **person** who … [ə ˌpɜ:sn 'hu:] eine
Person, die … ⟨**III U2**, 44⟩

personal pronoun [ˌpɜ:snl 'prəʊnaʊn] Personalpronomen °**III U1**, 16

personal ['pɜ:snl] persönlich II

personality [ˌpɜ:sn'æləti] Persönlichkeit;
Charakter **III U1**, 9

perspective [pə'spektɪv] Perspektive; Blickwinkel **III U4**, 102

to **persuade** [pə'sweɪd] überreden II

persuasive [pə'sweɪsɪv] überzeugend
°**III U2**, 48

pet [pet] Haustier I

phone [fəʊn] Telefon; Handy I
phone box ['fəʊn ˌbɒks] Telefonzelle
III U4, 105
phone call ['fəʊn ˌkɔ:l] Anruf; Telefonanruf I
phone number ['fəʊn ˌnʌmbə] Telefon-/
Handynummer I
rotary **phone** ['rəʊtri fəʊn] Telefon mit
Wählscheibe **III U2**, 53

photo ['fəʊtəʊ] Foto; Fotografie I
*to take **photos** [ˌteɪk 'fəʊtəʊz] fotografieren; Fotos machen I

to **photobomb** ['fəʊtəʊbɒm] ins Foto laufen
III U3, 75

to **photograph** (sb/sth) ['fəʊtəgrɑ:f] jmdn./
etw. fotografieren **III U3**, 66

photographer [fə'tɒgrəfə] Fotograf/-in II

photoshoot ['fəʊtəʊʃu:t] Fotoshooting;
Fotoaufnahmen **III U3**, 74

phrase [freɪz] Satz; Redewendung; Ausdruck **III U1**, 9

piano [pi'ænəʊ] Klavier; Piano I

pic (= picture) [pɪk] Foto **III U2**, 45

to **pick** up [pɪk 'ʌp] abholen; mitnehmen;
aufheben II

picnic ['pɪknɪk] Picknick I

Picts [pɪkt] Pikten (schottischer
Volksstamm) **III U3**, 63

pie [paɪ] Kuchen; Pastete I

piece [pi:s] Stück I
a **piece** of … [ə 'pi:s əv] ein Stück … I
piece of junk [ˌpi:s əv 'dʒʌŋk] Stück
Schrott **III U1**, 21
piece of advice [ˌpi:s əv əd'vaɪs] Rat;
Ratschlag; Hinweis II

pier [pɪə] Pier; Hafendamm I

piercing ['pɪəsɪŋ] Piercing **III U1**, 19

pig [pɪg] Schwein I
guinea **pig** ['gɪni ˌpɪg] Meerschweinchen I

piggy bank ['pɪgi bæŋk] Sparbüchse; Spardose; Sparschwein I

*to give sb a **piggyback** [gɪv ə 'pɪg bæk]
jmdn. Huckepack nehmen **III U4**, 104

pill [pɪl] Pille; Tablette II

pillow ['pɪləʊ] Kopfkissen II

pineapple ['paɪnæpl] Ananas **III U3**, 77

pink [pɪŋk] pink; rosa I

pipe [paɪp] Rohr; Rohrleitung II; Pfeife
III U3, 69
clay **pipe** ['kleɪ ˌpaɪp] Tonpfeife II

pirate ['paɪrət] Pirat/-in; Seeräuber/-in II

pitch [pɪtʃ] Spielfeld; Platz II

pizza ['pi:tsə] Pizza I

place [pleɪs] Ort; Stelle; Platz I
starting **place** ['stɑ:tɪŋ ˌpleɪs] Startpunkt II
*to take **place** [ˌteɪk 'pleɪs] stattfinden II

plan [plæn] Plan; Entwurf I
to **plan** [plæn] planen II

plane [pleɪn] Flugzeug **III U4**, 94

planet ['plænɪt] Planet II

planner ['plænə] Handbuch; Kalender I

plant [plɑ:nt] Pflanze II

plaster cast ['plɑ:stə kɑ:st] Gipsverband
III U3, 74

plate [pleɪt] Teller **III AC1**, 34

platform ['plætfɔ:m] Plattform; Bahnsteig
II

play [pleɪ] Theaterstück **III U3**, 68
to **play** [pleɪ] spielen I
to **play** a trick (on) [pleɪ ə 'trɪk ɒn] einen
Streich spielen I

player ['pleɪə] Spieler/-in; Mitspieler/-in II

playground ['pleɪgraʊnd] Schulhof; Pausenhof; Spielplatz II

to **please** [pli:z] jmdm. gefallen
⟨**III TMS1**, 32⟩

Please. [pli:z] Bitte. I

pleasure ['pleʒə] Freude; Vergnügen
⟨**III TR2**, 112⟩

plumber ['plʌmə] Installateur/-in; Kl-
empner/-in II

plumbing ['plʌmɪŋ] Sanitärarbeiten II

pocket ['pɒkɪt] Tasche; Hosentasche
III U2, 50
pocket money ['pɒkɪt ˌmʌni] Taschengeld I

podcast ['pɒdkɑ:st] Podcast **III U1**, 10

poem ['pəʊɪm] Gedicht I
shape **poem** ['ʃeɪp ˌpəʊɪm] Formgedicht;
Gestaltgedicht **III TMS1**, 26

poet ['pəʊɪt] Dichter/-in **III TMS1**, 26

poetry ['pəʊɪtri] Lyrik; Poesie; Dichtung;
Gedichte **III TMS1**, 26

point [pɔɪnt] Punkt II
*to have a **point** [ˌhæv ə 'pɔɪnt] nicht ganz
Unrecht haben **III U1**, 18
point of view [ˌpɔɪnt əv 'vju:] Standpunkt;
Ansicht; Perspektive II
to the **point** [tə ðə 'pɔɪnt] prägnant;
treffend **III AC2**, 57
turning **point** ['tɜ:nɪŋ ˌpɔɪnt] Wendepunkt
III U1, 22
to **point** at [pɔɪnt] zeigen auf II

poker ['pəʊkə] Poker **III TMS1**, 28

polar bear ['pəʊlə ˌbeə] Eisbär II

police [pə'li:s] Polizei II

polite [pə'laɪt] höflich I

political [pə'lɪtɪkl] politisch **III U3**, 65

poll [pəʊl] Abstimmung; Umfrage °**III U1**, 17

pollution (no pl) [pə'lu:ʃn] Verschmutzung
II

pony ['pəʊni] Pony I
pony trekking ['pəʊni ˌtrekɪŋ] Ponyreiten
im Gelände II

the **poor** [ðə 'pʊə] die Armen II

poor [pɔ:; pʊə] arm **III U1**, 21

pop [pɒp] Pop (Musik) **III TMS1**, 26

the **Pope** [ðə 'pəʊp] der Papst **III U3**, 65

popular ['pɒpjələ] beliebt; populär I

port [pɔ:t] Hafen **III U4**, 96

positive ['pɒzətɪv] positiv II

possessive pronoun [pəˌsesɪv 'prəʊnaʊn]
Possessivpronomen °**III TR2**, 112

possibility [ˌpɒsə'bɪləti] Möglichkeit II

possible ['pɒsəbl] möglich **III U1**, 18

post [pəʊst] Post (Eintrag im Internet) I

post office ['pəʊst ˌɒfɪs] Postamt I
to **post** [pəʊst] online stellen; posten II

postal address ['pəʊstl əˌdres] Postanschrift
III TMS2, 81

postcard ['pəʊstkɑ:d] Postkarte II

poster ['pəʊstə] Poster I

postman ['pəʊstmən] Briefträger/-in II

potato, potatoes (pl) [pə'teɪtəʊ; pə'teɪtəʊz]
Kartoffel **III U3**, 66
mashed **potatoes** (pl) [ˌmæʃt pə'teɪtəʊz]
Kartoffelpüree; Kartoffelbrei **III U2**, 44

pound (£) [paʊnd] Pfund (brit.
Währungseinheit) I

to **pour** [pɔ:] gießen; schütten; einschenken **II**

power [pauə] Kraft; Macht; Stärke ⟨**III TR2**, 112⟩

power cut ['pauə ˌkʌt] Stromausfall **II**

powerful ['pauəfl] stark; mächtig **II**

practical ['præktɪkl] nützlich **II**; praktisch **III U4**, 102

practice ['præktɪs] Übung; Training **III U1**, 8

to **practise** ['præktɪs] üben; trainieren **I**

prediction [prɪ'dɪkʃn] Vorhersage; Voraussage **II**

to **prefer** [prɪ'fɜ:] vorziehen; bevorzugen **III TMS1**, 30

prehistoric [ˌpri:hɪ'stɒrɪk] vorgeschichtlich **II**

to **prepare** [prɪ'peə] vorbereiten; zubereiten **II**

prepared [prɪ'peəd] vorbereitet ⟨**III TR1**, 111⟩

prescription [prɪ'skrɪpʃn] Rezept (für Arzneimittel) **II**

present ['preznt] Geschenk **I**; Gegenwart; Präsens **II**

present perfect [ˌpreznt 'pɜ:fɪkt] das Perfekt °**III U2**, 44

to **present** [prɪ'zent] präsentieren; vorstellen **III TMS1**, 29

present ['preznt] heutig; Gegenwarts- **III U2**, 48

presentation [ˌprezn'teɪʃn] Präsentation; Vortrag **I**

presenter [prɪ'zentə] Moderator/-in **II**

to **press** [pres] drücken; pressen **III U4**, 105

peer **pressure** ['pɪə ˌpreʃə] Gruppenzwang **III U1**, 22

to **pretend** [prɪ'tend] tun als ob; vortäuschen **III TMS1**, 27

pretty ['prɪti] hübsch **III U1**, 21

price [praɪs] Preis **II**

princess [prɪn'ses] Prinzessin **II**

print [prɪnt] gedruckt; Druck- **II**

prison ['prɪzn] Gefängnis **II**

prisoner ['prɪznə] Gefangene/-r; Häftling; Sträfling **III U4**, 102

private ['praɪvɪt] privat; Privat- **II**

prize [praɪz] Preis; Gewinn **I**

pro [prəu] Argument dafür **II**

probably ['prɒbəbli] möglicherweise; wahrscheinlich **II**

problem ['prɒbləm] Problem; Schwierigkeit **I**

to **produce** [prə'dju:s] produzieren; erzeugen; herstellen **III U1**, 10

product ['prɒdʌkt] Produkt; Erzeugnis **III U1**, 10

profile ['prəufaɪl] Profil; Porträt **II**

programme ['prəugræm] Programm; Sendung **II**

project ['prɒdʒekt] Projekt **I**

promise ['prɒmɪs] Versprechen **II**

to **promise** ['prɒmɪs] versprechen **II**

prompt card ['prɒmpt kɑ:d] Stichwortkarte; Rollenkarte **II**

object **pronoun** [ɒbdʒɪkt 'prəunaun] Objektpronomen °**III U1**, 16

personal **pronoun** [ˌpɜ:snl 'prəunaun] Personalpronomen °**III U1**, 16

possessive **pronoun** [pəˌsesɪv 'prəunaun] Possessivpronomen °**III TR2**, 112

reflexive **pronoun** [rɪˌfleksɪv 'prəunaun] Reflexivpronomen °**III U1**, 15

relative **pronoun** [ˌrelətɪv 'prəunaun] Relativpronomen °**III U3**, 68

pronunciation [prəˌnʌnsi'eɪʃn] Aussprache **II**

proofreading ['pru:fri:dɪŋ] Korrekturlesen °**III U1**, 19

prop [prɒp] Requisite **II**

prop word ['prɒp ˌwɜ:d] Stützwort °**III U3**, 63

to **protect** [prə'tekt] schützen **II**

proud (of) ['praud (ˌəv)] stolz (auf) **II**

to **provide** [prə'vaɪd] zur Verfügung stellen; liefern ⟨**III TMS2**, 86⟩

pub [pʌb] Kneipe; Gasthaus ⟨**III TR3**, 114⟩

public ['pʌblɪk] öffentlich **II**

public transport (no pl) [ˌpʌblɪk 'trænspɔ:t] öffentliche Verkehrsmittel **II**

pudding ['pudɪŋ] Pudding; Nachtisch **I**

to **pull** [pul] ziehen **I**

to **pull** down [pul 'daun] abreißen **III U2**, 42

pure [pjuə] rein; pur ⟨**III TMS1**, 32⟩

purple ['pɜ:pl] violett; lila **I**

purpose ['pɜ:pəs] Ziel; Absicht; Zweck **III TMS2**, 81

to **push** [puʃ] stoßen; schieben; schubsen **II**

to **push** oneself ['puʃ wʌn,self] sich alles abverlangen; sich Mühe geben **III U1**, 15

*to **put** (in) [put (ˌɪn)] setzen; hineinstellen; hineinlegen **I**

*to **put** away [put ə'weɪ] wegstellen; weglegen **I**

*to **put** on [put 'ɒn] anziehen **III U1**, 20

*to **put** up [put 'ʌp] aufhängen; errichten; aufstellen **II**

puzzle ['pʌzl] Rätsel; Puzzle **I**

pyjamas (pl) [pɪ'dʒɑ:məz] Schlafanzug; Pyjama **II**

Q

quality ['kwɒləti] Qualität **I**

quarter past/to ['kwɔ:tə pɑ:st/tə] Viertel nach/vor **I**

queen [kwi:n] Königin **I**

drama **queen** (coll) ['drɑ:mə ˌkwi:n] Tussi (abwertend); Zicke (abwertend) **III U3**, 74

question ['kwestʃən] Frage **I**

question mark ['kwestʃən ˌmɑ:k] Fragezeichen °**III U2**, 52

queue [kju:] Schlange; Warteschlange **I**

to jump the **queue** [ˌdʒʌmp ðə 'kju:] sich vordrängeln **I**

quiche [ki:ʃ] Quiche **II**

quick [kwɪk] schnell **I**

quickly ['kwɪkli] schnell **II**

quiet [kwaɪət] still; ruhig; leise **I**

quill [kwɪl] Federkiel **III U3**, 72

quite [kwaɪt] ziemlich; ganz; völlig **II**

quite a few [ˌkwaɪt ə 'fju:] ziemlich viele **II**

quiz [kwɪz] Quiz; Rätsel **I**

quotation marks [kwə'teɪʃn ˌmɑ:ks] Anführungszeichen °**III U2**, 52

R

rabbit ['ræbɪt] Kaninchen **I**

race [reɪs] Wettlauf; Rennen **II**

camel **racing** ['kæml ˌreɪsɪŋ] Kamelrennen **II**

racquet ['rækɪt] Schläger **II**

radio ['reɪdiəu] Radio **I**

raffle ['ræfl] Tombola **I**

rain [reɪn] Regen **III U1**, 11

to **rain** [reɪn] regnen **II**

raincoat ['reɪnkəut] Regenmantel **II**

rainwater ['reɪnˌwɔ:tə] Regenwasser **III U1**, 11

to **raise** money [ˌreɪz 'mʌni] Geld sammeln **II**

firing **range** ['faɪrɪŋ ˌreɪndʒ] Schießplatz ⟨**III TR1**, 110⟩

to **rap** [ræp] rappen **I**

rat [ræt] Ratte **I**

flat **rate** ['flæt reɪt] Flatrate; Einheitspreis **III TMS1**, 29

to **rate** [reɪt] bewerten; einstufen **II**

I'd **rather** [aɪd 'rɑ:ðə] ich würde lieber **III U3**, 77

rather than ['rɑ:ðə ðən] eher als **III U3**, 65

rating ['reɪtɪŋ] Bewertung; Rating **II**

raven ['reɪvn] Rabe **II**

raven master ['reɪvn ˌmɑ:stə] Aufseher über die Raben **II**

raw material [ˌrɔ: mə'tɪəriəl] Rohstoff; Rohmaterial **III U3**, 65

RE (= Religious Education) [ɑ:'ri:; rɪˌlɪdʒəs edʒu'keɪʃn] Religion (Schulfach) **II**

to **reach** [ri:tʃ] erreichen; dran kommen **II**

to **react** [ri'ækt] reagieren **III U1**, 15

reaction [ri'ækʃn] Reaktion **II**

*to **read** [ri:d] lesen **I**

*to **read** out loud [ˌri:d/sɪŋ aut 'laud] laut vorsingen °**III TMS1**, 31

reader ['ri:də] Leser/-in **II**

reading ['ri:dɪŋ] Lesen **I**

ready ['redi] fertig; bereit **II**

*to get **ready** [ˌget 'redi] sich vorbereiten; sich fertig machen **III TMS1**, 26

ready meal [ˌredi 'mi:l] Fertiggericht **I**

real [rɪəl] echt; richtig **II**

to **realise** ['rɪəlaɪz] erkennen; realisieren **III U2**, 50

realistic [ˌrɪə'lɪstɪk] realistisch **II**

really ['rɪəli] wirklich **I**

reason ['ri:zn] Grund **II**

rebel yell ['rebl jel] Kampfschrei ⟨**III TMS1**, 27⟩

*to **rebuild** [ˌriːˈbɪld] wieder aufbauen **III U3**, 69

to **receive** [rɪˈsiːv] erhalten; bekommen; empfangen **II**

recipe [ˈresɪpi] Rezept **III U2**, 46

recipient [rɪˈsɪpiənt] Empfänger/-in **III TMS2**, 81

to **recommend** [ˌrekəˈmend] empfehlen **III U1**, 10

record [ˈrekɔːd] Schallplatte **II**

recorder [rɪˈkɔːdə] Flöte **III U1**, 15

recording [rɪˈkɔːdɪŋ] Aufnahme; Aufzeichnung **I**

   recording studio [rɪˈkɔːdɪŋ ˌstjuːdiəʊ] Aufnahmestudio; Tonstudio **I**

to **recycle** [ˌriːˈsaɪkl] recyceln; wiederverwerten **II**

recycling [ˌriːˈsaɪklɪŋ] Recycling; Wiederaufbereitung **III U1**, 11

red [red] rot **I**

to **reef** the sails [ˌriːf ðə ˈseɪlz] die Segel einholen **I**

reflexive pronoun [rɪˌfleksɪv ˈprəʊnaʊn] Reflexivpronomen °**III U1**, 15

refugee [ˌrefjʊˈdʒiː] Flüchtling **III U4**, 106

region [ˈriːdʒn] Region; Gegend **II**

register [ˈredʒɪstə] Sprachebene; Register °**III TMS2**, 86

registration [ˌredʒɪsˈtreɪʃn] Anwesenheitskontrolle **II**

to **regret** sth [rɪˈgret] etw. bedauern **II**

regulation [ˌregjəˈleɪʃn] Vorschrift; Regelung; Regulierung **III U4**, 99

to **rehearse** [rɪˈhɜːs] proben °**III AC1**, 35

reign [reɪn] Herrschaft; Regierungszeit **III U3**, 65

to **reign** [reɪn] herrschen; regieren **III U3**, 72

*to be **related** to [bi rɪˈleɪtɪd tə] sich beziehen auf; verwandt sein mit **III TMS2**, 80

relation [rɪˈleɪʃn] Verbindung; Verhältnis ⟨**III TMS1**, 32⟩

relationship [rɪˈleɪʃnʃɪp] Beziehung **II**

defining **relative** clause [dɪˌfaɪnɪŋ ˈrelətɪv ˌklɔːz] notwendiger Relativsatz °**III U3**, 63

   relative pronoun [ˌrelətɪv ˈprəʊnaʊn] Relativpronomen °**III U3**, 68

to **relax** [rɪˈlæks] sich entspannen; sich ausruhen; sich beruhigen **II**

relaxed [rɪˈlækst] entspannt; locker; gelassen **III U3**, 66

reliable [rɪˈlaɪəbl] verlässlich; zuverlässig; vertrauenswürdig ⟨**III TMS1**, 32⟩

relief [rɪˈliːf] Erleichterung; Linderung **III U4**, 99

religious [rɪˈlɪdʒəs] religiös; gläubig **II**

to **rely** (on) [rɪˈlaɪ (ˌɒn)] sich verlassen (auf); vertrauen (auf) **III U1**, 12

to **remain** [rɪˈmeɪn] bleiben ⟨**III U2**, 47⟩

to **remember** [rɪˈmembə] sich erinnern (an); sich merken; denken an **I**

   Remember? [rɪˈmembə] Erinnerst du dich?; Erinnert ihr euch? **II**

to **remind** (sb of sth/sb) [rɪˈmaɪnd (ˌəv)] (jmdn. an etw./jmdn.) erinnern **III TMS1**, 30

to **remove** [rɪˈmuːv] entfernen **II**

to **rent** (out) [ˌrent (ˈaʊt)] mieten **III U2**, 54

to **repeat** [rɪˈpiːt] wiederholen **III TMS1**, 29

repetition [ˌrepɪˈtɪʃn] Wiederholung **III TMS1**, 31

to **replace** (by/with) [rɪˈpleɪs] ersetzen (durch) ⟨**III U2**, 55⟩; **III TMS2**, 84

reply [rɪˈplaɪ] Antwort; Erwiderung; Entgegnung **II**

to **reply** (to) [rɪˈplaɪ] antworten; erwidern; entgegnen **II**

report [rɪˈpɔːt] Bericht; Meldung **II**

   travel **report** [ˌtrævl rɪˈpɔːt] Reisebericht **II**

reporter [rɪˈpɔːtə] Reporter/-in **II**

to **require** [rɪˈkwaɪə] benötigen; erfordern **III U4**, 103

rescue [ˈreskjuː] Rettung **II**

research (no pl) [rɪˈsɜːtʃ] Recherche; Forschung; Untersuchung **III U4**, 10ˉ

respect [rɪˈspekt] Respekt **III TMS1**, 30

responsibility [rɪˌspɒnsəˈbɪləti] Verantwortung **III TMS1**, 30

responsible [rɪsˈpɒnsəbl] verantwortlich; zuständig **III U4**, 104

the **rest** [rest] der Rest **III U4**, 108

restaurant [ˈrestrɒnt] Restaurant; Gaststätte **I**

result [rɪˈzʌlt] Ergebnis; Resultat **II**

return [rɪˈtɜːn] Rückkehr ⟨**III TR1**, 110⟩

   return ticket [rɪˈtɜːn ˌtɪkɪt] Hin- und Rückfahrkarte **II**

to **return** [rɪˈtɜːn] zurückkehren; zurückfahren **II**

review [rɪˈvjuː] Rezension; Kritik **II**

reviewer [rɪˈvjuːə] Kritiker/-in **II**

revolution [ˌrevlˈuːʃn] Revolution **III U3**, 63

rhyme [raɪm] Reim **III TMS1**, 31

   nursery **rhyme** [ˈnɜːsri ˌraɪm] Kinderreim; Kinderlied **III TMS1**, 26

   rhyme scheme [ˈraɪm skiːm] Reimschema **III TMS1**, 31

to **rhyme** [raɪm] (sich) reimen **III TMS1**, 31

rhyming [ˈraɪmɪŋ] Reim-; sich reimend °**III TMS1**, 29

rhythm [ˈrɪðm] Rhythmus **III TMS1**, 29

rhythmic [ˈrɪðmɪk] rhythmisch; gleichmäßig **III TMS1**, 29

rich [rɪtʃ] reich **III U1**, 12

*to **ride** [raɪd] fahren; reiten **II**

rigging [ˈrɪgɪŋ] Takelage **I**

right [raɪt] richtig; korrekt; (nach) ˉechts; rechte-/-r/-s **I**; direkt; genau ⟨**III TR3**, 114⟩

*to be **right** [bi ˈraɪt] Recht haben **I**

on the **right** [ɒn ðə ˈraɪt] auf der rechten Seite; rechts **I**

   right away [ˌraɪt əˈweɪ] sofort; gleich **I**

   right here [ˌraɪt ˈhɪə] genau hier **I**

   right now [ˌraɪt ˈnaʊ] im Momenˉ; gleich jetzt; sofort **II**

ring [rɪŋ] Ring **III U3**, 65

   key **ring** [ˈkiː ˌrɪŋ] Schlüsselbund; Schlüsselanhänger **III U2**, 51

*to **ring** [rɪŋ] klingeln; läuten **I**

ice **rink** [ˈaɪs ˌrɪŋk] Eisbahn; Schlittschuhbahn **II**

*to **rise** [raɪz] sich erheben; aufstehen; steigen **III U3**, 63

river [ˈrɪvə] Fluss **I**

road [rəʊd] Straße **I**

robber [ˈrɒbə] Räuber/-in **II**

rock [rɒk] Rock (Musik) **III TMS1**, 26

to **rock** [rɒk] schaukeln **III U4**, 104

rocky [ˈrɒki] felsig; steinig **II**

role [rəʊl] Rolle **II**

   role model [ˈrəʊl ˌmɒdl] Vorbild **III U1**, 10

bread **roll** [ˌbred ˈrəʊl] Brötchen **III AC1**, 34

to **roll off** [rəʊl] hinunterrollen; herunterrollen **II**

   to **roll** one's eyes [ˌrəʊl wʌnz ˈaɪz] die Augen verdrehen **III U3**, 74

Roman [ˈrəʊmən] Römer/-in; römisch **II**

romance [ˈrəʊmæns] Liebesgeschichte; Liebesfilm **III U4**, 107

roof [ruːf] Dach **II**

room [ruːm; rʊm] Zimmer; Raum **I**; Platz **II**

   living **room** [ˈlɪvɪŋ rʊm] Wohnzimmer **I**

   side **room** [ˈsaɪd ˌrʊm] Nebenraum **III U4**, 99

rope [rəʊp] Seil **III U2**, 51

rotary phone [ˈrəʊtri fəʊn] Telefon mit Wählscheibe **III U2**, 53

round of boxing [ˌraʊnd əv ˈbɒksɪŋ] Boxrunde **II**

round [raʊnd] rund **III U3**, 63

round [raʊnd] um … herum **II**

   *to go **round** in circles [gəʊ ˌraʊnd ɪn ˈsɜːklz] sich im Kreis drehen **III U2**, 50

route [ruːt] Strecke; Route **II**

routine [ruːˈtiːn] Routine **I**

royal [ˈrɔɪəl] königlich **I**

rubber [ˈrʌbə] Radiergummi **I**

rubbish [ˈrʌbɪʃ] Müll; Gerümpel **I**

rude [ruːd] unhöflich; unverschämt **I**

rugby [ˈrʌgbi] Rugby **II**

to **ruin** [ˈruːɪn] ruinieren; zerstören **II**

rule [ruːl] Regel **I**; Herrschaft; Regierungszeit **III U3**, 63

ruler [ˈruːlə] Lineal **I**

run [rʌn] Rennen; Lauf **II**

*to **run** [rʌn] rennen; laufen **I**

   *to **run** away [ˌrʌn əˈweɪ] wegrennen **I**

runner [ˈrʌnə] Läufer/-in **II**

running [ˈrʌnɪŋ] Laufen; Rennen **II**

S

sad [sæd] traurig **I**

safe [seɪf] sicher; ungefährlich **II**

to **reef** the **sails** [ˌriːf ðə ˈseɪlz] die Segel einholen **I**

sailing boat [ˈseɪlɪŋ ˌbəʊt] Segelboot **II**

sailor [ˈseɪlə] Seemann; Matrose **I**

patron **saint** ['peɪtrn ˌseɪnt] Nationalheiliger ⟨III TR3, 115⟩

salad ['sæləd] Salat I

sale [seɪl] Verkauf II

the **same** [ðə 'seɪm] der-/die-/dasselbe; der/die/das gleiche I

sandal ['sændl] Sandale III U3, 65

sandwich ['sænwɪdʒ] Sandwich; belegtes Brot I

sandy ['sændi] sandig; Sand- II

Saturday ['sætədeɪ] Samstag I

sauce [sɔːs] Soße III U2, 44

sausage ['sɒsɪdʒ] Wurst; Bratwurst III AC1, 34

to **save** [seɪv] retten; bergen; sparen I
  *to be **saved** by the bell [bi 'seɪvd baɪ ðə ˌbel] noch mal Glück haben III U1, 15

sax ['sæks] Saxofon I

Saxon ['sæksn] Sachse/Sächsin; sächsisch III U3, 65
  Anglo-**Saxon** [ˌæŋgləʊ'sæksn] Angelsachse; Angelsächsin; angelsächsisch III U3, 63

saxophone ['sæksəfəʊn] Saxofon I

*to **say** [seɪ] sagen; aufsagen; sprechen I
  … **says** ['sez] auf/in … steht II
  *to **say** goodbye (to) [ˌseɪ gʊd'baɪ (tə)] sich verabschieden (von) III U3, 63
  *to **say** hello (to) [ˌseɪ hel'əʊ (tə)] grüßen I

saying ['seɪɪŋ] Sprichwort; Redensart III U1, 8

*to be **scared** (of) [bi 'skeəd ˌəv] Angst haben (vor) I

scary ['skeəri] unheimlich; gruselig; beängstigend II

scene [siːn] Szene; Schauplatz II

rhyme **scheme** ['raɪm skiːm] Reimschema III TMS1, 31

school [skuːl] Schule I
  school fees (pl) ['skuːl fiːz] Schulgeld; Schulgebühren III U3, 77

schoolbag ['skuːlbæg] Schultasche I

science [saɪəns] Naturwissenschaften II
  science fiction [ˌsaɪəns 'fɪkʃn] Science-Fiction (Zukunftsdichtung) III U4, 107

scientist ['saɪəntɪst] Wissenschaftler/-in III U2, 43

scone [skɒn] Scone (eine Art süßes Brötchen) II

score [skɔː] Punktestand; Spielstand II

Scot [skɒt] Schotte/Schottin III U2, 43

Scotch egg [skɒtʃ 'eg] hart gekochtes Ei in Wurstbrät I

Scottish ['skɒtɪʃ] schottisch II

gorge **scrambling** ['gɔːdʒ ˌskræmblɪŋ] Schluchtenklettern II

to **scream** [skriːm] schreien; kreischen II

screen [skriːn] Bildschirm ⟨III TMS2, 86⟩

screwdriver ['skruːˌdraɪvə] Schraubenzieher II

script [skrɪpt] Drehbuch; Skript II

sea [siː] Meer I

sea level ['siː ˌlevl] Meeresspiegel III U3, 63

to **seal** [siːl] geschlossen; fest verschließen; versiegeln °III TMS1, 28

search [sɜːtʃ] Suche; Such- II
  search engine ['sɜːtʃ ˌendʒɪn] Suchmaschine II

seasick ['siːsɪk] seekrank III U4, 94

seaside ['siːsaɪd] Küste; Meeresküste III U3, 65

season ['siːzn] Saison; Jahreszeit II

seat [siːt] Sitz; Sitzplatz II

second ['seknd] Sekunde III TMS1, 30

secondly ['sekndli] zweitens II

secret ['siːkrət] Geheimnis II
  in **secret** [ɪn 'siːkrət] heimlich II

secret ['siːkrət] geheim; Geheim- ⟨III TR3, 114⟩

*to **see** [siː] sehen I
  a must-**see** [ə ˌmʌst 'siː] unbedingt empfehlenswert III U4, 102
  See you! ['siː jə] Bis dann!; Bis … I
  See you soon! [ˌsiː jə 'suːn] Bis bald! II
  Wait and **see**! [ˌweɪt ˌənd 'siː] Warte ab! I

self [self] das Selbst III U1, 9

self-critical ['selfˌkrɪtɪkl] selbstkritisch II

selfie ['selfi] Selfie II

*to **sell** [sel] verkaufen I

seller ['selə] Verkäufer/-in (auf einem Flohmarkt) I

semi- ['semi] halb-; Halb- III TMS2, 83

*to **send** [send] schicken; senden II

sender ['sendə] Absender/-in III TMS2, 82

sense of humour (no pl) [ˌsens əv 'hjuːmə] Sinn für Humor III U1, 23

sentence ['sentəns] Satz I
  conditional **sentence** [kənˌdɪʃnl 'sentəns] Bedingungssatz °III U1, 9

separate ['seprət] separat; getrennt; verschieden II

September [sep'tembə] September II

sequel ['siːkwl] Fortsetzung; Folge II

sequence ['siːkwəns] Sequenz; Szene III U3, 77

series ['sɪəriːz], **series** ['sɪəriːz] (pl) Reihe °III TMS1, 30

serious ['sɪəriəs] ernsthaft; ernst II

*to take sth **seriously** [teɪk 'sɪəriəsli] etw. ernst nehmen II

set [set] Aufnahmeort; Drehort II

*to **set** [set] setzen; aufstellen ⟨III TMS1, 32⟩
  *to be **set** in [bi 'set ˌɪn] spielen in III U4, 107
  *to **set** off fireworks [set ˌɒf 'faɪəwɜːks] ein Feuerwerk zünden III U2, 43
  *to **set** out [ˌset ˌaʊt] anordnen; gestalten; darstellen ⟨III TMS2, 87⟩

setting ['setɪŋ] Schauplatz; Rahmen II
  account **settings** [əˈkaʊnt ˌsetɪŋz] Profileinstellungen III U1, 23

to **settle** ['setl] siedeln; sich niederlassen III U3, 67

seven ['sevn] sieben I

several ['sevrl] einige; mehrere; verschiedene °III AC1, 35

shall [ʃæl] sollen II

shape poem ['ʃeɪp ˌpəʊɪm] Formgedicht; Gestaltgedicht III TMS1, 26

tc **share** [ʃeə] teilen II

shark [ʃɑːk] Hai III U4, 104

she [ʃiː] sie I

sheep, sheep (pl) [ʃiːp; ʃiːp] Schaf I

shelf, shelves (pl) [ʃelf; ʃelvz] Regal; Regalbrett II

shell [ʃel] Schale; Muschel III TMS1, 27

sheriff ['ʃerɪf] Sheriff ⟨III TR2, 112⟩

*to **shine** [ʃaɪn] glänzen; scheinen III U3, 69

ship [ʃɪp] Schiff I

shipbuilding ['ʃɪpbɪldɪŋ] Schiffsbau III U2, 42

shirt [ʃɜːt] Hemd; Shirt I

shoe [ʃuːz] Schuhe I
  in … **shoes** [ɪn 'ʃuːz] an … Stelle III U1, 13

shop [ʃɒp] Geschäft; Laden I
  charity **shop** ['tʃærɪti ʃɒp] Second-Hand-Laden I
  pawn **shop** ['pɔːn ʃɒp] Pfandhaus; Pfandleihe III U3, 77

shopping ['ʃɒpɪŋ] Einkaufen; Einkäufe I
  *to do the **shopping** [ˌduː ðə 'ʃɒpɪŋ] einkaufen; einkaufen gehen III U2, 53
  *to go **shopping** [ˌgəʊ 'ʃɒpɪŋ] einkaufen gehen I

shore [ʃɔː] Ufer; Küste II

short [ʃɔːt] kurz II

shorts (pl) [ʃɔːts] Shorts; kurze Hose II

shot [ʃɒt] Aufnahme II

should [ʃʊd] sollte/-est/-t/-n I
  shouldn't ['ʃʊdnt] sollte(n) nicht II

shoulder ['ʃəʊldə] Schulter II

to **shout** [ʃaʊt] schreien; rufen I

show [ʃəʊ] Show; Schau; Aufführung I
  comedy **show** ['kɒmədi ˌʃəʊ] Comedy Show II
  slide **show** ['slaɪd ʃəʊ] Diashow °III U2, 40
  talent **show** ['tælənt ˌʃəʊ] Talentwettbewerb I

*to **show** [ʃəʊ] zeigen I
  to **show** off [ʃəʊ ˌɒf] angeben II

shower ['ʃaʊə] Dusche I

show-off ['ʃəʊˌɒf] Angeber/-in III U1, 23

shy [ʃaɪ] schüchtern II

*to be **sick** [bi 'sɪk] sich übergeben II
  *to feel **sick** [ˌfiːl 'sɪk] Übelkeit verspüren; sich schlecht fühlen II

side [saɪd] Seite II
  side room ['saɪd ˌrʊm] Nebenraum III U4, 99
  by my **side** [baɪ maɪ 'saɪd] an meiner Seite ⟨III TMS1, 30⟩

sights [saɪts] Sehenswürdigkeiten II

sightseeing ['saɪtsiːɪŋ] Sightseeing-; Besichtigungs- II

sign [saɪn] Schild; Zeichen II
  sign language [saɪn] Gebärdensprache; Zeichensprache II

a **sign** that … [ə ˌsaɪn 'ðæt] ein Schild, das … ⟨**III U2**, 51⟩

to **sign** [saɪn] unterschreiben; unterzeichnen **III TMS1**, 27

to **sign** up [ˌsaɪn 'ʌp] sich anmelden **II**

signal ['sɪɡnl] Empfang; Signal; Zeichen **III U2**, 50

signature ['sɪɡnətʃə] Unterschrift **III TMS2**, 82

silence (no pl) ['saɪləns] Stille; Schweigen; Ruhe **III U3**, 69

silly ['sɪli] Dummkopf **II**

silly ['sɪli] dumm; doof; albern **I**

silver ['sɪlvə] Silber **II**

similarity [ˌsɪmɪ'lærəti] Ähnlichkeit; Gemeinsamkeit; Parallele ⟨**III TMS1**, 33⟩

simile ['sɪmɪli] Vergleich; Gleichnis **III TMS1**, 31

simple ['sɪmpl] einfach; simpel **III U1**, 18

since (+ Zeitpunkt) [sɪns] seit; seitdem **II**

Yours **sincerely,** [ˌjɔːz sɪn'sɪəli] Mit freundlichen Grüßen, **III TMS2**, 80

*to **sing** [sɪŋ] singen **I**

*to **sing** along [ˌsɪŋ ə'lɒŋ] mitsingen **III TMS1**, 29

*to **sing** out loud [ˌriːd/sɪŋ ˌaʊt 'laʊd] laut vorsingen °**III TMS1**, 31

singer ['sɪŋə] Sänger/-in **I**

singing ['sɪŋɪŋ] Gesang; Singen **I**

single ['sɪŋgl] einzige/-r/-s °**III U2**, 52

single ticket ['sɪŋgl ˌtɪkɪt] einfache Fahrkarte **II**

sister ['sɪstə] Schwester **I**

half-**sister** ['hɑːf̩sɪstə] Halbschwester **I**

sisterhood ['sɪstəhʊd] Zusammenhalt unter Frauen; Solidarität unter Frauen ⟨**III TMS1**, 30⟩

*to **sit** [sɪt] sitzen **I**

Sit! [sɪt] Sitz! (Befehl für Hunde); Platz! (Befehl für Hunde) **I**

*to **sit** down [ˌsɪt 'daʊn] sich hinsetzen; sich setzen **I**

site [saɪt] Website **II**

situation [ˌsɪtju'eɪʃn] Situation **III U1**, 8

six [sɪks] sechs **I**

size [saɪz] Größe; Kleidergröße **I**

to **skate** [skeɪt] Inlineskates fahren; Schlittschuh laufen **I**

skateboard ['skeɪtbɔːd] Skateboard **I**

skateboarding ['skeɪtbɔːdɪŋ] Skateboardfahren **I**

skates (pl) [skeɪts] Inlineskates; Rollschuhe; Schlittschuhe **I**

skating ['skeɪtɪŋ] Schlittschuhlaufen **II**
(inline) **skating** ['ɪnlaɪn ˌskeɪtɪŋ] Inlineskatefahren **I**

skill [skɪl] Fertigkeit; Geschick; Fähigkeit **III U1**, 10

skirt [skɜːt] Rock **I**

sky [skaɪ] Himmel **III U2**, 50

*to **sleep** [sliːp] schlafen **I**

sleepover ['sliːpˌəʊvə] Übernachtung; Pyjama-Party **II**

sleeve [sliːv] Ärmel ⟨**III TR3**, 115⟩

to **slice** [slaɪs] in Scheiben schneiden **II**

slide [slaɪd] Rutschbahn **I**

slide show ['slaɪd ʃəʊ] Diashow °**III U2**, 40

water **slide** ['wɔːtə ˌslaɪd] Wasserrutsche **I**

slogan ['sləʊɡən] Slogan; Werbespruch **II**

slow [sləʊ] langsam **I**

small [smɔːl] klein **I**

small talk ['smɔːl ˌtɔːk] Smalltalk **III AC2**, 56

smart [smɑːt] schlau; klug; intelligent **III U1**, 9

smart type ['smɑːt ˌtaɪp] Lerntyp; Intelligenztyp **III U1**, 9

smartcard ['smɑːtkɑːd] Chipkarte; Smartcard **II**

smartphone ['smɑːtfəʊn] Smartphone **I**

to **smash** [smæʃ] zerschlagen; zerschmettern **III U4**, 104

*to **smell** [smel] riechen; duften ⟨**III TR1**, 110⟩

smile [smaɪl] Lächeln **I**

to **smile** [smaɪl] lächeln **II**

smuggler ['smʌɡlə] Schmuggler/-in **III U4**, 104

snack [snæk] Snack; Imbiss **I**

snack bar ['snæk ˌbɑː] Café; Imbissstube **I**

to **sneak** around [ˌsniːk ə'raʊnd] herumschleichen **II**

snowy ['snəʊi] Schnee- ⟨**III TMS1**, 32⟩

so [səʊ] so; also **I**

so (that) [ˌsəʊ 'ðæt] damit; so dass **II**

so far [ˌsəʊ 'fɑː] bis jetzt **II**

social media [ˌsəʊʃl 'miːdiə] soziale Netzwerke **III U1**, 10

social network [ˌsəʊʃl 'netwɜːk] soziales Netzwerk **II**

society [sə'saɪəti] Verein; Gesellschaft **II**

sofa ['səʊfə] Sofa; Couch **I**

soldier ['səʊldʒə] Soldat/-in **III U2**, 47

solution [sə'luːʃn] Lösung **II**

to **solve** [sɒlv] lösen **II**

Somali [sə'mɑːli] Somali; somalisch **III U4**, 105

some [sʌm; səm] einige; ein paar; etwas **I**

somebody ['sʌmbədi] jemand **I**

someone ['sʌmwʌn] jemand **II**

something ['sʌmθɪŋ] etwas **I**

sometimes ['sʌmtaɪmz] manchmal **I**

somewhere ['sʌmweə] irgendwo **II**

son [sʌn] Sohn **III U2**, 42

song [sɒŋ] Song; Lied **I**

songwriter ['sɒŋˌraɪtə] Liedermacher/-in; Songschreiber/-in **III TMS1**, 26

soon [suːn] bald **II**

as **soon** as [əz 'suːn ˌəz] sobald **II**

Get well **soon**! [ˌget wel 'suːn] Gute Besserung! **III TMS2**, 85

Sorry! ['sɒri] Entschuldigung!; Tut mir leid! **I**

*to be **sorry** [bi 'sɒri] leid tun **I**

*to feel **sorry** for [ˌfiːl 'sɒri fɔː] Mitleid haben mit; bedauern **III U1**, 23

I'm **sorry!** [aɪm 'sɒri] Tut mir leid! **I**

to **sort** [sɔːt] sortieren **III U4**, 109

sound [saʊnd] Ton; Geräusch; Klang **I**

to **sound** [saʊnd] klingen **II**

source [sɔːs] Quelle **II**

south [saʊθ] Süden; Süd- **II**

south [saʊθ] südlich; im Süden **III U2**, 45

(the) **southwest** [ˌsaʊθ'west] (der) Südwesten; im Südwesten; südwestlich **II**

souvenir [ˌsuːvn'ɪə] Souvenir; Andenken **II**

sovereign ['sɒvrɪn] historische Münze **I**

Spanish ['spænɪʃ] spanisch; Spanisch; die Spanier **III U3**, 65

*to **speak** (to) ['spiːk (tə)] sprechen (mit) **I**

speaker ['spiːkə] Redner/-in; Sprecher/-in **I**

spear [spɪə] Speer **II**

special ['speʃl] besonders; speziell **I**

special offer [ˌspeʃl 'ɒfə] Sonderangebot **I**

with **special** needs [wɪð ˌspeʃl 'niːdz] mit Behinderung; mit speziellen Bedürfnissen **II**

specially ['speʃli] besonders; vor allem **II**

species, species (pl) ['spiːʃiːz, 'spiːʃiːz] Art; Spezies **II**

specific [spə'sɪfɪk] spezifisch; speziell **III U4**, 107

spectacular [spek'tækjələ] spektakulär **II**

indirect **speech** [ˌɪndɪrekt 'spiːtʃ] indirekte Rede ⟨**III TR3**, 115⟩

*to **spell** [spel] buchstabieren **I**

*to **spend** [spend] ausgeben (Geld) **I**; verbringen (Zeit) **II**

spider ['spaɪdə] Spinne **I**

sponge [spʌndʒ] Rührkuchen; Biskuit(kuchen) **II**

spontaneous [spɒn'teɪniəs] spontan **II**

spoon [spuːn] Löffel **I**

sport [spɔːt] Sport; Sportart **I**

spring [sprɪŋ] Frühling **I**

spring break ['sprɪŋ breɪk] Frühlingsferien **I**

I **spy** with my little eye [aɪ spaɪ wɪð ˌmaɪ lɪtl 'aɪ] Ich sehe was, was du nicht siehst **II**

squirrel ['skwɪrəl] Eichhörnchen **I**

stadium ['steɪdiəm] Stadion **II**

stage [steɪdʒ] Bühne **I**

stage direction ['steɪdʒ dɪˌrekʃn] Regieanweisung **III AC2**, 57

stairs (pl) [steəz] Treppe **III U2**, 50

stall [stɔːl] Stand; Bude **III U4**, 102

stamp [stæmp] Briefmarke **III TMS2**, 82

*to **stand** [stænd] stehen **I**

stanza ['stænzə] Strophe **III TMS1**, 30

star [stɑː] Star; Stern **I**

to **stare** [steə] starren; anstarren **I**

start [stɑːt] Anfang; Start **II**

to **start** [stɑːt] anfangen; beginnen; starten **I**; hier: gründen **III U2**, 43

starting place ['stɑːtɪŋ ˌpleɪs] Startpunkt **II**

statement ['steɪtmənt] Aussage; Behauptung; Erklärung **II**

station ['steɪʃn] Bahnhof; Haltestelle; Station **II**; Sender **III U2**, 43

bus **station** ['bʌs ˌsteɪʃn] Busbahnhof **I**

to **stay** [steɪ] bleiben **I**; untergebracht sein; wohnen **II**
  to **stay** away from [ˌsteɪ_ə'weɪ frəm] fernbleiben von; meiden **II**
  to **stay** in touch (with) [ˌsteɪ ɪn 'tʌtʃ wɪð] in Kontakt bleiben (mit) **II**
  to **stay** with ['steɪ wɪð] wohnen bei **II**
  Stay the way you are. [ˌsteɪ ðə weɪ ju 'ɑː] Bleib wie du bist. **III U1**, 16
steady ['stedi] kontinuierlich; unaufhörlich **III U4**, 105
steak [steɪk] Steak **I**
*to **steal** [sti:l] stehlen **II**
steam [sti:m] Dampf; Dampf- **III U2**, 43
  steam engine ['sti:m‿endʒɪn] Dampfmaschine **III U2**, 43
step [step] Stufe; Schritt **II**
  step-by-**step** [ˌstepbaɪ'step] Schritt-für-Schritt- **II**
stepmum ['stepmʌm] Stiefmutter **I**
stew [stju:] Eintopf ⟨**III TR3**, 114⟩
*to **stick** [stɪk] kleben; stecken **III TMS1**, 30
still [stɪl] Standbild °**III AC1**, 34
still [stɪl] reglos; bewegungslos; still; ruhig **II**
  *to keep one's feet or hands **still** [ˌki:p wʌnz 'fi:t‿ɔː 'hændz stɪl] die Beine und Hände ruhig halten **III TMS1**, 29
still [stɪl] noch; immer noch **I**; dennoch **II**
stomach ['stʌmək] Magen; Bauch **II**
stomachache ['stʌməkeɪk] Bauchschmerzen; Bauchweh **II**
stone [stəʊn] Stein; Stein- **III U2**, 50
bus **stop** ['bʌs ˌstɒp] Bushaltestelle **I**
to **stop** [stɒp] aufhören (mit); anhalten; stoppen **I**
  Stop it! ['stɒp ɪt] Mach/Macht das aus!; Hör/Hört auf! **I**
stop [stɒp] Halt; Stopp **I**
storm [stɔːm] Sturm **I**
stormy ['stɔːmi] stürmisch ⟨**III TMS1**, 32⟩
story, **stories** (pl) ['stɔːri; 'stɔːriz] Story; Geschichte; Erzählung **I**
storyboard ['stɔːribɔːd] Szenenbuch; Storyboard **III U1**, 19
straight [streɪt] gerade; direkt; geradewegs **III U4**, 105
  straight on [streɪt 'ɒn] geradeaus **I**
hair **straightener** ['heə ˌstreɪtnə] Haarglätter **I**
strange [streɪndʒ] fremd; seltsam; merkwürdig **I**
stranger ['streɪndʒə] Fremde/-r **III TMS1**, 30
street [stri:t] Straße (in der Stadt) **I**
  in the **street** [ˌɪn ðə 'stri:t] auf der Straße **I**
  the high **street** [ðə 'haɪ ˌstri:t] die Haupteinkaufsstraße **III U1**, 20
*to be **stressed** out [bi ˌstrest 'aʊt] völlig gestresst sein **III U1**, 12
strong [strɒŋ] stark **II**
structure ['strʌktʃə] Struktur; Aufbau; Gliederung **III TMS1**, 31
stud [stʌd] Stecker **III U1**, 19

student ['stju:dnt] Schüler/-in; Student/-in **I**
  exchange **student** [ɪks'tʃeɪndʒ ˌstju:dnt] Austauschschüler/-in **III AC1**, 34
  student exchange [ˌstju:dnt ɪks'tʃeɪndʒ] Schüleraustausch **III AC2**, 57
studies (pl) ['stʌdiz] …wissenschaft; …wissenschaften **II**
studio ['stju:diəʊ] Studio; Atelier **II**
  recording **studio** [rɪ'kɔːdɪŋ ˌstju:diəʊ] Aufnahmestudio; Tonstudio **I**
to **study** ['stʌdi] lernen; studieren **III U1**, 12
studying ['stʌdiɪŋ] Lernen; Studieren **I**
stuff (no pl) [stʌf] Zeug **I**
stupid ['stju:pɪd] dumm; blöd **II**
style [staɪl] Stil °**III U3**, 68
subject ['sʌbdʒɪkt] Betreff in E-Mails etc.; Thema **I**; Schulfach **II**; Subjekt; Satzgegenstand °**III U3**, 70
to **subscribe** [səb'skraɪb] abonnieren **III U1**, 10
success [sək'ses] Erfolg **III U1**, 12
successful [sək'sesfl] erfolgreich **III U1**, 14
suddenly ['sʌdnli] plötzlich; auf einmal **II**
sugar ['ʃʊɡə] Zucker **I**
to **suggest** [sə'dʒest] vorschlagen **II**
suggestion [sə'dʒestʃn] Vorschlag; Anregung **II**
suitcase ['su:tkeɪs] Koffer **III U4**, 95
to **sum** up [ˌsʌm‿'ʌp] zusammenfassen °**III U1**, 14
sun [sʌn] Sonne **II**
Sunday ['sʌndeɪ] Sonntag **I**
sunny ['sʌni] sonnig **I**
superhero ['su:pəˌhɪərəʊ] Superheld **II**
supermarket ['su:pəˌmɑːkɪt] Supermarkt **I**
supernatural [ˌsu:pə'nætʃrl] übernatürlich **III U4**, 107
to **support** [sə'pɔːt] unterstützen **II**
sure [ʃʊə; ʃɔː] sicher **I**
  *to be **sure** [bi 'ʃʊə] sicher sein **II**
  *to make **sure** [meɪk 'ʃɔː] sichergehen; achten auf **III U1**, 10
(wind) **surfing** ['(wɪnd) sɜːfɪŋ] (Wind-)Surfen **II**
surgery ['sɜːdʒəri] Arztpraxis; Praxis; Praxisräume **I**
surname ['sɜːneɪm] Nachname **I**
surprise [sə'praɪz] Überraschung **I**
to **surprise** [sə'praɪz] überraschen **II**
*to be **surprised** [bi sə'praɪzd] überrascht sein **II**
surprising [sə'praɪzɪŋ] überraschend **I**
survey ['sɜːveɪ] Umfrage; Studie **I**
to **survive** [sə'vaɪv] überleben **III U4**, 104
suspense [sə'spens] Spannung **II**
swan [swɒn] Schwan **I**
sweet [swi:t] süß **I**
sweets (pl) [swi:ts] Süßigkeiten; Bonbons **I**
*to **swim** [swɪm] schwimmen **I**
swimming ['swɪmɪŋ] Schwimmen **I**
  swimming things (pl only) ['swɪmɪŋ ˌθɪŋz] Schwimmsachen **II**
switch [swɪtʃ] Schalter **III U2**, 53

to **switch** [swɪtʃ] wechseln °**III U4**, 98
sword [sɔːd] Schwert **II**
syllable ['sɪləbl] Silbe **III TMS1**, 32
system ['sɪstəm] System **III U4**, 109

T

table ['teɪbl] Tisch **I**
tablet ['tæblət] Tablet **I**
tae [tə] um zu ⟨**III U2**, 47⟩
tail [teɪl] Schwanz; Schweif **I**
*to **take** [teɪk] nehmen; mitnehmen; wegnehmen; bringen; mitbringen; dauern; (Zeit) brauchen **I**
  *to **take** a message [ˌteɪk ə 'mesɪdʒ] eine Nachricht entgegennehmen; jmdm. etw. ausrichten **I**
  *to **take** care of sb/sth [teɪk 'keər‿əv] sich um jmdn./etw. kümmern; für jmdn. sorgen **III U3**, 74
  *to **take** off [teɪk 'ɒf] abnehmen; herunternehmen; ausziehen **II**
  *to **take** part (in) [teɪk 'pɑːt (ɪn)] teilnehmen (an) **II**
  *to **take** photos [teɪk 'fəʊtəʊz] fotografieren; Fotos machen **I**
  *to **take** place [teɪk 'pleɪs] stattfinden **II**
  *to **take** sth seriously [teɪk 'sɪəriəsli] etw. ernst nehmen **II**
  *to **take** turns [teɪk 'tɜːnz] sich abwechseln **II**
talent ['tælənt] Talent **I**
  talent show ['tælənt ˌʃəʊ] Talentwettbewerb **I**
small **talk** [ˌsmɔːl ˌtɔːk] Smalltalk **III AC2**, 56
to **talk** [tɔːk] sprechen; reden **I**
  to **talk** about ['tɔːk əbaʊt] sprechen über; erzählen von **I**
  to **talk** to ['tɔːk tə] reden mit **I**
talker ['tɔːkə] Sprecher/-in **III AC2**, 56
tall [tɔːl] groß; hoch **II**
tap [tæp] Wasserhahn **III U1**, 11
to **tap** [tæp] antippen **II**
tartan ['tɑːtn] Schottenkaro (bestimmtes Muster eines Clans); karierter Schottenstoff **III U2**, 41
to **taste** [teɪst] probieren; kosten; schmecken ⟨**III TR1**, 110⟩
tasty ['teɪsti] lecker; schmackhaft **III U4**, 102
tattoo [tæt'u:] Tattoo; Tätowierung **III U1**, 19
taxi ['tæksi] Taxi **II**
tea [ti:] Tee **I**
  cream **tea** [ˌkri:m 'ti:] Cream Tea (südwestenglische Spezialität: Tee mit süßen Brötchen, die mit stichfestem Rahm und Marmelade serviert werden) **II**
teabag ['ti:bæg] Teebeutel **III U3**, 77
*to **teach** [ti:tʃ] unterrichten; lehren; beibringen **II**
  *to **teach** somebody a lesson [ˌti:tʃ ə 'lesn] jmdm. eine Lehre/Lektion erteilen **II**
teacher ['ti:tʃə] Lehrer/-in **I**

head **teacher** [ˌhed ˈtiːtʃə] Schulleiter/-in III TMS2, 80

team [tiːm] Team; Gruppe II

*to **tear** apart [ˌteər ə'pɑːt] auseinanderreißen; zerreißen ⟨III TMS1, 30⟩

to **tease** sb [tiːz] jmdn. aufziehen; jmdn. hänseln; jmdn. ärgern III U1, 23

technical [ˈteknɪkl] technisch; fachlich; handwerklich III U1, 10

technology [tekˈnɒlədʒi] Computerunterricht; Technik II

teen [tiːn] Jugend- II

teenager [ˈtiːnˌeɪdʒə] Teenager; Jugendliche/-r II

telephone [ˈtelɪfəʊn] Telefon II

television [ˈtelɪvɪʒn] Fernsehen; Fernseher III U2, 43

*to **tell** [tel] erzählen; sagen; mitteilen I
I was just **telling** [ˌaɪ wəz dʒast ˈtelɪŋ] ich habe gerade gesagt ⟨III U1, 15⟩
Tell me about … [ˈtel miː əˌbaʊt] Erzähle/ Erzählt mir von … I

ten [ten] zehn I

tennis [ˈtenɪs] Tennis I

tense [tens] Zeit (grammatisch); Zeitform (grammatisch) °III U1, 11

tent [tent] Zelt ⟨III TR1, 110⟩

term [tɜːm] Begriff II; Trimester; Semester; Halbjahr III U3, 66

terms [tɜːmz] Bestimmungen; Bedingungen III TMS1, 29

terrible [ˈterəbl] furchtbar; schrecklich; schlimm ⟨III TR2, 112⟩

test [test] Test; Klassenarbeit; Prüfung I

text [tekst] Text; Kurznachricht; SMS II
text (message) [ˈtekst ˌmesɪdʒ] SMS; Kurznachricht I

to **text** [tekst] eine SMS schicken I

than [ðæn] als (bei Vergleichen) II
rather **than** [ˈrɑːðə ðən] eher als III U3, 65
more … **than** [ˈmɔː ðən] mehr … als I

Thank you very much! [ˈθæŋk ju veri ˈmʌtʃ] Vielen Dank!; Herzlichen Dank! III U1, 10
Thank you. [ˈθæŋk ju] Danke. I
Thanks. [θæŋks] Danke. I

thankful [ˈθæŋkfl] dankbar I

that much [ðæt ˈmʌtʃ] so viel III AC1, 35

that [ðæt; ðət] dass II
so (**that**) [ˌsəʊ ˈðæt] damit; so dass II

that [ðæt] das; jenes I
after **that** [ˌɑːftə ˈðæt] danach I
like **that** [ˌlaɪk ˈðæt] so I
That was close! [ˌðæt wəz ˈkləʊs] Das war knapp! I
that's how [ˌðæts ˈhaʊ] so I
That's what friends are for. [ˌðæts wɒt ˈfrendz ɑː ˌfɔː] Dafür sind Freunde da. I
That's … [ˌðæts] Das macht … I

that [ðæt] der; dem; den; die; das (Relativpronomen) III U3, 66
a sign **that** … [ə ˌsaɪn ˈðæt] ein Schild, das … ⟨III U2, 51⟩

the [ðə; ði] der; die (auch Pl.); das I

the same [ðə ˈseɪm] der-/die-/dasselbe; der/die/das gleiche I

the … **the** [ðə ðə] je … desto II

theatre [ˈθɪətə] Theater I

their [ðeə] ihr/-e (Pl.) I

theirs [ðeəz] ihre-/r/-es ⟨III TR2, 112⟩

them [ðem] sie (Pl.); ihnen I

theme [θiːm] Thema; Motto II

themselves [ðəmˈselvz] sie (selbst); sich (selbst); selbst; selber III U1, 9

then [ðen] dann; danach I
back **then** [bæk ˈðen] damals II
just **then** [ˌdʒʌst ˈðen] genau in dem Moment I

there [ðeə] da; dort; dahin; dorthin I
over **there** [ˌəʊvə ˈðeə] da drüben; dort drüben; nach dort drüben I
there's (= there is) [ðeəz] es gibt I
there is/are [ðər ˈɪz/ɑː] es gibt I

these [ðiːz] diese (hier) I
these days [ˌðiːz ˈdeɪz] heute; heutzutage; zurzeit III U1, 20

they [ðeɪ] sie (Pl.) I
It's …/**They**'re … [ɪts/ðeə] Es kostet …/ Sie kosten … I

thick [θɪk] dick (nicht für Personen) ⟨III U2, 47⟩; dick III U2, 50

thing [θɪŋ] Ding; Sache I

thingy [ˈθɪŋi] Dingsda ⟨III TR3, 115⟩

*to **think** [θɪŋk] denken; nachdenken; glauben; finden (= der Meinung sein) I
*to **think** of [ˈθɪŋk əv] halten von; denken über I
*to **think** of [ˈθɪŋk əv] (sich) ausdenken; sich etwas einfallen lassen II

thirdly [ˈθɜːdli] drittens II

thirteen [ˌθɜːˈtiːn] dreizehn I

this [ðɪs] dies; diese-/r/-s I
like **this** [ˌlaɪk ˈðɪs] so II
this afternoon [ðɪs ɑːftəˈnuːn] heute Nachmittag II
this early [ˈðɪs ˌɜːli] so früh III AC1, 35

thistle [ˈθɪsl] Distel III U2, 54

those [ðəʊz] diese dort; jene I

thought [θɔːt] Gedanke II

thousands of [ˈθaʊzndz əv] tausende (von) III U2, 42

three [θriː] drei I

through [θruː] durch I

*to **throw** (at) [θrəʊ] werfen (nach) I
*to **throw** away [ˌθrəʊ əˈweɪ] wegwerfen I

thunder (no pl) [ˈθʌndə] Donner II

thunderous [ˈθʌndrəs] donnernd ⟨III TMS1, 32⟩

Thursday [ˈθɜːzdeɪ] Donnerstag I

ticket [ˈtɪkɪt] Los; Ticket; Eintrittskarte I; Fahrschein II
one-way **ticket** [ˈwʌnweɪ ˌtɪkɪt] einfache Fahrkarte II
return **ticket** [rɪˈtɜːn ˌtɪkɪt] Hin- und Rückfahrkarte II
single **ticket** [ˈsɪŋgl ˌtɪkɪt] einfache Fahrkarte II

ticket office [ˈtɪkɪt ˌɒfɪs] Kartenausgabestelle; Vorverkaufsschalter; Fahrkartenschalter III U2, 50

tide [taɪd] Flut II
high **tide** [ˈhaɪ ˌtaɪd] Flut II
low **tide** [ˈləʊ ˌtaɪd] Ebbe II

to **tidy** (a room) [ˈtaɪdi] aufräumen; in Ordnung bringen I
to **tidy** (up) [ˌtaɪdi ˈʌp] sauber machen II

to **tie** (to) [ˈtaɪ (tə)] binden (an); festbinden (an) III U2, 51

'**til** (= until) [tɪl] bis ⟨III TMS1, 27⟩

till [tɪl] bis I

time [taɪm] Zeit I; Mal II
all the **time** [ˌɔːl ðə ˈtaɪm] die ganze Zeit II
at the same **time** [ət ðə ˌseɪm ˈtaɪm] gleichzeitig; zur selben Zeit II
free **time** (no pl) [ˌfriː ˈtaɪm] Freizeit I
local **time** [ˈləʊkl ˌtaɪm] Ortszeit III U4, 96
on **time** [ɒn ˈtaɪm] pünktlich II
at this **time** [ət ðɪs ˈtaɪm] zu dieser Zeit III U3, 65
I can't wait till next **time**. [aɪ kɑːnt ˌweɪt tɪl nekst ˈtaɪm] Ich kann es bis zum nächsten Mal kaum erwarten. II
Time to get up! [ˌtaɪm tə ˌget ˈʌp] Es ist Zeit aufzustehen! I
What **time**? [ˌwɒt ˈtaɪm] Um wie viel Uhr? I
What's the **time**? [ˌwɒts ðə ˈtaɪm] Wie spät ist es?; Wie viel Uhr ist es? I

opening **times** [ˈəʊpnɪŋ ˌtaɪmz] Öffnungszeiten II

timetable [ˈtaɪmˌteɪbl] Stundenplan; Fahrplan I

tin [tɪn] Zinn II; Dose; Büchse ⟨III TR1, 110⟩
tin can [ˈtɪn kæn] Blechdose III U2, 53

tin whistle [ˈtɪn ˌwɪsl] Blechflöte ⟨III TR3, 114⟩

tinned [tɪnd] Dosen-; aus der Dose II

tiny [ˈtaɪni] klein; winzig III U2, 48

tip [tɪp] Tipp; Ratschlag II

to **tiptoe** [ˈtɪptəʊ] auf Zehenspitzen gehen II

tired [taɪəd] müde I

title [ˈtaɪtl] Titel; Überschrift III TMS1, 27

to [tʊ; tə] zu; nach; auf; in; an; vor (bei Uhrzeitangaben) I
from … **to** [frəm tə] von … bis I
quarter past/**to** [ˈkwɔːtə pɑːst/tə] Viertel nach/vor I
to the point [tə ðə ˈpɔɪnt] prägnant; treffend III AC2, 57
to this day [tə ðɪs ˈdeɪ] bis heute III U3, 65

toast [təʊst] Toast I

tobacco (no pl) [təˈbækəʊ] Tabak III U3, 66

today [təˈdeɪ] heute I

together [təˈgeðə] zusammen; miteinander; gemeinsam I

toilet [ˈtɔɪlət] Toilette I

tomato, tomatoes (pl) [təˈmɑːtəʊ; təˈmɑːtəʊz] Tomate I

tomorrow [təˈmɒrəʊ] morgen I

too [tuː] auch; zu I
me **too** [mi ˌtuː] ich auch I
Too bad! [ˌtuː ˈbæd] Zu dumm!; Schade! I

You **too**? [juː 'tuː] Du auch?; Ihr auch? **I**
tool [tuːl] Werkzeug; Gerät **II**
to **top** up [tɒp ˌʌp] aufladen **II**
top [tɒp] Spitzen-; oberste/-r/-s; beste/
-r/-s **I**
on **top** [ɒn 'tɒp] oben; obendrauf **II**
topic ['tɒpɪk] Thema **III U1**, 10
torch [tɔːtʃ] Taschenlampe; Fackel **II**
to stay in **touch** (with) [ˌsteɪ ɪn 'tʌtʃ wɪð] in
Kontakt bleiben (mit) **II**
tour [tʊə] Tour; Fahrt; Rundgang **I**
package **tour** ['pækɪdʒ ˌtʊə] Pauschalreise **III U4**, 102
tour operator ['tʊər ˌɒpreɪtə] Reiseveranstalter **III U4**, 102
tourism ['tɔːrɪzm] Tourismus **II**
tourist ['tɔːrɪst] Tourist/-in **I**
tourist information centre [ˌtɔːrɪst
ɪnfə'meɪʃn ˌsentə] Touristeninformation **I**
towards [tə'wɔːdz] in … Richtung; auf …
zu; darauf zu **II**
tower [taʊə] Turm **III U2**, 50
town [taʊn] Stadt **I**
toy [tɔɪ] Spielzeug **I**
tradition [trə'dɪʃn] Tradition **II**
traditional [trə'dɪʃnl] traditionell **III U2**, 40
traffic ['træfɪk] Verkehr **III U4**, 100
traffic light ['træfɪk ˌlaɪt] Ampel **I**
trail [treɪl] Weg; Pfad ⟨**III TR1**, 110⟩
train [treɪn] Zug **I**
to **train** [treɪn] trainieren **II**
trainer ['treɪnə] Trainer/-in **II**; Turnschuh
III U1, 14
to **translate** [trænz'leɪt] übersetzen **II**
transport ['trænspɔːt] Verkehrsmittel;
Transport **I**
means of **transport** (sg or pl) [ˌmiːnz əv
'trænspɔːt] Transportmittel; Verkehrsmittel **III U4**, 95
public **transport** (no pl) [ˌpʌblɪk
'trænspɔːt] öffentliche Verkehrsmittel **II**
travel ['trævl] Reise- **III U4**, 95
travel agent's ['trævl ˌeɪdʒnts] Reisebüro
II
travel report [ˌtrævl rɪ'pɔːt] Reisebericht
II
to **travel** ['trævl] fahren; reisen **II**
travelling (no pl) ['trævlɪŋ] (das) Reisen **II**
tray [treɪ] Tablett **I**
treasure ['treʒə] Schatz **II**
to **treat** [triːt] behandeln **III U1**, 21
palm **tree** ['pɑːm ˌtriː] Palme **II**
pony **trekking** ['pəʊni ˌtrekɪŋ] Ponyreiten im
Gelände **II**
trial [traɪəl] Qualifikation **II**
tribe [traɪb] Stamm; Volksstamm **III U3**, 63
trick [trɪk] Trick; Streich **I**
to play a **trick** (on) [ˌpleɪ ə 'trɪk ɒn] einen
Streich spielen **I**
trifle ['traɪfl] Trifle (britischer Nachtisch) **II**
trip [trɪp] Trip; Reise; Ausflug; Fahrt **I**
triphelper ['trɪphelpə] Triphelfer/-in **II**

trouble ['trʌbl] Ärger; Probleme; Schwierigkeiten **I**
*to get into **trouble** [ˌget ɪntə 'trʌbl] in
Schwierigkeiten geraten **III U1**, 20
*to make **trouble** [ˌmeɪk 'trʌbl] Ärger
machen; in Schwierigkeiten bringen **I**
trousers (pl) ['traʊzəz] Hose **I**
trowel ['traʊəl] Kelle **II**
true [truː] wahr **II**
trust [trʌst] Vertrauen **III TMS1**, 30
to **trust** [trʌst] vertrauen **III U1**, 10
truth [truːθ] Wahrheit **III U4**, 101
to **try** [traɪ] versuchen; probieren **I**
to **try** on [ˌtraɪ 'ɒn] anprobieren **II**
to **try** out [ˌtraɪ 'aʊt] ausprobieren
°**III TMS2**, 87
T-shirt ['tiːʃɜːt] T-Shirt **I**
Tudor ['tjuːdə] Tudor; Tudor- **III U3**, 65
Tuesday ['tjuːzdeɪ] Dienstag **I**
tuna ['tjuːnə] Thunfisch **II**
tunnel ['tʌnl] Tunnel **I**
It's your **turn**. [ˌɪts 'jɔː tɜːn] Du bist dran. **I**
*to take **turns** [teɪk 'tɜːnz] sich abwechseln **II**
to **turn** (into) [tɜːn 'ɪntə] einbiegen; abbiegen **I**
to **turn** around [tɜːn ə'raʊnd] (sich)
umdrehen; wenden **II**
to **turn** back [tɜːn 'bæk] umkehren;
zurückgehen **III U3**, 69
to **turn** down [tɜːn 'daʊn] abdrehen;
niedriger stellen **III U1**, 11
to **turn** in [ˌtɜːn 'ɪn] sich stellen
⟨**III TR2**, 112⟩
to **turn** off [tɜːn 'ɒf] abschalten; ausschalten **II**
to **turn** on [ˌtɜːn 'ɒn] einschalten **II**
to **turn** to ['tɜːn tə] sich wenden an; sich
zuwenden **II**
turning point ['tɜːnɪŋ ˌpɔɪnt] Wendepunkt
III U1, 22
tutor ['tjuːtə] Klassenlehrer/-in **I**
tutor group ['tjuːtə ˌgruːp] Klasse (in einer
englischen Schule) **I**
tutorial [tjuː'tɔːriəl] Tutorium; Tutorial **II**
TV [ˌtiː'viː] Fernsehen; Fernseher **I**
on **TV** [ɒn ˌtiː'viː] im Fernsehen **II**
to watch **TV** [ˌwɒtʃ tiː'viː] fernsehen **I**
twelve [twelv] zwölf **I**
twin [twɪn] Zwilling; Zwillings- **II**
to **twist** [ˌtwɪst jɔːr 'æŋkl] sich verrenken **II**
to **twist** your ankle [ˌtwɪst jɔːr 'æŋkl] sich
den Knöchel verrenken **II**
two [tuː] zwei **I**
the **two** of them [ðə 'tuː əv ðəm] beide **II**
two of which ['tuː əv wɪtʃ] zwei davon **II**
type [taɪp] Typ; Art; Sorte **III U1**, 9
smart **type** ['smɑːt ˌtaɪp] Lerntyp; Intelligenztyp **III U1**, 9
to **type** [taɪp] tippen **II**
typical ['tɪpɪkl] typisch **II**

U

u (= you) [juː; jə] du; Sie; ihr **I**
ugly ['ʌgli] hässlich; scheußlich; übel
III U1, 14
umbrella [ʌm'brelə] Regenschirm **III U3**, 78
uncle ['ʌŋkl] Onkel **I**
under ['ʌndə] unter **I**
underground ['ʌndəgraʊnd] U-Bahn
III U1, 25
*to **understand** [ʌndə'stænd] verstehen **II**
understanding [ʌndə'stændɪŋ] Verständnis
II
unfair [ʌn'feə] unfair **II**
unfamiliar [ʌnfə'mɪliə] nicht vertraut; unbekannt **III AC1**, 34
unfinished [ʌn'fɪnɪʃt] unvollendet
°**III TMS1**, 31
unforgettable [ʌnfə'getəbl] unvergesslich
III U4, 102
unfriendly [ʌn'frendli] unfreundlich **II**
uniform ['juːnɪfɔːm] Uniform **I**
unknown [ʌn'nəʊn] unbekannt
⟨**III TMS1**, 32⟩
*to be **unlucky** [bi ʌn'lʌki] Pech haben **II**
unmarked [ʌn'mɑːkt] nicht gekennzeichnet
⟨**III TR1**, 110⟩
unnecessary [ʌn'nesəsri] unnötig; überflüssig; verzichtbar **III TMS2**, 81
unofficial [ʌnə'fɪʃl] inoffiziell **III U2**, 47
unreal [ʌn'rɪəl] unwirklich **III U4**, 107
until [ʌn'tɪl] bis; erst wenn **II**
to **unwrap** [ʌn'ræp] auswickeln; auspacken
II
up [ʌp] hinauf; (nach) oben **II**
to end **up** [ˌend 'ʌp] enden; landen **II**
*to get **up** [ˌget 'ʌp] aufstehen (aus dem
Bett) **I**
*to give **up** [gɪv 'ʌp] aufgeben **III U1**, 13
to look **up** [ˌlʊk 'ʌp] nachschlagen; nachschauen **II**; aufschauen; hochschauen
III U2, 50
What's **up**? [wɒts 'ʌp] Was ist los? **III U1**, 15
update ['ʌpdeɪt] Aktualisierung; Update
III U2, 45
ups and downs [ˌʌps ən 'daʊnz] Höhen und
Tiefen **III TMS1**, 27
*to **upset** [ʌp'set] aus der Fassung bringen
III AC1, 35
upset [ʌp'set] aufgebracht; bestürzt **II**
upstairs [ʌp'steəz] nach oben; im Obergeschoss; oben **II**
us [ʌs] uns **I**
to **use** [juːz] benutzen; verwenden; gebrauchen **I**
*to be **used** to [bi 'juːs tə] gewöhnt sein
an; gewohnt sein **III AC1**, 35
useful ['juːsfl] nützlich; hilfreich **II**
useless ['juːsləs] nutzlos **III U4**, 105
user ['juːzə] Benutzer/-in **II**
usual ['juːʒl] üblich **III U1**, 21
usually ['juːʒli] normalerweise; gewöhnlich; meistens **I**

V

valid ['vælɪd] gültig III U4, 99
valuable ['væljuəbl] wertvoll III U3, 64
vegetable ['vedʒtəbl] Gemüse III U2, 42
vegetarian [ˌvedʒɪ'teəriən] Vegetarier/-in III U2, 42
vegetarian [ˌvedʒɪ'teəriən] vegetarisch III U2, 44
verse [vɜːs] Vers; Strophe III TMS1, 31
version ['vɜːʃn] Version II
versus (vs.) ['vɜːsəs] gegen III U2, 53
very ['veri] sehr I
  very much [ˌveri 'mʌtʃ] sehr I
vet [vet] Tierarzt/Tierärztin I
Victorian [vɪk'tɔːriən] viktorianisch; Viktorianer/-in III U3, 65
video ['vɪdiəʊ] Video II
  video chat ['vɪdiəʊ ˌtʃæt] Videochat II
view [vjuː] Ansicht; Einstellung; Standpunkt III U3, 65; Aussicht; Sicht; Ausblick; Blick ⟨III TR1, 111⟩
  point of **view** [ˌpɔɪnt əv 'vjuː] Standpunkt; Ansicht; Perspektive II
viewer ['vjuːə] Zuschauer/-in II
Viking ['vaɪkɪŋ] Wikinger III U3, 63
village ['vɪlɪdʒ] Dorf II
villain ['vɪlən] Bösewicht II
visa, visas (pl) ['viːzə, 'viːzəz] Visum, Visa (Pl.); Einreisebewilligung III U4, 95
visit ['vɪzɪt] Besuch I
to **visit** ['vɪzɪt] besichtigen; besuchen I
visitor ['vɪzɪtə] Besucher/-in I
visual ['vɪʒuəl] visuell; optisch °III TMS1, 28
vitamin ['vɪtəmɪn] Vitamin III U3, 77
vlog (video blogging) [vlɒg] Vlog (Videoblog) °III U3, 64
vocabulary [və'kæbjəlri] Vokabular; Wortschatz II
voice [vɔɪs] Stimme I
  voice message ['vɔɪs ˌmesɪdʒ] Sprachnachricht I
volleyball ['vɒlibɔːl] Volleyball I
to **vote** [vəʊt] abstimmen; wählen II

W

to **wait** (for) [weɪt] warten (auf) I
  I can't **wait** till next time. [aɪ kɑːnt ˌweɪt tɪl nekst 'taɪm] Ich kann es bis zum nächsten Mal kaum erwarten. II
  Wait and see! [ˌweɪt ənd 'siː] Warte ab! I
*to **wake up** [ˌweɪk 'ʌp] aufwachen; aufwecken III U3, 77
*to go for a **walk** [ˌgəʊ fər ə 'wɔːk] spazieren gehen II
night **walk** ['naɪt wɔːk] Nachtwanderung II
to **walk** [wɔːk] gehen; laufen I
walking ['wɔːkɪŋ] Wandern II
  walking boot ['wɔːkɪŋ ˌbuːt] Wanderschuh II
wall [wɔːl] Wand; Mauer I; Online-Pinnwand III U1, 23

to **want** (to) ['wɒnt (tə)] wollen; mögen II
to **want** (to) ['wɒnt tə] wollen; mögen II
to **want** sb to do sth [ˌwɒnt tə 'duː] wollen, dass jmd. etw. tut III U1, 12
wanna (= want to) (infml) ['wɒnə] will/wollen I
wardrobe ['wɔːdrəʊb] Kleiderschrank I
to **warm** [wɔːm] aufwärmen ⟨III TR1, 110⟩
warm [wɔːm] warm II
to **warn** [wɔːn] warnen I
warrior ['wɒriə] Krieger II
to **wash** [wɒʃ] waschen; sich waschen I
to **wash** up [wɒʃ'ʌp] angespült werden II
washing machine ['wɒʃɪŋ məˌʃiːn] Waschmaschine II
waste [weɪst] Abfall; Müll; Verschwendung III U1, 10
to **waste** [weɪst] verschwenden II
wasteful ['weɪstfl] verschwenderisch III U4, 102
watch [wɒtʃ] Armbanduhr II
to **watch** [wɒtʃ] beobachten; (sich) ansehen; zuschauen I
  to **watch** TV [ˌwɒtʃ tiː'viː] fernsehen I
water ['wɔːtə] Wasser I
  water slide ['wɔːtə ˌslaɪd] Wasserrutsche I
wave [weɪv] Welle I
wax figure ['wæks ˌfɪgə] Wachsfigur II
way [weɪ] Weg I; Art und Weise II
  *to be in the **way** [bi ˌɪn ðə 'weɪ] im Weg sein/stehen I
  *to be on one's **way** [ˌbi ɒn wʌnz 'weɪ] auf dem Weg sein; unterwegs sein I
  *to get in the **way** [ˌget ɪn ðə 'weɪ] stören; im Weg stehen II
  Get out of his **way**. [get ˌaʊt əv hɪz 'weɪ] Geh ihm aus dem Weg. I
  in other **ways** [ɪn ˌʌðə weɪz] auf andere Weise II
  No **way**! [ˌnəʊ 'weɪ] Auf keinen Fall!; keineswegs I
we [wiː; wi] wir I
  We did it! [wi 'dɪd ˌɪt] Wir haben es geschafft! II
  We're from … ['wɪə frɒm] Wir sind aus … I
*to **wear** [weə] anhaben; tragen (Kleidung) I
weather ['weðə] Wetter I
  weather forecast ['weðə ˌfɔːkɑːst] Wettervorhersage II
web [web] Netz; Spinnennetz III U2, 47
  web designer ['web dɪˌzaɪnə] Webdesigner III U1, 15
  web page ['web ˌpeɪdʒ] Website; Internetauftritt II
website ['websaɪt] Website; Internetauftritt I
Wednesday ['wenzdeɪ] Mittwoch I
wee bit ['wiː bɪt] klitzeklein ⟨III U2, 47⟩
week [wiːk] Woche I
weekday ['wiːkdeɪ] Wochentag I
weekend [ˌwiːk'end] Wochenende I

  at the **weekend** [ət ðə ˌwiːk'end] am Wochenende I
Welcome! ['welkəm] Willkommen! II
to **welcome** ['welkəm] willkommen heißen II
  You're **welcome**. [jɔː 'welkəm] Bitte schön.; Nichts zu danken.; Gern geschehen. I
Get **well** soon! [get wel 'suːn] Gute Besserung! III TMS2, 85
well [wel] tja; nun I
Welsh [welʃ] walisisch; Walisisch; Waliser/-in II
west [west] Westen; West- I
western ['westən] westlich; West- III U3, 63
wet [wet] nass II
wetsuit ['wetsuːt] Neoprenanzug II
what [wɒt] was I
  What about … ? ['wɒt əˌbaʊt] Was ist mit …?; Wie wär's mit …? I
  What colour is …? [ˌwɒt 'kʌlər ˌɪz] Welche Farbe hat …? I
  what else [ˌwɒt 'els] was sonst; was noch II
  What luck! [wɒt 'lʌk] Was für ein Glück! III U3, 69
  What on earth …? [ˌwɒtː ˌɒn 'ɜːθ] Was um alles in der Welt …? II
  what the man looked like [ˌwɒt ðə mæn 'lʊkt laɪk] wie der Mann aussah II
  What time? [wɒt 'taɪm] Um wie viel Uhr? I
  What was … like? [ˌwɒt wɒz 'laɪk] Wie war … ? III U3, 32
  What's up? [ˌwɒts'ʌp] Was ist los? III U1, 15
  What's your favourite …? ['wɒts jə ˌfeɪvrɪt] Was ist dein/-e Lieblings …? I
  What's your name? [ˌwɒts jə 'neɪm] Wie heißt du?; Wie heißen Sie? I
  What's the matter? [ˌwɒts ðə 'mætə] Was ist los?; Was hast du? II
  What's the time? [ˌwɒts ðə 'taɪm] Wie spät ist es?; Wie viel Uhr ist es? I
  What's wrong? [ˌwɒts 'rɒŋ] Was ist los?; Was stimmt nicht? II
  … **what** to do. ['wɒt tə duː] … was … tun soll/-st/-t/-en II
wheel [wiːl] Rad; Steuerrad; Steuer I
wheelchair ['wiːltʃeə] Rollstuhl II
when [wen] wenn; wann; als I
whenever [wen'evə] wann immer; jedes Mal, wenn; so oft II
where [weə] wo; wohin I
  Where … from? [ˌweə 'frɒm] Woher …? I
  where I belong [ˌweər aɪ bɪ'lɒŋ] wo ich hingehöre III U4, 104
  … **where** to go. [ˌweə tə 'gəʊ] … wohin ich gehen kann. II
I go **wherever** the wind takes me. [aɪ ˌgəʊ weəˌrevə ðə wɪnd 'teɪks miː] Ich lasse mich treiben. III U4, 107
which [wɪtʃ] der (Relativpronomen); die (Relativpronomen); das (Rela-

tivpronomen); dem *(Relativpronomen);* den *(Relativpronomen)* **III U3**, 66

a **while** [ə ˈwaɪl] eine Weile **I**

while [waɪl] während; solange **II**

to **whip** [wɪp] schlagen **II**

whisky [ˈwɪski] Whisky **III U2**, 42

to **whisper** [ˈwɪspə] flüstern **II**

tin **whistle** [ˈtɪn ˌwɪsl] Blechflöte ⟨**III TR3**, 114⟩

white [waɪt] weiß **I**

who [huː] wer; wem; wen **I**
  Who … for? [ˌhuː ˈfɔː] Für wen …? **I**
  Who's in? [huːz ˈɪn] Wer macht mit?; Wer ist dabei? **II**

who [huː] der *(Relativpronomen);* dem *(Relativpronomen);* den *(Relativpronomen);* die *(Relativpronomen)* **III U3**, 66
  a person **who** … [ə ˌpɜːsn ˈhuː] eine Person, die … ⟨**III U2**, 44⟩
  the only person **who** … [ðiˌəʊnli ˌpɜːsn ˈhuː] der einzige Mensch, der … ⟨**III U1**, 20⟩

whole [həʊl] ganz **I**

whom [huːm] der; die; das **III U3**, 67

whoosh [wʊʃ] wusch **I**

whose [huːz] dessen *(Relativpronomen);* deren *(Relativpronomen)* **II**

why [waɪ] warum **I**

wide [waɪd] breit; weit; ausgedehnt **II**

wife, wives *(pl)* [waɪf, waɪvz] Ehefrau **II**

the **wild** [ðə ˈwaɪld] Wildnis; freie Wildbahn ⟨**III TR1**, 110⟩

wild [waɪld] wild **II**

wildlife *(no pl)* [ˈwaɪldlaɪf] Tierwelt *(in freier Wildbahn)* **II**

will [wɪl] werden **II**

*to **win** [wɪn] gewinnen; siegen **II**

wind [wɪnd] Wind **II**
  I go wherever the **wind** takes me. [aɪ ˌgəʊ weəˌrevə ðə wɪnd ˈteɪks miː] Ich lasse mich treiben. **III U4**, 107

window [ˈwɪndəʊ] Fenster **I**

wine [waɪn] Wein **I**

winner [ˈwɪnə] Gewinner/-in; Sieger/-in **I**

winter [ˈwɪntə] Winter **II**

wise [waɪz] weise ⟨**III TR2**, 112⟩

wish [wɪʃ] Wunsch **II**
  *to make a **wish** [ˌmeɪk ə ˈwɪʃ] sich etwas wünschen **II**
  Best **wishes**, [ˌbest ˈwɪʃɪz] Viele Grüße,; Herzliche Grüße, **III TMS2**, 83

witch [wɪtʃ] Hexe **II**

with [wɪð] mit; bei **I**
  with me [wɪð ˈmiː] mit mir; bei mir **I**

within [wɪˈðɪn] innerhalb (von) ⟨**III TR1**, 111⟩

without [wɪˈðaʊt] ohne **I**

witness [ˈwɪtnəs] Zeuge/Zeugin **II**

wizard [ˈwɪzəd] Zauberer **II**

wobbly [ˈwɒbli] wackelig **II**

woman, women *(pl)* [ˈwʊmən; ˈwɪmɪn] Frau **I**

to **wonder** [ˈwʌndə] sich Gedanken machen; sich fragen **II**

wonderful [ˈwʌndəfl] wunderbar **II**

wood [wʊd] Holz **III U2**, 51

wooden [ˈwʊdn] hölzern; aus Holz **III U2**, 50

Woof! [wʊf] Wau! **I**

word [wɜːd] Wort **I**
  linking **word** [ˈlɪŋkɪŋ ˌwɜːd] Bindewort °**III U2**, 48
  prop **word** [ˈprɒp ˌwɜːd] Stützwort °**III U3**, 63
  word bank [ˈwɜːd ˌbæŋk] Wortsammlung °**III AC1**, 34

work [wɜːk] Arbeit **I**

to **work** [wɜːk] arbeiten **I**; funktionieren **II**
  to **work** out [wɜːk ˈaʊt] funktionieren; klappen **III U1**, 23

workshop [ˈwɜːkʃɒp] Workshop **I**

world [wɜːld] Erde; Welt **II**

worm [wɜːm] Wurm **I**

*to be **worried** [bi ˈwʌrid] beunruhigt sein; besorgt sein **II**

to **worry** [ˈwʌri] sich Sorgen machen **II**
  Don't **worry**! [ˌdəʊnt ˈwʌri] Keine Sorge! **I**

worse [wɔːs] schlimmer; schlechter **II**

the **worst** [ðə ˈwɜːst] der/die/das schlimmste; der/die/das schlechteste **II**

*to be **worth** [bi ˈwɜːθ] wert sein **I**

would [wʊd] würde-/st/-n/-t **II**
  would have happened [ˌwʊd həv ˈhæpnd] wäre passiert ⟨**III U4**, 105⟩
  would have sent [ˌwʊd həv ˈsent] hätten geschickt ⟨**III U4**, 105⟩
  would like [wʊd ˈlaɪk] würde-/st/-n/-t gern; hätte-/st/-n/-t gern **I**
  would love [wʊd ˈlʌv] würde-/st/-n/-t sehr gern; hätte-/st/-n/-t sehr gern **II**

wounded [ˈwuːndɪd] verletzt; verwundet **III U2**, 50

Wow! [waʊ] Wow! **I**

to **wrap** [ræp] einwickeln; einpacken **II**

wrapping [ˈræpɪŋ] Verpackung; Hülle **II**

wrist [rɪst] Handgelenk **II**

*to **write** [raɪt] schreiben **I**

writer [ˈraɪtə] Autor/-in; Verfasser/-in **II**

written [ˈrɪtn] schriftlich °**III U3**, 67

wrong [rɒŋ] falsch **I**
  *to be **wrong** [bi ˈrɒŋ] unrecht haben; sich irren **I**
  *to go **wrong** [ˌgəʊ ˈrɒŋ] schiefgehen **II**
  What's **wrong**? [ˌwɒts ˈrɒŋ] Was ist los?; Was stimmt nicht? **II**

X

XOXO [ˌhʌgz ən ˈkɪsɪz] Umarmungen und Küsse *(am Ende von E-Mails und SMS)* **I**

Y

yeah *(infml)* [jeə] ja **I**

year [jɪə] Jahr **I**
  11-**year**-old [ɪˌlevnˈjɪərəʊld] 11-Jährige/-r **II**
  18-**year**-old [ˌeɪtiːn ˈjɪərˌəʊld] 18-jährig **II**
  New **Year's** Eve [ˌnjuː ˌjɪəzˈiːv] Silvester **III U2**, 43

yearbook [ˈjɪəbʊk] Jahrbuch **II**

rebel **yell** [ˈrebl jel] Kampfschrei ⟨**III TMS1**, 27⟩

yellow [ˈjeləʊ] gelb **I**

yes [jes] ja **I**

yesterday [ˈjestədeɪ] gestern **II**

yet [jet] schon; noch **II**
  not … **yet** [nɒt ˈjet] noch nicht **II**

yoghurt [ˈjɒgət] Joghurt **I**

you [juː; jə] du; ihr; Sie **I**
  Are **you** …? [ˈɑː ju] Bist du … ?; Sind Sie …?; Seid ihr … ? **I**
  You too? [juː ˈtuː] Du auch?; Ihr auch? **I**
  You're welcome. [jɔː ˈwelkəm] Bitte schön.; Nichts zu danken.; Gern geschehen. **I**
  You're … [jɔːr] Sie sind …; Du bist … **I**

young [jʌŋ] jung **I**

your [jɔː; jə] dein/-e; euer/eure; Ihr/-e **I**
  What's **your** name? [ˌwɒts jə ˈneɪm] Wie heißt du?; Wie heißen Sie? **I**

yours [jɔːz] dein/-er/-e/-es; eure/-r/-s; Ihr/-e **II**
  Yours sincerely, [ˌjɔːz sɪnˈsɪəli] Mit freundlichen Grüßen, **III TMS2**, 80

yourself [jɔːˈself] du (selbst); dir (selbst); dich (selbst); Sie (selbst); sich (selbst); selber **II**

yourselves [jɔːˈselvz] ihr/euch/Sie/sich (selbst); selber **III U1**, 16

yummy [ˈjʌmi] lecker ⟨**III TR3**, 114⟩

Z

zero [ˈzɪərəʊ] null **I**

zone [zəʊn] Zone **II**

zoo [zuː] Zoo; Tierpark **II**

to **zoom** in (on) [zuːm ˈɪn (ɒn)] heranzoomen (auf) **III U3**, 74

Boys' names

Abdi [ˈæbdi] **III U4**, 104

Abdirahman [ˌæbdirəˈmɑːn] **III U4**, 105

Ahmed [ˈæmed] **III U4**, 104

Amir [ɑːˈmiːr] **II**

Andrew [ˈændruː] **I**

Benjamin [ˈbendʒəmɪn] **III U4**, 96

Bob [bɒb] **I**

Carlo [ˈkɑːləʊ] **I**

Charlie [ˈtʃɑːli] **III U4**, 96

Damian [ˈdeɪmiən] **I**

Dave [deɪv] **I**

David [ˈdeɪvɪd] **I**

Desmond [ˈdezmənd] **I**

Dhanu [ˈdɑːnuː] **III U4**, 99

Ethan [ˈiːθn] **III U2**, 42

Filip [ˈfɪlɪp] **I**

Finn [fɪn] **III U1**, 20

Frank [fræŋk] **II**

Hamid [ˈhæmɪd] **II**

Harold [ˈhærəld] **III U3**, 65

Henry [ˈhenri] **I**

Jack [dʒæk] I
Jago ['dʒeɪɡəʊ] II
Jahangir [dʒə'hʌŋɡɪə] I
James [dʒeɪmz] III U2, 42
Jamie ['dʒeɪmi] III TMS1, 30
Jan [jan] I
Jay [dʒeɪ] I
Jim [dʒɪm] III U3, 74
Jinsoo ['dʒɪnzu:] I
John [dʒɒn] II
Jon [dʒɒn] II
Logan ['ləʊɡən] III U2, 41
Luke [lu:k] I
Marley ['mɑ:li] I
Masud [mə'su:d] III U4, 100
Matt [mæt] III U1, 18
Max [mæks] III U1, 20
Michael ['maɪkl] II
Mike [maɪk] II
Nathan ['neɪθn] I
Nick [nɪk] II
Oliver ['ɒlɪvə] III TMS1, 30
Peter ['pi:tə] II
Rafiq [ræ'fɪk] III U4, 99
Robert ['rɒbət] III U1, 10
Sam [sæm] I
Sean [ʃɔ:n] III U1, 23
Shahid [ʃɑ:'hi:d] I
Steve [sti:v] I
Terry ['teri] I
Thomas ['tɒməs] III U3, 78
Tim [tɪm] I
Tony ['təʊni] I
Will [wɪl] II
William ['wɪljəm] III U3, 65

Girls' names

Alicia [ə'lɪsɪə; ə'lɪʃə] I
Alva ['ælvə] III U2, 53
Amalia [ə'mɑ:lɪə] III U1, 10
Amber ['æmbə] I
Amy ['eɪmi] ⟨III TR2, 112⟩
Amy ['eɪmi] III U4, 102
Anna ['ænə] I
Annie ['æni] III U2, 44
Ayla ['eɪlə] I
Carol ['kærəl] I
Catherine ['kæθrɪn] II
Ceri ['keri] II
Ciara [s'jærə] III U4, 107
Claire ['kleə] I
Elizabeth [ɪ'lɪzəbəθ] III U3, 65
Emily ['emɪli] II
Emma ['emə] I
Fowsia [faʊ'zi:ə] III U4, 104
Frances ['frɑ:nsɪs] I
Gwen [gwen] II
Haley ['heɪli] III U4, 107
Helen ['helɪn] II
Holly ['hɒli] I
Irina [ɪ'ri:nə] I
Ivy ['aɪvi] III U1, 14

Jeanette [dʒə'net] III TMS2, 80
Karen ['kærən] ⟨III TR3, 114⟩
Kate [keɪt] III U2, 45
Khadija [kə'di:dʒə] III U4, 104
Kim [kɪm] III U1, 25
Kirsty ['kɜ:sti] III U2, 42
Laura ['lɔ:rə] I
Lauren ['lɔ:rən] II
Lilian ['lɪlɪən] III U2, 55
Lily ['lɪli] I
Lisa ['li:sə] I
Lou [lu:] I
Lucy ['lu:si] I
Maisie ['meɪzi] I
Marian ['mærɪən] II
Mary ['meəri] III U3, 65
Maryan ['mærjən] III U4, 104
Megan ['megən] II
Merlina [mə:'li:nə] II
Mila ['mi:lə] I
Mina ['mi:nə] II
Olivia [ɒl'ɪvɪə] I
Parule [pə'ru:lə] I
Pauline ['pɔ:li:n] III U4, 108
Pia ['pi:ə] I
Polly ['pɒli] II
Rose [rəʊz] I
Ruby ['ru:bi] II
Sabra ['sæbrə] III U4, 104
Sadia ['seɪdjə] III U4, 99
Sally ['sæli] I
Seeta ['si:tə] I
Sophia [sə'fi:ə] II
Sue [su:] III U2, 55
Tamara [tə'mɑ:rə] II
Violet ['vaɪələt] III U3, 77
Vivien ['vɪvjən] II

Surnames

Ashton ['æʃtən] II
Azad [ə'zɑ:d] I
Baines [beɪnz] I
Bates [beɪts] I
Bayram ['beɪrəm] II
Beckett ['bekət] I
Clarkson ['klɑ:ksn] III U4, 96
Dylan ['dɪlən] III U1, 14
Elliot ['elɪət] I
Evans ['evnz] III TMS2, 81
Francis ['frɑ:nsɪs] III U1, 14
Fraser ['freɪzə] I
Green [gri:n] I
Karp [kɑ:p] III U1, 24
Lassiter ['læsɪtə] III U4, 102
Mahmoud [mæ'mu:d] III U4, 105
Miller ['mɪlə] I
Mussa ['mu:sə] III U4, 104
Preston ['prestən] I
Reed [ri:d] III U1, 16
Richardson ['rɪtʃədsn] I
Simons ['saɪmənz] II
Swindon ['swɪndən] I

Thompson ['tɒmsən] II
Walker ['wɔ:kə] I
Wilson ['wɪlsn] III TMS2, 80
Zajac ['zeɪdʒæk] I

Place names

Aberdeen [ˌæbə'di:n] III U2, 40
Angleland ['æŋglænd] III U3, 63
Bankside ['bæŋksaɪd] Stadtteil von London III U3, 72
Bath [bɑ:θ] III U3, 64
Bradford ['brædfəd] II
Brick Lane [brɪk 'leɪn] II
Brook Lane [brʊk 'leɪn] II
Caerphilly [keə'fɪli] walisische Stadt II
Camden Lock Market ['kæmdən lɒk ˌmɑ:kɪt] III U4, 102
Camden Town Station ['kæmdən ˌtaʊn 'steɪʃn] II
College Way [ˌkɒlɪdʒ 'weɪ] I
Cologne [kə'ləʊn] Köln I
Covent Garden [ˌkɒvnt 'gɑ:dn] II
Cracow ['krækɒv; 'krɑ:kaʊ] Krakau I
Dhaka ['dɑ:kə] III U4, 99
Dubai [du:'baɪ] III U4, 104
Dublin ['dʌblɪn] ⟨III TR3, 114⟩
Dunrossness [dʌnrɒs'nes] III U2, 48
Eden Project ['i:dn ˌprɒdʒekt] II
Edinburgh ['edɪnbrə] II
Enfield [en'fi:ld] I
Glasgow ['glɑ:zgəʊ] III U2, 41
Greenwich ['grenɪdʒ] Stadtteil von London I
Greenwich Park [ˌgrenɪdʒ 'pɑ:k] I
Greenwich Pier [ˌgrenɪdʒ 'pɪə] I
Heathrow [ˌhi:θ'rəʊ] Flughafen in London III U4, 101
Inverness [ˌɪnvə'nes] ⟨III TR1, 111⟩
Kidbrooke Gardens [ˌkɪdbrʊk 'gɑ:dnz] I
King William Walk [ˌkɪŋ 'wɪljəm ˌwɔ:k] I
Lanchester ['læntʃestə] III U1, 25
London ['lʌndən] I
Mary King's Close [ˌmeəri kɪŋz 'kləʊs] III U2, 44
Nelson Road [ˌnelsn 'rəʊd] I
Nottingham ['nɒtɪŋəm] ⟨III TR2, 112⟩
Oxford Street ['ɒksfəd ˌstri:t] II
Panitania [ˌpænɪteɪnɪə] III U4, 109
Redruth [ˌred'ru:θ] II
Rosendale Road [ˌrəʊzndeɪl 'rəʊd] II
South Street ['saʊθ ˌstri:t] I
Southend [saʊθ'end] II
St Agnes [ˌseɪnt 'ægnəs] II
St Austell [ˌseɪnt 'ɔstel] II
Stratford-upon-Avon [ˌstrætfədəpɒn'eɪvn] Geburtsort Shakespeares III U3, 68
Tower Hill [ˌtaʊə 'hɪl] II
Victoria Park [vɪktɔ:rɪə 'pɑ:k] II
Waterloo Station [ˌwɔ:təlu: 'steɪʃn] II
York [jɔ:k] Stadt im Norden Englands I

Geographical names

Africa ['æfrɪkə] Afrika II
America [ə'merɪkə] III U3, 67
Aragon ['ærəgən] III U3, 65
Atlantic Ocean [ət,læntɪk 'əʊʃn] Atlantischer Ozean II
Austria ['ɔːstrɪə] Österreich II
Bangladesh [,bæŋglə'deʃ] Bangladesch III U4, 99
Ben Nevis [ben 'nevɪs] *Berg in Schottland* II
Bodmin Moor [,bɒdmɪn 'mɔː] *Hochmoorlandschaft im nordöstlichen Cornwall* II
Britain ['brɪtn] Großbritannien I
British Empire [,brɪtɪʃ'empaɪə] britisches Königreich III U3, 65
British Isles [,brɪtɪʃ'aɪlz] Britische Inseln II
Cairngorm Mountain [,keəngɔːm 'maʊntɪn] ⟨III TR1, 111⟩
Calton Hill [,kɔːltn 'hɪl] III U2, 55
Canberra Road [,kænbrə 'rəʊd] III TMS2, 80
Cape Wrath [,keɪp 'rɔːθ] ⟨III TR1, 110⟩
China ['tʃaɪnə] China I
City Hall [,sɪti 'hɔːl] III U4, 102
Cornwall ['kɔːnwɔːl] I
England ['ɪŋglənd] England I
Europe ['jʊərəp] Europa I
European Union (EU) [jʊərəpɪən 'juːnjən; iːjuː] Europäische Union III U3, 65
Fort William [,fɔːt 'wɪljəm] ⟨III TR1, 110⟩
France [frɑːns] Frankreich III U3, 65
Galumphia [gə'lʌmfɪə] III U2, 44
Germany ['dʒɜːməni] Deutschland I
Great Britain (GB) [,greɪt 'brɪtn] Großbritannien II
the Highlands [ðə 'haɪləndz] ⟨III TR1, 110⟩
Ireland ['aɪələnd] Irland II
Isle of Dogs [,aɪl əv 'dɒgz] I
Italy ['ɪtəli] Italien II
Kent [kent] *Grafschaft im Südosten Englands* II
Kenya ['kenjə] Kenia III U4, 104
Loch Awe [,lɒx 'ɔː] III U2, 46
Loch Lomond [,lɒx 'ləʊmənd] *See in Schottland* III U2, 45
Loch Ness [,lɒx 'nes; ,lɒk 'nes] *See in Schottland* III U2, 41
the Lowlands [ðə 'ləʊləndz] *schottische Landschaft* III U2, 45
Napada [nə'pɑːdə] III U4, 109
Normandy ['nɔːməndi] die Normandie III U3, 65
North Carolina [,nɔːθ kær'laɪnə] III U3, 67
North Sea [,nɔːθ 'siː] Nordsee II
Northern Ireland [,nɔːðn 'aɪələnd] Nordirland II
Pakistan [,pɑːkɪ'stɑːn] I
Panville ['pænvɪl] III U4, 109
Park Street [,pɑːk 'striːt] III TMS2, 81
Poland ['pəʊlənd] Polen I
Republic of Ireland [rɪ,pʌblɪk əv 'aɪələnd] Republik Irland II
River Liffey [,rɪvə 'lɪfi] ⟨III TR3, 114⟩

Roanoake Island [,rəʊənəʊk 'aɪlənd] III U3, 67
Russia ['rʌʃə] Russland I
Scandinavia [,skændɪ'neɪvɪə] Skandinavien III U2, 44
Scotland ['skɒtlənd] Schottland II
Sherwood Forest [,ʃɜːwʊd 'fɒrɪst] ⟨III TR2, 112⟩
the Shetland Islands [ðə 'ʃetlənd ,aɪləndz] die Shetlandinseln III U2, 48
Somalia [sə'mɑːlɪə] Somalia III U4, 104
South America [,saʊθ ə'merɪkə] Südamerika III U3, 65
Syria ['sɪrɪə] Syrien I
Thames [temz] I
Turkey ['tɜːki] Türkei I
United Kingdom (UK) [juː'keɪ] Vereinigtes Königreich von Großbritannien und Nordirland II
USA (United States of America) [,juːes'eɪ; juː,naɪtɪd ,steɪts əv ə'merɪkə] USA (Vereinigte Staaten von Amerika) II
Wales [weɪlz] II

Other names

Auld Lang Syne [,ɔːld læŋ 'saɪn] *schottisches Volkslied* III U3, 43
Balmoral Castle [bæl,mɒrəl 'kɑːsl] *schottische Residenz der britischen Königsfamilie* III U2, 45
Battle of Hastings [,bætl əv 'heɪstɪŋz] III U3, 65
Battle of Trafalgar [,bætl əv trə'fælgə] III U3, 63
Bayeux Tapestry [,baɪjɜː 'tæpɪstri] Wandteppich von Bayeux III U3, 65
Beefeater ['biːfiːtə] *königlicher Leibgardist* II
Best Young Tech Entrepreneur [,best jʌŋ ,tek ɒntrəprə'nɜː] III U1, 24
Big Ben [,bɪg 'ben] II
Black Death [,blæk 'deθ] III U3, 63
Brexit ['breksɪt] III U3, 65
British Airways [,brɪtɪʃ'eəweɪz] *Fluggesellschaft* III U4, 101
British Museum [,brɪtɪʃ mjuː'ziːəm] II
Buckingham Palace [,bʌkɪŋəm 'pælɪs] II
Business Week ['bɪznɪs wiːk] *Wirtschaftszeitung* III U1, 24
Church of England [,tʃɜːtʃ əv 'ɪŋglənd] III U3, 65
Civil War [,sɪvl 'wɔː] Bürgerkrieg III U3, 63
Comic Relief [,kɒmɪk rɪ'liːf] *wohltätige Organisation* II
Crossharbour ['krɒs,hɑːbə] II
Cutty Sark [,kʌti 'sɑːk] I
Docklands Light Railway (DLR) [,dɒklændz ,laɪt 'reɪlweɪ] *Regionalbahn im Osten Londons* I
Dunnottar Castle [dʌn,ɒtə 'kɑːsl] III U2, 40

Edinburgh Fringe Festival [,edɪnbrə ,festɪvl 'frɪndʒ] *jährliches Kulturfestival in Edinburgh* III U2, 41
Elephant & Castle ['elɪfənt ən kɑːsl] II
Emerald Isle ['emrld ,aɪl] ⟨III TR3, 115⟩
Emigration Museum [emɪ,greɪʃn mjuː'ziəm] ⟨III TR3, 114⟩
Fan Museum [,fæn mjuː'ziːəm] I
Feast of Samhain [,fiːst əv 'saʊɪn] III U3, 63
Flower of Scotland [,flaʊər əv 'skɒtlənd] III U2, 47
the Globe Theatre [ðə ,gləʊb 'θɪətə] III U3, 68
God Save the Queen ['gɒd seɪv ðə ,kwiːn] Gott schütze die Königin *(britische Nationalhymne)* III U2, 47
Great Fire of London [,greɪt faɪər əv 'lʌndən] III U3, 63
Greenwich Foot Tunnel [,grenɪdʒ 'fʊt ,tʌnl] I
Hadrian's Wall [,heɪdrɪənz 'wɔːl] III U3, 63
Halloween [,hæləʊ'iːn] *Tag vor Allerheiligen* III U3, 63
Hamlet ['hæmlət] III U3, 68
the Highland Games ['haɪlənd geɪmz] III U2, 45
Hogmanay ['hɒgməneɪ] *traditionelles schottisches Neujahrsfest* III U2, 43
Hogwarts ['hɒgwɔːts] II
Hogwarts Express ['hɒgwɔːts ɪk,spres] II
Horse Guards Parade [,hɔːs 'gɑːdz pə,reɪd] II
the Houses of Parliament [ðə ,haʊzɪz əv 'pɑːləmənt] *britisches Parlamentsgebäude* II
HTML [,eɪdʒtiː'emel] III U1, 12
Ice Age ['aɪs ,eɪdʒ] Eiszeit III U3, 63
Industrial Revolution [ɪn,dʌstrɪəl revl'uːʃn] die industrielle Revolution III U3, 65
Instagram ['ɪnstəgræm] III TMS1, 26
Jewel House [,dʒuːəl 'haʊs] II
Jubilee ['dʒuːbɪliː] II
London Dungeons [,lʌndən 'dʌndʒnz] II
London Eye [,lʌndən_'aɪ] II
London Wall [,lʌndən 'wɔːl] II
London Zoo [,lʌndən 'zuː] II
Madame Tussauds [,mædəm tʊ'sɔːdz] II
Magna Carta [,mægnə 'kɑːtə] III U3, 63
Meridian Line [mə,rɪdɪən 'laɪn] Nullmeridian I
Millennium Bridge [mɪ,lenɪəm 'brɪdʒ] II
Millennium Footbridge [mɪ,lenɪəm 'fʊtbrɪdʒ] II
Mizscorpio [mɪz'skɔːpɪəʊ] III TMS1, 30
Mother's Day ['mʌðəz ,deɪ] Muttertag III TMS1, 26
Mudchute Farm [,mʌdʃuːt 'fɑːm] I
Natural History Museum [,nætʃrl 'hɪstri mjuː,ziːəm] II
Oxford Circus [,ɒksfəd 'sɜːkəs] II
Oyster card ['ɔɪstə ,kɑːd] II
Red Nose Day [,red nəʊz 'deɪ] II
Roman Empire [,rəʊmən 'empaɪə] Römisches Reich III U3, 63
Royal Observatory [,rɔɪəl əb'zɜːvətri] I

Royal Shakespeare Company [ˌrɔɪəl ˈʃeɪkspɪə ˌkʌmpəni] III U3, 68

Second World War [ˌseknd ˌwɜːld ˈwɔː] Zweiter Weltkrieg III U3, 65

Shakespeare's Globe [ˌʃeɪkspɪəz ˈgleʊb] II

Shetland Crofthouse Museum III U2, 48

Spanish Armada [ˌspænɪʃ ɑːˈmɑːdə] Spanische Flotte III U3, 66

St Patrick's Day [sn ˈpætrɪks ˌdeɪ] ⟨III TR3, 115⟩

Tandoori [tænˈdʊəri] I

Temple Bar [ˈtempl ˌbaː] III TR3, 114

The Pier [ðə ˈpɪə] II

Thomas Tallis School (= TTS) [ˌtɒməs ˈtælɪs ˌskuːl] I

Titan Clydebank [ˌtaɪtən ˈklaɪdbæŋk] III U2, 48

the Tower of London [ðə ˌtaʊər əv ˈlʌndən] II

Transport Museum [ˌtrænspɔːt mjuːˈziːəm] II

TTS planner [ˌtiːtiːˌes ˈplænə] Handbuch für TTS-Schülerinnen und -Schüler I

the Tube [ðə ˈtjuːb] die Londoner U-Bahn II

Tumblr [ˈtʌmblə] III U1, 24

Twinkle, twinkle, little star! [ˌtwɪnkl ˈtwɪnkl lɪtl ˈstaː] III TMS1, 30

Twitter [ˈtwɪtə] III TMS1, 26

Venn diagram [ˈven ˌdaɪəgræm] III TMS1, 33

Victoria [vɪkˈtɔːriə] II

Weezer [ˈwiːzə] III U4, 98

Whitehall [ˈwaɪthɔːl] Straße in London II

World Heritage Site [ˌwɜːld ˌherɪtɪdʒ ˈsaɪt] Welterbestätte (von der UNESCO anerkanntes Weltkulturerbe) III U3, 64

World Heritage Site [ˌwɜːld ˌherɪtɪdʒ ˈsaɪt] Weltkulturerbe (von der UNESCO anerkanntes Weltkulturerbe) III U3, 64

Famous names

Adam Hunter [ˌædəm ˈhʌntə] III U2, 48

Alexander Cumming [ˌælɪgzaːndə ˈkʌmɪŋ] III U3, 78

Alexander Fleming [ˌælɪgzaːndə ˈflemɪŋ] III U2, 43

Andy Murray [ˌændi ˈmʌri] schottischer Tennisspieler III U2, 44

Anne Boleyn [ˌæn ˈbɒlɪn] Mutter von Elizabeth I. III U3, 65

Boudicca [ˈbuːdɪkə] II

Julius Caesar [ˌdʒuːliəs ˈsiːzə] III UΞ, 63

Captain Cook [ˌkæptɪn ˈkʊk] III U3, 63

Charles Macintosh [tʃaːlz ˈmækɪntɒʃ] III U2, 43

Miley Cyrus [ˌmaɪli ˈsaɪrəs] III TMS1, 27

Daniel Craig [ˌdænjəl ˈkreɪg] II

Darwin [ˈdaːwɪn] II

Guy Fawkes [ˌgaɪ ˈfɔːks] III U3, 63

Harry Potter [ˌhæri ˈpɒtə] II

James Bond [ˌdʒeɪmz ˈbɒnd] II

James Watt [ˌdʒeɪmz ˈwɒt] III U2, 43

John Henry Holmes [ˌdʒɒn ˌhenri ˈhəʊmz] III U2, 53

John Logie Baird [ˌdʒɒn ˌləʊgi ˈbeəd] III U2, 43

King Arthur [ˌkɪŋ ˈaːθə] König Artus II

King Edward [kɪŋ ˈedwəd] III U2, 47

Lenny Henry [ˌleni ˈhenri] britischer Comedian II

Miss Marple [mɪs ˈmaːpl] II

Hannah Montana [ˌhænə mɒnˈtænə] III TMS1, 27

Queen Victoria [ˌkwiːn vɪkˈtɔːriə] brit. Königin (1837–1901) I

Robert Hooke [ˌrɒbət ˈhʊk] III U2, 53

Robert the Bruce [ˌrɒbət ðə ˈbruːs] III U2, 47

Robin Hood [ˌrɒbɪn ˈhʊd] II

Robin Hood and his Merry Men [ˌrɒbɪn ˈhʊd ən hɪz ˌmeri ˈmen] ⟨III TR2, 112⟩

Sherlock Holmes [ˌʃɜːlɒk ˈhəʊmz] II

Sir Arthur Conan Doyle [sɜː ˌaːθə ˌkəʊnən ˈdɔɪl] III U2, 43

Sir Francis Drake [sɜː ˌfraːnsɪs ˈdreɪk] III U3, 65

Sir Walter Raleigh [sɜː ˌwɔːltə ˈrɔːli] III U3, 65

Thomas Edison [ˌtɒməs ˈedɪsn] amerik. Erfinder (1847–1931) III U3, 78

the Virgin Queen [ðə ˌvɜːdʒɪn ˈkwiːn] die jungfräuliche Königin (Elizabeth I. wurde so genannt, weil sie nie heiratete.) III U3, 67

William Shakespeare [ˌwɪljəm ˈʃeɪkspɪə] englischer Dramatiker (1564–1616) III U3, 66

William the Conqueror [ˌwɪljəm ðə ˈkɒŋkrə] II

German-English

A

abbiegen to turn (into) I

abblocken to block II

abbrechen to drop out (of) III U1, 12

abbrennen *to burn down III U3, 72

abchecken to check out (coll) III AC2, 56

abdecken to cover III U4, 105

abdrehen to turn down III U1, 11

Abend evening I; night II
heute Abend 2nite (= tonight) I

Abendessen dinner I

abends in the evenings I

abends (Uhrzeit) p.m. I

Abenteuer adventure II

aber but I

abfahren *to leave I; to depart II

Abfall waste III U1, 10

Abflughalle departure lounge III U4, 95

Abgang exit III U3, 65

abgeschlossen locked II

abhalten *to hold III U2, 45

abhängen von to depend (on) II

Abhängigkeit addiction II

abholen to pick up II; to fetch III U4, 105

abkürzen to abbreviate III TMS2, 84

Abkürzung abbreviation I

ablaufen to expire III U4, 99

abonnieren to subscribe III U1, 10

abreißen to pull down III U2, 42

Absatz paragraph III TMS2, 81

abschalten to turn off II

abschneiden *to cut (off) II

sich abschotten von to close oneself away from III U4, 104

Absender/-in sender III TMS2, 82

Absicht purpose III TMS2, 81

absolut absolutely III TMS2, 83

Abstammung origin III U4, 107

abstimmen to vote II

abstürzen to crash II

sich alles abverlangen to push oneself III U1, 15

sich abwechseln *to take turns II

außer Acht lassen to ignore III U1, 21

acht eight I

achten auf *to make sure III U1, 10

Acker field II

Action action II

addieren to add I

Adresse address I

Adverb adverb II

AG club I

aggressiv aggressive II

Ähnlichkeit similarity ⟨III TMS1, 33⟩

Keine Ahnung. No idea. I

Akku battery II

Aktion action II

Aktivität activity I

Aktualisierung update III U2, 45

Akzent accent II

akzeptieren to accept III U4, 104

albern silly I

Album album III TMS1, 29

alle everyone I; everybody II
alle/-s all I
  wir **alle** all of us II
allein alone I; on one's own III U4, 105
alles everything I
alles klar alright (= all right) (III TMS1, 27)
allgemein overall III U4, 102
Alphabet alphabet II
alphabetisch alphabetical II
als (bei Vergleichen) than II
als when I
also so I
alt old I
  Wie **alt** bist du? How old are you? I
  Wie **alt** sind Sie? How old are you? I
  Wie **alt** seid ihr? How old are you? I
Alter age III U1, 12
ältere/-r/-s elderly III U2, 53
Alternative alternative III U4, 103
am on I
  am besten best I
  am Wochenende at the weekend I
Amerikaner/-in American II
Amerikanisch American II
amerikanisch American II
Ampel traffic light I
sich **amüsieren** *to have fun I; to enjoy
  oneself III U1, 15
an on; at; to I; by II
  an Bord aboard I
  an Stelle von instead of III U3, 67
  an meiner Seite by my side (III TMS1, 30)
  an sein *to be on II
Ananas pineapple III U3, 77
anbauen *to grow III U1, 12
anbieten to offer II
andauern to last III TMS1, 30; to continue
  III U4, 99
(die) **anderen** (the) others II
andere/-r/-s other I; else II
  ein/-e **andere/-r/-s** another I
Einerseits …, (aber) **andererseits** … On
  the one hand …, (but) on the other hand
  … II
seine Meinung **ändern** to change one's
  mind III U4, 104
  (sich) **ändern** to change II
anders different; other I
Änderung change II
Andeutung hint III AC2, 57
Anfang beginning; start II
anfangen to start I; *to begin III U3, 63
anfeuern to cheer on II
anführen *to lead III U4, 104
Anführer/-in leader III U3, 65
angeben to show off II
Angeber/-in show-off III U1, 23
Angebot offer I
angekleidet dressed III U3, 69
Angeln fishing II
Angelsachse Anglo-Saxon III U3, 63
Angelsächsin Anglo-Saxon III U3, 63
angelsächsisch Anglo-Saxon III U3, 63

angemessen appropriate III AC1, 35
die **Angesagten** in-crowd III U1, 20
von **Angesicht** zu **Angesicht** face-to-face II
angezogen dressed III U3, 69
angreifen to attack III U3, 63
Angst fear II
  Angst haben (vor) *to be scared (of) I
  Ich habe (keine) **Angst** vor … I'm (not)
  scared of … I
anhaben *to wear I
anhalten to stop I
Anhänger/-in follower III U1, 10; fan
  III AC3, 89
anhören to listen (to) I
anklicken to click on II
ankommen to arrive II
ankommend inward II
Ankündigung announcement II
Ankunft arrival III U4, 102
Ankunftshalle arrivals hall III U4, 95
Anlass occasion III TMS1, 26
anlocken to attract III U1, 10
anmalen to paint I
sich **anmelden** to sign up II
Anmerkung note II
annähernd nearly II
annehmen to guess III AC3, 88; to accept
  III U4, 104
Annehmlichkeit convenience III U4, 95
anonym anonymous II
anordnen *to set out (III TMS2, 87)
anprobieren to try on II
Anregung suggestion II
Anruf phone call I
anrufen to call I
anschauen to look at; *to have a look (at) I
  jmdn. komisch **anschauen** *to give sb
  funny looks III U1, 15
  jmdn. schief **anschauen** *to give sb funny
  looks III U1, 15
anschließen to connect (to) III U3, 62
  sich **anschließen** to join II
ansehen to look at I
(sich) **ansehen** to watch I
Ansicht point of view II; opinion
  III U1, 15; view III U3, 65
jmdn. **ansprechen** to appeal to sb III U2, 49
anstarren to stare I
anstatt instead of III U3, 67
antippen to tap II
Antwort reply; answer II
antworten to answer I; to reply (to) II
Anweisung instruction III AC2, 57
Anwendung app (= application) II
Anwesenheitskontrolle registration II
Anzahl number III U3, 65
anziehen to attract III U1, 10; *to put on
  III U1, 20
Apfel apple I
App app (= application) II
Apparat machine I
April April II
Ära era III U4, 107

Arbeit job; work I
arbeiten to work I
Areal area II
Ärger trouble I
  Ärger machen *to make trouble I
ärgerlich annoying II
jmdn. **ärgern** to tease sb III U1, 23
Argument dafür pro II
  Argument dagegen con II
Arm arm II
arm poor III U1, 21
Armband bracelet I
Armbanduhr watch II
die **Armen** the poor II
Armee army (III U2, 47)
Ärmel sleeve (III TR3, 115)
Art kind (of); species, species (pl) II; type
  III U1, 9
  Art und Weise way II
Arzt/Ärztin doctor II
Arztpraxis surgery I
Atelier studio II
athletisch athletic (III TMS1, 32)
atmen to breathe II
Atmosphäre flair; atmosphere II
Attraktion attraction II
Aua! Ouch! II
auch too I; also II
  auch nicht not … either II
  Du **auch**? You too? I
  ich **auch** me too I
  Ihr **auch**? You too? I
Audio- audio I
auf on; at; to I
  auf der anderen Seite von across;
  opposite I
  auf der Straße in the street I
  auf einmal suddenly II
  auf Wiedersehen goodbye I
  auf … hinauf onto II
  auf … zu towards II
  auf/in … steht … says II
Aufbau structure III TMS1, 31
wieder **aufbauen** *to rebuild III U3, 69
aufbewahren *to keep II
aufführen to perform III U1, 14
Aufführung show I
Aufgabe exercise; job I
aufgeben *to give up III U1, 13
aufgebracht upset II
aufgeregt excited I; nervous II
aufgeschlagen open I
aufgeschlossen open-minded (III TMS1, 32)
aufhalten *to hold open III AC3, 88
aufhängen *to put up II
aufheben to pick up II
jmdn. **aufheitern** to cheer sb up III U1, 23
aufhellen to lighten III U3, 76
aufhören to stop I; to finish II
  Hör/Hört auf! Stop it! I
aufklaren to clear (III TR1, 111)
aufladen to top up II
auflösen *to break down (III TMS1, 30)

aufmachen to open **I**
aufmerksam sein *to pay attention **III U1**, 24
Aufmerksamkeit attention **II**
Aufnahme recording **I**; shot **II**
Aufnahmeort set **II**
Aufnahmestudio recording studio **I**
aufpassen to look out **II**; *to pay attention **III U1**, 24
    aufpassen auf to look after **I**
aufräumen to tidy (a room) **I**
aufrechterhalten etw. *to keep sth going **II**
aufregend exciting **I**
Aufregung excitement (no pl) **III U1**, 22
aufsagen *to say **I**
aufschauen to look up **III U2**, 50
aufstehen *to rise **III U3**, 63
aufstehen (aus dem Bett) *to get up **I**
    Es ist Zeit **aufzustehen**! Time to get up! **I**
aufstellen *to put up **II**; *to set ⟨**III TMS1**, 32⟩
auftauchen to appear **II**
aufteilen (in) to divide (up/into) **III U3**, 63
auftreten to perform **III U1**, 14
Auftritt gig **III U2**, 51
aufwachen *to wake up **III U3**, 77
aufwärmen to warm ⟨**III TR1**, 110⟩
aufwecken *to wake up **III U3**, 77
aufweisen to feature **II**
Aufzeichnung recording **I**
jmdn. **aufziehen** to tease sb **III U1**, 23
Auge eye **II**
    die **Augen** verdrehen to roll one's eyes **III U3**, 74
    Ich traute meinen **Augen** nicht. I couldn't believe my eyes. **II**
Augenblick moment **II**
Augenzeuge/Augenzeugin eyewitness **II**
August August **II**
aus from **I**
    aus Cornwall Cornish **II**
ausblasen *to blow out **II**
Ausblick view ⟨**III TR1**, 111⟩
auschecken to check out (coll) **III AC2**, 56
(sich) **ausdenken** *to think of **II**
Ausdruck phrase **III U1**, 9
ausdrücken to express **II**
auseinanderreißen *to tear apart ⟨**III TMS1**, 30⟩
Auseinandersetzung conflict **III U1**, 18; argument **III U1**, 20
Ausfahrt exit **III U3**, 65
ausflippen *to go crazy **II**
Ausflug trip **I**; day out **II**
ausfüllen to fill in **II**
Ausgang exit **III U3**, 65; gate **III U4**, 101
ausgeben (Geld) *to spend **I**
ausgedehnt wide **II**
ausgehen *to go out **II**
sich **ausgeschlossen** fühlen *to feel left out **II**
aushelfen to help out **III U2**, 53
ausländisch foreign **III U4**, 95
auslassen *to leave out **III TMS1**, 31
ausleihen to hire **III U3**, 71

(sich) **ausleihen** to borrow **II**
auslöschen to destroy **III U3**, 66
auspacken to unwrap **II**
auspusten *to blow out **II**
ausräumen to clear out **I**
jmdm. etw. **ausrichten** *to take a message **I**
sich **ausruhen** to relax **II**
Ausrüstung equipment **II**
Aussage statement **II**
ausschalten to turn off **II**
ausscheiden to drop out (of) **III U1**, 12
aussehen to look **I**
Aussehen looks (pl) **III U1**, 12
außer Acht lassen to ignore **III U1**, 21
außer except **II**
außerhalb outside; out **I**
außerirdisches Wesen alien **II**
Außerirdische/-r alien **II**
äußerst extremely **III U2**, 48
Aussicht view ⟨**III TR1**, 111⟩
Aussprache pronunciation **II**
Ausstattung equipment **II**
aussteigen *to get out of **II**; to drop out (of) **III U1**, 12
    aussteigen (aus einem Bus/Zug) *to get off (a bus/train) **II**
Ausstellung display; exhibition **II**
Ausstoß emission **III U4**, 95
Austausch exchange **II**
Austausch- exchange **II**
Austauschschüler/-in exchange student **III AC1**, 34
Auswahl choice **II**
auswählen *to choose **II**
auswendig lernen *to learn … by heart **III TMS1**, 26
auswickeln to unwrap **II**
Auszeichnung award **II**
ausziehen *to take off **II**
Auto car **I**
Automat machine **I**
Autor/-in writer **II**; author **III TMS1**, 32
Axt axe **III U3**, 65

B

Baby baby **II**
Background- backing **III U1**, 12
Backgroundtänzer/-in backing dancer **III U1**, 12
Backstage backstage **III U3**, 70
Bad bath **I**
Badewanne bath **I**
Badezimmer bathroom **I**
Badminton badminton **I**
Bahnhof station **II**
Bahnsteig platform **II**
bald soon **II**
Ball ball **I**
Banane banana **I**
Band band **III U2**, 50
Bank bench **III U1**, 23
bannen to ban **III U2**, 44

Bär bear **II**
basierend auf based on **III U4**, 103
Basketball basketball **I**
Batterie battery **II**
Bauch stomach **II**
Bauchschmerzen stomachache **II**
Bauchweh stomachache **II**
bauen *to build **II**
Bauer/Bäuerin farmer **II**
Bauernhof farm **I**
jmdn./etw. **beachten** *to pay attention **III U1**, 24
Beachtung attention **II**
Beamter/Beamtin official **III U4**, 105
beängstigend scary **II**
beantragen to apply for **III U4**, 99
beantworten to answer **I**
Becher mug **III AC1**, 34
bedauern *to feel sorry for **III U1**, 23
    etw. **bedauern** to regret sth **II**
bedecken to cover **III U4**, 105
bedeckt cloudy **II**
bedeuten *to mean **I**
Bedeutung meaning **II**
Bedingungen terms **III TMS1**, 29
bedrückend depressing **III U4**, 105
mit speziellen **Bedürfnissen** with special needs **II**
bedürftig in need **II**
sich **beeilen** to hurry **II**
beeindruckt sein *to be impressed **II**
beenden to finish **II**; to end **III U1**, 18
sich **befassen** (mit) *to deal (with) **II**
Befehlsform imperative **II**
befestigen to fix **II**
befolgen to follow **I**
befördern to carry ⟨**III TR1**, 110⟩
befragen to interview **II**
Befragung interview **I**
befreien to free **III TMS1**, 28
Befürchtung fear **II**
begeistert excited **I**
Begeisterung enthusiasm **III U4**, 96
Beginn beginning **II**
beginnen to start **I**; *to begin **III U3**, 63
begreifen *to get ⟨**III TR3**, 114⟩
Begriff term **II**
behalten *to keep **II**
behandeln to treat **III U1**, 21
Behauptung statement **II**
beherrschen to control **III U3**, 67
mit **Behinderung** with special needs **II**
bei with; at **I**; by **II**
    bei mir with me **I**
beibringen *to teach **II**
beide both **II**; the two of them **II**
Bein leg **II**
    die **Beine** und Hände ruhig halten *to keep one's feet or hands still **III TMS1**, 29
beinahe almost **II**
beinhalten to include **II**
beiseite aside ⟨**III TMS1**, 27⟩
Beispiel example **II**

zum **Beispiel** for example II
Beitrag input III U4, 103
beitreten to join II
bekannt sein (als) *to be known (as) III U2, 55
bekommen *to get I; to receive II
etw. aus dem Kopf **bekommen** *to get sth out of one's head III TMS1, 29
belebt busy I
Beleg evidence (no pl) III TMS1, 31
beliebt popular I
die **Beliebten** in-crowd III U1, 20
bellen to bark I
bemerken to notice II
Benehmen behaviour (no pl) III AC3, 88; manners (pl) III AC3, 89
sich **benehmen** to behave III U1, 15
Bengale/Bengalin Bengali III U4, 101
bengalisch Bengali III U4, 101
benötigen to need I; to require III U4, 103
benutzen to use I
Benutzer/-in user II
beobachten to watch I
bequem comfortable III U1, 14
bereit ready II
bereits already I
Berg mountain; hill II
hoher **Berg** ben III U2, 46
Bergbau mining II
bergen to save I
Bericht report II
Beruf career III U1, 12
beruhend auf based on III U4, 103
sich **beruhigen** to calm down; to relax II
berühmt famous II
jmdn. **beschäftigen** to entertain sb III TMS1, 26
beschäftigt busy I
beschreiben to describe II
Beschreibung description III U3, 72
beschuldigen to blame III U1, 18
besichtigen to visit I
Besichtigungs- sightseeing II
besiegen *to beat II; to defeat III U2, 47
besitzen *to have got I
Besitzer/-in owner I
besonders special I; specially II; especially III U1, 10
besorgt sein *to be worried II
besorgt sein (um) *to be concerned (about) III U1, 10
besser better II
Gute **Besserung**! Get well soon! III TMS2, 85
(der/die/das) **Beste** (the) best II
bestehen (auf) to insist (on) III U4, 99
bestehen aus *to be made of III U3, 64
besteigen to climb I
beste/-r/-s best; top I
am **besten** best I
bestimmend bossy III U1, 15
bestimmt definitely III U2, 51
Bestimmungen terms III TMS1, 29
bestürzt upset II

Besuch visit I
besuchen to visit I
Besucher/-in visitor I
beteiligt sein *to be involved III U1, 10
Beton concrete III U4, 105
betonen to emphasize II
betrachten to perceive ⟨III TR3, 115⟩
Betragen behaviour (no pl) III AC3, 88
Betreff in E-Mails etc. subject I
betreten to enter III U4, 99
Betreuer/-in instructor II
Bett bed I
ins **Bett** gehen *to go to bed I
beunruhigt sein *to be worried II
beunruhigt sein (wegen) *to be concerned (about) III U1, 10
beurteilen to judge III U1, 8
bevor before I
bevorzugen to prefer III TMS1, 30
(sich) **bewegen** to move II
Bewegung move II
bewegungslos still II
Beweis evidence (no pl) III TMS1, 31
Beweismaterial evidence (no pl) III TMS1, 31
sich **bewerben** um to apply for III U4, 99
bewerten to rate II; to judge III U1, 8
Bewertung rating II
bewölkt cloudy II
bezahlen *to pay (for) I
Bezahlung payment III TMS2, 81
sich **beziehen** auf *to be related to III TMS2, 80
Beziehung relationship II
Bibel bible III U3, 63
Biene bee I
bieten to offer II
Bild picture I
bildhafte Sprache metaphor III TMS1, 31
Bildschirm screen ⟨III TMS2, 86⟩
Bildung education (no pl) II
billig cheap I
binden (an) to tie (to) III U2, 51
biografisch biographical III U3, 72
Bis … See you! I
Bis bald! See you soon! II
Bis dann! See you! I
bis jetzt so far I
von … **bis** from … to I
bis auf except II
bis heute to this day III U3, 65
bis till I; until II; 'til (= until) ⟨III TMS1, 27⟩
Biskuit(kuchen) sponge II
ein **bisschen** a bit II
Bitte. Please. I
Bitte schön! Here you go. I
Bitte schön. You're welcome.; Here you are. I
bitten to ask I
bitten um to ask for I
blasen *to blow II
Blatt leaf liːf, leaves liːvz (pl) ⟨III U2, 47⟩
blau blue I

Blechdose tin can III U2, 53
Blechflöte tin whistle ⟨III TR3, 114⟩
bleiben to stay I; to remain ⟨III U2, 47⟩
draußen **bleiben** (von) *to keep out (of) III U2, 50
Bleib wie du bist. Stay the way you are. III U1, 16
Bleistift pencil I
Blick look II; view ⟨III TR1, 111⟩
Blickwinkel perspective III U4, 102
Blitz lightning (no pl) II; flash III U3, 75
blockieren to block II
blöd stupid II
blond blond III U1, 20
bloß bare ⟨III U2, 47⟩
bloß only I
Blume flower II
Blut blood III U3, 69
Boarding boarding III U4, 101
Boden ground III TMS1, 27
Bogen bow II
Bonbons sweets (pl) I
Boot boat I
an **Bord** aboard I
an **Bord** gehen boarding III U4, 101
Bordkarte boarding card III U4, 95
böse angry; bad I
Bösewicht villain II
Boss boss III U1, 20
Botschaft message I
Bowling bowls III U3, 66
Bowlingbahn bowling alley II
Box box I
Boxrunde round of boxing II
Branche industry III U2, 42
Bratwurst sausage III AC1, 34
Brauch custom III AC3, 88
brauchen to need I
nicht **brauchen** needn't II
(Zeit) **brauchen** *to take I
braun brown I
brechen *to break II
brechend cracking III U2, 50
breit wide II
brennen *to burn III U3, 63
Brennholz firewood ⟨III TR1, 110⟩
schwarzes **Brett** noticeboard II
Brief letter II
Briefmarke stamp III TMS2, 82
Briefträger/-in postman II
Briefumschlag envelope III TMS2, 82
Brille glasses (pl) II
bringen *to bring; *to take; *to get I
in Schwierigkeiten **bringen** *to make trouble I
jmdn. dazu **bringen**, etw. zu tun *to make sb do something II
Brite/Britin British I
britisch British I
Bronzezeit (ca. 2200–800 v. Chr.) Bronze Age II
Broschüre brochure I; catalogue III U4, 103; booklet III U4, 109

Brot bread **I**
   belegtes **Brot** sandwich **I**
Brötchen bread roll **III AC1**, 34; bun **III U2**, 43
Brücke bridge **II**
Bruder brother **I**
buchen to book **II**
Buchhandlung bookshop **III TMS1**, 30
Büchse can **I**; tin ⟨**III TR1**, 110⟩
Buchstabe letter **II**
buchstabieren *to spell **I**
Bude stall **III U4**, 102
Bühne stage **I**
   hinter der **Bühne** backstage **III U3**, 70
bunt colourful **II**
Buntstift pencil **I**
Burg castle **II**
Bürgerkrieg Civil War **III U3**, 63
Bürgersteig pavement **I**
Büro office **I**
bürsten to brush **III U3**, 78
Bus bus **I**
Busbahnhof bus station **I**
Bushaltestelle bus stop **I**
Business business **III U1**, 24
Butter butter **III AC1**, 34

C

Café café; snack bar **I**
Cafeteria cafeteria **I**
campen to camp **II**
Cartoon cartoon **III AC2**, 56
CD CD **II**
Cent *(Währung)* cent **I**
Center centre **I**
Chance chance **III TMS1**, 27
   keine **Chance** mehr haben *to be out of
   chances **III TMS1**, 27
Chaos chaos **III U3**, 74
chaotisch chaotic **II**
Charakter character **II**; personality **III U1**, 9
Charme charm **III U3**, 67
Chat chat **II**
chatten *(sich online unterhalten)* to chat **I**
Chef boss **III U1**, 20
Chipkarte smartcard **II**
Christentum Christianity ⟨**III TR3**, 115⟩
nach **Christus** AD (= Anno Domini) **III U3**, 63
vor **Christus** BC (= before Christ) **III U3**, 63
circa about **I**
Clan clan **III U2**, 45
Cleverness cleverness **III TMS1**, 30
Clown clown **II**
CO₂ CO₂ (carbon dioxide) **III U4**, 95
Cola coke **I**
Comedian comedian **II**
Comedy Show comedy show **II**
Comic(heft) comic **II**
Comicheft comic **II**
Computer computer **I**
Computerunterricht technology **II**
cool cool **I**
Couch sofa **I**

Cousin/Cousine cousin **I**
Cover cover **III U1**, 8
Cowboy cowboy **II**
Creme cream **II**
Cricket cricket **II**
Curry *(Gewürz oder Gericht)* curry **I**

D

da because **I**; as **II**; 'cause ⟨**III TMS1**, 27⟩
da there **I**
   da drüben over there **I**
dabei sein *to be in **II**
Dach roof **II**
Dachboden loft **I**; attic **II**
Ich habe nichts **dagegen** (zu …) I don't
   mind *(+ …ing)* **III U1**, 18
dahin there **I**
damals back then **II**
Dame lady **II**
damit so (that) **II**
Dampf steam **III U2**, 43
Dampfmaschine steam engine **III U2**, 43
danach then; after that **I**
dankbar thankful **I**; glad **III AC3**, 89
Dankbarkeit gratitude **III AC1**, 35
Danke! Cheers! **III AC2**, 56
   Danke. Thank you.; Thanks. **I**
   Nichts zu **danken**. You're welcome. **I**
dann then **I**
darauf zu towards **II**
darstellen to illustrate **II**; *to set out
   ⟨**III TMS2**, 87⟩
das the **I**
das that **I**; whom **III U3**, 67
   Das macht … That's … **I**
   Das war knapp! That was close! **I**
das *(Relativpronomen)* which **III U3**, 66
dass that **II**
Datum date **II**
dauern *to take **I**; to last **III TMS1**, 30
die **Daumen** drücken *to keep your fingers
   crossed **I**
davonkommen *to get away with sth **II**
dazupassen to fit in **III U1**, 22
Deck deck **I**
Defekt flaw ⟨**III TMS1**, 32⟩
Definition definition **II**
definitiv definitely **III U2**, 51
dein/-e your **I**
dein/-er/-e/-es yours **II**
Dekoration decorations *(pl)* **II**
dekorieren to decorate **II**
dem *(Relativpronomen)* who; which
   III U3, 66
den *(Relativpronomen)* who; which
   III U3, 66
denken *to think **I**
   denken an to remember **I**
   denken über *to think of **I**
Denkmal monument **II**
dennoch still **II**
deprimierend depressing **III U4**, 105

der the **I**
der whom **III U3**, 67
der; dem; den; die; das *(Relativpronomen)*
   that **III U3**, 66
der *(Relativpronomen)* which; who **III U3**, 66
deren *(Relativpronomen)* whose **II**
der-/die-/dasselbe the same **I**
Desaster disaster **II**
Designer/-in designer **III U1**, 14
dessen *(Relativpronomen)* whose **II**
Dessert dessert **II**
Detail detail **II**
deutlich clear **I**
Deutsch German **I**
deutsch German **I**
Deutsche/-r German **I**
aus **Deutschland** German **I**
Dezember December **II**
Diagramm diagram **III U1**, 9
Dialekt dialect **II**
Dialog dialogue **III U2**, 54
dich (selbst) yourself **II**
Dichter/-in poet **III TMS1**, 26
Dichtung poetry **III TMS1**, 26
dick *(nicht für Personen)* thick ⟨**III U2**, 47⟩
die *(auch Pl.)* the **I**
die *(Relativpronomen)* who; which **III U3**, 66
Diele hall **II**
Dienstag Tuesday **I**
dies this **I**
diese (hier) these **I**
   diese dort those **I**
diese/-r/-s this **I**
digital digital **II**
Ding thing **I**
Dingsda thingy ⟨**III TR3**, 115⟩
Dinosaurier dinosaur (dino) **II**
dir (selbst) yourself **II**
direkt direct **III TMS2**, 80; straight
   III U4, 105; right ⟨**III TR3**, 114⟩
Discjockey DJ **III U1**, 21
Diskussion discussion **II**
Distanz distance **II**
Distel thistle **III U2**, 54
doch after all **II**
Dokument document **III U4**, 99
Dollar *(Währung)* dollar **III U1**, 24
ein Gespräch **dominieren** to hog a conver-
   sation **III AC2**, 56
Donner thunder *(no pl)* **II**
donnernd thunderous ⟨**III TMS1**, 32⟩
Donnerstag Thursday **I**
doof silly **I**
Doppel- double **I**
Dorf village **II**
dort there **I**
   dort drüben over there **I**
dorthin there **I**
Dose can **I**; tin ⟨**III TR1**, 110⟩
   aus der **Dose** tinned **II**
Drachen kite **I**
Drama drama **II**
dramatisch dramatic **II**

dran kommen to reach **II**
   Du bist **dran**. It's your turn. **I**
(jmdn.) **drangsalieren** to bully (sb) **II**
draußen outside **I**
   draußen bleiben (von) *to keep out (of)
   III U2, 50
   draußen halten (von) *to keep out (of)
   III U2, 50
   nach **draußen** out **I**
dreckig dirty **II**
Drehbuch script **II**
sich im Kreis **drehen** *to go round in circles
   III U2, 50
Drehort set **II**
drin inside **II**
drittens thirdly **II**
dröhnen to boom **II**
nach dort **drüben** over there **I**
Druck- print **II**
drücken to press **III U4**, 105
   die Daumen **drücken** *to keep your
   fingers crossed **I**
du you; u (= you) **I**
   Du auch? You too? **I**
   Du bist … You're … **I**
du (selbst) yourself **II**
   Du bist dran. It's your turn. **I**
Dudelsack bagpipes (pl) **III U2**, 41
duften *to smell ⟨**III TR1**, 110⟩
dumm silly **I**; stupid **II**
   Zu **dumm**! Too bad! **I**
Dummkopf silly **II**
dunkel dark **II**
Dunkelheit the dark; darkness **II**
durch through **I**
durchdrehen *to go crazy **II**
Durcheinander chaos **III U3**, 74
schmaler **Durchgang** close **III U2**, 44
durchhalten *to hang on **III TMS1**, 27
durchkommen mit *to get away with sth **II**
Durchsage announcement **II**
dürfen can; may **I**; *to be allowed to (do
   sth) **III U1**, 20; *to be able to (do sth)
   III U1, 21
   darf nicht can't **I**; cannot **II**
   dürfen nicht can't **I**; cannot **II**
   nicht **dürfen** mustn't **II**
Dusche shower **I**

E

Ebbe low tide **II**
echt real **II**
Ecke corner **II**
Effekt effect **III TMS1**, 29
egal no matter **III TMS1**, 30
Ehefrau wife, wives (pl) **II**
Ehemann husband **III TMS2**, 84
eher als rather than **III U3**, 65
ehrlich honest **III U1**, 22
Ei egg **I**
Eichhörnchen squirrel **I**
eifersüchtig jealous **II**

eigene/-r/-s own **I**
Eigenschaft characteristic **III U3**, 66
eigentlich actually **III U2**, 45; in fact **III U2**, 45
eilen to hurry **II**
Eimer bucket **II**
ein/eine one, ones (pl) **II**
ein/-e a; an **I**
   ein paar a couple of **I**
   ein wenig a little **I**
   ein/-e andere/-r/-s another **I**
   noch **ein**/-e another **I**
einander each other **II**; one another
   III TMS1, 32
Einband cover **III U1**, 8
einbiegen to turn (into) **I**
Einchecken check-in **III U4**, 95
eindeutig definitely **III U2**, 51
Eindruck impression **III TMS1**, 27
Einerseits …, (aber) andererseits … On
   the one hand …, (but) on the other hand
   … **II**
einfach easy **I**; simple **III U1**, 18
   einfache Fahrkarte one-way ticket; single
   ticket **II**
einfach just **I**
Einfall idea **I**
einfallen in to invade **III U3**, 66
   sich etwas **einfallen** lassen *to think of **II**
einfallsreich imaginative **III U1**, 9
Einfluss influence **III U3**, 65
Einflussnehmer/-in influencer **III U1**, 10
sich **einfügen** to fit in **III U1**, 22
Einführung introduction **III U4**, 103
Eingang entrance **III U2**, 50; lobby **III U4**, 102
eingängig catchy **III TMS1**, 29
eingeklemmt crushed **III U4**, 104
eingequetscht crushed **III U4**, 104
Einheimische/-r local **III U4**, 102
Einheitspreis flat rate **III TMS1**, 29
einige a few; some **I**
sich **einigen** to agree **III U1**, 9
Einkäufe shopping **I**
Einkaufen shopping **I**
einkaufen *to do the shopping **III U2**, 53
   einkaufen gehen *to go shopping **I**; *to do
   the shopping **III U2**, 53
einladen to invite **II**
Einladung invitation **II**
Einlass admission **II**
Einleitung introduction **III U4**, 103
einmal once **II**
einmarschieren (in) to invade **III U3**, 66
einpacken to wrap **II**
einprägsam catchy **III TMS1**, 29
Einreisebewilligung visa, visas (pl) **III U4**, 95
einreisen to enter **III U4**, 99
einsam lonely **II**
einschalten to turn on **II**
einschenken to pour **II**
einschlafen *to fall asleep **I**
einschließen to include **II**
einst once **II**
einsteigen *to get into **II**

einsteigen (in den Bus) *to get on (the
   bus) **II**
Einstellung opinion **III U1**, 15; view **III U3**, 65
einstufen to rate **II**
einstürzen *to fall down **III U2**, 50
Eintopf stew ⟨**III TR3**, 114⟩
Eintrag entry **II**
eintreten to enter **III U4**, 99
Eintritt entry **II**; entrance **III U2**, 50
Eintrittskarte ticket **I**
nicht **einverstanden** sein to disagree
   III U1, 9
Einwanderungsbeamter/-beamtin immigra-
   tion officer **III U4**, 99
einwickeln to wrap **II**
Einzelheit detail **II**
Einzelkind only child **I**
einziehen in to move in/into **II**
einzige/-r/-s only **II**
Eis ice cream; ice **II**
Eisbahn ice rink **II**
Eisbär polar bear **II**
Eiscreme ice cream **II**
Eiszeit Ice Age **III U3**, 63
ekelhaft disgusting **I**
Elektrik electrics **II**
Elektriker/-in electrician **II**
Elektrizität electricity **II**
Element element **II**
elf eleven **I**
Elisabethaner/-in Elizabethan **III U3**, 69
elisabethanisch Elizabethan **III U3**, 69
Eltern parents (pl) **I**
E-Mail email **II**
   per **E-Mail** schicken to email **II**
Emission emission **III U4**, 95
Emoji emoji **I**
Emotion emotion **III TMS1**, 26
Empfang signal **III U2**, 50
empfangen to receive **II**
Empfänger/-in recipient **III TMS2**, 81
Empfangsbereich lobby **III U4**, 102
empfehlen to recommend **III U1**, 10
unbedingt **empfehlenswert** a must-see
   III U4, 102
empfinden to perceive ⟨**III TR3**, 115⟩
Ende end; ending **I**
enden to end up; to finish **II**; to end
   III U1, 18
endlich at last **I**; finally **II**
Energie energy **II**
eng close **I**; narrow **III U2**, 44
aus **England** English **I**
Engländer/-in English **I**
Englisch English **I**
englisch English **I**
englischsprachig English-speaking **I**
Enkel/-in grandchild (sg) grandchildren (pl) **II**
Enkelkind grandchild (sg) grandchildren (pl) **II**
entdecken to discover **II**
Entdeckung discovery **III U2**, 43

auf **Entdeckungsreise** gehen to explore I
Ente duck I
entfernen to remove II
Entfernung distance II
entfliehen to escape III TMS1, 28
eine Nachricht **entgegennehmen** *to take a message I
entgegnen to reply (to) II
Entgegnung reply II
enthalten to contain III TMS2, 81
Enthusiasmus enthusiasm III U4, 96
entkommen to escape III TMS1, 28
entlang along II
entlanggehen *to go down I
entrümpeln to clear out I
(sich) **entscheiden** (für) to decide (on) III U1, 15
Entscheidung decision III U1, 18
Entschuldigen Sie! Excuse me … I
sich **entschuldigen** to apologise III U1, 23
Entschuldigung! Sorry!; Excuse me … I
entsetzt horrified I
sich **entspannen** to relax II
entspannt laid-back III U1, 12; relaxed III U3, 66
enttäuscht disappointed I
Enttäuschung disappointment II
entwerfen to design III U1, 12; *to draw up III U4, 103
(sich) **entwickeln** to develop III U1, 24
Entwurf plan I
er he I
Erdboden earth II; ground III TMS1, 27
Erde earth; world II
die **Erde** earth II
erdichtet fictional III U4, 109
Erdkunde geography II
Ereignis event II; occasion III TMS1, 26
erfahren *to learn II; to experience ⟨III TR1, 110⟩
erfahren über *to learn about III U1, 9
Erfahrung experience II
erfinden to create II; to invent III U2, 43
Erfinder/-in inventor III U2, 53
Erfindung invention III U2, 43
Erfolg success III U1, 12
erfolgreich successful III U1, 14
erforderlich necessary III U1, 18
erfordern to require III U4, 103
erforschen to explore I
ergänzen to add I
Ergebnis result II
ergreifen to grab II
erhalten to receive II
erhältlich available III TMS2, 81
sich **erheben** *to rise III U3, 63
(jmdn. an etw./jmdn.) **erinnern** to remind (sb of sth/sb) III TMS1, 30
sich **erinnern** (an) to remember I
Erinnerst du dich? Remember? II
Erinnert ihr euch? Remember? II
Erinnerung memory II
Erkältung cold II

erkennen to realise III U2, 50
erklären to explain I
Erklärung statement II
erkunden to explore I
erlauben to allow II
Erlaubnis permission III TMS2, 82
erleben to experience ⟨III TR1, 110⟩
Erleichterung relief III U4, 99
ernähren *to feed II
ernst serious II
etw. **ernst** nehmen *to take sth seriously II
ernsthaft serious II
erobern to conquer III U3, 63
erraten to guess III AC3, 88
erreichen *to get to I; to reach II
errichten *to put up II
erschaffen to create II
erscheinen to appear II
ersetzen (durch) to replace (by/with) III TMS2, 84
erst only I
erst wenn until II
erstaunlich amazing II
Erste-Hilfe-Kasten first aid kit I
erstens first II
erste/-r/-s first I
als **Erstes** first I
ertappt caught on camera II
Erwachsene/-r adult II
erwähnen to mention II
erwarten to expect II
erwidern to reply (to) II
Erwiderung reply II
erzählen *to tell I
erzählen von to talk about I
Erzähle/Erzählt mir von … Tell me about … I
Erzähler/-in narrator III U4, 106
Erzählung story, stories (pl) I
erzeugen to produce III U1, 10
Erzeugnis product III U1, 10
Erziehung education (no pl) II
es it I
Essen food I; meal II
essen *to eat I
etwa about I
etwas something; some; a little I
euer/eure your I
eure/-r/-s yours II
Euro (Währung) euro I
aus **Europa** European III U4, 101
Europäer/-in European III U4, 101
europäisch European III U4, 101
Europäische Union European Union (EU) III U3, 65
ewig forever II
extra extra I

F

Fabrik factory III U3, 65
fachlich technical III U1, 10
Fackel torch II
fähig sein zu *to be able to (do sth) III U1, 21
Fähigkeit skill III U1, 10
Fähre ferry III U4, 95
fahren *to go I; to travel; *to ride ; *to drive II
Fahrrad fahren to cycle I
Fahrer/-in driver II
Fahrgast passenger III U4, 95
einfache **Fahrkarte** one-way ticket; single ticket II
Fahrkartenschalter ticket office III U2, 50
Fahrplan timetable I
Fahrpreis fare II
Fahrrad bike I; bicycle II
Fahrrad fahren to cycle I
Fahrradmotocross (=BMX) bicycle motocross (BMX)
Fahrschein ticket II
Fahrt tour; trip I; journey II
fair fair I
Fakt fact II
für den **Fall**, dass … in case II
Auf keinen **Fall**! No way! I
fallen *to fall I
fallen (lassen) to drop II
falls if I; in case II
falsch wrong I; fake II
fälschen to fake II
Familie family I
Fan fan III AC3, 89
fangen *to catch II
Fantasie fantasy I; imagination III U1, 9
fantasievoll imaginative III U1, 9
fantastisch fantastic II
Fantasy fantasy III U4, 107
Farbe colour I; paint II
Welche **Farbe** hat …? What colour is …? I
farbenfroh colourful II
Farm farm I
aus der **Fassung** bringen *to upset III AC1, 35
fast almost; nearly II
faszinierend fascinating III U2, 48
Februar February II
Feder feather II
Federkiel quill III U3, 72
Federmäppchen pencil case I
Feedback feedback II
fehlend missing II
Fehler mistake II; flaw ⟨III TMS1, 32⟩
Feier party II
feiern to celebrate II
Feiertag holiday I; bank holiday ⟨III TR3, 114⟩
Feld field II
felsig rocky II
Fenster window I
Ferien holidays (pl) III U4, 95
Ferienhaus holiday home III U4, 96

fernbleiben von to stay away from **II**
(sich) **fernhalten** von *to keep away from **II**
Fernsehen TV **I**; television **III U2**, 43
fernsehen to watch TV **I**
Fernseher TV **I**; television **III U2**, 43
fertig ready **II**
   sich **fertig** machen *to get ready
   III TMS1, 26
Fertiggericht ready meal **I**
Fertigkeit skill **III U1**, 10
fertigstellen to finish **II**
Fest festival **II**
fest hard **II**
festbinden (an) to tie (to) **III U2**, 51
festhalten *to hold **I**
   (sich) **festhalten** an *to hold onto
   III U2, 51
Festival festival **II**
festnehmen to arrest **II**
Festung fort **III U3**, 63
Feuer fire ⟨**III TMS1**, 31⟩; ⟨**III TR1**, 110⟩
Fieber fever **II**
Figur character **II**
fiktional fictional **III U4**, 109
fiktiv fictional **III U4**, 109
Film film **I**
Filmemacher/-in filmmaker **II**
filtern to filter **II**
finden *to find **I**
   finden (= der Meinung sein) *to think **I**
Finger finger **I**
Fingerfood (Essen, das man mit den Fingern
   essen kann) finger food **I**
Firma company **III U1**, 10
Fisch fish, fish (pl) **I**
Fischen fishing **II**
Fischerei fishing **II**
Fitness fitness **II**
Fläche area **II**
Flair flair **II**
Flasche bottle **I**
Flashback flashback **III U3**, 76
Flatrate flat rate **III TMS1**, 29
Fleisch meat (no pl) **III U2**, 42
Fleischpastete pasty **II**
flexibel flexible **III U4**, 102
Fliegen flying **III U4**, 94
fliegen *to fly **III U4**, 99
fliehen to escape **III TMS1**, 28
fließen to flow **II**
Flohmarkt flea market **I**
Flöte recorder **III U1**, 15
flüchten to escape **III TMS1**, 28
Flüchtling refugee **III U4**, 106
Flug flight **III U4**, 98
Flugbegleiter/-in flight attendant **III U4**, 95
Flughafen airport **III U4**, 95
Flugsteig gate **III U4**, 101
Flugzeug plane **III U4**, 94
Flur hall **II**
Fluss river **I**
flüstern to whisper **II**
Flut high tide; tide **II**

fluten to flood **III U3**, 63
Flyer flyer **I**
Folge sequel **II**
folgen to follow **I**
Follower follower **III U1**, 10
formal formal **II**
formell formal **II**
Formgedicht shape poem **III TMS1**, 26
förmlich formal **II**
Formular form **II**
Forscher/-in explorer **III U3**, 67
Forschung research (no pl) **III U4**, 101
Forschungsreisende/-r explorer **III U3**, 67
Fort fort **III U3**, 63
fortfahren to continue **III U4**, 99
Fortsetzung sequel **II**
Forum forum **II**
Foto photo; picture **I**
   Fotos machen *to take photos **I**
   ins **Foto** laufen to photobomb **III U3**, 75
Fotoapparat camera **II**
Fotoaufnahmen photoshoot **III U3**, 74
Fotograf/-in photographer **II**
Fotografie photo **I**
jmdn./etw. **fotografieren** to photograph
   (sb/sth) **III U3**, 66
   fotografieren *to take photos **I**
Fotoshooting photoshoot **III U3**, 74
Frage question **I**
fragen to ask **I**
   fragen nach to ask for **I**
   sich **fragen** to wonder **II**
Französisch French **II**
französisch French **II**
Frau woman, women (pl) **I**
Frau (Anrede) Mrs **I**; Ms **III TMS2**, 81
Fräulein (veraltete Anrede) Miss **III U1**, 16
frei free **I**
   freie Wildbahn the wild ⟨**III TR1**, 110⟩
Freiheit freedom (no pl) **III U1**, 20
freilassen to free **III TMS1**, 28
Freiluft- outdoor **II**
Freitag Friday **I**
Freizeit free time (no pl); leisure (no pl) **I**
Freizeit- free-time **II**
Freizeitzentrum leisure centre **I**
fremd strange **I**; foreign **III U4**, 95
Fremde/-r stranger **III TMS1**, 30
Fremdsprache foreign language **III U4**, 94
Freude fun **I**; pleasure ⟨**III TR2**, 112⟩
sich **freuen** auf to look forward to **II**
Freund/-in friend **I**
   Dafür sind **Freunde** da. That's what
   friends are for. **I**
Freundin (in einer Paarbeziehung) girlfriend
   II
freundlich friendly **I**; kind **II**
   Mit **freundlichen** Grüßen, Yours sincerely,
   III TMS2, 80
Freundschaft friendship **II**
   Freundschaft schließen *to make friends **I**
Frieden peace **III U3**, 63
   in **Frieden** peaceful **III U3**, 63

friedlich peaceful **III U3**, 63
frisch fresh **II**
uns **frisieren** *to do our hair **II**
froh happy **I**; glad **III AC3**, 89
fröhlich happy; fun **I**
Frucht fruit **I**
früh early **I**
   so **früh** this early **III AC1**, 35
Frühling spring **I**
Frühlingsferien spring break **I**
Frühstück breakfast **I**
frühstücken *to have breakfast **I**
Frühstückszerealie cereal (no pl) **I**
fühlen *to feel **I**
   sich **fühlen** *to feel **I**
   sich ausgeschlossen **fühlen** *to feel left
   out **II**
   sich schlecht **fühlen** *to feel sick **II**
führen *to lead **III U4**, 104
Führer/-in guide **II**; leader **III U3**, 65
füllen to fill **III U2**, 44
Füller pen **I**
funktionieren to work **II**; to work out
   III U1, 23
für for **I**
   für sich on one's own **III U4**, 105
   Für wen …? Who … for? **I**
   für den Fall, dass … in case **II**
Furcht fear **II**
furchtbar awful **I**; horrible **II**; terrible
   ⟨**III TR2**, 112⟩
Fuß foot, feet (pl) **I**
   zu **Fuß** on foot **II**
Fußball football **I**
Fußboden floor **I**
Fußgelenk ankle **II**
Fußknöchel ankle **II**
füttern *to feed **II**

G

Gabel fork **I**
Galerie gallery **II**
Gälisch Gaelic **II**
gälisch Gaelic **II**
Gangart pace **III U4**, 102
ganz all; whole **I**; full **II**; quite **II**
Garage garage **I**
garstig nasty **II**
Garten garden **I**
Gast guest **II**
Gastfamilie host family **III AC1**, 34
Gasthaus pub ⟨**III TR3**, 114⟩
Gaststätte restaurant **I**
Gate gate **III U4**, 101
Gattung genre **III U4**, 107
Geächtete/-r outlaw **II**
Gebäckstück bun **III U2**, 43
Gebärdensprache sign language **II**
Gebäude building **I**
geben *to give **I**; to grant **III U2**, 43
   es **gibt** there is/are; there's (= there is) **I**
Gebiet area **II**

geboren werden *to be born **III U3**, 72
Ge- und Verbote dos and don'ts **III AC3**, 88
gebrauchen to use **I**
gebräuchlich common **III TMS1**, 31
gebrochen broken **I**
Gebühr charge; fee **II**
Geburtstag birthday **II**
    Alles Gute zum **Geburtstag**! Happy Birthday! **II**
    Herzlichen Glückwunsch zum **Geburtstag**! Happy Birthday! **II**
Gedächtnis memory **II**
Gedanke thought **II**
    sich **Gedanken** machen to wonder **II**
    von einem **Gedanken** loskommen *to get sth out of one's head **III TMS1**, 29
Gedicht poem **I**
Gedichte poetry **III TMS1**, 26
gedruckt print **II**
geduldig patient **II**
Gefahr danger **III U2**, 50
gefährlich dangerous **I**
jmdm. **gefallen** to please ⟨**III TMS1**, 32⟩; to appeal to sb **III U2**, 49
gefälscht fake **II**
Gefangene/-r prisoner **III U4**, 102
Gefängnis prison **II**
Gefühl feeling **II**; emotion **III TMS1**, 26
geführt guided **II**
gegen against **II**; versus (vs.) **III U2**, 53
Gegend area; region **II**
gegenseitig one another **III TMS1**, 32
sich **gegenseitig** each other **II**
Gegenstand object **III U3**, 63
gegenüber opposite **I**
Gegenwart present **II**
Gegenwarts- present **III U2**, 48
geheim secret ⟨**III TR3**, 114⟩
Geheim- secret ⟨**III TR3**, 114⟩
Geheimnis secret **II**; mystery **III U3**, 74
geheimnisvoll mysterious **II**
gehen *to go; to walk **I**
    an Bord **gehen** boarding **III U4**, 101
    ins Bett **gehen** *to go to bed **I**
    nach unten **gehen** *to go down **I**
    zu jmdm. nach Hause **gehen** *to go over to **II**
    Geh ihm aus dem Weg. Get out of his way. **I**
    Wie **geht** es dir/euch/Ihnen? How are you? **II**
    Wie **geht** es euch? How are you? **II**
    Wie **geht** es Ihnen? How are you? **II**
Gehirn brain ⟨**III U4**, 98⟩
gehören (zu) to belong (to) **II**
    zueinander **gehören** *to go together **I**
Geige fiddle ⟨**III TR3**, 114⟩
Geist ghost **II**
nicht **gekennzeichnet** unmarked ⟨**III TR1**, 110⟩
gekleidet dressed **III U3**, 69
gelangweilt bored **II**
gelassen relaxed **III U3**, 66

gelb yellow **I**
Geld money **I**
    Geld sammeln to raise money **II**
    Geld verdienen *to make money **I**
Gelegenheit occasion **III TMS1**, 26; chance **III TMS1**, 27
Gemälde painting **II**
gemein nasty **II**
gemein haben *to have in common **III TMS1**, 30
Gemeindezentrum community centre **I**
gemeinsam together **I**
Gemeinsamkeit similarity ⟨**III TMS1**, 33⟩
Gemüse vegetable **III U2**, 42
gemütlich cosy ⟨**III TR3**, 114⟩
genau exactly **III U1**, 15; right ⟨**III TR3**, 114⟩
    genau genommen in fact **III U2**, 45
    genau hier right here **II**
    genau in dem Moment just then **I**
Genehmigung permission **III TMS2**, 82
Genie genius **II**
genießen to enjoy **II**
Genre genre **III U4**, 107
Gentleman gentleman ˈdʒentlmən, gentlemen ˈdʒentlmen (pl) **III U2**, 45
genug enough **I**
genügend enough **I**
Geocaching geocaching **I**
geöffnet open **I**
Geografie geography **II**
Gepäck luggage (no pl) **III U4**, 94
Gepäckaufgabe check-in **III U4**, 95
gerade straight **III U4**, 105
gerade just; at the moment **I**
geradeaus straight on **I**
geradewegs straight **III U4**, 105
Gerät machine; device **I**; tool **II**; gadget **III U4**, 106
Geräusch sound **I**; noise **II**
gerecht fair **I**
germanisch Germanic **III U3**, 63
Gern geschehen. You're welcome **I**
gern haben to like **I**; to love **I**
    hätte/-st/-n/-t **gern** would like **I**
    hätte/-st-/-n/-t sehr **gern** would love **II**
    würde/-st/-n/-t **gern** would like **I**
    würde/-st/-n/-t sehr **gern** would love **II**
Gerümpel rubbish **I**
Gesamt- overall **III U4**, 102
Gesang singing **I**
Geschäft shop **I**; business **III U1**, 24
Geschäftsführer/-in manager **III TMS2**, 81
geschehen to happen **I**; *to go on **III AC3**, 88
Geschenk present; gift **I**
Geschichte story, stories (pl) **I**; history **II**
geschichtlich historical **II**
Geschick skill **III U1**, 10
geschlossen closed **III TMS1**, 28
Geschwindigkeit pace **III U4**, 102
Gesellschaft society **II**; company **III U1**, 10
Gesetzlose/-r outlaw **II**
Gesicht face **I**
Gesichtsausdruck facial expression **III U1**, 19

Gespenst ghost **II**
Gespräch conversation **II**; dialogue **III U2**, 54
    ein **Gespräch** dominieren to hog a conversation **III AC2**, 56
    ein **Gespräch** für sich in Beschlag nehmen to hog a conversation **III AC2**, 56
    hier: das **Gespräch** am Laufen halten *to keep the ball bouncing **III AC2**, 56
gestalten to design **III U1**, 12; *to set out ⟨**III TMS2**, 87⟩
Gestaltgedicht shape poem **III TMS1**, 26
gestatten to allow **II**
gestern yesterday **II**
völlig **gestresst** sein *to be stressed out **III U1**, 12
gesund healthy **I**
Gesundheit health **II**
Getränk drink **I**
getrennt separate **II**
gewähren to grant **III U2**, 43
gewaltig huge **III U2**, 48
Gewerbe industry **III U2**, 42
Gewinn prize **I**
gewinnen *to win **II**
Gewinner/-in winner **I**
gewiss certain **II**
Gewohnheit custom **III AC3**, 88
gewöhnlich common **III TMS1**, 31
gewöhnlich usually **I**
gewohnt sein *to be used to **III AC1**, 35
gewöhnt sein an *to be used to **III AC1**, 35
gießen to pour **II**
Gig gig **III U2**, 51
Gipsverband plaster cast **III U3**, 74
Gitarre guitar **III U4**, 107
Gitterstab bar ⟨**III TMS1**, 30⟩
glänzen *to shine **III U3**, 69
Glas glass **I**
glatzköpfig bald **III U3**, 66
glauben *to think; to believe **I**
gläubig religious **II**
der/die/das **gleiche** the same **I**
gleich right away **I**
    ganz **gleich** no matter **III TMS1**, 30
    gleich jetzt right now **II**
gleichmäßig rhythmic **III TMS1**, 29
Gleichnis simile **III TMS1**, 31
gleichzeitig at the same time **II**; at once ⟨**III TMS2**, 86⟩
Gliederung structure **III TMS1**, 31
Glocke bell **I**
Glück haben *to be lucky **I**
    noch mal **Glück** haben *to be saved by the bell **III U1**, 15
    Was für ein **Glück**! What luck! **III U3**, 69
glücklich happy **I**
glücklicherweise luckily **III U4**, 99
Glücksbringer lucky charm **I**
Glückszahl lucky number **I**
Glückwunsch! Congratulations! **III TMS2**, 85
Glühbirne light bulb **III U3**, 78
Gold gold **I**

Gold- golden ⟨III **U4**, 98⟩
golden golden ⟨III **U4**, 98⟩
  goldenes Zeitalter golden age III **U3**, 65
Golf golf II
GPS-Gerät GPS device I
Gratuliere! Congratulations! III **TMS2**, 85
grau grey I
grausam cruel II
greifen to grab II
Grenzschutzbeamter/-beamtin immigration
  officer III **U4**, 99
Griff knob II
groß big I; high; tall II; large III **U2**, 42
großartig great I; fantastic II; marvellous
  ⟨III **TMS1**, 32⟩; grand ⟨III **TR3**, 114⟩
Größe size I
Großeltern grandparents (pl) I
Großstadt city I
größtenteils mostly ⟨III **TMS1**, 32⟩
grün green I
Grund reason II
Grund- basic II
gründen to start III **U2**, 43; to found
  III **U3**, 63
Gründer/-in founder III **U1**, 24
grundlegend basic II
Gruppe group I; team II
Gruppenzwang peer pressure III **U1**, 22
gruselig scary II
Gruß greeting I
  Herzliche **Grüße** (am Briefende) Love
  … II
  Herzliche **Grüße**, Best wishes, III **TMS2**, 83
  Liebe **Grüße** (am Briefende) Love … II
  Mit freundlichen **Grüßen**, Yours sincerely,
  III **TMS2**, 80
  Viele **Grüße**, Best wishes, III **TMS2**, 83
grüßen *to say hello (to) I
gültig valid III **U4**, 99
Gürtel belt I
gut good; fine I
Gute Besserung! Get well soon! III **TMS2**, 85
  gut sein in *to be good at I
  gut umgehen können mit *to be good
  with ⟨III **TR2**, 112⟩
  Guten Morgen. Good morning. I
  Mir geht's **gut**. I'm fine. I
Güter goods (pl) III **U3**, 65
Guthaben credit II

H

Haar hair II
Haarbürste hairbrush III **U3**, 65
Haare hair II
  unsere **Haare** machen *to do our hair II
Haarglätter hair straightener I
haben *to have got; *to have I
  gemein **haben** *to have in common
  III **TMS1**, 30
  hätte/-st/-n/-t gern would like I
  hätte/-st-/-n/-t sehr gern would love II

nicht ganz Unrecht **haben** *to have a
  point III **U1**, 18
Ich **habe** nichts dagegen (zu …) I don't
  mind (+ …ing) III **U1**, 18
Hafen harbour II; port III **U4**, 96
Hafendamm pier I
Häftling prisoner III **U4**, 102
Hähnchen chicken I
Hai shark III **U4**, 104
Halb- semi- III **TMS2**, 83
halb half I; (bei Uhrzeitangaben) half past I
  eine **halbe** Stunde half an hour III **U3**, 75
halb- semi- III **TMS2**, 83
Halbjahr term III **U3**, 66
Halbschwester half-sister I
die **Hälfte** half (of), halves (pl) II
Halle hall II
Hallo. Hello.; Hi.; Hey! I
Halskette necklace III **U3**, 65
Halt stop I
halten *to hold I; *to keep II
  draußen **halten** (von) *to keep out (of)
  III **U2**, 50
  halten von *to think of I
Haltestelle station II
Hamburger burger I
Hand hand II
  von **Hand** by hand III **U3**, 65
Handbuch planner I
sich **handeln** um *to be about I
handeln von *to be about I
Handgelenk wrist II
handgeschrieben handwritten II
Handlung action II
Handlungsort location II
handschriftlich handwritten II
Handschuh glove II
handwerklich technical III **U1**, 10
Handy phone I; mobile II
Telefon-/**Handy**nummer phone number I
jmdn. **hänseln** to tease sb III **U1**, 23
Harmonie harmony III **TMS1**, 29
hart hard II
hassen to hate I
hässlich ugly III **U1**, 14
häufig often I
Haupt- main II; lead III **U1**, 12
die **Haupteinkaufsstraße** the high street
  III **U1**, 20
Hauptrolle lead part III **U1**, 12
hauptsächlich mostly ⟨III **TMS1**, 32⟩
Hauptstadt capital II
Haus house I
  nach **Hause** home I
  zu **Hause** at home I
  zu jmdm. nach **Hause** gehen *to go over
  to II
  rund ums **Haus** around the house I
  ums **Haus** herum around the house I
Hausarrest haben *to be grounded III **U1**, 20
Hausaufgabe(n) homework (no pl) I
Haustier pet I
Haustür front door II

He! Hey! I
Heft booklet III **U4**, 109
Heim home I
Heimatort hometown II
Heimatstadt hometown II
heimlich in secret II
heimwärts homeward ⟨III **U2**, 47⟩
Heimweh haben *to be homesick III **U4**, 106
heiraten to marry III **U3**, 65
heiß hot III **AC1**, 35
Ich **heiße** … My name is … I
  Wie **heißen** Sie? What's your name? I
  Wie **heißt** du? What's your name? I
Heizung heating III **U1**, 11
Held hero, heroes (pl) II
Heldin heroine II
helfen to help I
hell bright III **TMS1**, 30
Helm helmet I
Hemd shirt I
heranzoomen (auf) to zoom in (on)
  III **U3**, 74
heraus out I
herausfinden *to find; *to find out I
Herausforderung challenge II
herauskommen aus *to get out of II
herausschneiden to edit out III **U3**, 75
Herberge hostel ⟨III **TR1**, 111⟩
Herbst autumn ⟨III **U2**, 47⟩
Herd cooker I
herein in I
hereinkommen *to come in I
Herkunft origin III **U4**, 107
Herr (Anrede) Mr I; lord III **U3**, 65
herrisch bossy III **U1**, 15
Herrschaft rule III **U3**, 63; reign III **U3**, 65
herrschen to reign III **U3**, 72
herstellen to produce III **U1**, 10
  hergestellt sein aus *to be made of
  III **U3**, 64
um … **herum** around I
herumschleichen to sneak around II
sich **herumtreiben** (mit) *to hang out (with)
  (infml) III **U1**, 20
herunter down I
  von … weg/ab/**herunter** off I
herunterfallen *to fall off I
herunterkommen *to come down I
herunterladen (aus dem Internet) to
  download II
herunternehmen *to take off II
herunterrollen to roll off II
hervorheben to emphasize III **TMS1**, 29
Herz heart II
Herzlichen Dank! Thank you very much!
  III **U1**, 10
  Herzliche Grüße (am Briefende) Love
  … II
  Herzliche Grüße, Best wishes, III **TMS2**, 83
Herzog duke III **U3**, 65
heulend howling ⟨III **TR1**, 110⟩
heute today I; these days III **U1**, 20
  bis **heute** to this day III **U3**, 65

heute Abend 2nite *(= tonight)* I
heute Nachmittag this afternoon II
heutig present III **U2**, 48
heutzutage these days III **U1**, 20
Hexe witch II
Hi. Hi.; Hey! I
hier here I
genau **hier** right here II
Highlight highlight II
Hilfe help I
ohne fremde **Hilfe** alone I
hilflos helpless I
hilfreich helpful I; useful II
hilfsbereit helpful I
Himmel sky III **U2**, 50
hinauf up II
hinaus out I
hinausgehen *to go out II
hinein inside II
hineingehen to enter III **U4**, 99
hineingelangen *to get into II
hineinlegen *to put (in) I
hineinsetzen *to put (in) I
hineinstellen *to put (in) I
Hin- und Rückfahrkarte return ticket II
hinfallen *to fall over; *to fall I
wo ich **hingehöre** where I belong III **U4**, 104
hinkommen *to get here II
hinnehmen to accept III **U4**, 104
sich **hinsetzen** *to sit down I
hinter behind I
hinter der Bühne backstage III **U3**, 70
du stehst **hinter** mir you've got my back III **TMS1**, 27
Hintergrund background II
Hintergrund- backing III **U1**, 12
hinterhergehen to follow I
hinüber over; across I
hinübergehen zu *to go over to II
hinunter down I
hinunterfallen *to fall off I; *to fall down III **U2**, 50
hinuntergehen *to go down I
hinunterrollen to roll off II
Hinweis clue; piece of advice II; hint III **AC2**, 57
hinzufügen to add I
historisch historical II; historic III **U2**, 40
Hobby hobby, hobbies *(pl)* I
hoch high; tall II
jmdn. **hochleben** lassen *to give sb the bumps II
hochschauen to look up III **U2**, 50
Hockey hockey II
Hofdame lady-in-waiting III **U3**, 66
hoffen to hope I
Hoffnung hope II
hoffnungsvoll hopeful I
höflich polite I
Höhen und Tiefen ups and downs III **TMS1**, 27
Höhepunkt highlight II; climax III **U2**, 52
hoher Berg ben III **U2**, 46

Höhle cave II
holen *to get I; to fetch III **U4**, 10
Holz wood III **U2**, 51
aus **Holz** wooden III **U2**, 50
hölzern wooden III **U2**, 50
Homepage homepage I
Honig honey III **AC1**, 34
Hoppla! Oops! I
Hör- audio I
horchen auf to listen for I
hören *to hear I
Ich habe **gehört**, dass … I hear … I
Hose trousers *(pl)* I
kurze **Hose** shorts *(pl)* II
Hosentasche pocket III **U2**, 50
Hospital hospital III **U3**, 75
Hotel hotel III **U4**, 102
hübsch beautiful II; pretty III **U1**, 21
Huch! Oops! I
jmdn. **Huckepack** nehmen *to give sb a piggyback III **U4**, 104
Hügel hill II
Huhn chicken I
Hülle wrapping II
Humor humour *(no pl)* III **U1**, 23
Sinn für **Humor** sense of humour *(no pl)* III **U1**, 23
Hund dog I
hundemüde dog-tired I
hunderte (von) hundreds of III **U2**, 44
hungrig hungry II
hüpfen to bounce III **AC2**, 56
Hurra! Hooray! III **TMS2**, 85
Husten cough II
Hut hat II
hüten to look after I

I

ich I I
ich auch me too I
Ich heiße … My name is … I
Ich möchte … I'd like to … *(= I would like to)* I
Ich sehe was, was du nicht siehst I spy with my little eye II
Ich weiß (es) nicht! I don't know! I
ich würde lieber I'd rather II **U3**, 77
Idee idea I
sich **identifizieren** (mit) to identify (with) III **U3**, 77
Idiot/-in idiot II
ignorieren to ignore III **U1**, 21
ihm him I
ihn him I
ihnen them I
ihr you; u *(= you)* I
Ihr/-e your I; yours II
ihr/-e her; its I
ihr/-e *(Pl.)* their I
ihre/-r/-es theirs III **TR2**, 112
Ikone icon III **TMS2**, 84
illustrieren to illustrate II

im Fernsehen on TV II
im in; on I
im Innern inside II
im Moment at the moment I; right now II
im Weg sein/stehen *to be in the way I
Imbiss snack I
Imbissstube snack bar I
immer always I
für **immer** forever II
immer noch still I
immerhin after all II
Imperativ imperative II
Impression impression III **TMS1**, 27
in in; on; at; to; into I; inside II
in Cornwall Cornish II
in der Nähe von near I
in … hinein into I
auf/**in** … steht … says II
in Ordnung OK; fine I
Inder/-in Indian I
indirekte Rede indirect speech 〈III **TR3**, 115〉
indisch Indian I
Industrie industry III **U2**, 42
Influencer/-in influencer III **U1**, 10
Informatik IT *(= Information Technology)* III **U1**, 12
Information information *(no pl)* I
Informationen information *(no pl)* I
Informationstechnik IT *(= Information Technology)* III **U1**, 12
informell informal III **TMS2**, 80
informieren to inform III **TMS2**, 80
Ingenieur/-in engineer III **U2**, 48
Inhalt content II
Inlineskates skates *(pl)* I
Inlineskates fahren to skate I
Inlineskatefahren inline skating I
inmitten among III **AC3**, 88
innen inside II
innerhalb (von) within 〈III **TR1**, 111〉
inoffiziell unofficial III **U2**, 47; informal III **TMS2**, 80
Input input III **U4**, 103
Insel island II
insistieren to insist (on) III **U4**, 99
Installateur/-in plumber II
Instruktion instruction III **AC2**, 57
Instrument instrument III **TMS1**, 29
intelligent smart III **U1**, 9
Intelligenztyp smart type III **U1**, 9
interessant interesting I
Interesse interest II
sich **interessieren** (für) *to be interested in; to care (about) II
interessiert sein an *to be interested in II
international international II
Internet internet I
Internetauftritt website I; web page II
interpretieren to interpret 〈III **TMS1**, 32〉
Interview interview I
interviewen to interview II
involviert sein *to be involved III **U1**, 10
inzwischen by now II

irgendein/-e/-er any **I**
irgendetwas anything **II**
irgendjemand anyone; anybody **II**
irgendwelche any **I**
irgendwo anywhere; somewhere **II**
Irisch Irish **II**
irisch Irish **II**
sich **irren** *to be wrong **I**
Italien Italy **II**

J

ja yes; yeah (infml) **I**
Jacke jacket **I**
jagen to chase **I**; to hunt ⟨**III TR2**, 112⟩
Jahr year **I**
Jahrbuch yearbook **II**
Jahreszeit season **II**
Jahrhundert century **II**
18-**jährig** 18-year-old **II**
11-**Jährige**/-r 11-year-old **II**
Jahrzehnt decade **III U2**, 44
Januar January **II**
Japanisch Japanese **III TMS1**, 32
japanisch Japanese **III TMS1**, 32
Jazz (Musik) jazz **III TMS1**, 26
je … desto the … the **II**
Jeans jeans (pl) **I**
jedenfalls anyway **II**
jede/-r/-s every **I**; each **II**
jeder everyone **I**; everybody **II**
    jede Menge lots (of) **I**; loads (of)
    III TMS2, 84
    jeder (beliebige) anyone; anybody **II**
    jedes Mal, wenn whenever **II**
jedoch however **III U3**, 65
jemals ever **II**
jemand somebody; someone **II**
    jemand anderes anyone else **II**
jene those **I**
jenes that **I**
jetzt now **I**
    gleich **jetzt** right now **II**
Job job **I**
Joghurt yoghurt **I**
jubeln to cheer on **II**
Jugend- teen **II**
Jugendliche/-r teenager; kid **II**
Juli July **II**
jung young **I**
Junge boy **I**
Juni June **II**

K

Kaffee coffee **I**
Käfig cage **III TMS1**, 28
kahl bald **III U3**, 66
Kaiserreich empire **III U3**, 63
Kalender planner **I**; calendar **III U3**, 65
kalt cold **I**
    etw. **kalt** stellen *to leave sth to cool **II**
    Mir ist **kalt**. I'm cold. **I**

Kamelrennen camel racing **II**
Kamera camera **II**
    mit der **Kamera** festgehalten caught on
    camera **II**
Kamin chimney **II**
Kampf fight **II**; battle **III U3**, 65
kämpfen *to fight **II**
Kampfschrei rebel yell ⟨**III TMS1**, 27⟩
Kanal (TV) channel **III U1**, 10
Kaninchen rabbit **I**
Kapitän/-in captain **I**
Kapitel chapter **III AC3**, 89
Kappe cap **II**
kaputt broken **I**
Karaoke karaoke **II**
Karotte carrot **I**
Karriere career **III U1**, 12
Karte card **I**
Kartenausgabestelle ticket office **III U2**, 50
Kartoffel potato , potatoes (pl) **III U3**, 66
Kartoffelbrei mashed potatoes (pl) **III U2**, 44
Kartoffelchip crisp **I**
Kartoffelpüree mashed potatoes (pl)
    III U2, 44
ein **Karton** … a box of … **I**
Käse cheese **I**
Kasten box **I**
Katalog catalogue **III U4**, 103
Katastrophe disaster **II**
Kategorie category **II**
Katze cat **I**
kaufen *to buy **I**
Käufer/-in buyer **I**
Kaugummi chewing gum **I**
kaum hardly ⟨**III TR1**, 110⟩
Keine Ahnung. No idea. **I**
kein/-e no **I**
    Keine Sorge! Don't worry! **I**
kein/-e/-en not … any **I**
keineswegs No way! **I**
Keks biscuit **I**
Kelle trowel **II**
Kelte/**Keltin** Celt **III U3**, 63
keltisch Celtic **II**
kennen *to know **I**
    kennen lernen *to get to know **III AC2**, 56
Kerl guy **II**
Kerze candle **II**
Kerzenlicht candlelight (no pl) **II**
Kfz-Mechaniker/-in mechanic **II**
Kilometer kilometre (km) **II**
Kilt kilt **III U2**, 41
Kind child, children (pl) **I**; kid **II**
Kinderlied nursery rhyme **III TMS1**, 26
Kinderreim nursery rhyme **III TMS1**, 26
Kino cinema **I**
Kirche church **I**
Kiste box **I**
    eine **Kiste** … a box of … **I**
Klang sound **I**
klappen to work out **III U1**, 23
klar clear **I**
Klasse class; group **I**

Klasse (in einer englischen Schule) tutor
    group **I**
Klassenarbeit test **I**
Klassenkamerad/-in classmate **I**
Klassenlehrer/-in tutor **I**
Klassenzimmer classroom **I**
klatschen to clap **II**
Klavier piano **I**
Klebstoff glue **III TMS1**, 30
Kleid dress **III U1**, 14
Kleider clothes (pl) **I**
Kleidergröße size **I**
Kleiderschrank wardrobe **I**
Kleidung clothes (pl) **I**; outfit **II**
klein little; small **I**; tiny **III U2**, 48
Klempner/-in plumber **II**
Kletter- climbing **II**
Klettern climbing **II**
klettern to climb **I**
Klick click **II**
Klicken click **II**
Kliff cliff **II**
Klima climate **III U4**, 106
Klimaanlage air-conditioning **III U4**, 105
Klimawandel climate change **III U1**, 10
Klingel bell **I**
klingeln *to ring **I**
klingen to sound **II**
Klippe cliff **II**
klitzeklein wee bit ⟨**III U2**, 47⟩
klonen to clone **III U2**, 43
Klub club **I**
klug clever **I**; smart **III U1**, 9
Klugheit cleverness **III TMS1**, 30
Knacken crack **III U2**, 51
knackend cracking **III U2**, 50
knapp close **I**
    Das war **knapp**! That was close! **I**
Kneipe pub ⟨**III TR3**, 114⟩
sich den **Knöchel** verrenken to twist your
    ankle **II**
Knopf knob **II**; button **III U4**, 105
Koch-AG cooking club **II**
Kochen cooking **I**
kochen to cook **II**
Koffer suitcase **III U4**, 95
Kofferraum boot **III U3**, 75
Kohle coal **III U2**, 43
Kohlendioxid CO_2 (carbon dioxide) **III U4**, 95
Kokosnuss coconut **II**
Kollektion collection **II**
Köln Cologne **I**
Kolonie colony **III U3**, 65
Kolonist/-in colonist **III U3**, 67
Komfort convenience **III U4**, 95
komfortabel comfortable **III U1**, 14
Komiker/-in comedian **II**
komisch funny **III U1**, 15; odd **III AC3**, 88
    jmdn. **komisch** anschauen *to give sb
    funny looks **III U1**, 15
kommen *to come **I**
    kommen nach *to get to **I**
    kommen zu *to get to **I**

Komm jetzt! Come on! **I**
Komm schon! Come on! **I**
Komm/Kommt rein. Come in. **I**
Kommentar comment **II**
kommentieren to comment (on) **II**
Kommunikation communication **III U2**, 53
kommunizieren to communicate **III U1**, 9
Komödie comedy **II**
Kompass compass ⟨**III TR1**, 110⟩
komplett complete **III U3**, 63
Kompromiss compromise **II**
  einen **Kompromiss** eingehen to compromise **III U1**, 9
Konfitüre jam **II**
Konflikt conflict **III U1**, 18
konfus confused **III U1**, 22
König king **I**
Königin queen **I**
königlich royal **II**
Königreich kingdom **III U3**, 63
konkurrieren (mit) to compete (with) **III U1**, 9
können can **I**; *to be able to (do sth) **III U1**, 21
konnte/-n could **II**
  kann nicht can't **I**; cannot **II**
  können nicht can't **I**; cannot **II**
  könnte/-n (vielleicht) might **II**
  (vielleicht) **können** may **I**
Kontakt contact **II**
  in **Kontakt** bleiben (mit) to stay in touch (with) **II**
kontaktfreudig outgoing **III U4**, 107
jmdn. **kontaktieren** to contact sb **II**
kontinuierlich steady **III U4**, 105
Kontrolle control **III U4**, 95
kontrollieren to check **I**; to control **III U3**, 67
Kontrollpunkt checkpoint **III U4**, 104
Konversation conversation **II**
(sich) **konzentrieren** (auf) to focus (on) **III U1**, 10; to concentrate (on) **III U4**, 105
Konzert concert **III TMS1**, 26
Kopf head **I**
  etw. aus dem **Kopf** bekommen *to get sth out of one's head **III TMS1**, 29
Kopfhörer headset; headphones (pl) **II**
Kopfkissen pillow **II**
Kopfschmerzen headache **II**
Kopfweh headache **II**
Korbball netball **I**
Koreaner/-in Korean **II**
Koreanisch Korean **II**
koreanisch Korean **II**
Körper body **III U1**, 9
  menschlicher **Körper** human body **II**
Körpersprache body language **III U1**, 19
korrekt right **I**; correct **III U1**, 11
Korridor hall **II**
kosten *to cost **I**; to taste ⟨**III TR1**, 110⟩
  Es **kostet** …/Sie **kosten** … It's …/They're … **I**
  Wie viel **kostet/kosten** …? How much is/are …? **I**

kostenlos free **I**
köstlich delicious **II**
Kostüm costume; fancy dress (no pl) **II**
Krachen crack **III U2**, 51
Kraft energy **II**; force **III U4**, 107; power ⟨**III TR2**, 112⟩
Krampf cramp **II**
Kran crane **III U2**, 48
Krankenhaus hospital **III U3**, 75
Krankenpfleger nurse **III U3**, 75
Krankenschwester nurse **III U3**, 75
Krankenwagen ambulance **III U3**, 75
Krankheit illness **III U4**, 102
kreativ creative **II**
Kreis circle **II**
  sich im **Kreis** drehen *to go round in circles **III U2**, 50
kreischen to scream **II**
Kresse cress **II**
Kreuz cross **II**
kreuzen to cross **I**
Krieger warrior **II**
Kriminalität crime **II**
Kriterium, **Kriterien** (Pl.) criterion, criteria (pl) **III U4**, 103
Kritik review **II**
Kritiker/-in reviewer **II**
Krone crown **II**
Kronjuwelen crown jewels **II**
Küche kitchen **I**
Kuchen cake; pie **I**
Küchenschrank cupboard **I**
Kuh cow **I**
Kühlschrank fridge **I**
Kultur culture **I**
Kummerkastentante agony aunt **II**
sich **kümmern** (um) to look after **I**; to care (about) **II**
  sich um jmdn./etw. **kümmern** *to take care of sb/sth **III U3**, 74
Kunst art **I**
Kunstgalerie gallery **II**
Künstler/-in artist **II**
Kunstunterricht art **I**
Kurs course **II**
  einen **Kurs** belegen *to do a course (in) **II**
kurz short **II**
Kurznachricht text (message) **I**; text **II**
kuschelig cosy ⟨**III TR3**, 114⟩
Kuss kiss **III TMS2**, 85
sich **küssen** to kiss **III U2**, 55
Küste shore; coastline **II**; seaside **III U3**, 65; coast **III U4**, 96
Küstenverlauf coastline **II**
Küstenweg coastal path **II**

L

Lächeln smile **I**
lächeln to smile **II**
Lachen laugh **III TMS1**, 27
lachen to laugh **I**
Laden shop **I**

Lady lady **II**
Lage location **II**
geheimes **Lager** cache **I**
Lamm lamb **I**
Lämmchen lamb **I**
Lampe light **I**
Land country, countries (pl); land **I**; countryside **II**
landen to end up **II**; to land **III AC3**, 89
Landkarte map **I**
Landschaft landscape **II**
Landwirt/-in farmer **II**
lang long **I**
  (nicht) **länger** (not) any longer ⟨**III TR1**, 110⟩
langsam slow **I**
langweilig boring **I**
Laptop laptop **II**
Lärm noise **II**
lassen *to leave **I**; *to let **II**
  Lass/Lasst uns … Let's … **I**
Lassi lassi **II**
lästig annoying **II**
Latein Latin **III U3**, 63
lateinisch Latin **III U3**, 63
Lauf run **II**
Laufbahn career **III U1**, 12
Laufen running **II**
laufen *to run; to walk **I**; *to be on **II**
  ins Foto **laufen** to photobomb **III U3**, 75
Läufer/-in runner **II**
Laune mood **II**; humour (no pl) **III U1**, 23
laut loud **I**
läuten *to ring **I**
Leben life, lives (pl) **II**
zum **Leben** erwecken *to bring to life **II**
leben to live **I**
Lebensmittel food **I**
Lebensstil lifestyle **III U3**, 79
lecker tasty **III U4**, 102; yummy ⟨**III TR3**, 114⟩
Leder leather **III U3**, 63
leer empty **II**
legal legal **III TMS1**, 29
legen *to put (in) **I**
Legende legend **II**
Leggings leggings (pl) **I**
jmdm. eine **Lehre/Lektion** erteilen *to teach somebody a lesson **II**
lehren *to teach **II**
Lehrer/-in teacher **I**; instructor **II**
leicht easy **I**; light **III AC2**, 56
leid tun *to be sorry **I**
Tut mir **leid**! Sorry!; I'm sorry! **I**
leihen *to lend (to) **II**
leise quiet **I**
jmdm. eine Lehre/**Lektion** erteilen *to teach somebody a lesson **II**
Lernen studying **I**
lernen *to learn **I**; to study **III U1**, 12
  auswendig **lernen** *to learn … by heart **III TMS1**, 26
Lerntyp smart type **III U1**, 9
Lesen reading **I**

lesen *to read I
Leser/-in reader II
letzte/-r/-s last I; final III U2, 48
letztlich finally II
leuchtend bright III TMS1, 30
Leute people (pl) I
Lexikon encyclopedia II
Licht light I
Lichtblitz flash III U3, 75
lieb nice I; dearly ⟨III U2, 47⟩
    Lieber … Dear … I
    Liebe … Dear … I
    Liebe Grüße (am Briefende) Love … II
Liebe love II
lieben to love I
lieber better II
    ich würde lieber I'd rather III U3, 77
Liebesfilm romance III U4, 107
Liebesgeschichte romance III U4, 107
Lieblings- favourite I
    Mein Lieblings… ist … My favourite …
    is … I
    Was ist dein/-e Lieblings …? What's your
    favourite …? I
Lied song I
Liedermacher/-in songwriter III TMS1, 26
liefern to provide ⟨III TMS2, 86⟩
liegen *to lie ⟨III U2, 47⟩
Lifestyle lifestyle III U3, 79
lila purple I
Limonade lemonade I
Linderung relief III U4, 99
Lineal ruler I
Linie line I
Link link II
linke/-r/-s left I
    auf der linken Seite on the left I
links on the left I
    (nach) links left I
Liste list II
Literatur literature III TMS1, 26
live live ⟨III TR3, 114⟩
locker laid-back III U1, 12; relaxed
    III U3, 66; easy-going III U4, 107
Löffel spoon I
Logik logic III U1, 9
lokal local II
Londoner/-in Londoner II
Lord lord III U3, 65
Los ticket I
los sein *to go on III AC3, 88
löschen to delete III U1, 23
lösen to solve II
von einem Gedanken loskommen *to get
    sth out of one's head III TMS1, 29
loslassen *to let go (of) II
Lösung solution II
Luft air ⟨III TR1, 110⟩
Lüge lie III TMS1, 28
lügen to lie II
Lupe magnifying glass (no pl) II
lustig funny; fun I
Lyrik poetry III TMS1, 26

M

machen *to do; *to make I
    Fotos machen *to take photos I
    gemacht sein aus *to be made of III U3, 64
    sauber machen to tidy (up) II
    das macht nichts It doesn't matter.
    III U1, 8
    Mir macht es nichts aus (zu …) I don't
    mind (+ …ing) III U1, 18
Macht force III U4, 107; power ⟨III TR2, 112⟩
mächtig powerful II
Mädchen girl I
Magen stomach II
Magie magic III U4, 107
magisch magical II
Magnet magnet III TMS1, 30
Mahlzeit meal II
Mai May II
mailen to email II
Mal time II
Malen painting II
malen to paint I
Malerei painting II
Mama mum I; mummy III U1, 21
Mami mummy III U1, 21
Manager/-in manager III TMS2, 81
manchmal sometimes I
Manga (japanischer Comic) manga II
Mangel flaw ⟨III TMS1, 32⟩
Mango mango I
Manieren manners (pl) III AC3, 89
Mann man, men (pl) I
Mannschaftsführer/-in captain I
manuell by hand III U3, 65
Mäppchen pencil case I
Marathon marathon II
markiert highlighted ⟨III TMS2, 86⟩
Markt market I
Marmelade jam II
März March II
Maschine machine I
Maske mask III U4, 104
Match match II
Mathe maths II
Mathematik maths II
Matrose sailor I
Mauer wall I
Maus/Mäuse mouse, mice (pl) I
Mechaniker/-in mechanic II
Medien media (pl) II
Meer sea I
Meeresküste seaside III U3, 65
Meeresspiegel sea level III U3, 63
Meerschweinchen guinea pig I
mehr more I
    (nicht) mehr (not) any longer ⟨III TR1, 110⟩
    mehr … als more … than I
meiden to stay away from II
Meile (brit. Längenmaß) mile II
mein/-e my I
    Mein Lieblings… ist … My favourite …
    is … I

    (meine) Schuld (my) fault II
mein/-er/-e/-es mine I
meinen *to mean I
Meinung opinion III U1, 15
    anderer Meinung sein to disagree
    III U1, 9
    einer Meinung sein to agree III U1, 9
    seine Meinung ändern to change one's
    mind III U4, 104
die meisten (the) most II
der/die/das meiste (the) most II
meistens usually I; mostly ⟨III TMS1, 32⟩
Meldung report II
melken to milk II
eine Menge a lot of I
jede Menge lots (of) I; loads (of) III TMS2, 84
Mensch person, people (pl) I
Menschen people (pl) I
Menschenmenge crowd II
menschlicher Körper human body II
sich merken to remember I
typisches Merkmal characteristic III U3, 66
merkwürdig strange I; funny III U1, 15
sich messen (mit) to compete (with)
    III U1, 9
Messer knife, knives (pl) I
Metall metal III U3, 63
Metapher metaphor III TMS1, 31
Meter metre II
mich me I
mieten to rent (out) III U2, 54; to hire
    III U3, 71
Milch milk I
militärisch military ⟨III TR1, 110⟩
Milliarde a billion III U1, 24
Million a million III U1, 12
    Ich habe das schon eine Million Mal
    gemacht. I've done this a million times
    before. II
Millionär/-in millionaire III U1, 12
mindestens at least ⟨III TR1, 111⟩
Mine mine II
Mineral mineral II
Mini- mini II
Minute minute I
mir me I
    Mir geht's gut. I'm fine. I
mischen to mix (up) III U3, 74
Mischung mix III U4, 102
missverstanden misunderstood III U1, 18
mit with I; on II
mit (dem Fahrrad) by (bike) I
    mit mir with me I
    Mit freundlichen Grüßen, Yours sincerely,
    III TMS2, 80
mitbekommen (ugs.) *to catch III AC2, 56
mitbringen *to bring; *to take I
miteinander together I; each other II
Mitglied member II
mithalten (mit) *to keep up (with) II
mitkriegen (ugs.) *to catch III AC2, 56
Mitleid haben mit *to feel sorry for III U1, 23
mitmachen *to be in II; to enter III U4, 99

mitnehmen *to take **I**; to pick up **II**
Mitschüler/-in classmate **I**
mitsingen *to sing along **III TMS1**, 29
Mitspieler/-in player **II**
Mittagessen lunch **I**
Mittagspause lunch break **I**
Mitte middle **II**
mitteilen *to tell **I**
Mittel means (pl only) **III U4**, 95
Mittelalter Middle Ages **III U3**, 63
mittelalterlich medieval **II**
mitten in in the middle of **II**
Mitternacht midnight **III U2**, 43
mittlerweile by now **II**
Mittwoch Wednesday **I**
(jmdn.) mobben to bully (sb) **II**
Mobiltelefon mobile **II**
Mode fashion **I**
Model model **I**
Modell model **I**
Modeln modelling **III U1**, 12
Moderator/-in presenter **II**
modern modern **II**
mögen to like; to want (to); *to be into **I**
  gern **mögen** to love **I**
  nicht **mögen** to hate **I**
  Ich **möchte** … I'd like to … (= I would like to) **I**
möglich possible **III U1**, 18
möglicherweise probably **II**
Möglichkeit possibility **II**; chance **III TMS1**, 27; option **III U2**, 44
Möhre carrot **I**
Moment moment **II**
  im **Moment** at the moment **I**; right now **II**
  genau in dem **Moment** just then **I**
Monarch/-in monarch **III U3**, 65
Monat month **II**
Mondlicht moonlight **III U2**, 50
Monster monster **I**
Montag Monday **I**
montags on Mondays **I**
Monument monument **II**
Mord murder **III U3**, 69
Morgen morning **I**
  Guten **Morgen**. Good morning. **I**
morgen tomorrow **I**
morgens (Uhrzeit) a.m. **I**
Motto theme **II**
Mountainbikefahren mountain biking **II**
müde tired **I**
sich **Mühe** geben to push oneself **III U1**, 15
Müll rubbish **I**; waste **III U1**, 10
  Müll herumliegen lassen to litter **III AC3**, 88
Münze coin **I**
murmeln to mumble **III U4**, 96
Muschel shell **III TMS1**, 27
Museum museum **I**
Musical musical **III U4**, 108
Musik music **I**
Musik- musical **III U2**, 42
musikalisch musical **III U2**, 42

Musiker/-in musician **II**
Musikgruppe band **III U2**, 50
Müsli muesli **III AC1**, 34
müssen must **I**; *to have to **II**
  nicht **müssen** needn't **II**
  (tun) **müssen** to need to (do) **I**
Muster pattern **III AC2**, 56
mutig brave **II**
Mutter mother **I**
Muttertag Mother's Day **III TMS1**, 26
Mutti mum **I**; mummy **III U1**, 21
Mütze cap **II**
mysteriös mysterious **II**

N

nach to **I**
  nach dort drüben over there **I**
  nach draußen outside; out **I**
  nach drinnen inside **II**
  nach Hause home **I**
  nach unten down **I**; downstairs **II**
  (**nach**) oben up **II**
nach (bei Uhrzeitangaben) past **I**
nach (zeitlich) after **I**
nach oben upstairs **II**
Nachbar/-in neighbour **I**
Nachbarschaft neighbourhood **III U2**, 53
nachdenken *to think **I**
nachjagen to chase **I**
Nachmittag afternoon **I**
  heute **Nachmittag** this afternoon **II**
nachmittags (Uhrzeit) p.m. **I**
Nachname surname **I**
Nachricht message **I**
  eine **Nachricht** entgegennehmen *to take a message **I**
Nachrichten news (sg) **I**
nachschauen to look up **II**
nachschlagen to look up **II**
Nachspeise dessert **II**
nächste/-r/-s next **I**
  der/die **Nächste(n)** next **I**
  als **Nächstes** next **I**
  am **nächsten** Tag the next day **II**
Nacht night **II**
  die ganze **Nacht** all night **II**
  über **Nacht** overnight **III U1**, 21
Nachtisch pudding **I**
Nachtwanderung night walk **II**
nackt bare **III U2**, 47
Nahaufnahme close-up **II**
in der **Nähe** von near **I**
nahe near **I**; close **II**
Name name **I**
Nase nose **II**
  die **Nase** voll haben (von) *to be fed up (with) **III U1**, 20
nass wet **II**
Nation nation (**III U2**, 47)
Nationalheiliger patron saint (**III TR3**, 115)
Nationalhymne national anthem **III U2**, 47
Natur nature **II**

Natur- natural **III U2**, 54
natürlich natural **III U2**, 54
natürlich of course **I**
Naturwissenschaften science **II**
Nebel fog (**III TR1**, 111)
neben next to **I**; besides; by **II**
(von) nebenan next door **III AC2**, 56
Nebenraum side room **III U4**, 99
negativ negative **II**
nehmen *to take **I**
  (ein Bonbon) **nehmen** *to have (a sweet) **I**
  etw. ernst **nehmen** *to take sth seriously **II**
neidisch jealous **II**
nein no **I**
benennen to name **III U2**, 44
nennen to call **I**; to name **III U2**, 44
Neoprenanzug wetsuit **II**
jmdm. auf die **Nerven** gehen *to get on somebody's nerves **I**
nervös nervous **II**
nett nice; friendly **I**; kind **II**
Netz net **I**; web **III U2**, 47
soziale **Netzwerke** social media **III U1**, 10
soziales **Netzwerk** social network **II**
neu new **I**
neueste/-r/-s latest **III U2**, 45
Neuigkeiten news (sg) **I**
neutral neutral **III TMS2**, 86
nicht not **I**
  auch **nicht** not … either **II**
  nicht mehr not any more **I**
  nicht mögen to hate **I**
  noch **nicht** not … yet **II**
nicht- non- **II**
nichts not … anything **I**; nothing **II**
  Nichts zu danken. You're welcome. **I**
nie never **I**
niederbrennen *to burn down **III U3**, 72
sich **niederlassen** to settle **III U3**, 67
niederreißen *to break down (**III TMS1**, 30)
niedlich cute **I**
niedrig low **II**
  niedriger stellen to turn down **III U1**, 11
niemals never **I**
niemand nobody **II**
  niemand anderes nobody else **II**
Nieselregen drizzle **III U4**, 105
nirgendwo nowhere **II**
nirgendwohin nowhere **II**
noch still **I**; yet **II**
noch (+ Komparativ) even (+ comparative) **II**
  noch ein/-e another **I**
  noch einmal again **I**
  noch mal again **I**
  noch nicht not … yet **II**
  noch mal Glück haben *to be saved by the bell **III U1**, 15
Nord- north **I**
Norden north **I**
  im **Norden** north **III U2**, 48
nördlich north **III U2**, 48
Nordsee North Sea **II**

normal normal **II**
normalerweise usually **I**
Normanne/Normannin Norman **III U3**, 65
normannisch Norman **III U3**, 65
in **Not** in need **II**
Note mark **III U1**, 12
Notfall emergency **III U4**, 109
nötig necessary **III U1**, 18
Notiz note **II**
Notlage emergency **III U4**, 109
notwendig necessary **III U1**, 18
November November **II**
Nudeln pasta **I**
null zero **I**
   null *(bei Telefonnummern und Uhrzeit-angaben)* oh **I**
Nummer number **I**
nun now **I**
nun well **I**
nur only; just **I**
nuscheln to mumble **III U4**, 96
Nuss nut **I**
nützlich useful; practical **II**
nutzlos useless **III U4**, 105

O

O! Oh! **I**
o.k. OK **I**
ob if **I**
oben on top; upstairs **II**
   (nach) **oben** up **II**
oben above **II**
obendrauf on top **II**
im **Obergeschoss** upstairs **II**
oberhalb (von) above **II**
oberste/-r/-s top **I**
Objekt object **III U3**, 63
Obst fruit **I**
oder or **I**
offen open **I**
öffentlich public **II**
offiziell official **III U2**, 47
offline offline **II**
öffnen to open **I**
Öffnungszeiten opening times **II**
oft often; a lot **I**
   so **oft** whenever **II**
ohne without **I**
   ohne fremde Hilfe alone **I**
Ohr ear **III TMS1**, 28
Oje! Oh dear! **II**
Öko- Eco **II**
Ökologie ecology **II**
Oktober October **II**
Oma grandma; granny **I**
Omi grandma; granny **I**
Onkel uncle **I**
Online-Pinnwand wall **III U1**, 23
   online stellen to post **II**
online online **II**
Opa grandad **I**; grandpa **II**
Opi grandad **I**; grandpa **II**

optimistisch optimistic **III U1**, 23
Option option **III U2**, 44
Orange orange **I**
orange orange **I**
Orangenmarmelade marmalade **III AC1**, 34
Ordnung order **II**
   in **Ordnung** fine **I**; alright (= all right) ⟨**III TMS1**, 27⟩
   in **Ordnung** bringen to tidy *(a room)* **I**
organisieren to organise **I**
Ort place **I**
örtlich local **II**
Ortsansässige/-r local **III U4**, 102
Ortszeit local time **III U4**, 96
Ost- east **I**
Osten east **I**
Outdoor- outdoor **II**
Outfit outfit **II**

P

Paar pair **I**
ein **paar** a few; some; a couple of **I**
Päckchen packet **I**; parcel **II**
Packung packet **I**
Paket packet **I**; parcel **II**
Palast palace **III U3**, 63
Palme palm tree **II**
Papa dad **I**
Papagei parrot **II**
Papier paper **II**
der **Papst** the Pope **III U3**, 65
Parade parade ⟨**III TR3**, 115⟩
Paradies paradise **II**
Paragraf paragraph **III TMS2**, 81
Parallele similarity ⟨**III TMS1**, 33⟩
paraphrasieren to paraphrase **II**
Park park **I**
Partner/-in partner **I**
   mit einem **Partner**/einer Partnerin in pairs **I**
Party party **II**
Pass passport **III U4**, 95
Passagier/-in passenger **III U4**, 95
zueinander **passen** *to go together **I**
passieren to happen **I**
Passwort password **II**
Pasta pasta **I**
Pastete pie **I**
patentieren patent **III U3**, 78
Pauschalreise package tour **III U4**, 102
Pause break **I**
   eine **Pause** machen *to have a break **I**
Pausenhof playground **II**
Pech haben *to be unlucky **II**
peinlich embarrassing **II**
Pence *(brit. Währungseinheit)* penny, pence *(pl)* **I**
Penicillin penicillin **III U2**, 43
Penny *(brit. Währungseinheit)* penny, pence *(pl)* **I**
perfekt perfect **I**
Periode period **III U3**, 62

Person person, people *(pl)* **I**
   pro **Person** each **I**
persönlich personal; face-to-face **II**
Persönlichkeit personality **III U1**, 9
Perspektive point of view **II**; perspective **III U4**, 102
Pfad trail ⟨**III TR1**, 110⟩
Pfandhaus pawn shop **III U3**, 77
Pfandleihe pawn shop **III U3**, 77
Pfannkuchen pancake ⟨**III TR3**, 114⟩
Pfeife pipe **III U3**, 69
Pfeil arrow **II**
Pferd horse **I**
Pflanze plant **II**
Pfund *(brit. Währungseinheit)* pound (£) **I**
Piano piano **I**
Picknick picnic **I**
Pier pier **I**
Piercing piercing **III U1**, 19
Pikten *(schottischer Volksstamm)* Picts **III U3**, 63
Pille pill **II**
pink pink **I**
Online-**Pinnwand** wall **III U1**, 23
Pirat/-in pirate **II**
Pizza pizza **I**
Plan plan **I**
planen to plan **II**
Planet planet **II**
Plattform platform **II**
Platz place **I**; room; pitch **II**
Platz! *(Befehl für Hunde)* Sit! **I**
plaudern to chat **I**
plötzlich suddenly **II**
Podcast podcast **III U1**, 10
Poesie poetry **III TMS1**, 26
Poker poker **III TMS1**, 28
Polen Poland **I**
politisch political **III U3**, 65
Polizei police **II**
Pommes frites chips *(pl)* **I**
Pony pony **I**
Ponyreiten im Gelände pony trekking **II**
Pop *(Musik)* pop **III TMS1**, 26
populär popular **I**
Porträt profile **II**
positiv positive **II**
Post *(Eintrag im Internet)* post **I**
Postamt post office **I**
Postanschrift postal address **III TMS2**, 81
Poster poster **I**
Postkarte postcard **II**
prächtig grand ⟨**III TR3**, 114⟩
prägnant to the point **III AC2**, 57
praktisch practical **III U4**, 102
Präsens present **II**
Präsentation presentation **I**
präsentieren to present **III TMS1**, 29
Praxis surgery **I**
Praxisräume surgery **I**
Preis price; prize **I**; award **II**
preiswert cheap **I**
pressen to press **III U4**, 105

Prinzessin princess **II**
privat private **II**
Privat- private **II**
pro per **II**
  pro Person each **I**
  pro Stück each **I**
probieren to try **I**; to taste ⟨**III TR1**, 110⟩
Problem problem **I**
Probleme trouble **I**
Produkt product **III U1**, 10
produzieren to produce **III U1**, 10
Profil profile **II**
Profileinstellungen account settings
  III U1, 23
Programm programme **II**
Programm (Radio) channel **III U1**, 10
Projekt project **I**
Prospekt brochure **I**
Prozent per cent **III U1**, 17
prüfen to check **I**; to check out (coll)
  III AC2, 56
Prüfung test **I**
Publikum audience **II**
Pudding pudding **I**
Pulli jumper **I**
Pullover jumper **I**
Punkt point **II**
Punktestand score **II**
pünktlich on time **II**
pur pure ⟨**III TMS1**, 32⟩
pusten *to blow **II**
putzen to clean **II**
Puzzle puzzle **I**
Pyjama pyjamas (pl) **II**
Pyjama-Party sleepover **II**

Q

Qualifikation trial **II**
Qualität quality **I**
Quelle source **II**
quer durch across **I**
Quiche quiche **II**
Quiz quiz **I**

R

Rabe raven **II**
Rad wheel **I**
Radfahren cycling **I**
Radiergummi rubber **I**
Radio radio **I**
Rahmen setting **II**
rappen to rap **I**
Rat advice (no pl) **I**; piece of advice **II**
raten to guess **III AC3**, 88
  Rate mal! Guess what! **III U3**, 70
Ratschlag advice (no pl) **I**; tip; piece of
  advice **II**
Rätsel puzzle; quiz **I**; mystery **III U3**, 74
Ratte rat **I**
Räuber/-in robber **II**
Raum room **I**

reagieren to react **III U1**, 15
Reaktion reaction **II**
realisieren to realise **III U2**, 50
realistisch realistic **II**
Recherche research (no pl) **III U4**, 101
Recht haben *to be right **I**
rechte/-r/-s right **I**
  auf der **rechten** Seite on the right **I**
  rechts on the right **I**
  (nach) **rechts** right **I**
rechthaberisch bossy **III U1**, 15
rechtlich legal **III TMS1**, 29
Rechts- legal **III TMS1**, 29
recyceln to recycle **II**
Recycling recycling **III U1**, 11
indirekte **Rede** indirect speech ⟨**III TR3**, 115⟩
reden to talk **I**
  reden mit to talk to **I**
Redensart saying **III U1**, 8
Redewendung phrase **III U1**, 9
Redner/-in speaker **I**
Refrain chorus **III TMS1**, 29
Regal shelf, shelves (pl) **II**
Regalbrett shelf, shelves (pl) **II**
Regel rule **I**
Regelung regulation **III U4**, 99
Regen rain **III U1**, 11
Regenmantel raincoat **II**
Regenschirm umbrella **III U3**, 78
Regenwasser rainwater **III U1**, 11
Regieanweisung stage direction **III AC2**, 57
regieren to reign **III U3**, 72
Regierung government **III U2**, 43
Regierungszeit rule **III U3**, 63; reign **III U3**, 55
Region region **II**
reglos still **II**
regnen to rain **II**
Regulierung regulation **III U4**, 99
Reich empire **III U3**, 63
reich rich **III U1**, 12
Reihenfolge order **II**
Reim rhyme **III TMS1**, 31
(sich) **reimen** to rhyme **III TMS1**, 31
Reimschema rhyme scheme **III TMS1**, 31
rein pure ⟨**III TMS1**, 32⟩
rein in **I**
reinigen to clean **II**
Reise trip **I**; journey **II**
Reise- travel **III U4**, 95
Reisebericht travel report **II**
Reisebüro travel agent's **II**
Reisebus coach **II**
Reiseführer guide; guide book **II**
(das) **Reisen** travelling (no pl) **I**
reisen to travel **II**
Reisepass passport **III U4**, 95
Reiseplan itinerary **III U4**, 95
Reiseroute itinerary **III U4**, 95
Reiseveranstalter tour operator **III U4**, 102
Reiseweg itinerary **III U4**, 95
Reiseziel destination **III TMS2**, 30
reiten *to ride **II**
jmdn. **reizen** to appeal to sb **III U2**, 49

Religion (Schulfach) RE (= Religious Educa-
  tion) **II**
religiös religious **II**
Rennen race; running; run **II**
rennen *to run **I**
reparieren to fix **II**
Reporter/-in reporter **II**
Requisite prop **II**
reservieren to book **II**
Respekt respect **III TMS1**, 30
der **Rest** the rest **III U4**, 108
Restaurant restaurant **I**
Resultat result **II**
retten to save **I**
Rettung rescue **II**
Rettungsboot lifeboat **I**
Rettungsring lifebuoy **I**
Revolution revolution **III U3**, 63
Rezension review **II**
Rezept recipe **III U2**, 46
Rezept (für Arzneimittel) prescription **II**
rhythmisch rhythmic **III TMS1**, 29
Rhythmus rhythm **III TMS1**, 29
richtig right **I**; real **II**; correct **III U1**, 11
in … **Richtung** towards **II**
riechen *to smell ⟨**III TR1**, 110⟩
riesengroß huge **III U2**, 48
riesig large **III U2**, 42; huge **III U2**, 48
Rinderhirte cowboy **II**
Ring circle **II**; ring **III U3**, 65
Ritter knight **II**
Rock skirt **I**
Rock (Musik) rock **III TMS1**, 26
Rohmaterial raw material **III U3**, 65
Rohr pipe **II**
Rohrleitung pipe **II**
Rohstoff raw material **III U3**, 65
Rolle role **II**; part **III U1**, 12
  es spielt keine **Rolle** It doesn't matter.
  III U1, 8
Rollenkarte prompt card **II**
Rollschuhe skates (pl) **I**
Rollstuhl wheelchair **II**
Rolltreppe escalator **I**
Römer/-in Roman **II**
römisch Roman **II**
rosa pink **I**
rot red **I**
Route route **II**
Routine routine **I**
Rückblende flashback **III U3**, 76
Rücken back **III U1**, 21
Rückenschmerzen backache **II**
Rückenweh backache **II**
Hin- und **Rückfahrkarte** return ticket **II**
Rückkehr return ⟨**III TR1**, 110⟩
Rückmeldung feedback **II**
Rucksack backpack **II**
Rückseite back **III U1**, 21
rufen to shout; to call **I**; to cry **II**
Rugby rugby **II**
Ruhe silence (no pl) **III U3**, 69
ruhig quiet **I**; still **II**

die Beine und Hände **ruhig** halten *to keep one's feet or hands still **III TMS1**, 29

Rührkuchen sponge **II**

ruinieren to ruin **II**

rumhängen (mit) *to hang out (with) *(infml)* **III U1**, 20

rund round **III U3**, 63

Rundgang tour **I**

die Stirn **runzeln** to frown **III U4**, 99

Rutschbahn slide **I**

S

Saal hall **II**

Sache thing **I**

sachlich factual **II**

Sachse/Sächsin Saxon **III U3**, 65

sächsisch Saxon **III U3**, 65

Saft juice **I**

Sage legend **II**

sagen *to tell; *to say **I**

sagenhaft mythical **III U4**, 107

sagenumwoben mythical **III U4**, 107

Sahne cream **II**

Saison season **II**

Salat salad **I**

Salbe ointment **II**

sammeln to collect **II**

Geld **sammeln** to raise money **II**

Sammlung collection **II**

Samstag Saturday **I**

Sand- sandy **II**

Sandale sandal **III U3**, 65

sandig sandy **II**

Sandwich sandwich **I**

Sänger/-in singer **II**

Sanitärarbeiten plumbing **II**

Satz sentence **I**; phrase **III U1**, 9

sauber clean **II**

sauber machen to tidy (up) **II**

säubern to clean **II**

sauer sein (auf) *to be fed up (with) **III U1**, 20

Säugling baby **II**

Saxofon saxophone; sax **I**

Schach chess **II**

Schachtel box **I**

eine **Schachtel** … a box of … **I**

Schade! Too bad! **I**

Schaf sheep, sheep *(pl)* **I**

schaffen to create **II**

Wir haben es **geschafft**! We did it! **II**

Schälchen bowl **II**

Schale bowl **II**; shell **III TMS1**, 27

Schallplatte record **II**

Schalter switch **III U2**, 53; desk **III U4**, 95

Schatz treasure **II**

schauen to look **I**

Schau/Schaut mal! Look! **I**

schaukeln to rock **III U4**, 104

Schauplatz scene; setting **II**

Schauspielen acting **II**

Schauspieler/Schauspielerin actor/actress **III U3**, 69

in **Scheiben** schneiden to slice **II**

sich **scheiden** lassen to divorce **III U3**, 65

scheinen *to shine **III U3**, 69

schenken *to give **I**

scherzen to joke **II**

scheußlich ugly **III U1**, 14

schicken *to send **II**

schieben to push **II**

Schiedsrichter/-in official **II**

jmdn. **schief** anschauen *to give sb funny looks **III U1**, 15

schiefgehen *to go wrong **II**

schießen to kick **II**

Schießplatz firing range ⟨**III TR1**, 110⟩

Schiff ship **I**

Schiffsbau shipbuilding **III U2**, 42

Schiffsjunge cabin boy **I**

Schiffsoffizier mate **I**

Schild sign **II**

Schinken ham **III AC1**, 34

Schinkenspeck bacon **I**

Schlacht fight **II**; battle **III U3**, 65

Schlafanzug pyjamas *(pl)* **II**

schlafen *to sleep **I**; *to be asleep **II**

Schlafzimmer bedroom **I**

Schlag beat **III TMS1**, 29

schlagen *to hit **I**; to whip; *to beat **II**

Schläger racquet **II**

Schlamm mud **II**

schlammig muddy **II**

Schlange queue **I**

schlau clever **I**; smart **III U1**, 9

Schlauheit cleverness **III TMS1**, 30

der/die/das **schlechteste** the worst **II**

sich **schlecht** fühlen *to feel sick **II**

schlecht bad **I**

schlechter worse **II**

schließen to close **I**

Schließfach locker **II**

schließlich at last; in the end **I**; after all; finally **II**

der/die/das **schlimmste** the worst **II**

schlimm terrible ⟨**III TR2**, 112⟩

schlimm (ugs.) bad **I**

schlimmer worse **II**

Schlittschuhe skates *(pl)* **I**

Schlittschuh laufen to skate **I**

Schlittschuhbahn ice rink **II**

Schlittschuhlaufen skating **II**

Schloss castle **II**

Schlucht glen **III U2**, 46

Schluchtenklettern gorge scrambling **II**

Schluss end **I**

zum **Schluss** in the end **I**; finally **II**

Schluss *(einer Geschichte)* ending **I**

Schlüssel key **II**

Schlüsselanhänger key ring **III U2**, 51

Schlüsselbund key ring **III U2**, 51

schmackhaft tasty **III U4**, 102

schmal narrow **III U2**, 44

schmaler Durchgang close **III U2**, 44

schmecken to taste ⟨**III TR1**, 110⟩

Schmerz pain **II**

Schmuck jewellery **I**; decorations *(pl)* **II**

schmücken to decorate **II**

Schmuggler/-in smuggler **III U4**, 104

schmutzig dirty **II**

Schnäppchen bargain **I**

schnappen to grab **II**

Schnee- snowy ⟨**III TMS1**, 32⟩

schneiden *to cut (off) **II**

in Scheiben **schneiden** to slice **II**

schnell fast; quick **I**

schnell quickly **II**

Schokolade chocolate **I**

schön nice; fine **I**; beautiful **II**

schon already **I**; yet **II**

schon einmal before **II**

Schornstein chimney **II**

Schotte/Schottin Scot **III U2**, 43

Schottenkaro *(bestimmtes Muster eines Clans)* tartan **III U2**, 41

Schottenrock kilt **III U2**, 41

karierter **Schottenstoff** tartan **III U2**, 41

schottisch Scottish **II**

Schottland Scotland **II**

Schrank cupboard **I**

Schranke bar ⟨**III TMS1**, 30⟩

Schraubenzieher screwdriver **II**

schrecklich awful **I**; horrible **II**; terrible ⟨**III TR2**, 112⟩

schreiben *to write **I**

Schreibtisch desk **III U4**, 95

schreien to shout **I**; to scream; to cry **II**

Schritt step **II**

Schritt halten (mit) *to keep up (with) **II**

Schritt-für-**Schritt**- step-by-step **II**

Stück **Schrott** piece of junk **III U1**, 21

schubsen to push **II**

schüchtern shy **II**

Schuhe shoe **I**

(meine) **Schuld** (my) fault **II**

Schule school **I**

Schüler/-in student **I**

Schüleraustausch student exchange **III AC2**, 57

Schülerversammlung assembly **II**

Schulfach subject **II**

Schulferien holidays *(pl)* **III U4**, 95

Schulgebühren school fees *(pl)* **III U3**, 77

Schulgeld school fees *(pl)* **III U3**, 77

Schulhof playground **II**

Schulklasse class **I**

Schulleiter/-in head teacher **III TMS2**, 80

Schulstunde lesson **I**

Schultasche schoolbag **I**

Schulter shoulder **II**

Schüssel bowl **II**

schütten to pour **II**

schützen to protect **II**

Schwan swan **I**

Schwanz tail **I**

schwarz black **I**

schwarz werden *to go black **II**

schwarzes Brett noticeboard **II**
schweben to drift ⟨**III U4**, 98⟩
Schweif tail **I**
Schweigen silence (no pl) **III U3**, 69
Schwein pig **I**
schwer hard; heavy **II**
Schwert sword **II**
Schwester sister **I**
schwierig difficult **I**; hard **II**
Schwierigkeit problem **I**
   in **Schwierigkeiten** geraten *to get into
   trouble **III U1**, 20
Schwierigkeiten trouble **I**
   in **Schwierigkeiten** bringen *to make
   trouble **I**
Schwimmen swimming **I**
schwimmen *to swim **I**
Schwimmsachen swimming things (pl
   only) **II**
Science-Fiction (Zukunftsdichtung) science
   fiction **III U4**, 107
Second-Hand-Laden charity shop **I**
See lake **I**
seekrank seasick **III U4**, 94
Seemann sailor **I**
Seeräuber/-in pirate **II**
Segelboot sailing boat **II**
sehbehindert partially sighted **II**
sehen *to see; to look **I**
Sehenswürdigkeit attraction **II**
Sehenswürdigkeiten sights **II**
sehr very; very much **I**; extremely **III U2**, 48
Seil rope **III U2**, 51
sein *to be **I**
   beeindruckt **sein** *to be impressed **II**
   ist nicht ain't (= isn't/aren't) ⟨**III TMS1**, 27⟩
   los **sein** *to go on **III AC3**, 88
   sind nicht ain't (= isn't/aren't)
   ⟨**III TMS1**, 27⟩
wie jmd./etw. **sein** *to be like sb/sth
   III U2, 40
sein/-e his; its **I**
seit since (+ Zeitpunkt) **II**
seitdem since (+ Zeitpunkt) **II**
Seite page; side **II**
   auf der anderen **Seite** von across;
   opposite **I**
   auf der linken **Seite** on the left **I**
   auf der rechten **Seite** on the right **I**
   an meiner **Seite** by my side ⟨**III TMS1**, 30⟩
Sekunde second **III TMS1**, 30
selber yourself; myself; himself **II**; themselves **III U1**, 9; ourselves; yourselves
   III U1, 16
das Selbst self **III U1**, 9
selbst even **I**
er/sich (selbst) himself **II**
   ihr/euch/Sie/sich **(selbst)** yourselves
   III U1, 16
ich/mir/mich (selbst) myself **II**
(sich) selbst itself **III U1**, 16
(sie) selbst herself **III U1**, 15
selbstbewusst confident **II**

selbstkritisch self-critical **II**
selbstsicher confident **II**
selbstverständlich of course **I**
Selfie selfie **II**
seltsam strange **I**; funny **III U1**, 15; odd
   III AC3, 88
Semester term **III U3**, 66
senden *to send **II**
Sender station **III U2**, 43
Sendung programme **II**
separat separate **II**
September September **II**
Sequenz sequence **III U3**, 77
Sessel chair **I**
setzen *to put (in) **I**; *to set ⟨**III TMS1**, 32⟩
   sich **setzen** *to sit down **I**
Sheriff sheriff ⟨**III TR2**, 112⟩
die **Shetlandinseln** the Shetland Islands
   III U2, 48
Shirt shirt **I**
Shorts shorts (pl) **II**
Show show **I**
   Comedy **Show** comedy show **II**
sich each other **II**
sich (selbst) yourself **II**; herself **III U1**, 15
   für **sich** on one's own **III U4**, 105
sicher sure **I**; certain; safe **II**
   sicher sein *to be sure **II**
sichergehen *to make sure **III U1**, 10
Sicht view ⟨**III TR1**, 111⟩
Sie you; u (= you) **I**
sie she; her **I**
sie (Pl.) them **I**
sie (Pl.) they **I**
Sie (selbst) yourself **II**
sie (selbst) themselves **III U1**, 9
siedeln to settle **III U3**, 67
Siedler/-in colonist **III U3**, 67
siegen *to win **II**
Sieger/-in winner **I**
Sightseeing- sightseeing **II**
Signal signal **III U2**, 50
Silbe syllable **III TMS1**, 32
Silber silver **II**
Silvester New Year's Eve **III U2**, 43
simpel simple **III U1**, 18
Singen singing **I**
singen *to sing **I**
Sinn meaning **II**
   Sinn für Humor sense of humour (no pl)
   III U1, 23
Sippe clan **III U2**, 45
Sitte custom **III AC3**, 88
Situation situation **III U1**, 8
Sitz seat **II**
Sitzbank bench **III U1**, 23
Sitz! (Befehl für Hunde) Sit! **I**
sitzen *to sit **I**
Sitzplatz seat **II**
Skandinavien Scandinavia **III U2**, 44
Skateboard skateboard **I**
Skateboardfahren skateboarding **I**
Skript script **II**

Slogan slogan **II**
Smalltalk small talk **III AC2**, 56
Smartcard smartcard **II**
Smartphone smartphone **I**
SMS text **II**
   eine **SMS** schicken to text **I**
Snack snack **I**
so so; that's how; like that **I**; like this **II**
   so dass so (that) **II**
   so früh this early **III AC1**, 35
   so oft whenever **II**
   so … wie as … as **I**
   so viel that much **III AC1**, 35
sobald once; as soon as **II**
Sofa sofa **I**
sofort right away **I**; right now **II**; at once
   ⟨**III TMS2**, 86⟩
sogar even **I**
Sohn son **III U2**, 42
solange while **II**
Soldat/-in soldier **III U2**, 47
sollen shall **II**
   sollte(n) nicht shouldn't **II**
sollte/-est/-t/-n should **I**
Somali Somali **III U4**, 105
somalisch Somali **III U4**, 105
Sonderangebot special offer **I**
Song song **I**
Songschreiber/-in songwriter **III TMS1**, 26
Sonne sun **II**
sonnig sunny **I**
Sonntag Sunday **I**
sonst noch else **II**
Sonst noch etwas? Anything else? **I**
Keine **Sorge!** Don't worry! **I**
sich **Sorgen** machen to worry **II**
für jmdn. **sorgen** *to take care of sb/sth
   III U3, 74
sorgfältig careful **II**
Sorte kind (of) **II**; type **III U1**, 9
sortieren to sort **III U4**, 109
Soße sauce **III U2**, 44
Souvenir souvenir **II**
sowieso anyway **II**
soziale Netzwerke social media **III U1**, 10
soziales Netzwerk social network **II**
Sozialwissenschaften humanities (pl) **II**
die **Spanier** Spanish **III U3**, 65
Spanisch Spanish **III U3**, 65
spanisch Spanish **III U3**, 65
spannend exciting **I**
Spannung suspense **II**
Sparbüchse piggy bank **I**
Spardose piggy bank **I**
sparen to save **I**
Sparschwein piggy bank **I**
Spaß fun **I**
   Spaß haben *to have fun **I**; to enjoy
   oneself **III U1**, 15
   Es macht **Spaß**. It's fun. **I**
spät late **I**
   zu **spät** late **I**
   zu **spät** kommen *to be late **I**

Wie **spät** ist es? What's the time? **I**
zu **spät** dran sein *to be late **I**
später later **I**
spazieren gehen *to go for a walk **II**
Speck bacon **I**
Speer spear **II**
spektakulär spectacular **II**
sperren to ban **III U2**, 44
speziell special **I**; specific **III U4**, 107
   mit **speziellen** Bedürfnissen with special
   needs **II**
Spezies species, species *(pl)* **II**
spezifisch specific **III U4**, 107
Spiegel mirror **III U3**, 65
Spiel game **I**; match **II**
spielen to play **I**; to perform **III U1**, 14
spielen *(Theater)* to act **II**
   spielen in *to be set in **III U4**, 107
   einen Streich **spielen** to play a trick (on) **I**
   es **spielt** keine Rolle It doesn't matter.
   III U1, 8
Spieler/-in player **II**
technische **Spielerei** gadget **III U4**, 106
Spielfeld field; court; pitch **II**
Spielkarte card **I**
Spielplatz playground **II**
Spielstand score **II**
Spielzeug toy **I**
Spind locker **II**
Spinne spider **II**
Spinnennetz web **III U2**, 47
Spitzen- top **I**
spontan spontaneous **II**
Sport sport **I**
Sportart sport **I**
Sporthalle gym(nasium) **II**
Sportunterricht PE (= Physical Education) **II**
Sprache language **II**
   bildhafte **Sprache** metaphor **III TMS1**, 31
Sprachnachricht voice message **I**
sprechen *to say; to talk **I**
   sprechen (mit) *to speak (to) **I**
   sprechen über to talk about **I**
Sprecher/-in speaker **I**; talker **III AC2**, 56
Sprechgesang chant **II**
Sprichwort saying **III U1**, 8
springen to jump **I**; to bounce **III AC2**, 56
spülen to flush **III U1**, 11
Spur clue **II**
Stadion stadium **II**
Stadt town; city **I**
Stadtplan map **I**
Stadtteil part **I**
Stamm tribe **III U3**, 63
stammen aus to date back to **III U3**, 63
Stand stall **III U4**, 102
ständig always **I**
Standort location **II**
Standpunkt point of view **II**; view **III U3**, 65
Star star **I**
stark hard; heavy; strong; powerful **II**
Stärke power ⟨**III TR2**, 112⟩
starren to stare **I**

Start start **II**
starten to start **I**
Startpunkt starting place **II**
Station station **II**
statt instead of **III U3**, 67
stattdessen instead **III U1**, 20
stattfinden *to take place **II**
Steak steak **I**
stecken *to stick **III TMS1**, 30
Stecker stud **III U1**, 19
stehen *to stand **I**
   stehen auf *to be into **I**
   auf/in … **steht** … says **II**
   du **stehst** hinter mir you've got my back
   III TMS1, 27
stehlen *to steal **II**
steigen to climb **I**; *to rise **III U3**, 63
Stein stone **III U2**, 50
Stein- stone **III U2**, 50
steinig rocky **II**
Stelle place **I**
   an **Stelle** von instead of **III U3**, 67
   an … **Stelle** in … shoes **III U1**, 13
stellen *to put (in) **I**
   online **stellen** to post **II**
   sich **stellen** to turn in ⟨**III TR2**, 112⟩
   zur Verfügung **stellen** to provide
   ⟨**III TMS2**, 86⟩
sterben to die **III U2**, 44
Stern star **I**
Steuer wheel **I**
steuern to control **III U3**, 67
Steuerrad wheel **I**
Stichwortkarte prompt card **II**
Stickerei embroidery **III U3**, 62
Stiefel boot **I**
Stiefmutter stepmum **I**
still quiet **I**; still **II**
Stille silence *(no pl)* **III U3**, 69
Stimme voice **I**
Was **stimmt** nicht? What's wrong? **II**
Stimmung mood; atmosphere **II**; humour
   (no pl) **III U1**, 23
die **Stirn** runzeln to frown **III U4**, 99
stolz (auf) proud (of) **II**
Stopp stop **I**
stoppen to stop **I**
stören *to get in the way **II**
Story story, stories *(pl)* **I**
Storyboard storyboard **III U1**, 19
stoßen to push **II**
Sträfling prisoner **III U4**, 102
strahlend bright **III TMS1**, 30
Strand beach **II**
Straße road **I**; *(in der Stadt)* street **I**
   auf der **Straße** in the street **I**
Strecke route **II**
Streich trick **I**
   einen **Streich** spielen to play a trick (on) **I**
Streit fight **II**; argument **III U1**, 20
(sich) **streiten** *to fight **II**
streng mit jmdm. sein *to be hard on sb
   III U1, 16

Strickjacke cardigan **I**
Strom electricity **II**
Stromausfall power cut **II**
strömen to flow **II**
Strophe stanza **III TMS1**, 30; verse
   III TMS1, 31
Struktur structure **III TMS1**, 31
Stück piece **I**
   ein **Stück** … a piece of … **I**
   pro **Stück** each **I**
   Stück Schrott piece of junk **III U1**, 21
Student/-in student **I**
Studie survey **I**
Studieren studying **I**
studieren to study **III U1**, 12
Studio studio **II**
Stufe step **II**
Stuhl chair **I**
Stunde hour **I**
   eine halbe **Stunde** half an hour **III U3**, 75
Stundenplan timetable **I**
Sturm storm **I**
stürmisch stormy ⟨**III TMS1**, 32⟩
Sturz fall **III U2**, 54
Such- search **II**
Suche search **II**
suchen nach to look for **I**
Suchmaschine search engine **II**
Sucht addiction **II**
Süd- south **II**
Südamerika South America **III U3**, 65
Süden south **II**
   im **Süden** south **III U2**, 45
südlich south **III U2**, 45
(der) **Südwesten** (the) southwest **II**
im **Südwesten** (the) southwest **II**
südwestlich (the) southwest **II**
super great; cool **I**
Superheld superhero **II**
Supermarkt supermarket **I**
(Wind-)**Surfen** (wind) surfing **II**
süß cute; sweet **I**
Süßigkeiten sweets *(pl)* **I**
Symbol icon **III TMS2**, 84
System system **III U4**, 109
Szene scene **II**; in-crowd **III U1**, 20; se-
   quence **III U3**, 77
Szenenbuch storyboard **III U1**, 19

T

Tabak tobacco *(no pl)* **III U3**, 66
Tablet tablet **I**
Tablett tray **I**
Tablette pill **II**
Tag day **I**
   am nächsten **Tag** the next day **II**
   eines **Tages** one day **I**
Tagebuch diary **III U3**, 66
Tagebucheintrag diary entry **II**
täglich daily ⟨**III TR1**, 110⟩
Takt beat **III TMS1**, 29
Talent talent **I**

Talentwettbewerb talent show **I**
Talisman lucky charm **I**
Tante aunt **I**
Tanz dancing **I**; dance *(no pl)* **II**
tanzen to dance **I**
Tänzer/-in dancer **III U1**, 12
Tanzschritt dance move **I**
Tanzveranstaltung dance *(no pl)* **II**
tapfer brave **I**
Tasche bag **I**; pocket **III U2**, 50
Taschengeld pocket money **I**
Taschenlampe torch **II**
Tasse cup **III AC1**, 34
   eine **Tasse** … a cup of … **I**
Tätowierung tattoo **III U1**, 19
Tatsache fact **II**
tatsächlich actually; in fact **III U2**, 45
Tattoe tattoo **III U1**, 19
tausende (von) thousands of **III U2**, 42
Taxi taxi **II**
Team team **II**
Technik technology **II**
Techniker/-in engineer **III U2**, 48
technisch technical **III U1**, 10
   technische Spielerei gadget **III U4**, 106
Tee tea **I**
Teebeutel teabag **III U3**, 77
Teenager teenager **II**
Teil part **I**
teilen to share **II**
teilnehmen (an) *to take part (in) **II**
Telefon phone **I**; telephone **II**
Telefon-/Handynummer phone number **I**
   Telefon mit Wählscheibe rotary phone
   III U2, 53
Telefonanruf phone call **I**
Telefonzelle phone box **III U4**, 105
Teller plate **III AC1**, 34
Tennis tennis **I**
Test test **I**
teuer expensive **I**
Text text; line **II**
Theater theatre **I**; drama **II**
Theaterstück play **III U3**, 68
Thema subject **I**; theme **II**; topic **III U1**, 10
Thunfisch tuna **II**
Ticket ticket **I**
tief deep **II**
   Höhen und **Tiefen** ups and downs
   III TMS1, 27
Tier animal **I**
Tierarzt/Tierärztin vet **I**
Tierpark zoo **II**
Tierwelt *(in freier Wildbahn)* wildlife *(no pl)* **II**
Tipp tip **II**; hint **III AC2**, 57
tippen to type **II**
Tisch table **I**
Titel heading **I**; title **III TMS1**, 27
Titelseite cover **III U1**, 8
tja well **I**
Toast toast **I**
Tochter daughter **III U3**, 65

Tod death **III U4**, 102
Toilette toilet **I**
toll great **I**; amazing **II**
Tomate tomato, tomatoes *(pl)* **I**
Tombola raffle **I**
Ton sound **I**
Tonmodell model **I**
Tonpfeife clay pipe **II**
Tonstudio recording studio **I**
Tor goal **II**
Torte cake **I**
tot dead **II**
töten to kill **III U3**, 66
Tour tour **I**
Tourismus tourism **II**
Tourist/-in tourist **I**
Touristeninformation tourist information centre **I**
Tradition tradition **II**
traditionell traditional **III U2**, 40
tragen to carry **II**
   mit sich **tragen** to carry ⟨**III TR1**, 110⟩
tragen *(Kleidung)* *to wear **I**
Trainer/-in coach **I**; trainer **II**
trainieren to practise **I**; to train **I**
Training practice **III U1**, 8
Transport transport **I**
Transportmittel means of transport *(sg or pl)* **III U4**, 95
Ich **traute** meinen Augen nicht. I couldn't believe my eyes. **II**
Traum dream **I**
Traum- fantasy; dream **I**
träumen *to dream **II**
traurig sad **I**
(sich) treffen *to meet **II**
   sich auf halbem Weg **treffen** *to meet halfway **III U1**, 18
   sich **treffen** *to meet **I**
treffen *to meet; *to hit **I**
treffend to the point **III AC2**, 57
treiben to drift ⟨**III U4**, 98⟩
   Ich lasse mich **treiben**. I go wherever the wind takes me. **III U4**, 107
Treppe stairs *(pl)* **III U2**, 50
treten to kick **II**
Trick trick **I**
Trimester term **III U3**, 66
trinken *to drink **I**
Trip trip **I**
Triphelfer/-in triphelper **II**
trocknen to dry ⟨**III TR1**, 111⟩
trotzdem anyway **II**
tschüss bye **I**
T-Shirt T-shirt **I**
Tudor Tudor **III U3**, 65
tun *to do; *to make **I**
   tun als ob to pretend **III TMS1**, 27
   was man **tun** und was man nicht **tun** sollte dos and don'ts **III AC3**, 88
Tunnel tunnel **I**
Tür door **I**
Turm tower **III U2**, 50

Turnhalle gym(nasium) **II**
Turnier competition **II**
Turnschuh trainer **III U1**, 14
Turteltauben lovebirds *(pl)* **II**
Tussi *(abwertend)* drama queen *(coll)* **III U3**, 74
Tüte bag **I**
   eine **Tüte** … a bag of … **I**
Tutorial tutorial **II**
Tutorium tutorial **II**
Typ guy **II**; type **III U1**, 9; *(ugs.)* bloke **III U1**, 20
typisch typical **II**
   typisches Merkmal characteristic **III U3**, 66
(jmdn.) tyrannisieren to bully (sb) **II**

U

U-Bahn underground **III U1**, 25
   die Londoner **U-Bahn** the Tube **II**
übel ugly **III U1**, 14
Übelkeit verspüren *to feel sick **II**
üben to practise **I**
über about; over; across **I**; above **II**
   über Nacht overnight **III U1**, 21
überall everywhere **I**
   überall (in) all over ⟨**III TR2**, 112⟩
   überall (egal, wo) anywhere **II**
überflüssig unnecessary **III TMS2**, 81
überfluten to flood **III U3**, 63
überfüllt crowded **III AC3**, 89
sich **übergeben** *to be sick **II**
überhaupt (nicht) (not) at all **II**
überladen overloaded **III U4**, 104
überleben to survive **III U4**, 104
Übernachtung sleepover **II**
übernatürlich supernatural **III U4**, 107
überprüfen to check **I**
überqueren to cross **I**
überraschen to surprise **II**
überraschend surprising **I**
überrascht sein *to be surprised **II**
Überraschung surprise **I**
überreagieren to overreact **II**
überreden to persuade **II**
Überschrift heading **I**; title **III TMS1**, 27
überschwemmen to flood **III U3**, 63
übersetzen to translate **I**
etw. **überstehen** to get through sth **II**
überzeugend convincing **III U2**, 49
üblich usual **III U1**, 21; common **III TMS1**, 31
übrig left **I**
Übung exercise **I**; practice **III U1**, 8
Übungsheft exercise book **I**
Ufer bank; shore **II**
Uhr clock; *(Zeitangabe bei vollen Stunden)* o'clock **I**
   Um wie viel **Uhr**? What time? **I**
   Wie viel **Uhr** ist es? What's the time? **I**
um *(bei Uhrzeitangaben)* at **I**
   um … herum around **I**; round **II**
   Um wie viel Uhr? What time? **I**

umarmen to hug **I**
Umarmung hug **III TMS2**, 85
umbringen to kill **III U3**, 66
(sich) umdrehen to turn around **II**
Umfrage survey **I**
Umgebung environment **II**
umgehen (mit) *to deal (with) **II**
  gut umgehen können mit *to be good
  with ⟨**III TR2**, 112⟩
Umhang cape **II**
umher around **I**
umkehren to turn back **III U3**, 69
umkippen *to fall over **I**
sich umschauen to explore **I**
Umschlag envelope **III TMS2**, 82
umschreiben to paraphrase **II**
umsteigen (in) to change (onto) **II**
Umwelt environment **II**
umweltfreundlich environmentally friendly
  III U4, 95
Umweltprobleme environmental issues
  III U1, 10
umziehen to move (house) **II**
Umzug parade ⟨**III TR3**, 115⟩
unabhängig independent **III U3**, 65
Unabhängigkeit freedom (no pl) **III U1**, 20
unaufhörlich steady **III U4**, 105
unbedingt empfehlenswert a must-see
  III U4, 102
unbekannt unknown ⟨**III TMS1**, 32⟩; unfamiliar **III AC1**, 34
und and **I**
unfair unfair **II**
Unfall accident **II**
unfreundlich unfriendly **II**
ungefähr about **I**
ungefährlich safe **II**
Ungeheuer monster **I**
unglaublich amazing **II**
Unglück disaster **II**
unheimlich scary **II**
unhöflich rude **I**; impolite **III AC1**, 35
Uniform uniform **I**
unkompliziert easy-going **III U4**, 107
unmittelbar direct **III TMS2**, 80
unnötig unnecessary **III TMS2**, 81
unordentlich messy **III U1**, 15
Unordnung chaos **III U3**, 74
nicht ganz Unrecht haben *to have a point
  III U1, 18
  unrecht haben *to be wrong **I**
uns us **I**
unscharf out of focus **III U3**, 75
unser/-e our **I**
unser/-er/-e/-es ours ⟨**III TR2**, 112⟩
unsichtbar invisible **III U4**, 105
unten downstairs **II**
  nach unten down **I**
  nach unten gehen *to go down **I**
unten below **III U2**, 51
unter under **I**; below **III U2**, 51; among
  III AC3, 88
unterbrechen to interrupt **II**

Unterbringung accommodation
  ⟨**III TR3**, 114⟩
untergebracht sein to stay **II**
im Untergeschoss downstairs **II**
unterhalb (von) below **III U2**, 51
jmdn. unterhalten to entertain sb
  III TMS1, 26
Unterhaltung conversation **II**; entertainment (no pl) **III U3**, 72
Unterkunft accommodation ⟨**III TR3**, 114⟩
Unternehmen company **III U1**, 10
Unterricht lesson **I**; class **II**
unterrichten *to teach **II**
Unterrichtsstunde lesson **I**; class **II**
Unterschied difference **II**
  einen Unterschied machen *to make a
  difference **II**
unterschiedlich different **I**
unterschreiben to sign **III TMS1**, 27
Unterschrift signature **III TMS2**, 82
unterstützen to support **II**
Untersuchung research (no pl) **III U4**, 101
unterwegs out and about **I**; on the move
  III U4, 94
  unterwegs sein *to be on one's way **I**
unterzeichnen to sign **III TMS1**, 27
unvergesslich unforgettable **III U4**, 102
unverschämt rude **I**
unvoreingenommen open-minded
  ⟨**III TMS1**, 32⟩
unwirklich unreal **III U4**, 107
Update update **III U2**, 45
üppig lavish **III U4**, 107
Urkunde document **III U4**, 99
Urlaub holiday **I**
Ursprung origin **III U4**, 107
usw. (= und so weiter) etc. (= et cetera) **II**

V

Vanillepudding custard **II**
Vanillesoße custard **II**
Vater father **I**
Vati dad **I**
Vegetarier/-in vegetarian **III U2**, 42
vegetarisch vegetarian **III U2**, 44
sich verabschieden (von) *to say goodbye
  (to) **III U3**, 63
etw. verändern *to make a difference **II**
Veränderung change **II**
veranschaulichen *to bring to life; to
  illustrate **II**
Veranstaltung event **II**
verantwortlich responsible **III U4**, 104
  verantwortlich machen to blame **III U1**, 18
Verantwortung responsibility **III TMS1**, 30
  die Verantwortung tragen (für) *to be in
  charge (of) **III U1**, 15
jmdn. verärgern *to make sb angry
  III AC1, 35
verärgert angry **I**
(sich) verbessern to improve **III U2**, 48
verbieten to ban **III U2**, 44

verbinden to join **II**
  verbinden (mit) to connect (to) **III U3**, 62
Verbindung link; connection **II**; relation
  ⟨**III TMS1**, 32⟩
  sich mit jmdm. in Verbindung setzen to
  contact sb **II**
Ge- und Verbote dos and don'ts **III AC3**, 88
Verbrechen crime **II**
(weit) verbreitet common **III TMS1**, 31
verbrennen *to burn **III U3**, 63
verbringen (Zeit) *to spend **II**
verdienen to earn **I**; to deserve **II**
  Geld verdienen *to make money **I**
die Augen verdrehen to roll one's eyes
  III U3, 74
Verein club **I**; society **II**
Verfasser/-in writer **II**
verfügbar available **III TMS2**, 81
zur Verfügung stellen to provide
  ⟨**III TMS2**, 86⟩
Vergangenheit past **II**
vergeben *to forgive **II**
vergessen *to forget **I**
Vergleich simile **III TMS1**, 31
vergleichen (mit) to compare (with/to) **II**
Vergnügen pleasure ⟨**III TR2**, 112⟩
Vergütung payment **III TMS2**, 81
verhaften to arrest **II**
Verhalten behaviour (no pl) **III AC3**, 88
sich verhalten to behave **III U1**, 15
Verhältnis relation ⟨**III TMS1**, 32⟩
verhandeln to bargain **III U4**, 100
verheiratet married **III TMS2**, 81
sich verirren *to get lost **II**
Verkauf sale **II**
verkaufen *to sell **I**
Verkehr traffic **III U4**, 100
Verkehrsmittel transport **I**; means of transport (sg or pl) **III U4**, 95
  öffentliche Verkehrsmittel public transport (no pl) **II**
Verkleidung costume; fancy dress (no pl) **II**
Verkürzung contraction ⟨**III TMS2**, 87⟩
verlassen *to leave **I**
  sich verlassen (auf) to rely (on) **III U1**, 12
verlässlich reliable ⟨**III TMS1**, 32⟩
verlegen embarrassed **II**
verleihen *to lend (to) **II**
verletzen *to hurt **II**
verletzt hurt **II**; wounded **III U2**, 50
Verletzung injury **II**
verlieren *to lose **II**
verloren lost ⟨**III U2**, 47⟩; ⟨**III TR1**, 111⟩
  verloren gehen *to get lost **II**
vermieten to rent (out) **III U2**, 54
vermischen to mix (up) **III U3**, 74
vermissen to miss **II**
vermitteln to mediate **II**; to connect (to)
  III U3, 62
verneint negative **II**
vernichten to destroy **III U3**, 66
Verpackung wrapping **II**
verpassen to miss **III U4**, 94

sich den Knöchel **verrenken** to twist your ankle **II**
sich **verrenken** to twist **II**
verrückt crazy **I**; mad **II**
   verrückt werden *to go crazy **II**
Vers verse **III TMS1**, 31
versäumen to miss **III U4**, 94
verschieden different **I**; separate **II**
Verschiedenheit diversity **II**
verschmutzen to litter **III AC3**, 88
Verschmutzung pollution (no pl) **II**
verschwenden to waste **II**
verschwenderisch wasteful **III U4**, 102; lavish **III U4**, 107
Verschwendung waste **III U1**, 10
verschwinden to disappear **III U3**, 63
verschwinden (von/aus) *to get out (of) ⟨**III TR2**, 112⟩
verschwommen blurred **III U3**, 77
verschwunden missing **II**
   verschwunden sein *to be gone **II**
Version version **II**
Verspätung delay **II**
Versprechen promise **II**
versprechen to promise **II**
Verstand brain ⟨**III U4**, 98⟩
sich **verständigen** to communicate **III U1**, 9
Verständnis understanding **II**
Versteck cache **II**
(sich) **verstecken** *to hide **II**
verstehen *to understand **II**; *to get ⟨**III TR3**, 114⟩
versuchen to try **I**
Vertrauen trust **III TMS1**, 30
vertrauen to trust **III U1**, 10
   vertrauen (auf) to rely (on) **III U1**, 12
vertrauenswürdig reliable ⟨**III TMS1**, 32⟩
nicht **vertraut** unfamiliar **III AC1**, 34
verunreinigen to litter **III AC3**, 88
verursachen to cause **II**
verwandt sein mit *to be related to **III TMS2**, 80
verwenden to use **I**
verwirrt confused **III U1**, 22
verwischt blurred **III U3**, 77
verwundet wounded **III U2**, 50
Verzeichnis directory **II**
verzeihen *to forgive **II**
verzichtbar unnecessary **III TMS2**, 81
verzieren to decorate **II**
Verzögerung delay **II**
Video video **II**
Videochat video chat **II**
viel/-e lots (of); a lot of **I**; loads (of) **III TMS2**, 84
   so **viel** that much **III AC1**, 35
   Viele Grüße, Best wishes, **III TMS2**, 83
viel much; a lot **I**
Vielen Dank! Thank you very much! **III U1**, 10
viele many **I**
Vielfalt diversity **II**
vielleicht maybe **I**; perhaps **III U2**, 50
Vielvölker- multi-ethnic **II**

Viertel nach/vor quarter past/to **I**
Viktorianer/-in Victorian **III U3**, 65
viktorianisch Victorian **III U3**, 65
violett purple **I**
Visum, Visa (Pl.) visa, visas (pl) **III U4**, 95
Vitamin vitamin **III U3**, 77
Vogel bird **I**
Vogelbeobachtung birdwatching **II**
Vokabular vocabulary **II**
Volk people (pl) **III U3**, 63
Volksstamm tribe **III U3**, 63
voll (mit/von) full (of) **I**
Volleyball volleyball **I**
völlig complete **III U3**, 63
völlig quite; completely **II**; absolutely **III TMS2**, 83
vollkommen perfect **I**
vollständig full **II**; complete **III U3** 63
von from; of; about **I**; by **III U2**, 43
   von Hand by hand **III U3**, 65
   von … bis from … to **I**
   von … weg/ab/herunter off **I**
vor outside **II**
vor in front of **I**; ahead **III U4**, 96
vor (bei Uhrzeitangaben) to **I**
   vor allem specially **II**; especially **III U1**, 1C
   vor (zeitlich) before **I**; ago **II**
voraus ahead **III U4**, 96
Voraussage prediction **II**
vorbei (an) past **I**
vorbeigehen to pass ⟨**III TMS1**, 32⟩
vorbereiten to prepare **II**
   sich **vorbereiten** *to get ready **III TMS1**, 26
vorbereitet prepared ⟨**III TR1**, 111⟩
Vorbild role model **III U1**, 10
sich **vordrängeln** to jump the queue **I**
etw. **vorführen** to perform **III U1**, 14
Vorführung exhibition **II**
vorgeschichtlich prehistoric **II**
Vorhang curtain **II**
vorher before **II**
Vorhersage prediction **II**
Vormittag morning **I**
vormittags (Uhrzeit) a.m. **I**
vorn ahead **III U4**, 96
Vorname first name **I**
Vorrichtung device **I**
Vorschlag suggestion **II**
vorschlagen to suggest **II**
Vorschrift regulation **III U4**, 99
vorsichtig careful **II**
Vorsingen audition **III U1**, 14
Vorsprechen audition **III U1**, 14
vorstellen to introduce **II**; to present **III TMS1**, 29
   sich (etwas) **vorstellen** to imagine **II**
   Stell dir **vor**! Guess what! **III U3**, 70
Vorstellungskraft imagination **III U1**, 9
Vortanzen audition **III U1**, 14
Vortänzer/-in lead dancer **III U1** 12
vortäuschen to fake **II**; to pretend **III TMS1**, 27
Vortrag presentation **I**

vortragen to perform **III U1**, 14
vorüber (an) past **I**
vorurteilsfrei open-minded ⟨**III TMS1**, 32⟩
Vorverkaufsschalter ticket office **III U2**, 50
vorziehen to prefer **III TMS1**, 30

W

wach awake **III U4**, 99
Wache guard **II**
wachsen *to grow **III U1**, 12
Wachsfigur wax figure **II**
Wächter/-in guard **II**
wackelig wobbly **II**
Wahl choice **II**; option **III U2**, 44
wählen *to choose; to vote **II**; to dial **III U4**, 96
wahr true **II**
während (+ Nomen) during (+ noun) **II**; while **II**
Wahrheit truth **III U4**, 101
wahrnehmen to notice **II**; to perceive ⟨**III TR3**, 115⟩
Wahrnehmung perception ⟨**III TR1**, 110⟩
wahrscheinlich probably **II**
Währung currency **III U4**, 95
Wald forest **II**
Waliser/-in Welsh **II**
Walisisch Welsh **II**
walisisch Welsh **II**
Wand wall **I**
Wanderer/-in hiker ⟨**III TR1**, 110⟩
Wandern walking; hiking **II**
Wanderschuh walking boot **II**
wann when **I**
   wann immer whenever **II**
Waren goods (pl) **III U3**, 65
warm warm **II**
warnen to warn **I**
warten *to hang on **III TMS1**, 27
   Warte ab! Wait and see! **I**
   warten (auf) to wait (for) **I**
Warteschlange queue **I**
warum why **I**
was what **I**
   Was für ein Glück! What luck! **III U3**, 69
   Was hast du? What's the matter? **II**
   Was ist dein/-e Lieblings …? What's your favourite …? **I**
   Was ist los? What's wrong?; What's the matter? **II**; What's up? **III U1**, 15
   Was ist mit …? What about …? **I**
   was noch what else **II**
   was sonst what else **II**
   Was stimmt nicht? What's wrong? **II**
   Was um alles in der Welt …? What on earth …? **II**
   … **was** … tun soll/-st/-t/-en … what to do. **II**
waschen to wash **I**
   sich **waschen** to wash **I**
Waschmaschine washing machine **II**
Wasser water **I**

Wasserhahn tap **III U1**, 11
Wasserrutsche water slide **I**
die **Wasserspülung** betätigen tc flush
   III U1, 11
Wau! Woof! **I**
Webdesigner web designer **III U1**, 15
Website website **I**; web page; site **II**
Wechsel change **II**
wechseln to change **II**
Weg way **I**; means (pl only) **III U4**, 95; trail
   ⟨**III TR1**, 110⟩
   im **Weg** sein/stehen *to be in the way **I**
   im **Weg** stehen *to get in the way **II**
   auf dem **Weg** sein *to be on one's way **I**
   Geh ihm aus dem **Weg**. Get out of his
   way. **I**
weg away **I**
   von … **weg**/ab/herunter off **I**
   weg sein *to be gone **II**
   Es ist **weg**. It's gone. **II**
wegen because of; for **II**
wegfahren *to drive off **III U3**, 75
weglassen *to leave out **III TMS1**, 31
weglegen *to put away **I**
wegnehmen *to take **I**
wegrennen *to run away **I**
wegstellen *to put away **I**
wegwerfen *to throw away **I**
weh tun *to hurt **II**
wehen *to blow **II**
Weide field **II**
Weihnachten Christmas **III TMS1**, 26
weil because **I**; as **II**; 'cause ⟨**III TMS1**, 27⟩
eine **Weile** a while **II**
Wein wine **I**
weinen to cry **III U2**, 50
auf andere **Weise** in other ways **II**
weise wise ⟨**III TR2**, 112⟩
weiß white **I**
weit far; wide **II**
weiter (weg) further **III U2**, 48
   weit weg far away **I**
weitere more; other **I**
weitergeben to pass (on) **II**
weitergehen to pass ⟨**III TMS1**, 32⟩
weitermachen to continue **III U4**, 99
Welche Farbe hat …? What colour is …? **I**
Welle wave **I**
Welt world **II**
   Was um alles in der **Welt** …? What on
   earth …? **II**
Weltkulturerbe (von der UNESCO anerkanntes Weltkulturerbe) World Heritage
   Site **III U3**, 64
wem who **I**
wen who **I**
   Für **wen** …? Who … for? **I**
wenden to turn around **II**
   sich **wenden** an to turn to **II**
Wendepunkt turning point **III U1**, 22
wenig little ⟨**III TR2**, 112⟩
   ein **wenig** a little **I**; a bit **II**
wenige a few **I**; few **II**

wenigstens at least ⟨**III TR1**, 111⟩
wenn when; if **I**
wer who **I**
   Wer ist dabei? Who's in? **II**
   Wer macht mit? Who's in? **II**
Werbespruch slogan **II**
werden *to become; *to get; will **II**; gonna
   (= going to) (coll) **III TMS2**, 84
würde/-st/-n/-t would **II**
werfen (nach) *to throw (at) **I**
Werk factory **III U3**, 65
Werkzeug tool **II**
wert sein *to be worth **I**
wertvoll valuable **III U3**, 64
West- west **I**; western **III U3**, 63
Westen west **I**
westlich western **III U3**, 63
Wettbewerb contest **I**; competition **II**
   in **Wettbewerb** treten (mit) to compete
   (with) **III U1**, 9
wetten *to bet **II**
Wetter weather **I**
Wettervorhersage weather forecast **II**
Wettkampf contest **I**
Wettlauf race **II**
Whisky whisky **III U2**, 42
wichtig important **I**
   wichtig nehmen to care (about) **II**
   das ist nicht **wichtig** It doesn't matter.
   III U1, 8
widerlich disgusting **I**
wie like **I**; as **II**
   wie ich like me **I**
   Wie war … ? What was … like? **III U3**, 62
wie how **I**
   Wie viele …? How many …? **I**
   Wie alt bist du? How old are you? **I**
   Wie alt seid ihr? How old are you? **I**
   Wie alt sind Sie? How old are you? **I**
   Wie geht es dir/euch/Ihnen? How are
   you? **II**
   Wie geht es euch? How are you? **II**
   Wie geht es Ihnen? How are you? **II**
   Wie heißen Sie? What's your name? **II**
   Wie heißt du? What's your name? **I**
   wie man … how to … **I**
   Wie spät ist es? What's the time? **I**
   Wie viel (kostet/kosten) …? How much
   is/are …? **I**
   Wie viel Uhr ist es? What's the time? **I**
   Wie wär's mit …? What about …? **I**
wieder again **I**
Wiederaufbereitung recycling **III U1**, 11
wiederholen to repeat **III TMS1**, 29
Wiederholung repetition **III TMS1**, 31
auf **Wiedersehen** goodbye **I**
wiederverwerten to recycle **II**
Wiese field **II**
Wikinger Viking **III U3**, 63
wild wild **II**
freie **Wildbahn** the wild ⟨**III TR1**, 110⟩
Wildnis the wild ⟨**III TR1**, 110⟩
Willkommen! Welcome! **II**

willkommen heißen to welcome **II**
Wind wind **II**
Winter winter **II**
winzig tiny **III U2**, 48
wir we **I**
   Wir haben es geschafft! We did it! **II**
wir (selbst) ourselves **III U1**, 16
wirklich really **I**; actually **III U2**, 45
Wirkung effect **III TMS1**, 29
wirr confused **III U1**, 22
wissen *to know **I**
   Ich **weiß** (es) nicht! I don't know! **I**
Wissenschaftler/-in scientist **III U2**, 43
Witz joke **I**
witzig funny; fun **I**
wo where **I**
   wo ich hingehöre where I belong
   III U4, 104
Woche week **I**
Wochenende weekend **I**
   am **Wochenende** at the weekend **I**
Wochentag weekday **I**
Woher …? Where … from? **I**
wohin where **I**
   … **wohin** ich gehen kann. … where to
   go. **II**
Wohlfahrt charity **I**
wohltätige Zwecke charity **I**
Wohltätigkeitsverein charity **I**
wohnen to live **I**; to stay **II**
   wohnen bei to stay with **II**
Wohnung flat **I**
Wohnzimmer living room **I**
Wolke cloud **II**
wollen to want (to) **I**
   wollen, dass jmd. etw. tut to want sb to
   do sth **III U1**, 12
Workshop workshop **I**
Wort word **I**
Wörterbuch dictionary **II**
Wortschatz vocabulary **II**
Wow! Wow! **I**
wunderbar wonderful; beautiful **II**; marvellous ⟨**III TMS1**, 32⟩
wundervoll marvellous ⟨**III TMS1**, 32⟩
Wunsch wish **II**
sich etwas **wünschen** *to make a wish **II**
würde/-st/-n/-t gern would like **I**
würde/-st/-n/-t sehr gern would love **II**
Wurm worm **I**
Wurst sausage **III AC1**, 34
wusch whoosh **I**
Wut anger (no pl) **III U1**, 21
wütend angry **I**
   jmdn. **wütend** machen *to make sb angry
   III AC1, 35

Z

z.B. (= zum Beispiel) e.g. (= for example) **I**
Zahl number **I**; figure **III U3**, 72
zählen (auf) to count (on) **II**
Zauber- magic; magical **II**

Zauberei magic **III U4**, 107
Zauberer wizard **II**
Zaun fence ⟨**III TR1**, 110⟩
auf **Zehenspitzen** gehen to tiptoe **II**
Zeichen sign **II**; signal **III U2**, 50
Zeichensprache sign language **II**
Zeichentrickfilm cartoon **III AC2**, 56
zeichnen *to draw **I**
zeigen *to show **I**; to feature **II**
Zeile line **I**
Zeit time **I**
   (**Zeit**) brauchen *to take **I**
   zur selben **Zeit** at the same time **II**
   die ganze **Zeit** all the time **II**
   Es ist **Zeit** aufzustehen! Time to get up! **I**
   zu dieser **Zeit** at this time **III U3**, 65
Zeitalter age **III U1**, 12; era **III U4**, 107
   goldenes **Zeitalter** golden age **III U3**, 65
Zeitraum period **III U3**, 62
Zeitschrift magazine **I**
Zeitspanne period **III U3**, 62
Zeitung newspaper **I**
Zelt tent ⟨**III TR1**, 110⟩
zelten to camp **II**
zentral central **II**
Zentral- central **II**
Zentrum centre **I**; heart **II**
zerbrechen *to break **II**
zerreißen *to tear apart ⟨**III TMS1**, 30⟩
zerschlagen to smash **III U4**, 104
zerschmettern to smash **III U4**, 104
zerstören to ruin **II**; *to break down
   ⟨**III TMS1**, 30⟩; to destroy **III U3**, 66
Zeug stuff (no pl) **I**
Zeuge/**Zeugin** witness **II**
Zicke (abwertend) drama queen (coll)
   III U3, 74
Ziege goat **I**
ziehen to pull **I**
Ziel goal **II**; destination **III TMS2**, 80; purpose **III TMS2**, 81
Ziellinie finish line **II**
ziemlich quite **II**

ziemlich viele quite a few **II**
Ziffer figure **III U3**, 72
Zimmer room **I**
Zinn tin **II**
Zitrone lemon **II**
zögern to hesitate **III U4**, 105
Zoll customs (sg) **III U4**, 95
zollfrei duty-free **III U4**, 95
Zone zone **II**
Zoo zoo **II**
Zorn anger (no pl) **III U1**, 21
zornig angry **I**
zu closed **III TMS1**, 28
zu too **I**
   Zu dumm! Too bad! **I**
zu to **I**
   zu guter Letzt last but not least
   ⟨**III TR3**, 114⟩
   zu Hause at home **I**
   zu dieser Zeit at this time **III U3**, 65
zubereiten to prepare **II**
züchten *to grow **III U1**, 12
Zucker sugar **I**
zudecken to cover **III U4**, 105
zuerst first **I**; at first **II**
Zug train **I**
Zuhause home **I**
zuhören to listen (to) **I**
Zuhörer/-in listener **II**
auf jmdn. **zukommen** *to come up to sb
   III U1, 21
Zukunft future **II**
zukünftig future **III U4**, 107
Zukunfts- future **III U4**, 107
zum for **I**
   zum Beispiel for example **II**
zumachen to close **I**
zumindest at least ⟨**III TR1**, 111⟩
zunächst at first **II**
zupassen to pass **II**
zur Verfügung stellen to provide
   ⟨**III TMS2**, 86⟩

(ein Foto) **zurechtschneiden** to crop (a
   photo) **III U3**, 75
zurück back **I**
zurückfahren to return **II**
zurückgehen to turn back **III U3**, 69
   zurückgehen auf *to go right back to **II**; to
   date back to **III U3**, 63
zurückkehren to return **II**
zurücklassen *to leave behind **III U2**, 44
zurzeit these days **III U1**, 20
jmdm. **zusagen** to appeal to sb **III U2**, 49
zusammen together **I**
zusammenfallen *to fall down **III U2**, 50
zusammenstoßen (mit) to crash (into)
   III U3, 75
Zusammenziehung contraction
   ⟨**III TMS2**, 87⟩
zusätzlich extra **I**; additional **II**
zuschauen to watch **I**
Zuschauer crowd **II**
Zuschauer/-in viewer **II**
zuspielen to pass **II**
zusprechen to grant **III U2**, 43
zuständig responsible **III U4**, 104
   zuständig sein (für) *to be in charge (of)
   III U1, 15
zustimmen to agree **III U1**, 9
Zutat ingredient **II**
Zutritt admission **II**
zuverlässig reliable ⟨**III TMS1**, 32⟩
zuvor before **II**
sich **zuwenden** to turn to **II**
zwanglos informal **III TMS2**, 80
Zweck purpose **III TMS2**, 81
Zweckmäßigkeit convenience **III U4**, 95
zwei davon two of which **II**
Zweifel doubt **III U1**, 9
zweimal double **I**
zu zweit in pairs **I**
zweitens secondly **II**
Zwilling twin **II**
Zwillings- twin **II**
zwischen between **II**;

In the classroom

Asking for help and information

Can you help me, please?	Kannst du / Können Sie mir bitte helfen?
How do you do this exercise?	Wie macht man diese Übung?
How do you spell … , please?	Wie schreibt man … , bitte?
Is this right? I'm not sure.	Ist das richtig? Ich bin mir nicht sicher.
Is it OK to …?	Ist es in Ordnung, wenn ich / wir …?
Is it true or false?	Ist das richtig oder falsch?
Sorry, I don't know. Ask …	Tut mir leid, das weiß ich nicht. Frag …
Sorry. Can you say that again, please?	Wie bitte? Können Sie das bitte wiederholen?
What does … mean?	Was bedeutet …?
What's for homework?	Was haben wir als Hausaufgabe auf?
What's that in English / German?	Was heißt das auf Englisch / Deutsch?

Vocabulary for instructions and activities

Act one of the scenes. / Act the dialogues.	Spiele eine der Szenen. / Spiele die Dialoge.
Add more words / ideas.	Füge weitere Wörter / Ideen hinzu.
Ask your partner questions.	Stelle deinem Partner / deiner Partnerin Fragen.
Answer your partner's questions.	Beantworte die Fragen deines Partners / deiner Partnerin.
Check your answers with a partner.	Überprüfe deine Antworten mit einem Partner / einer Partnerin.
Choose one part of the story.	Wähle einen Teil der Geschichte aus.
Collect ideas.	Sammle Ideen.
Compare your answers / ideas / notes.	Vergleicht eure Antworten / Ideen / Notizen.
Complete the sentences / dialogue / text.	Vervollständige die Sätze / den Dialog / den Text.
Copy the grid / the mind map.	Schreibe die Tabelle / das Wörternetz ab.
Correct the wrong sentences.	Korrigiere die falschen Sätze.

Decide …	Entscheide / Entscheidet …
Describe …	Beschreibe / Beschreibt …
Design a flyer / a poster.	Entwerfe / Gestalte einen Flyer / ein Poster.
Discuss.	Diskutiert (darüber).
Draw a picture.	Zeichne ein Bild.
Exchange your …	Tausche dein/e … aus.
Explain why or why not.	Erkläre warum oder warum nicht.
Explain your answer.	Erkläre deine Antwort.
Fill in …	Fülle … aus.
Find the rule / the right word order.	Finde die Regel / die richtige Satzstellung.
Finish your brochure.	Stelle deine Broschüre fertig.
Get organised.	Organisiere dich. / Organisiert euch.
Give feedback.	Gib Feedback / Rückmeldung.
Guess the new words.	Errate die neuen Wörter.
Improve your partner's text.	Verbessere den Text deines Partners / deiner Partnerin. / Mache Verbesserungsvorschläge.
Learn your text by heart.	Lerne deinen Text auswendig.
Listen to the sentences / the dialogue.	Höre dir die Sätze / den Dialog an.
Look at the picture / the examples.	Schau dir das Bild / die Beispiele an.
Make a poster / a grid / a mind map.	Fertige ein Poster / eine Tabelle / ein Wörternetz an.
Make notes.	Mache dir Notizen.
Make sentences.	Bilde Sätze.
Match the sentence parts. / Match each of them.	Ordne die Satzteile einander zu. / Ordne jede/r/s zu.
Name …	Nenne …
Note down …	Notiere … / Schreibe … auf.
Peer-edit each other's work.	Kontolliert / Überprüft gegenseitig eure Arbeit.
Plan the scenes.	Plane die Szenen.
Play a game.	Spiele ein Spiel.
Practise your scenes / the dialogues.	Übe deine Szenen / die Dialoge.
Present the information from your text.	Präsentere die Informationen aus deinem Text.
Put in the correct forms.	Setze die richtigen Formen ein.
Read your text out loud.	Lies deinen Text laut vor.
Record your report / dialogue.	Nehmt euren Bericht / Dialog auf.
Repeat the sentences / the dialogues.	Wiederhole die Sätze / die Dialoge.
Say the words / the sounds.	Sage die Wörter / die Laute.
Share your ideas.	Tauscht euch über eure Ideen aus.
Show the class your brochure.	Zeige der Klasse deine Broschüre.
Start. / Start like this.	Fange an. / Fange so an.
Sum up the information / the text.	Fasse die Informationen / den Text zusammen.
Swap roles.	Tauscht die Rollen.

Take a card.	Nimm eine Karte.
Take notes.	Mache dir Notizen.
Take turns.	Wechselt euch ab.
Talk about yourself.	Sprich über dich selbst.
Talk to your partner.	Sprich mit deinem Partner / deiner Partnerin.
Tell your partner about …	Erzähle deinem Partner / deiner Partnerin von …
Think about the story.	Denke über die Geschichte nach.
Translate the words / sentences.	Übersetze die Wörter / Sätze.
Use the ideas / the vocabulary.	Verwende die Ideen / die Vokabeln.
Watch the film.	Schau dir den Film an.
Work on your own.	Arbeite in Einzelarbeit. / Arbeite für dich.
Work with a partner or in a group.	Arbeite mit einem Partner / einer Partnerin oder in einer Gruppe.
Write dialogues / a short text.	Schreibe Dialoge / einen kurzen Text.
Write about your friends.	Schreibe über deine Freunde.
Write down …	Schreibe … auf.

Vocabulary for media activities

Can I have a charger, please?	Kann ich bitte ein Ladegerät / Ladekabel haben?
Click play / pause.	Klicke auf Abspielen / Pause.
Close the document / file.	Schließe das Dokument / die Datei.
Copy and paste the text / picture.	Schneide den Text / das Bild aus und setze ihn/es wieder ein.
Insert the text / picture.	Füge den Text / das Bild ein.
Mark / Highlight …	Markiere … / Hebe … hervor.
Open a new document / file.	Öffne ein neues Dokument / eine neue Datei.
Play …	Spiele … ab.
Print the document / file.	Drucke das Dokument / die Datei aus.
Record …	Nimm … auf.
Save the document / file (as …).	Speichere das Dokument / die Datei (als …).
Send the document / file.	Verschicke das Dokument / die Datei.
Share the document / file.	Teile das Dokument / die Datei.
Spell check your text.	Überprüfe die Rechtschreibung deines Textes.
Start a (new) folder.	Erstelle einen (neuen) Ordner.
Save the file to your folder.	Speichere die Datei in deinem Ordner.
The battery is flat.	Die Batterie / Der Akku ist leer.
Turn on / off …	Schalte ein / aus …
Type your text.	Tippe deinen Text.
Where's the plug?	Wo ist die Steckdose?

Useful words

activity	Aktivität	presentation	Präsentation; Vortrag
answer	Antwort	prompt card	Stichwortkarte; Rollenkarte
(main) character	(Haupt-)Figur	pros and cons	Vor- und Nachteile
column	Spalte	puzzle	Rätsel; Puzzle
description	Beschreibung	question	Frage
detail	Detail; Einzelheit	quiz	Quiz; Rätsel
diagram	Diagramm	quote	Zitat
dialogue	Dialog	reaction	Reaktion
dice	Würfel	report	Bericht
dictionary	Wörterbuch	rhyme	Reim
draft	Entwurf; Konzept	role play	Rollenspiel
drawing	Zeichnung	rule	Regel
example	Beispiel	scene	Szene
expert puzzle	Expertenpuzzle	section	Abschnitt; Paragraf
fact	Tatsache; Fakt	skill	Fertigkeit
folder	Ordner; Mappe	song	Lied
game	Spiel	sounds and spelling	Laute und Rechtschreibung
gist	das Wesentliche	statement	Aussage; Behauptung; Erklärung
grammar	Grammatik	story	Geschichte; Erzählung
grid	Gitter; Tabelle; Raster	summary	Zusammenfassung
heading	Überschrift	task	Aufgabe
information	Information(en)	theme	Thema; Motto
key word	Schlüsselwort; Stichwort	timeline	Zeitstrahl
line	Zeile	tip	Tipp
material	Material	title	Titel; Überschrift
mind map	Wörternetz	topic	Thema
(alphabetical) order	(alphabetische) Reihenfolge	unit	Lektion; Kapitel
phrase	Satz; Redewendung; Ausdruck	useful phrases	nützliche Ausdrücke
picture story	Bildergeschichte	vocabulary	Vokabular; Wortschatz
point of view	Standpunkt; Ansicht; Perspektive	word order	Wortstellung; Satzstellung

Irregular verbs

infinitive	simple past	past participle	German
be [biː]	was [wɒz] / were [wɜː]	been [biːn]	sein
beat [biːt]	beat [biːt]	beaten ['biːtn]	schlagen; besiegen
become [bɪ'kʌm]	became [bɪ'keɪm]	become [bɪ'kʌm]	werden
begin [bɪ'gɪn]	began [bɪ'gæn]	begun [bɪ'gʌn]	beginnen; anfangen
bet [bet]	bet [bet]	bet [bet]	wetten
bite [baɪt]	bit [bɪt]	bitten ['bɪtn]	beißen
blow [bləʊ]	blew [bluː]	blown [bləʊn]	blasen; pusten
break [breɪk]	broke [brəʊk]	broken ['brəʊkn]	(zer)brechen; kaputt machen
bring [brɪŋ]	brought [brɔːt]	brought [brɔːt]	(mit)bringen
build [bɪld]	built [bɪlt]	built [bɪlt]	bauen
burn [bɜːn]	burnt [bɜːnt] / burned [bɜːnd]	burnt [bɜːnt] / burned [bɜːnd]	(ver)brennen
buy [baɪ]	bought [bɔːt]	bought [bɔːt]	kaufen
catch [kætʃ]	caught [kɔːt]	caught [kɔːt]	fangen
choose [tʃuːz]	chose [tʃəʊz]	chosen ['tʃəʊzn]	(aus)wählen
come [kʌm]	came [keɪm]	come [kʌm]	kommen
cost [kɒst]	cost [kɒst]	cost [kɒst]	kosten
cut [kʌt]	cut [kʌt]	cut [kʌt]	schneiden
deal (with) [diːl]	dealt (with) [delt]	dealt (with) [delt]	sich befassen (mit); umgehen (mit)
do [duː]	did [dɪd]	done [dʌn]	machen; tun
draw [drɔː]	drew [druː]	drawn [drɔːn]	zeichnen; ziehen
dream [driːm]	dreamt [dremt]	dreamt [dremt]	träumen
drink [drɪŋk]	drank [dræŋk]	drunk [drʌŋk]	trinken
drive [draɪv]	drove [drəʊv]	driven ['drɪvn]	fahren
eat [iːt]	ate [et]	eaten ['iːtn]	essen
fall [fɔːl]	fell [fel]	fallen ['fɔːlən]	(hin)fallen
feed [fiːd]	fed [fed]	fed [fed]	füttern; ernähren
feel [fiːl]	felt [felt]	felt [felt]	fühlen
fight [faɪt]	fought [fɔːt]	fought [fɔːt]	kämpfen; (sich) streiten
find [faɪnd]	found [faʊnd]	found [faʊnd]	finden
fit [fɪt]	fit [fɪt] / fitted ['fɪtɪd]	fit [fɪt] / fitted ['fɪtɪd]	passen
fly [flaɪ]	flew [fluː]	flown [fləʊn]	fliegen
forget [fə'get]	forgot [fə'gɒt]	forgotten [fə'gɒtn]	vergessen
forgive [fə'gɪv]	forgave [fə'geɪv]	forgiven [fə'gɪvn]	vergeben; verzeihen
freeze [friːz]	froze [frəʊz]	frozen ['frəʊzn]	gefrieren; erstarren
get [get]	got [gɒt]	got [gɒt]	bekommen; erhalten
give [gɪv]	gave [geɪv]	given ['gɪvn]	geben
go [gəʊ]	went [went]	gone [gɒn]	gehen; fahren
grow [grəʊ]	grew [gruː]	grown [grəʊn]	wachsen; anbauen; züchten
hang [hæŋ]	hung [hʌŋ]	hung [hʌŋ]	hängen
have [hæv]	had [hæd]	had [hæd]	haben
hear [hɪə]	heard [hɜːd]	heard [hɜːd]	hören
hide [haɪd]	hid [hɪd]	hidden ['hɪdn]	(sich) verstecken
hit [hɪt]	hit [hɪt]	hit [hɪt]	schlagen; treffen
hold [həʊld]	held [held]	held [held]	(fest)halten
hurt [hɜːt]	hurt [hɜːt]	hurt [hɜːt]	verletzen; sich weh tun
keep [kiːp]	kept [kept]	kept [kept]	(auf)bewahren; behalten

infinitive	simple past	past participle	German
know [nəʊ]	knew [nju:]	known [nəʊn]	kennen; wissen
lead [li:d]	led [led]	led [led]	(an)führen
learn [lɜ:n]	learnt [lɜ:nt] / learned [lɜ:nd]	learnt [lɜ:nt] / learned [lɜ:nd]	lernen
leave [li:v]	left [left]	left [left]	(ver)lassen
lend [lend]	lent [lent]	lent [lent]	(ver)leihen
let [let]	let [let]	let [let]	lassen
lie [laɪ]	lay [leɪ]	lain [leɪn]	liegen
lose [lu:z]	lost [lɒst]	lost [lɒst]	verlieren
make [meɪk]	made [meɪd]	made [meɪd]	machen; tun
mean [mi:n]	meant [ment]	meant [ment]	bedeuten; meinen
meet [mi:t]	met [met]	met [met]	treffen
pay [peɪ]	paid [peɪd]	paid [peɪd]	(be)zahlen
put [pʊt]	put [pʊt]	put [pʊt]	legen; setzen; stellen
read [ri:d]	read [red]	read [red]	lesen
ride [raɪd]	rode [rəʊd]	ridden ['rɪdn]	fahren; reiten
ring [rɪŋ]	rang [ræn]	rung [rʌŋ]	klingeln; läuten
rise [raɪz]	rose [rəʊz]	risen ['rɪzn]	steigen; sich erheben; aufstehen
run [rʌn]	ran [ræn]	run [rʌn]	laufen; rennen
say [seɪ]	said [sed]	said [sed]	sagen
see [si:]	saw [sɔ:]	seen [si:n]	sehen
sell [sel]	sold [səʊld]	sold [səʊld]	verkaufen
send [send]	sent [sent]	sent [sent]	senden; verschicken
set up [set ˈʌp]	set up [set ˈʌp]	set up [set ˈʌp]	erbauen; errichten
shine [ʃaɪn]	shone [ʃɒn]	shone [ʃɒn]	scheinen; glänzen
shoot [ʃu:t]	shot [ʃɒt]	shot [ʃɒt]	schießen
show [ʃəʊ]	showed [ʃəʊd]	shown [ʃəʊn]	zeigen
sing [sɪŋ]	sang [sæn]	sung [sʌŋ]	singen
sink [sɪŋk]	sank [sæŋk]	sunk [sʌŋk]	untergehen; sinken
sit [sɪt]	sat [sæt]	sat [sæt]	sitzen
sleep [sli:p]	slept [slept]	slept [slept]	schlafen
smell [smel]	smelt [smelt] / smelled [smeld]	smelt [smelt] / smelled [smeld]	riechen; duften
speak [spi:k]	spoke [spəʊk]	spoken ['spəʊkn]	sprechen
spell [spel]	spelt [spelt] / spelled [speld]	spelt [spelt] / spelled [speld]	buchstabieren
spend [spend]	spent [spent]	spent [spent]	ausgeben; verbringen
spill [spɪl]	spilt [spɪlt] / spilled [spɪld]	spilt [spɪlt] / spilled [spɪld]	verschütten; auslaufen
stand [stænd]	stood [stʊd]	stood [stʊd]	stehen
steal [sti:l]	stole [stəʊl]	stolen ['stəʊln]	stehlen
stick [stɪk]	stuck [stʌk]	stuck [stʌk]	kleben; stecken
swim [swɪm]	swam [swæm]	swum [swʌm]	schwimmen
take [teɪk]	took [tʊk]	taken ['teɪkn]	nehmen
teach [ti:tʃ]	taught [tɔ:t]	taught [tɔ:t]	unterrichten; lehren; beibringen
tell [tel]	told [təʊld]	told [təʊld]	erzählen
think [θɪŋk]	thought [θɔ:t]	thought [θɔ:t]	(nach)denken; glauben
throw [θrəʊ]	threw [θru:]	thrown [θrəʊn]	werfen
understand [ˌʌndəˈstænd]	understood [ˌʌndəˈstʊd]	understood [ˌʌndəˈstʊd]	verstehen
wake up [ˌweɪk ˈʌp]	woke up [ˌwəʊk ˈʌp]	woken up [ˌwəʊkn ˈʌp]	(auf)wachen; (auf)wecken
wear [weə]	wore [wɔ:]	worn [wɔ:n]	anhaben; tragen
win [wɪn]	won [wʌn]	won [wʌn]	gewinnen; siegen
write [raɪt]	wrote [rəʊt]	written ['rɪtn]	schreiben

Unit 1
Check-out

1 If I learn HTML, . . .
2. If I drop out of school, I will have more time for my business ideas.; **3.** But if I'm not successful, I will go back to school.; **4.** If I use a deep voice on the phone, people will not know how young I am.; **5.** I'll save money if I live at home for the first few years.; **6.** If my business is a big success, I will win awards and become rich.; **7.** I'll have more than a billion dollars if I sell my business.

2 Why I can't to go the school dance
1. If I **weren't** grounded, I**'d go** to the school dance.; **2.** If I **had** better marks, I **wouldn't be** grounded.; **3.** If I **paid** attention at school, I**'d have** better marks.; **4.** If I **enjoyed** class more, I**'d pay** attention.; **5.** If English **was/were** easier, we **wouldn't have to** learn so much grammar.; **6.** If the school **compromised** and didn't make me write texts, English **would be** so much easier.; **7.** I bet if I **asked** my teacher, she**'d disagree** with me.

3 Help! I can't do it myself!
1 me; **2** yourself; **3** her; **4** myself; **5** you; **6** you; **7** me; **8** myself

4 Different smart types
b) Street smart:
- every underground is almost the same → no map; just follow colours and numbers
- to go to lunch follow kids your age and eat what they have; don't follow tourists
- If a street looks like trouble, look for a different way that is safer.
- ask people for help or free tours

Book smart:
- know facts about the city: 625,000 people, more than a million people work in the city; big biscuit company
- know about times: underground trains leave every hour at half past; train station by famous architect
- lunch at 12 o'clock for £3
- the harbour is the biggest in the south of England and 20 ships arrive and depart every day

c) *individuelle Lösung*

Diff pool

1 Your turn: In what way are you smart?
individuelle Lösung

2 Your turn: In what way are you smart?
Lösungsvorschlag:
Gwen: good at running and finding her way → body smart, logic smart
Holly: looks after her guinea pigs → nature smart
Olivia: plays the sax, plays netball, likes cycling, writes for the yearbook → music smart, body smart, word smart
Dave: is into computers, helps people, solves conflicts → logic smart, people smart
Jay: good at singing and dancing → music smart, body smart
Luke: plays football, looks after his dog → body smart, nature smart

3 What will the future bring?
a) 1. If Olivia practises a lot, she'll play in front of a big audience.
2. If Holly studies hard, she'll become a vet.
3. If Luke pushes himself, he'll play in the Premier League.
4. If Dave saves his pocket money, he'll open a snack bar.

b) *individuelle Lösung*

4 What will the future bring?
1. If Olivia practises a lot, she'll play in front of a big audience.
2. If Holly studies hard, she'll become a vet.
3. If Luke pushes himself, he'll play in the Premier League.
4. If Dave saves his pocket money, he'll open a snack bar.

5 More advice for Jay
1 were; **2** wouldn't worry; **3** 'd/would worry; **4** was/were; **5** wouldn't earn; **6** would put; **7** didn't look; **8** was/were; **9** 'd/would make sure; **10** 'd/would stop

6 What would an adult say?
Lösungsvorschlag: Jay, if I were you, I'd practise hard to be a professional singer and dancer. If you want to be a super star, you'll have to learn a lot. There are just so many singers and dancers out there! I'm a professional dancer too, and there's a lot of competition. If you left school early, what would happen if you aren't successful? And if you don't have a good education, you'll have problems to find a good job after your career as a dancer. Nobody can dance forever!

7 Your turn: A forum for teenagers
Lösungsvorschlag: Dear …,
I understand how you feel. If my friends wanted to copy my homework, I would want to help them too because they're my friends. Maybe you can suggest that you do your homework together if they have problems at school. But they shouldn't let you do the work! Teachers give homework to students for them to practise and to find out what they can or can't do.
So next time they ask you, suggest that you do your homework together. If they still want you to do it for them, you should look for new friends.
Dear …,
I'm sorry to hear that your parents won't let you go out with your friends. Why don't you tell your parents why and where you want to meet your friends? It's important to explain what you want to do together. Why don't you promise to take your phone with you and not to turn it off? I hope you can find a compromise.

8 Ivy's model
1 didn't love; **2** wouldn't be; **3** 'd/would find; **4** was/were; **5** didn't like; **6** wouldn't work; **7** weren't; **8** 'd/would have

9 A German talent show
individuelle Lösung

10 Different jobs
1. model; **2.** influencer; **3.** dancer; **4.** designer

11 Different jobs
Lösungsvorschlag:
- **model:** self and picture smart I like to perform I love fashion I like travelling I work in a team
- **influencer:** good technical skills I communicate well I people and self smart I post videos I give advice
- **dancer:** body and self smart I practise hard I imaginative I confident I perform in front of an audience
- **designer:** creative I like drawing I good at working with his/her hands I people smart I good at working in a team

12 Compare two families: the Azads and the Frasers
Lösungsvorschlag:
Olivia: **Personality:** bossy; strong; serious; clever; likes to get organised; is good at everything; **Opinions:** school is

important; you must work hard and get good marks; you should teach yourself new things; **Problems:** can only focus on important things like school

Claire: **Personality:** strong; likes to have fun; is good at compromising; **Opinions:** hobbies are good for you; find time to enjoy yourself; **Problems:** –

Lucy: **Personality:** likes to play; messy; **Opinions:** find time to enjoy yourself; **Problems:** room is messy

Jay: **Personality:** clever; creative; is good at singing and dancing; likes to dream; likes to have fun; **Opinions:** hobbies are good for you; **Problems:** can't focus on important things like school; can't agree with parents; gets bad marks

Jay's parents: **Personality:** serious; strong; **Opinions:** school is important; you must work hard and get good marks; no good job without good marks; you're too laid-back; **Problems:** can only focus on important things like school

13 Act it out!
a) Picture 1: disappointed; Picture 2: happy / excited; Picture 3: shocked; Picture 4: angry; Picture 5: not sure what to do
b) *individuelle Lösung*

14 Before you read
individuelle Lösung

Grammar

G1 If your content is interesting, people will be interested in you.
1. If we **don't leave** now, we**'ll miss** our train.
2. If we **miss** our train, we**'ll be** late for the film.
3. If we**'re** late for the film, they probably **won't let** us in.
4. And I**'ll be** really upset if that **happens**.

G2 They wouldn't worry if they didn't care.
1 tried; 2 wouldn't fight; 3 wouldn't have; 4 worked; 5 got; 6 believed; 7 wouldn't worry; 8 weren't; 9 wouldn't have to

G3 You have to push yourself!
1 myself; 2 me; 3 yourself; 4 yourselves; 5 each other

Vocabulary

Sounds and spelling
a) 1. does; 2. now; 3. practice; 4. are; 5. phone; 6. idea
b) lice (3); bunny (5); hare (4); flea (6); doe (2); kangaroos (1)

Text and media smart 1
Diff pool

1 Understanding the song
laughs with you (l. 2); looks after you (l. 3); you enjoy his/her company (l. 4); is loyal (l. 5); is always there for you (l. 11, l. 30, ll. 32–33); is there to talk to (l. 14)

2 Understanding the song
In a song the writer often leaves out commas, full stops and letters (e.g. lookin' = looking, 'til = until). Each line or idea starts with a capital letter.

3 Focus on language
1 b); 2 c); 3 a)

4 Focus on language
friends stick together like glue: they stay together and help each other; a shoulder to cry on: listen to somebody's problems

and show understanding; speak the same language: can communicate easily with another person because you share similar opinions and experiences; know someone inside out: know somebody very well; be on the same page: agree with others about what they're trying to achieve

5 Be a songwriter!
left to right: **1** helps you to get back to your feet; **2/5** helps you to carry your burdens; **3** supports you when you are down; **4** helps you to reach your goals; **6/8** shares everything with you; **7** supports you so you can take the next step; **9** helps you to meet challenges, never leaves you when you are in trouble

6 Rhymes in poetry
c)

7 Writing a stanza
individuelle Lösung

8 Your turn: A friendship poem
individuelle Lösung

Revision A

1 The saxophone lesson
a) 1. Helen wants £45 for saxophone lessons. Her mother thinks that she doesn't practise enough and she doesn't want to pay.;
2. She thinks that practice makes progress and progress leads to more fun. She compares it with work and says that you sometimes have to do things even if you don't want to.;
3. Helen is going to stop lessons for three months. If she misses her sax and if she practises, she can take lessons again.
b) **Good:** Missing something shows you that it is important. Helen learns to practise and how important it is. **Bad:** She'll have no lessons at all. Maybe she won't go back to the lessons.
c) *individuelle Lösungen*

2 Follow or don't follow the crowd
a) *Lösungsvorschlag:*
   – Cartoon 1: The cartoon shows six men. They are walking in a circle, one behind the other. The men's faces look almost the same and they're wearing the same long shirt. On the back of each man, there's a sign. It says, "FOLLOW ME".
   – Cartoon 2: In the picture you can see a crowded room. It's probably a party because the people are wearing nice clothes, and some people are holding drinks in their hands. Almost everybody in the picture is crying and the caption of the cartoon says, "Crying is cool now."
b) *Lösungsvorschlag:*
   – Cartoon 1: In my opinion, the cartoon's message is that you shouldn't just follow other people. I think the cartoonist wants to show that it's important to have your own ideas and opinions. If everybody just followed the others, we'd all be the same and never be able to discover anything new. I agree / don't agree with the cartoon's message because …
   – Cartoon 2: In my opinion, the cartoon's message is that we shouldn't just follow the crowd but develop our own way of life. The cartoonist wants to make fun of the fact that if something is 'in' or 'cool', everybody starts doing it, even if it's something silly. I agree / don't agree with the cartoon's message because …

3 The dangers of social media

Direkte Interaktion:
- lernen soziale Beziehungen aufzubauen und zu kommunizieren (wichtig für Arbeitsleben)
- treffen sich mit Gleichaltrigen und erfahren, wie diese auf sie reagieren
- entwickeln ein Selbstwertgefühl, indem sie sagen, was sie denken, auch wenn andere eine andere Meinung vertreten
- Zeit für sich haben und nicht in ständigem Kontakt zu anderen sein

Digitale Interaktion:
- verbringen mehr Zeit am Bildschirm als im direkten Austausch mit anderen
- sehen nicht die Mimik und Gestik des Gesprächspartners
- weniger kontaktfreudig
- können sich verstecken oder eine andere Identität annehmen
- grausamer gegenüber anderen, weil sie nicht direkt anwesend sind und die Reaktion nicht gesehen wird
- erfinden ein perfektes Ich
- stehen in permanentem Wettbewerb mit anderen, um beliebt zu sein
- führt zu Problemen bei der Kommunikation und bei der Entwicklung des Selbstwertgefühls

4 Gaming parties

b) **1.** Dave can **sometimes** have a gaming party at home.; **2.** He and his friends **always** try to find a new game.; **3.** They have **never** played this game before.; **4.** The friends **usually** order pizzas for their gaming parties.; **5.** The pizzas **sometimes** don't arrive on time.; **6.** The parties at the Prestons' house have **already** become a big success.; **7.** One of the rules at the party is that the friends should **always** play fair.; **8.** They are **hardly ever** late for a party.

5 Is e-sport really a sport?

a) **1** love; **2** enjoy; **3** means; **4** is becoming; **5** aren't talking; **6** take part; **7** watch; **8** is changing; **9** include; **10** are thinking; **11** is moving

b) *individuelle Lösung*

6 Dave didn't win ...

Hi Luke,

Sorry I **missed** your call yesterday. That's because I **was** a player in an e-sport competition, and I **didn't have** my phone with me. I **played** three games. I **won** the first two games, but then I **lost** against a girl from Brighton. She **was** amazing! I **played** for about ten minutes, and then I **was** out of the competition. So I **didn't win** a prize, but I really **enjoyed** it!

How **was** your football match yesterday? You **didn't say** anything about it in your email. **Was** the weather OK? I hope it **wasn't** too cold! **Did** your team **win** the match?

Send me an email soon!

Dave

7 Let's dance

1 haven't been; **2** for; **3** haven't been; **4** since; **5** haven't seen; **6** since; **7** 's loved; **8** since; **9** 's danced; **10** since, **11** haven't heard; **12** for; **13** has she been; **14** 's been back; **15** since

8 Best friend?

1 felt; **2** studied; **3** told; **4** has ('s) ever got; **5** hung out; **6** ignored; **7** have ('ve) been; **8** listened

Unit 2
Check-out

1 Berlin then and now

2. In a survey Berlin was voted the most 'fun' city in the world.; **3.** 150 years ago there were no cars, so everything was pulled by horses.; **4.** In the 1800s industry was growing and a lot of machines were produced in Berlin.; **5.** Berlin is very popular and every year its sights are visited by millions of tourists.; **6.** 'Currywurst', a popular type of street food, was invented by Herta Heuwer.; **7.** To make extra money, many flats are rented out to tourists today.; **8.** The fall of the Berlin Wall is celebrated at the Brandenburg Gate each year.

2 Only in Scotland

Alan: Lots of people enjoyed the concert last night. But a storm interrupted our gig. We were really disappointed by the weather.

David: Oh, that doesn't matter. Most of us just ignored the storm.

Alan: Did the roof keep out the rain?

David: Most of it! A lot of people put on raincoats.

Alan: Were they rented out?

David: Yeah, they usually do that at concerts. What's going on at the Highland Games tomorrow?

Alan: A bagpipe contest has been planned by some people. And there's a new contest where people walk on thistles. Sounds dangerous!

David: Well, now we can say thistle-walking was invented by the Scots!

Alan: And listen to this – this is great! The winners of the bagpipe contest judge the thistle-walking contest. Funny, isn't it?!

David: Yes, you can only find that in Scotland!

3 At the ceilidh

1. They were having dinner when Holly's mobile rang.; **2.** While a band was playing music at a ceilidh, they started to dance.; **3.** When Ethan was singing, Amber went red.; **4.** When Ethan and Amber were kissing, Holly took photos of them.

4 Boring!

so nice – amazing; like I've been in this city many times before – at home here; come back to the same place where I started – go round in circles; typical Scottish clothes – traditional clothes; known around the world – world-famous; very big – huge; nice – fascinating; say it very quietly – whisper it; too many – thousands of

Diff pool

1 Typically German?

individuelle Lösung

2 Hogmanay

2. are cleaned; **3.** is celebrated; **4.** are rung, (are) set off; **5.** are held, is sung; **6.** are given; **7.** is brought; **8.** are granted

3 Famous Scots

Radar was invented by Robert Wattson-Watt.
Tunnels, canals and roads were built by Thomas Telford.
Scottish castles were designed by Robert Adams.
James Bond was played by Sean Connery.
Lots of money was given to charity by Andrew Carnegie.
Treasure Island was written by Robert Louis Stevenson.

4 Scottish heroes and heroines
1. have been told; 2. was put up; 3. has been told; 4. was kidnapped; 5. was brought; 6. was told; 7. is always described; 8. was defeated; 9. was hidden

5 Scottish heroes and heroines
1. have been told; 2. was put up; 3. has been told; 4. was kidnapped; 5. was brought; 6. was told; 7. is always described; 8. was defeated; 9. was hidden

6 Your turn: A different country
Lösungsvorschlag: You can find the country of Galumphia in a warm and sunny place in the Atlantic Ocean. Its people live in small houses in palm trees. They wear yellow hats with colourful flowers on them. Every day they go fishing, swimming or windsurfing in the sea. In the evenings they often have barbecues. The king of the country wears a crown made of flowers on his head. Flowers are the national symbol of Galumphia.
Everyone should go to Galumphia because it's a really beautiful country and its people are friendly and relaxed.

7 What were Olivia and her family doing?
Present progressive (left side): 3. are you using; 5. are looking
Past progressive (right side): 2. was tidying; 4. were preparing

8 When or while?
1. when; 2. When; 3. while; 4. While; 5. when; 6. While

9 A crazy day at home
Lösungsvorschlag: First, breakfast was crazy. While Mum was having breakfast, our dog Alfred tried to eat her breakfast! Then, while Mum and Dad were sitting in the garden, we started to make a cake in the kitchen. But when Mum and Dad came back, the kitchen was very messy. It was terrible, and they weren't happy about it. But where was Alfred? When we looked under the table, Alfred was eating all the sugar for our cake! What a crazy and messy day!

10 Strong adjectives
- **small:** little, tiny
- **good:** great, amazing, spectacular, fascinating, interesting, wonderful, exciting
- **nice:** great, beautiful, amazing, interesting, spectacular, fascinating, wonderful
- **big:** large, huge

11 It's amazing!
a) 1 world-famous; 2 tall; 3 largest; 4 most beautiful; 5 exciting; 6 enough; 7 very; 8 amazing
b) I'd choose picture C. In this picture you can see that the crane is really tall. Also, the sky is blue, and good weather makes people want to go outside and do and see things.

Grammar

G4 Is haggis made with meat?
was invented; was brought; has been played; is played

G5 What were they doing when Holly took the picture?
2. Were William and Kate visiting Edinburgh when Gwen and Holly saw them? – No, they weren't. They were visiting Glasgow.; 3. Was Gwen running in a / the park when she fell over? – No, she wasn't. She was running down the road.; 4. Were Holly and Gwen walking through a field when cows started to follow them? – No, they weren't. They were walking past it/the field.

Vocabulary
Sounds and spelling
●○○: vegetable; musical; shipbuilding
○●○: historic
○○●: entertain; impolite; interrupt; engineer
○●○○: traditional; historical; spectacular; communicate
○○●○: unofficial; competition

Revision B

1 Landscapes
a)+b) *individuelle Lösung*

2 Role play: I'm sorry
individuelle Lösung

3 Let's celebrate!
Lösungsvorschlag: There are different words for this festival in the different parts of Germany. It's called 'Fastnacht', 'Fasching' or 'Karneval'. Traditions and customs are different as well, but the parades are all held at the same time between 11th November and the day before Ash Wednesday. Even the Romans celebrated this festival and it has been celebrated for centuries in Germany. People celebrate 'Karneval' for different reasons. Some people are happy that the winter is over and some just want to have lots of fun before Lent. But everybody wants to be loud, to sing and dance, to be happy and celebrate in the streets. In some areas there are even school holidays during this time. In the first picture you can see a typical float from Cologne and in the second there are some masks. In the last picture you can see a very old mask.

4 Visit Edinburgh!
individuelle Lösung

5 Word puzzles
1 I understand; 2 mashed potatoes; 3 backpack; 4 bagpipes

6 At Balmoral Castle
1 easy; 2 warm; 3 safely; 4 confidently; 5 little; 6 expensive; 7 bravely; 8 perfect; 9 rudely; 10 sweetly 11 personally; 12 roughly; 13 quickly; 14 slowly; 15 quickly; 16 easily; 17 friendly; 18 successful

7 The comparison of adjectives
b) amazing – more amazing – (the) most amazing; hot – hotter – (the) hottest; happy – happier – (the) happiest; beautiful – more beautiful – (the) most beautiful; good – better – (the) best

8 The best of Scotland
Lösungsvorschlag:
1. A: Of all the inventions by a Scot I think the television was the most important.
   B: Really? I think that the invention of penicillin was more important than the invention of the TV.
2. A: Of all outdoor activities I think that mountain biking is the best.
   B: Really? I think climbing is better than mountain biking.
3. A: Of all the events in Edinburgh I think the Book Festival is the most popular.
   B: Really? I think that the Festival Fringe is more popular than the Book Festival.

9 Facts about Scotland
1. Life in the Highlands **is quieter than** life in the cities.; **2.** The weather this year **isn't as good as** last year.; **3.** The Scottish accent **is easier** to understand **than** most people think.; **4.** Mount Snowdon in Wales **isn't as high as** Ben Nevis in Scotland.; **5.** Glasgow **isn't as popular as** Edinburgh with tourists.

10 The comparison of adverbs
b) easily – more easily – (the) most easily; bad - worse – (the) worst; aggressively – more aggressively – (the) most aggressively; angrily – more angrily – (the) most angrily; hard – harder – (the) hardest; well – better – (the) best

11 How well did they do?
1 best; **2** more slowly; **3** more clearly; **4** simple / simpler; **5** little; **6** the most important; **7** well; **8** more interesting; **9** funnier; **10** the funniest; **11** the most friendly; **12** funny; **13** the fastest; **14** hard/harder

12 Dear Diary
1 because; **2** Before; **3** as soon as; **4** Whenever; **5** after; **6** and; **7** until

Unit 3
Check-out

1 Quiz time
a) **1.** whose; **2.** that/which; **3.** that/which; **4.** which; **5.** whose; **6.** (that/which)
b) **1.** Victoria; **2.** Buckingham Palace; **3.** armada; **4.** the Globe Theatre; **5.** Francis Drake; **6.** wood

2 Victorian inventions
1 who/that; **2** which/that; **3** whom; **4** (which/that); **5** who/that; **6** whose; **7** which; **8** (which/that); **9** (which/that); **10** (who/that); **11** who/that; **12** who/that; **13** whose; **14** which/that; **15** which/that

3 Tidying up the community centre
Olivia: So many glasses! I think people took a clean **glass / one** every time they wanted some more lemonade!
Holly: And these are just the **ones** I've brought into the kitchen. There are still some in the Roman room. And the Romans were the people who drank the most lemonade!
Olivia: Where should I put them, Claire?
Claire: The small **glasses / ones** go in the cupboard, and the big **ones** go on the shelf.
Olivia: Which shelf?
Claire: That **one** over there, next to the door.
Holly: I hope our Tudor photo is OK.
Claire: Well, it may not be the best **one** in the calendar, but Jim says it'll be good enough.
Holly: Gwen and I are smiling in it. I think the best **photos / ones** from the shoot are the **ones** which are more serious.
Claire: Well, it's the only **photo / one** we've got with you in your costumes. I'm sure it'll be fine.

4 Which one doesn't belong?
a) **1.** Roman, bath, empire, heating; **2.** entertainment, Globe Theatre, play, writer; **3.** (to) attack, Spanish Armada, battle, (to) defeat; **4.** Industrial Revolution, factory, British Empire, steam engine; **5.** lady-in-waiting, dress, (to) take care of, queen; **6.** Norman, William the Conqueror, food, French

b) *Lösungsvorschlag:*
1. The Romans wanted to make their empire bigger. Roman soldiers built baths and underfloor heating.; **2.** The Globe Theatre was a famous theatre. A writer wrote plays for the theatre groups and they acted them out for entertainment.; **3.** The Spanish Armada attacked Britain. The British Empire was strong enough to win the battle and defeat the Armada.; **4.** During the Industrial Revolution, lots of factories were built. The steam engine was invented and people travelled to other countries in the British Empire.; **5.** The lady-in-waiting took care of the queen. She helped her with her dress.; **6.** William the Conqueror was a Norman. People grew food for their lord. The Normans introduced French as a language in Britain.
c) *individuelle Lösung*

Diff pool

1 Vocabulary
a) **1.** win – lose; **2.** arrive – leave; **3.** appear – disappear; **4.** fight – make peace; **5.** marry – divorce
b) **1.** won; **2.** arrived; **3.** disappeared; **4.** fought; **5.** married
c) – group 1 (verb = noun): attack – attack; defeat – defeat; fight – fight; design – design
– group 2 (verb + ing): build – building; kill – killing; feel – feeling; paint – painting
– group 3 (verb + ion): invent – invention; protect – protection; connect – connection; decide – decision; invade – invasion

2 Vocabulary
a) **1.** win – lose; **2.** arrive – leave; **3.** appear – disappear; **4.** fight – make peace; **5.** marry – divorce
b) *Lösungsvorschlag:*
1. He's just **won** a battle.; **2.** By the time the Angels and Saxons **arrived** in Britain, there were already roads there.; **3.** They lost the battle and then **disappeared**.; **4.** Back then they **fought** over land.; **5.** King Henry VIII **married** six times.
c) – group 1 (verb = noun): attack – attack; defeat – defeat; fight – fight; design – design; paint – paint
– group 2 (verb + ing): build – building; kill – killing; feel – feeling; paint – painting
– group 3 (verb + ion): invent – invention; protect – protection; connect – connection; decide – decision; invade – invasion

3 Your turn: The five most important objects
a) I chose this object because it was my first cuddly toy. His name is Thomas and he's a brown bear. My grandparents gave him to me when I was a baby. I played with him a lot and I went to bed with him too. Thomas is really old now, but I still like him very much. He's a happy childhood memory.
b) *individuelle Lösung*

4 The oldest thing
Lösungsvorschlag:
The oldest thing in our house is this doll. It belonged to my grandma. It was very important to her because it was her only toy. She used to take it everywhere when she was a child and she never threw it away. Today it's sitting on our sofa in the living room – in memory of my grandma.

5 Find the rule: Relative pronouns
a)+b)

1. Olivia is in the Tudor period for the **calendar which** Claire is making. (thing); **2.** This is the **calendar whose** page themes are from different historical periods. (thing); **3.** Gwen and Holly are the **girls who** Olivia is going be photographed with. (people); **4.** They'll wear clothes like the **women whose** job it was to be with the queen all day and all night. (people); **5.** Jay has to choose the historical **person that** he wants to be. (people); **6.** Olivia needs to think about the **dress that** she's going to wear. (thing) *You use 'which' or 'that' for things. You use 'who' or 'that' for people. You use 'whose' for people or things.*

6 People from history
Francis Drake was the first Englishman **who** sailed around the world. On his way he attacked Spanish ships **which** carried gold and spices. In 1587 the Spanish were preparing to attack England, but it was Drake **who** led a surprise attack and burnt the Spanish ships. When the Spanish ships (known as the Armada) attacked in 1588, Drake was one of the people **who** defeated them in the English Channel. The battle was won by the side **whose** ships were lighter and faster. It was the first sea battle **which** involved large numbers of ships.

7 People from history
Lösungsvorschlag: siehe Lösung zu Übung 6

8 Sherlock Holmes
1. whose; **2.** that; **3.** who; **4.** that; **5.** which; **6.** which

9 Sherlock Holmes
a) 1. whose; **2.** which; **3.** who; **4.** who; **5.** which; **6.** which
b) 1.

10 At History Club
a)+b)

1. Last week we watched a modern film about Shakespeare **which** was very interesting.; **2.** Yesterday we went to a theatre **(that)** we really liked.; **3.** The guide told us that in the old days they needed light **which** came through an open roof.; **4.** He said that all the actors were men and boys **who** also played the roles of women and girls.; **5.** After the backstage tour we met an actor **(who)** we'll never forget.

11 Useful phrases for presenting facts and figures
- times and dates: in 1599, in the 16th century; 400 years ago, in just two hours, the following year
- description of places/objects: was used for, belonged to, was made of
- biographical information: was born in 1564, wrote, acted, moved to, reigned
- typical history verbs: was built, started, was rebuilt, was opened, burnt down, pulled down

Grammar

G6 I'm in the calendar which Claire is making.
1 which; **2** who; **3** which; **4** which; **5** which; **6** whose; **7** who

G7 Jay was in streets he didn't know.
4 (which); **5** (which); **7** (who)

G8 They heard a scream and then another one.
1 ones; **2** ones; **3** ones; **4** ones; **5** ones; **6** one; **7** one

Vocabulary
The phonetic alphabet
a) 1. B; **2.** A; **3.** D; **4.** E; **5.** C
b) 1. There's a flood when there has been too much rain.; **2.** No, there isn't a monarch in Germany.; **3.** You can get married in a church.; **4.** You can write important dates, times and meetings in a calendar. **5.** You need an umbrella when it rains.

Text and media smart 2
Diff pool

1 Types of messages
a) C, D
b) E
c) A, B

2 Write a reply
Lösungsvorschlag:
- **email (C):** Dear all,
   Thank you for your email. Sorry, but I forgot to send you my new mobile phone number. It's 0977 905844.
   Things are well with us in Cornwall. We've got a new member at Cooking Club. He's cool and the food he prepares tastes great!
   We're going to visit Granny Rose in Greenwich next month. Hope to see you too!
   Dave
- **text message (D):** Sorry, just left home. Will b there in 10 min. CU

3 Write a reply
Lösungsvorschlag:
- **email (C):** Dear all,
   Thank you for your email. Sorry, but I forgot to send you my new mobile phone number. It's 0977 905844.
   Things are well with us in Cornwall. We've got a new member at Cooking Club. He's cool and the food he prepares tastes great!
   We're going to visit Granny Rose in Greenwich next month. Hope to see you too!
   Dave
- **text message (D):** Sorry, just left home. Will b there in 10 min. CU
- **invitation (E):** Dear Emma,
   Thank you for inviting me to your party. I'm sorry, but I can't come. My grandma's birthday is on the same day. I hope you have a nice party.
   Love,
   Olivia

4 Formal emails
ll. 1–3 header; l. 4 greeting; ll. 5–8 reason for writing; l. 9 asking for information; ll. 10–11 giving information; ll. 12–14 ending

5 Mr Evan's reply
Lösungsvorschlag: Dear Ms/Mrs Fraser,
Thank you for your email. I am very interested in taking the photographs for the calendar. It sounds like a wonderful idea and I am happy to support the community centre without payment – just a nice cup of tea during the photoshoot would be fine.
I am available on Saturday, 9th April. If it is all right with you, I would like to visit the community centre before I take the photos.

That will help me to decide what equipment I will need to bring. I am looking forward to the project.
Yours sincerely,
Jim Evans

6 Mrs, Miss or Ms?
1 greeting; **2** formal; **3** recipient; **4** married; **5** surname; **6** Ms; **7** Miss/Mrs; **8** Mrs/Miss

7 Claire's reply to Mr Evans
Lösungsvorschlag: Dear Mr Evans,
Thank you very much for your email. I am happy to hear that you are going to support the calendar project.
You can come to the community centre any time it is open.
The times are shown on the following website / Please click here for the opening times: www.parkstreetcentre.org.uk.
All the best/Yours sincerely,
Claire Fraser

8 Parts of a letter
1 sender's address; **2** recipient's name and address; **3** date; **4** greeting; **5** main part of the letter; **6** ending; **7** signature; **8** sender's name and job

9 A semi-formal email
Hi Jay,
Thank you for your email and your offer to help. Could you come an hour before the photoshoot starts to help set up the rooms? That would be great!
See you,
Claire

10 Informal communication
- **Text messages:** incomplete sentences; no punctuation or punctuation like ?!/!!!, abbreviations like u, ur; no greeting, short forms, icons
- **Formal messages:** complete sentences, correct punctuation, abbreviations like Re:/Mr/Mrs, greeting; long forms

Revision C

1 At the museum
a) 1. pick up the audio guide **2.** test the audio guide **3.** ask the museum assistant to help if the audio guide doesn't work **4.** don't be too loud/noisy **5.** put things in locker **6.** look at museum map to find room **7.** listen to audio guide while looking at display **8.** complete worksheet **9.** take back audio guide **10.** meet at 4:00; don't be late
b) *individuelle Lösung*

2 Be a history detective
individuelle Lösung

3 What's new?
1 century; **2** known; **3** grown; **4** Spanish; **5** coffee; **6** popular; **7** Europe; **8** brought; **9** travelled; **10** Chocolate; **11** made; **12** produced

4 Who said it and why?
a) *Lösungsvorschlag:*
1. Das Zitat bedeutet, dass die ganze Welt eine Bühne ist. Shakespeare wollte damit sagen, dass die Menschen oft nur eine Rolle spielen.; **2.** Auf Deutsch würde man sagen: „Ich kam, sah und siegte." Cäsar schrieb diese Worte in einem Brief, um selbstbewusst seinen Sieg zu feiern.; **3.** Das Zitat

„Rom ist nicht in einem Tag erbaut worden" bedeutet, dass es Zeit braucht, um etwas Wichtiges zu erschaffen.; **4.** Mit diesem Zitat wollte Queen Victoria ausdrücken, dass sie wichtiger und einflussreicher als andere Personen ist, und dass es deshalb nicht von Bedeutung ist, was andere von ihr denken.; **5.** Mit dem Zitat wollte Orwell ausdrücken, dass es wichtig ist zu gewinnen. Er dachte, dass sich später niemand an Verlierer erinnern wird.; **6.** Bei diesem Zitat handelt es sich um ein Wortspiel. In *history* steckt das Wort *his*, was auf Deutsch „sein" bedeutet. Das Wort *her* bedeutet „ihr". Das Zitat soll ausdrücken, dass Frauen in der Geschichte genauso viel Bedeutung haben wie Männer, aber oft nicht erwähnt oder beachtet wurden und werden.
b) *individuelle Lösung*

5 French words in English
a) acteur – actor; arriver – (to) arrive; changer – (to) change; cousin – cousin; grands-parents – grandparents; départ – (to) depart; dialogue – dialogue; histoire – history; danser – (to) dance; excuser – (to) excuse; famille – family; différent – different; problème – problem; répéter – (to) repeat; visiteur – visitor; musique – music; théâtre – theatre; station – station

6 Plan a visit to a museum
a)+b) *individuelle Lösung*

7 Exciting news
b) 1 'll never guess; **2** is going to be; **3** is going to play; **4** 'll have; **5** 'm going to choose / 'll choose; **6** 'm going to ask / 'll ask; **7** 'll going to have

8 Before the class trip to the Globe
1 'm going to say, **2** 're going to catch; **3** 're going to take; **4** 'll have; **5** 'll be; **6** 're going to watch; **7** 'll be; **8** won't rain / isn't going to rain; **9** 'll be / 's going to be

9 A visit to Madame Tussauds
1. e); **2.** g); **3.** f); **4.** b); **5.** a); **6.** d); **7.** c)

10 An interview with a Celtic warrior
1 May / Can; **2** may / can; **3** Can / Could; **4** mustn't / shouldn't; **5** must; **6** mustn't; **7** needn't; **8** Can / Could; **9** could; **10** couldn't; **11** can't; **12** can / should; **13** could; **14** must; **15** mustn't; **16** can

Unit 4
Check-out

1 What is happening next week?
On Monday they arrive in the UK. On Tuesday morning Anna is going to school with me. School only starts at 10 a.m. that day. In the afternoon she's/they're visiting the leisure centre. On Wednesday we're/they're spending the whole day in London. The train departs at 7 a.m. We/They aren't coming back before 10 p.m. On Thursday morning she's/they're staying with the family/with us. In the evening they're/she's seeing a musical performance at the school theatre. On Friday they're/she's enjoying a day trip to the seaside. On Saturday they're/she's returning to Germany. The bus leaves from the front of the school at 5:30 a.m.!

2 The worst day of our trip
1 had to; **2** weren't allowed to; **3** will be able to / was able to; **4** was able to; **5** 'll be allowed to; **6** won't have to

3 Welcome to our home
1 Wir können die Fahrräder in der Garage benutzen, dürfen aber nicht vergessen, auf der linken Straßenseite zu fahren.; **2** Neben dem Telefon liegt eine Liste mit Telefonnummern für den Notfall.; **3** Falls wir eine schwarze Katze sehen, sollen wir sie verscheuchen. Sie darf nicht in den Garten oder ins Haus kommen, weil sie immer tote Mäuse bringt.; **4** Dienstags wird der Müll abgeholt. Die Nachbarn werden uns erklären, was in die grüne und gelbe Tonne gehört.; **5** Der Fernseher ist kaputt, aber wir können den Computer im Kinderzimmer benutzen und online Fernsehen schauen.

4 Travel advice
a) 1 foreign; **2** suggest; **3** flights; **4** land; **5** coast; **6** Passengers; **7** delays; **8** passport control; **9** purpose; **10** look; **11** traffic; **12** get in
b) *individuelle Lösung*

Diff pool

1 Vocabulary
1 journey; **2** train; **3** train station; **4** tickets; **5** taxi; **6** got on; **7** destination; **8** car

2 Ways of travelling
individuelle Lösung

3 Find the rule
1. simple present; **2.** present progressive

4 Simple present or present progressive
individuelle Lösung

5 What happened
Lösungsvorschlag: In Italy we wanted go to the beach by bus. We were a little bit late and when we arrived at the bus stop, the bus was just leaving. The next bus was only in one hour! Later when we were at the beach, somebody stole our clothes so we went back to our tent in our swimsuits. In the evening we were trying to sleep in our tent when a cow looked inside it. It was scary!

6 Travel situations
Lösungsvorschlag: During my last holiday, I went to Greece. It was really hot there. We had some fantastic days at the beach and went to see some amazing sights. The people were always very friendly to us and said hello to us when we walked by. I checked my guide and found that 'Kalimera' was Greek for 'Good morning'. But the next morning, when a woman said hello to me on my way to the beach, I replied 'Kalamari'. It was so embarrassing!

7 At passport control
Rafiq felt nervous when the man at passport control called somebody. / He was worried that he wouldn't be allowed to enter the country. / He felt lucky that he was allowed to call his aunt and uncle. / Rafiq was tired when he left the airport. / But he was happy because he would be able to enjoy his holiday after all.

8 After the holiday
1 wasn't able to; **2** had to; **3** don't have to; **4** were you able to; **5** was able to; **6** were you allowed to; **7** I'll be able to; **8** had to

9 After the holiday
1 wasn't able to; **2** had to; **3** don't have to; **4** were you able to; **5** was able to; **6** were you allowed to; **7** I'll be able to; **8** had to

10 Destinations for a school trip
individuelle Lösung

11 Reading between the lines
1 b); **2** c); **3** a); **4** c)

12 Reading between the lines
individuelle Lösung

Grammar

G9 The ferry arrives at 3:15 local time.
1 are you doing; **2** 'm meeting; **3** opens; **4** are you getting; **5** leaves; **6** takes; **7** is driving; **8** 's going

G10 Your passport photo has to look like you.
1 had to; **2** wasn't able to; **3** wasn't allowed to; **4** have to; **5** had to; **6** was allowed to; **7** have to / must

Vocabulary
Sounds and spelling
a) autumn; birds; castle; could; fascinating; foreign; frown; guess; ghost; island; know; lambs; local; travel
b) 1. island; **2.** ghost / castle; **3.** birds; **4.** Lambs / autumn; **5.** know / guess; **6.** foreign / travel; **7.** local; **8.** fascinating; **9.** frown / Could

⟨Trailer 1⟩
Grammar
G11 When we arrived, we felt fantastic.
1 new; **2** nice; **3** well; **4** quickly; **5** great; **6** happy; **7** fast; **8** carefully; **9** perfect; **10** terribly; **11** fantastic; **12** hard; **13** fantastic; **14** amazing

⟨Trailer 2⟩
Grammar
G12 He takes from people who have little to give, which makes me angry.
1 which makes it one of the most successful historical drama films; **2** which was great for his fans / which came as a surprise to his fans; **3** which came as a surprise to his fans / which was great for his fans; **4** which was too bad

G13 My children and I live in this house. It's ours.
1 mine; **2** yours; **3** mine; **4** Yours; **5** ours; **6** his

⟨Trailer 3⟩
Grammar
G14 She writes that she's in Dublin.
The woman says that she takes her dog to greyhound races because he likes to move. She says that the origin of the sport dates back centuries, and that in her family that tradition has been passed down from one generation to the next. She tells the reporter that her dog isn't dangerous / is nice and that most owners treat their greyhounds as friends. She says that she doesn't enter competitions to make money and if her dog didn't enjoy racing so much, she'd stop right away.

Bildquellennachweis

U1.1 Getty Images RF (Stefan Auth), München; **U1.2** plainpicture GmbH & Co. KG RF (RelaxImages/STUDD), Hamburg; **3.1** ShutterStock.com RF (suicidecrew), New York, NY; **3.2** ShutterStock.com RF (suicidecrew), New York, NY; **5.1** ShutterStock.com RF (suicidecrew), New York, NY; **5.2** ShutterStock.com RF (suicidecrew), New York, NY; **8.1** ShutterStock.com RF (Shawn Goldberg), New York, NY; **8.2** ShutterStock.com RF (PhotoByToR), New York, NY; **8.3** ShutterStock.com RF (suicidecrew), New York, NY; **9.1** Getty Images Plus (E+/SDI Productions), München; **9.2** ShutterStock.com RF (Monkey Business Images), New York, NY; **9.3–10** Thinkstock (comzeal), München; **9.3–10** stock.adobe.com (alexghidan89), Dublin; **9.3–10** Thinkstock (arabes), München; **9.3–10** Thinkstock (Nixken), München; **9.3–10** Thinkstock (nosopyrik), München; **9.3–10** Thinkstock (pking4th), München; **9.3–10** Thinkstock (Andrii_Oliinyk), München; **9.3–10** Thinkstock (nuranvectorgirl), München; **12.1** YERMAN FILMS (Andrea Artz), London; **12.2** YERMAN FILMS (Andrea Artz), London; **13.1** YERMAN FILMS (Andrea Artz), London; **14.1** Thinkstock (iStock/kadmy), München; **14.2** ShutterStock.com RF (George Dolgikh), New York, NY; **18.1** ShutterStock.com RF (cheapbooks), New York, NY; **19.1** ShutterStock.com RF (Rawpixel.com), New York, NY; **19.2** Avenue Images GmbH (Banana Stock), Hamburg; **20.1** Getty Images (Mark Scoggins/Corbis), München; **21.1** YERMAN FILMS (Andrea Artz), London; **23.1** February Films, London; **23.2** February Films, London; **23.3** February Films, London; **24.1** Getty Images (Bloomberg), München; **28.1** ShutterStock.com RF (Igor Zakowski), New York, NY; **32.1** ShutterStock.com RF (stoatphoto), New York, NY; **33.1** Getty Images Plus (CiydemImages), München; **33.2** ShutterStock.com RF (Dubova), New York, NY; **33.3** ShutterStock.com RF (Fabio Principe), New York, NY; **33.4** ShutterStock.com RF (Sofia Apkalikova), New York, NY; **34.1** ShutterStock.com RF (suicidecrew), New York, NY; **34.2** February Films, London; **34.3** February Films, London; **35.1** February Films, London; **35.2** February Films, London; **36.1** ShutterStock.com RF (SpeedKingz), New York, NY; **36.2** www.CartoonStock.com (Farris, Joseph), Bath; **36.3** www.CartoonStock.com (Madden, Chris), Bath; **37.1** Thinkstock (istock/bokan76), München; **38.1** ShutterStock.com RF (Gorodenkoff), New York, NY; **40.1** plainpicture GmbH & Co. KG (Fancy Images), Hamburg; **41.1** Getty Images (Panoramic Images), München; **41.2** Alamy stock photo (Ian Dagnall), Abingdon, Oxon; **41.3** iStockphoto (George Clerk), Calgary, Alberta; **41.4** iStockphoto (TT), Calgary, Alberta; **42.1** YERMAN FILMS (Andrea Artz), London; **43.1** stock.adobe.com (mmmg), Dublin; **43.2** Picture-Alliance (Reuters/Jeff J Mitchell UK), Frankfurt; **44.1** Getty Images (Anadolu Agency), München; **45.1** Mauritius Images (robertharding), Mittenwald; **45.2** iStockphoto (Mnieteq), Calgary, Alberta; **45.3** iStockphoto (Martin McCarthy), Calgary, Alberta; **45.4** Getty Images (Colin McPherson/Sygma), München; **45.5** iStockphoto (Gim42), Calgary, Alberta; **45.6** Alamy stock photo (Thornton Cohen), Abingdon, Oxon; **47.1** stock.adobe.com (mmmg), Dublin; **48.1** Getty Images (DEA / PUBBLI AER FOTO/De Agostini), München; **49.1** ShutterStock.com RF (gkrphoto), New York, NY; **49.2** Thomas Weccard Fotodesign BFF, Ludwigsburg; **49.3** Getty Images Plus (The Image Bank / Ed Bock), München; **53.1** February Films, London; **53.2** February Films, London; **56.1** ShutterStock.com RF (suicidecrew), New York, NY; **56.2** www.CartoonStock.com (McNeill, Geoff), Bath; **57.1** February Films, London; **57.2** February Films, London; **57.3** February Films, London; **57.4** February Films, London; **58.1** ShutterStock.com RF (Matyas Rehak), New York, NY; **58.2** ShutterStock.com RF (Rainer Albiez), New York, NY; **58.3** ShutterStock.com RF (Rainer Albiez), New York, NY; **59.1** ShutterStock.com RF (chrisdorney), New York, NY; **59.2** stock.adobe.com (zuzule), Dublin; **59.3** ShutterStock.com RF (360b), New York, NY; **60.1** ShutterStock.com RF (ColeTrickle), New York, NY; **62.1** Alamy stock photo (robertharding/Stuart Forster), Abingdon, Oxon; **62.2** akg-images (Science Photo Library/CLAUS LUNAU), Berlin; **62–63.3** laif (Alicia Canter/Guardian/eyevine/laif), Köln; **62–63.4** Bridgemanimages.com (Mzphoto), Berlin; **62.5** ShutterStock.com RF (suicidecrew), New York, NY; **64.1** Ullstein Bild GmbH (Archiv Gerstenberg), Berlin; **64.2** Getty Images (Stapleton Collection), München; **64.3** Getty Images (Getty Images Europe/ Jeff J Mitchell), München; **64.4** Bridgemanimages.com (© Look and Learn), Berlin; **66.1** ShutterStock.com RF (Stocksnapper), New York, NY; **67.1** ShutterStock.com RF (Everett - Art), New York, NY; **67.2** ShutterStock.com RF (Morphart Creation), New York, NY; **69.1** ShutterStock.com RF (suicidecrew), New York, NY; **69.1** ShutterStock.com RF (Pres Panayotov), New York, NY; **70.1** February Films (Andrew Kemp), London; **72.1** ShutterStock.com RF (Anneka), New York, NY; **73.1** Getty Images (Fine Art Images/Heritage Images), München; **75.1** YERMAN FILMS (Andrea Artz), London; **75.2** YERMAN FILMS (Andrea Artz), London; **76.1** YERMAN FILMS (Andrea Artz), London; **77.1** February Films, London; **77.2** February Films, London; **78.1** ShutterStock.com RF (Everett Historical), New York, NY; **81.1** ShutterStock.com RF (suicidecrew), New York, NY; **85.1** ShutterStock.com RF (suicidecrew), New York, NY; **85.2** ShutterStock.com RF (PremiumArt), New York, NY; **85.3** ShutterStock.com RF (Africa Studio), New York, NY; **85.4** ShutterStock.com RF (Alex Gorka), New York, NY; **85.5** ShutterStock.com RF (fatir29), New York, NY; **86.1** ShutterStock.com RF (panuwat phimpha), New York, NY; **87.1** YERMAN FILMS (Andrea Artz), London; **88.1** ShutterStock.com RF (suicidecrew), New York, NY; **89.1** February Films, London; **89.2** February Films, London; **89.3** February Films, London; **90.1** Thinkstock (Jupiterimages), München; **90.2** ShutterStock.com RF (CHANG JO-YI), New York, NY; **90.3** iStockphoto (miskolin), Calgary, Alberta; **90.4** iStockphoto (fcafotodigital), Calgary, Alberta; **90.5** ShutterStock.com RF (Sergios), New York, NY; **90.6** Thinkstock (Hemera Technologies), München; **91.1** ShutterStock.com RF (Radu Bercan), New York, NY; **92.1** ShutterStock.com RF (Ron Ellis), New York, NY; **93.1** ShutterStock.com RF (Kachalkina Veronika), New York, NY; **93.2** Alamy stock photo (Brickley Pix), Abingdon, Oxon; **94.1** Thinkstock (brians101), München; **95.1** Getty Images (Getty Images News/Marco Di Lauro), München; **95.2** Getty Images (E+), München; **95.3** Thinkstock (Creatas), München; **97.1** ShutterStock.com RF (wjarek), New York, NY; **97.2** ShutterStock.com RF (LanaG), New York, NY; **100.1** iStockphoto (Tarzan9280), Calgary, Alberta; **101.1** Alamy stock photo (David Gee), Abingdon, Oxon; **102.1** Alamy stock photo (Justin Kase zsixz), Abingdon, Oxon; **102.2** Alamy stock photo (robertharding), Abingdon, Oxon; **103.1** Alamy stock photo (Alibi Productions), Abingdon, Oxon; **107.1** February Films, London; **110.1** ShutterStock.com RF (Tom Eversley), New York, NY; **112.1** Alamy stock photo (Ross Aitken), Abingdon, Oxon; **113.2** Alamy stock photo (Jim Nicholson), Abingdon, Oxon; **114.1** Alamy stock photo (Anne-Marie Palmer), Abingdon, Oxon; **114.2** Alamy stock photo (Simon

Reddy), Abingdon, Oxon; **115.1** stock.adobe.com (sunt), Dublin; **118.1** akg-images, Berlin; **124.1** Mauritius Images (Cavan Images/Samantha Mitchell), Mittenwald; **126.1** ShutterStock.com RF (javi_indy), New York, NY; **127.1-5** iStockphoto (DenisZbukarev), Calgary, Alberta; **129.1** ShutterStock.com RF (Leremy), New York, NY; **130.1** Getty Images (Getty Images Europe/Jeff J Mitchell/Staff), München; **131.1** Getty Images (Hans Georg Eiben/Photolibrary), München; **131.2** Getty Images (Hans Georg Eiben/Photolibrary), München; **132.1** Getty Images (Sonya Hurtado), München; **132.2** Getty Images (Digital Vision), München; **133.1** Getty Images (De Agostini Editorial/DEA/ICAS94), München; **133.2** ShutterStock.com RF (Antony McAulay), New York, NY; **133.3** Alamy stock photo (John Peter Photography), Abingdon, Oxon; **134.1** ShutterStock.com RF (Stasia04), New York, NY; **134.2** ShutterStock.com RF (vlastas), New York, NY; **134.3** stock.adobe.com (vlad), Dublin; **134.4** ShutterStock.com RF (bedya), New York, NY; **134.5** ShutterStock.com RF (Jacob Lund), New York, NY; **135.1** Alamy stock photo (Roksana Bashyrova), Abingdon, Oxon; **135.2** Getty Images (Andreas von Einsiedel/Corbis Documentary), München; **136.1** Alamy stock photo (Science History Images), Abingdon, Oxon; **136.2** Alamy stock photo (Alan Wilson), Abingdon, Oxon; **144.1** Alamy stock photo (Ievgen Chabanov), Abingdon, Oxon; **145.1** stock.adobe.com (Michael Rogner), Dublin; **145.2** F1online digitale Bildagentur (MEV), Frankfurt; **147.1** Alamy stock photo (Image Source/Steve Prezant), Abingdon, Oxon; **151.1** ShutterStock.com RF (andromina), New York, NY; **151.2** ShutterStock.com RF (andromina), New York, NY; **151.3** ShutterStock.com RF (Rvector), New York, NY; **151.4** ShutterStock.com RF (Djent), New York, NY; **151.5** ShutterStock.com RF (Sissoupitch), New York, NY; **151.6** ShutterStock.com RF (Alexander Ryabintsev), New York, NY; **151.7** ShutterStock.com RF (Rvector), New York, NY; **151.8** ShutterStock.com RF (andromina), New York, NY; **151.9** ShutterStock.com RF (Alexander Ryabintsev), New York, NY; **151.10** ShutterStock.com RF (Alexander Ryabintsev), New York, NY; **151.11** ShutterStock.com RF (andromina), New York, NY; **151.12** ShutterStock.com RF (Alexander Ryabintsev), New York, NY; **151.13** Alamy stock photo (Aleksey Boldin), Abingdon, Oxon; **156.1** Nutzung des Screenshots Microsoft Word 2010 mit freundlicher Genehmigung der Microsoft Corporation; **157.1** iStockphoto (kizilkayaphotos), Calgary, Alberta; **157.2** Nutzung des Screenshots von Microsoft Excel 2016 mit freundlicher Genehmigung der Microsoft Corporation; **157.3** ShutterStock.com RF (Bloomicon), New York, NY; **158.1** ShutterStock.com RF (Datenschutz-Stockfoto), New York, NY; **158.2** ShutterStock.com RF (fizkes), New York, NY; **159.1** February Films (Elke Bock), London; **160.1** ShutterStock.com RF (Dmitry Kalinovsky), New York, NY; **160.2** Thomas Weccard Fotodesign BFF, Ludwigsburg; **162.1** stock.adobe.com (PixelShot), Dublin; **163.1** stock.adobe.com (Christian Schwier), Dublin; **170.1** YERMAN FILMS (Andrea Artz), London; **174.1** ShutterStock.com RF (Michaelpuche), New York, NY; **174.2** Thinkstock (Alan Crawford), München; **176.1** imago images (Inpho Photography), Berlin; **179.1** gemeinfrei; **179.2** stock.adobe.com (fotosd), Dublin; **179.3** gemeinfrei; **179.4** stock.adobe.com (fotosd), Dublin; **180.1** Alamy stock photo (Ian Rutherford), Abingdon, Oxon; **182.1** Alamy stock photo (Tracey Whitefoot), Abingdon, Oxon; **186.1** ShutterStock.com RF (Dean Drobot), New York, NY; **188.1** Alamy stock photo (Ross Aitken), Abingdon, Oxon; **189.1** Alamy stock photo (LMR Group), Abingdon, Oxon; **190.1** stock.adobe.com (wavebreak3), Dublin; **190.2** ShutterStock.com RF (Antonio Guillem), New York, NY; **191.3** ShutterStock.com RF (tommaso79), New York, NY; **197.1** ShutterStock.com RF (Production Perig), New York, NY; **200.1** ShutterStock.com RF (Pressmaster), New York, NY; **206.1** stock.adobe.com (konstan), Dublin; **206.2** iStockphoto (luoman), Calgary, Alberta; **206.3** Thinkstock (Vrabelpeter1), München; **206.4** iStockphoto (jeangill), Calgary; **Timeline.2** Alamy stock photo (CJG – UK), Abingdon, Oxon; **Timeline.3** iStockphoto (Andrew Gosling), Calgary, Alberta; **Timeline.4** Getty Images (Bettmann), München; **Timeline.5** Alamy stock photo (robertharding/Stuart Forster), Abingdon, Oxon

Textquellennachweis

27 Song: True Friend, Texter: Lurie, Jeannie Renee; Verlag: Walt Disney Music Co., Universal Music Publishing GmbH, Berlin; **30** ©2015, Mizscorpio; **32** ©2010, newwrittenobsession; **47** „Flower of Scotland" Text: (OT) Williamson, Roy, Copyright Variena Music Inc./Edition AIM Publishing; **91.1** As you like it, William Shakespeare †1616; **91.2** Julius Caesar, 46 BC; **91.3** from the medieval French, Li Proverbe au Vilain, 1190.; **91.4** Queen Victoria (1819-1901); **91.5** George Orwell, Tribune, 4 February 1944, **91.6** source unknown; **98** „ISLAND IN THE SUN" Text: CUOMO, RIVERS Copyright E O Smith Music, Melodie der Welt J. Michel GmbH & Co. KG Musikverlag, Frankfurt; **104–105** From Where I belong by Gillian Cross, Oxford University Press, April 2010; **115** https://theirishgifthouse.com; **116–117** First published by Utbildningsstaden AB, Sweden, 1995 (c) Dave Draper 1995; **165** FONS Schülerwörterbuch Englisch, 978-3-12-516236-5

Timeline of British history

A typical Celtic round house

We don't know much about **the earliest people** who lived in the British Isles, but we can still see some of the famous stone rings they built, like Stonehenge. We also know that their priests were called Druids.

From around 600 BC, the **Celts** came from Europe to live in the British Isles. They lived in round houses with fires in the middle and built high walls to keep out wild animals. They had many gods.

In 43 AD the Romans conquered the lands we now call England and Wales. They built Hadrian's Wall to keep the Picts out of their part of the island of Britain.

The **Angles** and **Saxons** began to attack Britain from about 400, but they didn't conquer the land until after Roman rule ended. The Angles gave England its name: It means 'Land of the Angles'.

At the Battle of Hastings, William, Duke of Normandy defeated Harold, King of the Saxons. The **Normans** ruled England for the next 88 years.

Industrialisation started in England in the 18th century. Factories with machines were built all over Britain and the invention of the steam engine meant that people could travel much more than before.

Powerful symbol of the Industrial Revolution: the steam train

The **House of Tudor** was important in English history. Henry VIII changed England from a Catholic to a Protestant country, and founded the Navy. His daughter Elizabeth was perhaps the biggest 'star' of the Tudor family. While she was queen, England became rich and powerful and started to colonise North America. It was a 'golden age' for music, literature and the theatre too.

Henry VIII and his six wives, as wax figures at Madam Tussauds

During the reign of **Queen Victoria**, Britain had so many colonies around the world that people said the sun always shone somewhere in the British Empire.

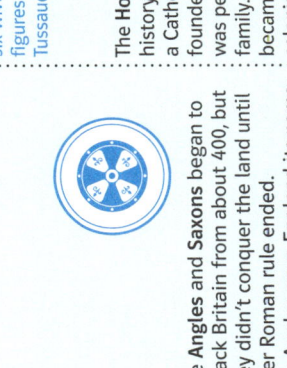

Queen Victoria reigned for almost 64 years

The UK joined the European Community (later the European Union), but the British kept their own money: the pound. In 2016 British people voted to leave the EU. 'Brexit' was finally done in 2020.

After the two world wars, Britain rebuilt itself, and people started to enjoy themselves again. British music and fashion became popular around the world. Even today, the music of the Beatles and Rolling Stones still has a major influence.

600

43–410 AD

5th, 6th cent.

1066–1154

1485–1603

18th, 19th

1837–1901

After

1973–2020

SCOTLAND

SHETLAND
ISLANDS

Atlantic Ocean

ORKNEY
ISLANDS

OUTER
HEBRIDES

Highlands

ISLE OF
SKYE

■ Inverness

Loch Ness

Aberdeen ■

Balmoral Castle ●

▲ Ben Nevis

Dunnottar Castle

Tay

Dundee ■

Firth of
Forth

Loch
Lomond

■ Glasgow

● Edinburgh

Edinburgh
Castle

Clyde

ARRAN

Tweed

North Sea